I N V E S T I G A Ç Ã O

I|U

EDIÇÃO
Imprensa da Universidade de Coimbra
Email: imprensa@uc.pt
URL: http//www.uc.pt/imprensa_uc
Vendas online: http://livrariadaimprensa.uc.pt

COORDENAÇÃO EDITORIAL
Imprensa da Universidade de Coimbra

CONCEÇÃO GRÁFICA
Imprensa da Universidade de Coimbra

IMAGEM DA CAPA
Imagem de Pete Linforth via Pixabay

INFOGRAFIA
Mickael Silva

EXECUÇÃO GRÁFICA
KDP

ISBN
978-989-26-2431-0

ISBN DIGITAL
978-989-26-2432-7

DOI
https://doi.org/10.14195/978-989-26-2432-7

ALEXANDRE DIAS PEREIRA

INTELLECTUAL PROPERTY, COMPETITION & NEW TECHNOLOGIES

I|U

SUMMARY

PREFACE

This book brings together a set of studies on intellectual property, competition and new technologies law, which corresponds to articles and other writings published in international journals and other publications mainly in English. The book is for students of Intellectual Property and Computer Law, but it can also be useful to all those interested, both in teaching and research, as well as in forensic practice and in the management of these rights.

Intellectual property covers not only industrial property (concerning invention patents, models and designs, trademarks and other distinctive signs, and trade secrets), but also copyright in literary and artistic works (including computer programs and video games) and the related rights of performers, phonographic and videographic producers, broadcasting organizations, and other special rights, such as the right of the producer of databases and the right of the organizer of sporting events.

Internationally, the protection of intellectual property is governed by WIPO/OMPI, a specialized UN agency that brings together around 90% of the world's countries and administers more than two and a half dozen international treaties. The protection of intellectual property under the terms of the TRIPS/ADPIC Agreement is also a goal of the WTO, thus constituting a pillar of mercantile globalization. In an economy of creativity, innovation and knowledge, in which intangible assets represent a substantial value for companies, the protection of these assets by intellectual property is considered a "powerful tool" for the competitiveness of companies in the European Union, having the European Parliament and the Council already approved around three dozen Directives and Regulations in this field, and there is a large body of jurisprudence of the Court of Justice of the European Union.

Internally, the importance of intellectual property and new technologies is also growing. Legislation has updated largely due to the normative production of the European Union. On the other hand, the jurisprudence is already significant and for more than a decade Portugal has a Court of Intellectual Property.

Intellectual property has developed largely in line with the challenges of new technologies, especially in the digital age. New technologies question other areas of law, from electronic contracting to the protection of personal data, computer security and cyber-crime, as well as the regulation of, and the defense of competition in the digital market. This work also includes some studies on the legal issues of the new economy, providing the study of intellectual property in the broader context of the information society and the digital economy.

Coimbra, January 2025

UPLOAD FILTERS FOR OBVIOUS COPYRIGHT INFRINGEMENTS*

Content filtering may be a good practice for commercial online sharing platforms to avoid liability for copyright infringement where it is obvious or manifest. However, what is an obvious or manifest infringement when consumers upload and share content on digital platforms? How to strike a fair balance between copyright enforcement and users' rights in online communication? This paper addresses such questions in the context of copyright law of the European Union.

1. The resilience of copyright in the digital world

The system of copyright and related rights is valid and effective in the digital world. To paraphrase the well-known words of MARK TWAIN, we could say that 'the news about the death of copyright has been grossly exaggerated'. This does not mean that copyright remains the same as it was in the days of analogue technology. Copyright has adapted to the challenges of digital technology by digitizing itself. In the sense that what digital technology has made possible, both in terms of new forms of creative expression and in terms of new ways of

* European Intellectual Property Review, vol. 45/5, p. 266-269, 2023, published by Sweet & Maxwell (imprint of Thomson Reuters).

exploiting works and other protected materials, as well as in the role of the end user, all this has been assimilated by the copyright system.

The most recent challenge concerns commercial platforms for online sharing of content uploaded by end users, the so-called web 2.0, which is featured by interactivity and often instantaneous sharing of user generated content. New business models have flourished under the *safe harbour* of internet service providers and in a context of relative legal uncertainty regarding copyright. The legislator of the European Union, in compliance with its duty to protect intellectual property and, at the same time, other fundamental rights also enshrined in the Charter of the Union, established in article 17 of Directive 2019/790[1] a regime that aims to strike a fair balance between the legitimate interests of all parties at stake.

This Directive puts forward the proposition according to which commercial online sharing platforms communicate or make publicly available the content uploaded by the platform's users. It aims to fix a gap of copyright protection resulting from the fact that traditional media (publishers, producers, broadcasters) channel a substantial part of their advertising revenue to copyright authorizations, while advertisers increasingly invest in new media, especially commercial platforms of sharing digital content, the responsibility of which for copyright infringement was far from clear under the legal framework previously in force.

Directive 2019/790 made it clear that such platforms require prior authorization from the right holders, even if through collective management or alternative schemes such as «Creative Commons» licenses. However, even if they do not have authorization, large platforms will not be responsible for copyright infringement if

[1] Directive (EU) 2019/790 of the European Parliament and of the Council of 17 April 2019 on copyright and related rights in the digital single market and amending Directives 96/9/EC and 2001/29/EC.

they meet various requirements, namely the implementation of best practices to prevent and stop infringement. These good practices mean, in particular, the use of content filters, which, however, can significantly restrict freedom of expression and creation in digital media. Between the manifest illegalities and those that are so by right holders' earmarking, irrespective of other considerations, there is a long way between two different perspectives on the role of copyright filters on digital platforms.

Indeed, it is not clear how these commercial platforms will have to filter content uploaded by users in order to avoid liability for copyright infringement. There are two different ways to implement these technical measures. On the one hand, the Commission seems to be more concerned with the protection of rights holders, since they could identify a priori everything they considered an obvious infringement, namely content that is particularly time sensitive. On the other hand, according to the Advocate-General and the Court of Justice of the European Union, users' rights justify that the automatic filtering of any content flagged by rights holders cannot replace human case-by-case assessment or control of the blocking or elimination of users' uploads.

The aim is to strike a fair balance between copyright and fundamental users' rights, such as freedom of expression and information. Finding this balance is an issue that has to be addressed by human intervention, rather than by machines acting mainly in the interests of rights holders. In the Opinion presented in the case of *Poland v. Parliament and Council*[2], the Advocate-General asserted two basic principles in this field. The first concerns the jurisprudence of the Court of Justice[3], according to which Article 17(2) of the Charter

---

[2] Opinion of Advocate General HENRIK SAUGMANDSGAARD ØE, delivered on 15 July 2021, C 401/19, Poland v. Parliament/Council, ECLI:EU:C:2021:613.

[3] Judgment of March 27, 2014, C 314/12, UPC Telekabel Wien, EU:C:2014:192, para. 61.

does not mean that intellectual property receives absolute protection. The second would lay in Article 15 of Directive 2000/31[4], providing the fundamental freedom of communication in the digital environment, which would bind not only Member States, but also the European Union legislator. In the Advocate-General's opinion, it would be contrary to the fundamental principle of freedom of communication to filter automatically any content shared online to prevent copyright infringements, in what would become a kind of copyright *ex machina* or absolute techno-digital property[5].

2. Communication or making available to the public works protected by copyright on content sharing platforms

Under Article 17 of Directive 2019/790, the offer to the public of access to works and other materials uploaded by users of online content sharing services is an act of communication to the public or making available to the public subject to the authorization of the respective rights holders. This authorization covers not only the activity of the platform, but also the acts performed by users of the services if they do not act with a commercial nature or if their activity does not generate significant revenue. The Directive affirms the principle of copyright sovereignty and contractual freedom, in the

[4] Directive 2000/31/EC of the European Parliament and of the Council of 8 June 2000 on certain legal aspects of information society services, in particular electronic commerce, in the internal market ('the Electronic Commerce Directive'). Meanwhile, Regulation (EU) 2022/2065 of the European Parliament and of the Council of 19 October 2022 on a single market for digital services "deleted" Articles 12 to 15 of Directive 2000/31/EC and replaced them by Articles 4, 5, 6 and 8 of the new Digital Services Regulation, which notwithstanding, according to Article 2(4)(b), is without prejudice to UE law on copyright and related rights.

[5] Alexandre Dias Pereira, 'Copyright Issues of Techno-Digital Property', in *Intellectual Property in the Digital Age: Challenges for Asia*, ed. C. Heath & A.K. Sanders, Kluwer: The Hague, 2001, p. 65-94.

sense that right holders are free to authorize, or not, this form of use, that is, right holders are not forced to authorize or license the use of their works by sharing platforms, as made clear by whereas (61) of the Directive.

As an activity subject to licensing, it does not benefit from the hosting providers' safe harbour of liability provided for in Directive 2000/31. In the absence of authorization, these commercial platforms are liable for copyright infringement, unless they prove that they have made a serious or diligent effort to obtain such authorization, do not make available works identified by the rights holders, or block or remove works that are the subject of notification by the right holders and prevent their future uploading. Compliance with these obligations, which involves the implementation of appropriate technical measures (i.e. content recognition technologies), is assessed in the light of the principle of proportionality, taking into account, *inter alia*, the type, target audience and size of the service, the type of content uploaded by users of the service, the availability of suitable and effective means, as well as the cost to service providers.

Bearing in mind that content control technologies (monitoring and filtering) can be ineffective and/or very expensive, it is considered necessary to assess, on a case-by-case basis, their burden to safeguard freedom of business and competition in the sector. Firstly, to avoid eliminating competitors at birth (start-ups), small or medium-sized companies, new to the sector (i.e. with less than three years of activity and an annual turnover of less than 10 million euros), must prove only that they made serious or diligent efforts to get authorization and, upon receipt of a notification, to block access to or remove protected content from their websites. With more than 5 million individual visitors, they will already have to prove that they have made serious efforts to avoid future uploads of works subject to notification by rights holders. Which in practice means that new platforms with more than 5 million individual visitors will have to resort to content recognition technologies, just like large-scale platforms do.

On the other hand, the control of user uploaded content must not prevent the use of works already in public domain nor the use of user-generated content for the purposes of quotation, criticism, analysis, as well as for the purposes of caricature or parody (the famous memes), under the protection of freedom of expression and information. In fact, these uses are now mandatory as individual rights of end users in the digital environment.

In addition, rights holders must duly justify their requests to block or remove content, and the platforms must provide users with a complaint and redress mechanism to resolve disputes about blocking access or removing content, the decisions of which remain subject to "human control".

This self-regulation mechanism does not prevent out-of-court dispute resolution mechanisms. Moreover, users may always resort to effective judicial remedies, namely through access to a court or other relevant jurisdictional body to claim the use of an exception or limitation. Online content sharing providers are required to implement responsible copyright policies, which means in special to inform end users about the possibility of using works under the exceptions or limitations to copyright and related rights provided for in law of the Union. In order to optimize these rules, Article 17 instructed the Commission to promote dialogue between stakeholders and issue guidelines on best practices, taking also into account fundamental rights and the use of exceptions and limitations.

3. Computer filtering tools as "best practices"

Although content recognition technologies are not found in the final wording of the Directive, both the Advocate-General and the

Court of Justice[6] as well as the Commission have already recognized that the system in place will largely require the use of monitoring and filtering digital technologies. The quest is to find the adequate level of machine automatic control.

In the *Guidelines*[7] on article 17 of Directive 2019/790 issued meanwhile, the Commission recognizes that 'in the current state of knowledge', no technology can assess, according to the standard required by law, whether the content that a user intends to upload corresponds to a violation or a legitimate use. However, this does not prevent the Commission from recommending that Member States implement the Directive in order to expressly provide for the possibility for automatic control to prevent, block and/or suppress the upload of manifestly illegal content, in particular situations of identical or equivalent full reproduction of protected works; the same goes for content marked by rights holders.

According to the Commission's *Guidelines*, filtering is tailored according to criteria such as the length/size of the copied file, the proportion of the copy in the user's work, the level of alteration of the work, the type of content, the business model, as well as the risk of significant economic damage to rights holders. In this order of ideas, 'exact matches of complete works or significant proportions of a work' will be manifestly infringing, as well as uploads of an original work, which has simply been technically altered/distorted to avoid its identification (for ex. adding an external frame to the image or rotating it 180°). Out of the notion of manifestly infringing would be content for which the rights holders have not given a blocking instruction to the provider of the platform, as well as partial uploading, in creative or parodical

[6] Judgment of June 22, 2021, C-682/18 and C-683/18, *Frank Peterson v. YouTube*, and *Elsevier v. Cyando*, ECLI:EU:C:2021:503.

[7] COM(2021) 288 final, Brussel, 4.6.2021, p. 23.

uses such as memes, or small excerpts under the right of quotation. With the exception, however, of the possibility to block time-sensitive content, such as the pre-release of songs or movies or highlights of recent sporting events broadcasts, which would require *ex ante* human analysis.[8]

For its part, in its *Opinion* in *Poland v. Parliament and Council*, the Advocate-General agreed with the possibility of filters for the first series of cases but opposed against the automatic control of any content marked by the rights holder, considering such control an excessive limitation on freedom of expression and information. In the Opinion of the Advocate-General, providers should not be able to block *ex ante* content by simply claiming a risk of significant economic damage by right holders, even if such content is not manifestly infringing.[9] On the contrary, users have the right to upload content under copyright exceptions or limitations provided by law, and this right could only be limited on a legal basis by the judiciary, rather than being subject to the discretion of platforms. In short, the Advocate-General argues for *in dubio pro libertate*, holding that, for the legislator, 'false positives', which consist of blocking legal content, are more serious than 'false negatives', i.e. letting certain illegal content through.[10]

4. Copyright in the context of digital human rights in perspective

The draft transposition of Article 17 into Portuguese domestic law did not incorporate the Commission's *Guidelines* on the functioning of content filters. Which is not necessarily bad, considering

[8] Cf. *ibidem*, p. 24-6.

[9] *Opinion*, cit., para. 223.

[10] *Ibidem*, para. 207.

the arguments of the Advocate-General in favour of a digital community in which the copyright system recognizes rights not only to traditional holders (creators, artists and producers), but also to end users, in the name of their fundamental freedoms of communication, especially in the context of digital human rights.

In fact, a fair balance between copyright and freedom of communication will not empower rights holders to require platforms to program filters to block or to remove any content in the name of their economic interest. It would seriously undermine freedom of communication online and ultimately compromise a pillar of free and democratic societies.

Automatic control is understood and accepted for manifestly illicit uses, although it is recognized that the technology does not yet provide fully right answers or beyond a reasonable doubt. Apart from obvious infringement situations where the work is fully or substantially reproduced, it would be excessive to prevent *ex ante* communication in digital media, without prejudice to *ex post* control, especially since the Artificial Intelligence systems at the service of copyright enforcement are still not sufficiently capable to distinguish legitimate uses from illegal uses under exceptions such as freedom of parody or the right to quote.[11]

The Portuguese Charter of Human Rights in the Digital Age[12] establishes in special freedom of expression and creation in a dig-

---

[11] The blocking obligations of service providers established by the German Act on the Copyright Liability of Online Content Sharing Service Providers of 31 May 2021 (Sec. 7 ff. UrhDaG) do not apply to uploads which are "presumably permitted under the law", even if potentially infringing. It includes, for ex., content flagged by the user as lawful under a copyright exception, uses of 160 characters per text, or 5 seconds per film work, moving picture or audio track. *A contrario*, it seems that uses which are not *prima facie* lawful require *ex ante* licensing or blocking. Although a system of presumptions is not provided by the Directive it may be a good solution to a complex problem. It is however disputable whether the provided number of characters or seconds will not excessively restrict free speech on the internet.

[12] Enacted by Law No. 27/2021 of 17 May (as amended by Law No. 15/2022, of 11 August, revoking provisions on disinformation control).

ital environment (Article 4), as well as the right to the protection of content by intellectual property rights, under special legislation which provides proportionate, adequate and effective measures to prevent access to or to remove content made available in manifest violation of copyright and/or related rights (Article 16/2).

In order to implement what 'manifest infringement' means, the legislator must consider the case-law of the Court of Justice of the European Union, in particular the judgment in *Poland v. Parliament/Council*. Endorsing the Advocate General's *Conclusions*, the Court of Justice holds that, by implicitly imposing the use of automatic recognition technologies and filtering tools, Article 17(4) of Directive 2019/790 entails a restriction on the exercise of the users' right to freedom of expression and information, which is guaranteed by Article 11 of the Charter. However, taking into account the exemption conditions provided for the Directive, the Court understands that this restriction was surrounded by the legislator with adequate guarantees to ensure the respect for the users' right to freedom of expression and information, as well as to strike a fair balance with the right to intellectual property, which is also protected by the Charter under Article 17(2). However, the Court reiterates its jurisprudence of not allowing 'filtering systems which are not capable to sufficiently distinguish between illegal and lawful content', so that lawful content is not blocked and freedom of communication on the Internet prevails as a matter of principle.[13]

Copyright in the context of digital human rights also leads us to support the Advocate-General's proposal to recognize users the right to flag their uploads of content under free or permitted uses, such as the right to quotation, freedom of parody or content in the public domain or event content not protected by copyright.

[13] Judgment of 22 June 2021, C-682/18 and C-683/18, cit., para. 99.

Copyright law will be all the stronger in the digital environment the more effective it becomes, not only enforcing authors' economic and moral rights, but also users' rights under copyright exceptions and limitations.

Nonetheless, in the current state of harmonization of copyright law of the Member States of the European Union, the development of filters, which also implement exceptions and limitations, may prove to be a real chimera for software developers. In fact, although European Union law has established a closed list of exceptions and limits, even if optional, it has only recently made some of them mandatory, so that the national legislations of Member States will still present significant differences. In this sense, the making of filters should look to the specificities of the national legislation of each Member State, in terms of exceptions and limitations.

Although this by no means is an impossibility, it does pose a great challenge to software programmers, which only in collaboration with lawyers will they be able to overcome. However, a mosaic of filters can be anticipated, and/or the use of geo-blocking. In the end, this just shows how copyright is an increasingly relevant legal sector for Internet companies, and as such it should be considered by regulators and corporations.

To end up with, a final suggestion, which consists of extending the system of fair compensation for private copying (the so-called copyright levies) to commercial platforms for online content sharing. A fair compensation for private uploading would compensate authors and other rights holders for possible damages arising out of uses not manifestly infringing and which, therefore, should not be blocked or frozen *ex ante* by content filters. Instead, it would pave the way to free flow of information and thus freedom of communication on the Internet, already established by the Court of Justice as a fundamental principle of the Digital Law of the European Union.

A COPYRIGHT 'HUMAN-CENTRED APPROACH' TO AI?*

The European Parliament (EP) resolution of 20 October 2020 on intellectual property rights for the development of artificial intelligence technologies argues for the need of 'a human-centred approach to AI that is compliant with ethical principles and human rights' (para. E). What does this mean in the field of copyright? *The resolution addresses a myriad of topics, but this Editorial will focus on the protection of AI-generated inventions (1) the use of copyrighted works to feed algorithms that produce works, (2) and the declared preference for an EU regulation over directives to achieve the desired goals.*

According to the EP resolution, a human-centred approach means, to begin with, compliance with the 'principle of originality, linked to a natural person', and with 'the concept of 'intellectual creation', addressing the author's personality' (para. 15). For this reason, and despite considering that 'works autonomously produced by artificial agents and robots might not be eligible for copyright protection', the EP resolution does not exclude this under 'common, uniform copyright provisions' based upon 'a horizontal, evidence-based and technologically neutral approach' (para. 15). Among such common, uniform provisions, the European Parliament 'recommends that

---

* GRUR International, vol. 70(4), 2021, p. 323–324 (Editorial), by permission of Oxford University Press.

ownership of rights, if any, should only be assigned to natural or legal persons that created the work lawfully' (para. 15).

Such recommended ownership of rights concerns only 'AI-generated creations' and not 'AI-assisted human creations', for which the EP resolution stresses that, 'the current IP framework remains applicable' (para. 14). However, where admitting the eligibility of AI-generated works for copyright protection and, at the same time, recommending ownership in such works for natural or legal persons who created the work lawfully, the EP resolution enters into contradiction. AI-generated works are, by definition, created by AI and not by natural or legal persons. Perhaps the EP resolution would solve this contradiction by admitting a legal personality to AI technologies. However, it expressly considers 'that it would not be appropriate to seek to impart legal personality to AI technologies' (para. 13), concerning the ownership of IPRs in content of an artistic nature generated by an AI autonomous creative process, pointing out 'the negative impact of such a possibility on incentives for human creators' (para. 13) and 'issues related to potential market concentration' (para. 14).

Arguably 'a human-centred approach to AI' would simply close the 'door' to AI-created works because they are not an intellectual creation of a natural person and therefore their origin cannot be traced in the personality of an author as an expression of his/her freedom of intellectual creation. In several jurisdictions, legal persons own copyright by contract or statutory provision. In particular, concerning the so-called 'collective work' (*oeuvre collective*) in *droit d'auteur* countries, copyright is vested in the natural or legal person that has directed the creation of the work and under which name it has been published. Copyright ownership of AI-created works as 'collective works' would probably provide 'reduction of complexity'. However, 'a human centred approach' to so-called collective works significantly limits the scope of application of this concept if the rights of human intellectual creators are complied with. In the end, it may be no more than a functional rule to assign the ownership of structures and titles of journals, periodicals or encyclopaedias, and/or a sort of 'fiduciary ownership' concerning anonymous works created within organisations, notably corporations.

Maintaining the principle of authorship does not mean that AI-generated works have no copyright protection. The EP resolution is aware of that, considering that 'technical creations generated by AI technology must be protected under the IPR legal framework'. Besides patent and trade secret law, copyright itself can protect AI-generated works by means of neighbouring rights, in particular those of phonograms or video producers. For example, under the Rome Convention (1961), a 'phonogram means any exclusively aural fixation of sounds of a performance or of other sounds', the producer being 'the person who, or the legal entity which, first fixes the sounds of a performance or other sounds' (Art. 3(b)(c)). The rights of the producer of sound recordings do not require originality of sounds as intellectual creations and, therefore, AI-generated works are likely to be protected under the right of the producer. It is not the same as authors' rights, notably the term of protection is shorter, identification of protection is required, but it does provide an incentive to invest in AI creations.

Then, concerning *the use of works by AI creations*, the EP resolution stresses that AI creations must respect copyright and therefore it is lawful 'only if authorisation has been granted by the copyright holder if copyright-protected material is being used, unless copyright exceptions or limitations apply' (para. 15). In this regard, where providing for an exception or limitation for reproductions and extractions of lawfully accessible works and other subject matter for the purposes of text and data mining, Directive 2019/790 may have transformed copyright into an *opt-out right*, as rightholders will have to expressly reserve such uses and only for purposes other than scientific research (Art. 4). Text and data mining implies reproductions and extractions of lawfully accessible works and other subject matter, which are crucial for AI-creations. Besides the mandatory privilege granted to research organisations and cultural heritage institutions, AI-creations are free to use copyrighted works by means of text and data mining, unless rightholders expressly reserve such uses 'in an appropriate manner, such as machine-readable means in the case of content made publicly available online' (Art. 4(3)). Copyright as an exclusive right becomes, where text and data mining is concerned, a right to oppose such uses and only for purposes other than scientific research. Therefore, to some extent, existing EU copyright law already paves the way to AI creations, placing the burden of reserving such uses on rightholders in general, instead of requiring their previous authorisation. Along with this copyright exemption, albeit non-mandatory, the EU resolution 'stresses the importance of facilitating access to data and data sharing, open standards and open source technology, while encouraging investment and boosting innovation' (para. 15), clearly pointing towards an AI-friendly legal environment.

Finally, the EP resolution considers that 'new common rules for AI systems should take the form of a regulation in order to establish equal standards across the Union' (para. F; see also para. 3). So far, the EU legislator has intervened in the field of copyright almost exclusively by means of directives, which by definition leave Member States with some room of implementation, in particular preserving their national acts or codes on copyright. Is a regulation the best method to regulate AI copyright at EU level? What will happen to national copyright? Certainly, EU law has already occupied many fields of copyright law, and the ECJ has become a sort of 'Copyright Supreme Court'.

Declaring a preference for a regulation in this field may be the announcement of an EU General Copyright Regulation, which, along with the General Data Protection Regulation, set an EU standard for the global digital market, complemented by the proposed *Digital Services Act* and *Digital Markets Act*. Instead of leaving technologies, code and AI to self-regulation and market driving forces, the EU affirms the primacy of the rule of law and 'a human-centred approach to AI that is compliant with ethical principles and human rights'. However, at the same time, the EP resolution may leave the door open to a 'brave new world' of *copyright ex machina* and '*techno-digital property*'. In particular, *new business models*, such as streaming services and online sharing platforms, have a major role in providing access to cultural and creative content. In view of this, the EP resolution highlights the importance of a 'transparent and responsible' use of algorithms, in order to guarantee access to content in various forms and different languages and impartial access to European works (para. 8). The configuration of AI algorithms should preserve cultural diversity and promote access to European works, and therefore the EP resolution points out the importance of 'evaluating human input regarding AI algorithmic data' (para. 9). The volume of content uploaded by users on sharing platforms makes it impossible to comply with 'high industry standards of professional diligence' without resorting to ID content technologies. The EP resolution points out that the machine task may not be left to AI only, and that a 'human review carried out on a case-by-case basis, in order to ensure the quality and fairness of decisions' is necessary, in line with whereas (70) and Art. 17(9) of Directive 2019/790. Algorithms are an important part of the process, providing real time control. Nonetheless, their design and functioning has to preserve cultural diversity and promote access to European works, as well as freedom of expression, as guaranteed by the European Convention of Human Rights and the Charter of Fundamental Rights of the Union. Leaving the control of free speech only to AI algorithms would be a shortcut to censorship ('cancel culture') and the return of some sort of *Index Librorum Prohibitorum* to digital content in general, as well as an obstacle to new business models and competition in the market of digital content and services.

FROM A ROCK TO A HARD PLACE? THE IMPLEMENTATION OF ENFORCEMENT INTERNATIONAL STANDARDS IN THE EUROPEAN UNION*

Abstract - What is the role of EU law in the implementation of international standards concerning the enforcement of intellectual property rights? This paper provides a concise overview of the regulatory framework of European Union law concerning the implementation of IP remedies provided by the Agreement on Trade Related Aspects of Intellectual Property Rights, including a survey of judgments of the EU Court of Justice on the interpretation of several provisions of the IP Enforcement Directive.

Introduction

Literary and artistic property is one of the branches of intellectual property along with industrial property. While the latter protects patents, industrial designs and models, in addition to trademarks and other distinctive signs (and, to some extent, unfair competition and trade-secrets), literary and artistic property

---

* Les recours en matière de droits d'auteurs, dir. Ysolde Gendreau, p. 443-460, 2019, Les éditions Thémis.

concerns literary and artistic works protected by copyright as well as artistic performances, phonograms, videos and broadcasts protected by related rights (and other sui generis rights such as the right of database producer).

The internet and the globalization of commerce significantly weaken literary and artistic property. If authors are not to be the *Misérables* of cyberspace - recalling the famous title of ALAI's founder Victor Hugo - it is necessary that their means of protection turn *law in the books* into *law in action*. In effect, the meaning and scope of intellectual property rights depend largely on their means of protection or remedies, which define how good is "the best substantive protection"[1]. However, at the same time, an excessive protection may arise out of a debate focused only on the interests of the IP holders, and therefore a balance must be achieved in establishing enforcement remedies[2].

---

[1] Thomas DREIER, «TRIPs and the Enforcement of Intellectual Property Rights», in Friedrich-Karl BEIER et Gerhard SCHRICKER (dir.), *From GATT to TRIPs – The Agreement on Trade-Related Aspects of Intellectual Property Rights*, Weinheim, VCH, 1999, p. 248, 255; see also e.g. Annette KUR, «The Enforcement Directive: Rough Start, Happy Landing?», (2004) 35/7 *IIC* 821, 830; Christopher HEATH, «Comparative Overview and the TRIPS Enforcement Provisions», in Christopher HEATH et Laurence PETIT (ed.), *Patent Enforcement Worldwide – A Survey of 15 Countries*, Oxford, Hart Publishing, 2005, p. 5; Annette KUR, & Henning G. RUSE-KHAN, «Enough is enough – the notion of binding ceilings in international intellectual property protection», in Annette KUR (dir.), *Intellectual property rights in a fair world trade system*, Cheltenham, Edward Elgar, 2011, p. 359; Sévérine DUSOLLIER, «Inclusivity in intellectual property», in Graeme B. DINWOODIE (dir.), *Intellectual Property and General Legal Principles: Is IP a Lex Specialis?*, Cheltenham, Edward Elgar, 2015, p. 101.

[2] Kimberlee WEATHERALL, «Provocations and challenges concerning enforcement and civil procedure in IP», in Graeme B. DINWOODIE (dir.), *Intellectual Property and General Legal Principles: Is IP a Lex Specialis?*, Cheltenham, Edward Elgar, 2015, p. 181, 194. The scope of intellectual property protection should not be enlarged by deterrent remedies, in special criminal remedies in the field of patents - Reto M. HILTY, «The Enforcement of Patents», in Reto M. HILTY et Kung-Chung LIU (dir.), *The Enforcement of Patents*, Alphen aan den Rijn, Kluwer Law International, 2012, p. 9, 22.

Harmonization of intellectual property remedies by the TRIPS Agreement

The means of protection of intellectual property have been the subject of part III of the Agreement on Trade-Related Intellectual Property Rights (TRIPS) under the WTO.[3] In general terms, this Agreement provides for "expeditious remedies intended to prevent infringements and remedies which constitute a deterrent against further offenses", with the proviso that their application "avoid creating obstacles to legitimate trade and to provide safeguards against their abusive use" (article 41).

TRIPS lays down rules on evidence, injunctions, calculation of compensation and other remedies, including the possibility for the courts to order the elimination or destruction of counterfeit or pirated goods, and it provides for expeditious and effective precautionary measures, in particular where delay is likely to cause irreparable damage to the right holder, or destruction of evidence. Furthermore, the Agreement provides border control measures, so that the customs authorities of the Contracting Parties may suspend the placement of counterfeit and pirated goods in the domestic circuit. Finally, Contracting Parties undertake to provide criminal protection against infringements of intellectual property, at least in cases of intentional trademark counterfeiting or copyright piracy on a commercial scale[4].

---

[3] See before TRIPS Articles 9 and 10 Paris Convention and Article 16 Berne Convention (seizure of counterfeited or pirated goods), and then also the Internet WIPO Treaties of 1996 on Copyright, Performances and Phonograms (Articles 14 and 23). On this provisions, Sam *RICKETSON* et Jane C. *GINSBURG*, *International Copyright and Neighbouring Rights: The Berne Convention and Beyond*, 2nd ed., Oxford, Oxford University Press, 2006, p. 661-3.

[4] On criminal remedies and their fragilities on the Internet, see e.g. Christophe GEIGER, «The Rise of Criminal Enforcement of Intellectual Property Rights... and its Failure in the Context of Copyright Infringements on the Internet», in Susy *FRANKEL* et Daniel J. *GERVAIS*, (dir.), *The Evolution and Equilibrium of Copyright in the Digital Age*, Cambridge, Cambridge University Press, 2014, p. 113-142.

In the European Union, protection of intellectual property is protected under the Charter of Fundamental Rights of the Union (Article 17/2) and is the subject of various legal instruments in its various domains[5]. A European Institute of Intellectual Property (EUIPO) has been established in Alicante, Spain, and it has estimated that piracy would cost about 790,000 jobs to the Union[6].

Implementation of international remedies by the European Union

The European Union has adopted two main instruments to promote a harmonized implementation of IP remedies provided by the TRIPS Agreement. In customs matters, it has adopted Council Regulation 1383/2003, replaced by Regulation N° 608/2013 of the European Parliament and of the Council[7]. On the other hand, the EU has adopted Directive 2004/48 (IPRED)[8], recital (1) of which

---

[5] See e.g. <https://ec.europa.eu/growth/industry/intellectual-property_pt>

[6] Cf. <https://euipo.europa.eu/ohimportal/pt/web/observatory/news/-/action/view/3361118>

In a joint study with the OECD, it is estimated that piracy concerns circa 2.5% of world GDP: OECD/EUIPO, *Trade in Counterfeit and Pirated Goods: Mapping the Economic Impact*, OECD Publishing, Paris. 2016 <http://dx.doi.org/10.1787/9789264252653-en>

[7] Regulation (EU) N° 608/2013 of the European Parliament and of the Council of 12 June 2013 concerning customs enforcement of intellectual property rights and repealing Council Regulation (EC) No. 1383/2003. For a commentary see Michel M. *WALTER*, «Product Piracy Regulation», in Silke *von LEWINSKI* et Michel M. *WALTER (dir.)*, *European Copyright Law: A Commentary*, Oxford, , Oxford University Press, 2010, p. 1365. The Regulation is complemented by the Commission Notice on the customs enforcement of Intellectual Property Rights concerning goods brought into the customs territory of the Union without being released for free circulation including goods in transit (2016/C 244/03), which incorporates the case-law from the Court of Justice from the European Union, notably judgment of 1 December 2011, joined cases C-495/09 e C-446/09, *Philips e Nokia*, ECLI:EU:C:2011:796.

[8] Directive 2004/48/EC of the European Parliament and of the Council of 29 April 2004 on the enforcement of intellectual property rights (read according to Corrigendum, OJ L 157, 30.4.2004)..

reads that the protection of intellectual property is an "essential element for the success of the internal market".

The Member States are Contracting Parties to the TRIPS Agreement, as well as - "with regard to matters within its competence" - the Union itself, which approved this Agreement by Council Decision 94/800/EC, as stated in recital (4) of Directive 2004/48. However, in the absence of direct effect of the TRIPS provisions[9], and in view of the "significant disparities in the means of enforcing intellectual property rights" then existing in Member States - recital (7) - the European Union has opted for the adoption of a directive on the harmonization of intellectual property enforcement remedies.

In view of the limited competences of the European Union, Directive 2004/48 does not establish criminal sanctions for intellectual property, but also does not prejudice *inter alia* "The obligations arising from international conventions, in particular the [TRIPS Agreement], including those related to criminal prosecutions and sanctions" (article 2/3-b)[10]. A proposal of Directive providing criminal remedies (IPRED II) has been discussed, but not adopted[11].

Principles of effective protection of intellectual property in Directive 2004/48

The fact that private law remedies of the TRIPS Agreement are implemented through a *directive* (rather than a *regulation*) means

[9] See e.g. CJEU judgment of 15 March 2012, case C-135/10, *SCF*, ECLI:EU:C:2012:140

[10] See Article 82 ff. Lisbon Treaty (TFUE).

[11] Amended proposal for a Directive of the European Parliament and of the Council on criminal measures aimed at ensuring the enforcement of intellectual property rights, COM(2006) 168 final, 24.04.2006.

that further implementation is required at national level[12]. In this regard, it is asked whether intellectual property remedies should be specific to those rights or whether they can be integrated into the general system of procedural and substantive civil remedies[13]. For example, in Portugal, instead of amending the Civil Code and / or the Code of Civil Procedure, Law 16/2008 of 1 April introduced changes in the special legislation on intellectual property, notably the Copyright and Related Rights Act, for one side, and the Industrial Property Act, on the other[14].

Directive 2004/48 lays down the general principle that intellectual property protection measures, procedures and remedies must be fair and equitable and must not be unnecessarily complex or burdensome and unjustifiably time-consuming (article 3/1), neither shall IP remedies be used abusively[15]. In practice, the application

---

[12] According to Article 288 TFUE (ex-Article 249 TEC), while regulations have general application, are binding in their entirety and directly applicable in all Member States, directives are binding, as to the result to be achieved, upon each Member State to which it is addressed, but leave to the national authorities the choice of form and methods.

[13] In principle, remedies should be provided under general legislation, unless obvious positive effects arise from specific regulation, as argued by Thomas JAEGER, «The framework for IP Rights Enforcement in the EU», in Christoph ANTONS (dir.), *The Enforcement of Intellectual Property Rights. Comparative perspectives from the Asia-Pacific Region*, Alphen aan den Rijn, Kluwer Law International, 2011, p. 47, 60.

[14] See Luís Menezes LEITÃO, «A transposição da Diretiva 2004/48/CE sobre a aplicação efetiva dos direitos de propriedade intelectual efetuada pela Lei 16/2008, de 1 de abril», in José de Oliveira ASCENSÃO (dir.), *Direito da Sociedade da Informação*, vol. VIII, Coimbra, Coimbra Editora, 2009, p. 277; Alberto Ribeiro de ALMEIDA, «Responsabilidade Civil pela violação de direitos subjetivos de Propriedade Intelectual – As influências anglo-saxónicas», (2014) 2 *RDI* 165, 187; Alexandre L. Dias PEREIRA, «Tutela efetiva da propriedade intelectual (*enforcement*), em especial a proteção dos direitos de autor e conexos contra a pirataria», (2017) 146/4003 *RLJ* 241, 266.

[15] On the use of IP remedies as possible abuse of dominant position under EU competition law, see CJEU judgment of 16 July 2015, case C-170/13, *Huawei v ZTE*, ECLI:EU:C:2015:477, fixing the requirements for the licensor of a standard dominant patent to apply for a interlocutory injunction against an infringer, so-called «FRAND» («fair, reasonable, and nondiscriminatory»). On this topic see e.g. Bjorn LUNDQVIST, «The interface between EU competition law and standard essential patents – from Orange-*Book-Standard* to the *Huawei* case», (2015) 5/2-3 *ECJ* 367.

of the remedies is subject by the EU Court of Justice to a fair and equitable balance of conflicting rights, in accordance with the principle of proportionality[16]. This has led the CJEU to play a "creative role" in determining the meaning and limits of intellectual property remedies, as in the case of the substantive definition of each authors' right under EU law, in particular the right of reproduction and the right of communication to the public[17].

Measures to obtain and protect evidence

Directive 2004/48 lays down rules on the obtaining and preservation of evidence under the control of the other party, which may include bank, financial or commercial documents in the case of commercial infraction, without prejudice to the protection of confidential information (article 6)[18].

Precautionary measures are also foreseen to preserve evidence, safeguarding the protection of confidential information (article 7). The so-called *Anton Piller* injunctions (similar to French *saisie-contrefaçon*) consist, for example, of the detailed description, with or without the taking of samples, or of the actual seizure of the disputed goods and, where appropriate, materials and instruments used in production and / or distribution of these assets and the documents

---

[16] CJEU judgment of 29 January 2008, case C-275/06, *Promusicae*, ECLI:EU:C:2008:54; see also Order of 19 February 2009, case . C-557/07, *LSG*, ECLI:EU:C:2009:107.

[17] See e.g. ALAI, *Report and Opinion on the making available and communication to the public in the internet environment – focus on linking techniques on the Internet*, adopted unanimously by the Executive Committee 16 September 2013 <http://www.alai.org/en/assets/files/resolutions/making-available-right-report-opinion.pdf>; Miguel PEGUERA, «Hyperlinking under the lens of the revamped right of communication to the public», (2018) 34/5 *CLSR* 1099, 1118.

[18] Holding that the court *a quo* may order the production of evidence which it deems necessary, see CJEU judgment of 15 November 2012, case C-180/11, *Bericap*, ECLI:EU:C:2012:717.

related thereto[19]. They may be ordered by the courts without hearing the other party in the case of danger in delay (*periculum in mora*) or destruction of such evidence, and subject to the provision of a security or other adequate guarantee to compensate losses suffered by the other party by virtue of the injunction. Evidence shall be revoked or lapse if the claimant does not bring a legal action on the merits within a reasonable time to be determined by the judicial authority ordering such measures under the law of the Member State or, failing that, within a period not exceeding 20 working days or 31 calendar days, whichever is longer.

Right to information

A right to information on the origin and distribution networks of pirated or counterfeit goods is provided (article 8). It is enforceable against *pirates* and / or their accomplices, and concerns in particular the names and addresses of producers, manufacturers, distributors or suppliers, as well as quantities produced, manufactured, delivered, received or ordered and the price obtained by the pirated goods. According to the Court of Justice, this right to information may prevail over banking secrecy[20] as well as justify the identification of Internet service subscribers to whom the intermediary has provided an IP address allegedly used in an infringement of intellectual property[21].

---

[19] In the UK law, injunctions have originated by the hand of the "Chancellor in equity", William CORNISH, David LLEWELYN, Tanya APLIN, *Intellectual Property: Patents, Copyright, Trade Marks and Allied Rights*, 8th ed., London, Sweet & Maxwell, 2013, p. 73.

[20] CJEU judgment of 6 December 2017, case C-230/16, *Coty Germany*, ECLI:EU:C:2017:941. See Dietrich KAMLAH, «Banking secrecy does not have unlimited priority over the protection of intellectual property», (2016) 11/1 *JIPL&P* 61, 63 ("The CJEU leaves no doubt that the claim for information has to apply in relation to banks as well, in principle.").

[21] CJEU judgment of 19 April 2012, case C-461/10, *Bonnier Audio*, ECLI:EU:C:2012:219.

Interim and precautionary measures

Directive 2004/48 establishes two types of provisional and precautionary measures (article 9). To begin with, it provides for interlocutory injunction measures to prevent an imminent infringement or to prevent the continuation of an alleged infringement, possibly subject to a penalty payment, or alternatively oblige the alleged infringer to lodge a security to ensure damages caused to the right holder.

On the other hand, injunctive relief is sought against any intermediary whose services are being used by a third party to infringe intellectual property rights, in line with injunctions against intermediaries already provided by Directive 2001/29 on copyright and related rights related on the information society[22].

These precautionary measures against Internet intermediaries have been interpreted by important judgments of the Court of Justice. In *Scarlet Extended*[23], the Court held that it was contrary to EU law for a national court to order an injunction against an Internet intermediary by requiring it to install, at its expense, on a preventive and indeterminate basis, computer filters intended to block the unauthorized circulation of files allegedly containing works protected by copyright and / or related rights. Then, in *Telekabel*[24], the Court of Justice would accept an unspecified court injunction prohibiting an internet broker from providing its clients with access to a website by making unlawfully available protected content, insofar as that

[22] Holding that the *tenant of market* halls who sublets the various sales points situated in those halls to market-traders, some of whom use their pitches in order to sell counterfeit branded products, falls within the concept of "an intermediary whose services are being used by a third party to infringe an intellectual property right" within the meaning of Article 11 of Directive 2004/48, see CJEU judgment of 7 July 2016, case C-494/15, *Tommy Hilfiger*, ECLI:EU:C:2016:528.

[23] CJEU judgment of 24 November 2011, case C-70/10, *Scarlet Extended*, ECLI:EU:C:2011:771; see also see CJEU judgment of 16 February 2012, case C-360/10, *Netlog*, ECLI:EU:C:2012:85.

[24] CJEU judgment of 27 March 2014, case C-314/12, *UPC Telekabel*, ECLI:EU:C:2014:192.

injunction does not prevent access to information and effectively prevents the infraction. Finally, in *McFadden*[25], the Court gave the green light to an access-blocking injunction the technical implementation of which would be left to the intermediary (for example through password control). It should also be noted in this connection that in the Communication "Guidance on certain aspects of Directive 2004/84" the Commission stresses the importance of wide and dynamic injunctions already existing in Ireland and the United Kingdom ("forward-looking, catalog- dynamic injunctions")[26].

The European Union wants to go further and require providers of information society services to control the public availability in sharing platforms of large amounts of protected works uploaded by their users (e.g. "YouTube"), and provide an effective and fair remedy to the so-called "value gap"[27]. It has been criticized in particular for

---

[25] CJEU judgment of 15 September 2016, case C-484/14, *McFadden*, ECLI:EU:C:2016:689.

[26] *Guidance on certain aspects of Directive 2004/48/EC of the European Parliament and of the Council on the enforcement of intellectual property rights*, COM(2017) 708 final, p. 20-1.

[27] Proposal for a Directive of the European Parliament and of the Council on copyright in the Digital Single Market, COM/2016/0593 final, Brussels, 14.9.2016. The qualification of online sharing platforms as users of copyrighted works uploaded by their users has been confirmed by the Court of Justice of the European Union in several cases - e.g. Silke von LEWINSKI, «Comments on Article 13 and related provisions in the JURI Committee Report for a Directive on Copyright in the Digital Single Market», *Kluwer Copyright Blog* (http://copyrightblog.kluweriplaw.com/).

The right of communication to the public, including the making available on the Internet, is broadly construed to include new uses, such as hyperlinks, peer-to-peer sharing platforms, or active cloud computing. At first, the Court of Justice of the European Union found that a communication to the public of copyrighted works would not take place by hyperlinks to works freely available on the Internet (CJEU judgment of 13 February 2014, case C-466/12, *Svensson*, ECLI:EU:C:2014:76; CJEU Order of 21 October 2014, case C-348/13, ECLI:EU:C:2014:2315). Later on, however, profit-making hyperlinks to works unlawfully made available on the Internet were considered communication to the public as the hyperlinking person would be presumed to know about the unlawfulness of the source (CJEU judgment of 8 December 2018, case C160/15, *GS Media* ECLI:EU:C:2016:644 - "Playboy")*;* the same was found for the sale of a multimedia player in which applications were pre-installed with links to Internet open sites in which copyrighted works were unlawfully made available to the public (CJEU judgment of 26 April 2017, case C527/15, *Stichting Brein*, ECLI:EU:C:2017:300), the provision and management on the Internet of a sharing platform which, through the indexation of metadata relating to protected works and the provision of a search engine, its users to find such works and share them within a decentralized (peer-to-peer) network (CJEU judgment of 14 June 2017, case C-610/15, *Stichting Brein II*, ECLI:EU:C:2017:456 - "The Pirate Bay"); and the supply to private individuals by a commercial company of a service of remote recording in the cloud of private copies of copyrighted works, through a computer system, actively intervening in the act of recording such copies without the authorization of the rights holder (CJEU judgment of 29 November 2017, case C265/16, *VCAST*, ECLI:EU:C:2017:913).

The proposal for a Directive of the European Parliament and of the Council on copyright in the digital single market (SWD (2016) 301 final) provides in Article 13 that, in order to communicate to the public works uploaded by users of its services, service providers information society need authorization from the authors, unless they are exempted from liability under Article 14 of Directive 2000/31 on electronic commerce (server-based storage). For this purpose, it is necessary to know whether, regardless of the means, providers of online sharing services play an active role, for ex. optimizing the presentation of the works. In addition to safeguarding free uses such as the right to quotation, the inclusion of short excerpts and uses for criticism or parody, the European Parliament stresses that the definition of an online content-sharing service provider should cover only providers of information society services whose main purpose is to store and allow public access to, or streaming, significant quantities of copyrighted content uploaded by their users, and which they optimize with profit purposes, namely by displaying, identifying, retaining and sequencing them, irrespective of the means used for that purpose. Where providers of sharing platforms play an active role they cannot benefit from the exemption from liability provided for in Article 14 of the Directive 2000/31/EC. Recital 37-A added by the European Parliament makes it clear that the definition of an online content-sharing service provider does not cover: (a) micro-enterprises and small enterprises within the meaning of Title I of the Annex to Commission Recommendation 2003/361/EC; b) non-commercial service providers, such as online encyclopaedias (e.g. the "Wikipedia" exception); c) on-line service providers when the content is loaded with the authorization of all right holders concerned, such as scientific or educational repositories; d) providers of cloud computing services for individual use that do not provide direct access to the public; e) open source software development platforms; (f) online markets whose main activity is the on-line retail sale of physical goods. In any case, the European Parliament asserts the principle that providers of online content sharing services communicate copyrighted works to the public by storing and allowing access to large quantities of works and other protected material uploaded by the their users, and should therefore enter into fair and adequate licensing agreements with rightholders (Article 13). Where rightholders do not authorize such use, such providers should cooperate to ensure that works are not available on their platforms, without prejudice to the free uses of copyrighted works, avoiding in any case the automatic blocking of content. The European Parliament refuses to impose on these providers the application of content recognition technologies (aka blocking filters), without prejudice of implementing best practices, which require due consideration for fundamental rights, the safeguard of exceptions and limitations, to ensure that the burden on SMEs remains adequate and, finally, to avoid automatic blocking of content (new Recital 39-A).

It should also be remarked that the proposal provides new compulsory exceptions: search of data and works for scientific research purposes (Article 3), distance learn-

bringing censorship to the internet by means of «copyright filters»[28]. Bots (software) would be liable for errors in implementing a "take-down and notice" policy. It is the whole problem of applying the rule of law to Code[29], and the regulation of Cyberspace, in which legislation is often based on existing self-regulation schemes, validating and enforcing them as a State law[30]. Notwithstanding, an explicit obligation to apply content recognition technologies upon sharing platforms has been removed by the European Parliament, which has introduced other substantial amendments to the proposal[31].

---

ing at school facilities or via secure electronic network accessible only by students, students and teaching staff (Article 4), and the preservation of the cultural heritage by institutions responsible for cultural heritage, such as libraries or museums accessible to the public, archives, institutions responsible for the cinematographic or sound heritage (Article 5). In the amendments adopted by the European Parliament on 12 September 2018, university libraries are «research bodies» for purposes of these exceptions. Finally, the European Parliament has added a new Art. 12-A enshrining a right for organizers or sports events (the ECJ has denied copyright protection to sporting events, including football matches, because they are governed by rules that leave no room for creative freedom - judgments of 4 October 2011, joined Cases C-403/08 and C-429/08, *Premier League*, ECLI:EU:C:2011:631), and has also established compulsory licensing for the use of copyrighted content by providers of information society services that perform automated image referencing services (so-called memes) that reproduce in publicly available protected works (Article 13-B).

[28] Similar concerns have been raised by the ACTA Treaty, see e.g. Michael D. TAYLOR, «The Global System of Copyright Enforcement: Regulations, Policies and Politics», in Irini A. STAMATOUDI (dir.), *Copyright Enforcement and the Internet*, Alphen an deen Rijn, Wolters Kluwers, 2010, p. 65-116; Henning G. RUSE-KHAN, «The Impact of the Anti-Counterfeiting Trade Agreement on the Legal Framework for IP Enforcement in the European Union», in Christoph GEIGER (dir.), *Constructing European Intellectual Property Law*, Cheltenham, Edward Elgar, 2013, p. 394; Christoph GEIGER, «Assessing the Implications of the Anti-Counterfeiting Trade Agreement for the European Union: Legitimate Aim but Wrong Means», in Pedro ROFFE et Xavier SEUBA (dir.), *The ACTA and the Plurilateral Enforcement Agenda: Genesis and Aftermath*, Cambridge, Cambridge University Press, 2014, p. 31.

[29] See Lawrence LESSIG, *Code 2.0*, New York, Basic Books, 2006.

[30] P. Bernd HUGENHOLTZ, «Codes of Conduct and Copyright Enforcement in Cyberspace», in Irini A. STAMATOUDI (dir.), *Copyright Enforcement and the Internet*, Alphen an deen Rijn, Wolters Kluwer, 2010, p. 303, 313.

[31] EUROPEAN PARLIAMENT, *Copyright in the Digital Single Market*. Amendments adopted by the European Parliament on 12 September 2018 on the proposal for a directive of the European Parliament and of the Council on copyright in the Digital Single Market (COM(2016)0593).

Technological remedies provided by the 1996 WIPO Treaties on Copyright and on the Rights of Artists and Producers of Phonograms on the Internet have been implemented in EU law by Directive 2001/29. They consist of a general prohibition of neutralization of effective technological measures for the protection of copyright and related rights, as well as of the removal or alteration of electronic information for the management of rights imbedded in digital files containing protected works and services. The prohibition against neutralization is not absolute, since neutralization can be justified. In *Nintendo*[32], the Court of Justice ruled that a system for protecting a gaming console could be lawful in certain circumstances, since the console manufacturer is protected against neutralization only if the protective measures intended to prevent the illegal use of video games.

Other precautionary measures

Directive 2004/48 provides other precautionary measures such as the seizure or order of delivery of goods suspected of infringing intellectual property rights, in order to prevent their entry into circulation in commercial circuits[33], and seizure of assets of the alleged infringer acting on a commercial scale, including the blocking of his bank accounts and the 'freezing' of other assets (the socalled *Mareva* injunction).

The court may order these measures without hearing the other party (*ex parte*), and subject them to the provision by the applicant of a guarantee or other equivalent guarantee that ensures the

---

[32] CJEU judgment of 23 January 2014, case C-355/12, *Nintendo*, ECLI:EU:C:2014:25

[33] Providers of online marketplaces should also be targeted by injunctions in the field of copyright, as the Court of Justice held concerning trademarks in judgment of 12 July 2011, case C-324/09, *L'Oréal,* ECLI:EU:C:2011:474.

compensation of damages suffered by the defendant by virtue of its application. The precautionary measures are revoked or lapse if the applicant does not bring the main action within a reasonable time, which may be 20 working days or 31 consecutive days, whichever is longer.

Merits of the case

Measures resulting from a decision on the merits of the case include corrective measures, injunctions, damages and costs.

Corrective measures concern pirated goods and materials used in their manufacture. They include, for example, the withdrawal from commercial channels or the destruction of property at the expenses of the pirate. The enforcement of these remedies shall respect the principle of proportionality, taking into account the seriousness of the infringement vis-à-vis the measures enacted and the interests of third parties.

Inhibitory and alternative measures (articles 11 and 12) consist in the prohibition of continuation of the infraction, subject to a periodic penalty payment intended to compel the defendant to comply with the injunction. Alternatively, the court may order payment of monetary compensation if the offense is innocent and the harm caused by the prohibition is disproportionate, provided that such payment is reasonably satisfactory. This is a 'strict liability' remedy, since even without fault the author of the unlawful act must compensate the right holder for the use made[34].

---

[34] Cf. Michael M. WALTER et Dominik GOEBEL, «Enforcement directive», in Silke *von LEWINSKI* et Michel M. *WALTER (dir.), European Copyright Law: A Commentary*, OUP, Oxford, 2010, p. 1193, 1298.

Calculation of damages

Under the TRIPS Agreement, compensation for damages must cover loss and expenses incurred by the successful party in connection with the proceedings, including attorneys' fees; in appropriate cases and where the offense is innocent, compensation shall include the profits made by the innocent infringer (account of profits) and / or the payment of statutory damages.

Directive 2004/48 does not entirely follow the TRIPS compensation scheme. Rather it provides in article 13 that the damage will correspond to actual loss, including economic damage and, in appropriate cases, moral harm; economic damages include both loss of profit and profits unjustly made by the offender, mixing indemnification (civil liability) and unjust enrichment[35]. Alternatively, a fixed amount can be awarded, including at least the remuneration that would have been paid if a license fee had been asked for. However, although the directive provides for this alternative, the Court of Justice held that the compensation may amount to unpaid royalties or fees plus moral harm[36], or twice the royalties[37]. In any event, according to the preamble to Directive 2004/48, recital (26), the purpose is not to introduce 'punitive damages', but rather to enable damages to be compensated on the basis of an 'objective criterion', which aims to encompass different traditions among

---

[35] Traditionally, in the UK, the injured would be entitled to compensation for damages actually suffered or, as an alternative, the right to a *reasonable royalty* corresponding to *account of profits* obtained by the infringer, to prevent the so-called "double counting" (William CORNISH, David LLEWELYN, Tanya APLIN, *Intellectual Property: Patents, Copyright, Trade Marks and Allied Rights*, 8th ed., London, Sweet & Maxwell, 2013, p. 108). Furthermore, the *account of profits*, as an *equitable discretionary remedy*, would not apply to *innocent infringers* – Charlotte SCOTT, «Damages Inquiries and Accounts of Profits in the IPEC», (2016) 38/5 *EIPR* 273, 277. However, the TRIPS Agreement and EU Directive 2004/48 seem to cumulate actual harm and account of profits, and does not exempt innocent infringement from account of profits.

[36] CJEU judgment of 17 March 2016, case C-99/15, *Liffers*, ECLI:EU:C:2016:173.

[37] CJEU judgment of 25 January 2017, case C-367/15, *OTK v SFP*, ECLI:EU:C:2017:36.

Member States concerning the calculation of damages, and which may set as the double or even the triple of the license fee.

On the other hand, as provided by the TRIPS Agreement, Directive 2004/48 allows Member States to provide compensation for cases of innocent breach, consisting in the recovery of the profits made by the offender or the payment of damages suffered (actual harm), which may be pre-established. This way the right holder can be compensated for unjust enrichment by means of the profits made by the other party[38] or by statutory damages and which correspond at least to unpaid royalties or fees, i.e., the so-called 'market price'[39].

On the other hand, Directive 2004/48 allows that court costs and other reasonable expenses incurred by the winner of the proceedings be borne by the unsuccessful party, as long as the court a quo finds it fair (article 14). In that regard, the Court of Justice has already decided that legal costs include costs relating to an exequatur procedure brought in a Member State[40]. It should be recalled that, under the TRIPS Agreement, attorneys' fees and / or consultants' fees are also eligible for compensation.

Finally, the court may order the publication, in full or in part, of judicial decisions, at the request of the claimant and at the expense of the violator (article 15).

Standing

Directive 2004/48 provides standing to those who present themselves in the work as its author (the presumption of authorship

[38] Phillip JOHNSON, «Damages in European law and the traditional accounts of profit», (2013) ¾ *Queen Mary Journal of Intellectual Property* 296, 296.

[39] Michael M. WALTER et Dominik GOEBEL, «Enforcement directive», in Silke *von LEWINSKI* et Michel M. *WALTER (dir.), European Copyright Law: A Commentary*, OUP, Oxford, 2010, p. 1193, 1310.

[40] CJEU judgment of 18 October 2011, case C-406/09, *Realchemie*, ECLI:EU:C:2011:668.

of the Berne Convention), the holders of licenses, professional rights advocacy bodies, and rights management collective bodies.[41] Collecting societies and professional bodies are not authors, but they are usually granted powers to enforce rights.

In *Guidance on certain aspects of Directive 2004/84*, the Commission refers to other remedies that could be adopted in the revision of the Directive[42]. One is a kind of negative declarative action, that is, a process that allows someone receiving a communication from the copyright holder alleging infringement of its rights, to obtain from the court a declaration of non-infringement (*protective brief*).

Conclusion

European Union law plays an important role in the implementation of international remedies for IP enforcement. In addition to the Customs Control Regulation, the IPRED harmonizes the means of protecting intellectual property rights. Without being a mere copy of the TRIPS Agreement, Directive 2004/48 envisages solutions that essentially meet the - and, in some areas, go beyond - the standards of the international agreement. It establishes measures to obtain and to preserve evidence, a right to information on the origin and networks of piracy, provisional measures and other precautionary measures, as well as remedies arising from decisions on the merits of the case, including remedial measures, injunctions and alternatives, damages, costs and publication of decisions.

Directive 2004/48 is not directly applicable. Instead, it requires transposition into the legal order of each Member State. In any case,

---

[41] Concerning trademarks, see CJEU judgment of 7 August 2018, case C-521/17, *SNB-REACT*, ECLI:EU:C:2018:639.

[42] *Guidance on certain aspects of Directive 2004/48/EC of the European Parliament and of the Council on the enforcement of intellectual property rights*, COM(2017) 708 final.

it has established a harmonized set of means of protection in the light of (but not limited to) the TRIPs Agreement, thereby contributing to the protection of intellectual property in the European Union effectively respecting international standards. The Court has played an important role in issuing judgments in a number of preliminary rulings on the interpretation of provisions of the Directive, and its rulings illuminate national courts where applying EU law.

The Enforcement Directive is under revision. The Commission intends to strengthen the "*Follow the Money*"[43] approach. The question of criminal protection is once again open for discussion. It is true that the TRIPS Agreement establishes criminal protection at least for copyright piracy and trademark counterfeiting in the case of commercial-scale activities. However, this apparent shortage of criminal protection is the result of the limited powers of the European Union, which has virtually no powers to intervene within the so-called sovereign functions of the Member States (political organization, defence and internal security, diplomatic relations and criminal justice). Criminal protection of intellectual property is a matter reserved to the legislation of each Member State, which will fully respond to the international standards set out in the TRIPS Agreement.

[43] *Towards a renewed consensus on the enforcement of Intellectual Property Rights: An EU Action Plan*, COM(2014) 392 final.

PATENT VALIDITY IN ARBITRATION? A *VEXATA QUAESTIO* CONCERNING GENERIC MEDICINES*

Abstract - In order to improve the use of generic drugs, Portugal has established mandatory arbitration for disputes between patent holders and applicants of generics. However, the scope of jurisdiction of this arbitration raises several questions, notably whether the arbitration court can, *inter partes* and *incidenter tantum,* invalidate such patents, and a divergence between the Supreme Court of Justice and the Constitutional Court of Portugal has emerged and is pending on this question.

Introduction

Portugal has established a court with specialized jurisdiction on matters of intellectual property, the Court of Intellectual Property.[1] At the same time, specific procedural remedies were set forth for the protection of pharmaceutical patents. The financial crisis urged Portugal to cut public spending on health care, notably by means of enabling generics to reach a market share similar to that of many EU Member States.

---

* European Intellectual Property Review, vol. 41/2, p. 107-110, 2019, published by Sweet & Maxwell (imprint of Thomson Reuters)

[1] Article 111(1)(c) of the Statue of Judiciary Organization enacted by Law No. 62/2013, of 26 August.

Law No 62/2011 of 12 December has expressly detached the administrative process of authorization to market generics from the existence and infringement of industrial property rights, in line with Articles 10(6) and 126 of Directive 2001/83[2] and the *Bolar* rule[3]; the same applies to subsequent assignments of authorizations to market generis.[4] Law No 62/2011 has also ammended the Statute of Medicines[5] and the general regulation of state co-payment of medicines[6], and provided that IP holders concerning reference medicines have to resort to (mandatory) arbitration to solve conflicts with applicants of approval of generic medicines. However, the scope of jurisdiction of this mandatory arbitration has raised controversial issues, in particular its scope of jurisdiction concerning patent validity.

On December 2016, the Portuguese Supreme Court of Justice ruled that mandatory arbitration courts established by Law 62/2011 cannot invalidate pharmaceutical patents because the Court of

---

[2] Directive 2001/83/EC of the European Parliament and of the Council of 6 November 2001 on the Community code relating to medicinal products for human use, OJ L 311, 28.11.2001. This was also the opinion given by the Supreme Administrative Court (STA) in several judgments, notably of 21 November 2013, case n. 08226/11, available at <www.dgsi.pt>.

[3] This rule prevents the artificial extension of the patent term so that generics can enter into the market immediately upon the expiry of a patent (or of a supplementary protection certificate) regarding a reference medicine. See J. Straus, 'The Bolar exemption and the supply of patented active pharmaceutical ingredients to generic drug producers: an attempt to interpret Article 10(6) of Directive 2004/270', *Journal of Intellectual Property Law & Practice* 9/11 (2014), p. 895-908. In 2000, a WTO Panel found that a similar provision introduced into Canadian law - the so-called exception for 'regulatory review' - complied with the TRIPS Agreement, in special with Article 30 on exceptions to the exclusive rights. Canada — Patent Protection of Pharmaceutical Products, Panel Report, WT/DS114/R (17 March 2000). Cf. G. Ritter, 'Recent Developments in WTO Dispute Settlement Dispute under the TRIPs Agreement', In *International Intellectual Property Law & Policy* - Vol. 7 ed. H. Hansen H, Juris Publishing Huntington, p. 73-11). In Portugal, see also Article 102(c) of the Industrial Property Code, enacted by Decree-Law No. 36/2003, of 5 March, as later amended.

[4] See more recently the STJ judgment of 17 May 2018, case no. 889/17.4YRLSB.S1, and the Lisbon Court of Appeal judgment of 24 April 2018, case no. 1334/17.2YRLSB-1.

[5] Decree-Law No 176/2006, of 30 August.

[6] Approved as Annex to Decree-Law No. 48-A/2010 of 13 May.

Intellectual Property has exclusive jurisdiction to revoke patents under Article 35 of the Industrial Property Code (IPC) and Article 111(1)(c) of the Statute of Judiciary Organization.[7]

A few months later, on May 2017, the Constitutional Court of Portugal followed the opposite position, holding that it would be unconstitutional to deny the mandatory arbitration court jurisdiction to invalidate *incidenter tantum* and *inter parties* a pharmaceutical patent, as it would excessively restrict the defendant's right of defence to a fair trial.[8]

On March 2018, the Supreme Court of Justice ruled again that the lack of jurisdiction of the mandatory arbitration court to invalidate *inter partes* and *incidenter tantum* a pharmaceutical patent does not disproportionally restrict the right of defence because the holder of a generic approval can bring nullity or annulment proceedings before the Court of Intellectual Property.[9]

Arguments against the competence of the arbitration courts to invalidate drug patents

Against the competence of the arbitration court to decide on patent validity there is a leading case of the Supreme Court of Justice concerning registered trademarks[10] and three main arguments.

---

[7] STJ judgment of 14 December 2016, case no. 1248/14.6YRLSB.S1.

[8] TC judgment of 24 May 2017, case no. 297/16.

[9] STJ judgment of 22 March 2018, case no. 1053/16.5YRLSB.S1.S1.

[10] STJ judgment of 3 February 1999, case n. 98A1093, concerning registered trademarks. See notably P. Sousa e Silva, *Direito Industrial (Noções Fundamentais)*, Coimbra, Almedina, 2011, p. 488, L. Couto Gonçalves, *Manual de Direito Industrial*, 5ª ed., Almedina, Coimbra, 2014, p. 317, n. 780; E. Mendes, 'Arbitragem Necessária. Invalidade de patente, direito a uma tutela jurisdicional efetiva e questões conexas', *Pi – Propriedades intelectuais* 3 (2015), p. 103-110; M Ohen Mendes, 'Breves considerações sobre a incompetência dos tribunais arbitrais portugueses para apreciarem a questão da invalidade das patentes e dos certificados complementares de proteção

To begin with, the presumption of validity of registered industrial rights (Article 4(2) IPC). Then, the wording of Article 35 IPC, according to which 'a declaration of nullity or annulment can result only from a judicial decision' (para. 1) in proceedings brought by the Public Prosecutor or by any interested party, and to which the holder of the right in question as well as all those who have applied for registration of derivative rights (e.g. licenses or securities), are given notice of (para. 2).[11] The rational of the exclusive jurisdiction of State courts lies upon the public interest in the system of statutory exclusive rights, which as monopoly-like rights entail limits to the freedom of entreprise of other operators, including competitors. i.e., it is a matter of economic public order.

In several cases, the Lisbon Court of Appeal has denied jurisdiction of arbitration to revoke patents[12], arguing that, otherwise, the parties would jointly exploit a patent, which the arbitration tribunal considers invalid, and therefore, they would be sharing a monopoly, which the State granted only to the patentee and which remains enforceable against third parties. It would be contrary to the public interest underlying the principle of the statutory exclusive rights. Moreover, legal certainty would not be compatible with divergent decisions on the validity of the patent. Finally, the defendant's right of defence remain unaffected since he can always raise the issue of patent invalidity before the IP state court.

---

para medicamentos', in *Estudos de Direito Intelectual em Homenagem ao Prof. Doutor José de Oliveira Ascensão,* ed. D. Moura Vicente et al., Coimbra, Almedina, 2015, p. 927-947; A. L. Dias Pereira, 'Da arbitragem necessária de litígios entre patentes e medicamentos genéricos no direito português', *Boletim da Faculdade de Direito da Universidade de Coimbra*, vol. 92/2 (2016), p. 827-848.

[11] The final decision is published on the Industrial Property Bulletin and registered - Article 33(4) IPC.

[12] See e.g. Lisbon Court of Appeal judgments of 4 February 2016, case n. 138-15.0YRLSB.L1-8, and, more recently, judgment of 21 June 2018, case no. 227/18.9YRLSB.L1-2.

Arguments pro the jurisdiction of the arbitration court to invalidate drug patents (*incidenter tantum* and *inter parties*)

Several authors[13] argued in favour of the jurisdiction of the arbitration court to invalidate patents. They maintain that the decision of the arbitral court would be limited to the parties (*inter partes*), and could be taken only where the issue of patent validity is raised as a defence or incidentally (*incidenter tantum*).

In favour of this opinion, to begin with, it is invoked the basic right of access to the courts, as a basic dimension of a fair and equitable process.[14] Because it is a mandatory arbitration court, and

---

[13] See notably D. Moura Vicente, 'O regime especial de resolução de conflitos em matéria de patentes (Lei n.° 62/2011)', *Revista da Ordem dos Advogados* 72/III (2012), p. 971-990; J.P. Remédio Marques, 'A apreciação da validade de patentes (ou certificados complementares de protecção) por tribunal arbitral necessário - Excepção *versus* reconvenção na Lei n° 62/2011', *Boletim da Faculdade de Direito de Coimbra* vol. 87 (2011), p. 197-212; Id., 'A arbitrabilidade da exceção de invalidade de patente no quadro da Lei n.° 62/2011', *Revista de Direito Intelectual* 2014/2, p. 211-257. Concerning international arbitration, with reference to several court decisions in comparative law, notably judgment of 28 February 2008 from the Court of Appeal of Paris in *Liv Hidravlika v. Diebolt* and holding that arbitration courts should have jurisdiction on patent validity, T. Cook & A.I. Garcia, *International Intellectual Property Arbitration*, Alphen aan den Rijn, Wolters Kluwer, 2010, p. 49-76. The Court of Appeal of Lisbon has also taken this position for ex. in judgment of 9 July 2015, case n. 336/15.6YRLSB.L1.-1.

[14] The basic right of access to the courts under Article 20 of the Portuguese Constitution was also at stake, concerning the nature of the term of 30-days to initiate arbitration proceedings after the publication of generic application for approval provided under Article 3 (1) of Law 62/2011. In several cases, the arbitral courts decided that it is a final term, in that it forfeits the right to oppose patents to the applicants of generics before not only State courts but also arbitration, concerning the same drug. The Lisbon Court of Appeal found in several cases that the duration of this term is final and that it complies with the basic right of access to the courts. It was not arbitrarily short nor unsuitable for the exercise of patent rights and therefore it did not infringe the relevant provisions of the TRIPs Agreement and of Directive 2004/48 on enforcement of intellectual property rights (judgment of 30 September 2014, case n. 512/14.9YRLSBA). However, asked to decide about the constitutionality of this interpretation, the Constitutional Court, in a first judgment, found that that the right of access to justice and to a fair and equitable procedure could not accept an interpretation of the 30-day term to initiate arbitration proceedings as a final term. Taking into account the particular complexity of the issues it would not be sufficient to afford judicial protection to intellectual property due to the lack of information available to the patentee at the time he would have to

taking into account the constitutional equivalence between state and arbitration courts[15], it should have jurisdiction to hear all questions necessarily submitted before it.[16] Otherwise, the principle of a fair and equitable process would be compromised as one of the parties would be prevented from carrying into the proceedings relevant arguments for the decision of the dispute. Moreover, in practice, arbitrators do not stay proceedings and do not wait for the judges of the IP court to rule on the validity of the patent. Accordingly, arbitrators would have to decide upon a patent, which they may consider invalid, in particular for lack of novelty or inventive step, despite the rebuttable presumption of validity of the registered right.

The Supreme Court of Justice says no

Apparently this question had been fixed by a judgment of the Supreme Court in December 2016[17], according to which the IP court has exclusive jurisdiction to invalidate patents and, therefore, mandatory arbitration cannot invalidate *inter parties* a pharmaceutical patent even where the issue is raised *incidenter tantum*. This case involved two pharmaceutical companies from different European

---

initiate arbitration proceedings (TC judgment n. 123/2015 of 12 February 2015, case n. 763/13). However, later on, the Lisbon Court of Appeal did not follow the ruling of the Constitutional Court, notably in its judgments of 22 October 2015, case n. 923-15.2YRLSB-8, and of 4 February 2016, case n. 138-15.0YRLSB.L1-8. Asked again about this question, the Constitutional Court decided that it is not against the Constitution to prevent the patent holder to sue the applicant of a generic medicine after the expiration of the 30 days term, in judgment no. 187/2018 of 10 April 2018, case n. 41/2017. In our opinion, this solution best serves the useful meaning of the 30-days term – A.L. Dias Pereira, 'Mandatory arbitration for patents vs. generics in Portuguese law', *Medicine and Law* vol. 35/4 (2016) p. 525-540.

[15] Article 209(2) of the Portuguese Constitution.

[16] Articles 91, 571, and 573(1) of Code of Civil Procedure.

[17] STJ judgment of 14 December 2016, case no. 1248/14.6YRLSB.S1 (full text and summary available at Kluwer IP Law Patent Cases).

countries and a manufacturer of generics established in Portugal. The plaintiffs and appellants asked the court to order the defendant to refrain, under Article 101 IPC, from producing, selling or otherwise using in trade a generic medicament containing a substance protected by a European patent. Moreover, they wanted the defendant to refrain from assigning to third parties the approval of the generic, under application of a penalty payment.

The defendant argued the invalidity of the disputed patent so that it could not prohibit the exploitation of the generic. The plaintiffs contested that the arbitration court does not have jurisdiction to revoke the patent and the arbitration court ultimately declined jurisdiction. The defendant appealed to the Court of Appeal of Lisbon, which has decided that the arbitration court has jurisdiction to invalidate patents but only *inter partes*. The main the argument is that Article 91(1) of the Code of Civil Procedure – which should apply to arbitration - provides that the power of the court to decide the main action also concerns all issues raised by the defendant as a means of defence.

The plaintiffs then appealed to the Supreme Court of Justice (STJ), which has denied jurisdiction to the arbitration tribunal to invalidate a patent as a registered right. The STJ found this solution proportional and adequate, holding that the rational of the exclusive jurisdiction of the IP court lies upon the nature of the disputed right, the constituting nature of the act of granting industrial property rights as well as systematic coherence and the public interest. The exception to the principle of civil procedure would not mean any deviation from the right of defence and the *audi alteram partem* principle, nor from the principle of a fair and equitable procedure.

In the opinion of the STJ, the applicant for a generic whiling to question the validity of a registered patent has to bring proceedings before the IP court, and ask the arbitration court to stay the proceedings until the issue is decided by the competent court. In the opinion of the STJ, these alternative procedural mechanisms are not an excessive burden to the applicant and are adequate to solve his right to question the validity of the patent that prevents the exploitation of the generic medicine. For these reasons, the necessary proceedings would not infringe the basic right of access to the court.[18]

The Constitutional Court says yes

A few months later, the Constitutional Court ruled that the impossibility of a generic applicant to argue, *incidenter tantum*, the invalidity of the patent, would not meet the constitutional guarantee of access to law and effective court protection, in particular the right to a fair hearing under Article 20 (4) of the Portuguese Constitution.[19]

The Court hold that the restriction to the right of defence may be justified by basic rights, public order and uniformity of criteria in the administration of justice, and that it may even be necessary and indispensable, as the defendant can challenge the patent before the IP court in proceedings to which interested third parties are called. Nevertheless, the impossibility to have the validity of the patent decided by the mandatory arbitration court would be an excessive burden. To begin with, in light of Article 272 of Civil Procedure Code, the arbitrators do not always stay the proceedings, and therefore they would have to decide in favour of the patent. Then, the generic applicant may not be interested in having the patent revoked, as it will also benefit competitors, and therefore, if the arbitration court

[18] For comments on this judgment see L. Couto Gonçalves, 'A questão da competência do tribunal arbitral necessário para apreciar a invalidade da patente com eficácia *inter partes*', *RDI - Revista de Direito Intelectual* 2017/1, p. 363-380 (concuring and hoping that it fixes 'case-law'); J.P. Remédio Marques, '*Bis in idem*: em torno da competência dos tribunais arbitrais necessários para apreciar a questão da invalidade da patente com efeitos *inter partes*', *Revista de Direito Intelectual* 2017/1, p. 305-362 (disagreeing).

[19] TC judgment no. 251/2017 of 24 May 2017, case no. 297/16 (full text and summary available at Kluwer IP Law Patent Cases).

could not invalidate the patent *inter parties*, the sacrifice caused to him would be much damaging than that caused to the patent holder.[20]

Arguably, this judgment disregards the guarantee of an appeal before the state court against the arbitration award and, to that extent, departs from previous decisions of the Constitutional Court itself on the constitutionality of the mandatory arbitration in sports as well as on IP and generic medicines.[21]

The Supreme Court of Justice says no, again

On March 2018, contrary to the ruling of the Constitutional Court, the Supreme Court of Justice ruled again that the mandatory arbitration court does not have jurisdiction to invalidate a patent, even if merely *inter parties* and *incidenter tantum*. The defence rights of generic sellers would not be disproportionally restricted because they can bring nullity or annulment proceedings before the Court of Intellectual Property.[22]

What does it mean to have a patent and why does the Court of Intellectual Property have exclusive jurisdiction to revoke it?

The granting of a patent 'implies a mere presumption of the legal requirements of its granting' (Article 4 (2) IPC). The rights

[20] A full summary of this case is available at Kluwer IP Law. The Lisbon Court of Appeal has later followed this ruling at least in two cases: judgments of 10 April 2018, case no. 861.16.1YRLSB.L1-1, and of 21 June 2018, case no. 2384/17.2YRLSB.L1-8.

[21] See A.L. Dias Pereira, 'Da invalidade da patente na arbitragem necessária relativa a medicamentos genéricos - Anotação ao acórdão do Tribunal Constitucional n.º 251/2017, de 24 de maio de 2017', *Revista de Legislação e Jurisprudência*, 147/4008 (2018), p. 198-210.

[22] STJ judgment of 22 March 2018, case no. 1053/16.5YRLSB.S1.S1.

conferred by the patent include the exclusive right to exploit the patented invention in any part of the Portuguese territory as well as the right to prevent third parties from making, offering, storing, placing on the market or using a patentable product or importing or possessing it for any of such purposes (Article 101 (1) and (2) IPC).

In order to be patented, an invention must be new, involve an inventive step, be capable of industrial application, and not be excluded from the limitations on the object (e.g. discoveries) and on the patent (e.g. public order and good customs), pursuant to Articles 51 to 57 of IPC, which incorporates international standards. The legal presumption of validity and effectiveness of the patent admits evidence to the contrary, pursuant to Article 350 (2) of the Civil Code. For this purpose, a judicial procedure of declaration of nullity or annulment is required (Article 35 and 36 IPC).

Exclusive rights are a matter of *economic public order*. They limit the freedom of enterprise of third parties. Reasons of legal certainty require registration of such rights to be enforceable *erga omnes*. Registration entails a presumption of validity. The legal protection of these rights means also that only State courts can revoke them and by means of a specific procedure, to which all interested parties are called to (for ex. licence holders).

Article 3(7) of Law 62/2011 guarantees an appeal from the arbitration award to a State Court of Appeal. The Constitutional Court, in its judgment no. 435/2016, of 13 July (case 744/15), ruled in favour of the mandatory arbitration established by Law no. 62/2011, because it gives State courts the last word in the resolution of these disputes. The same argument had already convinced the Constitutional Court concerning the constitutionality of the mandatory sports arbitration court.[23]

[23] TC judgment no. 230/2013, of 9 May 2013, case no. 279/2013.

Then, the argument of forcing the applicant to undergo a preventive defence or to defend the economic interests of competitors and the public interest can hardly be an 'excessive burden' to the defendant, because it is not reasonable to expect to benefit from an invalid patent as if it were valid. It is a matter of economic public order the existence or not of statutory exclusive rights such as those conferred by patents and other industrial property rights.[24] The registration of a patent grants a monopoly-like right, and a presumption of validity and effectiveness of the patent. The presumption exempts the proof of the right, but it does not prevent third parties from making a case against the patent.

The Court of Justice of the European Union interpreted the rule of exclusive jurisdiction of *forum rei sitae* provided in the Brussels Convention, and decided in *GAT* that the rule of exclusive jurisdiction[25] covers all disputes relating to the registration or validity of a patent, whether the question is raised by way of action or by way of exception.[26] This interpretation has been incorporated in Article 22 (4) of the Lugano Convention of 2007 on jurisdiction and the recognition and enforcement of judgments in civil and commercial matters ('whether the question is raised action by way of exception') and Article 24 (4) of Regulation Brussels I recast ('irrespective of whether the issue is raised by way of an action or as a defence').[27] The justification for the exclusive jurisdiction of the courts of the country of registration is, on the one hand, the granting of the

[24] Considering 'legally chocking' the judgment of the Constitutional Court for allowing an unreasonable and unproportional excessive defence, L. Couto Gonçalves, *Manual de Direito Industrial,* 7th ed. Coimbra, Almedina, 2017, p. 125-6, n. 292.

[25] Article 16 (4) of the Convention of 27 September 1968 on Jurisdiction and the Enforcement of Judgments in Civil and Commercial Matters.

[26] Judgment of 13 July 2006, case C-4/03, *Gesellschaft für Antriebstechnik mbH & Co. KG c. Lamellen und Kupplungsbau Beteiligungs KG*, ECLI:EU:C:2006:457.

[27] Regulation (EU) no.1215/2012 of the European Parliament and of the Council of 12 December 2012 on jurisdiction and the recognition and enforcement of judgments in civil and commercial matters (repealed and replaced Regulation 44/2001).

exclusive right as a manifestation of national sovereignty (the so-called *act of state doctrine*) and, on the other hand, the principles of good administration of justice and legal security.[28]

Detaching the procedure of approval of generic drugs from the existence and infringement of industrial property rights does not authorize selling generics before the expiration or revocation of the patent. The party willing to sell generic medicines involving patents can ask the arbitration court to stay the proceedings. The arbitration court will then check whether there is a preliminary ruling as well as the conditions for the suspension of proceedings, according to Article 272(2) of the Code of Civil Procedure. In principle, the defendant will not raise the question of validity without good reasons, and the patent holder will not resort to shame litigation, risking revokation of the patent.

It is up to the arbitration court to hear all questions submitted to it, but patent validity is a matter of economic public policy, which prevails over the convenience of the parties and justifies the exclusive jurisdiction of the IP court. Moreover, the guarantee of appeal to State courts is the «cornerstone' that constitutionally protects the different mechanisms of mandatory arbitration, and the same should should be valid concerning the question of patent validity.

Eventually mandatory arbitration courts could have full jurisdiction to revoke patents according to the procedure provided for revocation by the Code of Industrial Property. There would be appeal from the decisions of this court and therefore full respect for the right of access to State courts. However, such a broader jurisdiction for mandatory arbitration should be provided by Statute.

---

[28] D. Moura Vicente, *A tutela internacional da propriedade intelectual*, Coimbra, Almedina, 2008, p. 376-8. For an argument against the exclusive jurisdiction rule, see B. Ubertazzi, *Exclusive Jurisdiction in Intellectual Property*, Tübingen, Mohr Siebeck, 2012.

… Just before the end of 2018 and in order to implement Directive (EU) 2015/2436 of the European Parliament and of the Council of 16 December 2015 to approximate the laws of the Member States relating to trade marks (Recast), and Directive (EU) 2016/943 of the European Parliament and of the Council of 8 June 2016 on the protection of undisclosed know-how and business information (trade secrets) against their unlawful acquisition, use and disclosure, a new Industrial Property Code has been enacted by Decree-Law No 110/2018 of 10 December. This Act has also amended arts 2 and 3 of Law No. 62/2011, abolishing the mandatory arbitration for patents v. generics and allowing the invalidity of a patent to be argued and recognized in (voluntary) arbitration proceedings. From the new wording of art. 3(3) of Law 62/2011 it is clear that arbitrators can recognize *inter partes* the invalidity of a patent, but the competence to revoke it lies nevertheless with the Court of Intellectual Property according to art. 34(1) of the new Code of Industrial Property

ROBOTIC SOFTWARE & INTELLECTUAL PROPERTY*

Abstract - Software executed by robots is protected by intellectual property rights? If so, which branch of IP applies to robotic software: copyright, patents, tradesecrets, all together? This paper focus on robots generated by humans and increasingly provided with artificial intelligence (AI). Will IP be an obstacle to the development of artificial intelligence or rather a stimulus in the evolutionary process?

Introduction

The robot is, basically, an automaton whose functionality, mobility and ability to communicate and learn depends on the model. The meaning of the word robot ranges from the toy dog-robot to Sofia, passing through the automatons of industrial production, especially in the automotive, electronic or textile sectors.

Robots execute instructions programmed in the form of software. The software is the computer program, i.e. the set of instructions performed or executed by a computer device, namely a computer or

---

* *Law and Technology – E.Tec Yearbook*, ed. M.M. Carvalho, Braga, 2018, 19-26. English version of the paper presented by the author at the Workshop on Law & Robotics organized by the Institute for Legal Research (Group 3) of the Faculty of Law of the University of Coimbra, on 16 November 2017.

a smartphone. Software has a source code, written in programming language (e.g. Basic, Cobol, Pascal, C ++, Java, Python, etc.) and an object code or executable file (in machine or binary language). There are several kinds of software: firmware, which is software embedded in the machine (e.g. ROM, BIOS); operating systems (iOS, Android, Windows); and applications (Office, Antivirus, Browsers, Games). In broad sense, software also includes software algorithms and documentation (program description and instruction manual), as well as databases or broad-based information that it processes (so-called 'dataware').

In the field of robotics, software is the centre of operations or commands of the robot, and the degree of intelligence of the robot depends on the software it performs or executes. The robot is often designed according to the image and likeness of its human creator, both in physical appearance and in behaviour and communication. However, robots do not all look human-like. Compare, for example, the Astro-mechanical droid *R2-D2* with the *C-3PO*, the latter an android of protocol, with shapes closer to humans, and which is presented in the following terms: "I am C-3PO, cyborg of human relations and fluent in 6 million different languages and speeches."

These characters from George Lucas's epic fiction *Star Wars* are mechanical (as opposed to biological) beings endowed with intelligence. Intelligence will evolve not only in communicational and behavioural terms, but also physically, with the *Hasbro Transformers*, alien robots that are able to turn their bodies into other objects like motor vehicles. Many of these beings are not even human creations, instead they come from worlds yet undiscovered and may pose a threat to the survival of the human species...

This paper focus on robots generated by humans and increasingly provided with artificial intelligence (AI), although not necessarily in human form. AI is a branch of computer sciences that looks for computational methods or devices capable of emulating the rational capacity of the human being to solve problems, to think or, in general, to act intelligently. That is the case of IBM's *Watson*, with relevant applications in healthcare and the legal sector, as well as in water, energy or traffic management systems. There is even mention of *Watson* overcoming *Google*: it is able not only to search information in the web, but also to process it in terms similar to human thinking, and it can be used on a smartphone. Legal challenges posed by technological advances impact several fields of law, from civil law to labour law, as well as administrative and tax law.

The European Parliament has passed a resolution of 16 February 2017 with recommendations to the Commission on Civil Law Rules on Robotics. In particular, it states "general principles concerning the development of robotics and artificial intelligence for civil use", notably a principle on intelectual property rights according to which "there are no legal provisions that specifically apply to robotics, but that existing legal regimes and doctrines can be readily applied to robotics, although some aspects appear to call for specific consideration; calls on the Commission to support a horizontal and technologically neutral approach to intellectual property applicable to the various sectors in which robotics could be employed".[1]

Legal protection of robotic software

This paper focus the legal protection of software executed by the robot, i.e., whether robotic software can and should be protected, and if so on what terms.

Robotic software, as a computer program, can be, and is, protected under intellectual property. The question has been raised

[1] European Parliament resolution of 16 February 2017 with recommendations to the Commission on Civil Law Rules on Robotics (2015/2103(INL)), para. 18.

more than half a century ago and it has been widely discussed, to the point that an author exclaimed about papers on the legal protection of software: "Not another one!"[2]

Some argued that software by its very nature should be protected as a technical invention by patent law, while others argued for the protection of computer programs under copyright law. A third way would be to assign a new sui generis protection to software, a mixture of patent and copyright. Finally, it was also possible to resort to the protection of trade secrets or technological know-how.

However, in 1973, the Munich Convention on the European Patent excluded the computer program as such from the subject matter of patents, and this exclusion was laid down in the domestic legislation of the contracting parties to that convention. In 1980, the US Copyright Act has been amended to grant copyright to computer programs.[3] In 1985, virtually all G7 countries adopted legislation in the same direction. In 1991 the European Community also enshrined the copyright solution, as later did several international intellectual property instruments such as the 1994 TRIPS Agreement and the 1996 WIPO Treaties.[4]

Copyright in the Software

In Europe, the Council Directive 91/250 of 14 May 1991 (later replaced by Directive 2009/24/EC) has harmonized the legal protection

[2] DWORKIN, G., «Copyrights, Patents and/or 'Sui Generis': What Regime Best Suits Computer Programs», in: *International Intellectual Property Law and Policy* (ed. HANSEN, H), I, London, Sweet & Maxwell, 1996, p. 165.

[3] Cf. MILLER, Arthur, "Copyright protection for computer programs, databases, and computer-generated works: is anything new since CONTU?", *Harvard Law Review*, 106/5 (1993), p. 977-1073, 985 ss.

[4] See, PEREIRA, Alexandre Dias, *Informática, direito de autor e propriedade tecno-digital*, Coimbra Editora, 2001, e VIEIRA, José Alberto, *A proteção jurídica do programa de computador pelo direito de autor*, Lex, Lisboa, 2005.

of computer programs. It has been implemented in Portugal by Decree-Law No 252/94 of October 20, which has provided a kind of "anomalous" or "improper" copyright.

Instead of amending the Copyright (and Related Rights) Act, domestic legislation drew up a specific statute for software.[5] In short, computer programs which, in their form of expression - including their preliminary design material (e.g. diagrams) - have a creative character (i.e. when they constitute intellectual creations) are protected (DL 252/94, art. 1/2). However, copyright does not protect the principles or algorithms implemented in the program, nor its functionality, but only the way in which they are presented, namely in source code.

Copyright belongs in principle to its intellectual creator. However, it can be assigned to a third party by contract and the law assigns it to the principal, the employer or the company where software is created, respectively, for hire, by employees, or within a company as a collective work (DL 252/94 art. 3, Copyright Act, art. 19). The moral rights of the creator of computer programs appear reduced to the right of paternity as the right to claim the authorship of the program and identification in the work (DL 252/94, art. 9). The right to the integrity of the work is deleted from moral rights, as article 15 (2) of the Copyright Act is excluded from computer programs (DL 252/94, art. 3/5). Said Article of the Copyright Act reads that "The right to make changes to the work depends of the express agreement of its creator and can only be exercised under the terms agreed upon." However, the courts do not exclude the moral right to integrity of the work, so that employers or acquirers of the program are prevented from freely modifying it.

With regard to economic rights, a broad concept of reproduction, as confirmed by the courts, and the right to produce and sell copies

[5] Belgian has also adopted a specific Act, Law of 30 June 1994. Cf. STROWEL, Alain/ TRIAILLE, Jean Paul, *Le droit d'auteur, du logiciel au multimedia*, Bruxelles, Bruylant, 1997, p. 136 s.

are listed (subject to EU exhaustion). The duration of the copyright is governed by the general rule of 70 years *post mortem auctoris* or, where rights belong to a legal person (e.g. a company), from its dissemination (Copyright Act, art. 36). In free use, comparing with copyright law in general, no freedom of reproduction is foreseen for private use of computer programs.

An innovative aspect of copyright that the directive introduced concerns the rights of the legitimate user (or license holder), who is provided with the rights to reproduce and to study the program in the context of its use, to make a backup copy, to reproduce and to modify the program for the purpose of correcting errors, including in our view reverse engineering strictly necessary for interoperability with independent program, and the use, for those purposes, of the information thus obtained. Users' rights are mandatory and do not detract from other means of software protection, namely patent law and protection of trade secrets (DL 252/94 arts. 6 and 7).

Patents for inventions related to computer programs

Is robotic software eligible for patent law protection?

The assignment of patents depends on the application fulfilling certain requirements. Patents concern technical inventions, i.e., works of the spirit on technical problems and that are not just mathematical or logical formulas. Technical inventions must be novel in the light of the state of the art and result from an inventive step, in the sense that they are not obvious. Finally, the invention must be susceptible of industrial application, i.e., capable of use in industry or agriculture.

The patent object does not cover all the works of the mind. Discoveries, scientific theories and mathematical methods, materials or substances already existing in nature and nuclear material, aesthetic creations, designs, principles and methods of engaging in intellectual activities in the field of games or in the field of economic activities, computer programs as such, without any contribution, and presentations of information, are not eligible for patents, unless the object for which the patent is applied is limited to the elements mentioned in it (Industrial Property Code, art. 52).

The provisions of the Munich Convention on the European Patent underpinning said internal system have not prevented the European Patent Office from granting patents to inventions relating to computer programs, in particular in the sector of medical devices. In the case of robots, reference is made to patent EP 1169092 B1 on a telescopic fire-fighting robot, controlled manually or remotely, and automatically connected to the water-channeling system and hung in a monorail in tunnels. According to the summary of the disclosure of the invention, the *fire-fighting robot* serves to extinguish fires in tunnels. It hangs in a carriage that runs on a monorail to the tunnel vault. An oil-dynamic telescopic piston allows transport to be reduced to the road surface. This feature allows the robot to overcome any obstacle, protect people and transport people without traffic obstacles and fight the fire. To have a continuous extinguishing of fire, the robot is connected to the water conduit by a flexible tube with 30 meters with an automatic arm.[6]

In the USA, patents do not meet a standard similar to CPE. There are software patents, including robotic software. This is the case, for example, of patent US 8996429 B1: methods and systems for the development of the *robotic personality*. According to the patent summary, the patented technology consists of methods and systems of interaction of the robot with the user in order to generate a personality of the robot. The robot can access a user's device to determine or identify information about a user's identity and the

[6] https://patents.google.com/patent/EP1169092B1/sv

robot can be configured to the user's measure with the identifiable information. The robot can find data associated with the user's identity through voice or facial recognition. The robot can provide a personalized interaction or response to the user based on the user's specified information. In some instances, the personality or personalization of a robot can be transferred from one robot to another (machine), and the information stored in one robot can be shared with another robot through the cloud.[7]

Patenting the brains of robots and robotic prostheses?

Should there be software patents on the logical component of the robot? The Free Software Foundation, created by Richard Stallman, launched the GNU GPL (General Public License) licenses ensuring the freedom to reproduce, modify, and/or distribute software. The use of free software developed by this community would be free, conditioned only to the duty to provide the license together with the software and to share the same freedom that is received. The idea is to prevent copyright and patents from impeding the free development of software, which is considered a language subject to the constitutional imperatives of free speech. In the EU, there is a European version of the GPL, the European Union Public License. Will patents deter the development of AI and the evolution of Robots? The rational of patents is the opposite: patents provide a stimulus to innovation by granting inventors with a temporary monopoly over a new product or process. So, the case may be that patents in robotic software contribute to the evolution of Artificial Intelligence.

Another question is whether pieces of the robot that replicate parts of the human body can be patented. Article 54(c) of the Industrial

[7] https://www.lens.org/lens/patent/US_8996429_B1

Property Code provides that a new invention may be patented, where it involves an inventive step and is capable of industrial application, affecting any element isolated from the human body or otherwise produced by a technical process, including the sequence or partial sequence of a gene, even if the structure of that element is identical to that of a natural element, provided it is expressly observed and specifically set forth in the patent application, the industrial application of a sequence or a partial sequence of a gene. Therefore, robotic prostheses are arguably eligible for patent protection.

Trade Secrets

Robotic software can be protected as know-how or confidential business information. Article 318 of the Industrial Property Code protects trade-secrets or know-how as undisclosed information. It is a special form of unfair competition, i.e., acts of competition contrary to the honest standards and practices of any branch of economic activity. It is the disclosure, acquisition or use of business secrets of a competitor, without the consent of the competitor, where such information (1) is secret, in the meaning that it is not generally known or easily accessible in its entirety or in the exact configuration and connection of its constituent elements to persons in circles who normally deal with the type of information in question; (2) has commercial value because it is secret; (3) has been the subject of considerable diligence in the light of the circumstances of the person legally in control of the information to keep it secret.

In the European Union, the European Parliament and the Council have adopted Directive 2016/943 of 8 June 2016 on the protection of know-how and confidential business information (trade secrets). Protection is provided against the acquisition, use and disclosure of confidential business information, which is considered secret information in the sense that: (1) in its entirety or in the exact configuration and connection of its constituent elements, it is not generally known to those in circles who deal normally with the type of information in question, or is not easily accessible to such people; (2) with commercial value because it is secret; (3) and which has been the subject of reasonable action, in the light of the circumstances, to be kept secret by the person exercising his control by law.

Conclusion

Robotic software is an essential dimension of AI systems. This paper figured out several possibilities to protect robotic software under intellectual property law. The first way is copyright law, as computer programs are listed as eligible copyright subject-matter, yet with special rules. However, copyright is limited in scope and does not exhaust the legal protection of robotic software. In particular, the patent system may prove a relevant solution for robotic software to protect its functionality. Finally, regardless of copyright and/or patent law, trade-secret protection is also an important branch of legal protection for robotic software.

In any case, is it important to preserve freedom of innovation so that AI can be developed to the benefit of Mankind and Nature.

CONSUMER PROTECTION ONLINE, IN SPECIAL THE EXPECTED CHANGES TO E-COMMERCE FROM S-COMMERCE, VR-COMMERCE AND AR-COMMERCE*

Introduction

Which changes to e-commerce are expected to take place, and which relate to new forms of online business beyond e-commerce and m-commerce, specifically S-commerce, VR-commerce and AR-commerce?

These are a new field of concern regarding the position of the consumer, within the regulatory framework of e-commerce in the EU concerning consumer rights. Consumer confidence is a major factor to boost the growth of e-commerce, and it relies to a large extend upon effective protection, as we have argued almost two decades ago.[1]

In 1995, Amazon started a business as an online bookseller. Less than 10 years latter it was first of the Internet Retailer's annual top 400 list[2]. Digital wallets such as Apple Pay, Google Wallet, Samsung Pay, have turned common smartphones into instant payment processors, providing customers with fast and secure one-click checkouts.

---

* *Estudos de Direito do Consumidor*, 14 (2018), 9-19

[1] *Comércio eletrónico na sociedade da informação: da segurança técnica à confiança jurídica*, Coimbra, Almedina, 1999.

[2] https://www.cbsnews.com/news/amazon-e-commerce-success-story/

In the European online market, E-commerce reached 61.8 billion euros in the United Kingdom alone[3]

However, geographic and linguistic borders are still a relevant obstacle to e-commerce. In its Communication "A Digital Single Market Strategy for Europe"[4] the European Commission states that "61% of EU consumers feel confident about purchasing via the Internet from a retailer located in their own Member State while only 38% feel confident about purchasing from another EU Member State". This means that the digital single market is not realising its full value, as "EU consumers could save EUR 11.7 billion each year if they could choose from a full range of EU goods and services when shopping online".[5]

Which impact will Social networks (S), Virtual Reality (VR) and Augmented Reality (AR) have upon e-commerce? Will they change the way consumers act online purchasing goods and services?

1. S-Commerce (Social Commerce), VR-commerce (Virtual Reality) and AR-Commerce (Augmented Reality)

Social networks sites (mostly through the development in Web 3.0 technologies, smartphones and iPads) have a relevant impact on e-commerce. According to a recent survey, "Social Media Captures Over 30% of Online Time"[6], social interaction through online communities affects the consumers' decision-making. S-Commerce means using social networks to sell and buy goods, products or services. Consumers share experiences and information, and contribute to building trust in e-commerce.

---

[3] https://www.statista.com/statistics/453628/online-retail-revenue-by-country-europe/

[4] COM(2015) 192 final, Brussels, 6.5.2015.

[5] *A Digital Single Market Strategy for Europe*, cit. § 2.1

[6] http://blog.globalwebindex.net/chart-of-the-day/social-media-captures-30-of--online-time/

S-commerce also serves as a marketing tool to promote branding[7], and it empowers consumers. It is a new channel of trade in which firms have to invest to create value in social networks (brand reputation). Firms become social peers. Due to the popularity of social networks, firms use this new channel of communication to build trust and create commercial value in and from social media.

The question is whether peer evaluation or recommendation is similar to advertising for purposes of regulation. Is it social free speech or should it be treated like online advertising? It means, for example, that the use of comparisons should comply with the regulation of misleading and comparative advertising.[8]

The potential impact of VR and AR in online commerce is high, notably through - but not limited to - gamification. The sale of VR headsets is rising and the penetration in households is likely to have a range of 1% in 2020, mainly in the North America and Western Europe. VR headsets could overcome mobile interfaces as these have once replaced desktops. Therefore, they also bear unneglectable disruptive potential for sales to consumers.

These technologies will enable consumers to visualize or experience what they are about to purchase online. Examples of VR-commerce are the shopping experience called Buy+ introduced by the Chinese retail giant Alibaba, and integrated with Alipay's instrument of payment. With a smartphone and a VR headset like Google Cardboard[9] (cheaper than models such as Oculus Rift)[10],

---

[7] https://www.journals.elsevier.com/computers-in-human-behavior/call-for-papers/social-commerce-and-the-future-of-e-commerce

[8] Directive 2006/114/EC of the European Parliament and of the Council of 12 December 2006 concerning misleading and comparative advertising, OJ L 376, 27.12.2006, p. 21–27. On this topic, with more references, see our paper "Publicidade comparativa, em especial na internet", in Estudos de Direito do Consumidor N.° 13 (2017), p. 37-56.

[9] https://vr.google.com/cardboard/

[10] In 2016, the Samsung Gear VR sold 4.5 million Gear VR, followed by the Sony PSVR.

customers can browse items in a virtual shopping mall, which emulates real life stores such as Matsumoto Kiyoshi in Japan. Customers have a "brick-and-mortar experience" while buying at home as if they were shopping at a physical store nearby. Another example is the flying company Thomas Cook. Travelers can experience a 60-degree in-flight experience before booking: "try before you fly", with interactive video featured real pilots and cabin crew, and surprising characters like Lady Gaga.[11]

VR-commerce is a major opportunity not only for travel agents. For example, Vroom can make online shopping as realistic as visiting a dealership to test drive a car but without having to search massive lots. The purpose is to give potential customers the best experience possible so that they buy the product and recommend it to their peers, notably through social networks.[12]

Augmented Reality is a variation of VR or computer-mediated reality, consisting of viewing real-world elements augmented by computer-generated or extracted sensors such as sound, video, graphics or GPS data. A perception of reality is modified (reduced or augmented) by a computer. In augmented reality, perception of reality is enhanced, whereas in virtual reality it is simulated. One example of augmented reality is overlaying scores over a live video feed of a sporting event or object recognition in a real-time environment. The user has an interactive experience with the information about the surrounding environment, which he can manipulate. AR adds digital information to the perception of the real objects surrounding the person. Prospective customers can have a more informed perception of reality and objects for sale.

---

[11] Other examples of VR- commerce are notably Holoroom, ShelfZone, IKEA; WorldPay. See http://www.fifthtribe.com/2017/06/21/virtual-reality-ecommerce/

[12] Source: https://www.forbes.com/sites/michelleevans1/2017/03/07/vr-the-brands-that-are-imagining-a-new-commerce-reality/#4875d9523b9d

Having this in mind, VR and AR commerce raise the question of whether the right to withdraw from the contract provided in EU legislation[13] should apply where consumers have an experience akin to the "real thing"?

2. The proposals of the Commission concerning consumer's rights for the digital market

The Commission has submitted two Directive proposals concerning consumers' rights for the digital market. However, they do not appear to address S-commerce, VR-commerce and AR-commerce.

In order to improve consumer confidence in cross-border purchases, the Commission presented on 9 December 2015 a Proposal for a Directive on certain aspects concerning contracts for the supply of digital content[14] and a Proposal for a Directive on certain aspects concerning contracts for the online and other distance sales of godos.[15]

These proposals will add to the EU acquis on consumer protection in e-commerce provided by the e-Commerce Directive (2000/31)[16] and the Directive on consumer rights (2011/83/EU)[17]. They intend

[13] Directive 2011/83/EU of the European Parliament and of the Council of 25 October 2011 on consumer rights, amending Council Directive 93/13/EEC and Directive 1999/44/EC of the European Parliament and of the Council and repealing Council Directive 85/577/EEC and Directive 97/7/EC of the European Parliament and of the Council, OJ L 304, 22.11.2011, p. 64–88.

[14] Proposal for a Directive of the European Parliament and of the Council on certain aspects concerning contracts for the supply of digital content. COM(2015) 634 final, Brussels, 9.12.2015.

[15] Directive of the European Parliament and of the Council on certain aspects concerning contracts for the online and other distance sales of godos, COM(2015) 635 final Brussels, 9.12.2015.

[16] Directive 2000/31/EC of the European Parliament and of the Council of 8 June 2000 on certain legal aspects of information society services, in particular electronic commerce, in the Internal Market ('Directive on electronic commerce').

[17] Directive 2011/83/EU of the European Parliament and of the Council of 25 October 2011 on consumer rights. This Directive has replaced, as of 13 June 2014,

to reinforce consumer protection when buying and selling online or by other means at a distance. According to the supporting memorandum, the proposals built upon the experience gained in negotiating the Draft Regulation on the Common European Sales Law.

These proposals regulate only certain aspects considered essential for the proper functioning of the internal market in the view of consumer protection. In particular, existing differences in remedies are an obstacle to the completion of the internal market. Moreover, the advanced proposals aim to create a friendly legal environment for small and medium-sized enterprises.[18]

The proposed directive on digital content supply contracts aims to fill a marked gap in consumer protection in the digital market. Directive 2011/83 on consumer rights completely harmonized the pre-contractual information and the right of withdrawal, but did not regulate consumer rights (remedies), including the right to modify and terminate long-term contracts, which at the EU level is governed only by the Directive on unfair terms. In addition, digital content, as such, does not fall under the concept of consumer goods in the Directive on Consumer Guarantees. The proposal for a directive on

Directive 97/7/EC on the protection of consumers in respect of distance contracts and Directive 85/577/EEC to protect consumer in respect of contracts negotiated away from business premises. Directive 1999/44/EC on certain aspects of the sale of consumer goods and associated guarantees as well as Directive 93/13/EEC on unfair terms in consumer contracts remain in force. The Consumer Rights Directive (CRD) governs all contracts concluded between a "consumer" and a "trader", including e-commerce. Traders are required to provide information prior to the conclusion of consumer contracts. Concerning distance and off-premises contracts, it includes information about the functionality and interoperability of digital content. Then, the CRD regulates the right of withdrawal (length of the withdrawal period, procedure and effects of the withdrawal), including a standard withdrawal form (Annex I(B)) to be provided by traders and which may be used by consumers to give notice of the withdrawal from the contract. The CRD also regulates delivery and passing of risk in contracts for the sale of goods as well as the fees for the use of certain means of payment (e.g. credit or debit cards). It also provides a prohibition to use pre-ticked boxes on websites for charging extra payments in addition to the remuneration for the trader's main performance.

[18] On this issue see our contribution "Novos direitos do consumidor no mercado único digital", *Estudos de Direito do Consumidor* N.° 10 (2016), p. 155-174.

the provision of digital content therefore regulates the compliance of the digital content with the contract, establishing the rights of the creditor in the event of non-conformity with the contract, as well as certain aspects relating to the right to terminate long-term contracts and modification of digital content. In this sense, the proposal enshrines the right of withdrawal in case of non-delivery, the right to repair and reduce the price in case of defective supply (non-conformity with the contract). It also establishes the right to cancel long-term contracts, which may last up to 12 months, and it provides for rules on cross-border content portability so that the consumer can enjoy digital content acquired in another Member State in any Member State.[19]

Concerning the proposal for a consumer rights directive in distance selling contracts, it establishes rules on the conformity of goods, the rights of the creditor in the event of breach of contract (non-conformity) and the terms for the exercise of such remedies. It does not apply to service contracts, except for mixed contracts, and provides a broad concept of buying and selling, covering the promise of sale and the contract. However, the notion of good is restricted to tangible movables. In line with the EU acquis of consumer law, the proposal enshrines the concept of non-conformity with the contract but also covers defective installation of the purchased good. The consumer will therefore have the right to order the correct installation of the goods acquired at a distance.

In the event of non-conformity with the contract, the consumer is entitled to have the goods brought into conformity by the seller, free of charge, by repair or replacement, as he chooses. Alternatively, the consumer has the right to reduce the price or to terminate the

[19] Pointing out a lack of consumer protection in the supply of digital content, see our paper "Comércio eletrónico de conteúdos digitais: proteção do consumidor a duas velocidades?", *Estudos de Direito do Consumidor* N. 9 (2015), p. 177-207.

contract where repair or replacement is impossible or unlawful and the seller has not repaired or replaced within a reasonable period of time, and the seller has failed to place the goods in accordance with the contract within a reasonable term.

Moreover, pre-contractual information and advertising becomes part of the contract and purchased goods have to be free from third parties' rights, including intellectual property rights. Thus, the seller has the duty to guarantee to the consumer the authenticity of the products, and therefore not to supply counterfeit copies (e.g. sports clothing bearing trademarks without the authorization of their right holders).

In our opinion, the Commission's initiative will enhance consumer protection in the digital market by contributing to the creation of a legal environment pro confidence in online shopping and digital content. The consumer of digital content will also have the right of withdrawal, within a period of 14 days, although it is not free, but rather conditioned to the lack of conformity of the content with the contract. It is also worth remarking that, under the proposal, contracts for the use of remote computing services, such as e-mail accounts, social networks, etc., are no longer transactions for free or gifts, because the authorization for the use of personal data is a consideration for purposes of the contract. To that extent, personal data becomes *res intra commercium*.

On the other hand, it is necessary to consider the impact of the proposals on internal legislation of each Member States. For example, although the third party rights rule may contribute to the good faith of the consumer, it will nevertheless have implications for the marketing of third parties' goods. Perhaps this aspect goes beyond consumer protection, entering areas still significantly marked by differences among Member States. The provision is limited to sale of goods by consumers, but, nonetheless, it will not have an impact on the regulation of sale of goods from traders.

According to the findings of a study of the European Parliament, "the harmonisation of rules across Member States and sales channels would reduce the fragmentation of the legal framework and enhance the clarity and transparency of applicable rules to the benefit of both consumers and businesses. Most importantly, one single regime for online and face-to-face transactions could contribute to increased consumers' and traders' awareness and confidence in purchasing/ selling online and offline, domestically and across borders."[20]

Conclusion

The legal construction of the digital single market is underway. Consumer protection is a key-factor to build confidence and therefore take full potential of e-commerce. At the EU level, consumer protection has justified the adoption of several regulatory instruments, and impact on e-commerce and online business. Moreover, two directive proposals are taking the steps of the UE law-making procedure[21] and aim to enhance consumer protection in the digital environment.

However, markets and technologies keep walking and doing their path regardless of what the law may bring. The new realities of S-commerce, VR-commerce and AR-commerce are there to stay and it is not clear whether existing or proposed rules apply to these phenomena. Let us hope that the Law keeps up with the challenges ahead!

---

[20] *Online and other sales of goods – impact assessment of substantial amendments*, June 2017 < http://www.europarl.europa.eu/thinktank/>

[21] See e.g. the Report of the European Parliament of 27 November 2017, on the proposal for a directive of the European Parliament and of the Council on certain aspects concerning contracts for the supply of digital content (COM(2015)0634), disponível em <http://www.europarl.europa.eu/>

VERTICAL RESTRAINTS ON INTERNET SALES IN EU COMPETITION LAW*

Abstract - The internet is a worldwide channel of trade with risks and opportunities for businesses, and new challenges for competition law. This contribution addresses vertical restraints on internet sales under competition law, in particular how far can the distributor limit its freedom to conduct business online.

The prohibition of cartels and distribution agreements as acceptable restraints

The organization of distribution networks often involves the allocation of an exclusive territory to the distributor. This means that the producer or supplier undertakes not to sell its products directly or through other distributors to customers in that territory. Absolute territorial protection is a serious restraint to competition. Instead of competing with each other, producers and distributors divide the market territorially, distorting the proper functioning of the market and depriving consumers of the benefits generated by competition.[1]

---

* European Competition Law Review vol. 38 / 10 (2017), p. 478-482, published by Sweet & Maxwell (imprint of Thomson Reuters).

[1] Cf. A Pinto Monteiro, *Contratos de distribuição comercial* (Coimbra, Almedina, 2002, p. 50-59).

In line with EU law, the Portuguese Competition Act prohibits anti-competitive agreements, decisions of associations and concerted practices between undertakings[2]. The prohibition covers agreements or concerted practices having an anti-competitive object or effect. A number of sensitive groups of cases are listed: (a) price fixing (price cartels) or other transaction conditions, production control, distribution and technical development; (b) the distribution of markets or sources of supply; (c) discriminatory conditions; (d) tying the agreement to extra services not related to the main contract; (e) refusal to sell or purchase goods and services.

This is a matter of economic public order, as contracts or agreements infringing the prohibition of cartels ae deemed null and void[3]. Notwithstanding this, competition law does not fully prohibit distribution networks.

In *Pronuptia*[4], the ECJ ruled that the conformity of distribution licensing agreements, such as franchising agreements, with Article 85 of the EC Treaty (now Article 101 of TFEU) is not determined in abstract, but rather looking at the contract terms and the economic context of the agreement. Accordingly, it excluded a number of clauses from the notion of restriction to competition under the doctrine of ancillary restraints. Such exempted clauses include those which are necessary to prevent the know-how transmitted and the assistance provided by the licensor from benefiting its competitors, and those which provide the essential control for the preservation of the identity and the reputation of the network, in special its insignia. Likewise, the Court did not consider a restriction on competition the communication by the licensor to the licensee of the target prices, provided there is no concerted practice between the licensor and

---

[2] Article 9 of Law 19/2012, of 8 May

[3] Article 10(2) of Law 19/2012 and Article 102(2) TFEU.

[4] ECJ Judgment of 28 January 1986, case no. 161/84, ECLI:EU:C:1986:41.

the licensees between them, with a view to the effective application of those prices. The clauses establishing a market partition between the licensor and the licensees qualified as restriction to competition for the purposes of Article 85 (1), although they might qualify for exemption under Article 85 (3).

In addition, distribution systems such as commercial licensing and selective distribution have been exempted under this provision and later codified in the regulation of block exemptions for vertical agreements and concerted practices.[5] Block exemptions are subject to certain requirements. The parties may not have a market share over 30% and, on the other hand, agreements may not contain serious restrictions concerning resale prices, territory or customer area of the distributor, except for exceptions for exclusive or selective distribution, the prohibition of passive sales in exclusive distribution, the prohibition of sale to end users in selective distribution (although it may be limited to other authorized distributors), and the prohibition of the manufacturer of spare parts to sell to end users, independent repairers or service providers.

The challenge raised by the Internet to distribution networks

With the internet, geographical borders are blurred and the organization of distribution networks is affected. The internet provides both the producer and distributors with a new trade channel, which does not require the physical movement of customers to a physical

[5] Regulation (EC) No 2790/1999, replaced by Commission Regulation (EU) No 330/2010 of 20 April 2010 on the application of Article 101 (3) of the Treaty on the Functioning of the European Union to certain categories of vertical agreements and concerted practices, OJ L 102/1, 23.4.2010. An important hermeneutic tool is the Commission's Guidelines on vertical restraints, OJ C 130/01, 19.5.2010.

shop, while allowing them quick access to information on prices and qualities of the products they want.

Can the supplier prohibit the distributor from selling over the Internet? Can he prevent the distributor from negotiating with customers that belong to territories or areas of other distributors? Can he limit the quantities or require higher prices for products intended for sale online? Can he forbid the distributor from doing online advertising aimed at customers in the territory of other distributors, for example through advertising banners or search engines? Can he demand from the distributor to have a traditional establishment with physical facilities?

In order to illustrate the issues at hand, it is important to consider case relevant ruling from the Court of Justice of the European Union.[6]

The judgment from the CJEU in *Pierre Fabre*

A French cosmetic and personal hygiene company - *Pierre Fabre* - used a selective distribution system as a contractual clause under which sales of its products could take place in physical premises only and in the presence of a graduate in pharmacy. In practice, this clause prohibited the use of the Internet by the company's distributors.

The French competition authority considered the clause invalid as a restriction by objective. It was devoid of objective justification in view of the properties of the products in question (cosmetics and personal hygiene products). Internet sales do not require the physical movement of the customer. To exclude this new form of marketing it would considerably limit the possibility to sell prod-

[6] ECJ judgment of 13 October 2011, case C439/09, *Pierre Fabre DermoCosmétique*, ECLI:EU:C:2011:649.

ucts to customers outside the territory or the area of activity of the distributor. It would therefore be a restriction on competition prohibited by Article L. 420-4 (1) of the French Commercial Code (which incorporates competition law) and then Article 81 TEC (now Article 101 TFEU). [7]

Pierre Fabre claimed to use a selective distribution system not covered by the prohibition of Article 85 (1). Moreover, the company's market share would be less than 30% and would qualify for exemption under Article 4 (1) (c) of Regulation 2789/1999 on the application of Article 81(3) to categories of vertical agreements and concerted practices. Pierre Fabre justified the prohibition of Internet sales because it would contribute to improving the distribution of its cosmetic products, preventing the risks of counterfeiting and parasitism between authorized sites, by guaranteeing the presence of a graduate in pharmacy in outlet sales, the provision of advice and the coverage of the respective cost by each distributor.

However, the French competition authority recalled that cosmetics and personal hygiene products are not medicinal products and therefore it would not be justified to treat them at the distribution level as medicines, especially as pharmacy graduates are not competent to provide health diagnoses. To that end, the competition authority mobilized the ECJ ruling in *Deutscher Apotheker*.[8]

In the opinion of the French Authority, the effects of the use of the products would not be checkable at the time of sale, thus not justifying the physical presence of a graduate in pharmacy. In addition, an Internet site would not be a place of commercialization, but rather an alternative channel of sales, such as direct store selling or distance selling used by distributors with physical

[7] *Ibid.* paras 9 – 31.

[8] ECJ judgment of 11 December 2003, case C-322/01, *Deutscher Apothekerverband*, *ECLI*:EU:C:2003:664.

retail outlets. Therefore, it would not fall under Article 4 (c) of the Regulation 2789/1999. Finally, *Pierre Fabre* would not have shown proof of individual exemption under Article 81/3 EC and Article L. 4-4-4/1 of the French Commercial Code.

Pierre Fabre brought an action for annulment of that decision. The Court of Appeal of Paris stayed the proceedings and asked the CJEU: (a) whether the general and absolute prohibition on selling to end users imposed on distributors within a selective distribution network constitutes a serious restriction of competition within the meaning of Article 81 TEC (now Article 101 TFEU); (b) whether such a restriction is not covered by the block exemption under Regulation No 2790/1999 or by an individual exemption under Article 81 (3) TEC.

In essence, the Court CJEU upheld the grounds of the French competition authority's decision.

To begin with, the Court points out that the prohibition on cartels does not in fact cover selective distribution systems - characterized by a ban on the sale of products to unauthorized distributors - where they pursue legitimate objectives, since the organization of a distribution network can contribute to improving competition, where competition is not based solely on prices. However, in order not to fall under the prohibition certain requirements have to be met: (a) resellers must be selected on the basis of objective criteria of a qualitative nature, fixed uniformly for all potential resellers and applied in a non-discriminatory manner; (b) the properties of the product concerned require, in order to preserve quality and ensure its correct use, that there is a distribution network; and (c) the criteria do not go beyond what is necessary.

The Court points out that in other judgments it did not accept the arguments that the ban on internet sales would be justified by the need to provide personalized advice to the customer and to ensure that it is protected against misuse of the products in connection with the sale of medicines that are not subject to medical prescription (*Deutscher Apothekerverband*) as well as contact lenses (*Ker-Optika*[9]). On the other hand, the CJUE considers that preserving the prestige of such products is not a legitimate objective to restrict competition in relation to the sale of cosmetic products and personal hygiene, and therefore it does not justify such anti-competitive contract term.

In short, the ECJ found that, "in the context of a selective distribution system, a contractual clause requiring sales of cosmetics and personal care products to be made in a physical space where a qualified pharmacist must be present, resulting in a ban on the use of the internet for those sales, amounts to a restriction by object within the meaning of that provision where, following an individual and specific examination of the content and objective of that contractual clause and the legal and economic context of which it forms a part, it is apparent that, having regard to the properties of the products at issue, that clause is not objectively justified." [10]

Concerning Article 4 (c) of Regulation No 2789/1999, the Court pointed out that this exemption does not extend to vertical agreements aimed to restrict active or passive sales to end users by members of a selective distribution system operating at retail level, without prejudice to the possibility of prohibiting a distributor from operating from an unauthorized place of business. In the Court's view, the contractual clause at issue seeks, as a minimum, to restrict passive sales to end-users who wish to buy over the Internet and who are outside the physical location of their

---

[9] Judgment of 2 December 2010, case C-108/09, *Ker-Optika*, ECLI: EU: C: 2010: 725, para., according to which "Articles 34 TFEU and 36 TFEU and Directive 2000/31 (...] must be interpreted as precluding national legislation which authorises the selling of contact lenses only in shops which specialise in medical devices."

[10] *Pierre Fabre,* para 47 and conclusion.

distributor. It is a serious restriction, as a territorial limitation to the distributor's freedom of action, which does not benefit from the exemption.

On the other hand, the term "place of establishment" would mean points of sale where direct sales take place, so that a clause prohibiting in fact marketing via the Internet could not be a clause prohibiting selected distributors from operating from a place of establishment not authorized within the meaning of that notion. The term "place of establishment" would not require a broad interpretation because "an undertaking has the option, in all circumstances, to assert, on an individual basis, the applicability of the exception provided for in Article 101(3) TFEU".[11]

The clause may individually benefit from the application of the legal exception provided for in Article 101 (3) TFEU if the requirements of the economic balance assessment are met, i.e., it generates efficiency gains (a), is indispensable (b), equitably shares its benefits with consumers (c), and does not eliminate competition in the relevant market (d). In that regard, the CJEU referred to the Court of Appeal of Paris the verification, in this case, of those conditions, because it had not sufficient information to carry out that assessment.

So, concerning the second question, the ECJ concluded that "the block exemption provided for in Article 2 of that regulation [Commission Regulation (EC) No 2790/1999] does not apply to a selective distribution contract which contains a clause prohibiting *de facto* the internet as a method of marketing the contractual products. However, such a contract may benefit, on an individual basis, from the exception provided for in Article 101(3) TFEU where the conditions of that provision are met."[12]

---

[11] *Pierre Fabre* para. 57.

[12] Ibid. para 59 and conclusion.

The *Eturas* judgement

The ECJ case-law had further developments. In particular, more recently, the case *Eturas*[13], concerning the practice of the administrator of an information system enabling travel agents to sell travel products on their website using a uniform booking method to send such economic operators, via a personal electronic mailbox, a message warning that discounts on products sold through such a system will be limited.

The main disputed question was whether Article 101 (1) of TFEU covered that practice where, following the dissemination of that message, the system in question undergoes the technical changes necessary to implement that measure.

The answer of the ECJ was positive concluding that "where the administrator of an information system, intended to enable travel agencies to sell travel packages on their websites using a uniform booking method, sends to those economic operators, via a personal electronic mailbox, a message informing them that the discounts on products sold through that system will henceforth be capped and, following the dissemination of that message, the system in question undergoes the technical modifications necessary to implement that measure, those economic operators may — if they were aware of that message — be presumed to have participated in a concerted practice (...], unless they publicly distanced themselves from that practice, reported it to the administrative authorities or adduce other evidence to rebut that presumption, such as evidence of a systematic application of a discount exceeding the cap in question."[14]

---

[13] Judgment of 21 January 2016, case C-74/14, *Eturas*, ECLI: EU: C: 2016: 42.

[14] *Eturas,* para. 50. The Court added that, on the basis of national rules governing the assessment of evidence and the standard of proof, the referring court has jurisdiction to examine "whether, in view of all the circumstances before it, the dispatch of a message, such as that at issue in the main proceedings, may constitute sufficient

The Commission's Guidelines on vertical restraints and online sales

The Commission's Guidelines on vertical restraints address online sales of distributors.[15] Although not binding, they provide the basis for the decisions from the CJEU and therefore they have a significant interpretative value. In principle, the Commission interprets the regulations on block exemptions in the light of those Guidelines, which are therefore important for undertakings.

The distinction between active sales and passive sales is of particular relevance in this context. The Commission states, as a general principle, the freedom of Internet sales, as long as it allows the distributor to reach a wider and more diverse clientele. However, this freedom applies only to passive sales, i.e. when the customer visits the distributor's website and following that visit the customer contacts the distributor, resulting in a sale, or when a sale results from information received by the customer. For ex., where the costumer has chosen to receive the distributor's newsletter, regardless of the language options available on the website.[16]

In this sense, serious restrictions on passive sales are agreements between the supplier and the distributor under which:

---

evidence to establish that the addressees of that message were aware of its content. The presumption of innocence precludes the referring court from considering that the mere dispatch of that message constitutes sufficient evidence to establish that its addressees ought to have been aware of its content."

[15] SEC(2010) 411, < http://ec.europa.eu/competition/antitrust/legislation/guidelines_vertical_en.pdf>

[16] *Guidelines on vertical restraints*, para. 52. For purposes of Article 4(b) of the Block Exemption Regulation, 'active' sales 'mean actively approaching individual customers by for instance direct mail, including the sending of unsolicited e-mails, or visits; or actively approaching a specific customer group or customers in a specific territory through advertisement in media, on the internet or other promotions specifically targeted at that customer group or targeted at customers in that territory', and 'passive' sales are 'responding to unsolicited requests from individual customers including delivery of goods or services to such customers' (para. 51).

1. Customers located in another (exclusive) territory are prevented from viewing their website or are automatically forwarded to the websites of the manufacturer or other exclusive distributors, without prejudice to the distributor's website being able to propose additional links for the websites of other distributors and / or the supplier (blocking or re-routing restriction);
2. The exclusive distributor does not conclude sales to consumers via the Internet when the credit card information shows that the consumer does not belong to the distributor's exclusive territory;
3. The distributor has to limit the percentage of global sales over the Internet, without prejudice to off-line minimum (value or volume) obligations to ensure the efficient operation of the traditional establishment, nor the conformity requirements of the activity according to the vendor's distribution model;
4. Payment of higher prices for products destined for resale through the Internet, without prejudice to the requirement of a fixed charge, which however does not allow duality of prices. "In general, an agreement that a distributor shall pay a higher price for products intended to be resold by the distributor online than for products intended to be resold offline ('dual pricing') is a hardcore restriction [...]. However, in some specific circumstances, such an agreement may fulfil the conditions of Article 101(3). Such circumstances may be present where a manufacturer agrees such dual pricing with its distributors, because selling online leads to substantially higher costs for the manufacturer than offline sales. For example, where offline sales include home installation by the distributor but online sales do not, the latter may lead to more customer complaints and warranty claims for the manufacturer."[17]

[17] *Guidelines on vertical restraints*, para. 52.

Moreover, restrictions on the use of the Internet that lead to active sales are accepted. For ex. on-line advertising targeted specifically at certain customers, through territory-based advertising banners on third-party websites (e.g. a distributor of mobile phones located in Madrid buys advertising on the website of a Portuguese newspaper) or payment by search engine or an online advertising provider to advertise specifically to users in a specific territory (e.g. Google's *AdWorks* or *Facebook*).[18]

Other restrictions may be permitted such as those resulting from:

(a) the imposition on distributors of quality standards for the use of the website used for the resale of goods, as well as quality standards for traditional establishments and for promotion, including amendments to those standards, unless they are aimed at limiting distributors' online sales;

(b) the obligation to have one or more traditional establishments or exhibition halls;

(c) the prohibition on using third-party platforms to host the distributor's website or not allowing customers to visit it through a site that shows the name or logo of the third-party platform (this legitimate restriction is intended for distribution on platforms such as, e.g., *eBay, Facebook, YouTube*).[19] To understand the impact of this restriction it is important to consider the percentage of network traffic concerning social networks.

Selective distribution

As far as selective distribution is concerned, according to the Commission Guidelines, the distributor should remain free to sell

[18] Ibid. para. 53.

[19] Ibid. para. 54.

over the Internet, both passively and actively, to end users.[20] Selling restrains which find no equivalent in those of physical outlets are "hardcore restriction". Differences should only arise from the different nature of the two modes of distribution. The Commission illustrates this: "In order to ensure timely delivery of contract products, a supplier may impose that the products be delivered instantly in the case of offline sales. Whereas an identical requirement cannot be imposed for online sales, the supplier may specify certain practicable delivery times for such sales. Specific requirements may have to be formulated for an online after-sales help desk, so as to cover the costs of customers returning the product and for applying secure payment systems."[21]

On the other hand, a restriction on competition can be allowed if the cumulative requirements of the legal exception to the prohibition of cartels are met, i.e. if the restriction generates efficiency gains, it is indispensable, a fair share of the benefits reverts to consumers, and does not lead to the elimination of competition.[22] The requirement of higher prices for products for resale on line is in principle a serious restriction. However, the Commission admits that dual pricing may be justified under Article 101 (3) where online sales entail substantially higher costs for the manufacturer than offline sales.[23]

---

[20] See Silke Heinz, *Ban on sales via third-party internet platforms in Germany and Pierre Fabre – recent referral to the Court of Justice.* <http://kluwercompetitionlawblog.com/2016/06/06/ban-on-sales-via-third-party-internet-platforms-in-germany-and-the-impact-of-pierre-fabre-on-selective-distribution-referral-to-the-court-of-justice-in-coty/>

[21] *Guidelines on vertical restraints*, para. 56.

[22] Article 101 (3) TFEU and Article 10 of Law 19/2012. See the Communication from the Commission, Guidelines on the application of Article 81 (3) of the Treaty, OJ C 101, 27.4.2004, p. 97.

[23] *Guidelines on vertical restraints*, para. 64. Agreements and concerted practices of minor importance (de *minimis*) and those excluded by the 'no appreciable restriction to competition' are not covered by the prohibition. See Commission Notice on agreements of minor importance which do not appreciably restrict competition under Article 81(1) of the Treaty establishing the European Community (*de minimis*), OJ C 368, 22.12.2001, p. 13.

Conclusion

The absence of geographical borders on the internet challenges the organization of distribution networks, often designed according to political-administrative territories. In order to preserve the efficiency of the distribution network, the supplier may wish to prevent the distributor from selling over the internet by confining it to its territory. From the point of view of competition law, as set out in the TFEU and domestic law, and in particular in the case-law from the CJEU and the Commission's Guidelines on vertical guidelines, a complete ban on internet sales is in principle out of the question. The same applies to the imposition of quotas or higher prices on sales.

However, considering the distinction between active sales and passive sales, restrictions on the distributor's freedom of competition with respect to dealing with customers in other territories, in particular with respect to online advertising directed at such customers, are acceptable, along with the requirement that the distributor has an establishment with physical facilities. As for selective distribution, in which the distributor's source is limited to the supplier or other members of the network, the freedom to promote sales to customers outside its territory (active sales) is broader, without prejudice to restrictions concerning compliance with requirements of quality of the website and terms of service established by the supplier.

CLOUD COMPUTING (SERVICE LEVEL AGREEMENTS)*

Abstract - This paper addresses the regulatory framework of Service Level Agreements (SLA) in Cloud Computing. The context of the Portuguese cloud computing landscape, including the relevant market and the cloud environment, are presented as well as a short description of most commonly used service level terms for both standard and bespoke SLAs, including aspects of portability and liability. Finally, it suggests that an initiative at the European level, similarly to the European Union Public License, could be useful to promote the development of the single digital market.

Introduction

"'Cloud computing' in simplified terms can be understood as the storing, processing and use of data on remotely located computers accessed over the internet. This means that users can command almost unlimited computing power on demand, that they do not have to make major capital investments to fulfil their needs and that they can get to their data from anywhere with an internet connection. Cloud computing has the potential to slash

* *Boletim da Faculdade de Direito*, vol. 92/1 (2017), p. 367-401.

users' IT expenditure and to enable many new services to be developed. Using the cloud, even the smallest firms can reach out to ever larger markets while governments can make their services more attractive and efficient even while reining in spending."[1]

Cloud Computing has advantages and benefits. It allows data storage and processing by remote computers, real-time and ubiquitous access to data and to IT resources without significant start-up investment or the possibility to develop new services and to optimize resources for both Government and Corporations. However, in a world in which data are in fact an important '*res intra commercium*'[2], it does also have risks, such as failures of information security, breaches of data confidentiality, integrity and availability, unauthorized access by the cloud provider and third parties, migration to countries with low standards of data protection, or uncertainty over data ownership. In particular, concerning cloud service level agreements (SLAs), there is an actual risk to make clients dependent up on the provider along with difficulties in law enforcement.

This paper addresses some legal aspects of Service Level Agreements (hereinafter SLA) in Cloud Computing. It begins with the context of the Portuguese cloud computing landscape, including the relevant market and the cloud SLA environment. Then, it follows a short description of commonly used service level terms for both standard and bespoke SLAs.[3] Next, it gives

---

[1] *Unleashing the Potential of Cloud Computing in Europe*. Communication from the Commission to the European Parliament, the Council, the European Economic and Social Committee and the Committee of the Regions, COM(2012) 529 final, Brussels, 27.9.2012.

[2] FRANCESCHI, A., LEHMANN, M. Data as tradeable commodity and new measures for their protection. *The Italian Law Journal*, Vol. 1, N° 1 (2015), 51-72.

[3] For a comparative analysis see BRADSHOW, S.; MILLARD, C.; WALDEN, I. Contracts for clouds: a comparative analysis of terms and conditions for cloud computing services. *International Journal of Law and Information Technology*, Vol. 19, N° 3 (2011), 187-223; for the distinction between negotiated contracts and standard contracts in cloud computing, HON, W.K.; MILLAR, C., WALDEN, I. Negotiated Contracts for Cloud

an overview of some relevant legal aspects, including liability and situation of specific regulated sectors such as financial, health and the public administration.[4] It also analyses important issues such as audit, control and standard setting, and closes with some concluding remarks.

1. The Portuguese market of Cloud Computing and SLAs landscape

There are several cloud providers offering their services to Portuguese customers, most of them from the U.S. Cloud providers offer a wide range of services from Software as a Service (SaaS)[5] to Infrastructure as a Service (IaaS)[6] and Platform as a Service (PaaS).[7]

Services. In MILLAR, C. (ed.) *Cloud Computing Law*. Oxford: Oxford University Press, 2013, 73-82; HON, W.K., MILLAR, C., WALDEN, I. Public Sector Cloud Contracts. In MILLAR, C. (ed.). *Cloud Computing Law*. Oxford: Oxford University Press, 2013, 108-141.

[4] Data protection is also a very important issue in Cloud Computing, which often involves personal data processing through the generation and/or transmission of personal data. The issue of personal data protection in cloud computing has been addressed by several official documents, notably *Article 29 Working Party Opinion 05/2012 on Cloud Computing* (2012), and The Berlin International Working Group on Data Protection in Telecommunications, *Working Paper on Cloud Computing - Privacy and data protection issues* -"Sopot Memorandum" (2014). Despite it does not directly concern SLAs, reference will be made to this issue in the health sector. In literature see e.g. BLUME, P. Data Protection in the Cloud. *CRi - Computer Law Review International*, No 3 (2011), 76-80; SLOOT, B., BORGESIUS, F.Z. Google and Personal Data Protection. In LOPEZ-TARRUELA, A. (ed.). *Google and the Law. Empirical Approaches to Legal Aspects of Knowledge-Economy Business Models*. Hague: Asser/Springer, 2012, 75-111; WALDEN, I. Accessing Data in the Cloud: The Long Arm of the Law Enforcement Agent. In PEARSON, S., GEORGE, Y. (ed.). *Privacy and Security for Cloud Computing*. London: Springer, 2013, 45-71.

[5] Applications run on a cloud infrastructure, but customers do not have control over the underlying infrastructure, including network, servers, operating systems, storage, or even individual application capabilities (e.g. Gmail).

[6] The customer has control over operating systems, storage and deployed applications, and possibly limited control over select networking components such as host firewalls.

[7] The customer has control over the deployed applications and possibly configuration settings for the application-hosting environment; he does not manage nor

The main market players in the Portuguese B2B cloud computing market are: PT Empresas[8], Microsoft[9], IMB[10], Cisco Systems[11], Google[12], Apple, and Rackspace[13]. In particular, PT has made a significant investment in the Covilhã *DataCenter*[14], taking advantage of the climate as well as the strategic location of Portugal. It provides a wide range of different solutions such as Housing, Hosting and Storage (1), Managed IT Services (2), Private Servers (3), Security Operations System (4), Network Operation Center (5), and Disaster Recovery (6).

SLAs set up the specific parameters and minimum levels of the service, as well as remedies for failure to meet those requirements. Cloud computing services are usually provided upon standard terms, i.e. terms of service which are not open to negotiation. In general, customers can choose only from the menu the cloud services they wish, and then to accept the terms set-up by the cloud providers for each service. SLAs may be included within the terms of the cloud service or form a separate agreement linked to the contract. In any case, negotiation is usually not possible because they are offered as 'take-it or leave-it' standard terms of service.

control the underlying infrastructure including network, servers, operating systems or storage (e.g. Google App Engine).

[8] https://cloud.ptempresas.pt/Pages/Content/Default.aspx?key=DCC (last access 25 May 2016).

[9] http://www.microsoft.com/business/pt-pt/Solucoes/Solucoes-Cloud/Paginas/default.aspx#&panel2-1 (last access 25 May 2016).

[10] http://www.ibm.com/cloud-computing/?lnk=bucl&lnk2=learn (last access 25 May 2016).

[11] http://www.cisco.com/web/PT/solutions/trends/cloud/index.html (last access 25 May 2016).

[12] https://developers.google.com/cloud/ (last access 25 May 2016).

[13] http://www.rackspace.com/pt/ (last access 25 May 2016).

[14] https://cloud.ptempresas.pt/Pages/Datacenter/DCC.aspx (last access 25 May 2016).

2. Service level terms commonly used

SLAs are part of standard terms of Cloud Computing services usually drafted after publicly available SLAs or SLA templates[15], notably those of *Rackspace SLA*[16], *The Microsoft Azure Cloud Services SLA*[17], or *Google SLA*[18].

SLAs set the parameters of the service concerning:

1° Availability of the service (uptime, downtime) and conditions of measurement of the availability (weekly, monthly, yearly), which may depend upon the level of service chosen by the customer: e.g. The Microsoft Azure Cloud Services SLA guarantees 99.9% availability and Google Cloud SQL provides an SLA of a Monthly Uptime Percentage to Customer of at least 99.95%;

2° User support and incident response time;

3° Penalties for breach of SLAs: service credits are the primary remedy for service failure, and they are based upon a percentage (varying upon the provider) of the fees paid by the customer during the billing cycle;

4° Maximum Financial Credit to be requested by the customer: usually these fees do not exceed 100% of the paid fees, but other caps may apply;

5° SLAs exclusions, such as disclaimers of warranties as well as exclusions and limitations of liability: data back-up and restoration are usually excluded from the scope of the contract, in the sense that the service provider holds no liability for it

---

[15] http://www.slatemplate.com/ (last access 25 May 2016).

[16] http://www.rackspace.com/pt/information/legal/cloud/sla (last access 25 May 2016).

[17] http://azure.microsoft.com/en-us/support/legal/sla/ (last access 25 May 2016).

[18] http://www.google.com/apps/intl/pt-PT/terms/sla.html (last access 25 May 2016).

and that the customer is responsible for securing and backing up its own data.

6° SLAs may also assert ownership of data stored on the system of the cloud provider[19], define system infrastructure and security standards, and customer auditing rights, as well as the terms of location of data processing and storage.

3. Relevant legal framework in Portugal

3.1 Introduction

There is no statutory regulation specifically designed for cloud computing and, in particular, for SLAs. These are concluded under the general principle of freedom of contract[20] and they are governed by the common rules of contract law, notably those provided by the Civil Code on contracts as legal transactions (e.g. offer and acceptance and freedom of form) and as source of obligations (e.g. the principles of sanctity of contract and good-faith).

In general terms, cloud computing qualify as services contracts, which are governed by the special provisions of the agency/mandate contract.[21] Software licenses within cloud computing have to comply with the Software Copyright Act[22], which provides that

---

[19] On the issue on information ownership, REED, C., CUNNINGHAM, A. Ownership of Information in Clouds. CHRISTOPHER, M (ed.). *Cloud Computing Law*. Oxford: Oxford University Press, 2013, 142-164.

[20] Article 405 of Civil Code.

[21] Articles 1156 ff. of Civil Code.

[22] Decree-Law 252/94 of 20 October, implementing Council Directive 91/250/EEC of 14 May 1991 on the legal protection of computer programs (as amended by Directive 93/98/EEC), repealed and replaced by Directive 2009/24/EC of the European Parliament and of the Council of 23 April 2009 on the legal protection of computer programs.

the general principles of contract law as well as the regulations of typical contracts (e.g. sale, lease) apply, either directly or by analogy.[23] Moreover, some provisions of the Copyright Act are deemed applicable, such as Articles 40, 45 to 51, and 55.[24] This Act also provides for a right to put into circulation[25], which corresponds to the right of distribution, subject nonetheless to exhaustion concerning the resale of the licenses.[26]

Besides this, cloud computing SLAs have to comply with the Standard Terms Act[27], as they offer their services based upon standard terms. In general, customization is not possible, because

---

[23] Decree-Law No 252/94, Article 11(1).

[24] Decree-Law No 252/94, Article 11(2). A *contrario*, Article 41 of the *Código do Direito de Autor e dos Direitos Conexos* (hereinafter, Copyright Act) enacted by Decree-Law No 63/85 of March 1985, and as last amended by Law No 32/2015 of 24 April 2015, which provides the general conditions of authorizations to use copyrighted works, does not apply to software. Such conditions are notably that authorizations have to be granted in writing and are presumably onerous and non-exclusive; moreover, they have to specify the authorized uses of divulgation, publication and utilization, as well as the conditions of time, place and price. Instead of applying this regulation to software licenses the legislator provided methodological guidelines, including a general principle of interpretation according to which contract terms are to be interpreted in accordance with good-faith and within the justified purpose of the contract - Decree-Law No 252/94, Article 11(3).

[25] Decree-Law No 252/94, Article 8(1)(2).

[26] A much discussed topic, with implications in cloud computing, is the exhaustion of the distribution right concerning digital copies distributed online, as the Court of Justice of the European Union ruled in its judgment of 3 July 2012 (case C-128/11, *UsedSoft GmbH v Oracle International Corp,* ECLI:EU:C:2012:407). Some commentators have argued that it is not likely to apply to cloud computing services such as SaaS: LEISTNER, M. Europe's Copyright Law Decade: Recent Case Law of the European Court of Justice and Policy Perspectives. *Common Market Law Review*, Vol. 51 (2014), 559-600, 582; PEINTINGER, S. Widerrufsrechte beim Erwerb digitaler Inhalte. *MMR – MultiMedia und Recht*. N° 1 (2016), 3-8, 8. However, holding that "in relation to software, it remains to be seen how the ECJ will decide if could-computing cases arise in near future", HILTY, R.H., KÖKLÜ, K., HAFENBRÄDL, F. Software Agreements: Stocktaking and Outlook – Lessons from the UsedSoft v. Oracle case from a Comparative Law Perspective. *IIC - International Review of Intellectual Property and Competition Law*. Vol. 44 (2013), 263-292, 290.

[27] Decree-Law 446/85 of 25 October, as last amended by Decree-Law No 323/2001 of 17 December.

customers can choose only which cloud services they want[28] and to accept the terms of service set-up by the cloud providers.

Concerning voluntary norms as well as the development of standards in the area of cloud computing in Portugal, there are events and special organizations on Cloud Computing, which are aimed to promote best practices in the sector. Despite there is no 'official' set of norms and standards in the area of cloud computing, control and practice guidelines concerning audit, control and standards are usually taken into consideration by cloud providers and customers, notably those from the Cloud Security Alliance[29] or the Cloud Council.[30]

3.2 General terms in SLAs

SLAs focus on service availability (uptime and downtime), criteria to measure availability and procedures to report performance, remedies for failure to comply with the level of service (usually as financial credits in the service fee and their caps), and disclaimers with limitation or exclusion of liability. The main legal questions raised by Cloud SLA and herein addressed are: compliance with legislation on standard terms (a), security, integrity and reliability (b), portability (c), and liability of cloud providers (d)

Cloud computing are usually provided upon standard terms or general conditions of contracts ('take-it-or-leave-it' terms). Standard terms are general conditions drafted without previous individual negotiation and submitted or accepted by indeterminate proponents or

[28] For example, Google's Cloud services include Google Apps for Business, Google Apps for Government, Google Apps for ISP, Google Apps for Education, and Google Apps Vault.

[29] See https://cloudsecurityalliance.org (last access 25 May 2016)

[30] See http://www.cloud-council.org (last access 25 May 2016).

addressees, respectively, or terms inserted by the proponent in individual contracts as 'take-it or leave-it clauses'.[31] The use of standard terms must comply with duties of full and previous communication to the other party as well as the duty to inform her and to answer to her reasonable requests of clarification; otherwise such terms are be deemed excluded from the contract as 'surprise terms'.[32]

On the other hand, the content of standard terms or general conditions must comply with the 'dark' and 'grey' lists of forbidden terms applicable to B2B contracts. For example, disclaimers of warranty and liability are forbidden where they exclude or limit liability for damages caused to life, moral or physical integrity, or to a person's health, as well as liability for personal damages caused to the other party or to third parties. Such conditions are also forbidden where they exclude or limit liability for lack of, or defective performance, including delay, where the breach of contract is intentional or grossly negligent.[33]

Concerning *formal requirements* applicable to license contracts, there aren't specific requirements for software licenses. Copyright authorizations have to be granted in writing under general copyright law[34], but the Software Copyright Act seems to exclude the requirement of a written document for software licenses.[35] On the other hand, as commercial contracts, cloud services may be drafted in English language only under the principle of freedom of language in drafting commercial contracts provided by the Commercial Code.[36] Concerning contracts with consumers (B2C),

[31] Article 1(1)(2) of Decree-Law 446/85.

[32] Articles 5, 6 and 8 of Decree-Law 446/85.

[33] Article 18(a)(b)(c) of Decree-Law 446/85.

[34] Article 43 of Copyright Act.

[35] Article 11(2) of Decree-Law 252/94.

[36] Article 96 of Commercial Code, enacted by Royal Act of 28 June 1888.

the General Consumer Act[37] and the Portuguese Language Act[38] provide that information on products as well as contracts must be drafted in Portuguese.

3.3 Capping Liability

Cloud service providers usually limit or exclude liability through disclaimers in standard SLAs. For example, Google Apps SLA offers a 99.9% availability term on a monthly basis. The monthly percentage availability corresponds to the total amount of minutes in one month minus the number of minutes of unavailability (consisting of a 5% or higher percentage of errors), divided by the total minutes in one month. If Google does not comply with the availability level, customers are entitled only to service credits (free of charge) as follows: for availability <99.9% - >= 99.0%, credit of 3 days of service; for availability <99.0% - >= 95.0%, credit of 7-days service; for availability <95.0%, 15 days of credit of service.

Customers must request the credit within 30 days after becoming eligible to receive it, otherwise it expires. 15 days of service is the maximum number of service credits to be issued by Google concerning failures of availability within one month. Service credits cannot be exchanged for money, except for clients with a monthly invoicing plan.[39] Service credits do not apply to services which are not covered by the SLA (e.g. Google Gmail Labs or Voice and/or Video chats to Gmail) or to performance problems caused by

---

[37] Law No 24/96 of 31 July, as last amended by Decree-Law No 47/2014 of 28 July, Article 7(3).

[38] Decree-Law No 238/86 of 19 August, as later amended by Decree-Law No 42/88 of 9 February.

[39] For different terms see e.g. Rackspace's Cloud Big Data Platform SLA, http://www.rackspace.com/pt/information/legal/cloud/sla (last access 25 May 2016)

conditions of *force majeur* as listed by the cloud service contract or by the customer's or a third party's equipment or both if they are not under Google's main control.

Under Google Cloud Platform Terms of Service the amount of liability is limited to the maximum paid by the customer to Google during the twelve months prior to the event giving rise to liability (13.2).[40] The Google Cloud Platform Terms of Service also disclaims any warranty of any kind, notably warranties of merchantability, fitness for a particular use and non-infringement as well as warranties of error-free or uninterrupted operation of the software or the services. In particular, it is expressly stated that neither the software nor the services are designed, manufactured, or intended for high risk activities.

Liability exclusion or disclaimers may be unenforceable under Portuguese law. Cloud computing terms of service, including SLA, are, as standard terms, ruled by the Standard Terms Act. Therefore, the content of standard terms must comply with the catalog of forbidden clauses applicable to B2B contracts. Terms which offend good faith are prohibited[41], notably those included in the list of dark clauses (clauses which are absolutely deemed null and void), or in the list of grey clauses (i.e. clauses the validity of which depends upon the relevant standard business framework). Concerning B2B standard contracts, terms providing for penalty clauses which are not proportional to eligible damages, as well as clauses which allow one of the parties to terminate the contract, immediately or without sufficient notice and adequate compensation, where the contract

[40] Other cloud providers have a term of calculating the availability period starting 12 moths before the client actually receives the service with the assumption that during that period availability was 100%. See *White Paper Comparing Public Cloud Service Level Agreements* at http://cloud.dimensiondata.com/saas-solutions/about/resources/white-papers/comparing-public-cloud-service-level-agreements (last access 25 May 2016).

[41] Article 15 of Decree-Law 446/85.

has required from the other party considerable investments or expenses[42], are deemed *grey clauses*, meaning that their conformity with good-faith has to be assessed in according with the standard business framework (*quadro negocial padronizado*). Good-faith is here understood in objective sense meaning a general legal principle from which duties of honesty and loyalty arise, including a general obligation to refrain from abusive exploitation of weaker business partners and consumers.

Concerning disclaimers of warranty and exclusions of liability, they are prohibited where they exclude or limit liability for damages caused to life, moral or physical integrity, to a person's health, as well as liability for personal damages caused to the other party or to third parties. Such conditions are also forbidden where they exclude or limit liability for lack of, or defective performance, including delay, due to intentional fault or gross negligence[43]; a *contrario*, general terms excluding liability of service providers acting with excusable negligence may be accepted. In contract terms open to negotiation, the exclusion of liability can be allowed in the cases of excusable negligence, provided that they do not concern offences to mandatory rights, including rights of personality, or to the infringement of duties imposed by rules of public order.[44]

Concerning the law applicable to contractual obligations, under Regulation Rome I on the law applicable to contracts[45], the principle is that they are governed by the law chosen by the parties.[46] In the absence of choice, this Regulation provides specific criteria for

---

[42] Article 19(c) and (f) of Decree-Law 446/85.

[43] Decree-Law 446/85, Article 18(a)(b)(c) of Decree-Law 446/85.

[44] See MONTEIRO, A. Pinto. *Cláusulas limitativas e de exclusão de responsabilidade civil*. 2nd reprint. Coimbra, Almedina, 2011.

[45] Regulation (EC) N° 593/2008 of the European Parliament and of the Council of 17 June 2008 on the law applicable to contractual obligations (Rome I).

[46] Article 3(1) of Regulation Rome I.

different types of contracts, and those for the provision of services are governed by the law of the country of the service provider's habitual residence.[47]

However, *consumer contracts* - i.e. those 'concluded by a natural person for a purpose which can be regarded as being outside his trade or profession (the consumer) with another person acting in the exercise of his trade or profession (the professional)' - are governed by the law of the country of the consumer's habitual residence if the professional acts mainly in that country or, by any means, directs his/her activities to that country or to several countries including that country, and the contract falls within the scope of such activities.[48] Choice of law is only allowed if it does not deprive the consumer of the protection afforded to him by mandatory provisions of the law of the country of his habitual residence.[49]

3.4. Data portability & migration

SLAs are usually silent on this issue. Data portability or migration is not a matter specific of SLAs but probably a different section of the terms of service offered by cloud providers.

Data portability should not hinder the freedom of customers to seek new cloud providers and to migrate from cloud to cloud. However, legislation in force provides no special obligation upon cloud providers to guarantee data portability to their customers.[50]

---

[47] Article 4(1)(b) of Regulation Rome I.

[48] Article 6(1) of Rome Regulation I.

[49] Article 6(2) of Rome Regulation I.

[50] Interoperability of services is a major concern of the regulation of electronic communications, as provided under several provisions of the Electronic Communications Act (Law No 5/2004 of 10 January, later amended), notably Article 27(1)(a). More recently, the EU has adopted the Regulation (EU) 2015/2120 of the European Parliament and of the Council of 25 November 2015 laying down measures

This aspect will improve in order to preserve customer freedom and therefore competition in the cloud environment, notably with the so-called "right to data portability".[51]

Software copyright legislation provides the mandatory right of reverse engineering of computer programs for purposes of computer interoperability, so that legitimate customers are free to develop independent solutions that are compatible with reverse engineered software.[52] This right of reverse engineering gives some freedom to software customers in relation to providers. Arguably it should apply both to software and to data-ware.[53]

3.5 Backup facilities

SLAs usually contain disclaimers concerning the exclusion of liability of the cloud provider for loss of their customers' data. For instance, the Google Cloud Platform Terms of Service includes a Disclaimer under sec. 12 according to which "*Google and its suppliers are not responsible or liable for the deletion of or failure to store any customer data and other communications maintained or trans-*

---

concerning open internet access and amending Directive 2002/22/EC on universal service and users' rights relating to electronic communications networks and services and Regulation (EU) No 531/2012 on roaming on public mobile communications networks within the Union.

[51] Article 20 and whereas 68 and 73 of Regulation (EU) 2016/679 of the European Parliament and of the Council of 27 April 2016 on the protection of natural persons with regard to the processing of personal data and on the free movement of such data, and repealing Directive 95/46/EC (General Data Protection Regulation), applicable as of 25 May 2018. See also the Proposal for a Regulation of the European Parliament and of the Council on ensuring the cross-border portability of online content services in the internal market, COM(2015) 627 final 2015/0284 (COD), Brussels, 9.12.2015.

[52] The imperative of interoperability is also stated as a normative principle by Directive 2001/29/EC of the European Parliament and of the Council of 22 May 2001 on the harmonization of certain aspects of copyright and related rights in the information society.

[53] Cf. PEREIRA, A.L. Dias. *Direitos de autor e liberdade de informação*. Coimbra: Almedina, 2008.

mitted through use of the services. Customer is solely responsible for securing and backing up its application, project, and customer data."

The analysis of different cloud solutions offered by different cloud providers shows that backup may be a service offered by the cloud provider but it appears not to be considered an essential part of the cloud service as such. It means that backup is a service of the cloud, but there may be cloud services without backup.

The exclusion of liability of the cloud provider for the loss of their customers' data is probably one of the most sensitive issues in the field of cloud computing. It means that customers bear the risk of loss of data, and therefore it is said that: "If it's in the Cloud, get in on paper".[54]

Concerning licensed software in the cloud, copyright legislation provides customers with a mandatory right to make a backup copy for safety reasons.[55] Arguably cloud providers should have an obligation to provide backup of data for a minimum period of time, after which cloud providers could charge for extended backup facilities.

4. Cloud computing in sensitive sectors

In some sectors, such as health, public administration or financial/banking, cloud computing is a sensitive resource which may eventually not be allowed.

4.1 Cloud computing may represent significant costs reduction for banking by means of IT-Outsourcing. It is estimated that a group of banks (Deutsche Bank, Barclays, Finibanco, Millennium bcp,

---

[54] TRAPPLER, T. *If It's in the Cloud, Get It on Paper: Cloud Computing Contract Issues* (2010)

[55] Article 6 of Decree-Law No 252/94.

BPI, Santander Totta, BPN and BES) alone has outsourced to IBM the provision and management of IT infrastructures worth around €1000 million. This investment enhanced scalability of investments and reduced operating costs from circa 15% to 30%.[56]

There are no outsourcing guidelines specific of cloud computing. However, cloud computing may be considered a form of outsourcing. As such it is not prohibited, but it should allow to know and to control risks, and do not hinder supervision. The General Regulation of Credit Institutions and Financial Companies[57] provides that banks and other credit institutions have to comply with a number of requirements. For instance, an institution established in Portugal has to organize efficient procedures for the identification, management, supervision and communication of the risks to which it may be exposed.[58] So, the use of cloud computing by the financial sector may be prohibited where it is used to circumvent such obligation.

One of such risks is money laundering. The Bank of Portugal issued Regulation No 5/2013[59] to implement Article 39(1) of Law No 25/2008 of 5 June concerning the required conditions, mechanisms and procedures of compliance with obligations preventing money laundering and terrorism funding related to the provision of financial services submitted to the supervision of the Bank of Portugal. According to Article 3 of said regulation it applies to: (1) credit institutions (banks), investment and other financial companies, payment institutions and institutions of electronic money with headquarters in Portugal; (2) branches located in the Portuguese territory where

---

[56] COSTA, R.L. "O «outsourcing» dos sistemas de informação como factor de competitividade no sector da banca", Rev. Portuguesa e Brasileira de Gestão 9/3 (2010) 11-19.

[57] Decree-Law No 298/92 of 31 January, as later amended.

[58] Article 14 of Decree-Law No 298/92.

[59] Aviso do Banco de Portugal n.º 5/2013 http://www.bportugal.pt/sibap/application/app1/docs1/avisos/textos/5-2013a-c.pdf (last access 25 May 2016).

such institutions have headquarters in foreign countries, including external financial branches; (3) providers of post services inasmuch as they provide to the public financial services which are related to matters subject to the supervision of the Bank of Portugal.

In order to prevent money laundering and terrorism funding, the Bank of Portugal has competence to do inspections in any premises of financial institutions or of third parties being used to the exercise of the activity of financial institutions, with the power to demand the presentation of any information or clarifications which it may deem relevant, including the local examination of information elements, the extracting of copies of all pertinent documentation, and to call of any person for hearings and collecting information.

Under Article 49 and for purposes of said regulation, financial institutions have to keep copies or electronic data of any document presented to them by their clients or any other person. Records and supporting evidence of transactions must enable the supervision authority: (1) to fully track their past movements from the beginning until the end, even where there are third parties, notably agents or intermediaries, involved, and (2) to identify every person intervening in the circuit. Records and supporting evidence must be kept on paper or other durable record and be archived in adequate conditions for their preservation, easy location and immediate access to them whenever the information is requested by those in charge with compliance or auditing and by external auditors of financial institutions, as well as by competent judicial, police and supervision authorities.[60]

4.2. Data protection is a sensitive issue of cloud computing in the health sector. Storing electronic medical records (EMR) in the

[60] Failure to comply with said regulation is an infringement for purposes of Law No 25/2008 subject to penalty fines ranging from 2,500 to 5,000,000 euros depending on several factors, notably whether it is practiced by individuals or by legal persons (Article 57).

Cloud raises several issues such as the content of clinical files and several levels of control, notably access (who and from where), authenticity and integrity (who can edit EMR), confidentiality, security and back-up control (who is in charge?), interoperability and functionality, and control of data migration to third countries.[61]

Health data is deemed sensitive for purposes of the Portuguese Data Protection Act[62].[63] Therefore, the health sector needs to guaran-

---

[61] Article 8 of the EU Charter of Fundamental Rights, which has become legally binding, guarantees the fundamental right to the protection of personal data and it is enshrined in Article 16(1) of the Treaty on the Functioning of the EU (TFEU). Directive 95/46/EC is the general EU law on the protection of personal data, which sets the rights of data subjects and establishes criteria for the legitimacy of processing personal data, including "personal data on health". On the other hand, Directive 2002/58/EC lays down specific requirements in connection with the provision of publicly available electronic communications services in public communications networks to ensure confidentiality of communications and security of their networks. Directive 95/46/EC has been repealed by Regulation (EU) 2016/679 of the European Parliament and of the Council of 27 April 2016 on the protection of natural persons with regard to the processing of personal data and on the free movement of such data (General Data Protection Regulation) with effect from 25 May 2018 (Article 94). Concerning Directive 2002/58/EC, the "Regulation does not impose additional obligations on natural or legal persons in relation to processing in connection with the provision of publicly available electronic communications services in public communication networks in the Union in relation to matters for which they are subject to specific obligations with the same objective set out in Directive 2002/58/EC" (Article 95 of Regulation (EU) 2016/679). On the impact of this Regulation on electronic commerce, see WEIGL, Michaela. The EU General Data Protection Regulation's Impact on Website Operators and eCommerce – Essential changes for Privacy Statements, Consent, Direct Marketing and Cookies. *CRi - Computer und Recht International*. N. 4 (2016), 102-108.

[62] Law No 67/98 of 26 October, which implements Directive 95/46/EC of the European Parliament and of the Council of 24 October 1995 on the protection of individuals with regard to the processing of personal data and on the free movement of such data. For an analysis of the Portuguese legal framework see, notably, MARQUES, Garcia; MARTINS, Lourenço. *Direito da Informática*. 2.ª ed. Coimbra, Almedina, 2006, 129-313, 422-442, 330-391. GONÇALVES, M. Eduarda. *Direito da Informação - Novos Direitos e Formas de Regulação na Sociedade da Informação*. 2.ª ed. Coimbra: Almedina, 2003, 82-111, 173-183. CASTRO, C. Sarmento e. *Direito da informática, privacidade e dados pessoais - A propósito da legalização de tratamento de dados pessoais*. Coimbra: Almedina, 2005. See also the Commission Regulation No 611/2013 of 24 June 2013 providing notably the duty to notify breaches of personal data and the use of technological protection measures.

[63] Directive 95/46/EC prohibits the processing of personal data related to health unless certain conditions are fulfilled (Article 8). According to the European Court of Justice, the notion of "data concerning health" must be given a wide interpretation, so as to include information concerning all aspects, both physical and mental, of an

individual's health (judgment of 6 November 2003, case C-101/01, *Bodil Lindqvist*, ECLI:EU:C:2003:596, paras. 50 and 51). The Article 29 Data Protection Working Party provided further interpretation of this concept by recommending that health data should cover: a) any personal data closely linked to the health status of a person only, such as genetic data or data on consumption of medicinal products, alcohol or drugs; b) any other data contained in the medical documentation concerning the treatment of a patient – including administrative data (social security number, date of admission to hospital, etc.), so that any data that is not relevant for the treatment of the patient, should not be included in the medical files. On the protection of health information, see Article 29 Working Party *Working Document on the processing of personal data relating to health in electronic health records (EHR)*, 2007; Cloud Standards, Consumer Council, *Impact of Cloud Computing on Healthcare*, 2012. In Portuguese literature RAPOSO, V. Lúcia O Fim da "Letra De Médico": Problemas Suscitados pelo Processo Clínico Eletrónico em Sede de Responsabilidade Médica. *Lex Medicinae - Revista Portuguesa de Direito da Medicina*. N° 19 (2013), 51-78.

Legislation in force in Portugal establishes a dualistic system concerning health information, which has raised criticism among authors, notably PEREIRA, A. G. Dias. Dever de documentação, acesso ao processo clínico e sua propriedade: uma perspectiva europeia. *Revista Portuguesa do Dano Corporal*, N° 16 (2006); BARBOSA, Carla. Aspectos Jurídicos do Acesso ao Processo. *Lex Medicinae – Revista Portuguesa de Direito da Medicina*. N° 7 (2010) 107-140. Health data is sensitive data under Article 7(1) of Law No 67/98. It means that health data is subject to a qualified level of protection. Notwithstanding this, processing health data, including genetic data, is allowed, regardless of the person's authorization, if it is necessary for purposes of preventive medicine, medical diagnostic, provision of healthcare or management of health services, and provided it is carried out by health professionals or another person acting under the duty of professional confidentiality, it is given notice of to the Data Protection Authority, and adequate information security measures are given (Article 7(4) Law 67/98). Special security measures of control concern entry in the premises, data supports, editing, use, access, transmission, and transportation (Article 15 Law 67/98). Access to health data is assisted by a doctor chosen the data holder (Article 11(5) Law 67/98).

On the other hand, the Statute of personal health information (Law No 12/2005 of 26 January) provides that health information belongs to the concerning person and can only be used to provide health care and to conduct research or other purposes statutorily authorized (Article 3 Law 12/2005). The person has the right to know in full the clinical record, unless it is harmful to her, and access to health information is assisted by a doctor chosen by the information owner. The person liable for processing health information has certain specific obligations, notably to preserve confidentiality, security of the premises and equipment, access control, to hold secrecy, to prohibit undue access by third parties to clinical files and computer systems storing health information, to maintain security levels which prevent the destruction, modification, diffusion or unauthorized access or any other unlawful use of the information, and to do regular data back-up. However, anonymized data can be used for research purposes. The Statute of personal health information defines the clinical file (*processo clínico*) as any record, electronic or else, of health information of patients and their relatives, as complete as possible (Article 5 Law No 12/2005). Viewing and editing are restricted to doctors or other health professionals supervised by the doctor and subject to confidentiality.

tee a suitable level of protection with regard to the patient's personal data, as well as respect for the rights of the data subject. Migration to the cloud, where allowed, does not preclude the obligations of the health service provider concerning the protection of the patient's data, notably in what concerns security of data processing.[64]

On the other hand, the Portuguese Code of Medical Ethics[65] provides a specific regulation for telemedicine. Telemedicine is "the provision of healthcare services, through the use of ICT, in situations where the health professional and the patient (or two health professionals) are not in the same location. It involves secure transmission of medical data and information, through text, sound, images or other forms needed for the prevention, diagnosis, treatment and follow-up of patients"[66]. Examples of telemedicine services are teleradiology, teleconsultation, telemonitoring, teleophtalmology, telesurgery and teledermatology. In broad sense telemedicine also includes other e-health services, notably health information portals, online pharmacy,

---

In contrast with the Personal Data Protection Act and the statute of personal health information, the Statute of Access to Public Documents (Law No 46/2007, of 24 November) provides that access to nominative documents with health information is done by the concerning person or by a third person authorized in writing by the data holder, or by any third party evidencing a direct, personal and legitimate interest, provided it is sufficiently relevant under the principle of proportionality (Article 6(5) Law 46/2007). It means that electronic medical records held by public hospitals or other units of the health service could be accessed by third parties even without the consent of the person concerned. Moreover, communication of data is carried out by the doctor if the applicant requests it; in any case, personal notes, drafts and alike records are excluded from the notion of public documents (Articles 7 and 3(2)(a) of Law 46/2007). This Act has been repealed by Law No 26/2016 of 22 August, which nonetheless allows access by third parties without the data subject's consent but limited to the information strictly necessary for the direct, personal, legitimate and constitutionally protected interest that supports access (Article 7).

[64] Articles 14 and 15 of the Data Protection Act.

[65] Regulation No 707/2016 of 21 July (implements the World Medical Association Statement on Accountability, Responsibilities and Ethical Guidelines in the Practice of Telemedicine, adopted in Tel Aviv, Israel, October 1999).

[66] See Commission *Communication on telemedicine for the benefit of patients, healthcare systems and society*. COM(2008) 689 final; Commission *Staff Working document on the applicability of the existing EU legal framework to telemedicine services*. SWD(2012) 414 final, Brussels, 6.12.2012.

electronic health record systems, electronic transmission of prescriptions or referrals (e-prescription, e-referrals), and e-prescription.

According to the Code of Medical Ethics, telemedicine must respect the doctor-patient relationship and doctors are free and completely independent to decide whether to use or to refuse telemedicine. If they decide to use it, they have to make sure that the team in charge assures a level of quality sufficiently high which works in a proper way and complies with established regulations. In particular, doctors must use supporting systems, quality controls and evaluation procedures to monitor the accuracy and the quality of the received and transmitted information. Moreover, doctors can only use telemedicine once they have made sure that the system used and its users assure medical secret, namely by means of encryption of names and other identifying data. Doctors inform and clarify the patient, obtain his consent, and must assure the application of security measures established to protect the patient's confidentiality. Computerized methods of storage and transmission of the patient's data may be used only if enough measures have been adopted to protect confidentiality and security of stored or exchanged information.[67]

If Cloud Computing is used to provide telemedicine the above-mentioned requirements also have to be complied with. Telemedicine is allowed but it must respect the doctor-patient relation, as well as patient's security and confidentiality.

4.3. The acquisition of Cloud Computing by the Public Sector is also a sensitive matter.[68] It is regulated as an acquisition of services

[67] Articles 46 to 49 of the Code of Medical Ethics. Cf. PEREIRA, A.L. Dias, "Patient safety in e-health and telemedicine", *Lex Medicinae – Revista Portuguesa de Direito da Medicina*. Special Issue (2014), 95-106.

[68] See HON, W.K., MILLAR, C., WALDEN, I. Public Sector Cloud Contracts. In MILLAR, C. (ed.). *Cloud Computing Law*. Oxford: Oxford University Press, 2013, 108-141.

by the Code of Public Contracts (or Public Procurement Act).[69] It governs all public institutions, however part II does not apply to certain institutions, notably public workers, hospitals and universities

The Public Procurement Act is complemented notably by the Open Standards Act 2011[70], which mandates public bodies to contract computer software based upon open standards concerning digital information processing in the Public Administration with a view to promoting technological freedom of citizens and organizations and the interoperability of computer systems of the Government. Acts of public procurement which exclude solutions based upon open standards are deemed null and void.[71]

Cloud computing is an opportunity for the development of e-Government. Cloud providers render services specially designed for the public administration.[72] However, outsourcing of cloud computing shall not compromise data's safety and confidentiality. Despite the principle of open archive concerning access to documents in the public sector, there are exceptions to this principle notably for reasons of external and internal security (the State's classified information concerning for ex. military and diplomatic files), classified legal proceedings, business secrets (undisclosed confidential information given to public bodies), professional secrecy, and personal data (nominative documents, in particular personal information held by the national health system or by the tax administration).[73]

---

[69] *Código dos Contratos Públicos* (Public Procurement Act), enacted by Decree-Law No 18/2008 of 29 January, as last amended by Decree-Law No 214-G/2015, of 2 October.

[70] Law No 36/2011 of 21 June.

[71] See PEREIRA, A.L. Dias. Normas abertas nos sistemas informáticos do Estado. *Revista do CEDOUA*. Nº 29 (2012) 39-43.

[72] See eg http://www.cisco.com/web/strategy/docs/gov/brochure_cisco_cloud_government.pdf

[73] Law No 26/2016 of 22 August (approves the regime for access to administrative and environmental information and re-use of administrative documents, transposing Dir. 2003/4/EC and Dir. 2003/98/EC, as last amended by Dir. 2013/37/UE, of the European Parliament and of the Council).).

4.4. The Court of Justice of the European Union[74] declared the invalidity of the Decision of the Commission No 2000/520/CE of 26 July 2000, concerning the «Safe Harbor» principles for the transfer of data to the USA. Following this, the National Commission for Data Protection[75] adopted Deliberation No 1770/2015 of 10 November 2015, concerning the assessment procedure of Intra-Group Agreements (IGA) for transferring data outside the European Union, i.e. multilateral agreements among several companies of the same corporate group usually located in countries which do not afford an adequate level of data protection under EU standards.[76] Under such agreements (IGA) the parties bind themselves to comply with a set of rules to protect rights in personal data and the privacy of their holders. Transfer of data to such countries requires authorization of the National Commission of Data Protection and is granted provided that the controller of data processing guarantees enough mechanisms to protect private life and the people's basic rights and freedoms, as well its exercise under adequate contract terms. This Deliberation sets guidelines which companies should comply with when drafting their IGA for transferring data to third countries, including the USA after the said ruling of the Court of Justice in *Maximillian Schrems v Data Protection Commissioner* of 6 October 2015.

In order to streamline the procedure of analysis of Intra-Group Agreements (IGAs) notified to the National Commission of Data Protection (CNPD) concerning the transfer of personal data to third countries which do not afford an adequate level of data protection and so that the reply to the controllers of data is faster, the CNPD deliberates that, for purposes of Article 20(2) of the Data Protection

[74] Judgment of 6 October 2015, case C-362/14, *Maximillian Schrems v Data Protection Commissioner*, ECLI:EU:C:2015:650.

[75] Comissão Nacional de Proteção de Dados – www.cnpd.pt

[76] Deliberação n.º 1770/2015, de 10 de novembro de 2015, relativa ao procedimento de análise dos Acordos Intragrupo (IGA) para transferências de dados para fora da EU.

Act, a multilateral agreement among companies of the same corporate group (IGA) notified to the CNPD by the controller which thereby declares that the IGA is identical or in conformity with standard clauses approved by the European Commission according to the conditions set forth in this Deliberation.

According to the specific guidelines issued by the CNPD, IGA clauses are deemed to be in conformity with the EC standards where the only difference concerns the multilateral nature of the contract, but all parties and respective functions should be identified and they should sign the agreement. The same applies for clauses incidentally changed concerning superficial aspects like punctuation or translation without altering the meaning of the words used in standard terms. Terms with commercial nature, provided they do not conflict in any way with standard clauses, as well as those concerning jurisdiction of business litigation among the parties, damage compensation, right of return, as long as they do not affect the right to complain and the right to appeal of the data holder, are also cleared.

Concerning outsourcing, it includes terms stipulating the obligation to provide previous information to the data controller concerning any modification of the subcontractor (outsourcing provider), whenever the parties agree that the requested authorization of the data controller for outsourcing activities has a general scope rather than specific (i.e. authorization for each new outsourcing activity) so that the data controller can oppose to it.

In short, the only difference from the EC standard clauses is that they are multilateral (instead of bilateral), concern superficial aspects like punctuation or translation, do not affect the right to complain and the right to appeal of the data holder, and concerning outsourcing, the data controller can oppose further outsourcing.[77]

---

[77] As for penalties for failure to comply with the regulations, a fine from 250 to 15000 euros is provided, depending on whether it is committed by an individual

5. Security, trust, and ISP liability

Cloud computing, as computing in general, is subject to the Cybercrime Act of 2009[78], which provides several types of criminal offences, notably computer forgery, computer damage, computer sabotage, illegal access, unlawful interception, and illegal reproduction of computer program. The penalties for cybercrimes include prison and fines, they are relevant to deter potential infringers from committing offences against information security, including data authenticity, integrity and confidentiality.

On the other hand, concerning the liability of cloud computing providers as Internet Service Providers (ISP), the Electronic Commerce Act[79] provides in Chapter III a special liability regime for networking service providers, such as providers of mere conduit, caching and hosting, as well as providers of network content association services, such as search engines and hyperlinks, which are assimilated, for regulation purposes, to providers of hosting services[80]. Moreover, considering the urgent nature that a settlement *prima facie* may have, this Act provides schemes of provisional settlement of disputes that arise regarding the lawfulness of contents available on the network. This procedure of *notice and take down*

---

or by a legal entity. In case it concerns data for which previous control is required the limits of the administrative fines doubles (Article 37 Law 67/98). On the other hand, it is a criminal offence where companies do not notify or request authorization from the National Commission of Data Protection to transfer data to third countries which do not afford an adequate level of protection, as well as to provide false data in the requests or to change it in manners not allowed by law (Article 43(1)(a)(b) Law 67/98). It is punished with prison up to one year or fine up to 120 days. This criminal offence requires intent. Where it concerns sensitive data (e.g. health or political data) fines can reach the double of said penalties (Article 43(2) Law 67/).

[78] Law No 109/2009 of 15 September

[79] Decree-Law No 7/2004 of 7 January, which implements Directive 2000/31/EC of the European Parliament and of the Council of 8 June 2000, as last amended by Law No 46/2012 of 29 August.

[80] Articles 11 to 19 of Decree-Law No 7/2004.

is assigned to an administrative supervision entity, without prejudice to the final decision of the dispute being taken by the courts.

Concerning hosting and content aggregation[81], ISPs are not bound to remove the disputed contents or to disable access to the information on the grounds of a claim made by an interested party, where the illegality is not obvious. However, any interested party may appeal to the relevant supervision authority, that shall present a preliminary settlement within forty-eight hours and notify it immediately by electronic means to all those involved. The supervision authority can alter at any time the preliminary settlement of the dispute and whatever the decision may be it is exempted from liability for it; likewise, the intermediary service provider is not liable for having removed contents or disabled access based on a mere request, where the illegality is not obvious. The final dispute settlement is carried out via common procedures, recourse to which is without prejudice to the use by interested parties, at the same time, of common judicial means. On the other hand, whoever has a legal interest in maintaining that content online is likewise entitled to appeal to the supervision authority against a decision of the provider to remove or to disable access to that content, in order to obtain a preliminary dispute settlement.

The Electronic Commerce Act also provides a general principle of assimilation and special rules on intermediaries' liability.[82] Intermediaries are not liable for the information transmitted/hosted, where:

1° they only transmit information in a communication network, or provide access to a communication network, not having initiated the transmission, nor modified the contents of the

[81] Article 18 of Decree-Law No 7/2004.

[82] Article 11 of Decree-Law No 7/2004 ("The liability of online service providers is subject to the common regime, namely in the case of content aggregation, with the specifications arising from the following articles.")

messages transmitted, nor selected either the information or the receivers; or where they merely provide technological storage of the information transmitted, in so far as this takes place for the sole purpose of carrying out the transmission and provided that the information is not stored for any period longer than what is necessary for the transmission[83];

2° - they provide automatic and temporary storage of information, performed for the sole purpose of making more efficient and economical the information's onward transmission to recipients of the service upon their request, as long as they do not modify the contents of the messages transmitted, nor select either the information or the receivers, and comply with the conditions on access to the information, and the usual rules of the sector regarding the updating of the information, and the use of technology to obtain data on the use of the information.[84] If any of these requirements fails the caching exemption does not apply, as well as if the provider has obtained actual knowledge of the fact that the information has been removed from its initial source or access to it has been disabled, or that a court or an administrative authority with powers upon the provider who has originated the information has ordered an immediate enforcement action towards such removal or access disablement, and the provider does not act expeditiously to remove or disable access to the information.[85]

---

[83] Article 14 of Decree-Law No 7/2004 (*mere conduit*).

[84] Article 15 of Decree-Law No 7/2004 *(caching)*.

[85] Article 15(3) of Decree-Law No 7/2004. Article 75 of the Copyright Act (as amended by Law No 50/2004 of 24 August to implement Directive 2001/29/EC of the European Parliament and of the Council, of 22 May, on the harmonization of certain aspects of copyright and related rights in the information society) provides that the reproduction right shall not comprise the temporary acts of reproduction which are transient, incidental or accessory, and which represent an integral and essential part of a technological process and the sole purpose of which is to enable a transmission in a network between third parties by an intermediary, or a lawful

3º They provide server storage and have not knowledge of an obviously illegal activity or information or do act expeditiously to remove or to disable access to such information once they gain knowledge or, for civil liability, should be aware of the illegal nature of the information; for this exemption to apply the recipients of the service cannot act under the authority or the control of the provider.[86]

4º - Where they provide network content aggregation services, by means of search engines, hyperlinks or similar procedures that allow access to illegal contents, the hosting exemption applies, *mutatis mutandis*.[87]

Notwithstanding, it is clarified, concerning the relationship with the right to information, that: (1) content aggregation is not irregular on the grounds that there are illegal contents in the destination website, despite the awareness of this fact by the provider; (2) the link is legal if performed with objectivity and distance, and represents a way of exercising the right to information, but it is illegal if it consists of a way to adopt the illegal content being linked to as one's own. In order to assess the illegality of content aggregation, the circumstances of the case are to be considered, namely

---

use of a protected work and which have no independent economic significance, including, to the extent that they meet these conditions, the acts which enable browsing as well as caching to take place, as well as those which enable transmission systems to function efficiently, provided that the intermediary does not modify the information in the transmission and does not interfere with the lawful use of technology, according to the uses widely recognized by industry, to obtain data on the use of the information, and generally the merely technological processes of transmission. Moreover, an injunction may be applied against intermediaries whose services are used by a third party to infringe a copyright or a related right, without prejudice to the power of rights holders to notify intermediaries, previously and directly, of the unlawful acts, aiming at the non-production or ceasing of its effects (Article 227 of Copyright Act).

[86] Article 16 of Decree-Law No 7/2004 (*hosting*).

[87] Article 17 of Decree-Law No 7/2004 (*browsing, search engines, hyperlinks*)

the possible confusion of the contents of the origin and destination websites, the automatic or intentional character of the link, and the area of the destination website to which the link is made.[88]

Internet intermediaries have no general duty to monitor, filter and/or block as long as they have a passive role[89].[90] The Electronic

---

[88] Article 19 of Decree-Law No 7/2004.

[89] In *Scarlet v SABAM*, case C-70/10, Judgment of 24 November 2011 (ECLI:EU:C:2011:771) the European Court of Justice held that, in short: "Directives 2000/31/EC on electronic commerce, 2001/29/EC on internet copyright, 2004/48/EC on IP enforcement, 95/46/EC on personal data protection, 2002/58/EC on privacy in electronic communications, 'read together and construed in the light of the requirements stemming from the protection of the applicable fundamental rights, must be interpreted as precluding an injunction made against an internet service provider which requires it to install a system for filtering: all electronic communications passing via its services, in particular those involving the use of peer-to-peer software; which applies indiscriminately to all its customers; as a preventive measure; exclusively at its expense; and for an unlimited period, which is capable of identifying on that provider's network the movement of electronic files containing a musical, audio-visual or cinematographic work in respect of which the applicant claims to hold intellectual property rights, with a view to blocking the transfer of files the sharing of which infringes copyright." See also *SABAM v. Netlog* (judgment of 16 February 2012, case C-360/10, ECLI:EU:C:2012:85). More recently, in *Telekabel* (judgment of 24 March 2014, case C314/12, *UPC Telekabel Wien GmbH* v *Constantin Film Verleih GmbH,* Wega Filmproduktionsgesellschaft mbH, ECLI:EU:C:2014:192), the ECJ ruled that "The fundamental rights recognised by EU law must be interpreted as not precluding a court injunction prohibiting an internet service provider from allowing its customers access to a website placing protected subject-matter online without the agreement of the rightholders when that injunction does not specify the measures which that access provider must take and when that access provider can avoid incurring coercive penalties for breach of that injunction by showing that it has taken all reasonable measures, provided that (i) the measures taken do not unnecessarily deprive internet users of the possibility of lawfully accessing the information available and (ii) that those measures have the effect of preventing unauthorised access to the protected subject-matter or, at least, of making it difficult to achieve and of seriously discouraging internet users who are using the services of the addressee of that injunction from accessing the subject-matter that has been made available to them in breach of the intellectual "property right, that being a matter for the national authorities and courts to establish."

[90] Concerning personal data processing, search engines providers have to respect the European protection of personal data, notably the right of remove (also known as the 'right to be forgotten'), according to the standards set up by the European Court of Justice in *Google Spain, Google Inc. v AEPD, Costeja González*, case C-131/12, judgment of 14 May 2014 (ECLI:EU:C:2014:317), in interpreting EC Directive 95/46, in particular that "the activity of a search engine consisting in finding information published or placed on the internet by third parties, indexing it automatically, storing it temporarily and, finally, making it available to internet users according to a particular order of preference must

Commerce Act expressly provides that online intermediary service providers are not under the general obligation to monitor the information that they transmit or store, nor to investigate possible offences practiced within their scope.[91] Notwithstanding, several common duties of intermediary service providers are established towards the competent authorities. ISP have (1) to inform the competent authorities promptly when becoming aware of illegal activities undertaken via services rendered, (2) to meet requests for the identification of recipients of their services with whom they have entered into storage agreements, (3) to comply promptly with the instructions aiming to terminate or to prevent an offence, namely to remove or disable access to a given information, and (4) to supply lists of owners of hosted websites, where requested.

---

be classified as 'processing of personal data' within the meaning of Article 2(b) when that information contains personal data and, second, the operator of the search engine must be regarded as the 'controller' in respect of that processing, within the meaning of Article 2(d)", and that "the operator of a search engine is obliged to remove from the list of results displayed following a search made on the basis of a person's name links to web pages, published by third parties and containing information relating to that person, also in a case where that name or information is not erased beforehand or simultaneously from those web pages, and even, as the case may be, when its publication in itself on those pages is lawful." However, this obligation to remove will not apply if, "for particular reasons, such as the role played by the data subject in public life, that the interference with his fundamental rights is justified by the preponderant interest of the general public in having, on account of its inclusion in the list of results, access to the information in question." On this judgment and its implications, see with, more references, SPIECKER, I. A new framework for information markets: Google Spain. *Common Market Law Review*. Vol. 52 (2015), 1033-1058. It is important to remark that in *Costeja Gonzalez*, the ECJ ruled, concerning the jurisdiction of EU law over personal data processing by *Google Inc.*, that "Article 4(1)(a) of Directive 95/46 is to be interpreted as meaning that processing of personal data is carried out in the context of the activities of an establishment of the controller on the territory of a Member State, within the meaning of that provision, when the operator of a search engine sets up in a Member State a branch or subsidiary which is intended to promote and sell advertising space offered by that engine and which orientates its activity towards the inhabitants of that Member State." On the complex issue of asserting jurisdiction concerning data protection in cloud computing, see HON, W. K., HÖRNLE, J., MILLARD, C. Data Protection Jurisdiction and Cloud Computing – When Are Cloud Users and Providers Subject to EU Data Protection Law? The Cloud of Unknowing. *International Review of Law, Computers & Technology*. Vol. 26, Issue 2-3 (2012), 129-164.

[91] Article 12 of Decree-Law No 7/2004.

Conclusion

Major cloud players in Portugal provide their services with standard terms, including SLAs, where customization is not possible. Customers are only free to decide which cloud services they wish and to accept the terms of service offered by the cloud providers. SLAs focus on service availability (uptime and downtime), criteria to measure availability and procedures to report performance, remedies for incompliance with the level of service (usually as financial credits in the service fee and their caps), and disclaimers with limitation or exclusion of liability.

There is no legislation specific of cloud computing services, and the relevant industry did not produce binding codes of conduct or guidelines. Some SLAs templates are available on the Internet, and they correspond essentially to those offered by the major players (Amazon, Google, Azure Microsoft). There are events discussing cloud computing, but it seems that self-regulation of standard terms for cloud computing is yet to bring about such codes of conduct.

The legal vacuum is however merely apparent. To begin with, cloud computing SLAs are subject to general contract law as well as –notably where software is involved - to copyright legislation. Other statutory regulations have also an important role, notably those on data protection. Even in the field of contract law, the role of special legislation is to be noticed, in particular the Standard Terms Act which, similarly to German legislation, applies not only to B2C contracts but also to B2B contracts. Proponents of standard terms have to comply with duties of communication and information in the formation of the contract, and standard terms have to pass the test of conformity with good-faith, in particular the lists of 'black' and 'grey' terms, notably those concerning exclusion of liability and the possibility to terminate the contract without previous notice and adequate compensation.

In what concerns regulated sectors such as health, finance and the public sector, besides legislation applicable to B2C and to the protection of personal data, cloud computing has to comply with regulations, notably on supervision of financial institutions, eHealth and public procurement. In particular, it is remarked that telemedicine in Portugal is allowed under the Code of Medical Ethics and, in public procurement, tenders cannot exclude solutions based upon open standards.

Considering the cross-border nature of cloud computing services and the need to harmonize some sensitive issues such as adequacy of availability to the customer's specific needs, data portability, backup and transparency with a view to protect customers and competition, an active role of the EU would probably be desirable in the development of standard SLAs.[92] An European legal instrument could be adopted, similar to the initiative of drafting the European Union Public License concerning the use of open software[93], as a relevant tool for the 'digital single market', as proclaimed by the European Commission.[94]

[92] See Spark Legal Network & Time.Lex, *Study on standard terms and performance criteria in service level agreements for cloud computing services* (2015).

[93] See https://joinup.ec.europa.eu/software/page/eupl

[94] *Digital Single Market Strategy for Europe*. Communication from the Commission to the European Parliament, the Council, the European Economic and Social Committee and the Committee of the Regions. COM(2015) 192 final.

PRIVATE ENFORCEMENT OF COMPETITION LAW IN PORTUGAL - BEFORE AND AFTER THE DAMAGES DIRECTIVE*

Abstract - Private enforcement of competition law in Portugal is known in the books but almost inexistent in practice. The EU Damages Directive 2014/24 is likely to change the *status quo,* bringing *law in the books* closer to *law in action*. This paper provides a comparative analysis between internal law and the Directive, and argues for its implementation by means of special legislation rather than amendments to the Civil Code or the Code of Civil Procedure.

1. General framework of Portuguese competition law

One of the State's economic priorities is 'to assure the sound functioning of the markets, in order to guarantee a balanced competition among undertakings, to fight monopolies and abuses of dominant positions as well as other practices that harm the general interest'[1].

---

* Global Competition Litigation Review, vol. 2, p. 43-49, 2016, published by Sweet & Maxwell (imprint of Thomson Reuters).

[1] Article 81(f) of the Portuguese Constitution.

The statutory discipline of competition is provided by Law No 19/2012 of 8 May[2]. This Act applies to all anti-competitive practices taking place or producing its effects on Portuguese territory[3]. As anti-competitive practices it provides, in particular, the prohibition of cartels (agreements and concerted practices), abuse of dominant position, and abuse of economic dependence, on one hand[4], and merger control (both in substance and procedure), on the other.[5] Moreover, it governs procedural aspects of antitrust[6], as well as the activity of the Competition Authority, in particular concerning its powers of drafting recommendations, inspections and auditing, including state aid[7], and its procedure of decision-making in matters of infringements and fines[8].

The Competition Act is complemented by special legislation, such as the Leniency Act[9]. Concerning private enforcement of competition law, there is no specific statutory regulation or relevant case-law, and literature is not abundant[10]. Probably because competition law is still considered mainly as a tool of public regulation of markets rather than one of protection of individual interests. As one author puts it, "An antitrust regime should seek to compensate victims, but the primary goal should be to deter violations."[11]

---

[2] The 4th generation of Portuguese competition statutes: Law No 19/2012 replaced Law No 18/2003 of 11 June, which replaced Decree-Law No 371/93 of 29 October, which in turn replaced Decree-Law No 422/83 of 3 December.

[3] Article 2(2) of Competition Act.

[4] Articles 9 to 12 of Competition Act.

[5] Articles 36 to 59 CA. For a general introduction to the sources and principles of EU and national competition law, see Pereira 2013. For an article-by-article commentary to the Portuguese Competition Act see Porto et al 2013.

[6] Articles 13 to 35 of Competition Act.

[7] Articles 60 to 65 of Competition Act.

[8] Articles 67 to 93 of Competition Act.

[9] Law No 39/2006 of 25 August.

[10] See however Abreu 2011, Campos 2014, Anastacio 2015. In other languages, see e.g. Font i Ribas et al 2013, Gutta 2014, Lianos/Davis/Nebbia 2015.

[11] Ginsburg 2010, 57.

2. 'Antitrust torts' as civil liability for damages

Infringements to competition law fall within the scope of the 2nd modality of extra-contractual civil liability[12], as competition law also gives protection to individual interests: "Competition is a publicly-protected interest" but competition "also protects the individual interests of companies and consumers".[13] In short, civil liability is governed in substance by the Civil Code of 1966, and its procedural aspects by the Code of Civil Procedure.[14]

The function of civil liability is to compensate damages. Any person harmed by an antitrust infringement can stand before the court to claim damages[15]. Other remedies are also available for private enforcement such as the declaration of nullity of anti-competitive transactions[16] and the requirement of an injunction to do or not to do a certain action[17], the performance of which can be subject to a compulsory fine[18].

Before dissecting the requirements of civil liability applied to antitrust infringement, it is important to underline that EU antitrust law, consisting of the prohibition of cartels and the abuse of dominant position[19], is directly applicable by national competition authorities and the courts[20]. Direct applicability of EU antitrust

---

[12] Lima & Varela 1987, 472 (economic law, including competition rules - "regras disciplinadoras da concorrência"); Varela 1989, 507 ("regras da boa concorrência").

[13] Abreu 2011, 101.

[14] Código de Processo Civil, enacted by Law No 41/2013 of 26 June.

[15] Article 483 of Civil Code.

[16] Articles 280, 286 and 294 of Civil Code.

[17] Article 829 of Civil Code (*execução específica).*

[18] Article 829-A of Civil Code (*sanção pecuniária compulsória* or *astreinte*).

[19] Respectively, Articles 101 and 102 of Treaty on the Functioning of the European Union (TFEU)

[20] Article 3(1)(2) of Council Regulation (EC) No 1/2003 of 16 December 2002 on the implementation of the rules on competition laid down in Articles 81 and 82 of the Treaty.

law is considered a major step towards the development of private enforcement law in Europe[21], culminating with the adoption of the Antitrust Damages Directive in November 2014.[22]

This topic is not very relevant in Portuguese literature and case-law, but things are starting to change[23]. There are no public records of 'antitrust torts' ruled by Portuguese courts, which is in fact "surprising", probably because "the general culture of competition law and civil liability has still not been properly established".[24] And so far no special statutory measures have been adopted to implement the Directive, the deadline of which is the 27 December of 2014[25]. It is not clear, to begin with, how should the implementation be carried out, either by adding new provisions to the Civil Code and to Code of Civil Procedure, or amending the Competition Act, or even enacting a special statute, such as, for example, the Leniency Act.

3. The impact of European case-law on competition

Notwithstanding this, particularly in matters of competition law, the existing legal framework is usually interpreted in accordance with the case-law of the European Court of Justice, which has been codified by the Damages Directive. Looking at some significant judgments, it means, in short, that:

---

[21] Goméz Ségade 2015, 849 ("autêntico hito en el desarollo del sistema de aplicación privada del derecho antitrust en el âmbito comunitário").

[22] Directive 2014/104/EU of the European Parliament and of the Council of 26 November 2014 on certain rules governing actions for damages under national law for infringements of the competition law provisions of the Member States and of the European Union.

[23] Anastacio 2015, 313-4.

[24] Abreu 2011, 103.

[25] Article 21 of Directive 2014/104/EU.

a) Antitrust damages are mandatory under EU competition law, but self-inflicted damage is not eligible[26];

b) Any person may argue nullity of cartels (including those on exchange of prices information) and seek compensation for damage which have an adequate link of causality with the cartel[27];

c) Domestic procedural rules cannot render impossible or extremely difficult the right to seek damages for antitrust torts... including limitation periods and criteria for damage quantification, which shall include *damnum emergens*, *lucrum cessans*, and interests[28];

d) Cartel participants cannot be exempted from damages caused by prices which a third party would not fix had the cartel not taken place[29];

e) Right of access to documents of leniency proceedings in favor of any person harmed by competition infringements[30];

f) To require the consent of all concerned parties in leniency proceedings does not satisfy the principle of effective enforcement[31]; and

g) The European Commission is entitled to act on behalf of Member States to seek compensation for antitrust damages[32].

---

[26] ECJ Judgment of 20 September 2001, C-453/99, *Courage & Crehan*, ECLI:EU:C:2001:465.

[27] ECJ Judgment of 13 July 2006, C-295/04 to C-298/04, *Manfredi*, ECLI:EU:C:2006:461.

[28] ECJ Judgment of 13 July 2006, C-295/04 to C-298/04, *Manfredi*, ECLI:EU:C:2006:461.

[29] ECJ Judgment of 5 June 2014, C-557/12, *Kone*, ECLI:EU:C:2014:1317.

[30] ECJ Judgment of 14 June 2011, C-360/09, *Pfleiderer*, ECLI:EU:C:2011:389.

[31] ECJ Judgment of 6 June 2013, C-536/11, *Donau Chemie*, ECLI:EU:C:2013:366.

[32] ECJ Judgment of 6 November 2012, C-199/11, *Otis*, ECLI:EU:C:2013:366.

4. Civil liability for antitrust damages

4.1. General principle and requirements of civil liability

The general principle of extra-contractual civil liability for unlawful acts (*torts*) means that 'anyone who, willfully or recklessly, unlawfully infringes another person's right or any statutory provision aimed at protecting someone else's interests, has the obligation to indemnify the injured person for damages arising from the infringement'[33].

Several requirements are embedded in the general principle of civil liability. In actions for damages the plaintiff has to argue an unlawful and faulty conduct (1), the actual damage suffered (2), and the nexus of adequate causality linking the unlawful conduct to the his/her damage (3).[34] The burden of proof lies with the claimant[35], including the defendant's fault which in case of *mera culpa* may justify reduction of damages by the court ruling on equity[36]. Fault may eventually be excluded in cases of involuntary parallelism or unintended participation in a cartel.

The plaintiff has a 3-year limitation term to bring an action for damages upon being aware of his right to a claim[37], within 20 years upon the production of damage[38].

In civil liability (*torts*), the rule is joint and several liability[39]. Any co-infringer is liable towards the claimant for the overall damage,

---

[33] Article 483(1) of the Civil Code (contributor's translation).

[34] Lima & Varela 1987, 470-6; Varela 1989, 489 ff.; Costa 2009 (civil liability).

[35] Articles 342 and 346 of Civil Code, and Article 414 of Code of Civil Procedure.

[36] Article 496 of Civil Code.

[37] Article 498 of Civil Code.

[38] Article 309 of Civil Code.

[39] Article 497(1) of Civil Code.

but he/she has the right to be reimbursed from the other co-infringers in the proportion of the fault and consequence each person, fault being statutorily presumed[40]. So far no exception is expressly provided for recipients of immunity in leniency proceedings[41], but nothing prevents considering participation in such proceedings as a factor of attenuation of fault.

4.2. Standing and jurisdiction

Standing in claims for damages is recognized to any natural or legal person who suffered harm because of an antitrust infringement[42]. It includes not only direct purchasers from cartelists and abusers of dominance, but also indirect purchasers (notably consumers), who may stand before the court to claim damages.

Standing is also recognized to any citizen or public interest association or foundation, as well as to municipalities and the Public Prosecutor in proceedings for the protection of 'diffuse interests'[43]. Portuguese law provides a special mechanism of collective redress, the so-called *ação popular (action popularis)*[44], i.e. recognizing the right to file an action to any citizen or legal person pursuing the general interest, including consumers' unions.[45]

---

[40] Article 497(2) of Civil Code.

[41] Holding that "it should [not] be any other way", Abreu 2011, 110 ("If the whistle-blower were to benefit from both a reduction in public sanctions as well as private sanctions, this would allow the infringing party to have a double benefit.").

[42] Articles 11 and 30 of Code of Civil Procedure.

[43] Article 31 of Code of Civil Procedure.

[44] Correia 2010, 111. On the constitutional meaning of this procedure as a remedy to protect basic rights, Canotilho 2003, 510-1.

[45] Article 52 of Portuguese Constitution and Law No 83/95 of 31 August. See also Abreu 2011 (holding that this Act confers the "*right to file class actions*" and that "the interests of consumers (also) protected by competition rules are diffuse interests" - 106).

In Portugal there is a court with specialized jurisdiction on competition, regulation and supervision.[46] However, it does not have jurisdiction to decide on civil matters, including torts.[47] These matters rest with general courts, the judicial hierarchy of which comprises courts of first instance, regional courts of appeal and the Supreme Court of Justice.

4.3. Discovery and Evidences

The general principle on evidences in civil procedure is that the judge takes all necessary measures to discover the truth of facts and to produce a just resolution of the conflict[48]. Anyway, as a general rule, evidences are only allowed if all concerned parties had the chance to contradict them before the court[49]. This applies also to experts, who can be appointed by the court but their expertise is freely accessed by the judge[50]. Expert evidence is particularly important concerning the quantification of damages as it usually requires a *complex* economic analysis.[51]

Of special relevance for evidence in antitrust damage actions is access to documents. The courts have the power, *ex officio* or upon request of any party, to order any of the parties or even third parties, including public authorities, to disclose documents which may be relevant for deciding a case[52]. Refusal to comply with must

[46] Established by Decree-Law No 67/2012 of 20 March. Article 83(3)(b) of Law No 62/2013 of 26 August (*Lei de Organização do Sistema Judiciário*).

[47] Article 112 of of Law No 62/2013 of 26 August.

[48] Article 411 of Code of Civil Procedure (*princípio do inquisitório*).

[49] Article 415 of Code of Civil Procedure.

[50] Article 467 ff. of Code of Civil Procedure; Articles 388 and 389 of Civil Code.

[51] Anastacio 2015, 318.

[52] Article 429 ff. of Code of Civil Procedure.

have legal ground, otherwise fines apply and the court may freely assess its meaning including the rehearsal of the burden of proof[53].

Concerning *follow-up litigation*, i.e., actions brought following a decision of the Competition Authority, the parties may have access to its files provided they are not under secrecy. The principle is publicity of proceedings, but the Competition Authority may determine secrecy until the final decision in the interests of the inquiry or the rights of the defendant. However, the Competition Authority may reveal the content of an act or document under secrecy where it does not jeopardizes the research of the facts and semes conveniente to the clarification of truth. [54]

In case of judicial secrecy third parties do not have access to the proceedings, and even the defendant can be denied access[55]. Concerning files classified as confidential by the Competition Authority, they can only be accessed under business or professional secrecy. As for documents presented by leniency applicants, consent of the applicant is required for access by third parties[56].

4.4. Quantification of damages and pass-on defense

The Civil Code provides regulation for the obligation to indemnify and criteria for the quantification of damages. It takes place by natural restoration or, in case of impossibility or hardship, by payment of monetary compensation[57]. The quantification of damage is done according to the theory of the difference, i.e. damage corresponds

[53] Articles 430 ff. and 417 Code of Civil Procedure; Article 344(2) Civil Code.

[54] Article 32 (1) to (5) of Competition Act.

[55] Article 33 of Competition Act.

[56] Article 81(3) of Competition Act.

[57] Articles 562 and 566 of Civil Code.

to the difference between the value of the claimant's assets after the antitrust infringement and what it would be had the infringement not taken place[58]. It includes *damnum emergens* (actual loss) and *lucrum cessans* (loss of profit)[59]. Interest will be due since the moment that the harm takes place until the moment of payment of the indemnity[60]. Civil liability does not have a punitive function and therefore punitive damages are not awarded.[61] It is argued that besides future damage, loss of chance and even moral damage might be claimed.[62] However, concerning moral damages, they must be serious (e.g. death and alike) to be eligible for compensation[63]. A possible example is a company undergoing bankruptcy because of the antitrust infringement.

In quantifying damage, if the exact amount of damages cannot be determined, the judge resorts to equity, within what was proved[64]. He also has to take into account the plaintiff's fault as it may reduce or even exclude compensation[65].

Victims of antitrust infringements are entitled to compensation for the actual prejudice they suffered as a result of the infringement. However, if they pass-on damage to third parties, either undertakings or consumers, then damage is not actual or effective. Compensation for pass-on damages would therefore originate unjust enrichment, which is deemed a quasi-tort under Portuguese law and gives rise to the obligation of restitution[66]. Nevertheless, damages transferred

---

[58] Articles 562 and 566(2) of Civil Code.

[59] Article 564 of Civil Code.

[60] Article 562 ff. of Civil Code.

[61] On this debate, concerning penalty clauses in contracts, see Monteiro 1990.

[62] Anastacio 2015, 319.

[63] Article 496 of Civil Code.

[64] Article 566(3) of Civil Code.

[65] Article 570 of Civil Code. Contingent fee or conditional fee is not allowed by the by-laws of the Bar Association, either as *palmarium* or as *quota litis* (Law No 15/2005 of 26 January, Article 101). Anastacio 2015, 319.

[66] Article 473 of Civil Code.

to third-parties are only excluded from compensation if the defendant gives evidence of pass-on. It may be used as a defense, but the party arguing it has the burden of proof or onus of evidence.

4.5. Follow-on litigation

The Courts and the Competition Authority are independent and separate bodies of the state[67]. Courts are the judiciary power. The Competition Authority is an independent administrative agency which nonetheless belongs to the executive branch.

Accordingly, concerning domestic competition law, civil proceedings do not require infringement proceedings before the Administrative Authority, i.e. there may be *stand alone* actions. Moreover, the decisions of the Competition Authority do not bind civil courts, but they may serve as *prima facie* evidence of infringement. Then, the Courts do not have to delay proceedings until a decision is given by the Competition Authority.[68] It means for example that the limitation period of the civil proceedings (3 years) may expire before the limitation period of administrative proceedings, which is a 5-year term[69].

4.6. Settlements and arbitration

Portuguese law provides for settlement procedures before and during court proceedings at any time[70]. Settlements concerning mandatory (non-disposable) mandatory rights and unlawful transactions

[67] Article 111 of Portuguese Constitution.

[68] Anastacio 2015.

[69] Article 74 of Competition Act.

[70] Article 283(2) ff. of Code of Civil Procedure.

are prohibited[71]. Written form is required, including public deed or notarized document where the legal effect produced by the settlement requires such form[72]. In court proceedings, it takes place by a transcript in the proceedings[73].

Antitrust damage claims are eligible for arbitration. Arbitration is governed by the Arbitration Act.[74] The parties, including under certain circumstances the State and other entities of public law, may agree in writing to refer to arbitration the decision of any dispute concerning economic interests unless the dispute is statutorily submitted to State courts or to mandatory arbitration. The referees decide according to statutory regulation, unless the parties agree to have a decision based on equity and the legal relationship at stake is disposable[75]. Decisions according to legislation or given *ex aequo et bono* have the same legal force as decisions of the court of first instance[76]. In arbitration the principle is confidentiality of proceedings, subject to some exceptions[77].

5. EU Directive 2014/104 of 26 November

Regulation No 1/2003 has provided direct application of Articles 101 and 102 of the Treaty on the Functioning of the European Union (TFUE). National Courts have been granted jurisdiction to award damages to any injured person (including undertakings, consumers

[71] Article 1249 of Civil Code.

[72] Article 1250 CC. It is, for the example, the case of a sale of real estate property under Article 879 of Civil Code.

[73] Article 290 of Code of Civil Procedure.

[74] Law No 63/2011 of 14 December.

[75] Article 1 of Arbitration Act.

[76] Article 39 of Arbitration Act.

[77] Articles 30**(5)** and 46 to 48 of Arbitration Act.

and public entities) due to infringements of such provisions. This raised the need to harmonize procedural aspects of private enforcement of EU and domestic competition law, as well as codification of relevant case-law of the European Court of Justice.

5.1. The right to seek full compensation

Directive 2014/104 on antitrust damages provides the right to seek full compensation for damages which have a causality link with competition torts, standing being recognized to all undertakings, consumers and public authorities[78]. Eligible damages necessarily include actual harm (*damnum emergens*) and loss of profits (*lucrum cessans*), as well as interests, either autonomously or as part of *damnum emergens* and *lucrum cessans*[79]. *Punitive damages* and *unfair enrichment* are prohibited[80], but damage may arguably include *loss of chance.*

The harmonization of private enforcement is based upon the principles of *effectiveness* and *equivalence* between EU and national antitrust torts[81]. These principles govern several topics of the regulation, notably the process of discovery (evidences), limitation periods, subjective liability, quantification of damage, and alternative resolution mechanisms.

5.2. Evidence / discovery

Concerning disclosure of evidence, the courts must have the power to order disclosure of relevant evidence, while at the same

---

[78] Article 3(1) of Directive 2014/104.

[79] Article 3(2) of Directive 2014/104.

[80] Article 3(3) of Directive 2014/104.

[81] Article 4 of Directive 2014/104.

time protecting sensitive information, notably trade-secrets and other confidential information including the attorney's privilege[82]. Then, evidences in proceedings before competition authorities are protected, so that access to files is ruled by the principle of proportionality and the so-called *prospective searches* are prohibited. Certain information is to be disclosed only after closing of proceeding[83], otherwise it is worthless as evidence[84]. Absolute protection is given to information concerning leniency statements and settlement proposals[85], which are in any case worthless as evidence[86]. Penalties are provided for nondisclosure and destruction of information requested by the court, as well as for violation of confidentiality, and abuse of privileged information.

5.3. Final decisions of national Competition Authority as irrebuttable evidence

The Antitrust Damages Directive binds the courts to the decisions of the competition authorities. In fact, final decisions of domestic competition authorities serve as *irrebuttable evidence* (or *iuris et the jure* presumption[87]) of antitrust infringement[88], even if limited in scope (subject matter, people involved, time and place). [89] In contrast, decisions of foreign authorities serve only as *prima facie* evidence of

[82] Article 5 of Directive 2014/104.

[83] Article 6(5) of Directive 2014/104.

[84] Article 7(2) of Directive 2014/104.

[85] Article 6(6) of Directive 2014/104.

[86] Article 7(1) of Directive 2014/104.

[87] Article 350(2) of Civil Code.

[88] Article 9(1) of Directive 2014/14.

[89] Before the adoption of the Damages Directive it was considered that a rule binding the national courts to the decisions of the Competition Authority "would possibly be unconstitutional in light of the provisions of Article 203 of the Constitution of the Portuguese Republic" (Abreu 2011, 103).

infringement[90]. This is the answer provided to the need to articulate the decisions of the Competition Authority with those of the Courts[91].

5.4. Limitation period of 5 years

In order to have a limitation period long enough for antitrust torts to be decided, it lasts at least 5 (five) years, and does not start to run before the infringement ceases and the plaintiff knows or should know about the infringing action, the damage suffered, and the identity of the infringer[92]. Moreover, limitation periods are suspended where a Competition Authority takes measures which concern a proceeding related to damages action.[93]

5.5. Joint and several liability, and exceptions

Concerning who is liable for antitrust damages, the rule is *joint and several liability* of every infringer, notwithstanding individual liability of each in internal relations[94]. Exceptions are provided for small or medium size undertakings to preserve their solvency[95] and *immunity recipients* to foster the useful effect of leniency proceedings[96].

---

[90] Article 9(2) of Directive 2014/14. In favor of this system, Goméz Ségade 2015, 859 ("La prejudicialidad que introduce la Directiva me parece muy positiva y constituye algo novedoso en el Derecho español"). Pointing out "the need to guarantee the interoperability between public and private enforcement and their synergetic interaction", Lianos/Davis/Nebbia 2015, 301.

[91] See e.g. Guillén Caramés 2013.

[92] Article 10(1)(3) of Directive 2014/104.

[93] Article 10(4) of Directive 2014/104.

[94] Article 11(1) of Directive 2014/104.

[95] Article 11(2) of Directive 2014/104.

[96] Article 11(4) of Directive 2014/104.

5.6. Passing-on of overcharges and the right to full compensation

The right to seek full compensation for damages, including actual harm, loss of profits and interests, should not give rise to unfair enrichment. "In order to avoid overcompensation... compensation for actual loss at any level of the supply chain does not exceed the overcharge harm suffered at that level"[97]. Therefore, the Directive provides the *passing-on defense*: the defendant in an action for damages can invoke the fact, which he has the burden of proving, that the claimant passed on the whole or part of the overcharge resulting from the infringement of competition law[98].

Moreover, *indirect purchasers* in claims for damages can argue to have been overcharged "taking into account the commercial practice that price increases are passed on down the supply chain"[99]. Actions for damages by claimants from different levels in the supply chain and provisions for the uniformity of judgments are also established[100].

Concerning the quantification of damages, theirs is a rebuttable presumption that cartels cause prejudice[101], notably by increasing or keeping prices high, *damnum emergens* being defined "as the difference between the price effectively paid and that which would have been paid in the absence of infringement"[102].

Courts always decide on the quantum of damages and can request assistance from national authorities[103]. Quantification of damage is a complex issue which also concerns notably the hypothetical evolution of the market in the absence of infringement. According

[97] Article 12(2) of Directive 2014/104.

[98] Article 13 of Directive 2014/104.

[99] Article 14 of Directive 2014/104.

[100] Article 15 of Directive 2014/104.

[101] Article 17(2) of Directive 2014/104.

[102] Whereas 39 of Directive 2014/104

[103] Article 17(1)(3) of Directive 2014/104.

to whereas 46 of Directive 2014/104, "Regard should be had to any information asymmetries between the parties and to the fact that quantifying the harm means assessing how the market in question would have evolved had there been no infringement. This assessment implies a comparison with a situation which is by definition hypothetical and can thus never be made with complete accuracy." The importance of the *Commission Guidelines* is therefore underlined in this concern.

5.7. Consensual dispute resolution

Resorting to consensual dispute resolution mechanisms, such as arbitration, suspends limitation periods for parties in such proceedings as well as court proceedings up to 2 years[104]. Moreover, compensation established in out-of-court proceedings is to be deduced from damage claims before court proceedings concerning other infringers who do take part of out-of-court proceedings, where such remaining compensation is to be claimed from them, unless they cannot pay it and it is not excluded by settlement[105].

6. Comparative outlook and conclusion

As it stands Portuguese law deals with antitrust damages as a situation of civil liability for infringement of statutorily protected interests. Despite the Competition Authority has found several antitrust infringements, there is no body of case-law on this issue, which is not also the hottest topic in academic debate and research.

---

[104] Article 18(1)(2) of Directive 2014/104.

[105] Article 19(1)(2)(3) of Directive 2014/104.

An overview analysis of the discipline provided for by Directive 2014/104 compared with the existing legal framework shows that its implementation will probably not require radical innovation transformation of Portuguese law.

To begin with, a presumption that antitrust infringement causes damages will make it easier for those suffering prejudice as a result of the infringement as it rehearses the burden of proof.

Next, exceptions to joint and several liability will be established concerning small and medium undertakings and well as recipients of immunity in leniency proceedings.

Moreover, the provision of the pass-on defense will prevent private enforcement of antitrust from giving rise to unfair enrichment, limiting compensation to actual and effective damage.

On the other hand, the scope of absolute confidentiality concerning documents held by the Competition Authority is limited to statements of immunity applicants in leniency proceedings as well as statements produced in settlement proceedings.

Finally, of greatest importance is also binding the courts to the decisions of the national Competition Authority, as they are already bound under Regulation 1/2003, and that administrative proceedings have a suspensive effect on the limitation periods concerning proceedings running before the courts.

Certainly, it will have an impact in modernizing Portuguese civil law so that victims of antitrust torts claim their right to compensation and have damage indemnified by antitrust law infringers. In our opinion, rather than amending the Civil Code and the Code of Civil Procedure, it would be better to deal with this matter within the Competition Act or, eventually, to make a special Act to implement the Directive on antitrust damages.[106]

---

[106] In favor of amending the Law of Civil Procedure in Spain, Gómez Ségade 2015, 855.

As pointed out by Goméz Ségade, the 'legal good protected by antitrust law is dual: on one hand public interest in keeping competition as a basis of market economy and implicitly the democratic political system; on the other hand, private interest of those taking part in the market as economic agents and consumers, who may experience damage as a consequence of infringement to antitrust law'.[107]

Having regard this *dual nature* of competition law probably it might be wiser to implement the Directive by means of competition specific legislation rather than amending the Civil Code and or the Code of Civil Procedure. The remedies and procedures established by the Damages Directive are tailored for 'antitrust torts' and therefore, by analogy with the implementation of the IP Enforcement Directive[108], they would be better placed within competition legislation.

References

Abreu, JM Coutinho (2011) Private enforcement of competition law in Portugal. Velasco San-Pedro, LA (dir.) Private enforcement of competition law, 101 (Lex Nova, Valladolid)

Anastacio, G (2015) Portugal. The Private Competition Enforcement Review, 8th ed. 313-325 (ed. Ilene Knable Gotts, Law Business Research Ltd, London)

Campos, FDC (2014) A reparação dos danos sofridos em violação das regras europeias da Concorrência (Universidade do Porto, Porto)

Canotilho, JJ Gomes (2003) Direito Constitucional e Teoria da Constituição (7th ed. Almedina, Coimbra)

Correia, JM Sérvulo (2010) The effectiveness and limitations of the Portuguese system of competition law enforcement by administrative and civil procedural means.

---

[107] Góméz Ségade 2015, 845; see also e.g. Abreu 2011, 101.

[108] Directive 2004/48/EC of the European Parliament and of the Council of 29 April 2004 on the enforcement of intellectual property rights, implemented by Law No 16/2008 of 1 April, amending the Copyright Act (*Código do Direito de Autor e dos Direitos Conexos*, enacted by Decree-Law No 63/85 of 15 March) and the Industrial Property Act (*Código da Propriedade Industrial*, enacted by Decree-Law No 36/2003 of 5 March).

Mateus, A, Moreira, T (ed.) Competition Law and Economics – Advances in Competition Policy Enforcement in the EU and North America, 85-121 (Edward Elgar, Cheltenham)

Costa, MJ Almeida (2009) Direito das Obrigações (12ª ed., Almedina, Coimbra)

Font i Ribas, A, Gómez Trinidad, S (coord) (2013) Competencia y acciones de indemnización. Actas del Congresso Internacional sobre daños derivados de ilícitos concurrenciales (Marcial Pons, Madrid)

Ginsburg, DH (2010) Costs and benefits of private and public antitrust enforcement: an American perspective. In Mateus, A, Moreira, T (ed.) Competition Law and Economics – Advances in Competition Policy Enforcement in the EU and North America, 39-58 (Edward Elgar, Cheltenham)

Goméz Ségade, JA (2015) Resarcimiento de los daños por infracciones del derecho de la competencia. In Vicente, D Moura et al. (Dir.) Estudos de Direito Intelectual em Homenagem ao Prof. Doutor José de Oliveira Ascensão, 843-864 (Almedina, Coimbra)

Guillén Caramés, J (2013) La cooperación entre jueces y autoridades administrativas en la aplicación privada del derecho de la competência. In Font i Ribas, A, Gómez Trinidad, S (coord) Competencia y acciones de indemnización. Actas del Congresso Internacional sobre daños derivados de ilícitos concurrenciales (Marcial Pons, Madrid)

Gutta, NB (2014) The Enforcement of EU Competition Rules by Civil Law (Maklu, Antwerpeen)

Lianos, I, Davis, P, Nebbia, P (2015) Damages claims for the infringement of EU competition law (Oxford University Press)

Lima, FA Pires de, Varela, Antunes (1987) Código Civil Anotado, vol. I (Artigos 1.° a 761.°) (col. M. Henrique Mesquita, 4.ª ed., Coimbra Editora, Coimbra)

Monteiro, A Pinto (1990) Cláusula penal e indemnização (Coimbra, Almedina)

Pereira, AL Dias (2013) Direito da concorrência e liberdade de empresa. Boletim da Faculdade de Direito, vol. 89/2, 97-131

Porto, M Lopes et al (2013) Lei da Concorrência Anotada - Comentário Conimbricense (Almedina, Coimbra)

Varela, JM Antunes (1989) Direito das obrigações, vol. I (6th ed., Coimbra, Almedina)

LEVIES IN EU COPYRIGHT LAW: AN OVERVIEW OF THE CJEU'S JUDGMENTS ON THE FAIR COMPENSATION OF PRIVATE COPYING AND REPROGRAPHY*

Abstract - The European Parliament has called for a 'virtuous system' of levies for private copying and the CJEU develops a model of 'fair compensation' based upon the notion of harm to right holders. This contribution provides an overview of the system of copyright levies in EU law as interpreted by the Court of Justice, and suggests its possible enhancement by means of tax-like measures upon the consumption of reproduction equipment and media to promote the freedom of cultural creation.

Introduction

On 27 February 2014, the European Parliament adopted a Resolution on *private copying levies*[1] calling on the Commission to submit a proposal of revision of Directive 2001/29[2] to set up,

---

* *Journal of Intellectual Property Law & Practice*, 12/7 (2017), p. 591-600, by permission of Oxford University Press.

[1] P7_TA(2014)0179.

[2] Directive 2001/29/EC of the European Parliament and of the Council of 22 May 2001 on the harmonisation of certain aspects of copyright and related rights in the information society.

notably, a 'virtuous system' of private copying levies. Considering that 'all European consumers should have the right to make private copies of legally acquired content' (n° 2), the European Parliament finds that it is necessary to harmonize the essential elements of the levy system, notably the concept of *fair compensation* and the concept of *harm to authors* resulting from private copying (recital G). In reply, the European Commission stated that it 'will assess the need for action to ensure that, when Member States impose levies for private copying and reprography to compensate right holders, their different systems work well in the *single market* and do not raise barriers to the *free movement of goods and services*.'[3]

The Commission had already obtained recommendations concerning the revision of the levy system, notably a 'uniform' definition of harm by reference to the value for consumers of private copying as 'lost profit' (n° 1)[4]. An active NGO on this sector has also argued a 'comprehensive reform' of compensation for private copying based upon the notion of 'actual and demonstrable harm'.[5]

Probably one of the reasons why the Commission was not sure about the 'need for action' is the number of requests for preliminary rulings submitted to the CJUE.

---

[3] *Towards a modern, more European copyright framework*, COM(2015) 626 final, at 9.

[4] A Vitorino, *Recommendations resulting from the Mediation on Private Copying and Reprography Levies (*Brussels, 31 January 2013).

[5] Digital Europe, *Private Copying: Assessing Actual Harm and Implementing Alternative Systems to Device- Alternative Systems to Device-Based Copyright Levies Based Copyright Levies* (Brussels, 22 June 2015). In scholarship see notably PB Hugenholtz, L Guibault and G van Sjoerd, *The Future of Levies in a Digital Environment (Final Report)* (Amsterdam IVIR 2003) 46, held the phasing out of levies 'not in function of actual use, but of availability of technical measures on the market place'.

I. FROM THE 'GERMAN LEVY SAGA' TO THE FAIR COMPENSATION IN EU COPYRIGHT LAW

A. The 'German Levy Saga'

The 'virtuous system' provided by Directive 2001/29, and as interpreted by the CJUE, finds its roots in the so-called 'German levy saga'[6]. The German Federal Court (BGH) hold in its judgments *Tonband*[7] and *Personalausweise*[8] that, despite private copying is contrary to the right of reproduction, copyright enforcement would be not only unfeasible but also invasive of users' privacy. The BGH suggested the statutory provision of a compensation for private copying, which took place under the German Copyright Act of 1965 by means of a levy system on recording equipment and devices. Later on, a similar mechanism has been set for reprography, following the judgment of the German Federal Court in *Kopierläden*[9].

The reproduction by natural persons for their private use became an accepted exception to the exclusive right of reproduction under the three-step test provided by Art. 9(2) of the Berne Convention introduced by the Act of Stockholm (1967), and later adopted by other international instruments (TRIPS Agreement 1994, WIPO Internet Treaties 1996).[10] This does not expressly incorporate the

---

[6] PB Hugenholtz, 'The Story of the Tape Recorder and the History of Copyright Levies' in B Sherman and L Wiseman (eds.) *Copyright and the Challenge of the New* (Wolters Kluwer, Alphen aan den Rijn 2012) 179-196, at 180.

[7] BGH, 18.05.1955 - I ZR 8/54, NJW (1955) 1276.

[8] BGH, 29.05.1964 - Ib ZR 4/63, NJW (1964) 2157.

[9] BGH, 09.06.1983 - I ZR 70/81, NJW (1984) 1106.

[10] See M Senftleben, *Copyright, Limitations, and the Three-Step Test. An Analysis of the Three-Step Test in International and EC Copyright Law* (Kluwer Law International, The Hague 2004).

requirement of fair compensation, but reference to it 'as an element of the third step' is found 'into the final report of the Conference'[11].

Nowadays, copyright levies exist not only in almost every Member State of the EU[12], but also in other countries, such as the USA, Canada, Japan and Russia, and they have amounted to € 804 million in 2014, Germany alone contributing with €281 million.[13]

According to the CJUE, the fair compensation for private copying established by Directive 2001/29 is mandatory in consideration for the (optional) private copy exception and its rational is to repair possible harm to right holders caused by consumers of reproduction devices, media and services[14]. Notwithstanding this, practical difficulties justify that those making such devices, media or services available to the public have to discharge a levy on the price of sale of their goods or services, which presumably they can pass-on to consumers. Inasmuch as the levy system exempts copies made

---

[11] PB Hugenholtz, 'The Story of the Tape Recorder and the History of Copyright Levies', at 191 (pointing out at 188 that 'The idea of a levy can actually be traced to the voluntary scheme developed by GEMA in the early 1950s, under which tape recorder manufacturers and importers were offered blanket licences for a one-time licence fee per recorder.').

[12] In Portugal, a levy system has been introduced in the Copyright Act of 1985 and implemented by Law No. 62/98. However, several provisions of this Law have been declared unconstitutional by the Constitutional Court [Judgment No. 616/2003 of 16 December 2003, case 340/99, (2004) 62 Diário da República I-A] due to failure to comply with tax-law principles, as copyright levies would be a tax-like measure (see also JO Ascensão, 'A «compensação»' (1990) 31 RFDUL 211-238). Law No. 50/2004 has established a fixed percentage on the price of sale to the public of reproduction equipment and a list of levied media and tariffs. It has been argued that Law No 50/2004 did not comply with Directive 2001/29 notably because it did not provide a reimbursement scheme: DM Vicente, 'Cópia privada e compensação equitativa: reflexões sobre o Acórdão Padawan' (2011) 36 CDP 22-35, at 30]. In order to fix this Law No 48/2015 has extended the levy to digital equipment and other media and expressly linked the compensation to the criterion of harm: see JO Ascensão, 'Lei nº 49/2015, de 5 de Junho, em matéria de cópia privada e compensação equitativa' (2015) 1 RDI 343-371; JA Vieira, 'A cópia privada e o seu regime de compensação' (2016) 1 RDI 51-64.

[13] WIPO, *International Survey on Private Copying Law & Practice* (Geneva, WIPO 2015) 22.

[14] M Leistner, 'Europe's Copyright Law Decade: Recent Case Law of the European Court of Justice and Policy Perspectives' (2014) 51 CMLR 559-600, at 586-7.

for purposes other than private use and provides mechanisms of reimbursement of such undue levies, it will ensure a fair balance between right holders and users of protected content.

The case-law from the CJUE raises the question of whether only a harm-based model of compensation is possible. Along with harm to rightholders it could also be argued unjust enrichment of manufacturers and sellers of reproduction equipment and media, with the argument that they charge prices for a function the value of which is mainly due to copyrighted works. Then, the system relies upon an irrefutable presumption of harm, as if the cause of damage was the private copy exception itself.

Linking the system to a presumed (and somehow fictitious[15]) harm, the case-law from the CJUE appears to exclude other possible valuable criteria to justify and to level it, such as for example the notion of remuneration for the private copying as a statutory license. If damage is due to the private copy exception, then the source of damage is legislation itself, and therefore Member States should have broader discretion to set-up funding schemes, including a tax or tax-like model.

In such an alternative or supplementary mechanism the fair compensation could arguably apply to any private copying, regardless of the lawfulness of its source and be funded by the state budget, at least as part of the VAT on such equipment and media, or by means of a broadcasting-like cultural fee[16]. Authors and other right holders could receive more funding for their creative and

---

[15] K Koelman, 'The Levitation of Copyright: An Economic View of Digital Home Copying, Levies and DRM' in E Huizer et al., *De toekomst van het auteursrecht - Bijdragen Symposium 15.10.2004* (Amsterdam, XS4ALL Bits of Freedom 2004) 39-59, at 42-44 (pointing out economic flaws of such approach); J Poort and JP Quintais, 'The Levy Runs Dry. A Legal and Economic Analysis of EU Private Copying Levies' (2013) 4(3) JIPITEC 205-224, at 214 ('lacking the relevant data, it becomes nearly impossible to establish a realistic baseline from which to calculate harm').

[16] See Digital Europe, para 2.3.

cultural activities, thus contributing to a high level of protection of intellectual property in the European Union, while at the same time safeguarding consumers from copyright infringement. In copyright scholarship, an alternative system of 'compensation without control' is considered, particularly in the field of non-commercial file-sharing, as one of 'the most promising approaches to take advantage of this new technology for authors and society at large'[17].

B. The fair compensation in EU legislation

Directive 2001/29/EC 'concerns the legal protection of copyright and related rights in the framework of the internal market, with particular emphasis on the information society'[18]. In special, it has harmonized the exclusive right of reproduction for authors, performers, phonogram and film producers, and broadcasters, based upon a 'broad definition' of this right[19]. Moreover, it has provided 'for an exhaustive enumeration of exceptions and limitations to the reproduction right'[20].

To begin with, 'certain acts of temporary reproduction, which are transient or incidental reproductions' (including routing, browsing and caching), are mandatorily exempted from the right of reproduction[21].

---

[17] A Peukert, 'A bipolar copyright system for the digital network environment', in A Strowel (ed) *Peer-to-Peer File Sharing and Secondary Liability in Copyright Law* (Edward Elgar, Cheltenham 2009) 148-195, at 193 (quoting Lessig); see also e.g. A Stazi, 'Digital copyright and consumer/user protection: moving toward a new framework', (2012) 2(2) QMJIP 158-174. Arguing for a 'middle way' DJ Gervais, 'Is There a 'Middle Way' in International Intellectual Property?' (2016) 47 IIC 135-137, at 137.

[18] Article 1(1) of Directive 2001/29.

[19] Article 2 and Recital 21 of Directive 2001/29.

[20] Recital 32 of Directive 2001/29.

[21] Recital 33 and Article 5(1) of Directive 2001/29. For the notion of 'transient act' see CJUE's Judgments of 16 July 2009, *Infopaq International*, case C-5/08,

Then, as exceptions and limitations to the reproduction right, it provides notably the *reprography exception*[22] and the *private copying exception*[23]. The private copy exception - or limitation, according to some commentators[24] - is possible 'on condition that the rightholders receive fair compensation' in order 'to compensate them adequately for the use made of their protected works or other subject-matter'[25].

Recital 35 of Directive 2001/29 provides a *set of guidelines* for the implementation of the fair compensation and puts forward a 'valuable criterion' to evaluate these circumstances ('the possible harm to the rightholders resulting from the act in question'). As relevant factors to level compensation, recital 35 points out (1) whether 'rightholders have already received payment in some other form, for instance as part of a licence fee', because in that case 'no specific or separate payment may be due', (2) 'the degree of use of technological protection measures', (3) and certain situations of minimal prejudice to the right holder in which 'no obligation for payment may arise'.

Recital 38 points out that 'Digital private copying is likely to be more widespread and have a greater economic impact', but it is not clear what means this 'greater economic impact'. Moreover, the 'form, detailed arrangements and possible level' of the fair compensation is a matter for each Member State. However, in several judgments, the CJUE has limited the national discretion in setting up the system.

ECLI:EU:C:2009:465, and of 5 June 2014, case C-360/13, ECLI:EU:C:2014:1195, para 63 ('the on-screen copies and the cached copies made by an end-user in the course of viewing a website').

[22] Article 5(2)(a) of Directive 2001/29.

[23] Article 5(2)(b) of Directive 2001/29.

[24] J Reinbothe and S von Lewinski, *The WIPO Treaties on Copyright: A commentary on the WCT, the WPPT, and the BTAP* (2.nd ed. Oxford: OUP 2015) 158.

[25] Recital 35 of Directive 2001/29.

III. THE RULINGS OF THE CJUE

The CJUE has answered a number of questions concerning the conformity of national laws with the relevant provisions of Directive 2001/29. The fair compensation is attached both in its rational and level to the possible harm to right holders caused by the use by consumers of copying equipment and media.

A. The rational of the fair compensation

In its landmark judgment *Padawan*[26], the Court of Justice clarified the rational of the fair compensation mechanism and the criteria to set it up in national legislation. The fair compensation is deemed 'an autonomous notion of European Union law'[27], the rational of which is to repair the possible harm to right holders arising from private copying[28]. Interpreting recitals 35 and 38 of Directive 2001/29 as binding provisions, the CJUE states that 'It is clear from those provisions that the notion and level of fair compensation are linked to the harm resulting for the author from the reproduction for private use of his protected work without his authorisation. From that perspective, fair compensation *must* be regarded as recompense for the harm suffered by the author'[29], which consumers have to remedy.[30]

However, practical reasons of enforcement and the fact that each single private copy is *per se* a minimal harm for which no payment is due[31], justify a mechanism of indirect payment by means of charging

[26] Judgment of 21 October, case C-467/08, ECLI:EU:C:2010:620.

[27] *Padawan*, paras 29, 33, 35, 37 and conclusion 1.

[28] *Padawan*, paras 39 to 42

[29] *Padawan*, para 40 (italics added).

[30] *Padawan*, paras 44 and 45.

[31] *Padawan*, para 46.

a levy on the sale of such equipment, devices and media discharged by those who make them available to end users. The rational is that these can pass on the levy in the charged price, and therefore, 'the burden of the levy will ultimately be borne by the private user who pays that price'[32]. Such levy system is deemed to meet the test of the 'fair balance' between the interests of right holders and of those who use protected subject-matter[33], 'inasmuch as they are able to pass on to private users the actual burden of financing it'[34].

In short, the criterion of the possible harm is *the* normative criterion of the fair compensation. A 'necessary link' between the levy and the use of devices and media for purposes of private copying is therefore required, as levies cannot charge devices and media regardless of their use[35], in particular where they are 'acquired by persons other than natural persons for purposes clearly unrelated to private copying'[36]. However, it is irrelevant whether private copies have actually been made because harm is deemed to occur merely by making available reproduction, equipment, media and services to consumers as these 'are rightly presumed to benefit fully from the making available of that equipment'[37]. The *possible harm* lies merely in the possibility to make use of the private copy exception[38]. I.e. the system relies upon a double absolute presumption: (1) natural persons use such equipment and media to make copies of copyrighted

---

[32] *Padawan*, para 48.

[33] *Padawan*, para 49.

[34] *Padawan*, para 50 and conclusion 2.

[35] *Padawan*, para 52.

[36] *Padawan*, para 53 (Spanish legislation charging devices and media manifestly used for purposes other than private copying was found incompatible with Directive 2001/29 – para. 59).

[37] *Padawan*, paras 54 and 55. The fair compensation also applies to the printing out of works on paper or their storage on a USB stick, carried out by users from dedicated terminals installed in publicly accessible libraries, according Judgment of 11 September 201, case C-117/13, *Eugen Ulmer*, ECLI:EU:C:2014:2196, conclusion 3, and paras 50 to 57.

[38] *Padawan*, paras 56 e 57.

works and (2) that these copies harm the legitimate interests of the author. However, we could also say that 'we seldom find detailed explanations on how the circulating figures have been calculated'[39].

B. The discharger of the fair compensation

In *Stichting de Thuiskopie*[40], the CJUE reaffirms that, for practical reasons, Member States may charge a levy on devices and media to be discharged by those who sell them 'since they are able to pass on the amount of that levy in the price paid by the final user for that service'[41]. Moreover, they have to ensure the effective recovery of the fair compensation for the harm suffered by the authors on their territory, even where consumers acquire equipment and media at a distance from sellers established in a different Member State.[42] The fair compensation is thus intrinsically linked to the notion of harm, which is deemed to occur in the territory of residence of consumers and to be caused by those who make available to consumers recording equipment and media, even where they are established abroad.

C. Authorship of cinematographic works and ownership of the fair compensation

In *Luksan*[43] the CJUE asserts the principle of authorship of *droit d'auteur* jurisdictions and holds that, under EU law,

---

[39] RM Hilty, 'The Enforcement of Patents', in K-C Liu and RM Hilty RM (eds), *The Enforcement of Patents* (Alphen aan den Rijn, Kluwer Law International 2012) 9-31, at p. 15.

[40] Judgment of 16 June 2011, case C-462/09, ECLI:EU:C:2011:397.

[41] *Stichting de Thuiskopie*, para 29 and conclusion 1.

[42] *Stichting de Thuiskopie*, paras 31-41 and conclusion 2

[43] Judgment of 8 February 2012, case C-277/10, ECLI:EU:C:2012:65.

the economic rights in cinematographic works belong to the principal director, because he is mandatorily the or one of the authors of such works. Member States cannot exclusively allocate the economic rights to the producer, but they can provide a rebuttable presumption of transfer of such rights, insofar as the principal director is able to agree otherwise.[44] However, national legislation cannot provide a rebuttable or non-rebuttable presumption of transfer of right to equitable compensation the producer[45] - by analogy with the prohibition to waive the right to receive equitable remuneration for the rental of copyrighted works[46] - as it would be contrary to the obligation to ensure effective recovery of the fair compensation[47].

---

[44] *Luksan*, conclusions 1 and 2.

[45] *Luksan*, conclusions 3 and 4.

[46] *Luksan*, paras 100-102. Despite different terminology, the equitable remuneration for the rental of copyrighted works 'is also designed to establish recompense for authors, since it arises in order to compensate for harm to the latter' – *Luksan*, para 103 (with reference to *VEWA*, C271/10). M Ficsor, *The Law of Copyright and the Internet: The 1996 WIPO Treaties, their Interpretation and Implementation* (Oxford: OUP 2002) at 275, points out that 'the remuneration may only be considered equitable if it corresponds more or less to the payment that the author might be able to agree upon through negotiations in the absence of compulsory licence'. Article 13(1)(b) of Directive 2004/48/EC of the European Parliament and of the Council of 29 April 2004 on the enforcement of intellectual property rights (IPRED), provides criteria to set up damages, including 'as a lump sum on the basis of elements such as at least the amount of royalties or fees which would have been due if the infringer had requested authorisation to use the intellectual property right in question'. However, private copying is not an infringement to the right of reproduction, but rather a lawful use under national legislation. Therefore, it would probably be better to consider the equitable compensation as a remuneration for such statutory licence, i.e., to give it a meaning autonomous from the concept of damages provided by the IPRED. See also P Johnson, 'Damages' in European law and the traditional accounts of profit', (2013) 3(4) QMJIP 296-306, at 300.

[47] *Luksan*, paras 106-109.

D. Effects of authorizations given by the right holder for acts covered by an exception or limitation and of the use of technological protection measures

In *VG Wort Kyocera*[48], the CJUE ruled that where national legislation provides the private copying exception, the authorization given by the right holder to make private copies is *irrelevant* for purposes of the harm caused to him and therefore has no impact upon the fair compensation. If there is no private copying exception, the harm which fair compensation aims to repair does not take place[49]. In short, the harm caused by the private copying exception is mandatory, irrefutable, and independent from authorisations given by the right holder.

It could give rise to double-payment, where private copies are directly licenced by the right holder[50]. It is questionable whether recital 35 of Directive 2001/29 has been taken into account, in particular where it reads that if 'rightholders have already received payment in some other form, for instance as part of a licence fee', then 'no specific or separate payment may be due'. In other words, it appears that the 'pricing-in model' is not enough justification to exclude the fair compensation.[51]

---

[48] Judgment of 27 June 2013, case C-457/11 to C-460/11, ECLI:EU:C:2013:426.

[49] *VG Wort*, paras 37, 39 and 40, and conclusion 2.

[50] See e.g. Poort and Quintais, cit., at 219 (holding that 'charging levies for copies that are licenced by rightholders would lead to double payment'); Digital Europe, para 2.1 *in fine* (streaming subscription services the ability to private copying 'is already included in the purchase price' and therefore 'does not cause any additional harm to rightholders').

[51] The UK has amended its Copyright Act to provide a narrow copying exception in terms of a pricing-in solution, and since only minimal damage would occur, it has not adopted a levy system: The Copyright and Rights in Performance (Personal Copies for Private Use) Regulations of 26 August 2014. However, 'in the absence of a compensation mechanism', the High Court of Justice ruled on 19 June 2015 the exception unlawful: [2015] EWHC 1723, Case No. CO/5444/2014.

Concerning the use of technological protection measures, as it is voluntary and cannot prevent effective application of the private copy exception where it is provided by the Member State[52], the Court found that it 'cannot render inapplicable the condition relating to fair compensation'.[53] But, taking into account recital 35, the level of fair compensation should take into account 'the degree of use of technological protection measures'.

E. Criterion to level the compensation where a printing involves the use of several devices

In *VG Wort*, the CJUE held that 'mediums which do not have comparable and equivalent qualities to those of paper do not come within the scope of the [reprography] exception'[54], which however covers the photographic technique and 'some other process having similar effects', i.e. 'the analogue representation of a protected work or other subject-matter'[55]. The reprography exception does not exclude the use of 'several devices, including those with a digital function'[56], provided, however, that 'the various elements [are] non-autonomous stages of that single process act or are carried out under the control of the same person and are all intended to reproduce the protected work or other subject-matter on paper or a similar medium'[57].

Moreover, the Court found that it is open to each Member State to put in place a system in which the fair compensation is paid by the persons in possession of a device contributing, in a non-autonomous

---

[52] *VG Wort*, paras 52-54.

[53] *VG Wort*, paras 57, 59 and conclusion 3.

[54] *VG Wort* para 66.

[55] *VG Wort*, para 68.

[56] *VG Wort*, para 72.

[57] *VG Wort*, para 70.

manner, to the single process of reproduction of the protected work or other subject-matter on the given medium, insofar as (1) they can pass on the cost of the levy to their customers and (2) the overall amount of the fair compensation owed as recompense for the harm suffered by the author at the end of that single process is not 'substantially different from the amount fixed for a reproduction obtained by means of a single device'[58].

It appears that where a PC and a printer are bundled and sold to consumers as a package both devices are charged because the PC is used not only for printing but also for digital private copying.

F. Reimbursement of levies charged at the first introduction in the market in the territory of a Member State regardless of the purpose of acquisition of recording media

In *Amazon.com International Sales*[59], the CJUE accepts charging levies regardless of the purpose of acquisition on the condition that, in particular, 'practical difficulties justify such a system of financing fair compensation and the right to reimbursement is effective and does not make repayment of the levies paid excessively difficult'[60]. The validity of a rebuttable presumption of private use of recording media where such media is sold to natural persons is confirmed, but on the condition that 'the presumption established does not result in the imposition of the private copying levy in cases where the final use of those media clearly does not fall within' the private copying exception[61].

---

[58] *VG Wort*, para 80 and conclusion 4.

[59] Judgment of 11 July 2013, case C-521/11, ECLI:EU:C:2013:515.

[60] *Amazon.com International Sales*, para 37 and conclusion 1.

[61] *Amazon.com International Sales*, conclusion 2.

Notwithstanding, the CJUE refused an exemption of levies where a comparable levy has already been paid in another Member State[62], holding that the place of establishment of the seller is irrelevant and that harm can be presumed to occur in the territory of the consumers' Member State of residence[63]. Therefore, the fact that the levy has already been discharged in one Member State does not preclude payment in the Member State of consumers' residence, but a mechanism of reimbursement must be available[64].

G. Attribution of half of the revenue to social and cultural institutions set up for the benefit of authors and other right holders

The statutory attribution of half of the levies revenue to social and cultural institutions set up for the benefit of authors and other right holders is accepted by the Court, but on the condition that 'those social and cultural establishments actually benefit those entitled and the detailed arrangements for the operation of such establishments are not discriminatory' [notably for reasons of nationality[65]][66].

The statutory attribution of half of such revenue to third parties is questionable. In principle, it is up to the person awarded damages to decide if and how she wants to assign the revenue to third parties. As the CJUE accepts to have half of the revenue given to third parties by the national legislator, the fair compensation can hardly be only a tool to repair harm suffered by individuals.

[62] *Amazon.com International Sales*, para 66 and conclusion 4.

[63] *Amazon.com International Sales*, paras 57-61.

[64] *Amazon.com International Sales*, para 62-65.

[65] *Amazon.com International Sales*, para 54.

[66] *Amazon.com International Sales*, para 55 and conclusion 3.

H. Lawfulness of the source of private copies

This question concerns the scope of application of the private copying exception. In *ACI Adam*[67], the Court recalls the principle of restrictive interpretation of exceptions or limitations to the exclusive rights and finds that the fair compensation does not apply to private copies made from an unlawful source.[68]

In the opinion of the Court 'the objective of proper support for the dissemination of culture must not be achieved by sacrificing strict protection of rights or by tolerating illegal forms of distribution of counterfeited or pirated works'.[69] An undifferentiated system would be contrary to the 'fair balance' between right holders and users, as it would overcharge with a 'non-negligible cost' purchasers of such equipment, devices and media[70].

This judgment corresponds to the opinion of several scholars[71], and it has been commented that the exclusion of copies made from unlawful sources would 'narrow the scope of the PC exception' and 'provide an increasingly weaker economic case for levies in the digital age'.[72] Apparently taking for granted a 'substitution effect'[73] between lawful and unlawful copies, the Court excludes the later from the private copying exception, while leaving unclear which

---

[67] Judgment of 10 April 2014, case C-435/12, ECLI:EU:C:2014:254.

[68] *ACI Adam*, para 37 and 58 and conclusion 1.

[69] *ACI Adam*, para 36 (adding that the circulation of pirated works adversely affect their normal exploitation works and unreasonably prejudices copyright holders - paras 39 and 40).

[70] *ACI Adam*, para 56.

[71] See e.g. Hugenholtz, Guibault and van Sjoerd, cit. at 46. Pointing out that, otherwise it would lead to the 'levitation of copyright' as an exclusive right, Koelman, cit. 53-5.

[72] Poort and Quintais cit. at 219.

[73] JP Quintais, 'Private Copying and Downloading from Unlawful Sources' (2015) 46(1) IIC 66-92, at 74 (pointing out 'some circularity' in the argument that unlawful copies would unreasonably prejudice the legitimate interests of right holders, as if the fair compensation was not designed to compensate them for such prejudice).

method will levy setting bodies use for this purpose. A box of *Pandora* may have been open in what concerns consumers' privacy[74] and possible criminal enforcement of copyright against them under the rule 'copyright is watching you'.

However, this ruling has a relevant economic effect: overall damages allegedly due to piracy, notably online piracy, and claimed by the copyright industries are, as such, not eligible for the fair compensation.

I. Multifunctional media (e.g. mobile telephone memory cards) irrespective of whether their main function

In *Copydan Båndkopi*[75] the CJUE ruled that multifunctional media (e.g. mobile telephone memory cards) are covered by the fair compensation, but on the condition that 'one of the functions of the media, be it merely an ancillary function, enables the operator to use them for that [reproduction] purpose'[76]. However, for purposes of determining the amount of payable compensation, it is necessary to consider 'whether the function is a main or an ancillary one and the relative importance of the medium's capacity to make copies', so that in case of minimal prejudice, 'the making available of such a function need not give rise to an obligation to pay fair compensation'[77]. The determination of what is the 'minimal prejudice' is a matter to decide, in respect for the principle of equal treatment, by Member States[78]. Once again the function of the fair

---

[74] See e.g. Quintais, cit. at 81 (pointing out 'the Court's failure to consider the impact of the fundamental right of privacy in the interpretation of the three-step test'– at 89).

[75] Judgment of 5 March 2015, case C-463/12, ECLI:EU:C:2015:144.

[76] *Copydan Båndkopi,* paras 26-29 and conclusion 1. With different opinion, Hugenholtz, Guibault and van Sjoerd cit. at 47.

[77] *Copydan Båndkopi*, para 29 and conclusion 1, 2nd per.

[78] *Copydan Båndkopi,* paras 61-62 and conclusion 4.

compensation justifies the application (and the level) of the levy, and its exclusion concerning reproduction equipment and media which cause only minimum harm.

J. Exemption of supply of components mainly designed to store copies for private use (e.g. internal memory of MP3 players)

The CJUE has not allowed the exemption of components mainly designed to store copies for private use[79]. The fact that a memory card is detachable is not deemed sufficient objective justification, but the Court left to national courts the possibility to assess other circumstances capable of providing such justification, such as, for example, where 'rightholders receive fair compensation in another form'[80]. Probably the Court considered that in order to storage copies in the internal memory of a MP3 reader, other devices and media, notably a PC or a smartphone, have to be used and therefore levying these devices would already allow right holders to receive the fair compensation for such copies.

On the other hand, the Court concludes that the levy system can apply to 'producers and importers who sell mobile telephone memory cards to business customers and are aware that those cards will be sold on by those customers but do not know whether the final purchasers of the cards will be individuals or business customers, on condition that:

[1] the introduction of such a system is justified by practical difficulties;

[2] the persons responsible for payment are exempt from the levy if they can establish that they have supplied the mobile

[79] *Copydan Båndkopi*, paras 32-33.

[80] *Copydan Båndkopi*, paras 40-41 and conclusion 2

telephone memory cards to persons other than natural persons for purposes clearly unrelated to copying for private use, it being understood that the exemption cannot be restricted to the supply of business customers registered with the organisation responsible for administering the levy;

[3] the system provides for a right to reimbursement of the private copying levy which is effective and does not make it excessively difficult to repay the levy paid and only the final purchaser of such a memory card may obtain reimbursement, by submitting an appropriate application to that organisation.'[81]

K. Copies made by or with the aid of a device belonging to third persons

For purposes of the scope of the private copy exception, it is only relevant the medium of reproduction, not the 'legal nature' of the connection between the natural person doing the reproduction and the device used.[82] The silence of the Directive on this issue would mean that private copies can be made 'by a natural person by or with the aid of a device which belongs to a third party'[83].

L. Beneficiaries of the 'reprography exception'

The 'reprography exception' concerns reproductions in paper or similar medium by means of photography technique or

[81] *Copydan Båndkopi*, para 55 and conclusion 3.

[82] *Copydan Båndkopi*, paras 81, 84-90.

[83] *Copydan Båndkopi*, para 91 and conclusion 8.

alike.[84] In *Hewlett-Packard*[85], the Court ruled that it benefits both categories of persons (businesses and consumers), while the 'private copy exception'[86] applies only to natural persons acting without direct or indirect commercial purposes.[87] The conceptual autonomy as well as the indemnification rational of the fair compensation apply also to the reprography exception for reasons of coherence in interpreting exceptions[88]. Nevertheless, because harm suffered by right holders is not identical in both situations a distinction between the reprographic reproduction in paper carried out by any user, or by a natural person for private use and without direct or indirect commercial purposes.[89] In other words, the reprography exception benefits any user, including legal persons acting for purposes other than private use, and therefore it causes more harm to right holders than if it would benefit consumers only.

M. Publishers as unlikely beneficiaries of the fair compensation

The compensation envisages paying authors for harm caused by the private copy exception. Publishers are not holders of the right of reproduction under Directive 2001/29. If publishers have no obligation to benefit authors from a substantial share of the compensation from which they are deprived, then they should not be entitled to receive such a share of the fair compensation.[90]

---

[84] Article 5(2)(a) of Directive 2001/29.

[85] Judgment of 12 November 2015, case C-572/13, ECLI:EU:C:2015:750.

[86] Article 5(2)(b) of Directive 2001/29.

[87] *Hewlett-Packard Belgium*, paras 29-34.

[88] *Hewlett-Packard Belgium*, paras 37-39.

[89] *Hewlett-Packard Belgium*, para 43 and conclusion 1.

[90] *Hewlett-Packard Belgium*, paras 44-49 and conclusion 2.

N. Reprography of sheet music and pirated copies

A system which applies the fair compensation to the copying of sheet music is refused because sheet music is excluded from the reprography exception and by extension from the private copy exception, without prejudice of 'limited and isolated situations' of unauthorized reproduction of sheet music where the prejudice to right holders is minimal[91]. On the other hand, the fair compensation does not cover pirated reproductions made from an unlawful source, including in the reprography sector.[92]

O. Remuneration for the reproduction device speed and for the number of copies produced

It is discussed a system of remuneration fixed prior to the reproduction operation by reference to the speed at which the device in question technically produces copies, combined with a remuneration fixed after the reproduction operation by reference to the number of copies produced.[93]

The Court holds that levies 'must necessarily be set as a lump sum', on the sole basis of the reproduction function of the device, because it 'cannot be fixed on the basis of the criterion of actual harm suffered, as the extent of that harm remains unknown at the moment at which the devices concerned are put into circulation on national territory'[94]. However, considering that the use of a reproduction device for private copying is different from its use

[91] *Hewlett-Packard Belgium*, paras 50-56.

[92] *Hewlett-Packard Belgium*, paras 57-61, and paras 62-63.

[93] *Hewlett-Packard Belgium*, para 66.

[94] *Hewlett-Packard Belgium*, paras 71-2.

for commercial or other purposes, the Court refuses a lump-sum remuneration fixed solely by reference to the technical copying speed of the device[95].

Notwithstanding this, a system which combines the proportional remuneration for copies produced with the lump-sum remuneration fixed in advance is not found incompatible, a priori, with the fair compensation provided that it enables levies to correspond, in essence, to the actual harm suffered by the right holders[96]. This means that such a system has to provide, notably, a mechanism for reimbursement designed to correct any occurring 'overcompensation' detrimental to particular categories of users[97], therefore safeguarding a fair balance between the rightholders and the users of protected subject-matter[98].

P. For jurisdiction purposes, the payment of the fair compensation is a matter of tort or delict

In *Austro-Mechana*[99], the Court recalls that the scope of application of the special rule of jurisdiction in matters relating to tort, delict or quasi-delict (Art. 5(3) of Brussels I[100]) is defined in negatives terms, as covering any action of civil liability in matters not relating to a contract[101]. Matters relating to a contract do not

[95] *Hewlett-Packard Belgium*, para 77.

[96] *Hewlett-Packard Belgium*, para 84.

[97] *Hewlett-Packard Belgium*, para 85 (referring by analogy to *Amazon.com*).

[98] *Hewlett-Packard Belgium*, para 86.

[99] Judgment of 21 April 2016, case C-572/14, ECLI:EU:C:2016:286.

[100] Article 5 of Council Regulation (EC) No 44/2001 of 22 December 2000 on jurisdiction and the recognition and enforcement of judgments in civil and commercial matters, replaced by Regulation (EU) No 1215/2012 of the European Parliament and of the Council of 12 December 2012 as from 10 January 2015 (Brussels I Regulation recast).

[101] *Austro-Mechana*, para 32.

necessarily require the conclusion of a contract, but they do not cover 'a situation in which there is no obligation freely assumed by one party towards another'[102]. The payment of the fair compensation is not a matter related to contract because it does not arise from an agreement freely consented by the debtor, but rather its source is a statutory provision concerning the distribution with commercial purposes of reproduction devices and media[103]. On the other hand, concerning the link of causality, the non-payment of the levy imposed to fund the fair compensation is the relevant cause of harm, even if payment is due to a copyright collecting society and not directly to right holders[104].

There is not much justification to this finding, but it means probably that the levy system concerns primarily the intermediaries, despite right holders and end-users are the (virtual) main creditors and debtors of the fair compensation.

On the other hand, harm occurs if levies are not actually paid, thus adding a new dimension of harm to the system, so as to include actual harm along with statutorily presumed harm.

Q. Funding the fair compensation by the State Budget,

In *EGEDA*[105], the Court accepts that, as a matter of principle, the funding of the fair compensation can take place by the General State Budget of a Member State, instead of by a system of levies[106].

---

[102] *Austro-Mechana*, para 35, with reference to CJUE Judgment of 14 March 2013, *Česká spořitelna*, case C419/11, EU:C:2013:165, para 46.

[103] *Austro-Mechana*, paras 37-38.

[104] *Austro-Mechana*, paras 39 to 46.

[105] Judgment of 9 June 2016, case C-470/14, ECLI:EU:C:2016:418.

[106] *EGEDA*, paras 24 to 25. Besides Spain, other countries like Finland and Norway have established funding of the fair compensation by means of the State Budget: Digital Europe, cit. para 2.2.

However, the rational of the fair compensation is to repair possible harm caused by the beneficiaries of the private copy exception (consumers), who are therefore the indirect debtors of levies, and the beneficiaries of the private copying exception are only natural persons acting for private purposes (consumers), legal persons being therefore exempted from the levies[107]. For these reasons the Court does not accept that there is no 'definite allocation of revenue — such as revenue from a specific levy — to particular expenditure'[108], nor a particular measure allowing tax payers to request exemption from contributing to the financing of the compensation or, at least, to seek reimbursement[109].

Such alternative scheme is not accepted because it cannot 'ensure that the cost of that compensation is borne by the users of private copies' (only)[110]. Nevertheless, this ruling appears to accept a tax on consumption of reproduction equipment and media (for ex. a percentage of VAT over such goods).

CONCLUSION

A 'virtuous system' of private copying levies called for by the European Parliament is still far from being established. From *Padawan* to *EGEDA*[111], the Court of Justice figured out a model according to which the fair compensation is mandatory for Member States providing the (optional) private copy exception. The rational of the fair compensation is to repair possible harm caused to right

---

[107] *EGEDA*, paras 26-36.

[108] *EGEDA*, para 39.

[109] *EGEDA*, paras 39 and 40.

[110] *EGEDA*, paras 41-2 and conclusion.

[111] See later CJUE Judgment of 22 September 2016, case C-11/15, *Microsoft Mobile Sales International and Others*, ECLI:EU:C:2016:326.

holders by consumers who acquire copying devices and media or services based thereupon.

However, harm caused by each consumer is probably minimal and therefore irrelevant, and it would be intrusive to the consumers' privacy as well as unfeasible to seek damages by means of court enforcement of copyright against each individual consumer. Harm is merely presumed and potential: it is not necessary to prove that consumers make copies nor that they actually harm right holders. As the Court of Justice recognized, 'the extent of that harm remains unknown at the moment at which the devices concerned are put into circulation'[112].

Due to practical difficulties, the fair compensation can be a levy scheme: national legislation may charge levies from persons making reproduction devices and media available to consumers upon the price of sale to the public of such equipment and media. A third presumption is added: businesses can pass-on the levy to consumers, who remain the actual - yet indirect - debtors of the fair compensation. For this reason, the levy system has to exempt copies made for purposes other than private use and to provide reimbursement of levies paid by non-consumers, and the private copying exception does not apply to copies made from unlawful sources. Massive harm claimed by right holders due to online piracy is thus excluded from the compensation. At the same time, the authorization given by the right holder to make private copies does not exclude the fair compensation, and the same applies to the use of technological protection measures.

The CJUE has figured out a model of fair compensation based upon the recitals of Directive 2001/29 and has consistently applied it in a number of cases. Is it the one and only 'virtuous system'?

[112] *Hewlett-Packard Belgium*, paras 71-2.

Are Member States not allowed to set up different systems upon other valuable rationale and criteria, notably a tax-like instrument.

The CJUE has not denied the possibility to fund the fair compensation by the State Budget, if there is 'definite allocation of revenue to particular expenditure' and exemption and/or reimbursement provisions[113]. The criterion however remains the same: to compensate possible harm due to lawful private copying. Harm caused by and passed-on to consumers. The *substitution effect* is deemed irrefutable.

However, the economic effect of 'margin compression' for sellers of copying equipment and media appears neglected, especially in a market also governed by Moore's law, and which along with the business models of licensing, streaming and cloud computing may end-up 'phasing-out' the levy system.

Any revision of the system might consider a combination of the levy scheme with a tax-like special contribution allocated to fund activities of cultural creation. The fair compensation would then have two and equally valuable rationale and operating systems: to compensate harm, possibly by means of a levy scheme, and to promote cultural creation through a tax or tax tax-like instrument.

[113] *EGEDA*, paras 39 and 40.

BROADCAST WORKS IN BARS AND RESTAURANTS: «RESISTANT» CASE-LAW TO THE CJUE'S RULINGS*

Abstract - The use of radio or TV sets in bars and restaurants making broadcast works enjoyable by customers is a disputed issue in copyright law. The Supreme Court of Justice of Portugal has been called to render a judgment of uniformity of case-law, in which it has ruled that said actions do not infringe copyright, even where extra loudspeakers are used, but provided that it does not amount to a public show. The Court decided that such acts do not fall under the right of communication to the public and therefore there is also no obligation to pay remuneration to authors. It contrasts with the relevant case-law of the CJUE, in particular the preliminary ruling in ***Premier League Football Association*** and later the Order in *Sociedade Portuguesa de Autores*. This paper provides an overview of the issue and submits that Portuguese law provides a statutory license to use radio or TV sets in bars and restaurants, but requires payment of equitable compensation to copyright holders.

* Queen Mary Journal of Intellectual Property, vol. 6/4 (2016), p. 525–535. Imprint Edward Elgar Publishing.

Introduction

In the case *Sociedade Portuguesa de Autores*[1] (SPA), the CJUE issued a preliminary ruling, by reasoned order, concerning the interpretation of the notion of 'communication to the public' in the EC Directive 2001/29. However, later on, the referring national court (*Tribunal da Relação de Coimbra*)[2] has decided several similar cases according to a different interpretation given by the Portuguese Supreme Court of Justice.[3] This paper addresses the conflict between the case-law of the CJEU and the «resistant case-law» of Portuguese courts.

Preliminary ruling (Order)

The facts concern the use of radio or TV sets with loudspeakers to make broadcasts perceptible by customers in bars, restaurants and shops open to the public. The question is whether it is an act of communication to the pubic in the meaning of Article 3 (1) of the EC Directive 2001/29.[4]

SPA, the Portuguese Authors' Society, argues that the answer is positive and that the people in charge of bars or restaurants in which such communication to the public takes place are liable for

---

[1] Judgment of 14 July 2015, case C-151/15, ECLI:EU:C:2015:468 (available in French and Portuguese). On this case-law see also P Malaquias, 'CJEU issues reasoned order on communication to the public' (2016) 11 *Journal of Intellectual Property Law & Practice*, 9-11; S Filgueiras, 'Case Note on "Loudspeakers in Bars" and "Sociedade Portuguesa de Autores"' (2016) 47 *IIC - International Review of Intellectual Property and Competition Law*. 125-31.

[2] Judgments of 14 October 2015 (case no. 35/12.0PFVIS.C1) and of 16 January 2016 (case no. 36/13.1PFVIS.C1) – decisions available at www.dgsi.pt

[3] Case no. 124/11.9GAPVL.G1-A.S1, Cons. Maia Costa, in (2013) 243 *Diário da República* – I série, of 16 December 2013.

[4] Directive 2001/29/EC of the European Parliament and of the Council of 22 May 2001 on the harmonisation of certain aspects of copyright and related rights in the information society (OJ L 167, p. 10).

copyright infringement, which is a criminal offence (*usurpação*). In the case in question the Court of first instance acquitted the defendants and therefore SPA brought an appeal before the *Tribunal de Relação* in Coimbra, which stayed the proceedings and referred to the CJUE the following questions (paras. 5-7):

1) The notion of communication to the public of Article 3(1) of Directive 2001/29 covers the transmission of broadcast works in public houses, such as bars, coffee-shops or restaurants, by means of TV sets with loudspeakers and/or amplifiers, and therefore a new use of copyrighted works takes place?
2) The answer to that question depends upon the use of loudspeakers and/or amplifiers, i.e., technical devices different from the receiver TV set, to amplify the reception of sound?

The CJUE replied by reasoned order, under Article 99 of the Rules of Procedure, because it found that the answer could be clearly derived from its case-law, in particular the ruling in *Football Association Premier League*[5] (para. 8-9), in which three conditions are required.

Broad notion of communication

To begin with, the CJUE considers that its case-law concerning the transmission of broadcasts in bars and restaurants by TV sets is also

[5] Judgment of 4 October 2011, joined cases C403/08 & C429/08, EU:C:2011:631. See also judgment of 27 February 2014, Case C-351/12, *OSA*, ECLI:EU:C:2014:110 (the right of communication to the public includes the communication of works, by a spa establishment business, through the intentional distribution of a signal by means of television or radio sets in the bedrooms of the spa's patients) and judgment of 31 May 2016, Case C-117/15, *Reha Training*, ECLI:EU:C:2016:379 (the broadcast of television programmes by means of television sets that the operator of a rehabilitation centre has installed in its premises is an act of communication to the public for purposes of copyright and related rights).

valid where it takes place by means of radio sets (para. 10). The Court recalls that the main purpose of Directive 2001/29 is to assure a high level of protection for authors, so that they get an adequate remuneration for the use of their works, notably where it takes place by means of communication to the public. This notion is to be understood in *broad sense*, as stated in Recital 21 of the Directive and previous case-law (para. 12), as comprehending any transmission of protected works regardless of the technical means or procedures used (para 13). In special the CJUE recalls in para. 14 its ruling in *Football Association Premier League* according to which: "'Communication to the public' within the meaning of Article 3(1) of Directive 2001/29 must be interpreted as covering transmission of the broadcast works, via a television screen and speakers, to the customers present in a public house."

The Court finds this situation 'comparable' to the facts of the case before the referring court, as they go beyond the mere facilitation of technical means to guarantee or to improve the original broadcast in the zone of reception (paras. 15 and 16). The use of loudspeakers or amplifiers does not make a difference because the relevant criterion is whether the customers present in the bar or restaurant can, by themselves, enjoy the broadcast works without the radio or TV sets installed by the person running the house (para 17).

The notion of new public

Then, customers of a bar-restaurant are deemed a public, for purpose of Article 3(1) of the Directive, because, like hotel clients, they represent a potential, fast-changing and quiet important number of indeterminate recipients (paras. 18-20, quoting also its judgment of 7 December 2006 in *SGAE*[6]). Moreover, it is deemed a

[6] C306/05, EU:C:2006:764.

new public as it is not included in the scope of the authorization to broadcast, which is found limited to individual recipients or to the reception in a private or family environment (para. 21-22). For these reasons the CJUE recalls that, as already declared in *Football Association Premier League*, customers in a pub are a new public if broadcasts are transmitted by its owner using TV screens (para. 23). Moreover, the new public is not present where the communications originate, as there is no direct and physical contact between the recipients and the broadcast works transmitted by means of TV screens and loudspeakers (paras. 24 and 25, recalling *SGAE* and *Football Association Premier League*[7]).

The lucrative purpose

Finally, the Court recalls that the lucrative purpose of the communication to the public is not irrelevant and that it takes place because such communication is capable to attract clients who are interested in the transmitted works and therefore it has an impact in the number of customers and in the economic results of the business (para. 26-27).

For the above reasons, the CJEU concludes that the transmission by a radio set with loudspeakers and/or amplifiers, undertaken by people running a bar-restaurant, of musical and literary-musical works radio broadcasts, to the customers present therein, is covered by the notion of communication to the public, in the meaning of

---

[7] See also judgment of 24 November 2011, case C283/10, Circul Globus, ECLI:EU:C:2011:772 ("Article 3(1) (...) must be interpreted as referring only to communication to a public which is not present at the place where the communication originates, to the exclusion of any communication of a work which is carried out directly in a place open to the public using any means of public performance or direct presentation of the work.").

Article 3 (1) of Directive 2001/29 (para. 28 and operative decision). In short, 'communication to the public' is a broad concept which includes the transmission of broadcast works by means of a TV screen or radio set to customers staying at pub or bar-restaurants. Without the intervention of the person who runs the establishment customers could not enjoy the broadcast works even if they can be received in the same broadcasting zone, and therefore there would not be a new public attracted to the establishment nor economic advantages to the bar-restaurant.

Discussion

Arguably with the exception of football, nowadays people seldom go to a bar or restaurant to watch TV or to listen to radio music or other programs. Moreover, bars and restaurants often hire communication services in a full package including phone and internet and if they want special channels, notably sports, they have to pay an extra fare which normally takes in consideration whether it is for home or business purposes. However, the use of radio or TV sets in bars and restaurants by people running these businesses remains a relevant issue, and probably the main copyright issue in Portugal.

Some hold that it is an act of communication to the public of broadcast works, according to Article 11*bis* of the Berne Convention and Articles 9, 68(2)(e), 108(2), 149(2)(3) and 155 of the *Código do Direito de Autor e dos Direitos Conexos*[8] (hereinafter, Copyright Code). It is understood that each use of copyrighted works requires authorization and payment, and that a communication to the public takes place *ipso facto* by the use of radio or TV broadcasting receiv-

[8] Enacted by Decree-Law No 63/85 of March 1985, as last amended by Law No 32/2015 of 24 April.

er sets in public places, such as bars, restaurants and shops.[9] The only exempted place of reception would be at home in a family or similar environment, and arguably individual reception in public places by means of headphones would also be excluded.

Others stand for freedom of reception of broadcast works in private as well as in public places, where it takes place spontaneously or without any further modification.[10] There would be no communication to the public by merely receiving broadcasting signals sent to the radio spectrum, authorization and payment being done at the source by broadcasters and receivers free to enjoy the broadcast. A further act of communication to the public would only take place if special technical means are used and the organization of an event similar to a public show takes place. The use of loudspeakers *per se* would not be relevant provided that it only improves the conditions of reception and does not amount to a public show.

For a long time, case-law of Courts of Appeal went into both directions.[11] But the Public Prosecutor found that the Court of Appeal of Guimarães has given opposite rulings for the same legal

---

[9] Cf. LF Rebello, 'O problema da comunicação de emissões de rádio e televisão em lugares públicos na perspectiva do direito de autor' in LF Rebello (ed), *Comunicação Pública de Emissões de Rádio e Televisão*, cit., 11-32, A Ferrer Correia, A de Sá, 'Direito de Autor e Comunicação Pública de Emissões de Rádio e Televisão', (1994) 70 *Boletim da Faculdade de Direito*, 1-96.

[10] J Oliveira Ascensão, *Direito civil - Direito de autor e direitos conexos* (Coimbra Editora, Coimbra, 1992) 310-3. Procuradoria-Geral da República, 'Parecer no. 4/92 de 28 de Maio' (1993) 63 *Diário da República* - II série, 16 March 1993. P Cordeiro, *Direito de autor e radiodifusão* (Almedina, Coimbra, 2004) 472-3. A Sá e Mello, *Manual de Direito de Autor* (Almedina, Coimbra, 2014) 189-90. In 2013 the Portuguese Ombudsman (*Provedor de Justiça*) has recommended legislative action to set free the exhibition of broadcast works in bars and restaurants - Provedor de Justiça, R-0871/10, of 9 September 2013 <http://www.provedor-jus.pt/?idc=67&idi=15271> accessed 29 April 2016

[11] For a survey of contradictory court decisions see AL Dias Pereira, 'Direitos de autor e comunicação pública de obra radiodifundida em estabelecimento comercial (Anotação ao Acórdão de Uniformização de Jurisprudência do S.T.J. n. 15/2013, de 13 de novembro)', (2015) 144-3990 *Revista de Legislação e de Jurisprudência*, 215-44 (with analysis of comparative law, including the UK as well as the USA Copyright Act § 110(5)(a) and (a) which regulates items such as the size and number of screens and the room area).

question[12], as in one case the use of radio and/or TV sets with loudspeakers in bars and restaurants was deemed a communication to the public of broadcast works and therefore authorization and payment were required, while in the other case concerning similar facts the same Court found that there was no copyright infringement.

The Supreme Court of Justice confirmed the (questionable) opposition of judgments, accepted the case to uniform case-law[13], and rendered judgment no. 15/2013 of 13 November 2013 (*acórdão de uniformização de jurisprudência*) according to which:

> *"The application, to a TV set, of amplifiers of sound, diffused by means of a TV channel in a commercial establishment does not amount to a new use of the transmitted work, and therefore its use does not require authorization of the author of the work and such act does not consequently correspond to the crime of usurpation provided for and punished under Articles 149, 195 and 195 of the Code of Copyright and Related Rights."*[14]

The main argument is that there is no re-use or recreation of the broadcast works because the "reception in bars or coffee-shops open to the public, without paid entry, of establishments which are traditionally places of meeting and social life, mainly but not only in small villages, in which the reception of TV programs may occasionally work as a decoy, but which normally only serve regular

[12] Judgment of 2 July 2007 (case no. 974/07-2) would have been contradicted by its later judgment of 7 January 2013 (case no. 124/11.9GAPVL.G1).

[13] Portuguese courts must consider 'analogous cases' (Article 8(3) of the Civil Code), but there is not rule of binding precedent, not even for the so-called judgments of uniformity (*acórdãos de uniformização de jurisprudência*) which are given by the Supreme Court of Justice in case of two conflicting rulings of the same Court of Appeal concerning the same legal question (Article 445(3) of the Code of Criminal Procedure).

[14] Case 124/11.9GAPVL.G1-A.S1 (*supra* fn. 3).

customers, for whom it is no special attraction" (translation by the contributor). For this reason, despite the Supreme Court agreed with the CJUE in *SGAE Rafael Hoteles*[15], it has expressly diverged from the application of the *Premier League* case-law to bars and restaurants, and for that reason it has received strong criticism.[16]

Judgments of uniformity are not binding, but in case of contradictory decisions the Public Prosecutor has to bring an appeal, *ex officio*, to the Supreme Court of Justice (STJ).[17] The Court of Appeal of Coimbra[18] has remained faithful to the STJ case-law, and the Court of Appeal of Porto partially followed it, but did not exempt the use of loudspeakers.[19] However, in a similar case concerning the transmission in bars and restaurants of broadcast phonograms by radio or TV sets, the Court of Appeal of Lisbon held that it requires the authorization of the phonogram's producer[20], taking into account the order of the CJUE in *Sociedade Portuguesa de Autores*.[21]

---

[15] Judgment of 7 December 2006, *Sociedad General de Autores y Editores de España (SGAE) v Rafael Hoteles SA*, case C-306/05, ECLI:EU:C:2006:764 ("the distribution of a signal by means of television sets by a hotel to customers staying in its rooms, whatever technique is used to transmit the signal, constitutes communication to the public within the meaning of Article 3(1) of" Directive 2001/29"). A similar ruling, concerning TV and radio sets in the rooms of spa establishments, has been given by the CJUE in its judgment of 27 February 2014, case C351/12, OSA, ECLI:EU:C:2014:110 (there is communication to the public where works are communicated "by a spa establishment which is a business, through the intentional distribution of a signal by means of television or radio sets in the bedrooms of the establishment's patients").

[16] V Castro Rosa, 'Comentário ao Acórdão do STJ no. 15/2013 de 13.11.2013', (2014) 1 *Propriedades intelectuais*, 55-67; N Sousa e Silva, 'Communication to the public or 'freedom to receive'? A Portuguese bitter-sweet symphony' (2014) 9-4 *Journal of Intellectual Property Law & Practice*, 272-3; M Ohen Mendes ('O Triângulo das Bermudas da "Comunicação ao Público" das obras e prestações radiodifundidas – Comentário de Jurisprudência' (2015) 2 *Revista de Direito Intelectual*, 179-195.

[17] Article 446(2) of the Portuguese Code of Criminal Procedure.

[18] See supra fn. 2.

[19] Judgment of 27 November 2014, case no. 2299/11.8TJVNF.P1.

[20] Judgment of 4 February 2016, case no. 216-15.5YHLSB.L1-6.

[21] See supra fn. 1.

The ruling of the STJ has to be understood in the context of the proceedings, the main question of which is whether said facts are a criminal offence (copyright usurpation). The STJ has expressly followed the proposal of the Public Prosecutor, and its arguments are largely found in Opinion No 4/92 of the General Public Prosecutor, holding that there is no copyright infringement in merely receiving broadcast works in bars and restaurants. If the Public Prosecutor has no reasons to make a criminal charge because it considers that the facts do not match the criminal type, then in principle the Court will hardly find a crime where the Public Prosecutor sees none (*in dubio pro libertate*).

Different levels of protection for broadcast works

However, the STJ gave an excessively narrow interpretation of the right of communication to the public of broadcast works.[22] If radio or TV sets had no economic value for bars, restaurants and other businesses probably they would not be used there, at least as sound ambiance or visual dynamic decoration. However, it is important to understand how Portuguese law protects broadcast works.

Broadcasting makes the work perceptible in many and distant places and by many people not present at the place of transmission.[23] To begin with, it enables individual and private reception, which is free[24], without prejudice to the legal protection of technological

---

[22] Cf. AL Dias Pereira, 'Direitos de remuneração equitativa pela comunicação pública de obras e prestações' in D Moura Vicente and others (eds.) *Estudos de Direito Intelectual em Homenagem ao Prof. Doutor José de Oliveira Ascensão – 50 Anos de Vida Universitária* (Almedina, Coimbra, 2015) 57-75.

[23] LF Rebello, *Código do Direito de Autor e dos Direitos Conexos Anotado* (3rd ed. SPA/D. Quixote, Lisboa, 2002) 206-7.

[24] Article 108(2) of the Copyright Code. Cf. with international standards in J Reinbothe and S von Lewinski, *The WIPO Treaties on Copyright: A Commentary on the WCT, the WPPT, and the BTAP* (2.ª ed. Oxford University Press, Oxford, 2015) 133.

measures concerning services consisting of or based upon conditional access. Next, broadcasting makes possible further retransmissions of works by different broadcasters, which are subject to the rights holders' authorization.[25] Then, broadcasting makes possible public shows consisting of or based upon the communication to the public of broadcasts, for which authorization and payment are also required[26] (for example, transmission of broadcast sport events or musical concerts by means of large screens and sound amplifiers, with or without paid access, but usually accompanied with drinks and food facilities). Finally, broadcasting enables the perception of broadcast works in public places like bars and restaurants by means of radio or TV sets which are used to please customers, but which do not, as such, amount to a public show. For the later situation Article 155 of the Copyright Code provides a special right of remuneration: "it is equally due compensation to the author for the public communication of broadcast work by loudspeaker or by any similar device which transmits signs, sounds or images" (contributor's translation).

In general, this last situation is not identified by the courts. The STJ case-law reads that "There will be reuse of the work only if technical means are used that recreate by any manner the diffusion of the work, producing a show different from the broadcast one" (contributor's translation). In such case authorization and payment and required, but if no reuse of the work takes place, as it is found to be the case in bars and restaurants using TV or radio sets to make broadcast works enjoyable by customers, then neither authorization nor payment are required, according to the STJ.

---

[25] Article 149(1) of Copyright Code. The right of retransmission by cable is mandatorily exercised by copyright collecting societies – Article 7 of Decree-Law No 333/97 of 27 November.

[26] Article 122(3) *ex vi* Article 156(2) of the Copyright Code (Article 187(1)(2) thereof provides broadcasters with the exclusive right of communication to the public of their broadcasts where carried out in public places and with paid entries).

A statutory license allowed under the Berne Convention?

Nevertheless, broadcast works can be used by means of public communication regardless of a public show taking place and, moreover, the exclusive right can be statutorily derogated from, without prejudice to the right to remuneration, concerning secondary uses. That is what happens with the communication to the public of broadcast works provided that it does not amount to a public show.[27]

Portuguese legislation conforms with Article 11*bis* (1)(2) of Berne Convention (as amended by the Brussels Act of 1948). Article 11*bis*(1) (iii) includes the use of radio or TV receivers in bars, restaurants and other public houses; Article 11(2) allows Berne members to discipline the exercise of this right provided that the authors' moral right is not harmed and an equitable compensation is paid.[28] The Portuguese Copyright Act of 1966 excluded from the authors' exclusive right the reception in public places of broadcast works, granting them in return a right to remuneration.[29] Arguably the

[27] Another case is public lending under Article 6 of Decree-Law No 332/97 de 27 November.

[28] Cf. W Nordemann, K Vinck, PW Hertin, *Droit d'auteur international et droits voisins dans les pays de langue allemande et les Etats membres de la Communauté Européenne – Commentaire* (trad. J. Tournier. Larcier, Bruxelles, 1983) 124-5 (holding that the truly minimum right guaranteed by the Convention is the right to equitable remuneration). S von Lewinski, *International Copyright Law and Policy* (Oxford University Press, Oxford, 2008) 165-6. P Goldstein, B Hugenholtz, *International Copyright – Principles, Law, and Practice* (2nd ed. Oxford University Press, Oxford, 2010) 328. MV Rocha, 'Obra radiodifundida e comunicação pública' (2013/2014) 34 *Actas de Derecho Industrial y de Derecho de Autor*, 397-404.

[29] In 1969 the General State Prosecutor, asked to provide legal opinion concerning the interpretation of Articles 155 and 160 of the former Copyright Code of 1996, held that as allowed under Article 11*bis* (2) of the Berne Convention the reception of broadcast works, as such, would not require authorization from right holders, but they would be entitled to receive an equitable remuneration to be paid by the holders of bars, restaurants and businesses alike for the economic advantage that they might be get from it - Procuradoria-Geral da República, 'Parecer n.º 35/69, de 8 de agosto de 1969' in LF Rebello (ed), *Comunicação Pública de Emissões de Rádio e Televisão*, cit. *supra* fn. 9, 75-92. According to Article 195(1) of the Copyright Code of 1985 copyright usurpation requires the use of a work by any manner provided

Copyright Code of 1985 did not bring a change, thereby keeping the statutory license in return for an equitable remuneration. It appears similar to the legislation of Italy[30] or Japan[31].

According to the STJ case-law, copyright only subsists where the person running a bar or restaurant uses the reception of broadcast works to attract clients in conditions similar to a public show, i.e., according to the Court, "where the reception becomes itself a show, organized in public establishments, around sports or musical event, with or without paid entrance" (contributor's translation). However, history as well as systematic and teleological reasons justify reading Article 155 as a provision with its own normative content, instead of just a redundancy. Its useful meaning is that the use of radio and TV sets in bars, restaurants and alike to make broadcast works enjoyable by customers is not equivalent to a public show. However, in return for the statutory license, authors are entitled to payment of remuneration.

Therefore, the STJ should single-out the authentic meaning of Article 155, which provides authors with a right to remuneration for the public communication of broadcasts, including where it takes place, according to the CJEU, by means of a TV screen and loudspeakers to customers staying in a pub or a bar-restaurant. In order to satisfy the specific subject-matter of the copyright, as identified by the CJEU, and to assure a high level of copyright protection, an equitable remuneration, as guaranteed by the Berne Convention and adopted by the Portuguese legislation, is due to right holders. Therefore, where exempting the payment of equitable remuneration to authors, the STJ does not give a balanced interpretation of

for under the Code but provided that the right holders' authorization is required. In case it is not, notably where a statutory license exists, then the right holders are entitled only to remuneration and they cannot prohibit such use of their works.

[30] Article 58 of Legge sul diritto d'autore (L. 633/1941) <http://www.altalex.com/> accessed 29 April 2016

[31] Article 68(2) of the Copyright Law of Japan <http://www.cric.or.jp/english/clj/cl2.html> accessed 29 April 2016

Article 155 of the Copyright Code and places Portugal in a situation of possible not compliance with international and, in particular, European Union law.

Full harmonization of the authors' right to communication to the public?

It may be argued that the EC Directive 2001/29 has fully harmonized the right of communication to the public as an exclusive right and therefore Member States cannot keep statutory licenses which do not comply with it, even if they are permitted under Berne. However, the main purpose of the Directive is to implement the WIPO Treaties of 1996, which have introduced a new right to make available to the public on the internet within the authors' right of communication to the public leaving basically unaltered the discipline of this right in what concerns broadcasting and other traditional forms of communication to the public.

Article 8 of the WIPO Copyright Treaty provides a general exclusive right of communication to the public, "including any communication to the public". Notwithstanding, the Agreed Statement concerning Article 8 reads that "nothing in Article 8 precludes a Contracting Party from applying Article 11*bis* (2)." I.e., in setting "the conditions under which the rights mentioned in the preceding paragraph may be exercised" Contracting Parties may keep or establish statutory licenses for the exercise of this right.[32]

---

[32] J Reinbothe and S von Lewinski, *The WIPO Treaties on Copyright* (cit. supra fn. 24) 133-4. The WTO Panel concerning the conformity of the US 'home-style' and 'business' exemptions with Article 11*bis*(1) (ii) and (iii) of the Berne Convention hold that the later, introduced by the *Fairness in Music Licensing Act* (1998), did not comply with the three-step test of Article 13 TRIPS, while the former would be allowed under the minor exemptions doctrine of the Berne Convention also valid under TRIPs – cf. G Ritter, 'Recent Developments in WTO Dispute Settlement Dispute under the TRIPs

Nevertheless, it has been remarked that "the Agreed Statement arguably does not apply to the communication to the public of wireless broadcasts, since Article 11*bis*(1)(iii) of the Berne Convention is not included in the reservation clause of Article 8 of the WCT".[33] Moreover, it has been argued that all permitted exceptions and limitations to copyright are listed by Directive 2001/29 and, as it does not provide the communication of broadcasts in bars and restaurants, Member States would be preempted from using the possibility left open by Article 11*bis* (2) of the Berne Convention.[34]

If that is the case, as Portugal did not amend its legislation in this regard, there would be defective implementation of the Directive. However, it is not clear whether the notion of communication to the public used by Directive 2001/29 should fully expand to traditional media. For some reason these instruments are usually called the WIPO Internet Treaties and the Info-Soc. Directive. But if this is not the case, there is at most defective implementation of the Directive, because national law has not been amended by revoking Article 155 of the Copyright Code.

The issue is at least controversial. Not to mention that the broad notion of communication to the public used in Article 3(1) of Directive 2001/29 has not prevented the CJUE from excluding hyperlinking and

---

Agreement' and N Netanel, 'TRIPs interpretation and dispute settlement Panel Report on U.S. Copyright Act § 110(5)' both in H Hansen (ed.) *International Intellectual Property Law & Policy - Vol. 7* (Juris Publishing Huntington, 2002) respectively at 73-5/8 and 74-5. S Ricketson, JC Ginsburg, *International Copyright and Neighbouring Rights – The Berne Convention and Beyond – Vol. I* (2nd ed. Oxford University Press, Oxford, 2006) 738, fn. 126. For a critical assessment of the Panel's decision, in special due to failure to comply with Article 13 TRIPS "in accordance with the general rule of treaty interpretation, codified by the VCLT" [Vienna Convention on the Law of Treaties, May 23, 1969], EB Rodrigues Jr. *The General Exception Clauses of the TRIPS Agreement. Promoting Sustainable Development* (Cambridge University Press, Cambridge, 2012) 127.

[33] M Walter, 'Article 3 Right of communication to the public', in M Walter and S von Lewinski (eds), *European Copyright Law. A Commentary* (Oxford University Press, Oxford, 2010) 977.

[34] M Ohen Mendes, supra fn. 16, 183-4, n. 25 (suggesting however that the provision of a *de mininis* exemption could be fair for small family-size businesses –187).

framing[35] as well as, concerning a similar concept used in Article 8(2) of Directive 92/100, the broadcasting of phonograms in dentist offices[36], where the issue is limited to payment of remuneration to phonogram producers.

Conclusion

Probably where the STJ said too much (the remuneration right was not the issue) has the CJUE said too little (concerning the articulation of the Info-Soc. Directive with the Berne Convention and the WCT). One may also wonder whether this is not another situation in which "the ECJ seems to have succumbed to the temptation to fill certain gaps that exist in the harmonized EU copyright landscape."[37]

The European Commission has published its Communication *Towards a modern, more European copyright framework*.[38] The keywords are digital single market, portability, online availability, text-and-data mining (TDM). But it also talks about "ensuring wid-

[35] See judgment of 13 February 2014, case C-466/12, Svensson, ECLI:EU:C:2014:76 ("the provision on a website of clickable links to works freely available on another website does not constitute an 'act of communication to the public'") and Order of 21 October 2014, case C348/13, BestWater, ECLI:EU:C:2014:2315 (framing is not considered a communication to the public because the work is not transmitted to a new public nor communicated by a specific technical way different from that of the communication of origin).

[36] Judgment of 15 March 2012, case C-135/10, *Consorzio Fonografici*, ECLI:EU:C:2012:140 (Article 8(2) of Directive 92/100 "does not cover the broadcasting, free of charge, of phonograms within private dental practices engaged in professional economic activity, such as the one at issue in the main proceedings, for the benefit of patients of those practices and enjoyed by them without any active choice on their part.").

[37] A Kur and T Dreier, *European Intellectual Property Law. Text, Cases & Materials* (E Elgar, Cheltenham, 2013) 291.

[38] Communication from the Commission to the European Parliament, the Council, the European Economic and Social Committee and the Committee of the Regions, *Towards a modern, more European copyright framework*. COM(2015) 626 final. Brussels, 9.12.2015.

er access to creative content" and points out the "lack of clarity" concerning the definition of the right of communication to the public[39]. For that person trying to make a living out of running a bar or restaurant in the southwestern coast of Europe, copyright uncertainty reigns, like a sword of *Damocles* over her head, due to the possible – and, arguably, ethically fragile[40] - criminal consequences of such disputed copyright infringement.

In this contributor's opinion, unless a public show takes place, Portuguese law provides a statutory license against payment of an equitable remuneration. This mechanism appears in conformity with the applicable international instruments and complies with Directive 2001/29, as it guarantees adequate remuneration to authors. As restated in *Sociedade Portuguesa de Autores*, the main purpose of this Directive is to assure a high level of protection for authors, so that they get an adequate remuneration for the use of their works (para. 12). In these situations, copyright is limited to a right to equitable remuneration, instead of providing use exclusivity or *erga omnes* protection. Whether it is adequate and proportional or not in the framework of EU law, is something the CJUE may be called to decide on.

---

[39] Pointint out that the case-law "seems fairly unstable", M Leistner, 'Europe's Copyright Law Decade: Recent Case Law of the European Court of Justice and Policy Perspectives' in *Common Market Law Review* (2004) 51, 559-600, at 572.

[40] J Oliveira Ascensão, 'Direito penal de autor' in *Estudos em Homenagem ao Professor Doutor Manuel Gomes da Silva* (Coimbra Editora, Coimbra, 2001) 460-1.

SOFTWARE INTEROPERABILITY, INTELLECTUAL PROPERTY AND COMPETITION LAW: COMPULSORY LICENSES FOR ABUSE OF MARKET DOMINANCE?*

Abstract - Innovation is a shared purpose of both intellectual property (IP) and competition law. However, sometimes competition law conflicts with the interests of IP holders. This paper searches for an adequate criterion of practical concordance, which consists of evaluating, in the concrete situation, which of those regulations best performs the purpose of promoting innovation. It is considered that requirements of competition law shape IP regulations, but the internal limits of protection therein identified are not enough to safeguard concerns of competition law. In particular, European courts held that, in exceptional circumstances, IP holders with market dominant position can be compelled to grant licenses of IP protected goods, such as copyrighted information and software. Such lifting of the IP exclusion power finds its rationale in preserving competition and promoting innovation, which is particularly sensitive within the dynamic software market.

Introduction

Intellectual property rights and competition law share a common purpose of promoting innovation. It has been called the 'innovation

* Computer Law & Security Review, vol. 27 / 2, p. 175-179, 2011, imprint of Elsevier.

nexus' between competition and intellectual property[1]. However, sometimes competition law collides with the interests of IP holders making it necessary to find an adequate criterion to solve such conflict. On one hand, IP rights mean a restriction to competition which is deemed necessary to stimulate competition itself and, therefore, to achieve the innovation policy and consumer welfare with new and enhanced products. On the other hand, IP rights have limits concerning their scope and content of protection which are intended to safeguard freedom of innovation and competition. Besides those limits expressly provided for in IP regulations, the case-law of the European courts scrutinizes the conformity of the exercise of IP rights with the European primary law. And, in case of incompatibility, the courts lift the exclusion power conferred by such exclusive rights. In particular, the European courts have established in several cases (e.g. *Magill*, *IMS,* and *Microsoft*) that the refusal to grant IP licenses may constitute, in exceptional circumstances, an abuse of dominant position by preventing access to an indispensable good to technical progress in a secondary market, thereby eliminating competition and harming consumers. Moreover, despite the existence of IP rights, competition law has justified the imposition of compulsory licenses upon such dominant undertakings.

The Promotion of Innovation as a Common Justification for Intellectual Property and Competition Law

Intellectual property, as well as competition law, is not neutral[2]. In fact, an economy based upon knowledge and innovation uses

[1] Ghidini (2007).

[2] Ascensão (2006), p. 165.

both competition law and intellectual property to achieve *consumer welfare*.[3] However, sometimes these legal tools collide[4] and it is necessary to find out a criterion for accessing which of those instruments shall have precedence.

In fact, IP rights restrict competition as the owners of these rights, such as patents, trademarks or copyrights, have the exclusive right of economic exploitation of the protected goods (e.g. technological inventions, distinctive signs, literary works including software and databases) during the term of protection.

Because of their incorporeal nature, these goods are not subject to consumer rivalry[5]. Nonetheless, the IP holder is in principle entitled to exclude any other, direct or indirect, competitor from their economic exploitation. It means that IP rights, as market exclusives, are obstacles to entry into the market, thereby restricting competition. But, how are such rights to be justified in a market economy with free competition?

To begin with, IP rights are not monopolies in themselves as the economical inter-changeability of goods typical of monopolies does not necessarily result from an IP right[6]. Then, at the economical and mercantile level, these rights are justified by the policy of promoting innovation and knowledge. For example, the first Copyright Act in England (the Act of Queen Anne, 1710) justifies copyright with a view to encourage learning, and the U.S. Constitution grants legislative power to the Congress 'to Promote the Progress of Science and useful Arts, by securing for limited Times to Authors and Inventors the exclusive Right to their respective Writings and Discoveries" (Art. 1, § 8, cl. 8.).

---

[3] European Commission (2004), p. 2, par. 7.

[4]Säcker (2008), p. 5, 35, 50-1.

[5] Stiglitz (1999), p. 309.

[6] Colston/Middleton (2005), p. 33; Säcker (2008), pp. 61-2.

So, the restriction to competition implied by IP rights is justified by the positive effects they produce in terms of innovation and knowledge, i.e., IP is a restriction to competition deemed necessary and adequate to stimulate competition itself and to better achieve innovation and consumer welfare. In fact, it is common understanding that, without IP protection, the investment in R&D would hardly be compensated as any *free-rider* could take advantage of new and enhanced products 'instead of striving to better them'[7].

On the other hand, the same result could not be achieved by the repression of unfair competition[8], as this protection grants no exclusive right opposable *erga omnes*. At the same time, such a system of protection would not safeguard the competition freedom that the concept of public domain safeguards under IP regulations.

Competition as a Restriction to the Existence and the Content of Intellectual Property

The previous considerations show that IP rights also protect competition, and no claim for more IP protection can find natural justification under IP rationale. The principle of Natural law does not provide any safe haven for expansionism of IP protection, as it is always and *ab initio* necessary to take into consideration concerns of competition law, regarding the negative or positive effects that such increase in IP protection may produce in terms of innovation and knowledge[9].

As a matter of fact, competition concerns are to be found at several levels of IP regulations. They represent, to begin with, the

[7] Turner (2010), p. 3.

[8] Dutfield/Suthersanen (2008), pp. 50-1.

[9] See Drexl (2008), Pereira (2008).

endogenous limits at the scope of protection, such as for example all those intellectual goods that are excluded from the object of patents, trademarks or copyrights, even if by chance they could meet the requirements, respectively, of novelty and inventive activity, distinctive capacity or originality.

The legal impossibility of IP appropriation of such intellectual goods is justified by the added value that is recognised to their collective free use[10]. Imagine what it would mean if a scientific theory or a certain mathematical method with industrial utility could be exploited only by one single enterprise. That would represent a market monopoly over an intellectual infrastructure.

On the other hand, a term of protection for IP makes it possible the liberation of goods for free use, therefore opening room for competition. Moreover, the requirements of novelty and inventive activity, distinctive capacity and originality do not only promote innovation but also they prevent the appropriation of intellectual goods that belong to the public domain, making it possible for every competitor to take advantage of them. And that's why the increase in the term of copyright protection, both in Europe and the USA, has been criticized[11]. One of the consequences of such increase of the term of protection was to prevent Disney's *Mickey Mouse* from falling into public domain[12].

Furthermore, the exclusive rights conferred by IP regulations meet several limits and exceptions, such as the rule of exhaustion of the right of distribution and a list of free uses which open space for competition through innovation (e.g. software reverse engineering). In all these situations, IP does not grant a power of exclusion because in the viewpoint of the law maker, the policy of innovation

---

[10] Stiglitz (1999), pp. 320-1.

[11] See e.g. Keeling (2003), p. 266.

[12] Landes/Posner (2003), p. 210 ff.

and knowledge is best served by free use of such goods, even if conditioned to fair remuneration.

In what concerns IP nuclear protection, IP regulations provide compulsory licenses which can be activated under certain circumstances. For example concerning patents, Portuguese law provides such compulsory licenses for reasons of public interest in case the holder of the patent does not explore it nor allows others to do it (Code of Industrial Property, Article 110). However, competition is not listed within the 'express grounds'[13] of public interest.

Competition Law as a Restriction to the Exercise of IP Rights: the Refusal of IP Licensing as a Possible Abuse of Dominant Position

Even though no compulsory license for reasons of competition is expressly provided for, the European courts have confirmed several decisions adopted by the European Commission, acting as the guardian of the Treaties. Commentators wonder whether competition law should limit IP rights for reasons of economic policy and criticize the legal uncertainty arising of such a 'vague test' as it would harm investment in R&D induced by IP[14].

Nonetheless, European authorities submit the exercise of IP rights to the requirements of primary Community law, in particular competition law. Under exceptional circumstances, the refusal of IP licenses may be considered an abuse of dominant position, as competition law intervenes as a last resource to control the potential monopolistic power of IP holders[15].

---

[13] See Marques (2007), pp. 187, 209.

[14] Korah (2007), p. 178.

[15] Cornish (2004), p. 28.

Following European case-law concerning the refusal of access to an essential element of the productive process[16], there is a series of decisions of the European courts concerning the refusal of licensing information protected under copyright law as abuse of dominant position, such as, cases *Magill*[17], *IMS*[18] and more recently, in what concerns the refusal of providing competitors access to the information on software interoperability, *Microsoft*[19].

In this last decision, dated of 17 September 2007, the Court of first instance has confirmed the 'controversial'[20] decision of the Commission concerning the infringement of the prohibition of abuse of dominant position provided for Article 82 of the Treaty of Rome (now Article 102 of the Treaty on the Functioning of the European Union - TFEU) and to order Microsoft to disclose interoperability information to undertakings willing to develop and distribute operative systems for group servers and to authorize them to use such information in reasonable and non discriminatory conditions[21].

According to the Court, the refusal by a dominant undertaking to license interoperability information may constitute an abuse of dominant position where such information is indispensable for the exercise of an activity in a neighbouring or related market (1), the refusal is capable of eliminating all effective competition (2) and prevents the introduction into the market of a new product for which there is potential consumer demand, including the limitation of technical development in prejudice of consumers

---

[16] See Cases 6-7/73 (*ICI/Commercial Solvents*), ECR 1974, 223; Case 238/87 (*Volvo/Veng*), ECR 1988, 6211; Case 7/97 (*Oscar Bronner/Mediaprint*), ECR 1998, I-7791.

[17] C-241/91 P, C-242/91 P, RTE/ITP (*Magill*), ECR 1995, I-0743.

[18] C-418/01 (*IMS Health/NDC Health*), ECR 2004, I-5039.

[19] T-201/04 (*Microsoft/Commission*), ECR 2007, II-03601, par. 797-799.

[20] Korah (2007), p. 185.

[21] See e.g. Andermann (2004), Hart (2006).

(3), unless the refusal has objective justification which cannot however result merely from the existence of IP rights in such information (4).

The Impact of European Case-Law on R&D Investment in Software

The Microsoft decision has been criticized on grounds that an excessively broad application of the prohibition of abuse of dominant position and the compulsory provision of access to an essential infrastructure or the compulsory licensing of IP rights could harm the capacity of undertakings to take advantage of the benefits of their R&D investments and, therefore, it would prejudice their investments in innovation[22].

Nonetheless, according to the European case-law, competition requirements only prevail over IP rights where the refusal to licensing harms consumers by preventing the development of a neighbouring market, as the competitor is willing to offer new products or enhanced products for which there is consumer demand[23], despite the IP holder is also acting in such secondary market. The promotion of innovation by the removal of a legal obstacle is targeted not only to products not yet available in the market but also to already existing - yet capable of enhancement - products, with the exclusion of mere replicas without added value, in order to protect the competition process in the *downstream market*[24].

More recently, in its paper on *exclusionary abuses*, the European Commission indicates that the benefits that competition allows to

---

[22] See Korah (2007), p. 178, Noonan (2008), p. 113, Eagles/Longdin (2008), p. 205; Curley (2009), p. 496.

[23] Säcker (2008), p. 64.

[24] Eilmansberger (2008), pp. 1172-3, 1175.

consumers are lower prices, better quality and a wider variety of new or enhanced products or services, and that, concerning exclusionary abuses, the most important is to protect a truthful competition process rather than the mere protection of competitors[25].

Although no legal exception is provided for concerning abuse of dominant position, the Commission outlines that a dominant undertaking can justify its behaviour by showing that either it is objectively necessary or that it produces substantial efficiency gains which compensate any anti-competition effect for consumers; however, this will be hard to prove in situations of near monopoly, and it means that the dominant undertaking 'bears the initial burden of proof, if it is to negate a finding of abuse'[26].

Moreover, the Commission is aware that compulsory licensing may dissuade dominant undertakings from investing in innovation and that competitors may feel tempted to free-ride on the investments done by the dominant undertaking, without benefits, in the long term, for consumers. Therefore the Commission clarifies that, according to consolidated case-law, three requirements must be met for compulsory licensing to be justified. First, the objective need of the production factor due to inexistence of, or impossibility of access to, an alternative source. Second, the elimination of effective competition (the probability of which is directly related with the market share of the dominant undertaking in the downstream market). Third, consumer harm as competitors are prevented from introducing new or innovated products or where it is likely that subsequent innovation will be hindered.

Nonetheless, the Commission acknowledges that efficiency gains arising out of the licensing refusal can be an objective justification for the behaviour of the dominant undertaking, in particular

[25] European Commission (2009), §§ 6 ff.

[26] Turner (2010), p. 92; Pereira (2010), p. 253.

when the refusal is a condition of compensation of the investment essential to production, or when the obligation to license affects the capacity to innovate of the dominant undertaking and their competitors.[27]

It is argued that the 'more economic approach' used by the Commission to assess the objective justification of the refusal to license proprietary information 'makes it difficult to predict the outcome'[28]. Moreover, it's wondered whether exclusive rights such as copyright are not reduced by reasons of competition to mere rights to remuneration[29].

Open-Source Compulsory Licenses?

Will undertakings stop investing in innovation, taking into account that their IP exclusive rights can be reduced by the courts to mere rights to remuneration?

To begin with, it should be noted that, taking requirements of copyright protection seriously[30], the existence of IP rights over software interoperability information, despite not disputed by the European authorities, is at least fragile. The same was the case concerning lists of TV programs in *Magill*. Moreover, despite *Microsoft* argued software patents issued by the European Patent Office[31], the European Patent Convention excludes computer programs, as such, from the object of patents[32].

[27] See European Commission (2009), §§ 75-90.

[28] Brown (2009), p. 439.

[29] Daum (2010), p. 67.

[30] Pereira (2008), pp. 397-402.

[31] Curley (2009), p. 492, n. 20 (European patent 0438571 B1 'Method and system for open file caching in a networked computer system').

[32] See Blind/Edler/Friedewald (2005).

However, regardless of the issue of the existence of IP rights, what seems to be more sensitive for the European authorities is the near monopolistic position of the dominant undertaking (*Microsoft*) and the power that enables it to eliminate competition in a downstream market taking into account its specific features[33].

It is curious to remark that the US Supreme Court, in *eBay Inc v. MercExchange*, despite not refusing patent protection to Internet business methods (according to previous a decision in *State Street*), has however denied the power of exclusion to such IP right. This decision comes in line with other decisions of US Courts (e.g. *z4 Technologies, Inc. v. Microsoft Corp.*, and *Paice v. Toyota Motor Corp.*, Texas 2006)[34]. In comparison, the European courts establish a kind of compulsory license limited to a neighbouring market in order to prevent the creation of a situation of near monopoly, submitting the dominant undertaking to competition pressure by removing an obstacle to competition that prevented access to software interoperability information.

In short, the European courts provide that dominant undertakings cannot use IP rights as *anti-competition shields* in order to prevent innovation and to eliminate competition in neighbouring markets, as IP rights (even where protected under international treaties) must comply with primary community law[35]. This case-law of the European courts is particularly relevant in the dynamic software market as undertakings acting on a proprietary basis compete with free and open-source software undertakings.

In fact, dominant undertakings which carry out their activities on a proprietary basis may be compelled to license interoperability information and therefore to provide open-source licenses to compet-

[33] T-201/04 (*Microsoft/Commission*), ECR 2007, II-03601, par. 561-2.

[34] Lee (2008), p. 104.

[35] See T-201/04 (*Microsoft/Commission*), ECR 2007, II-03601, par. 797799.

itors in a downstream market. This open-source compulsory license is however limited to competing works in neighbouring markets and may be imposed only where the IP holder is a dominant undertaking which makes use of its economic power to hinder or to eliminate competition. Moreover, competition law seems to appear as a last resource to achieve the imperative of interoperability which justifies the legal mandatory right of reverse engineering of copyrighted software.

It means that competition law does not provide a general blanket for transforming proprietary software into open-source software, as competitors are not entitled to replicate the software of the dominant undertaking nor to free-ride on it either by cloning or updating it[36]. Rather, competitors are only entitled, on a reasonable paid basis, to get access to and to make use of interoperability information that is essential for improving the performance of their own software when functioning together with the software of the dominant undertaking. Accordingly, the dominant undertaking's right to derivate works cannot hinder the innovation in independent software that otherwise competitors would not be capable of developing, with the result of depriving consumers of access to innovated products and the elimination of competition.

In short, dominant undertakings bear the special responsibility of not hiding behind IP rights and exercising them in a manner that forecloses secondary markets and eliminates competition therein. The criteria established by the case-law and the guidelines of the European authorities may not be make it easy to predict the outcome in all situations, but they provide dominant undertakings with the existing legal framework concerning the interoperability between intellectual property and competition law, making it clear that the abuse of market dominance can justify compulsory licenses in the name of innovation and consumer welfare.

[36] Govära (1996), p. 247.

References

Andermann, S.: Does the Microsoft Case Offer a New Paradigm for the Exceptional Circumstances Test and Compulsory Copyright Licenses under EC Competition Law?. The Competition Law Review 1(2), pp. 7-22 (2004)

Ascensão, J.O.: Propriedade Intelectual e Internet [Intellectual Property and Internet]. In: Direito da Sociedade da Informação [Information Society Law], VI, pp. 145-165. Coimbra Editora, Coimbra (2006)

Blind, K., Edler, J., Friedewald, M.: Software Patents: Economic Impacts and Policy Implications. Cheltenham/Northampton, Edward Elgar (2005)

Brown, A.E.: Intellectual Property, Competition and the Internet. In: Edwards, L., Waelde, C. (eds.): Law and the Internet, 3rd ed., pp. 417-440. Oxford/Portland, Hart Publishing (2009)

Colston, C., Middleton, K.: Modern Intellectual Property Law, 2nd ed. London, Cavendish (2005)

Cornish, W.: Intellectual Property: Omnipresent, Distracting, Irrelevant?. Oxford University Press, Oxford (2004)

Curley, D.: Value Judgments. European Intellectual Property Review 31, pp. 491-496 (2009)

Daum, F.: Copyright, European Competition Law, and Free Movement of Goods and Services. In: Walter, M.M., Lewinski, S. von (eds.): European Copyright Law: A Commentary, pp. 50-70. Oxford, Oxford University Press (2010)

Drexl, J. (ed.): Research Handbook on Intellectual Property and Competition Law. Cheltenham/Northampton, Edward Elgar, (2008)

Dutfield, G., Suthersanen, U.: Global Intellectual Property Law. Edward Elgar, Cheltenham/Northampton (2008)

European Commission: Commission Notice, Guidelines on the application of Article 81 of the EC Treaty to technology transfer agreements. OJ 2004/C 101/02, 27.04.2004 (2004)

European Commission: Communication from the Commission, Guidance on the Commission's enforcement priorities in applying Article 82 of the EC Treaty to abusive exclusionary conduct by dominant undertakings. OJ 2009/C 45/02, 24.2.2009 (2009)

Eagles, I., Longdin, L.: Microsoft's Refusal to Disclose Software Interoperability Information and the Court of First Instance. European Intellectual Property Review 30(5), pp. 205-208 (2008)

Eilmansberger, T.: Article 82. In: Hirsh, G., Montag, F., Säcker, F.J. (gen.eds.) Competition Law: European Community Practice and Procedure - Article-by-Article Commentary, pp. 1056-1240. London, Sweet & Maxwell (2008).

Ghidini, G.: Intellectual Property and Competition Law: The Innovation Nexus. Cheltenham/Northampton, Edward Elgar (2007)

Govâre, I.: The Use and Abuse of Intellectual Property Rights in E C Law. London, Sweet & Maxwell (1996)

Hart, R.: Interoperability and the Microsoft Decision. European Intellectual Property Review 28(7), pp. 361-365 (2006)

Keeling, D.T.: Intellectual Property and EU Law. Volume I. Free Movement and Competition Law, Oxford/New York, Oxford University Press (2003)

Korah, K.: An Introductory Guide to EC Competition Law and Practice. 9th ed., Hart Publishing, Oxford (2007)

Landes, W., Posner, R.: The Economic Structure of Intellectual Property Law. Cambridge Mass., Harvard University Press, (2003)

Lee, P.: 'The Evolution of Intellectual Infrastructure', Washington Law Review 83, pp. 39-122 (2008)

Marques, J.P.R.: Biotecnologia(s) e Propriedade Intelectual [Biotechnologies and Intellectual Property], II. Almedina, Coimbra (2007)

Noonan, C.: The Emerging Principles of International Competition Law. Oxford University Press, Oxford (2008)

Pereira, A.L.D.: Inovação tecnológica, propriedade intelectual e concorrência [Technological innovation, intellectual property and competition]. In: Wachowicz, M., Moreno, G.P. (coord.): Propriedade Intelectual: Inovação e Conhecimento [Intellectual Property: Innovation and Knowledge], pp. 241-260. Curitiba, Juruá (2010)

Pereira, A.L.D.: Direitos de Autor e Liberdade de Informação [Copyright and Freedom of Information]. Coimbra, Almedina (2008)

Säcker, F.J.: Basic Principles. In: Hirsh, G., Montag, F., Säcker, F.J. (gen.eds.) Competition Law: European Community Practice and Procedure - Article-by-Article Commentary, pp. 1-83. London, Sweet & Maxwell, London (2008)

Stiglitz, J.: Knowledge as a Global Public Good. In: Kaul, I., Grunberg, I., Stern, M., (eds.) Global Public Goods – International Cooperation in the 21st Century, pp. 308-325. Oxford/New York, Oxford University Press (1999)

Turner, J.D.C.: Intellectual Property and EU Competition Law. Oxford, Oxford University Press (2010)

MEDIA RIGHTS AND ONLINE BETTING IN FOOTBALL MATCHES UNDER PORTUGUESE LAW*

Abstract - Football is a major point of interest for media and entertainment industries. More recently, the market evolved to online betting in webcasted football matches. This phenomenon challenges the ability of the legal system to cope with the evolution of technologies. This paper addresses legal issued raised by online betting in football matches under Portuguese law, such as, notably, the protection of football matches under copyright and related rights and the rights of image of sports professionals concerned with football broadcasts, as well as the relation between exclusive media rights in sports events and freedom of information, competition law concerns, and the specific regulation of online betting services. In general, despite many issues have not yet been harmonized at the European level, the Portuguese legal framework is similar to other Member States of the European Union. Notwithstanding, for the improvement of the digital single market, it might be useful to have common regulations concerning exclusive media rights and the exploitation of online betting in football matches.

---

* The International Sports Law Journal, vol. 14 / 3-4, p. 167–178, 2014, Springer Nature.

1. Football matches, copyright and related rights

In media speech football plays and players are sometimes called 'works of art' and 'artists'. However, for purposes of copyright law, football matches as well as sport events in general are not recognized as copyrightable works.

1.1. Literary and artistic creations and broadcasting works

Copyright law protects original works, i.e., according to the general notion provided for by the Copyright Act (CA)[1], intellectual creations in any literary, artistic or scientific field, by any means exteriorized, regardless of merits or purpose (Articles 1 and 2 CA)). The legal concept of work is illustrated by a catalog of examples (e.g. books, music, stage arts), and it is open to unnamed works; copyright law protects also derivative works and creative compilations (Article 3 CA).

Football matches – as well as sporting events in general - are not listed in the catalogue of examples, which illustrate the legal concept of copyrightable works. Despite artistic and scientific dimensions of football and sports in general, football matches as such - as well as sporting events in general – do not match any legal example of works (e.g. stage arts), nor the legal concept of work, and they are not, *per se*, derivative works or compilations. In short, football teams, coaches and players are not usually recognized as authors of literary or artistic intellectual creations.[2] Therefore, uploading of independently recorded

[1] Código do Direito de Autor e dos Direitos Conexos, enacted by Decree-Law No 63/85 of March 1985, as last amended by Law No 82/2013 of 6 December.

[2] See also ECJ judgment of 4 October 2011 (C-403/08 and C-429/08, Football Association Premier League), ruling that the FAPL cannot claim copyright in the Premier League matches themselves, as those sporting events cannot be considered to be an author's own intellectual creation and, therefore, to be 'works' for the purposes of copyright in the European Union.

videos by individuals who attend and record the event is not likely to be infringement of copyright and/or related rights in Portugal, because football games per se and as such are not copyrighted.

Nonetheless, football matches can be the 'raw material' of 'broadcasted works', i.e. works created according to the special conditions of use by audio and/or visual broadcasting as well as adaptations to such media of works originally created for a different type of use (Article 21(1) CA). Despite the level of creativity may not always be fulfilled as broadcasts are bound to a faithful transmission of the event, original broadcasted works, as such, are protected by copyright law. Broadcasted works are deemed joint works the authors of which are the director (e.g. scene selection) and the authors of texts and music (Article 21(2) CA).

1.2. Broadcasters' related rights

Title III of the Copyright Act protects four categories of persons/entities: performers, phonogram producers, film producers and broadcasting organizations. Portuguese copyright law provides as related rights the rights of performing artists, producers of phonograms, producers of films, and broadcasting organizations (Article 176 CA). A sui generis right is also provided for producers of databases[3].

Related rights are independent from copyright and they can exist even where no copyrighted work is used. However, performing artists are only protected where literary or artistic works are performed. In fact, performing artists are 'actors, singers, musicians, dancers and others who act, sing, recite (...) or otherwise perform literary or artistic works' (Article 176(2) CA).

[3] Decree-Law No 122/2000 of 4 July, implementing EC Directive 96/9 on the legal protection of databases.

Sport players as such are generally not considered performing artists for purposes of this related right. Notwithstanding their value in entertainment industries, the role of sport players is not literary or artistic but rather to serve the team with sporting skills executing strategies or tactics established by the coach and under the disciplinary authority of the Club and the League.

Concerning broadcasting organizations as well as sound and/or film producers, a related right to copyright subsists regardless of a literary or artistic work being broadcasted or produced. Therefore, broadcasting organizations which broadcast football matches have (related) exclusive rights in their emissions (Article 187 CA) despite football matches as such are not considered literary or artistic works.

1.3. A *right to show («direito ao espetáculo»)?*

Portuguese copyright law provides that the organizer of a show in which a work is performed has the right to authorize any broadcast, recording, reproduction and/or displaying of the performed work (Article 117 CA).

This special right of the organizer of shows is designed for stage performance of works. However, it requires the existence and performance of a work. Football matches – as well as sporting events in general – are not, as such, recognized as literary or artistic works. Football matches are not listed in the catalogue of examples of copyrightable works (e.g. books, music, performing arts on stage). Despite unlisted works are admitted for copyright protection, sport events, as 'random events', are not usually considered literary or artistic works.

In legal doctrine it has been argued that Article 117 of the Copyright Code reflected a right of customary basis generally conferred on the organizer of shows, and with special importance for sport events. The so-called right to show (*direito ao espetáculo*), which would be absolute but ephemeral as limited to acts of public communication.[4]

This right to sport show would have been indirectly established by the Basic Regulation of the Sport System[5]. It provided on the free entry into sport grounds the right of access for media professionals in the course of their profession, within the limitations justified notably for reasons of protection of the 'right to show' of organizers of sport events (Article 19). This Basic Regulation was replaced by the new Basic Regulation of Sports[6] which it kept a similar formula (Article 84(2)).

However, the Regulation of Physical Activities and Sports of 2007[7] revoked the Basic Regulation of 2004 and discontinued reference to the 'right of show'. It merely provides on access to sport shows that consumer protection measures are defined by legislation concerning notably the protection of economic interests and the right to previous information about the value of entries into sport shows during the season (Article 47).

Notwithstanding, the Lisbon Court of Appeals[8] and the Supreme Court of Justice[9] held that football matches are shows and that the owners of shows have a right to their economic exploitation by means of broadcasting. The courts rely on doctrine to elaborate the right to show as an ephemeral intellectual right which applies to broadcasting (but including preparatory acts).

---

[4] Ascensão 1987, p. 41-55, Id. 1988, p 15-35, Id. 1992, p. 590; Leitão 2011, p. 270-4.

[5] Law No 1/90 of 13 January (Lei de Bases do Sistema Desportivo).

[6] Law No 30/2004 of 21 July (Lei de Bases do Desporto).

[7] Law No 5/2007 of 16 January (Lei de Bases da Actividade Física e do Desporto).

[8] Judgment of 17 December 2008, Proc. 3599/2008-6.

[9] Judgment of 25 January 2009, Proc. 4986/06.3TVLSB.S1.

1.4. 'Exclusive' media rights in football regulations

References to the 'right of show' are to be found in the Regulation of Competitions organized by Portuguese League of Professional Football[10], notably Article 38(13). As last revised in 2012, it provides that Clubs are individually holders of the rights of transmission of games and summaries (Article 68(2)). But it is up to the Executive Committee of the League to establish the number of games to be broadcasted by TV, the schedules, the number of games for each team, to authorize the TV transmission of games within official competitions organized by the League and to establish the fees of such transmission (Article 68(1)).

Moreover, this Regulation provides that the images of games of competitions organized by the League can only be collected by the League itself or by the broadcaster(s) which has been expressly authorized by the League (Article 74(1)). Hosting clubs must authorize visiting clubs to collect images, but these can't divulgate, by any means, such images (Article 74(2)).

The League Regulation confers on the clubs and the League itself a 'right to show' for matches disputed in their own stadiums within the competition organized by the League. However, the nature of this right is not clear. Is it an absolute right, i.e. a right which the League and/or the teams can invoke against third parties, or a right which can be opposed only in the relations between the League and the teams and among the teams themselves?

In a dispute involving television rights in football matches, the Lisbon Court of Appeals ruled that the effects of the UEFA Regulations are limited to the parties to such regulations, and therefore they cannot be opposed against third parties, notably broadcasters operating without authorization from the League.[11]

---

[10] Regulamento das Competições Organizadas pela LPFP - http://www.lpfp.pt/

[11] Judgment of 10 November 2009, Proc. 4292/1999.L1-7.

This decision has been upheld by the Supreme Court of Justice[12] ruling also that the exercise of the right to TV broadcast of a football match acquired by contract is not abusive where it frustrates mere expectations of fact such as an expected income in ticket sales.

1.5. The legal protection of economic interests in public shows under the Television Act

Under the Television Act[13], organizers of public shows or events and holders of exclusive rights therein cannot oppose to the transmission of short informative extracts, and broadcasters may use their own technical means for that purpose. This right would not make much sense if the organizers of shows (and the holders of exclusive rights therein) could not control the full transmission of the shows, and its scope of protection is likely to target both traditional broadcasters and webcasters.

However, the legal provision does not establish a property right in the sense of a right opposable against all persons. Instead, it provides a legal protection of economic interests of both organizers of events and of broadcasters that acquire by contract exclusive media rights in the events.

Consequently, broadcasting companies do not have a property right against uploaders on the basis of copyright and/or related rights, but they can invoke a 'quasi-property' remedy based upon the exclusive acquisition of an interest protected under legislation and football regulations. This 'quasi-property' remedy entitles broad-

[12] Judgment of 24 May 2010, Proc. 4292/1999.L1.S1.

[13] Law No 27/2007 of 30 July (Lei da Televisão), and as last amended by Law 8/2011 of 11 April which implements EU Directive 2007/65.

casting companies to ask compensation for damages under tort law and unjust enrichment.[14]

Despite there is no copyrighted and/or related right in football matches as such, organizers of sport events can grant exclusive media rights to broadcasters concerning such events. However, privity of contract means that such exclusive rights cannot be opposed to third parties as property rights if there's no property right in the broadcasting of the event.

The provision of the Television Act which confers the right to short informative extracts does not provide the organizer of shows or public events with an intellectual property right in such events. The scope of protection of such provision is not to create a transferable property right but rather to protect the economic interest of the organizer of shows and of broadcasters which have been granted exclusive media rights in the events.

1.6. Conclusion: a quasi-property right to show

The right to show, as recognized and enforced by the courts as an ephemeral protection, is limited to acts of broadcasting and preparatory acts. The Portuguese League of Professional Football is entitled by the Football Regulations to a right to record the game in its capacity of organizer of the sport event, but this right is enforceable only against the members of the League. Concerning the broadcaster's exclusive right to record (and distribute) the matches, it would be infringed by uploaders's recording as such if such recording are used for real-time uploading ('webcasting').

---

[14] Articles 483 and 473 of the Portuguese Civil Code, enacted by Decree No 47344 of 25 November 1966.

On the other hand, if no organization of a show with access control takes place, the right to show is likely no to be recognized. In fact, concerning an amateur league organizing its matches on municipal (i.e. publicly owned) sporting grounds that are open for free to the general public, there would probably be no economic interest in protecting exclusive media rights under the 'right to show' provided by the Television Act and the Regulations of professional football. The relevant interest belongs to the organizer of the event (the League or the Federation concerning official competitions) and the media (as derivative acquirer). Ownership of the sporting grounds is not relevant per se.

As for the fact that attendance to matches requires the purchase of tickets or any other form of payment or registration, it plays a role on this matter, even if the sport was not football but a different one. In fact, a price or equivalent is required to enjoy the show in real-time or live and therefore the organizer of the show has an economic interest which may be affected by free-riding broadcasts.

In this direction seems to point the Statute of Journalists[15] where providing that journalists have the right of access to public places for information purposes, but concerning shows and other events with paid access in which the number of spectators justifies limitations to access, systems of accreditation of journalists may be established for each media (Article 9(1)(3)).

Nonetheless, the Supreme Court of Justice[16] held that the organizer of football events have merely a *de facto* expectation concerning ticket sales, so that where a broadcaster transmits a match under a contract with the Club but disregarding the UEFA Regulation it does not entitle the organizer to compensation.

---

[15] Estatuto do Jornalista, enacted by Law No 1/99 of 13 January, as last amended by Law No 64/2007 of 6 November.

[16] Judgment of 24 May 2010, Proc. 4292/1999.L1.S1.

2. Exclusive media rights in sports events and freedom of information

2.1. Freedom of information is protected by the Portuguese Constitution, as well as the journalist's right to access to information sources (Articles 37 and 38(2)(b)).[17]

According to the Television Act[18], holders of exclusive rights in shows and other public events cannot oppose to the transmission of short extracts, with informative nature, by a service of programs made available by any domestic or foreign TV broadcaster (Article 33(1)). In order to exercise this right to information, broadcasters may use the signal issued by the holders of exclusive rights, bearing the costs that eventually result from making the signal available, or, in alternative, broadcasters may use their own technical means under the regulation of access by media bodies to public places (Article 33(2)). Moreover, broadcasters under Portuguese jurisdiction holding exclusive rights to transmit, for the national territory, events taking place within the territory of another Member State of the European Union must provide access to their signal to domestic broadcasters interested in transmitting short extracts of informative nature about those events (Article 33(3)).

2.2. Limits to the right of informative extracts

Without prejudice of agreement for different use, such extracts shall:

[17] See Pereira 2008.

[18] Law No 27/2007 of 30 July.

a) be limited to the duration strictly indispensable to the perception of the essential content of the events, having regard their nature, provided it does not exceed 90 seconds;
b) be transmitted exclusively in regular programs of general information nature;
c) be transmitted within 36 hours after the end of the event, unless their future inclusion in reports of current events is justified by the scope of information;
d) identify the source of images in case they are transmitted upon the signal issued by the holder of the exclusive - Article 33(4).

Article 33(4) of the Television Act allows agreements for different use. However, such agreements should not provide terms of use more limited than the minimums provided by the Television Act. Portuguese legislation did not yet implement Directive 2010/13/EU of the European Parliament and of the Council of 10 March 2010 on the coordination of certain provisions laid down by law, regulation or administrative action in Member States concerning the provision of audiovisual media services (Audiovisual Media Services Directive).

Concerning relevant copyright and/or related rights limitations, the Copyright Act provides - in line with Directive 2001/29/EC on the harmonization of certain aspects of copyright and related rights in the information society – that informative extracts of the broadcasting works and emissions can be used for reporting of current news as well as quotation for criticism review - Articles 75(2)(b)(d)(g) and 189(1)(b). The concrete use of copyright limitations is subject to control by the 'three-step test' – Article 75(4).

2.3. Events of high public interest

The right of domestic broadcasters to have access to the signal of other broadcasters applies to 'events taking place within the territory of another Member State of the European Union', regardless of their high public interest. Notwithstanding, a concept close to events of high public interest is relevant concerning TV broadcasters that operate on a conditional access basis or without national coverage and acquire exclusive rights to transmit events of 'general public interest'. The Television Act provides that such broadcasters have to provide, in non-discriminatory and within the normal conditions of the market, access to other interested broadcasters that operate by Hertzian terrestrial via with national coverage and unconditional access (Article 32(2)). In case the holder of exclusive TV rights and other interested broadcasters do not reach an agreement, parties may request a binding arbitrage by the Media Authority (Article 33(3)). A list of events of 'general public interest' is established by Ministerial Order. The list in force does not include UEFA Champions League.[19]

The Television Act provides that organizers of shows and other public events and holders of exclusive rights in such events cannot oppose to the transmission of short extracts, with informative nature, by a service of programs made available by any TV broadcaster (Article 33(1)). In order to exercise this right to information, broadcasters may use their own technical means under the regulation of access by media bodies to public places (Article 33(2)).

On the other hand, the League Regulation provides that, without prejudice to the right of sport show as emerging by exclusive granting the full transmission of games and image collecting for further emission in summaries, journalists and image and sound operators of other TV broadcasters have the right to collect short informative extracts according to the applicable legal provisions (Article 38(13)).

---

[19] Ministerial Order (Portaria) No 14004/2012 of 24 October 2012.

In this regard, the Statute of Journalists[20] provides the right of access to public places for information purposes. However, concerning shows and other events with paid access in which the number of spectators justifies limitations to access, systems of accreditation of journalists may be established for each media (Article 9(1)(3)). Moreover, recording images in the margin of the event such as interviews with the players is likely to exceed the right to informative extracts. As for recording images of the public, it may be justified to provide factual information on the attendance to the match.

3. Rights of image of sports professionals

The right of image of sports professionals (workers) is regulated under the Civil Code as a personality right, and under the Sport Labor Act. As personality rights, it is notably absolute, can't be waived, and has no term.

3.1. The of image as a right of personality

The right to image is recognized in the Civil Code as a special right of personality (Article 79). The principle is that each person has the right to authorize the reproduction, the exhibition or the introduction in commerce of his/her portrait (Article 79(1)).

The Civil Code allows the use of a person's image (portrait) without his/her authorization where it is justified by his/her condition of celebrity or performed job, requirements of security or justice, scientific, learning or cultural purposes, or where the reproduction of image occurs in public places, or within facts of public interest

[20] Law No 1/99 of 13 January, as last amended by Law No 64/2007 of 6 November.

or which have publicly occurred, and provided that the reproduction, exhibition or introduction in commerce of the image does not cause harm to the honor, reputation or simply discretion of the person (Article 79(3)).

Within the limits of public order, each person can freely exercise his/her right of image (Article 81(1)). Notwithstanding, agreements on the right of image are revocable at any time, but the person has the obligation to compensate damages caused to the legitimate expectations of the other party (Article 81(2)).

3.2. Image rights under the Sport Labor Act

The right of image of professional sport workers has special regulation under the Sport Labor Act[21], which provides that professionals of sports have the right to use their public image in connection with sports and the right to oppose against third parties from unlawfully using their image for commercial exploitation or other economic purposes, notwithstanding the right of use of collective image of the team, which can be regulated by collective or class contracts (Article 10).

In short, professionals of sports have individual image rights: the right to use their image in connection with sports and the right to authorize the use of their image for commercial exploitation or other economic purposes, except where the lawfulness of such use is provided by the law, notably under the right to information. The right of image of sports professionals does not extend to the use of collective image of the team, which is a matter left to collective negotiation.

The collective agreement concluded between the Portuguese League of Professional Football and the Portuguese Union of

[21] Law No 28/98 of 27 June, as amended by Law No 114/99 of 2 August.

Professional Football Players (SJFP)[22] has a provision on the right to image according to which each football player has the right to use his/her own public image in connection with football activities and the right to prevent others from unlawfully using it for commercial or any other economic purposes (Article 38(1)). At the individual level, the right to use and to explore the image of the player belongs to himself, who may assign this right to the team during the term of the contract (Article 38(2)). The right to use the collective image of the team's players remains with the team or sports company (Article 38(3)). The commercial exploitation of the image of football players as a professional collectivity is managed by the Players' Union (SJFP), which is therefore entitled to receive circa one thousand euro for the television broadcasting of matches of national championships in open signal (Article 38(4)(5)).

4. Sales of football media rights and competition law

The right to collectively sell the media rights concerning the Portuguese League is granted to the Portuguese League of Professional Football by the Regulation of competitions organized by this League.[23] It provides that Clubs are individually holders of the rights of transmission of games and summaries (Article 68(2)). But it is up for the Executive Committee of the League to authorize TV transmissions of games within official competitions organized by the League and to fix the fees of such transmissions (Article

[22] Contrato colectivo entre a Liga Portuguesa de Futebol Profissional e o Sindicato dos Jogadores Profissionais de Futebol - http://www.lpfp.pt/

[23] Regulation adopted pursuant Article 29 of the Regulation of Sports Federations enacted by Decree-Law 248-B/2008 of 31 December. Disciplinary penalties are provided for teams which allow television transmissions of games by Article 114 of the Discipline Regulation (Regulamento Disciplinar das Competições Organizadas pela Liga Portuguesa de Futebol Profissional) - http://www.lpfp.pt/

68(1)). Moreover, this Regulation provides that the images of games of competitions organized by the League can only be collected by the League itself or by the broadcaster(s) which has been expressly authorized by the League (Article 74(1)).

4.1. The League and the Clubs as undertakings and the League Regulation as a decision by an association of undertakings

For purposes of competition law, both the teams and the League itself are considered undertakings that exercise economic activities, such as, according to the Commission's White Paper on Sports, 'the sale of tickets for sport events, advertising activities, the sale of media rights for sport events and the transfer of athletes in return for transfer fees'[24].

As for the Regulation of Competitions, it is likely to be considered a decision by an association of undertakings, which constitutes a prohibited (null and void) anti-competitive agreement within the meaning of Article 9 of the Portuguese Competition Act.[25] These agreements can be justified if the association of undertakings provides evidence that the agreements contribute to improving production or distribution of goods or services or to promoting technical or economic progress where cumulatively they: allow the users of these goods or services an equitable part of the resulting benefit (a); do not impose on the undertakings concerned any restrictions which are not indispensable to the attainment of these objectives (b); do not afford such undertakings the possibility of eliminating competition from a substantial part of the market for the goods or services at issue (c).

---

[24] European Commission 2007.

[25] Law No 19/2012 of 8 May 2012 (Lei da Concorrência).

In *Benfica v. Olivedesportos*, the Court of Appeals of Lisbon[26] declared null and void a clause of exclusivity of an agreement of sale of television rights between a Portuguese football team and a company operating in the sector of sport events and advertising. The Court applied a provision of the former Competition Act (Decree-Law No 371/93) similar to Article 81 EC (now Article 101 TFEU) and ruled that granting to the company the exclusive rights of transmission of football matches infringes the prohibition of anti-competitive agreements because it leaves no room for other undertakings (notably broadcasters) to conclude contracts with teams for the transmission of football matches. The Court held that the appealed company did not produce evidence that the agreement complied with the requirements of the legal exception to be accepted under competition law. There was no appeal from this judgment as the case terminated by settlement.

The Competition Authority takes into account the judgments of national courts, but the interpretation of competition law is usually referred to European case-law and decision-making. Accordingly, the Competition Authority would probably accept: selling exclusive rights for a period no longer than three years (a) and exclusivity bonus for multiple or full packages as alternative to the highest bid, provided it is objective and non-discriminatory (2). For the public tender procedure to be objective and non-discriminatory the conditions of granting the exclusive media rights should be available in advance to all bidders.[27] Concerning preferential renewal clauses[28] for subsequent seasons they are likely to introduce a discriminatory element towards competitors and to find no objective justification.

[26] Judgment of 2 November 2000, p. 75-6.

[27] According to Article 459(1) of the Civil Code, a public offer (*promessa pública*) binds the offeror to the terms of the offer.

[28] Preferential agreements are regulated in Articles 414 to 423 of the Civil Code.

4.2. Abuse of dominant position

Collective sales of media rights conducted by the national League may fall under the prohibition of abuse of a dominant position. The exercise of monopoly-like powers in football events by the League may give rise to exploitation abuses, for example by 'imposing, directly or indirectly, unfair purchase or selling prices or other unfair trading conditions', 'applying dissimilar conditions to equivalent transactions with other trading parties, thereby placing them at a competitive disadvantage', or 'making the conclusion of contracts subject to acceptance by the other parties of supplementary obligations which, by their nature or according to commercial usage, have no connection with the subject of such contracts.' Cases of abuse of exclusion with anticompetitive effects are also conceivable in collectively selling media rights, for example by 'limiting production, markets or technical development to the detriment of consumers', or 'refusing access to an essential facilities that it controls' without reasonable justification – Article 11 of the Competition Act.

Moreover, abuses of economic dependence are also prohibited by the Portuguese Competition Act. According to Article 12(3) of this Act, a situation of economic dependence exists where equivalent alternatives are not available for business partners, suppliers or customers, so that efficient competition cannot take place in the market. An undertaking is deemed not to have an equivalent alternative in case the supply of the goods or services at issue, specifically at the point of distribution, is controlled by a restricted number of undertakings (1) and the undertaking cannot find identical conditions from other commercial partners within a reasonable time scale (2).

In what concerns the prohibition of clubs to individually license TV broadcasts of football matches within competitions organized by the Professional League, the Competition Authority is likely to accept it and therefore clubs should refrain from exercising their individual contracts if they want to play in competitions organized by the

Professional League. In fact, according to the Federation Statutes[29], Clubs have to be members of the League to compete in the first division, i.e. the First League (Article 7(3)). Then, the League Statutes[30] provide that participation is mandatory for clubs promoted to the First League (Article 7(1)). Membership of the League requires application of entry and acceptance and compliance with its Statutes (Article 8(3)).

Clubs know beforehand that in order to compete in the First League they have to comply with the League's policy on commercial activities, including selling media rights. It applies to each and every club and it is justified as a means necessary to have the League operating in sustainable conditions from a financial solidarity viewpoint. Therefore, it is likely to be found objective, transparent and non-discriminatory by the Competition Authority.

Where contracting on an individual basis with promoted Clubs the exclusive broadcasting rights for their home games, it is (or should be) no surprise to the parties that their contracts may not be enforced due to the League Regulations. Promotion to the First League could be considered a tacit condition of termination of such contracts.[31]

5. Media rights and access to the market of online betting

5.1. Acquisition by betting operators of media rights

Portuguese law provides no specific limitation on the acquisition by betting operators of non-exclusive rights to exploit for betting

---

[29] Estatutos da Federação Portuguesa de Futebol - http://www.fpf.pt/

[30] Estatutos da Liga Portuguesa de Futebol Profissional - http://www.lpfp.pt/

[31] In Portugal, second division football matches are also organized by the Professional League and therefore the TV transmission of such games has also to be authorized by the League.

purposes live transmissions of football matches via a website, mobile application or digital interactive TV. However, where such live transmissions are considered equivalent to TV broadcasting and available to the national territory, there is case-law holding that companies which are not licensed to operate as TV broadcasters cannot acquire broadcasting rights in sport events because the contract would be null and void for unlawfulness of the object and violation of public order.

In *Benfica v. Olivedesportos* one of the main questions in dispute was whether an organizer of sports events and advertising which was not authorized to operate as television broadcaster in Portugal could lawfully acquire from football clubs TV media rights for the transmission of football matches. The appellant, a top Portuguese football team, argued that the contract signed with the other party was null and void because *Olivedesportos* did not have authorization to operate as TV broadcaster. The court of first instance denied the claim, but *Benfica* appealed arguing that the constitutional principles and rules as well as the legislation on television activity provided a strict regulatory framework for the exercise of this activity, so that it would be contrary to mandatory rules and public order to acquire exclusive rights of television transmission of sport events without having a license to operate as TV broadcaster. The Lisbon Court of Appeals ruled that such contracts would be null and void due to legal impossibility and illegality of their object as well as for infringing public order. [32]

Despite the issue in controversial, there was no appeal to the Supreme Court as the parties closed the case by settlement. In case other judgments would follow this jurisprudence, organizers of sport events could not sell media rights to companies which are not authorized to operate as TV broadcasters in Portugal. However, they might conclude such contracts with companies which do not operate in Portugal, including betting operators.

---

[32] Judgment of 2 November 2000, p.72-5.

5.2. The monopoly of online betting services in Portugal

On the other hand, the organizer of a domestic football competition could conclude contracts with regulated betting operators authorized in one or more EU Member States concerning live transmissions of matches for betting purposes, but such betting services cannot be available to the Portuguese territory. The League might grant betting operators the exploitation of live transmissions of matches of its competitions for betting purposes, be it via a website, mobile application or digital interactive TV. However, online betting services and advertising can't be made available to the national territory. The regulated operator within Portugal (*Santa Casa da Misericórdia de Lisboa*) has the exclusive right to explore mutual bets both online and offline, but case-law referred to supra would prevent it from acquiring TV rights.

As a matter of fact, the Regulation of the League Cup, provided in Annex III of the Regulation of Competitions organized by the Professional League[33], provides that competing clubs exclusively hold the broadcasting rights of the matches of this competition, including by any electronic means (Article 19); nevertheless, the exploitation of these rights must comply with agreements concerning the commercial and advertising exploitation of the competition (League Cup) concluded by the League, which has the exclusive rights therein and the power of attorney to negotiate and to manage such rights on behalf of the participating clubs (Article 22).

The Gaming Act[34] provides that the right to explore gambling activities is reserved to the State and that it can only be exploited by entities which have been granted by the Government an administrative gambling concession. The exploitation and practice of

---

[33] Regulamento das Competições Organizadas pela LPFP - http://www.lpfp.pt/

[34] Decree-Law No 422/89 of 2 December (Lei dos Jogos de Fortuna ou Azar).

gambling can only in principle be permitted within existing casinos in zones of permanent or temporary gambling established by decree-law of the Government.

The Act on 'Social Games'[35] provides that the State reserves to itself the right to promote mutual bets and grants to 'Santa Casa de Misericórdia de Lisboa' (SCML) the exclusive right to organize and to exploit mutual betting for all the national territory via its Gambling Department - Article 1(1).[36] Mutual bets contests are considered to be all those in which betters forecast results of one or more competitions or of lotteries of number to win the right to prize-money or to any other rewards (Article 1(2)). 'Totobola' is a betting contest for football sport competitions (Article 2(2)). Administrative penalties are provided for the infringement of the exclusive right granted to the SCML as well as for the introduction, selling, distribution or advertising of tickets for foreign mutual bets (Articles 22 and 23).

The Electronic Betting Regulation[37] establishes the legal framework for the exploitation, in electronic medium, of lotteries and mutual bets as well as any other gambling granted to SCML. It includes notably the Internet, mobile phone, and television (Article 1). This Regulation provides that the exploitation by electronic means of lotteries and mutual bets is granted in exclusive terms for the entire national territory (including the radio-electric space, the Hertzian spectrum - analogue and digital -, and the Internet as well as any other public network of telecommunications) to the SCML, through its Gambling Department (Article 2). Administrative penalties - and collateral sanctions - are provided for the infringe-

---

[35] Decree-Law No 84/85 of 28 March.

[36] Article 24 and Annex II of the Statutes of SCML, enacted by Decree-Law No 322/91.

[37] Enacted by Decree-Law 282/2003 of 8 November.

ment of the exclusive right granted to SCML (Articles 11 to 13). *Gambling brokers* of lotteries and mutual bets need authorization from the SCML, concerning its lotteries and bets, and they have to comply with several requirements[38].

A detailed description of the legal framework of games of chance in Portugal, including the provision of 'social games' via the Internet, is provided by the European Court of Justice in its judgment *Liga Portuguesa de Futebol Profissional* (LPFP) and *Bwin International Ltd* (Bwin) versus *Departamento de Jogos da Santa Casa da Misericórdia de Lisboa* (SCML)[39]:

"In Portugal games of chance are, in principle, prohibited. However, the State has reserved the right to authorise, in accordance with the system which it deems most appropriate, the operation of one or more games directly, through a State body or a body controlled directly by the State, or to grant the right to operate such games to private entities, whether profit-making or not, by calls for tender conducted in accordance with the Code of Administrative Procedure.

Games of chance in the form of lotteries, lotto games and sports betting are known in Portugal as games of a social nature ('jogos sociais') and the operation of such games is systematically entrusted to Santa Casa.

Each type of game of chance organised by Santa Casa is instituted separately by a decree-law and the entire organisation and operation of the various games offered by it, including the amount of stakes, the system for awarding prizes, the frequency of draws, the specific percentage of each prize, methods of collecting stakes, the method of selecting authorised distributors, and the methods and periods for payment of prizes, are covered by government regulation.

---

[38] Ministerial Order No 216/2012 of 18 July.

[39] Judgment of 8 September 2009, Case C-42/07, para 3 to 11.

The first type of game in question was the national lottery (Lotaria Nacional), which was established by a royal edict of 18 November 1783, and a concession was awarded to Santa Casa, the concession being renewed regularly thereafter. Today that lottery consists in the monthly drawing of numbers by lot.

Following a number of legislative developments, Santa Casa acquired the right to organise other games of chance based on the drawing of numbers by lot or on sporting events. This led to the introduction of two games involving betting on football matches called 'Totobola' and 'Totogolo', respectively enabling participants to bet on the result (win, draw or loss) and the number of goals scored by the teams. There are also two lotto games, namely Totoloto, in which six numbers are chosen from a total of 49, and EuroMillions, a type of European lotto. Players of Totobola or Totoloto may also take part in a game called 'Joker', which consists in the drawing of a single number by lot. Lastly, there is also the Lotaria Instantânea, an instant game with a scratch card, commonly called 'raspadinha'.

[...]

In 2003 the legal framework governing lotteries, lotto games and sports betting was adapted in order to take account of technical developments enabling games to be offered by electronic means, in particular the internet. Those measures feature in Decree-Law No 282/2003 of 8 November 2003 (*Diário da República* I, Série A, No 259, 8 November 2003). They seek essentially, first, to license Santa Casa to distribute its products by electronic means and, secondly, to extend Santa Casa's exclusive right of operation to include games offered by electronic means, in particular the internet, thereby prohibiting all other operators from using those means.

Article 2 of Decree-Law No 282/2003 confers on Santa Casa, through its Departamento de Jogos (Gaming Department), exclusive rights for the operation by electronic means of the games in question and for any other game the operation of which may be entrusted to Santa Casa, and states that that system covers all of the national territory, and includes, in particular, the internet.

Under Article 11(1) of Decree-Law No 282/2003 the following are classed as administrative offences:

'(a) the promotion, organisation or operation by electronic means of games [the operation of which has been entrusted to Santa Casa], in contravention of the exclusive rights granted by Article 2 [of the present Decree-Law], and also the issue, distribution or sale of virtual tickets and the advertisement of the related draws, whether they take place within national territory or not;

(b) the promotion, organisation or operation by electronic means of lotteries or other draws similar to those of the Lotaria Nacional or the Lotaria Instantânea, in contravention of the exclusive rights granted by Article 2, and also the issue, distribution or sale of virtual tickets and the advertisement of the related draws, whether they take place within national territory or not;

...'.

Article 12(1) of Decree-Law No 282/2003 sets the maximum and minimum fines for the administrative offences laid down in, inter alia, Article 11(1)(a) and (b) of that Decree-Law. For legal persons, the fine is to be not less than EUR 2 000 or more than three times the total amount deemed to have been collected from organising the game in question, provided that the triple figure is greater than EUR 2 000 but does not exceed a maximum of EUR 44 890."

The LPFP/BWIN v. SCML judgment consists of reference for a preliminary ruling concerning the interpretation notably of Article 49 EC. It has been made in the course of proceedings between, on the one hand, the Portuguese League of Professional Football (Liga Portuguesa de Futebol Profissional - 'the Liga') and Bwin International Ltd ('Bwin'), and, on the other, the Gaming Department of the Santa Casa (Departamento de Jogos da Santa Casa da Misericórdia de Lisboa) concerning fines imposed on the Liga and Bwin by the directors of Santa Casa on the ground that they had infringed the Portuguese legislation governing the provision of certain games of chance via the internet.

The ECJ summarizes the basic facts of the case as follows (paras 20, 22 to 28):

"Bwin is an on-line gambling undertaking which has its registered office in Gibraltar. It offers games of chance on an internet site. (...) Bwin offers a wide range of on-line games of chance covering sports betting, (...) and games based on drawing numbers by lot which are similar to the Totoloto operated by Santa Casa.

Betting is on the results of football matches and other sporting events. The different games offered include bets on the result (win, draw or loss) of football matches in the Portuguese championship equivalent to the Totobola and Totogolo games operated exclusively by Santa Casa. Bwin also offers on-line betting in real time, in which the odds are variable and change as the sporting event in question unfolds. Information such as the match score, the time elapsed, yellow and red cards given, and so on, are displayed in real time on the Bwin internet site, thus enabling gamblers to place bets interactively as the sporting event unfolds.

The order for reference states that the Liga is a private-law legal person with the structure of a nonprofitmaking association, made up of all the clubs taking part in football competitions at professional level in Portugal. It organises, inter alia, the football competition corresponding to the national First Division and is responsible for the commercial operation of that competition.

The Liga and Bwin stated in the observations which they submitted to the Court that a sponsorship agreement, concluded by them on 18th August 2005 for four playing seasons starting in 2005/2006, made Bwin the main institutional sponsor of the First Football Division in Portugal. Under the terms of that agreement, the First Division, previously known as the 'Super Liga', changed its name first to the Liga betandwin.com, and then subsequently to the Bwin Liga. In addition, the Bwin logos were displayed on the sports kit worn by the players and affixed around the stadiums of the First Division clubs. The Liga's internet site also included references and a link allowing access to Bwin's internet site, making it possible for consumers in Portugal and other States to use the gambling services thus offered to them.

Subsequently, in exercising the powers conferred on them by Decree-Law N 282/2003, the directors of the Gaming Department of Santa Casa adopted decisions imposing fines of EUR 75000 and EUR 74500 respectively on the Liga and Bwin in respect of the administrative offences referred to in Article 11(1)(a) and (b) of that Decree-Law. Those sums represent the aggregated amounts of two fines imposed on each of the Liga and Bwin for promoting, organising and operating, via the internet, games of a social nature reserved to Santa Casa or such similar games, and also for advertising such gambling.

The Liga and Bwin brought actions before the national court for annulment of those decisions, invoking, inter alia, the relevant Community rules and case-law.

In those circumstances, the Tribunal de Pequena Instância Criminal do Porto (Local Criminal Court, Oporto) (Portugal) decided to stay the proceedings and to refer [a] question to the Court for a preliminary ruling.

The ECJ defines *the scope of the question referred for a preliminary ruling as follows (paras 49 and 50)*:

"The dispute in the main proceedings concerns the marketing in Portugal of a number of games of chance played on an electronic medium, namely the internet. Bwin, a private operator established in another Member State, offers games of chance in Portugal exclusively via the internet, and the administrative offences laid down in Article

11(1)(a) and (b) of DecreeLaw No 282/2003, of which the Liga and Bwin are accused in the main proceedings, concern exclusively conduct in relation to games of chance organised by electronic means.

The question referred by the national court must therefore be construed as asking in essence whether Article 49 EC precludes legislation of a Member State, such as that at issue in the main proceedings, which prohibits operators, such as Bwin, which are established in other Member States, in which they lawfully provide similar services, from offering games of chance via the internet within the territory of that first Member State."

The ECJ found that (Summary of the Judgment, paras 53-54, 67-73, operative part):

"Article 49 EC does not preclude legislation of a Member State which prohibits private operators established in other Member States, in which they lawfully provide similar services, from offering games of chance via the internet within the territory of that Member State.

Admittedly, such legislation gives rise to a restriction of the freedom to provide services enshrined in Article 49 EC, by also imposing a restriction on the freedom of the residents of the Member State concerned to enjoy, via the internet, services which are offered in other Member States.

However, in the light of the specific features associated with the provision of games of chance via the internet, the restriction at issue may be regarded as justified by the objective of combating fraud and crime. The grant of exclusive rights to operate games of chance via the internet to a single operator which is subject to strict control by the public authorities may confine the operation of gambling within controlled channels and be regarded as appropriate for the purpose of protecting consumers against fraud on the part of operators.

As to whether the system in dispute is necessary, the sector involving games of chance offered via the internet has not been the subject of Community harmonization [1]. A Member State is therefore entitled to take the view that the mere fact that a private operator lawfully offers services in that sector via the internet in another Member State, in which it is established and where it is in principle already subject to statutory conditions and controls on the part of the competent authorities in that State, cannot be regarded as amounting to a sufficient assurance that national consumers will be protected against the risks of fraud and crime, in the light of the difficulties liable to be encountered in such a context by the authorities of the Member State of establishment in assessing the professional qualities and integrity of operators [2]. In addition, because of the lack of direct contact between consumer and operator, games of chance accessible via the internet involve different and more substantial risks of fraud by operators against consumers compared with the traditional markets for such games [3]. Moreover, the possibility cannot be ruled out that an operator which sponsors some of the sporting competitions on which it accepts bets and some of the teams taking part in those competitions may be in a position to influence their outcome directly or indirectly, and thus increase its profits. [4]"

In accordance with the preliminary ruling of the ECJ the Oporto criminal court of first instance ruled on 6 January 2012 that domestic law was infringed both by the sponsorship agreement between LPFP and Bwin as a kind of advertising (1) and by the activities conducted by Bwin in or to Portuguese territory via the electronic medium (2).

After LPFP/Bwin v. SCML, advertising and sponsorship between the Portuguese League and Bwin has terminated. Betting is deemed a dangerous activity from the viewpoint of consumer protection and public policy. This is the reason why betting, including online betting services and related advertising, is reserved by the State which however confers an exclusive right to Santa Casa concerning the off-line and online exploitation of specific mutual bets related with sports available at the national territory.

The prohibition/monopoly is protected by administrative offences against betting operators regardless of their place of establishment. In fact the *Electronic Betting Regulation* provides administrative penalties and collateral sanctions for the infringement of the exclusive right granted to Santa Casa (Articles 11 to 13), and the 'Gaming Department has the powers of an administrative authority to open, institute and prosecute proceedings concerning offences involving the illegal operation of games of chance in relation to which Santa Casa has the exclusive rights, and to investigate such offences. Decree-Law No 282/2003 confers upon the directors of the Gaming Department, inter alia, the necessary administrative powers to impose fines as provided for under Article 12(1) of that Decree-Law'.

However, due to the 'passivity' of the competent authorities the prohibition becomes, according to the European Parliament, a 'passive permission'. Online sport betting sites are well available to computers connected to the web from the national territory and in practice it seems that 'there is no mechanism controls concerning illegal operators and the black-market on online sport bets, as criminal law is not applicable to gambling providers without establishment in our country'[40].[41]

With a view to put an end to this apparent situation of online anarchy, and at the same time to put the tax hand of the State in this growing market, the Government considered regulations with different configurations, the most consensual of which would be to allow betting houses to operate under the regulation and authority of Santa Casa. Current regulation already allows gambling brokers of lotteries and mutual bets to operate under the authorization of Santa Casa, concerning its lotteries and bets, and provided they comply with several requirements.[42]

---

[40] http://www.desportonews.com/lei-nas-apostas-on-line/ (free translation).

[41] The Electronic Commerce Regulation (enacted by Decree-Law 7/2004 of 7 January) does not apply to game of fortune, including lotteries and bets (Article 2(1)(e)).

[42] Ministerial Order No 216/2012 of 18 July.

5.3. Advertising of betting services

Concerning exploitation rights, other than the digital live rights above mentioned, the organizer of a domestic football competition or an organizer of an international sports event could license to betting operators advertising rights, notably sponsorship of the organization of the football competition. However, it could not be the essential part of messages available to the national territory, as the exclusive rights of the regulated betting operator extend also to advertising.

Organizers of domestic football competition hold other exploitation rights besides the live transmission of matches. In particular, they have advertising and merchandising rights. Sponsorship is one of the most important advertising and commercial rights, notably sponsorship by which the League names the competition upon the commercial name of the sponsor. However, the Advertising Act[43] prohibits all kinds of advertising where games of luck and chance are the essential part of the message, except for games of chance promoted by SCML (Article 21).

5.4. Horse racing

The Regulation of horse-racing betting[44] provides special regulation for mutual bets in horse-races. Betting in horse-races conducted in foreign countries is not allowed (Article 1(2)). Exploitation of betting in domestic horse-races requires prior authorization and it is granted by exclusive administrative concession upon public tender (Article 4). In practice, horse-racing is not relevant in Portugal, if it exists at all.

---

[43] Decree-Law No 330/90 of 23 October 1990, as last amended by Law 8/2011 of 11 April.

[44] Decree-Law 268/92 of 28 November (Apostas mútuas hípicas).

5.5. Sports funding by betting operators

Under the existing legal framework in Portugal, regulated sports betting operators are statutorily required to contribute to the funding of grass-root sports (across all disciplines). The Gaming Regulation of 1985[45] provides that 50% of the exploitation results of 'Totobola' should be distributed to the promotion and development of football (Article 16(3)(a)). This amount is delivered to the *Fundo de Fomento Desportivo* (Sports Development Fund) which then distributes it to the Portuguese Football Federation (Article 17-A). Sports entities would also be entitled to receive a percentage of the results of exploitation of non-sport betting such as 'Totoloto' (Article 16(4)(e) and Article 17(3)).

More recently, Decree-Law 56/2006 of 15 March[46] introduced new rules for the distribution of the net exploitation results of lotteries and mutual bets organized by SCML. Percentages are distributed to promote sports activities and infrastructures, to promote and develop football, or to fund students' sport and investments in educational sport infra-structures (Article 3).

Conclusion

Online betting in football matches is an important and growing sector of the entertainment industry. There are however several legal issues the clarification of which is necessary for this sector to get out of some legal darkness. This paper, originally drafted as national contribution to the Study on sports organizers' rights in the European Union[47], provides an insight of the Portuguese legal

[45] Decree-Law 84/85 of 28 March.

[46] Decree-Law No 56/2006 of 15 March.

[47] ASSER Institute & IVIR (2014).

framework concerning notably the protection of football matches under copyright and related rights and the rights of image of sports professionals concerned with football broadcasts, as well as the relation between exclusive media rights in sports events and freedom of information, competition law concerns, and the specific regulation of online betting services. This field of law does probably justify European harmonization of the legal framework concerning notably exclusive media rights and the exploitation of online betting in football matches, in the absence of which it is likely that a mosaic of national legislations will not make it easy for the single electronic market in the online entertainment sector to get out of the shadow.

References

Ascensão JO (1987) O direito ao espectáculo. BMJ 366: 41-55

Ascensão JO (1998) Direito à informação e direito ao espectáculo. ROA 48/1: 15-35

Ascensão JO (1992) Direito Civil - Direito de Autor e Direitos Conexos. Coimbra Editora.

Leitão LMTM (2011) Direito de Autor. Almedina, Coimbra.

Pereira ALD (2008) Direitos de Autor e Liberdade de Informação. Almedina, Coimbra.

European Commission (2007) White Paper on Sport.

http://eur-lex.europa.eu/legal-content/EN/TXT/?uri=CELEX:52007DC0391. Accessed 2 June 2014

ASSER Institute & IVIR (2014) Study on sports organisers' rights in the European Union, organized by the ASSER Instituut and the Institute for Information Law of the University of Amsterdam for the European Commission. Final Report published on February 2014

http://ec.europa.eu/sport/news/2014/study-on-sport-organisers-rights_en.htm - Accessed 2 June 2014

Tribunal da Relação de Lisboa (2000) Acórdão de 2 de Novembro de 2000. CJ V: 71-8.

Lisbon Court of Appeals, Judgments of 17 December 2008 (Proc. 3599/2008-6) and of 10 November 2009 (Proc. 4292/1999.L1-7). http://ww.dgsi.pt.

Supreme Court of Justice, Judgments of 25 January 2009 (Proc. 4986/06.3TVLSB. S1), and of 24 May 2010 (Proc. 4292/1999.L1.S1). http://ww.dgsi.pt.

C-42/07, judgment of 8 September 2009 (Bwin).

http://curia.europa.eu/juris/liste.jsf?language=en&num=C-42/07. Accessed on 2 June 2014.

MEDIA CONCENTRATIONS AND PLURALISM IN PRESS, BROADCASTING AND INTERNET*

Introduction

1. Notion of media and technological convergence

The word 'media' is often used to refer undertakings that operate means or channels of social communication, information or entertainment, including press, radio, television, and online communication, as well as, in a broader sense, cinema, advertising, publishing, music, film and audiovisual production, and distribution (press, books, cinema, etc).

Technological convergence and changes brought by the Internet may require the concept of media to be redefined, in the sense that the internet offers a single online digital medium as a complement, or as a substitute, to a variety of means of communication. As Walden puts it,

---

* RBMAD - *Revista Brasileira de Meio Ambiente Digital e Sociedade da Informação* (2014), nº 1, vol. 1, pp. 2-25. Orig. National report on 'Plurality of Political Opinions and the Concentration of Media', XVIII International Congress of Comparative Law, AICD/IACL (Academie Internationale de Droit Comparé / International Academy of Comparative Law) and American Society of Comparative Law (ASCL), July 25 to August 1 2010, Washington D.C.

> 'the development of the internet is causing a fundamental shift in the nature of the media industry and, as a consequence, calling into focus the suitability of existing governing laws and regulation, including media ownership rules. It can be argued, for example, that given an individual's potential capability to reach a global audience through the internet, ownership controls no longer make sense as a tool of pluralism.'[1]

Nonetheless, despite the impact of the Internet on traditional media and in particular the migration to the electronic environment, media are still operating through the traditional channels.

2. *Sources that guarantee the preservation of the plurality of the 'media' in Portugal*

The preservation of the plurality of the 'media' in Portugal is guaranteed by several legal sources.

To begin with, the Constitution of the Portuguese Republic provides for in Article 38(4) on freedom of press and other media that the State guarantees freedom and independence of media from political and economic power, and establishes the principle of specialty for undertakings that hold bodies of general information and treating and supporting them in a non discriminatory way and preventing their concentration namely through multiple and cross participations. Moreover, the Constitution also provides for in Article 39 that media regulation, concerning namely concentrations, is implemented by an independent

[1] Ian Walden, 'Who Owns the Media? Plurality, Ownership, Competition and Access', in *Media Law and Practice*, ed. David Goldberg, Gavin Sutter and Ian Walden, Oxford University Press, 2009, 19-55, at 54.

administrative authority, the ERC (*Entidade Reguladora para a Comunicação Social*)[2].

Then, plurality of the media is addressed by several media statutes, namely the provisions of the former Television Act on media concentration and ownership transparency[3], which are still in force as they have not been repealed by the new Television Act[4], as well as the Press Act[5], and the Radio Act[6].

At the EU level, the respect for the preservation of the plurality of the media is provided for the Charter of Fundamental Rights (Art. 11(2)).

At the international level, Portugal has approved and ratified the Convention on Cultural Diversity, adopted in Paris on 20 October 2005, which provides that the Parties have the sovereign right to adopt policies and measures to protect and to promote the diversity of cultural expressions within their territories, including the stimulation of media diversity.

3. *Rationale of the plurality of the media*

Pluralism of the media is an essential condition of basic civil rights in a democratic society[7] such as the right to information and freedom of expression and confrontation of opinions, as well as an important means of preservation of language and cultural diversity.

---

[2] Law 53/2005 of 8 November (Lei nº 53/2005, de 8 de Novembro), Article 2.

[3] Law 32/2003 of 22 August (Lei n.º 32/2003, de 22 de Agosto).

[4] Law 27/2007 of 30 July (Lei n.º 27/2007, de 30 de Julho), Article 98(2).

[5] Law 2/99 of 13 January 1999 (Lei n.º 2/99, de 13 de Janeiro).

[6] Law 4/2001 of 23 February (Lei n.º 4/2001, de 23 de Fevereiro).

[7] See C. Edwin Baker, *Media Concentration and Democracy – Why Ownership Matters*, Cambridge University Press, 2007; Dieter Dörr, Christine Heer-Reissmann, 'Meinungsvielfatssicherung und Wettbewerbsrecht', in *Handbuch Medienrecht: Recht der elektronischen Massenmedien*, Hrsg. von Dieter Dörr, Johannes Kreile und Mark D. Cole, Frankfurt am Main : VR&W Verlag Recht und Wirtschaft, 2008, pp. 185-232.

Media plurality is generally conceived as information independence and confrontation of opinions, mainly on political and economical issues, and it is seen as an 'internal plurality' in the sense that each newspaper and radio or television operator is supposed to be independent and to assure pluralism of ideas and opinions.

Part I. Media Regulations and 'Anti-Concentration' Measures

4. *Anti-concentration measures in Portugal: background and rationale*

In Portugal there are anti-concentration measures specific of the media sector which are aimed to implement the basic principles and rules of the Constitution.

Concerning TV undertakings, the Media Regulatory Authority (ERC) issues a previous binding opinion in mergers assessed by the Competition Authority. However, those binding opinions can only be negative in case merger operations present grounded risks for freedom of expression and plurality of opinion[8]. A similar solution had already been provided for concerning mergers of press undertakings[9].

Concentrations of radio broadcasting undertakings require a previous authorization from the Media Regulatory Authority[10], and they are to be denied in case it manifestly affects freedom of expression and plurality of opinion.

---

[8] Former Television Act (Law 32/2003), Article 4(2), provision still in force as not repealed by the new Television Act (Law 27/2007 of 30 July, Art. 98(2)).

[9] Press Act (Law 2/99), Article 4(3).

[10] Radio Act (Law 4/2001), Articles 7(2) and 18.

Reference to a person's right to information, as opposed to the mere assertion of the principle of the freedom of expression, is not expressly provided for as an alternative justification for anti-concentration measures.

5. *Scope of application*

The Constitution provides basic principles for media regulation (Arts. 37 to 40), and texts specific to the media sector are limited to some media, in particular to those known as traditional media (press, radio and television).

The Press Act aims to guarantee the constitutional freedom of press[11], including the right to inform, to get information and to be informed without impediment or discrimination, including the prohibition of any sort of censorship[12]. Limits to freedom of press can only be imposed in order to safeguard rigor and objectivity of information, to guarantee personality rights (e.g. name, privacy, image), and to defend the public interest and democratic order[13].

On the other hand, the new Television Act[14] provides for that the television activity is aimed at: contributing to the information, formation and entertainment of the public (a), and promoting the right to inform, to get information and to be informed, in rigorous and independent conditions and without impediment nor discriminations (b), promoting citizenship and democratic participation and to respect political, social and cultural plural-

[11] Portuguese Constitution, Article 37.

[12] Press Act, Article 1.

[13] Press Act, Article 49.

[14] Law 27/2007 of 30 July.

ism (c), and diffusing and promoting Portuguese language and culture, as well as Portuguese creators, artists and scientists, and the values that express national identity[15].

6. *Requirements of application of measures anti-concentration measures*

The conditions to the application of the media anti-concentration measures are generally the same as the conditions to the application of the merger control provided for by the Competition Act[16]. The notion of concentration is linked to the notion of control, which refers to both direct and indirect control, including the power to determine influence. According to the Portuguese Competition Act[17], control shall be constituted by any act, irrespective of the form which it takes, which, separately or jointly and having regard to the circumstances of fact or law involved, implies the ability to exercise a determinant influence on an undertaking's activity, in particular: acquisition of all or part of the share capital (a); acquisition of rights of ownership, use or enjoyment of all or part of an undertaking's assets (b); acquisition of rights or the signing of contracts which grant a decisive influence over the composition or decision-making of an undertaking's corporate bodies (c).

Moreover, according to a (still in force) provision of the former TV Act, acquisitions of shareholdings in legal TV operator undertakings, or applicants to a TV license, by other TV operator undertakings have to be notified to the Media Regulatory Authority, where they do not represent a concentration operation subject to

[15] Television Act, Article 9(1).

[16] Law 18/2003 of 11 July (Lei nº 18/2003, de 11 de Julho).

[17] Competition Act, Article 8(3).

previous notification under competition law[18]. However, despite an obligation to notify is imposed on the undertakings, the Media Authority is not expressly empowered to authorize or to prohibit this type of concentrations.

On the other hand, the Radio Act provides additional anti-concentration measures. For example, the number of radio operators in which a person may hold a share is limited to 5 and no company can own more than a 25% share in two or more stations that operate in the same municipality[19]. Transactions that change the control of a radio licensed undertaking can only take place 3 years after the issuance of the license or one year after its last renovation and it is subject to previous authorization from the Media Regulatory Authority[20]. The existence of undertaking control is assessed by the possibility to exercise a determinant influence over its activity, namely through the existence of rights of disposal over any of its assets or rights that grant the power to determine the composition or the decisions of its bodies[21].

Then, in order to implement the constitutional principle of transparency of media ownership[22], media specific statutes also provide for measures concerning transparency ownership of media undertakings[23]. For example, for purposes of the TV regulation, a qualified shareholding is deemed to exist when it enables a significant influence over the undertaking management, and it is presumed to exist where it corresponds to 10% of the capital of the company or to 10% voting of the voting rights therein[24].

---

[18] Law 32/2003, Article 4(3).

[19] Radio Act, Article 7(3).

[20] Radio Act, Article 18(1).

[21] Radio Act, Article 18(3).

[22] Portuguese Constitution, Article 38(3).

[23] Press Act, Article 16, Radio Act, Article 8, and Law 32/2003, Article 5.

[24] Law 32/2003, Article 5(3)(5).

Finally, concerning communication conglomerates, it should also be added that ownership of media undertakings holding bodies of general information is subject to the constitutional principle of specialty, meaning that their operations are limited to the media sector[25].

7. *Implementation and enforcement competence*

Those specific media regulations are implemented in first instance by the sector-specific authority, the Media Regulatory Authority (ERC). Nonetheless, merger control of media undertakings is enforced by the Competition Authority, which must take into account the previous binding opinion of the Media Regulatory Authority (ERC). This binding opinion can only deny a media merger where it places serious risks to freedom of expression and confrontation of different trends of opinion.

8. *Sanctions for non-compliance*

Aside competition law sanctions, there are provisions specific to the media. To begin with, an administrative fine between ten thousand and one hundred Euros is provided for those who exceed the maximum amount of shareholdings in radio operators, as well as to radio operator undertakings involved in concentration or transfer of shares operations that do not comply with the obligations to communicate such operations to the Media Authority[26].

Then, concerning TV operators, undertakings that do not comply with the obligation to notify operations of transfers of shares to

[25] Portuguese Constitution, Article 38(4).

[26] Radio Act, Article 68(d).

the Media Authority were subject to an administrative fine between twenty thousand and one-hundred and fifty thousand Euros[27].

Part II. Other Ways to Guarantee the Plurality of the Media

9. *Obligations of contents (variety of programs, broadcasting quotas, broadcast access right, reply right ...) on the operators*

Operators have to comply with obligations of content concerning namely variety of programs, broadcasting quotas, broadcast access right, right of reply, etc. For example, the Television Act provides for limits to the freedom of programming (Art. 27), acquisition of exclusive rights (Art. 32), as well as a set of general obligations concerning broadcasting of diversified and plural programs, objective information, diffusion of creative works or European origin, including in Portuguese, and to guarantee namely the right of reply (Art. 34). Moreover, limits to advertising are also provided for (Art. 40).

10. *Allocation of public funds and the respect of plurality.*

The Constitution provides for in Article 38(5) that the State guarantees the existence and functioning of a radio and television public service.

Concerning television, there is a system of allocation of public funds in order to finance the broadcasting public service in proportional and transparent conditions and with a refunding

---

[27] Law 32/2003, Article 70(1). However, it is not clear whether this provision is still force, as the new Television Act that did not expressly safeguarded it.

control mechanism[28]. It is limited to what is strictly necessary to the functioning of the public service and a refunding control mechanism is provided for, as well as the statutory provision that the concession contract of the public service must prevent the concessionaire from adopting practices that are not justified by the rules of the market and which lead to the increase of costs or to the reduction of income[29].

Despite the allocation of public funds is not expressly subject to the respect of plurality of requirements, it does actually contribute to the respect of the plurality or at least participate in guaranteeing the respect of plurality, as one of the basic principles that justifies the existence of a public service is to guarantee media pluralism[30].

As far as press and radio are concerned, there is a system of allocation of public funds to promote in non discriminatory terms the possibilities of expression and confrontation of different trends of opinion[31].

Part III. Competition Law

11. *Competition Law in Portugal: background and constitutive parts*

The Portuguese Competition Act is provided for Law 18/2003 of 11 July[32]. In Portugal there is a Competition Act since 1983. It has been enacted by Decree-Law 422/83 of 3 December[33]. This statute

---

[28] Television Act, Article 57.

[29] Television Act, Article 57(4).

[30] Television Act, Article 50.

[31] Press Act, Article 4(1), and Radio Act, Article 11.

[32] Lei n.° 18/2003, de 11 de Junho.

[33] Decreto-Lei n.° 422/83, de 3 de Dezembro.

has been repealed by Decree-Law 370/93 of 29 October[34], which has later been repealed by the currently in force competition regulation enacted by Law 18/2003 of 11 July (Competition Act).

The main constitutive parts of Portuguese competition law are anti-competitive behavior (cartels, i.e. agreements, decisions of associations and concerted practices of undertakings, and trusts, i.e. abuse of dominant position) and mergers (concentrations). A provision on state aid is also provided for in the Competition Act.

Moreover, as a member State of the European Union (EU), Portugal is bound to the EU competition rules[35] concerning competitive behavior (cartels, i.e. agreements, decisions of associations and concerted practices of undertakings), trusts (i.e. abuse of dominant position), and state aid, as well as EC merger control, in special the Merger Regulation[36].

12. *Enforcement of competition rules.*

The Competition Authority (Autoridade da Concorrência) is in charge of implementing national competition rules regarding both anti-competitive behavior and merger control[37], as well as EU competition rules concerning anti-competitive behavior[38].

Nonetheless, concerning areas subject to sector-specific regulation, the Competition Authority and the sector-specific regulatory authorities work together to apply the competition legislation, in accordance with Chapter III of the Competition Act[39].

---

[34] Decreto-Lei n.º 370/93, do 29 do Outubro.

[35] Treaty on the Functioning of the European Union (TFUE), Article 101 et seq. (and applicable Competition Regulations).

[36] Regulation 139/2004 of 20 January 2004.

[37] Competition Act, Article 14.

[38] Council Regulation 1/2003 of 16 December 2002, Article 3.

[39] Competition Act, Articles 15; see also Articles 27(4), 29 and 39.

13. *Application of competition rules to the various media (press, radio, television, Internet)*

In principle, Portuguese competition rules can be applied to the various media (press, radio, television, internet...) as the Competition Act 'is applicable to all economic activities carried out on a permanent or occasional basis in the private, public or co-operative sectors'[40]. Moreover, several media statutes provide for the application of the competition regulation[41].

However, concerning merger control, the Competition Authority asks the respective regulatory authority to state its opinion, within a reasonable period and without affecting the exercise by the sector regulatory authorities of the powers that, within the scope of their specific duties, are legally conferred on them in relation to the concentration in question[42].

Concerning TV undertakings, the decision of the Competition Authority is bound to the binding previous opinion to be issued by the Media Regulatory Authority (ERC), which nonetheless can only be negative in case such merger operations present grounded risks for freedom of expression and plurality of opinion[43]. A similar solution had already been provided for mergers of press undertakings[44]. Concentrations of radio broadcasting undertakings require a previous authorization to be issued by the Media Regulatory Authority[45], which is to be denied in case freedom of expression and plurality of opinion is seriously at stake.

---

[40] Law 18/2003, Article 1(1).

[41] Press Act, Article 4(3), Radio Act, Article 7(1), former Television Act (Law 32/2003), Article 4(1) (still in force as not repealed by the new Television Act (Law 27/2007, Art. 98(2)).

[42] Law 18/2003, Article 39(1)(2).

[43] Former Television Act (Law 32/2003), Article 4(2).

[44] Press Act, Article 4(3).

[45] Radio Act, Articles 7(2) and 18.

14. *Type of merger control implemented in Portugal*

A compulsory prior control is provided for concentrations which either create or reinforce a share exceeding 30% of the national market for a particular good or service or for a substantial part of it or when in the preceding financial year, the group of undertakings taking part in the concentration have recorded in Portugal a turnover exceeding € 150 million, net of directly related taxes, provided that the individual turnover in Portugal of at least two of these undertakings exceeds two million euro[46].

Such concentrations are to be notified to the Competition Authority within seven working days of conclusion of the agreement or, where relevant, by the publication date of the announcement of a takeover bid, an exchange offer or a bid to acquire a controlling interest.

Moreover, a concentration subject to prior notification cannot be put into effect before it has been notified and explicitly or tacitly decided in terms of non-opposition[47].

15. *Notion of 'concentration' (determining influence or control)*

Portuguese competition law provides for a notion of concentration which includes not only mergers between two or more previously independent undertakings but also those cases where one or more individuals who already have control of at least one or more undertakings acquire control, directly or indirectly, of the whole or parts of one or several other undertakings[48].

---

[46] Competition Act, Article 9.

[47] Competition Act, Article 11(1).

[48] Competition Act, Article 8(1).

Portuguese competition law seems to favor a broad conception of concentration. Despite it is based on the notion of control, this notion refers to both direct and indirect control, including the power to determine influence. In fact, control shall be constituted by any act, irrespective of the form which it takes, which, separately or jointly and having regard to the circumstances of fact or law involved, implies the ability to exercise a determining influence on an undertaking's activity, in particular: acquisition of all or part of the share capital (a); acquisition of rights of ownership, use or enjoyment of all or part of an undertaking's assets (b); acquisition of rights or the signing of contracts which grant a decisive influence over the composition or decision-making of an undertaking's corporate bodies (c)[49].

The acquisition of shareholdings or assets under the terms of a special procedure of corporate rescue or bankruptcy, the acquisition of a shareholding merely as a guarantee, and the acquisition by credit institutions of shareholdings in non-financial undertakings, where such acquisition is not covered by the prohibition in Article 101 of the General Regulation on Credit Institutions and Financial Institutions[50], are not held to constitute a concentration between undertakings[51].

16. *Assessment of joint ventures and other alliances*

A joint venture is assessed as a merger in case the establishment or acquisition of a joint undertaking is deemed a concentration between undertakings, i.e. provided that the joint undertaking ful-

[49] Competition Act, Article 8(3).

[50] Enacted by Decree-Law No. 298/92 of 31 December.

[51] Competition Act, Article 8(4).

fils the functions of an independent economic entity on a lasting basis[52]. Otherwise, joint ventures and other alliances are assessed with regard to rules on cartels[53].

17. *Assessment test?*

Market dominance is the criterion of the assessment test laid down by the Portuguese Competition Act. Concentrations that neither create nor strengthen a dominant position that results in significant barriers to effective competition in the Portuguese market or in a substantial part of it are to be authorized (a) where those that create or strengthen a dominant position that results in significant barriers to effective competition in the Portuguese market or in a substantial part of it are to be prohibited (b)[54].

In order to appraise the effects of notified concentrations on the competition structure, with a view to preserve and develop effective competition in the Portuguese market, in the interests of the intermediate and final consumer, the Competition Authority takes into account several factors, namely: the structure of the relevant markets and the existence or absence of competition from undertakings established in such markets or in distinct markets (a); the position of undertakings participating in the relevant market or markets and their economic and financial power, in comparison with their main competitors (b); the potential competition and the existence, in law or in fact, of entry barriers to the market (c); the opportunities for choosing suppliers and users (d); the access of the different undertakings to supplies and markets (e); the structure

[52] Competition Act, Article 8(2).

[53] See also Competition Act, Article 12(6).

[54] Competition Act, Article 12(3).

of existing distribution networks (f); supply and demand trends for the products and services in question (g); special or exclusive rights granted by law or attached to the nature of the products traded or services provided (g); the control of essential infrastructure by the undertakings in question and the access opportunities to such infrastructure offered to competing undertakings (i); technical and economic progress provided that it is to the consumer's advantage and does not create an obstacle to competition (j); the contribution that the concentration makes to the international competitiveness of the Portuguese economy (l).

18. *Relevance of the use of commitments as remedies*

The Competition Authority may decide not to oppose to the concentration provided that the authors of the notification accept commitments and establish conditions and obligations intended to guarantee compliance with such commitments with a view to ensuring that effective competition is maintained[55]. Such commitments can be either structural or behavioral.

19. *Sanction for the failure to notify a merger subject to prior control*

Merger control is actually implemented as mergers are usually notified to the Competition Authority. This has a significant record of merger control decisions, including in the media sector[56].

[55] Competition Act, Article 35(3).

[56] Ver http://www.concorrencia.pt.

Failure to notify a concentration subject to prior notification is deemed an administrative offence with a fine that may not exceed 1% of the previous year's turnover for each of the undertakings[57].

Part IV. Relationships between Media Specific Rules and Competition Rules: Anti-Concentration Measures and Merger Control

20. *Mode of implementation of the various sets of rules (media-specific rules, Competition Law rules)*

Media-specific rules and competition law rules are concurrently implemented where a merger is subject to previous notification to the Competition Authority. In these cases the Competition Authority has to request a previous binding opinion from the Media Authority.

However, acquisitions of shareholdings in legal TV operator undertakings, or applicants to a TV license, by other TV operator undertakings have to be notified to the Media Regulatory Authority, where they do not represent a concentration operation subject to previous notification under competition law, according to a still in force provision of the former TV Act (Art. 4(3)). The same applies concerning transactions that change the control of a radio licensed undertaking which are subject to previous authorization from the Media Regulatory Authority (Art. 18(1)).

[57] Competition Act, Articles 9 and 43(3)(a)).

21. *Role of the enforcement authorities*

If the only applicable regulation is the sector-specific regulation and no issue that may constitute an infringement to the Competition Act is assessed, the Competition Authority is not entitled to intervene on even a consultative basis.

In the case of a concurrent implementation, the Media Authority is the first to intervene. There is concurrent implementation where mergers are subject to previous notification to the Competition Authority. Nonetheless, the Competition Authority cannot decide without and against the previous binding of opinion of the Media Regulatory Authority (see supra 15).

On the other hand, in the case of a concurrent implementation, the Competition Act provides rules that allow the Competition Authority to 'communicate' with the Media Authority as a sector regulatory authority (Art. 15). To begin with, concerning anti-competitive practices (cartels and trusts), the Media Regulatory Authority, as an independent administrative authority, has the duty to inform the Authority if it becomes aware of facts which may be described as restrictive competitive practices (Art. 24(2)). Then, the Competition Authority has to request the prior opinion of the Media Regulatory Authority, which is to be delivered within either a maximum of five working days concerning interim measures (Art. 27(4)) or a reasonable period of time prescribed by the Competition Authority concerning completion of the evidence-taking (Art. 28(2)).

Moreover, Article 29 of the Competition Act provides specific rules of co-ordination with sector regulatory authorities. On one hand, whenever the Competition Authority is aware of facts occurring in the media sector, as an area subject to sector regulation, which may be described as practices restricting competition, it shall immediately report such facts to the Media Regulatory Authority for the subject matter, for the Media Authority to state its opinion within a reasonable period of time, to be set by the Competition Authority (Art. 29(1)). On the other hand, whenever, within the scope of its attributions and without prejudice to the provisions of Article 24(2), the Media Regulatory Authority officially or at the request of regulated bodies assesses issues that may constitute an infringement to the Competition Act, it shall immediately inform the Competition Authority of the case and supply the essential facts (Art. 29(2)). And before reaching its final decision, the Media Regulatory Authority informs the Competition Authority of its draft proposals, so that the Competition Authority may state its opinion within a reasonable period of time prescribed by the Media Authority.

Concerning mergers, Article 39 of the Competition Act provides detailed rules of co-ordination with the Media Authority as a sector regulatory authority. To begin with, whenever a concentration of undertakings affects a media market, before reaching a decision before or after an in-depth investigation, the Competition Authority must ask the Media Authority to state its opinion, within a reasonable period prescribed by the Authority. According to the Press and Television Acts, the opinion of the Media Authority is binding, and it shall be negative in case the merger causes grounded risks to freedom of expression and plurality of opinion; a similar criterion is provided for in the Radio Act, by which the Media Authority is empowered to authorize mergers (see supra 15).

22. *Examples of mergers in the media sector examined at the European level*

Several mergers in the media sector have been examined by the European authorities[58]. In the sector of book publishing and sales reference goes to the case Lagardère / Natexis / VUP case, in which the merger was approved subject to conditions imposed by the Commission to ensure effective competition in the French-language publishing market.

[58] http://ec.europa.eu/competition/sectors/media/overview_en.html

Moreover, in the case of Sony / BMG, a joint venture combining the recorded music businesses of Sony and Bertelsmann, the European Commission approved the creation of the joint venture, after it concluded that it did not have sufficiently strong evidence to oppose the deal. However, this decision was later overturned by a European Court, when the Court of First Instance upheld a complaint from a group of independent record labels, saying the union of Sony Music and BMG required more scrutiny'.

Another example is the Télé2 decision. Under the EU Merger Regulation, the European Commission has approved the purchase of the fixed telephony and Internet access businesses of Télé2 France by the French mobile telephony operator SFR. This operation raised serious competition concerns in pay- TV markets in France and the Commission launched an in-depth investigation. These concerns have been addressed by commitments guaranteeing DSL operators equal treatment with the new entity as regards access to television content owned by the Vivendi group, of which SFR forms part. Based upon these commitments, the Commission authorized the merger, concluding that it would not significantly impede effective competition in the European Economic Area (EEA) or any substantial part of it.[59]

23. Use of the provision of the EU regulation that allows the protection of justifiable interests (art. 21, § 4, Regulation n° 139/2004)

The corresponding provision of the previous Merger Regulation[60], which allowed also for the protection of justifiable interests, has been used by the Portuguese authorities not in the media but in the

---

[59] http://ec.europa.eu/comm/competition/mergers/cases/index/m90.html#m_4504.

[60] Regulation (CEE) 4064/89 of the Council of 21 December 1989, Art. 21(3).

financial sector, in the case BSCH/Champalimaud, concerning the acquisition of a controlling interest in the Champalimaud group by Banco Santander Central Hispano (BSCH) of Spain. However, the Commission considered that the measures adopted by the Portuguese authorities to veto this acquisition on grounds of national interest had violated EU Internal Market and competition rules and therefore sued Portugal before the ECJ. Nonetheless, as Portugal withdrew the measures in question, the European Commission decided to close the two infringement procedures it had opened in 1999 against Portugal in the so-called *Champalimaud* affair.

V. Other Rules that Guarantee the Plurality of the Media and Competition Rules

24. *Assessing the obligations (e.g. production and broadcasting quotas, 'media chronology') that curtail competition ... in the name of competition protection.*

Obligations that may curtail competition, such as production and broadcasting quotas and 'media chronology', are aimed at protecting other values such as cultural diversity and plurality of opinion. Therefore, they can hardly be assessed in the name of competition protection, as they are grounded upon different values of public interest.

25. *Allocation of public funds to guarantee the plurality of the media and its compatibility with competition requirements.*

The Portuguese Competition Act provides that 'aid granted to undertakings by a state or any other public body must not significantly restrict or affect competition in the whole or in part of the market' (Art. 13(1)). However, 'compensatory payments made by the state in return for the provision of a public service, whatever the form of such payments, shall not be considered aid' (Art. 13(3)). The Portuguese State makes compensatory payments to RTP in return for the provision of the TV and radio broadcasting public service as provided for by Law 30/2003 of 22 August.

Accordingly, the allocation of public funds that consist of compensatory payments made by the state in return for the provision of the broadcasting public service are not considered state aid and therefore fall outside the scope of application of the state aid provision of the Competition Act.

In what concerns the allocation of public funds that do not consist in such compensatory payments, they can be treated as state aid, meaning that they should not significantly restrict nor affect competition in the whole or in part of the market even if aimed to guarantee the plurality of the media.

Nonetheless, the control mechanism provided for under the Competition Act to assess the conformity of such allocation of public funds with competition requirements is rather fragile, as the Competition Authority is only empowered to, at the request of any interested party, 'scrutinize any aid or aid project and formulate such recommendations for the Government as it deems necessary to eliminate the negative effects on competition of such aid'[61]. Consequently, the Competition Authority cannot but to formulate recommendations to the Government and provided that any interested party has requested them.

However, concerning the EU state aid control mechanism, the allocation of public funds to media undertakings may be deemed state aid for purposes of Article 107(1) of the TFUE (and related

[61] Competition Act, Art. 31(2).

regulations) even if they consist of compensatory payments made by the state in return for the provision of the broadcasting public service.[62] However, the assessment of this state aid must take into account that the undertaking is charged with a service of general economic interest as provided for under Article 106(2) of the Treaty.

Part VI. Implementation of the Regulation

26. *Recent cases in the media sector examined by the Portuguese competition authority*

The Competition Authority has examined several cases in the media sector. A more recent case concerning various areas is PRISA/ MEDIA CAPITAL (Proc. 54/2006).

The merger, notified on 7 November 2006, consisted of the projected acquisition of sole control of Grupo Media Capital SGPS, SA ('MEDIA CAPITAL') by Promotora de Informaciones SA ('PRISA'), by means of a bid to purchase the shares representing its registered capital.

PRISA was a Spanish-registered company listed on the stock exchange, which, as a holding company of Grupo Prisa, controlled a group of companies operating mainly in the sectors covering communications, education, culture and entertainment, mostly in Spain, but also in France and Latin America. In Portugal, Grupo Prisa operated in the sectors covering cable channel distribution, through Grupo Sogecable; school book publishing, through Constância Editores SA; and promotional marketing, through Prisa Innova SA.

On the other hand, MEDIA CAPITAL was a listed company, under Portuguese law, which, as a holding company of Grupo Media

[62] Case 10/5/2000, Proc. T-46/97 (SIC v Commission).

Capital, held a group of companies that operated essentially in the sectors involving television, radio, outdoor advertising, as well as press and internet services in Portugal.

Under Article 35 (1) (b) of the Competition Act, the Council of the Competition Authority has decided, on 29 December 2006, not to oppose the merger on the grounds that it was not likely to create or to reinforce a dominant position that might result in significant barriers to effective competition in the following markets: (i) the national market for advertising on open-signal television; (ii) the national radio advertising market; (iii) the national market for the supply of outdoor advertising space and (iv) the national market for music publishing and distribution.'

27. *Specific problems regarding the demarcation of markets and the analysis of the organisation of markets*

The Competition Authority faced specific problems regarding the demarcation of operated markets.

To begin with, concerning TV broadcasting, the Authority distinguished free access (open signal) from conditional access TV taking into account different sources of income (advertising v. user subscription). The Competition Authority rejected the existence of an autonomous market for end viewers of TV open signal as a commercial connection was only established with advertisers. Therefore the relevant market in free access (open signal) TV consisted only of the advertising market.

The Competition Authority identified also the market of acquisition of broadcasting rights. However, considering the residual presence of Media Capital in this market, as its own contents were sold mainly intra-group, the Competition Authority excluded this market from its analysis, and focused on the market of advertising in open signal TV. Moreover, for reasons of cultural diversity, language and regulatory specificities, the Competition Authority limited the geographical market to the Portuguese territory.

Concerning radio broadcasting, the Competition Authority also limited the relevant market to advertising in radio broadcasting, as the relevant commercial transactions consisted of broadcasters selling advertising 'air time' to advertisers. The Competition Authority considered this to be an autonomous market from other advertising markets for technical and price reasons. Moreover, the Competition Authority held that, despite some radio operators of Media Capital had local or regional limited broadcast, the advertising effect had national reach and therefore the geographical market should be delimited by the Portuguese territory.

Concerning outdoor advertising, the Competition Authority held this to be an autonomous and unitary market despite the diversity of means of outdoor advertising, reasoning that all those different means have in common to present an advertising message at a public place to a public in movement. The geographical scope of this market was also limited to the national territory because advertisers plan their advertising campaigns at national scale and the undertakings of this sector also operate at the national scale.

Moreover, for purposes of this operation, the Competition Authority demarked the market of musical edition and distribution as an autonomous market, with geographical scope corresponding to the Portuguese territory.

28. *Specific problems related to the low number of operators on the markets*

The market of advertising in open signal TV was considered to be concentrated, according to the IHH criterion, due to the low number of operators and the high share of Media Capital. Moreover, significant barriers to entry into this market existed as an administrative license to operate TV broadcasting both in open signal and cable distribution was required. Nonetheless, the Competition Authority considered that the operation consisted of a mere transmission of market shares between the merging undertakings without significantly affecting the market structure. In short, the merger was found not to create nor reinforce a dominant position which could cause significant impediments to competition within the market of advertising in open signal TV.

A similar reasoning was applied to the markets of advertising in radio broadcasting, outdoor advertising and musical edition and distribution, in which, despite the low number of operators, barriers to entry were found to be not so significant.

29. *The use of commitments as remedies considering the characteristics of the sector involved*

In the PRISA/MEDIA CAPITAL case no commitments have been used. In a different case, the projected merger Sonaecom/PT, the Competition Authority has conditioned the authorization of the concentration upon the acceptance of commitments. It was a case in the telecommunication sector but with ramifications into the media sector. In particular, the Authority conditioned the merger upon Sonaecom assuming a set of conditions concerning the media and content markets.

In an earlier decision (case 47/2003, - PPTV / PT CONTEÚDOS / SPORT TV), the Competition Authority decided not to oppose the concentration on the grounds that, subject to the imposition of conditions tied to monitoring obligations, the concentration would not create or reinforce a dominant position that might result in significant barriers to competition in the Portuguese market for the television broadcasting rights of football matches and match summaries involving national teams, the distribution market for pay-TV sports channels or the multimedia content market for football.

This concentration involved the acquisition by the undertakings PPTV – Publicidade de Portugal e Televisão, SA (marketing of advertising and television rights), and PT Conteúdos, SGPS, SA (management of equity investments in other enterprises), of joint control of the commercial enterprise SPORT TV Portugal, SA (activity of television and broadcasting, and the acquisition and resale of television broadcasting rights for events, to produce, make and market programs on sporting events, for reference to them, and advertising and any activities that raise the commercial value of individuals and objects related to the different types of sports and other activities connected with those referred to above). The acquisition took place by means of the purchase, in equal parts, of the total investment hitherto held by RTP (Rádio e Televisão de Portugal, SGPS, SA) in SPORT TV PORTUGAL, SA., accompanied by SPORT TV's acquisition and exclusive exercise of the broadcasting rights for the main division matches in the National Football Championship for the seasons 2004/2005 to 2007/2008.

In a more recent case - *Ongoing/Vertix* [63] -, the Media Authority issued a legal opinion against a projected merger which would result of the acquisition of a significant part of the shares (35%) of a relevant media company (*Media Capital*) by another one in the sector (*Ongoing*), which already had a dominant position in a third media company (*Impresa*).

The Media Authority held that in order to assure pluralism and diversity of opinion by means of controlling media concentrations, *Ongoing* could only acquire joint control of Media Capital in case it would hold less than 1% of *Impresa's* shares and refrain from directly or indirectly interfere in its internal affairs, either social, editorial or else.

---

[63] See non confidential version available at http://www.erc.pt.

The Media Authority found out that the sectors of open signal TV and information channels distributed by cable and the production of TV contents to be those in which the risks to diversity and plurality of media would be more sensitive, as *Ongoing* would be at the same time in a position of joint control of *Media Capital* and of privileged access to confidential information of *Impresa*, where both companies had a joint dominance of the market (for ex. 75% of advertising). The Media Authority based the imposition that Ongoing should have less than 1% of *Impresa*'s as a means to prevent the diversity of TV programs to be affected.

30. *Concurrent implementation of Competition Law (merger control) and the sector-specific regulation (anti-concentration measures)*

In PRISA/ MEDIA CAPITAL, both the ERC (Media Regulatory Authority) and the ANACOM (National Communications Authority) did not object to the projected merger, and the Competition Authority also cleared the merger from the viewpoint of competition law.

In the PPTV/PT CONTEÚDOS/SPORT TV case, the Media Authority held that the concentration would aggravate the situation of risk concerning external pluralism, as it would make harder and delay the possibility of entry of operators in the market due namely to the conditions imposed to RTP and the long term of the exclusive broadcasting rights. Nonetheless, the Media Authority decided not to issue a previous negative opinion on the concentration, reasoning that it would not cause a reduction of the number nor the quality of the events of general interest as sport events previously held by RTP would remain available on the market, and that the relevant provisions of the Television Act in force would not be infringed. Moreover, the Media Authority emphasized as a positive effect the socialization of those broadcasting rights previously held by RTP and now available on the market on an offer-and-demand basis.[64]

Taking into account the opinion of the Media Authority, in particular the danger for external plurality of media, the Competition Authority did not prohibit the concentration, but imposed commitments and obligations to ensure compliance with competition rules.

In a different recent case, IMPRESA, the media sector-specific authority (ERC) assessed whether the merger would affect the plurality of opinion. In particular, addressing the issue of external plurality, the ERC reasoned that a condition for such plurality of opinion to take place would be the existence of different autonomous undertakings operating in the market. The authority found that the projected merger would not reduce the number of players in the market as the acquirer undertaking was only replacing the acquired.[65]

31. *Conceptual convergences and divergences between Competition Law and sector-specific regulations*

The Media Authority establishes a close connection between (external) plurality of media and the structure of the market reasoning that a competitive structure of the market is a decisive factor for plurality of media. A point of divergence between competition law and sector-specific regulations may be found in the so-called internal plurality concerning quality and diversity of content which is not by itself guaranteed by competition law.

---

[64] See Decision of Council of the Competition Authority, at p. 14, at http://www.concorrencia.pt.

[65] See final decision in Portuguese, pp. 23-24, available at http://www.concorrencia.pt.

Part VI. Prospects and Improvements

32. *Efficiency of anti-concentration measures*

The decision praxis of the Media Authority seems to indicate that the media sector anti-concentration specific measures concerning the so-called external plurality are somehow redundant as media pluralism is closely connected with the competitive structure of the market. It is possible however that, despite the competitive structure of the market, a merger endangers freedom of expression and media pluralism from the viewpoint of the so-called internal pluralism.

33. *Towards a European anti-concentration regulation?*

In December 2007, the Audiovisual Media Services Directive[66] entered into force, extending the scope of the EU audiovisual regulation to emerging media services, but no anti-concentration measures specific to the media sector are provided therein. However: 'Responding to continuing political concerns about media concentration, and its possible effects on pluralism and freedom of expression, the Commission launched a three-step approach for advancing the debate on media pluralism across the European Union in 2007.'[67] And Directive 2010/13/EU of the European Parliament and of the Council of 10 March 2010, repealed Council Directive 89/552/EEC.

---

[66] Directive 2007/65/EC of the European Parliament and of the Council of 11 December 2007 amending Council Directive 89/552/EEC on the coordination of certain provisions laid down by law, regulation or administrative action in Member States concerning the pursuit of television broadcasting activities; OJ L 332 of 18 December 2007.

[67] http://ec.europa.eu/information_society/media_taskforce/pluralism/index_en.htm.

On the other hand, the Merger Regulation does provide that pluralism of media is a legitimate interest for the protection of which Member States can adopt adequate measures concerning a concentration with community dimension that has been declared compatible with the internal market by the European Commission (Regulation 134/2004, Art. 23(4)).

In Portugal, a new Act on Media Pluralism and Non Concentration has been approved by the Parliament but it has later been vetoed by the President[68].

34. *Requirements of internal plurality (e.g. variety of information sources, variety of the programming, variety in the production, speaking times of the various currents of thoughts) and/or anti-concentration measures specific to the media sector?*

Variety of information sources, programming and production as well as speaking times of the various trends of thought are crucial requirements of internal plurality of the media. These requirements of internal plurality appear to be decisive for the Media Authority, in the sense that a concentration that does not affect internal plurality did not receive a negative opinion from the Media Authority despite it aggravated the situation of risk concerning the so-called external plurality of the media (case PPTV / PT CONTEÚDOS / SPORT TV). In short, anti-concentration measures specific to the media sector aimed at guaranteeing structural (external) plurality of media do not seem to be determinant from the viewpoint of the Media Authority.

On the other hand, taking into account that the Media Authority usually assesses the risks to freedom of expression and (external) plurality of media posed by mergers upon the competitive structure

---

[68] See http://www.gmcs.pt.

of the market, the anti-concentration measures specific to the media sector appear somehow redundant. Nonetheless, anti-concentration measures are also aimed at controlling the internal plurality of media, which is not provided for by competition law itself.

In short, plurality of media is a sensitive issue and not only a competition law problem, as media regulation is aimed at preserving and promoting other values of public interest. This is acknowledged by the EC Merger Regulation according to which Member States may adopt adequate measures to protect legitimate interests, such as media pluralism, concerning mergers with community dimension which have been declared compatible with the internal market, provided such measures are proportionate and fully compatible with all aspects of Community law.

Literature

J.J. Gomes Canotilho, Vital Moreira, *Constituição da República Portuguesa Anotada*, I, 4.ª ed., Coimbra Editora, 2007

Jorge Miranda, *Manual de Direito Constitucional*, Tomo IV - *Direitos Fundamentais*, Coimbra Editora, 2008

Jónatas Machado, *Liberdade de Expressão*, Coimbra Editora, 2002

Ian Walden, 'Who Owns the Media? Plurality, Ownership, Competition and Access', in *Media Law and Practice*, ed. David Goldberg, Gavin Sutter and Ian Walden, Oxford University Press, 2009, 19-55

C. Edwin Baker, *Media Concentration and Democracy: Why Ownership Matters*, Cambridge University Press, 2007

Luís Brito Correia, *Direito da Comunicação Social,* reimp., Almedina, 2005

António Monteiro Cardoso, João Pedro Figueiredo, Alberto de Carvalho, *Direito da Comunicação Social - O regime jurídico da Comunicação Social em Portugal*, Casa das Letras, 2005

Fernando dos Reis Condesso, *Direito da Comunicação Social (Lições)*, Almedina, 2007

André Santini, *L'État et la Presse*, préf. Claude Puhl, Paris, Litec, 1990

Bertrand Cousin, *Le Droit de la Communication: presse écrite et audiovisuel*, Paris: Ed. du Moniteur, 1990

Denis Barrelet, *Droit Suisse des Mass-Media*, 2.ª éd. rev. et aug., Berne: Ed. Starp, 1987

Henri Blin [et al.], *Droit de la Presse*, dir. Jacques-Henri Robert, Paris: Litec, 1993

Wayne Overbeck, *Major Principles of Media Law*, Fort Worth: Harcourt College Publishers, 2009

Roy L. Moore, Michael D. Murray, *Media Law and Ethics*, 3rd ed. London/New York: Routledge, 2008

Jörg K. Fischer, *Medienrecht und Medienmärkte*, Heidelberg: Springer, 2008

Don R. Pember, Clay Calvert, *Mass Media Law*, Boston: MacGrawhill, 2007

Thomas Gibbons, *Regulating the Media*, 2nd ed. London: Sweet and Maxwell, 1998

Donald E. Lively [et al.], *Communications Law: Media, Entertainment and Regulation*, Cincinnati: Anderson Publishing, 1997

Eric Barendt (ed.), *Media Law*, New York: New York University Press, 1993

Martin Loeffler, Reinhart Ricker, *Handbuch des Presserechts*, 3. Aufl. München: C.H. Beck, 1994

William E. Francois, *Mass Media Law and Regulation*, 6th ed. Illinois: Waveland Press, 1994

Marian Paschke, *Medienrecht*, Berlin: Springer Verlag, 1993

Monroe E. Price, *Media and Sovereignty: The global Information - Revolution and its Challenge to State Power*, Cambridge: The MIT Press, 2002

Paul Levinson, *Digital McLuhan: A Guide to the Information Millennium*, London/New York: Routledge, 1999

Frank Fechner, *Medienrecht*, 7. Aufl. 2006

Daniel L. Brenner, *Law and Regulation of Common Carriers in the Communications Industry*, Boulder: Westview Press, 1992

David B. Winn, *European Community and International Media Law*, London: Graham & Trotsman, 1994

David Goldberg, *Regulating the Audiovisual Industry*, London: Butterworths, 1991

Lesley Ainsworth/Daniel Weston, 'Newspapers and UK media ownerships controls', *Media Law* 1(1995), 2-9

Lucas A. Power Jr., *The Fourth Estate and Constitution: Freedom of the Press in America*, Berkeley: UCP, 1991

Thomas Gibbows, *Regulating the Media*, London: Sweet & Maxwell, 1991

Albrecht Goetz von Olenhausen, *Handbuch des Medienrechts: Rundfunkrecht*, Freiburg: Hochschul Verlag, 1988

Gerhard Friedrich Holtmeier, *Presse -und Rundfunkfreiheit*, Frankfurt am Main: Peter Lang, 1991

Horst Von Hartlieb, *Handbuch des Film -, Fernseh -und Videorechts*, München: Beck, 1991

Joachim Wolf, Medienfreiheit und Medienunternehmen, Berlin: Dunker & Humblot, 1985

INTELLECTUAL PROPERTY AND MEDICAL BIOTECHNOLOGIES*

Abstract - Biotechnology offers relevant applications in the medical sector. In particular, genetic engineering provides new methods of diagnosis and therapeutic processes which are very important in such areas as preventing and fighting cancer. Concurrently, biomedical technologies are at the core of important economic activities, generally known as biotech industries. High-risk investment in research and development (R&D) activities is required, and companies claim intellectual property protection for their biotechnological assets, both as a shield and sword against free riders and pirates. Gene patenting is a sensitive issue, not only in what concerns the distinction between inventions and "products of nature" but also concerning implications of public morality and ordre public. This chapter discusses these issues, focusing on intellectual property (IP) protection of biotechnology, in special gene patents, under EU legislation [1].

Introduction

The value of human genes, as biotechnological corporate assets, is determined to a large extent by the existence of exclusive economic

---

* In: *Legal and Forensic Medicine,* ed. Roy Beran, p. 1735-1754, 2013, Springer Nature.

rights in genetic information. The question was relatively pacific until 29 March 2010, when the US District Court declared invalid patents, owned or licensed by Myriad Genetics, related to BRCA1 and BRCA2, concerning diagnostic methods for breast and ovarian cancers. Judge Robert W. Sweet found that genes are "unpatentable products of nature" and rejected the legal equivalency between DNA and "chemical compositions," like purified adrenaline (Parke-Davis v. Mulford, 1906), arguing that

> "The information encoded in DNA is not information about its own molecular structure incidental to its biological function, as is the case with adrenaline or other chemicals found in the body. . .this informational quality (of DNA) is unique among the chemical compounds found in our bodies, and it would be erroneous to view [1] DNA as 'no different' than other chemicals previously the subject of patents. . . DNA, in particular the ordering of its nucleotides, therefore serves as the physical embodiment of laws of nature – those that define the construction of the human body. . .the preservation of this defining characteristic of DNA in its native and isolated forms mandates the conclusion that the challenged composition claims are directed to unpatentable products of nature."

This decision was a setback to biotechnological corporations that expected their genetic engineering assets to be valued as intellectual property (IP), and it could be seen as a detour from a biotech friendly approach of US case law which goes back to Diamond v. Chakrabarty (1980), in which the US Supreme Court upheld, against the decision of the United States Patent Office (USPTO), a patent on a newly created living organism, a bacterium for digesting crude oil in oil spills. Judge Sweet's decision was appealed by Myriad, which had already won a similar battle in Europe for its BRCA patents. On 29 July 2011, the United States (US) Court of Appeals for the

Federal Circuit ruled that Myriads patents are valid, holding that isolated DNA molecules are eligible for patent protection because they are not products of nature [2–5].

Territoriality is a basic principle of intellectual property rights, and the purpose of this reference to US jurisprudence is only to introduce the question revived by the above-mentioned decisions: Are genes eligible for patent protection? Which line should be drawn with a view to achieve the "optimum balance between public and private ownership"? Gene patenting is a sensitive issue, not only in what concerns the distinction between inventions and "products of nature" but also concerning public morality and ordre public. This chapter provides a general discussion on these issues followed by an analysis of the relevant legal framework of biotechnological patents in the European Union (EU).

Biotechnologies, Intellectual Property, and Health Care From Fiction to Reality: The Impact of Biotechnology in the Health Sector

X-Men is a work of fiction, as well as Huxley's Brave New World, but sometimes fiction becomes reality, and a lot is taking place in the sector of biotechnology genetic engineering. Genetics "cracks" the source code of living organisms and opens new horizons for bioengineering. It promises to correct errors or defects of natural evolution and to introduce modifications into existing species and to cross them. The creation of new species and the rebirth of extinct ones are also envisaged.

Genetic engineering is one of the most important sectors of the so-called knowledge economy, in which, "information forms the raw material of progress and is the new form of wealth" [6]. This economy is based upon high R&D investment in scientific knowledge with a view to transform such knowledge into new useful technologies with industrial application, either as products or as processes of production, and to be traded as marketable commodities.

Biotechnology is a new mantra for health care, promising revolutionary technologies to improve the quality of life and the preservation of life itself. Using Dawkins' analogy with computer sciences, namely, DNA as software, genetics provide a kind of reverse engineering of life's "source code" [7, 8].

The Human Genome Project evidences the value of biotechnological genetic engineering for the health sector (On the Human Genome Project, gene patenting and its implications for medical research see [9, 10]. See also [11]). New cures and treatments are developed by establishing a cause-effect link between a gene and a disease and by finding the way to remove or neutralize such gene from the DNA. Another example is provided by the development, through biotechnologies, of compatible body parts, both internal and external. It may be possible to choose the color of the baby's eyes and to improve the quality and duration of life.

All these possibilities of technical progress are very interesting not only from a scientific perspective but also from an economic outlook. Bioengineering technologies make possible the introduction into the market of new products for which there is potential consumer demand, particularly in the health sector. A "brave new world" of therapies and medicinal products and devices becomes available, and new industries and jobs are established. As Gollin puts it, "Innovation drives history, creating and destroying businesses, ways of life, and societies" [12].

Biotechnologies and the Rationale of Intellectual Property

There already has been a virtuous cycle pattern, for economic development, in most advanced economies, leveraged by a system of IP rights which confers exclusive rights of economic exploitation, namely, in inventions and utility models (patents), literary and artistic works (copyright), and distinctive signs (trademarks). These exclusive rights are necessary to promote investment in R&D and creative activities, protecting the investment and assuring special reward for creative intellectual labor.

Patent law can be traced back to the Venetian Patent Decree of 1474, by which the venetians adopted the first known patent law, with many features of modern laws. At the international level, the system of IP rights has been established in the nineteenth century by several conventions, namely, the Paris Convention for the Protection of Industrial Property (1883), as revised by the Stockholm Act (1967), and the Berne Convention for the Protection of Literary and Artistic Works (1886), as revised by the Paris Act (1971). Other international instruments have been adopted later, namely, the International Convention for the Protection of Performers, the Producers of Phonograms and Broadcasting Organizations (1961, Rome Convention), the Patent Cooperation Treaty (1970), the European Patent Convention, signed at Munich on 5 October 1973 (revised in 2000), and finally the Agreement on Trade-Related Aspects of Intellectual Property Rights (TRIPs 1994), as a nuclear element of the World Trade Organization (WTO) law. In Europe, despite the discrete reference to industrial and commercial property within the Treaty on the Functioning of the EU (TFEU) – after the founding Rome Treaty – IP rights are increasingly harmonized by means of EU Directives and other EU law instruments, taking into account their importance for the internal market. Based upon the assumption that it is "essential for both techno-scientific research and economic development in Europe," a Directive has been adopted on the legal protection of biotechnological inventions – Directive 98/44/EC of 6 July 1998 [13].

Sensitive Ethical Issues in Biotechnology Patents

Despite the economic value of biotechnology, there are dark clouds on the horizon of bioengineering raised by sensitive ethical issues. The question is not whether human beings should be allowed to interfere with the natural creation of life but rather the level of such interference.

Few will contest that bioengineering can, and should, be used to meet the needs of the human species, not only in terms of its preservation but also in what we could argue to be a rational evolution in view of the so-called human emancipation. This emancipation has also shown humans to be the biggest predator and, time and again, ethical concerns are raised to preserve the natural order of life, not only human life but also concerning the life of other species as well as the preservation of biodiversity in general.

Human beings can transform – and to a certain extent dominate – nature, but, at the same time, they are a part of it. A basic sense of respect for Mother Nature, and life in general, emerges as a universal moral principle in today's complex societies.

Looking inside mankind, genetics make possible a deeper knowledge of human beings. More than fingerprints, DNA seems like a serial code, unique and unrepeatable. Genetic identity is not only a right (such as concerning paternity investigation or the right to natural instead of selected DNA) but also a duty (as for criminal research purposes).

Despite everyone having the right to his/her own DNA, it does not mean that one's DNA can be freely used. Technology could make possible human cloning; by means of genetic self-reproduction, this does not equate to a right of duplication of oneself, namely, to make copies of oneself to be used as robots or as organ and tissue banks.

Considering benefits offered by new technologies, does not the right to health justify overcoming some moral constraints, especial concerns granting patents for new biotechnological inventions? In case patents are to be granted, where should the line be drawn between patented inventions, as private goods, and the public domain of intellectual goods which are to be preserved for free collective use? [14].

The economic analysis of IP rights suggests a need for an adequate level of protection to be found so that there are incentives to invest in technological R&D to maintain competition in the relevant marketplace [15]. Information freedom and competition law go hand in hand with the search for optimal and efficient protection of IP. It is argued that competition is stronger when IP is weak and the preservation of freedom of research against totalitarian patents is advocated. In a more radical approach, it has been argued that the patent system is broken and endangers innovation and progress ([16]. On this debate see notably [17–25]). Are in fact patents "old bottles" for the "new wine" of biotechnology?

The Right to Health and the Role of Patents: Fixing Market Failures

Technologies and patents have a significant impact on health. The right to health is a fundamental right, which has both an individual and a social dimension. As an individual right, the right to health means that everyone has the right not to be injured in his/her physical and/or psychic integrity and to receive compensation for health damages either as tort or as contractual liability. As an individual right, the right to health also grounds certain rights and duties within special relations, such as parenthood.

As a social right, the right to health entitles everyone to demand the government to provide health care. In modern social welfare states, it is understood that health is not only an individual right but also a matter to be addressed by the community so that governments are empowered to set up a public health service with universal access and to collect taxes and other revenues to finance the system.

Quality of life and life itself rely heavily on health care. Concurrently, health care depends largely on available technologies.

The rationale of patents is to stimulate the invention of new technologies by means of conferring a limited industrial and commercial "monopoly." It is understood that an exclusive right of economic exploitation is a fair reward to those who develop new products and processes by means of investing time, money, and skills into such inventive and useful activity. This instrumental or utilitarian rationale of patents is reinforced by the "natural law" argument, according to which everyone should be entitled to own – even if only for purposes of industrial and commercial exploitation and for a limited period – the fruits of his/her intellectual labor.

There appears an inherent contradiction, within the relationship between public health innovation and intellectual property rights, between patents and the right to health, or are they "two sides of the same coin"? (see [26–29]). Patents promote the invention of new technologies, including the health-care sector. Patents can serve the right to health, as they increase the spectrum of available technologies along with their quality. Without patents, innovation in the sector of health technologies could arguably stagnate and people would not have access to new health products and services. They also provide for industrial and commercial monopolies, meaning that the patent holder has the exclusive right to manufacture and to trade his patented inventions. The patent holder is in a position to charge monopolistic prices for his patented goods, excluding from new health-care technologies those who cannot afford them. As an exclusive right, the patent holder is free to accommodate the exercise of the monopoly to his commercial strategy, namely, by means of entry, or not, into a particular market. It becomes problematic when states implement and enforce patent schemes and, concurrently, provide up-to-date social health care. It means that states confer monopolies on health technologies while also financing such monopolies through the health-care system.

This is a twofold government intervention into the market. Governments create monopolies which are legal barriers to entry into the market while also providing funding to such monopolies by means of social health care.

From a strictly theoretical economics approach, the "invisible hand of the market" fails strongly in the health-care sector. Monopoly-like exclusive rights are necessary to stimulate the production of goods which meet consumers' needs. In order to satisfy the same needs, governments have to implement a socialized healthcare system, which subsidizes such monopolies, together with the scientific and technological R&D activities upon which they are based.

Patents of Biotechnological Inventions

No international treaty on IP law expressly provides, or excludes, legal protection of biotechnological inventions. This is valid for the Paris Convention for the Protection of Industrial Property, the European Patent Convention, and the TRIPs. TRIPs establishes the principle of technological neutrality, meaning that patent protection must be guaranteed for products, as well as for processes, in all areas of technology. It means that biotechnologies cannot be excluded from patentability.

A very important international instrument in the sector of biomedicine is the Convention on Human Rights and Biomedicine (1997) – ([30]. See also [31]). No direct answer to the patentability of human genes is to be found in this convention, but it provides a few relevant principles, such as the primacy of the human being over the sole interest of society or science (Art. 2). This principle has some implications, namely, (a) predictive genetic tests may be performed only for health purposes or for scientific research linked to health purposes (Art. 12); (b) modification of the human genome may be undertaken only for preventive, diagnostic, or therapeutic purposes and only if its purpose is not to introduce any modification in the genome of any descendants (Art. 13); and (c) prohibition of financial gain and disposal of a part of the human body, as such (Art. 21). This convention leaves some room to consider the use of genetic engineering for purposes of health and scientific research related to health, as well as for preventive, diagnostic, or therapeutic purposes.

EU Directive on Biotechnological Inventions

The European Parliament and the Council of the EU have adopted Directive 98/44/ EC of 6 July 1998 on the legal protection of biotechnological inventions. This Directive establishes that biotechnological inventions can and shall be patented. For purposes of patentability, distinction, between what is patentable and what is not, is clarified. The simple discovery of one of the elements of the human body, including the sequence or partial sequence of a gene, is deemed not patentable. However, an element isolated from the human body or produced by means of a technical process, including the partial sequence of a gene, may constitute a patentable invention. It has been commented that Directive 98/44 establishes the patentability of genes in uncertain and dangerous terms [32].

In order to be patented, biotechnological inventions have to meet the substance requirements of patentability, namely, they have to be new, involve an inventive step, and be susceptible of industrial application. Thus, biotechnological inventions can be patented even if they concern a product consisting of, or containing, biological material – as biological material which is isolated from its natural environment or produced by means of a technical process may also be the subject of an invention.

Some inventions are not patentable where their exploitation would be contrary to public policy or morality, such as processes for cloning human beings, processes for modifying the germ line genetic identity of human beings, and uses of embryos for industrial or commercial purposes. These are among the so-called plagues and evils of the patentability of human genome, yet it is argued that the Pandora box should not be closed, concerning the discussion of the pros and cons of the economic exploitation of the results of scientific research and technological innovation [33].

Taking into account the sensitive nature of biotechnology, all of its aspects are evaluated by the Commission's European Group on Ethics in Science and New Technologies. Under Directive 98/44, the scope of patent protection covers, as derivatives, the use of patented self-reproducing material and material incorporating patented genetic information, limited by the exhaustion of the right of propagation or multiplication. Directive 98/44 also provides compulsory cross-licensing of patents for genetically modified plants.

The Legal Protection of Biotechnological Inventions as a European Industrial Policy Tool

Aware of the important role played by biotechnology and genetic engineering in a broad range of industries and in particular of the required high-risk investments in genetic engineering R&D, the protection of biotechnological inventions is deemed of "fundamental importance for the Community's industrial development" (Recitals 1 and 2). Harmonized adequate legal protection is considered crucial to promote investment in the field of biotechnology and to foster the proper functioning of the internal market (Recitals 3–7).

Biotechnological Inventions Are to be Protected Under National Patent Law

Instead of setting up a separate body of law, it is understood that, in order to accommodate technological developments involving biological material, it is only required, where necessary, to adjust the rules of national patent law which remain the essential basis for the legal protection of biotechnological inventions (Recital 8 and Art. 1(1) 2nd period).

Biotechnological inventions shall be protected under national patent law of each Member State (Art. 1(1)). The intervention of the EU legislation is deemed subsidiary, meaning that "the Community's legal framework for the protection of biotechnological inventions can be limited to laying down certain principles as they apply to the patentability of biological material as such, such principles being intended in particular to determine the difference between inventions and discoveries with regard to the patentability of certain elements of human origin, [or] to the scope of protection conferred by a patent" (Recital 13). It is made clear that certain elements of human origin, including genes, are not merely discoveries as they can qualify, for purposes of patent law, as inventions.

Patent Protection for Biotechnological Inventions Either as Products or as Processes

According to TRIPs – which this Directive is without prejudice to (Art. 1(2)) – patent protection must be guaranteed for products as well as for processes in all areas of technology (Recital 12). It is understood that "this Directive does not in any way affect the basis of current patent law, according to which a patent may be granted for any new application of a patented product" (Recital 28). Thus, new applications of patented products can be protected by new patents.

Novelty, Inventive Step, and Industrial Application as General Requirements of Patentability of Biotechnological Inventions

In order to be patentable, biotechnological inventions have to meet the three basic requirements, namely, they have to be new (1), need to involve an inventive step (2), and must be susceptible of industrial application (3). (Portuguese law provides definitions of novelty, inventive activity, and industrial application (Art. 55 et seq. of the Industrial Property Code): novelty means that the invention is new to the state of the art (a); it involves an inventive step if for an expert on the subject it is not obvious (b); and it is capable of industrial application if the object of the invention can be produced or used in any kind of industry or in agriculture (c). Concerning the state of the art, it comprises all that, inside or outside of the country, has been made available to the public before the date in which the patent application was filed, by description, use or any other way, as well as the content of patent and utility models applications filed before the patent application to produce effects in Portugal and not yet published (Art. 56 CPI)).

Directive 98/44 clarifies that biotechnological inventions are patentable "even ifthey concern a product consisting of or containing biological material or a process by means of which biological material is produced, processed or used" (Art. 3(1)). Biological material means "any material containing genetic information and capable of reproducing itself or being reproduced in a biological system" (Art. 2(1)(a)).

Knowledge of indigenous and local communities does not seem to qualify as invention, for purposes of patent protection, but it can be integrated as an element of a biological patented invention. Concerning biodiversity and the protection of knowledge of indigenous and local communities, it is necessary to develop a common appreciation of the relationship between IP rights and the relevant provisions of the TRIPs Agreement and the Convention on Biological Diversity. This is particularly so for issues relating to technology transfer and conservation; sustainable use of biological diversity; and the fair and equitable sharing of benefits, arising out of the use of genetic resources, including the protection of knowledge, innovations, and practices of indigenous and local communities embodying traditional lifestyles relevant for the conservation and sustainable use of biological diversity (Recital 56).

Patentability of Biological Material Isolated from Its Natural Environment or Produced by Means of a Technical Process

Biological material, which previously occurred in nature, may be the subject of a patentable invention where it "is isolated from its natural environment or produced by means of a technical process" (Art. 3(3)). The patentability of biological material is established as "no prohibition or exclusion exists in national or European patent law (Munich Convention) which precludes a priori the patentability of biological matter" (Recital 15).

Patentability of Processes for Treatment of the Human or Animal Body by Surgery or Therapy and Diagnostic Methods Practiced in the Human or Animal Body as a Matter of National Law

The exclusion from patentability, under national law of processes for treatment of the human or animal body by surgery or therapy and diagnostic methods practiced in the human or animal body, is not affected by the Directive (see Recital 35). On the same direction, see also TRIPs (Art. 27(3)) and the European Patent Convention

(Art. 53). For example, under Portuguese law, methods of surgery or therapeutic methods of treatment of human or animal body as well as methods of diagnosis applied to the human or animal body cannot be patented, but products, substances, or compositions used in any of those methods can be patented (Art. 52(2) of Portuguese Industrial Property Code).

The background for this exception of patentability subject matter is found in the conflict between doctors and lawyers concerning jurisdiction over medical technologies with doctors prevailing. According to *Piper* [34], this exclusion comes in line with the monopolization of medical activities and the emergence of the medical community, including scientific publications. It is also as a response to the previous "state of nature" which led to the establishment of professional bodies with higher education, deontological rules, and certification. In this process, patents, previously a matter for lawyers, were used by reference to the Crown, as means to advertise products as safe and functional but, in reality, without prior medical control. The abuse of this system would lead to the end of medical patents.

The exclusion of the medical activity from patentability has also been based upon the principle of medicine not being a business or industrial activity but rather as a service of public interest, to be submitted to deontological control as different from mere trade regulation. The interests of medicine justified the revelation of the medical findings and inventions instead of their being kept secret or monopolized.

The idea of medicine, as a team work, would be degenerated by the system of patents. The author remarks the "progressive hollowing out of the exception" and criticizes the exception itself:

"The distinctions drawn in law appear to many to be arbitrary, fruitless and driven with contradiction, as judges since the 1970s have observed. An example is the requirement that diagnosis must be performed on or in the body. This means that a diagnostic method of testing for allergies performed on the skin will be excluded from patentability, whereas a blood test to the same end will be patentable. It is unclear why apparatus and drugs are patentable but medical and diagnosis methods are not, particularly when both can be applied in or on the body. Further concerns are raised as to why doctors are given blanket protection from patents in the course of their 'life-saving' work, while other professions and trades the work of which is arguably as important to preserving life are not treated similarly. Examples are fire fighters and emergency workers, paraprofessional health workers, municipal water suppliers, sanitation and other public authorities" ([34], p. 440).

Elements Excluded from Patentability as Mere Discoveries Per Se (1): Plant and Animal Varieties and Essentially Biological Processes for the Production of Plants or Animals

Some elements are not patentable, such as "plant and animal varieties" (Art. 4(1) (a)) as well as "essentially biological processes for the production of plants or animals" (Art. 4(1)(b)), namely, processes which "consist entirely of natural phenomena such as crossing or selection" (Art. 2(2)). Plant and animal varieties cannot be patented, but "the concept of "plant variety" is defined by legislation protecting new varieties, pursuant to which a variety is defined by its whole genome and possesses individuality and is clearly distinguishable from other varieties" (Recital 30).

It asserted the patentability of unprotected plant grouping as well as technically feasible pools of plants and animals, excluding processes for producing new plant varieties by means of genetic modifications. In fact, "a plant grouping which is characterized by a particular gene (and not its whole genome) is not covered by the protection of new varieties and is therefore not excluded from patentability even if it comprises new varieties of plants" (Recital 31). Inventions concerning plants or animals can be patented provided the "technical feasibility," or the application of the invention is not technically confined to a single plant or animal variety (Art. 4(2) and Recital 29): (I)f an invention consists only in genetically modifying a particular plant variety, and if a new plant variety is bred, it will still be excluded from patentability even if the genetic modification is the result not of an essentially biological process but of a biotechnological process (Recital 32).

The exclusion of essentially biological processes is "without prejudice to the patentability of inventions which concern a microbiological [i.e. any process involving or performed upon or resulting in microbiological material" – Art. 2(1) (b)] or other technical process or a product obtained by means of such a process (Art. 4(3)).

Elements Excluded from Patentability as Mere Discoveries Per Se (2): the Human Body or One of Its Elements

Concerning the human body or one of its elements, it is understood that "patent law must be applied so as to respect the fundamental principles safeguarding the dignity and integrity of the person," and therefore it is asserted that "the principle that the human body, at any stage of its formation or development, including germ cells, and the simple discovery of one of its elements or one of its products, including the sequence or partial sequence of a human gene, cannot be patented" (Recital 16). This exclusion of patentability of the human body or one of its elements is found to be "in line with the criteria of patentability proper to patent law, whereby a mere discovery cannot be patented" (Recital 16, in fine). The human body, or any of its elements, is not an invention but rather a mere discovery, without prejudice to concepts of invention and discovery, as developed by national, European, and international law (Recital 34). Article 5(1) reads that "The human body, at the various stages of its formation and development, and the simple discovery of one of its elements, including the sequence or partial sequence of a gene, cannot constitute patentable inventions."

Patentability of Elements Isolated from the Human Body or Otherwise Produced by Means of a Technical Process, Including the Sequence or Partial Sequence of a Gene

Despite the human body or one of its elements being excluded from patentability, certain elements, isolated from the human body concerning new medicinal products, should not be peremptorily excluded from patentability. Recital 17 reads that "significant progress in the treatment of diseases has already been made thanks to the existence of medicinal products derived from elements isolated from the human body and/or otherwise produced, such medicinal products resulting from technical processes aimed at obtaining elements similar in structure to those existing naturally in the human body"; for these, it is found that "research aimed at obtaining and isolating such elements valuable to medicinal production should be encouraged by means of the patent system" – and the same applies mutatis mutandis to research and production of biotechnological medicines which are needed to combat rare or "orphan" diseases (Recital 18).

Distinguishing natural from artificial environments, it is "made clear that an invention based on an element isolated from the human body or otherwise produced by means of a technical process, which is susceptible of industrial application, is not excluded from patentability, even where the structure of that element is identical to that of a natural element, given that the rights conferred by the patent do not extend to the human body and its elements in their natural environment" (Recital 20).

Elements isolated from the human body, or otherwise produced, are the result of technical processes used to identify, purify, and classify them and to reproduce them outside the human body, and therefore, they are "techniques which human beings alone are capable of putting into practice and which nature is incapable of accomplishing by itself" (Recital 21). Article 5(2) provides that "An element isolated from the human body or otherwise produced by means of a technical process, including the sequence or partial sequence of a gene, may constitute a patentable invention, even if the structure of that element is identical to that of a natural element."

Artificial replication techniques of human genetic sequences can be patented but not the genes per se, recognizing that "the discussion on the patentability of sequences or partial sequences of genes is controversial." It is understood that the granting of a patent, for inventions which concern such elements, is to be subject to the same criteria as in all other areas of technology: novelty, inventive step, and industrial application (Recital 22).

Disclosure of the DNA Function

Disclosure of the DNA function is put forward as a basic requirement for the patentability of gene-related inventions. The operative part of the Directive adds that: "The industrial application of a sequence or a partial sequence of a gene must be disclosed in the patent application" (Art. 5(3) – for administrative and procedural provisions concerning deposit, access, and redeposit of a biological material, see Articles 13 and 14).

Rejecting the possibility of patents, without disclosure of the know-how embedded into the invention, it is understood that "a mere DNA sequence without indication of a function does not contain any technical information and is therefore not a patentable invention" (Recital 23). Protein production is a function of DNA sequences and Recital 24 reads "in order to comply with the industrial application criterion it is necessary in cases where a sequence or partial sequence of a gene is used to produce a protein or part of a protein, to specify which protein or part of a protein is produced or what function it performs" (Recital 24).

It seems that a DNA sequence, indicating as function the production of a certain protein, is not excluded from patentability, provided that the function of the protein is also disclosed.

Free and Informed Consent of the Person from Whose Body the Material is Taken

If an invention is based on biological material of human origin or if it uses such material, the person from whose body the material is taken must have had – where a patent application is filed – an opportunity of expressing free and informed consent thereto, in accordance with national law (Recital 26). Under Portuguese law, both health information and biological material are deemed to be the property of the person to whom it relates [Law 12/2005 of 25 January on personal genetic and health information, Articles 3(1), 18(2), and 19(13)] Patentability does not seem to be excluded where such material has been taken without its owner having had an opportunity of expressing free and informed consent thereto, who will have a future claim against the patent applicant.

Exclusion of Patentability of Inventions the Commercial Exploitation of Which Is Contrary to Ordre Public or Morality (1): The Prevalence of Ethical or Moral Principles

According to the TRIPs Agreement, members of the WTO may exclude from patentability inventions, the prevention within their territory of the commercial exploitation of which is necessary to protect ordre public or morality, including to protect human, animal, or plant life or health or to avoid serious prejudice to the environment, provided that such exclusion is not made merely because the exploitation is prohibited by their law (Recital 36 and Art. 6(1)).

It is understood that "ordre public and morality correspond in particular to ethical or moral principles recognized in a Member State, respect for which is particularly important in the field of biotechnology in view of the potential scope of inventions in this field and their inherent relationship to living matter" and that "such ethical or moral principles supplement the standard legal examinations under patent law regardless of the technical field of the invention" (Recital 39).

The primacy of ethical or moral principles is asserted over the economic interests of commercial exploitation of biotechnological inventions, regardless of the technical field of the invention.

The Commission's European Group on Ethics in Science and New Technologies is entrusted, as the Guardian of Basic Ethical Principles, to evaluate all ethical aspects of biotechnology (Art. 7) which has to assess such aspects at the "level of basic ethical principles, including where it is consulted on patent law" (Recital 44). It is asserted that fundamental rights, as guaranteed by the European Convention on Human Rights (ECHR) and as they result from constitutional traditions common to the Member States, as general principles of law, are to be respected by the EU (Recital 43).

It is stressed the "principle whereby inventions must be excluded from patentability where their commercial exploitation offends against order public or morality" (Recital 37). An illustrative list (not exhaustive) of these inventions is included in the operative part of the Directive in order to "provide national courts and patent offices with a general guide to interpreting the reference to ordre public and morality" (Recital 38).

As examples of inventions excluded from patentability due to their commercial exploitation being deemed contrary to ordre public or morality, Article 6(1)(2) expressly lists processes for cloning human beings (1), processes for modifying the germ line genetic identity of human beings (2), uses of human embryos for industrial or commercial purposes (3), and processes for modifying the gene identity of animals which are likely to cause them suffering without any substantial medical benefit to man or animal and also animals resulting from such processes (4).

This list provides two kinds of examples. The first being inventions which are absolutely excluded from patentability due to their exploitation being deemed contrary to ordre public or morality in any case, regardless of the benefits they could generate. The second being inventions which are relatively excluded from patentability, meaning that certain circumstances, may justify the limitation of the exclusion.

Absolute Exclusion of Patentability of Inventions the Commercial Exploitation of Which Is Contrary to Ordre Public or Morality (2): Processes to Produce Chimeras from Germ Cells or Totipotent Cells of Humans and Animals (a), Processes for Modifying the Germ Line Genetic Identity of Human Beings (b), and Processes for Cloning Human Beings (c)

It is understood that "processes, the use of which offend human dignity, such as processes to produce chimeras from germ cells or totipotent cells of humans and animals, are obviously excluded from patentability" (Recital 38, in fine). Due to the existing "consensus within the Community that interventions in the human germ line and the cloning of human beings offends against ordre public and morality," it is deemed "important to exclude unequivocally from patentability processes for modifying the germ line genetic identity of human beings and processes for cloning human beings" (Recital 40). The same applies to cloning human beings which is defined as "any process, including techniques of embryo splitting, designed to create a human being with the same nuclear genetic information as another living or deceased human being" (Recital 41).

Relative Exclusion of Patentability of Inventions the Commercial Exploitation of Which Is Contrary to Ordre Public or Morality (2): Uses of Human Embryos for Industrial or Commercial Purposes (a) and Processes for Modifying the Genetic Identity of Animals (b)

Directive 98/44 excludes from patentability uses of human embryos for industrial or commercial purposes. Recital 42 reads that this exclusion from patentability does not extend to inventions for therapeutic or diagnostic purposes which are applied to the human embryo and are useful to it[.]

On 18 October 2011, the Court of Justice of the European Union delivered a judgment in Case C-34/10, a reference for a preliminary ruling from the German Supreme Court of Justice (Bundesgerichtshof) concerning the interpretation of Article 6(2)(c) of Directive 98/44/EC which has been made in proceedings brought by Greenpeace e.V. ("Greenpeace") seeking annulment of the German patent held by Mr. Bruestle, which relates to neural precursor cells and the processes for their production from embryonic stem cells and their use for therapeutic purposes ([35]. See [36]).

The court ruled that Article 6(2)(c) of Directive 98/44/EC "must be interpreted as meaning that: any human ovum after fertilisation, any non-fertilised human ovum into which the cell nucleus from a mature human cell has been transplanted ['dolly method'], and any non-fertilised human ovum whose division and further development have been stimulated by parthenogenesis constitute a 'human embryo'; [and] it is for the referring court to ascertain, in the light of scientific developments, whether a stem cell obtained from a human embryo at the blastocyst stage constitutes a 'human embryo' within the meaning of Article 6(2)(c) of Directive 98/44." The court also ruled that "The exclusion from patentability concerning the use of

human embryos for industrial or commercial purposes set out in Article 6(2)(c) of Directive 98/44 also covers the use of human embryos for purposes of scientific research, only use for therapeutic or diagnostic purposes which are applied to the human embryo and are useful to it being patentable." This acknowledges that the exclusion from patentability, concerning the use of human embryos for industrial or commercial purposes, does not cover their use for therapeutic or diagnostic purposes which are applied to the human embryo and are useful to it. It implies a distinction between the human body and the human embryo, as according to Recital 35 of Directive 98/44, the legal protection of biotechnological inventions provided for does not affect the provisions of national patent law whereby processes for treatment of the human body by surgery or therapy and diagnostic methods practiced in the human body are excluded from patentability.

In addition, the court ruled that "Article 6(2)(c) of Directive 98/44 excludes an invention from patentability where the technical teaching which is the subject-matter of the patent application requires the prior destruction of human embryos or their use as base material, whatever the stage at which that takes place and even if the description of the technical teaching claimed does not refer to the use of human embryos." Consequently, patentability is excluded where the uses for therapeutic or diagnostic purposes which are applied to the human embryo and are useful to it require "the prior destruction of human embryos or their use as base material, whatever the stage at which that takes place and even if the description of the technical teaching claimed does not refer to the use of human embryos." German lawyers have argued that "the ECJ decision does not affect the patentability of iPS (induced pluripotency stem cells) cells which have ES-like pluripotency but which are derived from human reprogrammed adult cells" [Recital 37].

Uses of human embryos for industrial or commercial purposes are excluded from patentability. Recital 42 reads that this exclusion from patentability does not extend to inventions for therapeutic or diagnostic purposes which are applied to the human embryo and are useful to it. Processes for modifying the genetic identity of animals, which are likely to cause them suffering, are also excluded from patentability in case no substantial medical benefit in terms of research, prevention, diagnosis, or therapy to man or animal and also animals result from such processes (see Recital 45).

Scope of Protection (1): The Use of Patented Self-Reproducing Material

The Biotech Directive also addressed whether the scope of the patent protection is limited to the product or the process or extends to derivatives. It takes the view that the argument according to which "the function of a patent is to reward the inventor for his creative efforts by granting an exclusive but time-bound right, and thereby encourage inventive activities' justifies the entitlement to the holder of the patent to prohibit the use of patented self-reproducing material in situations analogous to those where it would be permitted to prohibit the use of patented, non-selfreproducing products, that is to say the production of the patented product itself" (Recital 46).

It is provided that "The protection conferred by a patent on a biological material possessing specific characteristics as a result of the invention extends to any biological material derived from that biological material through propagation or multiplication in an identical or divergent form and possessing those same characteristics (Art. 8(1)). The same applies mutatis mutandis to the protection conferred by a patent on a process that enables a biological material to be produced possessing specific characteristics as a result of the invention concerning biological material directly obtained through that process" (Art. 8(2)).

Scope of Protection (2): Material Incorporating Patented Genetic Information

Protection conferred by a patent on a product containing, or consisting of, genetic information extends to all material – except the human body or one of its elements, including the sequence or partial sequence of a gene – in which the product is incorporated and in which the genetic information is contained and performs its function (Art. 9). For purposes of interpreting rights conferred by a patent, when sequences overlap only in parts which are not essential to the invention, each sequence is considered as an independent sequence in terms of patent law (Recital 25).

Scope of Protection (3): Exhaustion of the Right of Propagation or Multiplication

The scope of protection extends to derivatives in patented self-reproducing material and material incorporating patented genetic information but does not extend to biological material obtained from the propagation or multiplication of biological material placed on the market in the territory of a Member State by the holder of the patent or with his consent, where the multiplication or propagation necessarily results from the application for which the biological material was marketed, provided that the material obtained is not subsequently used for other propagation or multiplication (Art. 10). The same applies mutatis mutandis to commercialization of plant propagating material or animal reproductive material to a farmer to use the product of his harvest for propagation or multiplication by him on his own farm or to use the protected livestock for an agricultural purpose (Art. 11; see Recitals 47–51).

Compulsory Cross-Licensing of Patents for Genetically Modified Plants

Instead of granting exclusive rights, patents are limited to remuneration rights in certain fields, namely, in the field of exploitation of new plant characteristics resulting from genetic engineering (or from new plant varieties in genetic engineering). In this field, guaranteed access, on payment of a fee, must be granted in terms of a compulsory license where, in relation to the genus or species concerned, the plant variety (or the invention) represents significant technical progress of considerable economic interest compared to the invention claimed in the patent (Recitals 52 and 53). The patent holder is not entitled to prevent the exploitation of a new plant variety which represents "significant technical progress of considerable economic interest compared to the invention claimed" in the patent the use of which is required.

It is provided that a breeder who cannot acquire or exploit a plant variety right, without infringing a prior patent, may apply for a compulsory license for nonexclusive use of the invention protected by the patent as the license is necessary for the exploitation of the plant variety to be protected, subject to payment of an appropriate royalty, and where such license is granted the holder of the patent that is entitled to a cross-license, on reasonable terms, to use the protected variety (Art. 12(1)). The same applies mutatis mutandis for holders of a patent concerning a biotechnological invention who cannot exploit it without infringing a prior plant variety right (Art. 12(2)).

As provided for in Article 12(3), applicants for such a compulsory license are required to demonstrate that they unsuccessfully have applied to the holder of the patent, or of the plant variety right, to obtain a contractual license (a) and that the plant variety or the invention constitutes significant technical progress of considerable economic interest, compared with the invention claimed in the patent or the protected plant variety (b).

Conclusion

Science moves forward and fiction becomes reality. Biotechnology provides significant benefits also for health purposes. Companies claim IP as a means to have exclusive protection of biotechnological assets. There are complex and sensitive moral issues involved. Patents play a role in promoting new health technologies, and, subsidized also by social health care, they fix market failures in the health sector. No international treaty on IP law expressly provides, nor excludes, the legal protection of biotechnological inventions. In the EU, Directive 98/44 established the legal protection of biotechnological inventions, as a tool of European industrial policy. Biotechnological inventions, either as products or as processes, are to be protected under national patent law and have to meet the requirements of novelty, inventive step, and industrial application. Biological material, isolated from its natural environment or produced by means of a technical process, is expressly eligible for patent protection (see in the US the Myriad Genetics case concerning patented methods to isolate BRCA1 and BRCA2).

Patentability of processes for treatment of the human or animal body, by surgery or therapy, and diagnostic methods practiced in the human or animal body is to be regulated under national law. Some elements are excluded from patentability, as mere discoveries per se, such as plant and animal varieties and essentially biological processes for the production of plants or animals (1) and the human body or one of its elements (2). This exclusion does not cover elements isolated from the human body or otherwise produced by means of a technical process, including the sequence or partial sequence of a gene. To meet the requirement of industrial application, the function of the DNA sequence has to be disclosed. Concerning biological material of human origin, the person from whose body the material is taken must have the opportunity to express his free and informed consent thereto.

Directive 98/44 asserts the predominance of ethical or moral principles over economic interests, excluding the patentability of inventions the commercial exploitation of which is contrary to ordre public or morality, by means of an illustrative catalog of examples which differentiate between absolute exclusion concerning processes to produce chimeras from germ cells or totipotent cells of humans and animals, processes for modifying the germ line genetic identity of human beings, and processes for cloning human beings and relative exclusion concerning uses of human embryos for industrial or commercial purposes (as interpreted by the ECJ in Br€ustle) and processes for modifying the genetic identity of animals.

References

1. See also Pereira ALD. Human genes as biotech corporate assets? Nature, morals and the role of intellectual property in healthcare innovation. Boletim da Faculdade de Direito 87(2011), p. 213–42.
2. United States Court of Appeals for the Federal Circuit. The Association for Molecular Pathology (Et al.) v. United States Patent and Trademark Office and Myriad Genetics, Inc. (Et. al.), July 29, 2011 – http://blogs.nature.com/news/myriad.pdf
3. See notably Williams-Jones B. History of a gene patent: tracing the development and application of commercial BRCA testing. Health Law J. 2002;10:123–46
4. Conley J, Vorhaus D. Pigs fly: federal court invalidates myriad's patent claims. Genomics Law Report, March 30; 2010.
5. Abbott A. Europe to pay royalties for cancer gene – BRCA1 patent decision may be ignored in clinics. Nature, 2 Dec 2008. http://www.nature.com/news/2008/081202/full/456556a.html
6. Colston C, Middleton K. Modern intellectual property law. New York: Cavendish Publishing; 2006. p. 31.
7. Dawkins R. The ancestor's tale. New York: Houghton-Mifflin; 2004.
8. Loureiro JC. O direito a` identidade gene´tica do ser humano. In: Portugal-Brasil Ano 2000. Coimbra: Coimbra Editora; 1999. p. 263.
9. World Health Organization. Genetics, genomics and the patenting of DNA. Review of potential implications for health in developing countries. Geneva: WHO Press; 2005.
10. WHO. Public health innovation and intellectual property rights. Geneva: WHO Press; 2006.
11. Yahong L. Human gene patenting and its implications to medical research. In: Yu, editor. Intellectual property and information wealth. Westport/London: Praeger; 2007. p. 347–76.
12. Gollin M. Driving innovation – intellectual strategies for a dynamic world. Cambridge: Cambridge University Press; 2008. p. 21.
13. Directive 98/44/EC of the European Parliament and of the Council of 6 July 1998 on the legal protection of biotechnological inventions, OJ L 213, 30.7.1998, p. 13–21.
14. Stiglitz J. Knowledge as a global public good. In: Kaul I, Grunberg I, Stern MA, editors. Global Public goods – international cooperation in the 21st century. Oxford/New York: Oxford University Press; 1999. p. 320–1.
15. Landes W, Posner R. The economic structure of intellectual property law. Cambridge, MA: Harvard University Press; 2003.
16. Jaffe A, Lerner J. Innovation and its discontents: how our broken patent system is endangering innovation and progress, and what to do about it. Princeton: Princeton University Press; 2004.
17. O'Rourke M. Toward a doctrine of fair use in patent law. Columbia Law Rev. 2000;100: 1177–250.
18. Heller M, Eisenberg R. Can patents deter innovation? The anticommons in biomedical research. Science. 1998;280:698–70.

19. Marques JPR. Introduc¸a˜o ao problema das invenc¸o˜es biotecnolo´gicas (algumas consideracões). In: Direito Industrial I, Coimbra: Almedina; 2001. p. 177–333.

20. Boyle J. Shamans software and spleens: law and the construction of the information society. Cambridge: Harvard University Press; 2003.

21. Opderbeck D. The penguins genome, or coase and open source biotechnology. Harvard J Law Technol. 2004;18:168–98.

22. Adelman DE. A fallacy on the commons in biotech patent policy. Berkeley Technol Law J. 2005;20:985–1030.

23. Bovenberg JA. Property rights in blood, genes & data: naturally yours. Boston: Martinus Nijhoff Academic Publishers; 2006.

24. Engel C. Innovationsanreize aus Wettbewerb und Kollusion. In: Ohly A, Klippel D, editors Geistiges Eigentum und Gemeinfreiheit. Tu¨bingen: Mohr Siebeck; 2007. p. 19–43.

25. Sumikura K. Intellectual property rights policy for gene-related inventions – toward optimum balance between public and private ownership. In: Castle D, editir. The role of intellectual property rights in biotechnology innovation. Cheltenham/Northampton: Edward Elgar; 2009. p. 73–97.

26. Yahong L. Intellectual property and public health: two sides of the same coin. Asian J WTO Int Health Law Policy. 2011; 6(2):390.

27. Caulfield T. Policy conflicts: gene patents and health care in Canada. Commun Genet 2005;8:223–27.

28. Heath A. Preparing for the genetic revolution – the effect of gene patents on healthcare and research and the need for reform. Canterbury Law Rev. 2005;11:59–90.

29. Marques JPR. Biotecnologia(s) e propriedade intelectual, 2 vols. Coimbra: Almedina; 2007.

30. Convention for the Protection of Human Rights and Dignity of the Human Being with regard to the Application of Biology and Medicine, Oviedo, 4.IV, 1997.

31. Additional Protocols to the Convention on Human Rights and Biomedicine, on the Prohibition of Cloning Human Beings (Paris, 12.I.1998), and concerning Genetic Testing for Health Purposes (Strasbourg, 27.XI.2008).

32. Ascensão JO. Intervencões no genoma humano. Revista da Ordem dos Advogados. 63, 2003: 25–49.

33. Marques JPR. Patentes de Genes Humanos. In: Direito Industrial, vol. III, APDI. Coimbra: Almedina; 2003. p. 143.

34. Piper T. Watch what you export: the history of medical exceptions from patentability. In: Castle D, editor. The role of intellectual property rights in biotechnology innovation. Cheltenham/Northampton: Edward Elgar; 2009. p. 437–55.

35. C-34/10 (Bru¨stle), 18/10/2011, European Court reports 2011. http://eur-lex.europa.eu/LexUriServ/LexUriServ.do?uri=CELEX:62010CJ0034:EN:HTML

36. Ertelt S. European union court bans stem cell patents if embryo destroyed. LifeNews.com, Luxembourg, 18 Oct 2011.

37. Bardehle/Pagenberg. ECJ: Exclusion from patentability of all human embryonic stem cell-related inventions in Europe (Bru¨stle v Greenpeace), 2011. http://www.bardehle.com/en/news/ip_news_and_information/release/article/ecj-exclusion-from-patentability-of-all-humanembryonic-stem-cell-related-inventions-in-europe-br.html.

LICENSE CONTRACTS, FREE SOFTWARE AND CREATIVE COMMONS IN PORTUGUESE LAW*

Abstract - Free and open source software (FOSS) is distributed in Portugal under the terms of licenses which are not 'legal free'. On the contrary, these licenses raise difficult legal issues concerning notably the law of contracts (e.g. formal requirements, standard terms and liability disclaimers), copyright law (e.g. statutory requirements of authorizations, equitable remunerations, and moral rights), competition law (e.g. abuse of dominant position) and the law of public procurement (notably the requirement of open standards). The same applies, mutatis mutandis, to Creative Commons licenses. This paper addresses such legal issues looking for the answers provided by Portuguese law, taking also into account legislation and case-law of the European Union.

1. Introduction – Licenses of Intellectual Property in Portugal and Free/Open Source Software (FOSS)

The Portuguese Civil Code provides that intellectual property is a special form of property with two autonomous regulato-

* In *Free and Open Source Software (FOSS) and other Alternative License Models - A Comparative Analysis*, ed. Axel Metzger, p. 357-370, 2016, Springer Nature.

ry branches (industrial property and copyright). The Code of Industrial Property[1] has special provisions on license contracts. By contrast, the Code of Copyright (Author's and Related Rights)[2] does not use the terminology licenses, but instead authorizations. However, this linguistic deviation does not have practical consequences. Industrial property licenses and copyright authorizations are integrated in the general category of licenses of intellectual property (IP).[3]

IP license contracts are temporary authorizations to use, usually against remuneration, goods protected under intellectual property rights (e.g. patented inventions, registered trademarks, copyrighted literary or artistic works, including software and databases).[4] IP licenses may qualify as legal types of contracts (notably lease of intangibles) and, in the absence of special provisions, general principles of contract law also apply to license contracts.

Concerning FOSS and other alternative licenses, notably Creative Commons[5], Portugal has enacted special provisions making open source mandatory in public procurement. The Open Standards Act[6] established the adoption of open standards for digital information in the Public Administration with a view to promoting technological freedom of citizens and organizations and the in-

---

[1] Código da Propriedade Industrial (CPI), enacted by Decree-Law No 36/2003 of 5 March, as last amended by Law No 46/2011 of 24 June.

[2] Código do Direito de Autor e dos Direitos Conexos (CDADC), enacted by Decree-Law No 63/85 of March 1985, as last amended by Law No 32/2015 of 24 April. Copyright regulation is complemented by special Acts, notably the Software Act (Decree-Law No 252/94 of 20 October) and the Databases Act (Decree-Law No 122/2000 of 4 July).

[3] Ascensão 2011; Almeida 2011; Pereira 2011a.

[4] Pereira 1999 (copyright); Marques 2008 (industrial property).

[5] On these licensing schemes in Portuguese literature see e.g. Pereira 2008, Leitão 2011.

[6] Law No 36/2011 of 21 June.

teroperability of computer systems in the State. In principle, acts of public procurement excluding open standards are not valid. Moreover, there is a Portuguese version of the European Union Public License (EUPL).[7]

2. FOSS licenses and the law of contracts

2.1. Licenses as contracts

FOSS licenses may be construed as contracts under Portuguese law. It means that offer and acceptance are required. However, the declaration of acceptance of the proposal may be waived by the nature or circumstances of the transaction (*Rechtsgeschäft*) or by the relevant usual practices, the contract being concluded where the use of the program under the terms of the FOSS license shows the will to accept the proposal[8].

On the other hand, the principles of contract law do not expressly provide for a consideration requirement. Several gratuitous transactions, such as donations (*donatio*) and loan for use (*comodatum*), are codified as legal types of contracts.[9] Nonetheless, the object of the contract has to be physically and egally possible, lawful (compliance with the relevant statutes as well as with public order and good morals) and ascertainable; otherwise the contract is null and void.[10]

---

[7] European Commission 2007.

[8] Civil Code, Article 234.

[9] Civil Code, Articles 940 and 1129.

[10] Civil Code, Article 280.

2.2. Formal requirements

The general principle of contract law is freedom of form[11]. However, industrial property licenses as well as copyright authorizations have to be granted in writing.[12] But the courts while considering that in copyright authorizations the written form is only an evidential requirement[13], regarding licenses of industrial property the written form is a requirement of validity of the transactions.[14]

Concerning licenses of copyrighted software, the Software Copyright Act[15] seems to exclude, by argumentum *a contrario sensu,* the requirement of a written document for software licenses.[16] Moreover, there are no specific requirements for alternative licenses.

2.3. Alternative licenses as standard terms and conditions

Alternative licenses are considered standard terms and conditions for purposes of the Standard Terms Act[17], i.e. where they are drafted without previous individual negotiation and where they are submitted or accepted by indeterminate proponents or addressees,

---

[11] Civil Code, Article 219.

[12] Code of Industrial Property, Article 32(2); Code of Copyright, Article 41(2).

[13] Supreme Court of Justice, judgment of 14 March 2006, proc. 06B231 - www.dgsi.pt; Rebello 2002. For a (critical) review of Portuguese literature and case-law on this issue, Pereira 2008.

[14] More recently, Supreme Court of Justice, 5 May 2013, proc. 7860/06.0TBCSC.L1.S1 - www.dgsi.pt. On this issue, Marques 2008, 2011.

[15] Decree-Law No 252/94, Article 11(2). See eg Ascensão 1990 ; Pereira 2004 ; Pereira 2001c.

[16] Rocha 1994; Cordeiro 1994; Pereira 2001, 2011a; Trabuco 2008b; Bessa 2012.

[17] Decree-Law No 446/85 of 25 October (drafted after the German Act on general contract terms), last amended by Decree-Law No 323/2001 of 17 December (EC Directive 93/13 on unfair standard terms).

respectively; or where they are inserted by the proponent in individual contracts as 'take-it' or 'leave-it' terms[18].

The use of standard terms must comply with duties of full and previous communication to the adherent as well as the duty to inform him and to answer to his requests of reasonable clarification; otherwise such terms are excluded from the contract as 'surprise clauses'[19]. Moreover, as standard terms, the content of the clauses has to comply with the dark and grey lists of forbidden clauses which apply both to B2C and to B2B contracts. For ex., typical FOSS licenses usually contain disclaimers or terms of exclusion of liability which are absolutely prohibited such as terms excluding or limiting, directly or indirectly, liability for damages caused to life, moral or physical integrity or to the health of individuals.[20]

2.4. Drafting language

The Commercial Code[21] provides the principle of freedom of language for commercial contracts. Therefore, where they qualify as commercial contracts, typical FOSS licenses may be drafted in English language only.

However, concerning consumer contracts (B2C), the General Consumer Act[22] and the Portuguese Language Act[23] provide that

---

[18] Decree-Law No 446/85, Article 1(1)(2)

[19] Decree-Law No 446/85, Articles 5, 6 and 8.

[20] Decree-Law No 446/85, Article 18(a).

[21] Article 96 of Commercial Code (enacted by Royal Act of 28 June 1888 as later amended), Article 96.

[22] Law No 24/96 of 31 July (as last amended by Decree-Law No 47/2014 of 28 July), Article 7(3).

[23] Decree-Law No 238/86 of 19 August (as amended by Decree-Law No 42/88 of 9 February).

information on products as well as contracts must be in Portuguese. Therefore contracts with consumers in principle have to be drafted in Portuguese if they qualify as commercial regarding the other party to the contract (e.g. a professional salesman selling a car to a consumer).

2.5. Interpretation rules

There is a rule of restrictive interpretation of copyright authorizations (*in dubio pro auctore*) as copyright licenses are formal contracts and the written authorizations must mandatorily specify the authorized uses as well their conditions of time, place and price.[24] In formal contracts the declaration of will cannot provide a meaning which does not have a minimum of correspondence in the wording of the drafted document, even if imperfectly expressed, unless it corresponds to the actual intent of the parties and the reasons which justify the formalization of the contract do not prevent it.[25]

However, these rules of interpretation do not apply to licenses of copyrighted software, as such, because they are excluded from the requirement of written from.

2.6. Warranty and liability disclaimers

In accessing the validity of warranty and liability disclaimers it may be relevant whether the license grant depends upon monetary consideration. In B2B sale contracts there is a warranty of good

[24] Code of Copyright, Article 41(3).

[25] Civil Code, Article 238.

functionning, meaning that regardless of the seller's fault or the buyer's error, the seller has the obligation to repair or to replace the good sold.[26] In B2C onerous contracts (sale, lease, work, etc), consumers who acquire a good which is not in conformity with the contract have the mandatory rights to repairing or replacement of the good (1), adequate reduction of the price (2) or termination of the contract with just case (3).[27]

However, FOSS licenses are usually granted for free. They may be construed as contracts of loan for use (*comodatum*), because the licensor is temporarily lending the licensed goods for free.[28] Accordingly, the lender does not have to warrant the use of the good and he is not liable for any defects or limitations of the right or of the good, unless he assumes such liability or acts with the intent to damage the other party.[29]

On the other hand, as standard terms, disclaimers of warranty and liability are forbidden where they exclude or limit liability for damages caused to life, moral or physical integrity, or to a person's health, as well as liability for uneconomic damages caused to the other party or to third parties. Such clauses are also forbidden where they exclude or limit liability for absolute non-performance, delay or defective performance in case of intentional fault or gross negligence[30]. As absolutely forbidden unfair standard terms, such clauses are deemed null and void.[31]

---

[26] Civil Code, Article 921.

[27] Decree-Law No 67/2003 of 8 April - implements EC Directive on the sale of consumer goods and associated guarantees (1999/44/EC) -, as amended by Decree-Law No 84/2008 of 21 May.

[28] It might also be construed as a donation, where the license confers a perpetual right to use the software, including the right to assign it to a third party.

[29] Civil Code, Articles 1133(1) and 1134.

[30] Decree-Law No 446/85, Article 18(a)(b)(c). See Monteiro 2011.

[31] Decree-Law No 446/85, Article 12.

Moreover, despite the immaterial nature of software, there is a trend in literature to consider computer programs as products for purposes of the Product Liability Act: product lieability is mandatory as it cannot be excluded or limited towards the injured person; disclaimers are deemed unwritten.[32]

2.7. Termination clauses for non-compliance with the license

Parties are due to perform their obligations in good faith[33] complying with accessory duties of performance which arise thereof. The termination of contracts may be based upon a termination clause, including failure to comply with the terms of the license, i.e. breach of contract[34], unless mandatory rules provide otherwise (e.g. lack of payment of the price does not justify termination for breach of contract[35]).

As standard terms in B2C contracts, termination clauses for breach of contract might be considered null and void as grey standard clauses, where they provide one of the parties with the right to freely terminate the contract without reasonable notice.[36] However, in principle, non-compliance with the terms of the license provides fair justification for the termination of the contract, the user being deemed to act with fault as a debtor in the relationship.[37]

---

[32] Article 10 of Decree-Law No 383/89 of 6 November (as last amended by Decree-Law No 131/2001 of 24 April) which implements Council Directive on product liability (85/374/EEC).

[33] Civil Code, Article 762(2).

[34] Civil Code, Article 432(2).

[35] Civil Code, Article 886.

[36] Decree-Law No 446/85, Article 22(1)b.

[37] Civil Code, Article 799(1).

3. Copyright law issues

3.1. The right to use the program

Typical FOSS licenses grant a non-exclusive license to copy and distribute the program with or without modifications, and usually they do not include or mention the mere use of the program, per se.

The mere use of copyrighted works (e.g. reading a book, watching a movie, listening to music) is traditionally outside the scope of copyright protection. However, acts of permanent or transitory reproduction of copyrighted programs belong to the copyright holder, even if such acts are for private use.[38] Therefore, in principle, lawful use requires a license as the mere use of the computer programs involves acts of reproduction.[39]

The Software Copyright Act provides that the limitations to copyright as provided under Article 75 of the Code of Copyright apply *mutatis mutandis* to computer programs, and that the analysis of software for purposes of scientific research or teaching is free[40]. Private use, however, requires a license. In other words, it is possible to use a program without a license agreement for the analysis of software for purposes of scientific research or teaching as well as, *mutatis mutandis*, for other purposes permitted as free use under Article 75 of the Code of Copyright. Private use, however, requires a license, the scope of which includes mandatory minimal rights for the legitimate user.

---

[38] Decree-Law No 252/94, Article 5(a) and Article 10.

[39] Decree-Law No 252/94, Article 6.

[40] Decree-Law No 252/94, Article 10(1)(2).

3.2. The requirement of specification of authorized uses

The Software Copyright Act provides that software licenses are regulated by the general principles of contract law as well as by the special provisions of typical contracts (e.g. sale, lease) either by direct qualification or by analogy.[41]

Moreover, some provisions of the Code of Copyright are deemed applicable, such as Articles 40, 45 to 51, and 55[42]. A *contrario sensu*, Article 41 of the Copyright Act, which provides the general conditions of authorizations to use copyright works, does not apply to software. Such conditions are notably that authorizations have to be granted in writing and are presumed onerous and non-exclusive; moreover, they have to mandatorily specify the authorized use of divulgation, publication and utilization, as well as its conditions of time, place and price.

Instead of applying this regulation to software licenses the legislator provided methodological guidelines, including a general principle of interpretation for software contracts according to which contract terms are to be interpreted in accordance with good-faith and within the justified purpose of the contract, similarly to the German *Zweckübertragungslehre* in copyright contracts.[43]

It should be remarked, nonetheless, that the copyright protection of computer programs is limited to the exclusive rights granted by the Software Act. Making available to the public is not expressly provided for as a specific act of the exclusive right in the Software Copyright Act, which however provides for a right to put into circulation subject to exhaustion.[44] This right to put into circulation

[41] Decree-Law No 252/94, Article 11(1).

[42] Decree-Law No 252/94, Article 11(2).

[43] Decree-Law No 252/94, Article 11(3).

[44] Decree-Law No 252/94, Article 8(1)(2).

is intended to correspond to the right of distribution. It may be construed as comprehending the act of making available to the public, subject nonetheless to exhaustion concerning the resale of the licenses.[45] As for sub-licenses, customers acquire rights under the applicable FOSS license and a grant of sub-licenses by the distributors is only possible provided it is allowed by the right holder.

3.3. Unknown manners of using the program

Under general copyright law unknown manners of using a work are included in copyright protection, but they cannot be covered by the authorization or license, because this has to specify the authorized uses.

However, the specification requirement does not apply to computer programs. Therefore, manners of using a computer program that are unknown at the time of the license grant may be covered by the license where, according to the mentioned interpretative principle, it shall be in accordance with good-faith and within the justified purpose of the contract[46] and provided that such new manners of using a work imply acts protected by copyright (e.g. reproduction, distribution or transformation).

---

[45] According to the European Court of Justice, judgment of 3 July 2012 (C-128/11, UsedSoft GmbH v Oracle International Corp), 'Articles 4(2) and 5(1) of Directive 2009/24 must be interpreted as meaning that, in the event of the resale of a user licence entailing the resale of a copy of a computer program downloaded from the copyright holder's website, that licence having originally been granted by that rightholder to the first acquirer for an unlimited period in return for payment of a fee intended to enable the rightholder to obtain a remuneration corresponding to the economic value of that copy of his work, the second acquirer of the licence, as well as any subsequent acquirer of it, will be able to rely on the exhaustion of the distribution right under Article 4(2) of that directive, and hence be regarded as lawful acquirers of a copy of a computer program within the meaning of Article 5(1) of that directive and benefit from the right of reproduction provided for in that provision.'

[46] Decree-Law No 252/94, Article 11(3).

3.4. Copyright revocation or rescission rights applicable to FOSS licenses

Authors of published works have the right to withdrawal (*direito de retirada*), i.e. the author can withdraw his work at any time from circulation and to put an end to its use, in any way it takes place, provided he has justified moral reasons and also compensates interested parties for damages they suffered because of the withdrawal.[47] This is one of the moral rights recognized under Portuguese law to authors of original works for their intellectual creations.

However, the protection of moral rights concerning authors of computer programs is a disputed legal issue. In particular, the application of the right to withdrawal in the field of software would be a non-sense.[48] Under the Software Copyright Act, authors of computer programs might only claim the right to identification of authorship and to paternity.[49] However, based upon different legal opinion[50], the Supreme Court of Justice considers that the protection of moral rights of authors of computer programs is not limited to the provisions of the Software Act and must comply with the principle to protect computer programs as literary works in the meaning of the Berne Convention.[51]

3.5. Statutory right for equitable remuneration

Authors have a statutory right for equitable remuneration under the copyright legislation of Portugal. Notwithstanding the special

---

[47] Copyright Act, Article 62.

[48] See Ascensão 1990, 1992; Cordeiro 1994; Rocha & Cordeiro 1995.

[49] Decree-Law No 252/94, Article 9.

[50] Vieira 1999, 2005; Pereira 2001; Marques & Martins 2006; Saavedra 1998.

[51] Judgment of 29 November 2012, Proc. 957/03.0TBCBR.C2.S1 - www.dgsi.pt

rules of authorship in computer programs (typical of corporate copyright), a special right of remuneration is conferred to the intellectual creator, where the intellectual creation clearly exceeds the performance of the task he has been committed to and/or where the work is used for or advantages are taken from which have not been included nor provided for within the agreed remuneration.[52]

However, the fact that FOSS licenses are granted for free arguably excludes this special remuneration. However, just because authors authorize that their copyrighted works may be used for free it should not be construed as an implied waiving of their special equitable claim to have a share in exceptional economic exploitations of their works by third parties.

3.6. Alternative licensing models and distribution of revenues by collecting societies

Participation in the distribution of revenues by collecting societies requires in principle compliance with their terms of service. Usually these include a term of non-competition, meaning that the author shall refrain from any act which may cause damage to the collecting society, including the licensing of works for free or in accordance with alternative licensing models (e.g. under Creative Commons).[53] According to the policy of the main collecting society in Portugal authors should inform whether they have permitted the use of their works under CC licenses, otherwise copyright will be enforced by the collecting society.[54]

---

[52] Decree-Law No 252/94, Article 3(4), and Code of Copyright, Article 14(4).

[53] See, for example, the registration form of the Portuguese Society of Authors (SPA) available at http://www.spautores.pt/assets_live/252/inscri_o.pdf

[54] http://www.spautores.pt/perguntas-frequentes/servico-juridicos

However, this is a matter of breach of contract, i.e. a problem between the author and the collecting society, the author remaining the copyright holder despite joining a collecting society. There are however uses under CC licenses which prevent users from any commercial use and therefore require authorization

Authors who grant licenses in accordance with an alternative licensing model will in principle be excluded from compensatory remuneration for private copying. Levies are designed to compensate damages suffered by copyright holders due to private copy as a statutory free use and not as use licensed by copyright holders. Under typical alternative licensing models private use is granted for free, and therefore the rational of levies does not apply.[55] In any case, under Portuguese law, compensation for private copying is statutorily excluded for computer programs and electronic databases.[56]

3.7. The moral right of integrity

Despite alternative licenses permit licensees to modify the work and to distribute adaptations, the author may still prohibit changes to the work that offend his moral rights. Under Portuguese copyright law the author's moral right of integrity cannot be waived from nor renounced to[57]. The purpose of this moral right, which is deemed a personality right, is to protect the honor and reputation of the author as intellectual creator of the work.

---

[55] Shortly, levies apply to statutory lawful uses, not to unlawful use or lawful use by agreement –European Court of Justice, judgment of 10 April 2014 (C435/12, ACI Adam v. Thuiskopie – cvria.eu).

[56] Law No 62/98 of 1 September (last amended by Law No 49/2015 of 5 June), Article 1(2).

[57] Code of Copyright, Article 56.

In the field of software authorship, the Software Copyright Act does not provide the moral right of integrity. In line with Directive 91/250 on the legal protection of computer programs (replaced by Directive 2009/24), transformation is deemed a pure economic right.[58]. The Software Act provides that Article 15(2) of the Code of Copyright does not apply to computer programs.[59] According to this provision, modification to the work requires express consent of its creator and can only be carried out as agreed. There is however a judgment of the Supreme Court of Justice holding that the silence of the Software Copyright Act concerning moral rights does not prevent the Courts from recognizing basic moral rights to software creators, as computer programs are deemed literary works in the meaning of the Berne Convention.[60] This judgment comes in line with our proposal of interpretation submitted in *Copyright and Freedom of Information*.[61]

3.8. Remedies for non-compliance with the license

The Code of Copyright provides several remedies, notably *interim measures* to prevent further infringement and compulsory penalties as well as compensation for damages, including moral damages.[62] Arguably the licensor might claim damages even though the license has been granted for free if a regular license under different terms would be granted in exchange for consideration.

---

[58] Decree-Law No 252/94, Article 5(a).

[59] Decree-Law No 252/94, Article 3(5).

[60] Supreme Court of Justice, judgment of 29 November 2012, proc. 957/03.0TBCBR.C2.S1 - dgsi.pt.

[61] Pereira 2008.

[62] Code of Copyright, Article 210-G and Article 211.

4. FOSS and competition law

The domestic legal framework, consisting basically of cartels, abuse of dominant position and merger control, is provided by the Portuguese Competition Act.[63] The relation between intellectual property rights and competition law usually concerns abuse of a dominant position by the holder of the intellectual property right, notably the copyright owner in computer software.[64] By contrast, FLOSS and other alternative licenses usually serve a pro-competition purpose which is to enable competitors to write compatible code, to fix bugs or to introduce new functionalities in existing programs, i.e. to update software.

However, *copyleft* provisions may also be deemed anti-competitive as abuse of dominant position, if they impose legal constraints on the licensee's freedom to dispose of its innovations. Under Portuguese competition law, which is drafted and interpreted in conformity with EU law (including case-law), an undertaking holding a dominant position may be tempted to abuse its position by keeping competitors out of the market. A practice is prohibited where several criteria are met.[65]

To begin with, the undertaking enjoys a dominant position on the market, i.e. it is capable of behaving independently from its competitors and customers in the relevant market. An undertaking holds a dominant position where its economic power enables it to operate on the market without caring for the reaction of its competitors or final consumers. In appraising a firm's economic power, it is taken into account its market share and other factors such as whether there are credible competitors, the firm has its own distribution network or

---

[63] Law No 19/2012 of 8 May.

[64] Trabuco 2008a; Pereira 2011b, 2014.

[65] Law No 19/2012, Article 11.

favorable access to raw materials, etc. The dominance of a company is evaluated with regard to various elements. The reference to the market share of the company for a specific product is a determinant element as well as a company owning products which are not interchangeable with other products on the market. Holding a technical advantage to lead a product development, or the ownership of an intellectual property right might be an important factor to establishing dominance even if they are not sufficient in themselves.

Secondly, the undertaking abuses of its dominant position on the relevant market in order to impose unfair and abusive conditions. Holding a dominant position is not wrong in itself if it is the result of the firm's own effectiveness. But if the undertaking exploits this power to stifle competition, this is an anti-competitive practice which constitutes abuse. Abuse of dominant position can be illustrated by several examples, such as, abuses on pricing, fidelity rebates, abuse of intellectual property rights, and tying clauses. Other types of abuse, which is an open concept, include the imposition of discriminatory and unfair conditions by the dominant company to any categories of users or any other company having contractual relationships with the dominant company.

The imposition of *copyleft* provisions to business partners by undertakings holding a dominant position may lead to an abuse of dominance where it has or is likely to have a market destructive or closing effect on the products of other undertakings.

5. Public procurement

The Open Standards Act[66] established the adoption of open standards for digital information in Public Administration with a view

[66] Law No 36/2011 of 21 June.

to promoting technological freedom of citizens and organizations and the interoperability of computer systems in the government. Acts of public procurement excluding open standards are, with few exceptions, invalid.[67]

In fact, the Open Standards Act has a provision on public contracts, according to which "it is null and without effect any act of contracting promoted by the Public Administration which provides the exclusion of open standards, as established in the Regulation"[68], i.e. the National Regulation of Digital Interoperability.[69] This special provision complements the regulation of public procurement provided for by the Code of Public Contracts.[70]

References

1. Legislation and Case-law

Code of Copyright - Código do Direito de Autor e dos Direitos Conexos (CDADC), enacted by Decree-Law No 63/85 of March 1985, as last amended by Law No 32/2015 of 24 April

Code of Industrial Property - Código da Propriedade Industrial (CPI), enacted by Decree-Law No 36/2003 of 5 March, as last amended by Law No 46/2011 of 24 June

Code of Public Contracts - Decree-Law No 18/2008 of 29 January, as last amended by Decree-Law No 149/2012 of 12 July

Competition Act - Law No 19/2012 of 8 May

Consumer Protection Act - Law No 24/96 of 31 July, as last amended by as last amended by Decree-Law No 47/2014 of 28 July

Copyright Databases Act -Decree-Law No 122/2000 of 4 July

[67] Pereira 2012.

[68] Law No 36/2011, Article 9.

[69] Decision of the Council of Ministers No 91/2012 of 8 November.

[70] Enacted by Decree-Law No 18/2008 of 29 January, as last amended by Decree-Law No 149/2012 of 12 July.

Copyright Levies Act- Law No 62/98 of 1 September, as last amended by Law No 49/2015 of 5 June

Copyright Software Act - Decree-Law No 252/94 of 20 October, later amended

European Court of Justice, judgment of 10 April 2014, C435/12, ACI Adam v. Thuiskopie, www.cvria.eu

European Court of Justice, judgment of 3 July 2012, C-128/11, UsedSoft GmbH v Oracle International Corp- www.cvria.eu

European Union (2009) Directive 2009/24/EC of the European Parliament and of the Council of 23 April 2009 on the legal protection of computer programs, OJ L 111, 5.5.2009, p. 16–22

Guarantees in Sale of Consumer Goods- Decree-Law No 67/2003 of 8 April, as amended by Decree-Law No 84/2008 of 21 May

Language Act - Decree-Law No 238/86 of 19 August, as amended by Decree-Law No 42/88 of 9 February

Open Standards Act - Law No 36/2011 of 21 June

Portuguese Civil Code (1966)

Portuguese Commercial Code (Royal Act of 28 June 1888)

Product Liability Act - Decree-Law No 383/89 of 6 November, as last amended by Decree-Law No 131/2001 of 24 April

Regulation of Open Standards - Decision of the Council of Ministers No 91/2012 of 8 November.

Supreme Court of Justice, 5 May 2013, proc. 786%6.0TBCSC.L1.S1 – www.dgsi.

Supreme Court of Justice, judgment of 14 March 2006, proc. 06B231 – www.dgsi.pt

Supreme Court of Justice, judgment of 29 November 2012, Proc. 957/03.0TBCBR. C2.S1 - www.dgsi.pt

Supreme Court of Justice, 5 May 2013, proc. 786%6.0TBCSC.L1.S1 – www.dgsi.pt

Unfair Standard Terms Act - Decree-Law No 446/85 of 25 October, as last amended by Decree-Law No 323/2001 of 17 December

2. Literature

Almeida, CF de, Gonçalves, LC, Trabuco, C (Eds.), Contratos de Direito de Autor e de Direito Industrial (Coimbra, Almedina).

Ascensão, JO (1990) 'A protecção jurídica dos programas de computador', 50 Revista da Ordem dos Advogados, Vol. I, 69-118

Ascensão, JO (1992) Direito Civil – Direito de Autor e Direitos Conexos (Coimbra, Coimbra Editora)

Ascensão, JO (2011) 'A «Licença» no Direito Intelectual'. Almeida, CF de, Gonçalves, LC, Trabuco, C (Eds.) Contratos de Direito de Autor e de Direito Industrial, 93-112 (Coimbra: Almedina)

Bessa, T (2012) 'Direito Contratual de Autor e Licenças de Exploração da Obra', 72 Revista da Ordem dos Advogados, IV, 1129-1246

Cordeiro, P.C. (1994) 'A lei portuguesa do «software»', 54 Revista da Ordem dos Advogados , II, 714-735

European Commission (2007), European Union Public License- EUPL v.1.1 (Bruxelas: IDABC)- (http://ec.europa.eu/idabc/eupl.html

Leitão, L.M.T.M. (2011) Direito de Autor (Coimbra, Almedina).

Marques, J.P.R (2008) As licenças (voluntárias e obrigatórias) de direitos de propriedade industrial (Coimbra, Almedina).

Marques, JPR (2011) 'Contrato de Licença de Patente'. Almeida, CF de, Gonçalves, L.C., Trabuco, C. (Eds.), Contratos de Direito de Autor e de Direito Industrial, 395-454 (Coimbra, Almedina).

Martins, L, Marques, G (2006) Direito da Informática (2.ª, Coimbra, Almedina).

Monteiro, AP (2011) Cláusulas limitativas e de exclusão de responsabilidade civil (2nd reprint, Coimbra, Almedina)

Pereira, ALD (1999) 'Programas de computador, sistemas informáticos e comunicações electrónicas: alguns aspectos jurídico-contratuais', 59 Revista da Ordem dos Advogados, III, 915-1000

Pereira, ALD (2001) Informática, direito de autor e propriedade tecnodigital (Coimbra, Coimbra Editora).

Pereira, ALD (2004) 'Software: sentido e limites da sua apropriação jurídica', Direito da Internet e da Informática, 73-136 (Coimbra, Coimbra Editora).

Pereira, ALD (2008) Direitos de Autor e Liberdade de Informação (Coimbra, Almedina).

Pereira, AL.D (2011a) 'Licenças de software e bases de dados', 110 Revista da ABPI – Associação Brasileira da Propriedade Intelectual, 23-32

Pereira, ALD (2011b) 'Software Interoperability, Intellectual Property and Competition Law: Compulsory Licenses for Abuse of Market Dominance'. 27 Computer Law & Security Review, 175-179

Pereira, ALD (2011c) 'Patentes de programas de computador e métodos de negociação na Internet'. In Ascensão, JO (ed.) Direito da Sociedade da Informação, IX, 111-123 (Coimbra, Coimbra Editora).

Pereira, ALD (2012) 'Normas abertas nos sistemas informáticos do Estado', 29 Revista do CEDOUA, 39-43.

Pereira, ALD (2014) 'Descompilação e direitos do utente de programas de computador', 2 Revista de Direito Intelectual, II, 95-122

Rebello, LF (2002) Código do Direito de Autor e dos Direitos Conexos – Anotado (2.ª ed. Lisboa, Âncora).

Rocha, ML (1994) 'Contratos de licença de utilização e contratos de encomenda de «software»'. Num Novo Mundo do Direito de Autor?, II, 695 (Lisboa: Cosmos/ Arco-Íris)

Rocha, ML, Cordeiro, P (1995) A protecção jurídica do software (2.ª ed. Lisboa, Cosmos).

Saavedra, R (1998) A protecção jurídica do software e a Internet (Lisboa, D.Quixote).

Trabuco, C (2008) 'A interoperabilidade entre o Direito de Autor e o Direito da Concorrência (Ac. do TPI de 17.09.2007, Proc. T- 201/04 - Microsoft Corp. v Commission of the European Communities)'. 21 Cadernos de Direito Privado, 28

Trabuco, C (2008) 'O direito de autor e as licenças de utilização sobre programas de computador: o contributo dos contratos para compreensão do direito' , 15 Themis, 139

Vieira, JA (2005) A protecção dos programas de computador pelo direito de autor (Lisboa, Lex)

Vieira, JAC (1999) 'Notas gerais sobre a protecção dos programas de computador em Portugal'. Direito da Sociedade da Informação, I (Coimbra, Coimbra Editora).

INTELLECTUAL PROPERTY, INTERNATIONAL JURISDICTION AND APPLICABLE LAW IN PORTUGAL*

Abstract - This paper corresponds to the Portuguese National Report on Jurisdiction and Applicable Law in Matters of Intellectual Property to the XVIII International Congress of Comparative Law, presented by the Academie Internationale de Droit Comparé / International Academy of Comparative Law and the American Society of Comparative Law, and hosted by the American University Washington College of Law, George Washington University Law School and Georgetown University Law Center (Washington D.C., July 25 to August 1, 2010). Structured upon the questionnaire submitted by the General Reporter, Prof. Toshiyuki Kono, this Report provides a general overview of the basic features of Portuguese law as it relates to cross-border enforcement of intellectual property rights, including the international and domestic legal sources concerning how intellectual property issues are addressed in the domestic statutes and what intellectual property rights can be granted, as well as the institutional (administrative/judicial) competence to apply them in the areas of intellectual

---

* *Intellectual Property and Private International Law – Comparative Perspectives*, ed. Toshiyuki Kono, p. 877-939, 2012, Hart Publishing, an imprint of Bloomsbury Publishing Plc.

property law. In particular, it provides an overview of Portuguese Industrial Property and Copyright Law as well as the legal framework laid down by Council Regulations Brussels I (on jurisdiction and the recognition and enforcement of judgments in civil and commercial matters and) and Rome I and II concerning conflict of laws regarding torts, contracts and transfer of rights. In Part II of this Report some hypothetical cases are dealt with in order to exemplify how intellectual property issues are addressed in conflict-of-law provisions and rules determining international jurisdiction in Portuguese law.

I. Sources and principles of intellectual property and jurisdiction in Portuguese law

1. Intellectual property

Intellectual property (*propriedade intelectual*), including authors' rights (copyright) and industrial property, is referred to in Article 1303 of the Portuguese Civil Code (*Código Civil Português*) as special kind of property regulated under special legislation, which consists of two main instruments.

On one hand, the Code of Industrial Property (Código da Propriedade Industrial)[1] , concerning patents and utility models, integrated circuits, models and designs, marks, logotypes (names and brands), rewards, denominations of origin and geographical indications, and unfair competition including the protection of undisclosed information.

---

[1] Approved by Decree-Law 36/2003 of 5 March, and as last amended by Decree-Law 52/2008 of 28 August.

On the other hand, the Code of Author's Right and Related Rights (Código do Direito de Autor e dos Direitos Conexos[2]) - *brevis causa* Copyright Act -, concerning artistic and literary works and performances of artists, sound/video recordings, and broadcasts; the regulation of copyright is complemented by specific legislation concerning namely certain categories of works (computer programs[3] and databases[4]), specific rights (rental and public lending[5], satellite broadcasting and cable retransmission[6]), copyright levies[7], or copyright collecting societies[8].

Portuguese intellectual property legislation implements several international treaties, in particular WIPO-Administered Treaties[9], ratified by Portugal as well as several Community instruments to which Portugal is bound as a Member State of the European Union.

Portugal has ratified several international treaties on intellectual property, such as: The Paris Convention for the Protection of Industrial Property (1883), as revised by the Stockholm Act (1967); The Berne Convention for the Protection of Literary and Artistic Works (1886), as revised by the Paris Act (1971); The International Convention for the Protection of Performers, Producers of Phonograms and Broadcasting Organizations, adopted at Rome on 26 October 1961 (Rome Convention); The European Patent Convention, signed at Munich on 5 October 1973 (revised in 2000); The Agreement on Trade-Related Aspects of Intellectual Property Rights (TRIPS 1994).

---

[2] Approved by Decree-Law 63/85 of March 1985, and as last amended by Law 16/2008 of 1 April.

[3] Decree-Law 252/94 of 20 October.

[4] Decree-Law 122/2000 of 4 July.

[5] Decree-Law 332/97 of 27 November.

[6] Decree 333/97 of 27 November.

[7] Decree-Law 62/98 of 1 September.

[8] Law 83/2001 of 3 August.

[9] http://www.wipo.int/treaties/en/.

Other international treaties include: The Patent Cooperation Treaty (1970); The Copyright Universal Convention (1952); The Budapest Treaty on international recognition of the deposit of microorganisms for purposes of the proceedings in matters of patents (1977, revised in 1980); The Treaty on Intellectual Property in Respect of Integrated Circuits, adopted at Washington on 26 May 1989 (Washington Treaty); The Hague Agreement on international deposit of industrial designs (1925, as revised in 1999); The Madrid Agreement on international registration of trademarks (1891, as revised in 1979); The Nice Agreement on the international classification of products and services in relation to trademarks (1957, as revised in 1977); Madrid Agreement for the Repression of False or Deceptive Indications of Source on Goods (1891); The Lisbon Agreement on the protection of denominations of origin and their international registration (1958, as revised in 1979); The International Convention for the Protection of Vegetable Products (1961, as revised in 1991).

Moreover, as a Member State of the European Union, Portugal is bound to the intellectual property related provisions of the Treaty of Rome as well as to the instruments of Community legislation[10] and the judgments given by the European courts over matters of intellectual property law covered by Community law[11].

As far as *industrial property* is concerned, Community law has not only harmonized the domestic legislation of the Member States but it has also established unitary Community rights.

Instruments of harmonization include: Council Directive 87/54/EEC of 16 December 1986 on the legal protection of topographies of semiconductor products *(OJ L 24, 27.1.1987, p. 36–40);* Directive 2008/95/EC of the European Parliament and of the Council of 22 October 2008 to approximate the laws of the Member States relating

[10] http://ec.europa.eu/internal_market/top_layer/index_52_en.htm.

[11] http://curia.europa.eu/jcms/jcms/j_6/.

to trade marks *(OJ L 299, 8.11.2008, p. 25–33, which repealed* Council Directive 89/104/EEC of 21 December 1988); Directive 98/44/EC of the European Parliament and of the Council of 6 July 1998 on the legal protection of biotechnological inventions *(OJ L 213, 30.7.1998, p. 13–21);* Directive 98/71/EC of the European Parliament and of the Council of 13 October 1998 on the legal protection of designs *(OJ L 289, 28.10.1998, p. 28–35);*

Instruments that create ***unitary Community rights*** are: Council Regulation (EC) No 2100/94 of 27 July 1994 on Community plant variety rights *(OJ L 227, 1.9.1994, p. 1–30) (as last amended by* Council Regulation (EC) No 15/2008 of 20 December 2007); Regulation (EC) No 1610/96 of the European Parliament and of the Council of 23 July 1996 concerning the creation of a supplementary protection certificate for plant protection products *(OJ L 198, 8.8.1996, p. 30–35);* Council Regulation (EC) No 6/2002 of 12 December 2001 on Community designs *(OJ L 3, 5.1.2002, p. 1–24);* Council Regulation (EC) No 207/2009 of 26 February 2009 on the Community trade mark *(OJ L 78, 24.3.2009, p. 1–42, which repealed* Council Regulation (EC) No 40/94, OJ L 11, 14.1.1994, p. 1). A proposal of Council Regulation on Community patent is under discussion[12].

As for *copyright and related rights*, several Community instruments of harmonization have been adopted, such as: Directive 2009/24/EC of the European Parliament and of the Council of 23 April 2009 on the legal protection of computer programs *(OJ L 111, 5.5.2009, p. 16–22, which repealed* Council Directive 91/250/EEC of 14 May 1991 on the legal protection of computer programs, OJ L 122, 17.5.1991, p. 42, as amended by Directive 93/98/EEC); Council Directive 93/83/EEC of 27 September 1993 on the coordination of certain rules concerning copyright and rights related to copyright applicable to satellite broadcasting and cable retransmission *(OJ L 248,*

[12] http://ec.europa.eu/internal_market/indprop/patent/index_en.htm.

6.10.1993, p. 15–21); Directive 96/9/EC of the European Parliament and of the Council of 11 March 1996 on the legal protection of databases *(OJ L 77, 27.3.1996, p. 20–28);* Directive 2001/29/EC of the European Parliament and of the Council of 22 May 2001 on the harmonization of certain aspects of copyright and related rights in the information society *(OJ L 167, 22.6.2001, p. 10–19);* Directive 2001/84/EC of the European Parliament and of the Council of 27 September 2001 on the resale right for the benefit of the author of an original work of art *(OJ L 272, 13.10.2001, p. 32–36);* Directive 2006/115/EC of the European Parliament and of the Council of 12 December 2006 on rental right and lending right and on certain rights related to copyright in the field of intellectual property *(OJ L 376, 27.12.2006, p. 28–35, which repealed* Council Directive 92/100/EEC, OJ L 346, 27.11.1992, p. 61, Council Directive 93/98/EEC, OJ L 290, 24.11.1993, p. 9, Article 11(2), and Directive 2001/29/EC of the European Parliament and of the Council, OJ L 167, 22.6.2001, p. 10, Article 11(1)); Directive 2006/116/EC of the European Parliament and of the Council of 12 December 2006 on the term of protection of copyright and certain related rights *(OJ L 372, 27.12.2006, p. 12–18, which repealed* Directive Council Directive 93/98/EEC, OJ L 290, 24.11.1993, p. 9).

A common Community instrument of harmonization has been adopted for both industrial property and copyright and related rights: Directive 2004/48/EC of the European Parliament and of the Council of 29 April 2004 on the *enforcement* of intellectual property rights *(OJ L 157, 30.4.2004, p. 45–86).*

Finally, other Community instruments of harmonization have an impact on intellectual property rights, notably Directive 2000/31/EC of the European Parliament and of the Council of 8 June 2000 on certain legal aspects of information society services, in particular electronic commerce, in the Internal Market (Directive on electronic commerce) (OJ L 178, 17.7.2000, p. 1).

2. Industrial property and copyright

Portuguese *industrial property* is codified in the 2003 Code of Industrial Property (hereinafter, CPI). Industrial property confers exclusive rights over patents, utility models and designs, trademarks, logotypes (brand names and insignia), rewards, denominations of origin and geographical indications. Moreover, the Code of Industrial Property provides for the regulation of unfair competition (including the protection of undisclosed information), which is complemented by the regulation of unfair business-to-consumer commercial practices[13].

Industrial property rights in patents, utility models, topographies of semiconductors, models and designs, and trademarks can be, in whole or in part, transmitted or licensed by contract concluded in writing (Arts. 31 and 32 CPI). These rights have to be applied for at the *Instituto Nacional da Propriedade Industrial* (Industrial Property Office) which issues a title of industrial property in case the requirements of attribution are met. Most industrial property rights are subject to the Community exhaustion (Arts. 103, 146, 166, 205, 259 CPI).

Infringements to industrial property rights are deemed criminal offenses (Arts. 321 to 330 CPI) and, as required by international treaties and Community legislation, the Code of Industrial Property lays down special enforcement provisions concerning namely collecting and preserving evidences and provisional measures (Arts. 308-C to 338-J CPI).

---

[13] Decree-Law 57/2008 of 26 March, which implements Directive 2005/29/EC of the European Parliament and of the Council of 11 May 2005 concerning unfair business-to-consumer commercial practices in the internal market and amending Council Directive 84/450/EEC, Directives 97/7/EC, 98/27/EC and 2002/65/EC of the European Parliament and of the Council and Regulation (EC) No 2006/2004 of the European Parliament and of the Council ('Unfair Commercial Practices Directive'), OJ L 149, 11.6.2005, p. 22–39.

Patents, models and designs

Patents are granted to protect inventions of products or processes, in all fields of technology, provided they are new to the state of the art, non-obvious ("involve an inventive step") and capable of industrial application; discoveries, scientific theories, mathematical methods and computer programs as such, as well as human cloning processes, cannot be patented (Arts. 51 et seq. CPI).

The right to patent an invention belongs to the inventor or inventors (Art. 58 CPI). In case the invention is done by an employee in the course of his contract, the right to patent belongs to the employer and the employee is entitled to remuneration in case it is not established in the contract (Art. 59(1) (2) CPI). The same applies to inventions made for hire by independent contractors (Art. 59(7) CPI). The inventor cannot waive his rights and he is entitled to be mentioned in the patent application and title (Arts. 59(9) and 60 CPI).

Patents have to be applied for at the *Instituto Nacional da Propriedade Industrial* (Industrial Property Office) and follow specific procedures: national, European, or the Patent Cooperation Treaty (Arts. 61 to 96 CPI). The Industrial Property Office issues a patent document, which describes the invention and entitles the patent holder for a non-renewable period of 20 years with an **exclusive right** of economic exploitation of the patent, including a bundle of rights to make, use, sale, and import, with the exception of certain acts such as namely private use without commercial purposes and acts for experimental purposes (Arts. 99, 101 and 102 CPI). Patent holders are required to explore the patent invention and under certain circumstances they are subject to compulsory licenses (Arts. 106, 110 and 111 CPI).

For patented medicinal products and plant protection products a supplementary protection certificate can be issued, which is to be applied for at the Industrial Property Office (Art. 115 et seq CPI; see also notably Council Regulation (EEC) No 1768/92 of 18 June

1992, as amended by Regulation (EC) No 1901/2006 of the European Parliament and of the Council of 12 December 2006 on medicinal products for paediatric use, and Regulation (EC) No 1610/96 of the European Parliament and of the Council of 23 July 1996).

Moreover, the protection of *utility models* follows closely the regulation of patents (Arts. 117 to 152 CPI). The term of protection is however limited to 6 years, which can be extended twice for periods of two years provided it does not exceed an overall 10 years term of protection (Art. 142 CPI). A more *sui generis* right concerning requirements of protection is provided for topographies of semiconductor products (Art. 155 CPI), but for most of the regulation patent provisions apply. However, the term of protection is limited to 10 or 15 years, depending on the circumstances (Art. 172 CPI).

Models and designs are the ornamental aspect of a useful article which may be constituted by elements which are three-dimensional (the shape of the article) or two-dimensional (lines, designs, colours) provided that they are not dictated solely or essentially by technical or functional considerations (Arts. 173 and 176 CPI). To be eligible for industrial property protection, industrial designs must be original or novel and must be registered at the Instituto Nacional da Propriedade Industrial (INPI) according to a certain application procedure (Arts. 184 ff. CPI). In case protection of an industrial design is granted, any person without consent of the right owner may not, for a period of 5 to 25 years, make, sell or import, or store for such purposes, articles bearing or embodying a design which is a copy, or substantially a copy, of the protected design, when such acts are undertaken for commercial purposes (Art. 201, 203 and 204 CPI).

Distinctive signs (marks, logotypes, rewards, denominations of origin and geographical indications)

Marks are signs (e.g. emblems), or combinations of signs (e.g. combinations of colours), capable of graphic representation, which can be protected if they are capable of distinguishing the goods or services of one undertaking from those of other undertakings (Art. 222 CPI). Certain elements, such as signs or indications that have become customary in current language, cannot be granted an exclusive use, unless the signs have acquired *distinctive character* in commercial practice (Art. 223(1) (2) CPI).

In general, effective protection requires registry of the mark at the Industrial Property Office according to the registration procedure (Arts. 233 ff. CPI). However, well-known and prestige unregistered trademarks also enjoy some protection (Arts. 241 and 242 CPI).

Moreover, to be registered a mark must comply with certain principles, such as veracity and distinctive capacity of the signs. Registration is made in respect of specified goods or services and therefore it will be refused if, e.g., the sign is deceptive or misleading, meaning that it is likely to mislead the public, namely with respect to the nature, qualities, usefulness or geographical origin of the product or service for which the trademark is to be used (Art. 238(4)(d) CPI). Moreover, despite registration is made in respect of specified products or services (the so-called 'princípio da especialidade'), it shall be denied in case the mark is equal or similar to a mark of prestige for different products or services where the new mark would take advantage of, or cause damage to, the distinctive power or prestige of such mark of prestige (Art. 242 CPI).

Registration of a mark confers to the mark owner the exclusive property right concerning the products or services to which the mark has been registered (Art. 224(1) CPI). The owner of the registered mark has the right to prohibit any other person from using an identical or similar mark in economical activities for identical or related products to those for which the mark has been registered, and that by virtue of such similitude between the signs or the products may lead to confusion or association in the minds of the public (Art. 258 CPI).

The exclusive right meets several limitations, namely the rule of exhaustion within the European economic area, as well as certain uses for informative purposes (Arts. 259 and 260 CPI).

Registration lasts for 10 years and may be renewed without limit for equal periods (Art. 255 CPI). Nonetheless, mark registration can be extinguished on grounds of nullity, preclusion, or caducity. Grounds of caducity include namely non serious use of the mark, or where the mark becomes generic or deceptive (Art. 269(1)((2) CPI).

Rewards are any prizes or demonstrations of preference with official origin (Art. 271 CPI). They can only be used for the products or services to which they have been conferred (Art. 272 CPI). In order to obtain a reward property right, a procedure is provided for (Arts. 274 to 277 CPI).

Moreover, the regulation of *brand names and insignia* has been unified under the designation *logotypes*. Logotypes can be composed of a sign or a combination of signs, namely nominative or figurative elements, or a combination thereof, provided they are capable of graphic representation. To be protected logotypes have to be adequate to distinguish an entity that provides services or trades products (Art. 304-A CPI), and have to follow a certain registration procedure (Arts. 304-D *et seq.* CPI). Several grounds of refusal of registration are provided for, such as namely where a logotype contains or offends symbols of the State, or uses deceptive signs concerning the activity of the applicant (Art. 304-H (3) CPI). Similar to marks, logotype registration lasts for 10 years and may be renewed without limit for equal periods (Art. 304-L CPI). The owner of the logotype right can prevent any person from using without his consent any identical or confusable sign which is a reproduction or imitation of his logotype (Art. 304-N CPI).

Denominations of origin and geographical indications are the names of a region, a place or even a country used to designate or identity a product from which it originates; where registered, denominations of origin and geographical indications are a common property of the people of such place and can be used with the authorisation of the registration holders by those who make the products in such place (Art. 305 CPI). A registration procedure is to be observed (Arts. 307 ff. CPI). Protection is not limited in time and in general it confers the exclusive right of economic exploitation of the denominations of origin or geographical indications (Art. 312 CPI). Registration can be extinguished by several causes, namely nullity or caducity (e.g. in case the denomination becomes a mere generic designation of a production system or certain type of products – Art. 315(1) CPI).

Unfair competition

The Code of Industrial Property also provides for the prohibition of unfair competition in a *general clause* comprehending any act of competition that is against the norms and honest usages of any economic activity (Art. 317 CPI). This general clause is illustrated by several typical acts of competition that are deemed to be, in certain circumstances, unfair competition, such as acts of confusion, misleading advertising, wrongful comparisons, and parasitism. The protection of undisclosed information is included within the framework of unfair competition (Art. 318 CPI). Unfair competition law does not grant an *erga omnes* exclusive right as it is opposable only to economic operators within the so-called relevant market.

Copyright and related rights

Portuguese copyright law belongs to the Civil Law family of *droit d'auteur* countries[14]. Portuguese copyright law is codified in the 1985 Copyright Act (*Código do Direito de Autor e dos Direitos*

[14] See A.L.D. Pereira, *Direitos de Autor e Liberdade de Informação,* Coimbra, Almedina, 2008, pp. 240 ff.

Conexos, hereinafter CDA), which implements the Berne principles of national treatment (prohibition of discrimination on grounds of nationality of authors), minimum standard of protection (minimal rights), and automatic protection regardless of formalities and regardless of protection in the country of origin (independence). This Code is the centerpiece of a web of Portuguese legislation on copyright.

Portuguese copyright law protects *original works*, i.e., intellectual creations in literary or artistic fields expressed in any perceptible form, regardless of their purpose or merits (Art. 1(1) CDA). *Originality* is the basis of protection. A work is considered original if it results of the author's own creative effort and not merely the appropriation of another person's creation. The normative concept of protected works is illustrated by an open catalogue of examples (Art. 2 CDA). Derivative works and compilations may also be protected as original works (Art. 3 CDA).[15]

Copyright protection starts as soon as the work is created and it is independent of any formalities, such as registration or deposit (Art. 12 CDA), except for the titles of works (Art. 4(3) CDA). Copyright protection does not extend to ideas, procedures, operational methods or mathematical concepts as such (Art. 1(2) CDA) nor to news or facts reports or political speeches (Art. 7(1) CDA).

Despite copyright is configured as a unitary right including both economic and *moral rights, economic rights* can be assigned, while moral rights, namely the right of paternity and the right of integrity, are always attached to the creator and cannot be waived or disposed of (Arts. 9, 42 and 52(2) CDA). Nonetheless, the right

[15] Notwithstanding, and despite the open notion of work, computer programs and databases are protected under special copyright legislation, namely Decree-Law 252/94 of 20 October (Software Copyright Act) and Decree-Law 122/2000 of 4 July (Database Intellectual Property Act), which include provisions not familiar to copyright, such as the regulation of software 'reverse engineering' and the establishment of a *sui generis* right for producers of databases, as required under Community intellectual property law.

of integrity is aimed to protect the honor and reputation of the intellectual creator as such (Art. 56(1) CDA), the author may agree an identification of authorship (Art. 28 CDA) and he can consent modifications to the work (Arts. 15(2) and 59 CDA). Other moral rights include the right not to publish the work as well as the right to withdraw the work from circulation (Art. 62 CDA). A right that cannot also be disposed of nor be waived is the *droit de suite* provided for certain artistic works (Art. 54 CDA).

Copyright belongs to the intellectual creator of the work, i.e., the author, who is in principle the person identified as such – *actor est quem opus demonstrat* (Arts. 11 and 27 CDA). However, in case of works created by employees or made for hire, the parties may agree the transmission of the economic rights, which is presumed if the name of the creator is not mentioned in the work or in the usual place for purposes of authorship identification (Art. 14(1)(3) CDA).[16] In case of transmission, the intellectual creator will be entitled to a special remunerative compensation (Art. 14(4), see also Art. 49 CDA). Concerning a work created by several persons, copyright belongs jointly to its creators, unless it is deemed a *collective work*, where copyright is assigned by law to the natural or legal person that organizes and directs its creation and in whose name it is published (Arts. 16 to 19 CDA). Certain types of works are deemed to be *joint works (*or works in collaboration), namely cinematographic works, so that authorship is accorded to several persons (Art. 22 CDA).

Copyright protection starts as soon as the work is created, no deposit or registration being required, and in principle it lasts during the life of the author plus 70 years *post mortem auctoris* (Art. 31 CDA). There are special criteria for certain categories of works,

[16] See also Law 1/99 of 13 January, as amended by Law 94/2007 of 6 November, concerning authorship and ownership of works of journalists (Art. 7-B).

namely joint works and orphan works (Arts. 32 to 34 CDA). After the term of protection, copyright expires and the work falls into public domain (Art. 38 CDA). However, a 'publisher copyright' (*rectius*, a related right to copyright) during 25 years is granted to the publisher of an unpublished work for which the term of protection has already expired (Art. 39 CDA).

Economic rights are exclusive and disposable rights: the copyright owner has not only the exclusive right to authorize the use of the work by third persons but also the right to transfer and to use as security, in whole or in part, the economic rights (Art. 40 CDA).

Authorizations (licenses) to use copyrighted works have to meet certain requirements, namely they have to be done in writing and specify the authorized uses and the conditions of time, place and payment thereof. Despite the regulation of the normative prototype of copyright contracts of authorization (copyright licenses) provides for that the edition contract is null and void in case it is not concluded in writing (Art. 87 CDA), it is however stable jurisprudence that the writing requirement for copyright authorizations has only proof value (formality *ad probationem*).[17]

Partial transfers of copyright are possible for specific economic rights but have to be done in writing and are subject to notary recognition of the signatures otherwise they are null and void (Art. 43(1)(2) CDA). Moreover, the complete and final transmission of economic rights can take place by contract, provided the work and the price are indicated and it is concluded by public deed (formality *ad substantiam*); otherwise it is null and void (Art. 44 CDA).

---

[17] Supremo Tribunal de Justiça (Supreme Court of Justice), Judgments of 31 April 1988 (summary available at www.dgsi.pt/jstj), of 15 December 1998 (482 *Boletim do Ministério da Justiça - BMJ* (1999) p. 266), and of 14 March 2006 (available at www.dgsi.pt/jstj). See also Tribunal da Relação de Coimbra (Coimbra Court of Appeals), Judgment of 29 October 1985 (IV *Colectânea de Jurisprudência – CJ* (1985) pp. 86-89), and Tribunal da Relação de Lisboa (Lisbon Court of Appeals), Judgment of 17 February 2005 (available at www.dgsi.pt/jtrl).

Portuguese jurisprudence does not extend this requirement of form to works made for hire[18], but the case of transmission of copyright in future works remains unclear (Art. 48 CDA).

Copyright confers an exclusive and disposable right of economic exploitation of the work in any form known or later developed (Arts. 67 and 68(1) CDA). The exclusive right comprehends a bundle of independent rights which cover the most typical uses such as, according to Article 68(2) CDA, the right to copy or otherwise reproduce the work (a), the right to distribute copies, including rental (b), the right to perform in public, particularly musical, dramatic or audiovisual works (c), the right to communicate to the public by cable and to broadcast, by radio, television or other wireless means (d), the right to make available to the public on computer network (e), the right to translate and the right to adapt (f). The regulation of these economic rights is complemented by special legislation concerning specific rights such as rental and public lending[19] as well as satellite broadcasting and cable retransmission.[20]

The Copyright Act provides for in chapter III a detailed regulation for special uses, such as edition, stage performance, production of audiovisual works, fixation and publication of phonograms and videos, broadcasting, communication to the public, and translations.

Economic rights can be exercised directly by the copyright holders or through *collective management* entities (Arts. 71 to 74 CDA)[21]. However, for certain situations, such as the right of cable retransmission[22], copyright collective management is compulsory.

---

[18] Supremo Tribunal de Justiça (Supreme Court of Justice), Judgment of 31 March 2005 (available at www.dgsi.pt/jstj).

[19] Decree-Law 332/97 of 27 November.

[20] Decree-Law 333/97 of 27 November.

[21] The regulation of copyright management and collecting entities is established by Law 83/2001 of 3 August.

[22] Decree-Law 333/97 of 27 November, Article 7(1).

The exclusive right meets certain *limitations* and *exceptions*. To begin with, the right of reproduction does not apply to the activity of mere conduit, caching, hosting, browsing and linking conducted by provider of information society services where acting as mere intermediaries (Art. 75(1) CDA, see also E-Commerce Act[23], Arts. 11 to 17). Then, private copy and other uses such as press reviews, quotations, teaching illustration, are examples of free uses listed under Article 75(2) CDA, i.e., they fall outside the scope of the exclusive right, provided however that such uses do not conflict with a normal exploitation of the work and do not unreasonably prejudice the legitimate interests of the right holder (Art. 75(4) CDA). These free uses are deemed **mandatory** user's rights, as they cannot be derogated from by contract (Art. 75(5) CDA). Moreover, copyright holders are entitled to *equitable compensation* for some of the free uses (Art. 76 CDA). In particular, a system of copyright levies is provided for concerning free reproductions for private use (Art. 82 CDA[24]).

Title III of the Copyright Act provides for the so-called *related rights* (*direitos conexos*). Artistic performers, phonogram producers, broadcasting organizations and entertainment organizers are granted related or neighbouring rights. These are economic rights similar to copyright, but the term of protection is limited to 50 years after the occurrence that originates them (Art. 183 CDA). Moreover, a limited moral right is conferred on to performers (Art. 182 CDA).

In addition to these 'typical' related rights, other related rights are identified such as the right to show (*direito do empresário do espectáculo*) conferred to the promoter of public shows (Art. 117 CDA). The *sui generis* right granted to the producer of a database

[23] Decree-Law 7/2004 of 7 January.

[24] The detailed regulation of copyright levies is provided for by Law 62/98 of 1 September 1998, as last amended by Law 50/2004 of 24 August.

to protect his substantial investments in the production of the database[25] could also be added to this list of 'atypical' related rights in the sense that it is not included within the framework of an international treaty.

Infringements to copyright and related rights are deemed criminal offenses (Arts. 195 to 202 CDA) and the Copyright Act lays down special enforcement provisions concerning namely collecting and preserving evidences and provisional measures (Arts. 209 to 211-B CDA). The same applies to the protection of technological protection measures and integrity of copyright management information (Title VI, Arts. 217 – 228 CDA). For example, it is a criminal offence to circumvent (or to facilitate the circumvention of) technological protection measures used by copyright and related rights holders, including the *sui generis* right of the database producer (Arts. 217 to 219 CDA). However, the protection of technological measures is limited by some of the mandatory user's rights (Art. 221 CDA).

3. The court of Intellectual Property

The Portuguese regulation of the organization and functioning of judicial courts[26] provides for in Article 74 that *juízos* ('sections') of *specialized jurisdiction* on intellectual property disputes can be created at *tribunais de comarca* (courts of first instance). In case such a specialized section (*juízo*) does not exist at the court of first instance, *juízos de comércio* (sections on commerce) have jurisdiction over proceedings on intellectual property (Art. 121(5)) to exercise the competences provided for in Article 122. Moreover, *Relações* (District courts of appeal) have sections in matters of commerce

[25] Decree-Law 122/2000 of 4 July, Chapter III, Articles 12 to 17.

[26] Law 52/2008 of 28 August.

and intellectual property according to the volume and complexity of the service to decide the appeals on these matters (Art. 57).

The law of judiciary organization has also amended the Code on Industrial Property in order to confer jurisdiction to the section on intellectual property of the *Tribunal de Comarca de Lisboa* (Lisbon court of first instance) to judge appeals of certain decisions of the *Instituto Nacional da Propriedade Industrial* (Industrial Property Office), unless such a section exists at the court of first instance of the domicile of the appellant (Art. 40(1) CPI).

Moreover, the *juízo* (section) on intellectual property of the Lisbon court of first instance (*Comarca*) and the Lisbon court of appeals (*Relação*) have jurisdiction in Portugal over proceedings concerning matters referred to in Articles 80 to 92 of Regulation 6/2002, and in Article 91 to 101 of Regulation 40/94 (now Regulation 207/2009).

4. International Jurisdiction

International jurisdiction of Portuguese courts is governed by several legal sources, notably: the Código de Processo Civil[27] (Code of Civil Procedure), Articles 65 and 65-A and Articles 1094 *et seq.*; The Brussels Convention on Jurisdiction and the Enforcement of Judgments in Civil and Commercial Matters, concluded on 27 September 1968 (Brussels Convention)[28]; the Lugano Convention on Jurisdiction and the Enforcement of Judgments in Civil and Commercial Matters, concluded on 16 September 1988 between Member States and EFTA States (revised in 2007), which is a parallel Convention to the 1968 Brussels Convention; Council Regulation

[27] Approved by Decree-Law 329-A/95 of 12 December 1995, and as last amended by Law 12/2009 of 29 June 2009.

[28] OJ L 299, 31.12.1972, p. 32, consolidated version in OJ C 27, 26.1.1998, p. 1

(EC) N° 44/2001 of 22 December 2000 on jurisdiction and the recognition and enforcement of judgments in civil and commercial matters (Brussels I)[29], which supersedes the Brussels Convention as between Member States with the exception of Denmark[30]; Council Regulation (EC) No 2201/2003 of 27 November 2003 concerning jurisdiction and the recognition and enforcement of judgments in matrimonial matters and the matters of parental responsibility, repealing Regulation (EC) No 1347/2000[31]. If and when The Hague Convention on Choice of Court Agreements, concluded on 30 June 2005, enters into force, Portugal will be bound by it by virtue of its conclusion by the European Community.

Concerning *supranational intellectual property rights*, international jurisdiction of Portuguese courts is governed by special legal sources, namely the Protocol on Jurisdiction and Enforcement annex to the European Patent Convention.

Concerning Community *unitary IP rights*, several instruments contain specific provisions on jurisdiction, notably Regulation 207/2009 on Community Trademark (refers to Brussels I), Regulation 2100/94 Community on Vegetable Products (refers to Lugano Convention), and Regulation 6/2002 Community Designs or Models (refers to Brussels Convention).

The Portuguese Code of Civil Procedure (*Código do Processo Civil*) provides for in Article 65 that, without prejudice to the

---

[29] OJ L 12, 16.1.2001, p. 1. Regulation as last amended by Regulation (EC) No 1791/2006, OJ L 363, 20.12.2006, p. 1.

[30] Denmark opted-out based on the 1997 Protocol No 5 on the position of Denmark annexed to the Treaty on European Union and to the Treaty establishing the European Community (OJ C 340 of 10.11.1997). However, on 19 October 2005 the Community concluded an agreement with Denmark on jurisdiction and the recognition and enforcement of judgments that extended the provisions of the Regulation to that country. The agreement was approved on behalf of the Community by a Council Decision of 27 April 2006 (OJ L 120 of 5.5.2006), and entered into force on 1 July 2007 (OJ L 94 of 4.4.207).

[31] OJ L 338, 23.12.2003, p. 1.

provisions of Community instruments or other international instruments, Portuguese courts have jurisdiction where: proceedings can be initiated in a Portuguese court according to the rules of territorial jurisdiction provided for under Portuguese law (i); the invoked right cannot be effective unless proceedings are initiated in Portuguese territory or where there is considerable hardship in initiating proceedings in a foreign court, provided that between the matter of the dispute and the Portuguese legal order a relevant element of connection, either real or personal, exists (ii).

Moreover, Portuguese courts have exclusive competence where, according to Article 65-A of this Code, such jurisdiction is provided for in Community regulations and other international instruments (a), proceedings over rights *in rem* in immovable property located in Portuguese territory (b), bankruptcy and proceedings relating to the winding-up of insolvent companies whose statutory seat in located in Portugal (c), matters of companies or other legal persons situated in Portugal (d), proceedings the main object of which is the validity of inscription in public registries of any rights subject to registry in Portugal (e).

These rules embed the following principles of international jurisdiction as summarized by the Supremo Tribunal de Justiça (Supreme Court of Justice): a) the principle of coincidence, meaning that proceedings are to be initiated in Portugal according to the territorial rules of jurisdiction provided for under Portuguese law; b) the principle of causality, i.e., the event upon which the action is found has occurred in Portugal; c) the principle of reciprocity, i.e., the possibility of Portuguese citizens to sue foreign citizens before Portuguese courts whenever the Portuguese citizen can be sued before the courts of the foreign country in which the foreign citizen is domiciled; d) the principle of necessity, i.e., the enforcement of the judgment is not possible unless proceedings are initiated before Portuguese courts. These principles are independent one from another.[32]

As safeguarded in any of these provisions of the Code of Civil Procedure, in ascertaining their international jurisdiction Portuguese courts should look first at Community instruments and other international instruments, in special Brussels I, which supersedes the Brussels Convention, as between Member States, and its parallel Lugano Convention in the relations with EFTA countries.

As we shall see, these instruments render Portuguese domestic law almost residual[33], as they will only apply, to matters covered by Brussels/Lugano, where the defendant is not domiciled in a Brussels/Lugano country nor has a branch therein, and provided it is not a matter of exclusive jurisdiction nor a situation of a defendant entering into an appearance without contesting jurisdiction, for which Brussels I still applies regardless of domicile. Moreover, as the Lugano Convention is a parallel Convention to the Brussels Convention and this Convention has been superseded by Regulation Brussels I as between Member States, the following analysis focus on Brussels I[34].

---

[32] STJ Judgment of 12 April 1997, Proc. 98B292 (available at www.dgsi.pt/jstj), based upon Manuel de Andrade, *Noções Elementares de Processo Civil*, Coimbra, 1979, pp. 92-93.

[33] According to the Supremo Tribunal de Justice (Supreme Court of Justice), the Brussels Convention had already replaced domestic provisions concerning the matters regulated under the Convention. STJ, Judgment of 3 October 2007, Proc. 07S922 (available at www.dgsi.pt/jstj). The ECJ had already decided that 'The Convention of 27 September 1968, which seeks to determine the jurisdiction of the courts of the contracting states in civil matters, must override national provisions which are incompatible with it' - Judgment of the Court (Fourth Chamber) of 15 November 1983, C-288/82, *Ferdinand M.J.J. Duijnstee v Lodewijk Goderbauer* [1983] *ECR* 03663.

[34] Council Regulation (EC) No 44/ 2001 of 22 December 2000 on jurisdiction and the recognition and enforcement of judgments in civil and commercial matters. See, e.g., D. Moura Vicente, «Competência Judiciária e Reconhecimento de Decisões Estrangeiras no Regulamento (CE) n.° 44/2001», *Scientia Iuridica* (2002), p. 347; A. Dias Pereira, «A Jurisdição na Internet segundo o Regulamento 44/2001 (e as alternativas extrajudiciais e tecnológicas)», *Boletim da Faculdade de Direito Universidade de Coimbra* LXXVII (2001), pp. 633-687.

Brussels I (Regulation 44/2001)

In order to overcome certain differences between national rules governing jurisdiction and recognition of judgments that hampered the sound operation of the internal market and the free circulation of judgments – which the ECJ already considered to be an objective of Brussels Convention[35] -, Brussels I lays down provisions that unify the rules of conflict of jurisdiction in civil and commercial matters, apart from certain well-defined matters, and simplify the formalities with a view to rapid and simple recognition and enforcement of judgments from Member States bound by this Regulation (Recital 2).

As stated in Recitals 11 to 13 of Brussels I, the rules of jurisdiction laid down in this Regulation are founded on the principle that jurisdiction is generally based on the *defendant's domicile* and jurisdiction must always be available on this ground except in a few well-defined situations in which the subject-matter of the litigation or the autonomy of the parties warrants a different linking factor. In addition to the defendant's domicile, this regulation establishes alternative grounds of jurisdiction based on a close link between the court and the action or in order to facilitate the sound administration of justice (e.g. in proceedings which have as their object rights *in rem* in immovable property). Finally, the weaker party in relation to insurance, consumer contracts and employment is protected by rules of jurisdiction more favorable to his interests than the general rules provide for.

Brussels I applies in civil and commercial matters whatever the nature of the court or tribunal; revenue, customs or administrative matters are excluded from the scope of application of this Regulation as well as certain matters such as the status or legal capacity of natural persons, rights in property arising out of a matrimonial rela-

---

[35] Judgment of 28 March 2000, C-7/98, *Dieter Krombach v André Bamberski*, [2000] *ECR* I-1935.

tionship, wills and succession (i), bankruptcy, proceedings relating to the winding-up of insolvent companies or other legal persons, judicial arrangements, compositions and analogous proceedings (ii), social security (iii), and arbitration (iv) (Art. 1(1) (2)).

Applying the framework provided for by Brussels I to Portuguese courts, these have general jurisdiction over proceedings in which the defendants are persons domiciled in Portugal, whatever their nationality (Art. 2(1) *actor sequitur forum rei)*. Companies or other legal persons or associations of natural or legal persons are deemed to be domiciled in Portugal in case this is the place where they have their statutory seat, central administration, or principal place of business (Art. 60(1)). Concerning natural persons, the judge applies its internal legislation (Art. 59(1)), and the Portuguese Código Civil (Civil Code) provides for that a person has domicile at the place of his usual residence (Art. 82(1)).

In *alternative*, Portuguese courts may have special jurisdiction over proceedings concerning persons domiciled in another Member State in special matters relating namely to: a *contract*, if the place of performance of the obligation in question is located in Portugal (Art. 5(1)); *tort*, delict or quasi-delict, if the place where the harmful event occurred or may occur is located in Portugal (Art. 5(3))[36]; a dispute arising out of the operations of a branch, agency or other establishment, if the branch, agency or other establishment is situated in Portugal (Art. 5(3)); to disputes where the person is one of a *number of defendants* and one of them is domiciled in Portugal,

[36] However, concerning ubiquitous infringement on the Internet, the mere accessibility of a website in a country may not be enough to establish jurisdiction in case the defendant does not direct his activity to that country nor engage in activities therein. According to the ECJ, 'the jurisdictional rules [are to be] interpreted in such a way as to enable a normally well-informed defendant reasonably to predict before which courts, other than those of the State in which he is domiciled, he may be sued' - Judgment of 17 June 1992, C-26/91, *Jakob Handte & Co. GmbH* v *Traitements Mécano-chimiques des Surfaces SA* [1992] ECR I-3967.

provided the claims are so closely connected that it is expedient to hear and determine them together to avoid the risk of irreconcilable judgments resulting from separate proceedings (Art. 6(1)), as previously ruled by the ECJ concerning the Brussels Convention[37].

Moreover, Portuguese courts may also have jurisdiction by virtue of special rules aimed at protecting the *weaker party* in relation to insurance, consumer contracts and employment. For example, concerning *consumer contracts*, Portuguese courts have jurisdiction over proceedings brought by a consumer against the other party in case either of the parties is domiciled in Portugal; where proceedings are brought by the other party against the consumer, Portuguese courts have exclusive jurisdiction if the consumer is domiciled in Portugal (Art. 16(1) and (2)). It is required however that the contract has been concluded by a person, the consumer, for a purpose which can be regarded as being outside his trade or profession (Art. 15(1)), with a person who pursues commercial or professional activities in the Member State of the consumer's domicile or, by any means, directs such activities to that Member State or to several States including that Member State, and the contract falls within the scope of such activities (Art. 15(1)(c)). Regardless of domicile, Portuguese courts may also have jurisdiction over consumer contracts in other restricted conditions, such as, for example, where they are chosen by an agreement of the parties entered into after the dispute has arisen (Art. 17(1)).

---

[37] Judgment of the Court (Fifth Chamber) of 27 September 1988, C-189/87, *Athanasios Kalfelis* v *Bankhaus Schröder, Münchmeyer, Hengst and Co. and others* [1988] *ECR* 05565 ('For Article 6(1) of the Convention of 27 September 1968 on Jurisdiction and the Enforcement of Judgments in Civil and Commercial Matters to apply, a connection must exist between the various actions brought by the same plaintiff against different defendants. That connection, whose nature must be determined independently, must be of such a kind that it is expedient to determine the actions together in order to avoid the risk of irreconcilable judgments resulting from separate proceedings'). See an application of the concept by the Tribunal da Relação de Lisboa (Lisbon Court of Appeals), Judgment of 18 January 2007 (available at www.dgsi.pt/jtrl).

Portuguese courts may also have jurisdiction, in principle exclusive, by virtue of a *choice of court* agreement by the parties, provided one or more of whom is domiciled in a Member State, to settle any disputes which have arisen or which may arise in connection with a particular legal relationship (Art. 23(1)). It is required that such an agreement conferring jurisdiction is either: a) in writing or evidenced in writing, with equivalence of any communication by electronic means which provides a durable record of the agreement (Art. 23(2); b) or in a form which accords with practices which the parties have established between themselves; c) or, in international trade or commerce, in a form which accords with a usage of which the parties are or ought to have been aware and which in such trade or commerce is widely known to, and regularly observed by, parties to contracts of the type involved in the particular trade or commerce concerned.[38] According to relevant ECJ jurisprudence, recently taken into consideration by the Portuguese Supremo Tribunal de Justiça (Supreme Court of Justice)[39], no other *formal requirements*, including language, can be provided under domestic law[40].

---

[38] The Supremo Tribunal de Justice (*Supreme Court of Justice*) has just decided that invoices with a standard term of jurisdiction can be considered a choice of court clause tacitly agreed (see Judgment of 8 October 2009, Proc. 5138/06.8TBSTS.S1, available at www.dgsi.pt/jstj). Before this judgment, Portuguese courts had decided that invoices with a standard term of jurisdiction cannot be considered a choice of court agreement due to lack of acceptance in writing by one the parties. See Tribunal da Relação de Coimbra (Coimbra Court of Appeals), Judgments of 12 June 2007 and 27 November 2007 (available at www.dgsi.pt/jtrc), Tribunal da Relação de Lisboa (Lisbon Court of Appeals), Judgment of 25 September 2008 (available at www.dgsi.pt/jtrl).

[39] Judgment of 8 October 2009, Proc. 5138/06.8TBSTS.S1 (available at ww.dgsi.pt/jstj).

[40] Judgment of 24 June 1981, C-150/80, *Elefanten Schuh GmbH* vs *Jacqmain* [1981] *ECR* 01671 ('Since the aim of article 17 of the Convention is to lay down the formal requirements which agreements conferring jurisdiction must meet, contracting states are not free to lay down formal requirements other than those contained in the Convention. When those rules are applied to provisions concerning the language to be used in an agreement conferring jurisdiction they imply that the legislation of a contracting state may not allow the validity of such an agreement to be called in question solely on the ground that the language used is not that prescribed by that legislation.').

Do disputes connected with a particular relationship include not only contractual obligations but also non-contractual obligations (e.g. torts, unjust enrichment)?[41] In Portugal, the scope of jurisdiction of the chosen court is controversial. In fact, it is disputed in Portuguese jurisprudence whether a choice of court agreement concerning an agency contract includes the issue of compensation for good-will of the agent after the termination of the contract[42]. Moreover, concerning intellectual property related contracts, there is Portuguese jurisprudence holding that a choice of court agreement for a license contract does not include litigations concerning the termination of the contract and *tort liability* caused by unlawful acts committed by the plaintiff in Portugal[43]. However, more recently the same Court grounded its jurisdiction over tort liability arising out of illegal termination of a concession contract and compensation for good-will under Article 5(1)(a) of Brussels I[44], and it has ruled, in a different case, that a choice of court agreement concerns any dispute that arises out of the main contract and therefore jurisdiction of the chosen court includes all issues, either contractual or tort, that result thereof[45].

On the other hand, it is understood in Portuguese jurisprudence that Brussels I does not provide the courts with the possibility to

---

[41] A positive answer is provided for in the Hague Convention on choice of court agreements (Art. 2(3)). It has been argued that the courts designated by the parties should also have jurisdiction over matters of validity of intellectual property rights which require registry or deposit, where they are raised as incidental questions and provided the decision would produce only *inter partes* effects. See D. Moura Vicente, *A Tutela Internacional da Propriedade Intelectual*, Coimbra, Almedina, 2009, pp. 387-399.

[42] Contra, Tribunal da Relação de Lisboa, Judgment of 24 October 2006 (available at www.dgsi.pt/jtrl). Pro, more recently, Tribunal da Relação do Porto (Oporto Court of Appeals, Judgment of 30 September 2008 (available at www.dgsi.pt/jtrp).

[43] Supremo Tribunal de Justiça (Supreme Court of Justice), Judgment of 12 April 1997, Proc. 98B292 (available at www.dgsi.pt/jstj).

[44] Judgment of 9 October 2008, Proc. 08B2633 (available at www.dgsi.pt/jstj).

[45] Judgment of 8 October 2009, Proc. 5138/06.8TBSTS.S1 (available at www.dgsi.pt/jstj).

control the grounds of jurisdiction of a court chosen by agreement[46], and that a party to a choice of court agreement can waive from such jurisdiction agreement in case it is provided for therein[47]. However, it should be considered the situation of *forum non conveniens*, and the fact that on one hand the court can declare null and void a choice of court agreement that is an unfair standard term[48], and that on the other hand, according to the ECJ, the court shall decline of its own motion the jurisdiction conferred on it by virtue of such an unfair term[49].

Regardless of domicile, Portuguese courts have *exclusive jurisdiction* in certain matters by virtue of Article 22. For example, in proceedings concerned with the *registration or validity* of patents, trademarks, designs, or other similar rights required to be deposited or registered[50], in case Portugal is the Member State in which the deposit or registration has been applied for, has taken place or is under the terms of a Community instrument or an international convention deemed to have taken place (Art. 22(4))[51]. Moreover, according to Article 24, regardless of domicile, a Portuguese court

---

46 Tribunal da Relação de Lisboa (Lisbon Court of Appeals), Judgment 21 May 2009, Proc. 8748/2008-6 (available at www.dgsi.pt/jtrl).

47 Supremo Tribunal de Justiça, Judgement of 17 December 2004, Proc. 04B4076 (available at www.dgsi.pt/jstj).

48 Unfair Standard Terms Act, approved by Decree-Law 446/85 of 25 October, Article 19(g).

49 Judgment of the Court of 27 June 2000, Joined cases C-240/98 to C-244/98, *Océano Grupo Editorial SA v Roció Murciano Quintero (C-240/98) and Salvat Editores SA v José M. Sánchez Alcón Prades (C-241/98), José Luis Copano Badillo (C-242/98), Mohammed Berroane (C-243/98) and Emilio Viñas Feliú (C-244/98)* [2000] *ECR* I-04941, para. 24, 29, 32. See A. Dias Pereira, «A via electrónica da negociação (alguns aspectos)», *Estudos de Direito do Consumidor* 8 (2006-2007), pp. 275 ff. (287-9).

50 See Judgment of the Court (Fourth Chamber) of 15 November 1983, C-288/82, *Ferdinand M.J.J. Duijnstee* v *Lodewijk Goderbauer* [1983] *ECR* 03663 (The term 'proceedings concerned with the registration or validity of patents' contained in Article 16(4) of the Convention of 27 September 1968 must be regarded as an independent concept intended to have uniform application in all the contracting states').

51 This rule of exclusive jurisdiction could apply to other rights subject to registration such as domain names. See A. Dias Pereira, op. cit. n. 14, pp. 368-71.

has jurisdiction if it is the court before which a defendant enters an appearance without contesting the jurisdiction[52] and provided no other court has exclusive jurisdiction by virtue of Article 22.

A Portuguese court may have jurisdiction over proceedings involving the same cause of action and between the same parties that are brought before the courts of different Member States (*lis pendens*), in case it is the court first seized, as any court other than the court first seized shall of its own motion stay its proceedings until such time as the jurisdiction of the court first seized is established and then decline jurisdiction in favor of that court (Art. 27(1) and (2)).

A Portuguese court may also have jurisdiction where, concerning *related actions* that are pending in the courts of different Member States, the Portuguese court is the court first seized and the other courts stay their proceedings, or if these actions are pending at first instance, those other courts, on the application of one of the parties, decline jurisdiction, provided the Portuguese court has jurisdiction over the actions in question and Portuguese law permits the consolidation thereof (Art. 28(1) and (2)). Actions are deemed to be related where they are so closely connected that it is expedient to hear and determine them together to avoid the risk of irreconcilable judgments resulting from separate proceedings (Art. 28(3)).

---

[52] See Judgment of 24 June 1981, C-150/80, *Elefanten Schuh GmbH* v *Jacqmain* [1981] *ECR* 01671 ('Article 18 of the Convention of 27 September 1968 must be interpreted as meaning that the rule on jurisdiction which that provision lays down does not apply where the defendant not only contests the court's jurisdiction but also makes submissions on the substance of the action, provided that if the challenge to jurisdiction is not preliminary to any defence as to the substance it does not occur after the making of the submissions which under national procedural law are considered to be the first defence addressed to the court seised'). Denying prorogation of jurisdiction under Article 24 of Brussels I in case the defendant contests the jurisdiction of the court and, then, in case such exception is not accepted, also contests the action, Supremo Tribunal de Justiça (Supreme Court of Justice), Judgment of 3 October 2007, Proc. 07S922 (available at www.dgsi.pt/jstj), and Tribunal da Relação de Lisboa (Lisbon Court of Appeals), Judgment of 13 January 2009 (available at www.dgsi.pt/jtrl).

Portuguese courts may have jurisdiction concerning such *provisional, including protective, measures* as may be available under Portuguese law, even if, under Brussels I, the courts of another Member State have jurisdiction as to the substance of the matter (Art. 31). Both the Portuguese Copyright Code and the Code of Industrial Property provide for such provisional measures as required by the TRIPS Agreement (Art. 50) and the Enforcement Directive 2004/48 (Art. 9).

Furthermore, Portuguese jurisprudence also accepts that an international arbitration agreement does not exclude the international jurisdiction of Portuguese courts concerning related interim provisional procedures[53].

Other international and Community instruments

The *Lugano Convention* (2007) provides rules similar to regulation Brussels I, which apply whenever the defendant is domiciled in Swiss, Norway or Island. The Lugano Convention also applies to proceedings concerning infringement to the Community protection law on vegetable varieties.

Concerning Community models or designs, Portuguese courts have jurisdiction in case the defendant is domiciled or established in Portugal (a), or in case the plaintiff is domiciled or established in Portugal and the defendant is not domiciled or established in any Member State (b), or in case they are elected by the parties by choice of court agreement (c) (Community Model and Design Regulation, Art. 79 ff.).

Community Trade Mark Regulation[54] (hereinafter CTM) lays down a jurisdiction framework concerning infringement and validity

---

[53] Tribunal da Relação de Lisboa (Lisbon Court of Appeals), Judgments of 2 December 2003 and 13 March 2007 (available at www.dgsi.pt/jtrl).

[54] Council Regulation (EC) No 207/2009 of 26 February 2009 on the Community trade mark, OJ L 78, 24.3.2009, p. 1–42 (which repealed Council Regulation (EC) No 40/94, OJ L 11, 14.1.1994, p. 1).

proceedings over Community trademarks. It is understood that, in order to prevent inconsistent decisions on the part of the courts and the Office and to ensure that the unitary character of Community trademarks is not undermined, decisions regarding their validity and infringement must have effect and cover the entire area of the Community (Recital 16).

To begin with, Community Trade Mark Regulation refers to the Brussels I concerning the jurisdiction and procedure in legal actions relating to Community trademarks and applications for Community trademarks, as well as to proceedings relating to simultaneous and successive actions on the basis of Community trademarks and national trade marks, unless the Community Trade Mark Regulation derogates from those rules (Art. 94(1)(2) CTM).

Member States are required to designate as limited a number as possible of national courts of first and second instance having jurisdiction in matters of infringement and validity of Community trade marks (Art. 95 CTM). Jurisdiction of Community trade mark courts over proceedings relating to infringement and validity is exclusive (Art. 96 CTM), and it is conferred to the courts of the Member State in which the defendant is domiciled or, if he is not domiciled in any Member State, in which he has an establishment (Art. 97(1) CTM); in case none of the these connections occur, jurisdiction is conferred to the courts of the Member State in which the plaintiff is domiciled or, if he is not domiciled in any Member State, in which he has an establishment (Art. 97(2) CTM); moreover, in case none of these connections occur, jurisdiction belongs to the courts of the Member State where the European Trademark Office has its seat, i.e., Spanish courts (Art. 97(3) CTM). However, in case any of the parties is domiciled in a Member State, jurisdiction belongs to the courts designated by the parties in a choice of court agreement or, in absence of such an agreement, if the defendant enters an appearance before a different Community trade mark court, according to requirements laid down respectively in Articles 23 and 24 of Brussels I (Art. 97(4)(a)(b) CTM).

In *alternative*, jurisdiction over infringement and validity proceedings, with the exception of actions for a declaration of non-infringement of a Community trade mark, can always be asserted to the courts of the Member State in which the act of infringement has been committed or threatened (Art. 97(5) CTM), but only in respect of facts committed or threatened within the territory of the Member State in which that court is situated (Art. 98(2) CTM).

Moreover, in order to avoid *contradictory judgments* in actions which involve the same acts and the same parties and which are brought on the basis of a Community trade mark and parallel national trade marks, two different ways are provided (Art. 104 CTM): on one hand, where the actions are brought in the same Member State, national procedural rules apply, on the other hand, where the actions are brought in different Member States, provisions similar to the rules on *lis pendens* and related actions of Brussels I are provided for (Arts. 27 ff CTM). However, in case 'the Community trade mark court stays proceedings it may order provisional and protective measures for the duration of the stay' (Art. 104(3) CTM).

Then, similar to Brussels I, the courts of a Member State have jurisdiction over *provisional and protective measures* in respect of a Community trade mark as may be available under the law of that State in respect of a national trade mark, even if, under the Community Trade Mark Regulation, a Community trade mark court of another Member State had jurisdiction as to the substance of the matter (Art. 103(1) CTM). However, Community trademark courts whose jurisdiction is based on Article 97(1), (2), (3) or (4) CTM have *exclusive jurisdiction* to grant provisional and protective measures which, subject to a necessary procedure for recognition and enforcement pursuant to Title III of Brussels I Regulation, are applicable in the territory of any Member State.

5. Conflict of Laws/Choice-of-Law

There are several sources of conflict of laws / choice-of-law provisions, notably: Código Civil Português (Portuguese Civil Code), Articles 14 to 65; special instruments of legislation may also contain relevant provisions, namely the Agency Contract Act[55], Article 38; the 1980 Convention on the Law Applicable to Contractual Obligations (Rome Convention)[56]; Regulation (EC) N° 593/2008 of the European Parliament and of the Council of 17 June 2008 on the law applicable to contractual obligations (Rome I)[57]; Regulation (EC) No 864/2007 of the European Parliament and of the Council of 11 July 2007 on the law applicable to non-contractual obligations (Rome II)[58].

Portuguese law has a codified system of conflict of laws, i.e. legal provisions that designate the applicable law as the law which, in the perspective of the law chosen by the law-maker, has the most relevant territorial connection (or most significant relationship) to the disputed questions. This system implements a complex set of general principles such as the principles of international harmony, material harmony, efficacy of judgments, sound administration of justice, and parity of treatment[59].

The Civil Code (hereinafter CC) regulates such general issues as qualification, *renvoi*, or *ordre public* (Arts. 15, 17, 22 CC). Nationality is the general connection to establish the personal law of natural per-

---

[55] Decree-Law 178/86 of 3 July 1986, as amended by Decree-Law 118/93 of 13 March 1993.

[56] OJ C 334, 30.12.2005, p. 1.

[57] OJ L 177, 4.7.2008, p. 7.

[58] OJ L 199, 31.7.2007, p. 40.

[59] Cf. A. Ferrer Correia, *Direito Internacional Privado – Alguns Problemas,* Coimbra, 1997. For an outline in English of sources and general principles of Portuguese international private law see D. Moura Vicente, «Sources and General Principles of Portuguese International Private Law: An Outline», *Yearbook of Private International Law* – YPIL IX (2007), pp. 257 ff.

sons, which applies notably to the status or legal capacity of natural persons, family relationships, wills and succession, and rights of personality (Arts. 25, 27 and 31 CC). The personal law of companies and other legal persons is the law of the country in which their central administration or principal place of business is located (Art. 33(1) CC).

The law applicable to contracts and *contractual obligations* is in principle the law designated by the parties (Art. 41(1) CC). In the absence of choice, unilateral transactions are governed by the law of the country in which the person by whom it was done has habitual residence; concerning contracts, the law of the country of common residence of both parties (Art. 42(1) CC); in case there is no common residence, the law of habitual residence of the donator in gratuitous contracts, or the law of the place of conclusion in the other situations (Art. 42(2) CC).

Tort liability is in principle regulated by *lex loci delicti commissi*, i.e. the law of the country in which the main harmful activity occurred (Art. 45(1) CC). In case the agent is not considered liable under this specified legislation but deemed liable under *lex loci damni*, this legislation applies provided the agent should predict the harmful result of his action or omission in that country (Art. 45(2) CC). Concerning other non-contractual obligations specific rules are provided for such as, e.g., the law upon which the transfer of the patrimonial value took place in favor of the enriched concerning unjust enrichment (Art. 44 CC).

Then, rights *in rem* in immovable property are regulated by the law of the country in which the property is located (*lex rei sitae*) (Art. 46(1) CC). Intellectual property is subject to a special provision (Art. 48 CC), according to which: the law applicable to copyright is the law of the first publication of the work and, in case it is not published, the personal law of the author, without prejudice of special legislation; the law applicable to industrial property is the law of the country of its creation.

Family relationships are governed by several laws depending on the subject-matter. For example, while the capacity to marry is governed by the personal law of each party (Art. 49 CC), the form of the marriage is in principle governed by the law of the country in which it takes place (Art. 50 CC); the relationship between the consorts is governed firstly by their common national law, secondly by the law of their common habitual residence, and thirdly by the law of the country which family life is more closely connected with (Art. 52 CC).

Successions/wills are governed by the personal law of the deceased/testator at the time of his death/testament (Art. 62 and Article 63(1) CC). This law also applies to the formal validity of the will in case it requires a special form as a condition of validity or efficacy (Art. 65 CC).

These domestic provisions on conflict of laws does not apply where an international or Community instrument provides otherwise, such as the specific provisions provided for under international intellectual property treaties, the Rome Convention on the law applicable to contractual obligations, and most significantly, Regulation Rome I (contractual obligations) and Regulation Rome II (non-contractual obligations), which have precedence over domestic legislation. Therefore, the following analysis will focus on these Community instruments.

Regulation *Rome II* on the law applicable to *non-contractual obligations* is binding in its entirety and directly applicable in the Member States of the European Union, with exception of Denmark which did not take part in its adoption and is not bound by it or subject to its application (Recital 40, Article 1(4)). Rome II applies, in situations involving a conflict of laws, to non-contractual obligations in civil and commercial matters. Revenue, customs or administrative matters and claims arising out of *acta iure imperii,* such as claims against officials who act on behalf of the State and liability for acts of public authorities, including liability of publicly appointed office-holders, are excluded from the **scope of application** of Rome

II (Art. 1(1)). Moreover, this Regulation does not apply to non-contractual obligations arising out of, namely, family relationships (a), matrimonial property regimes, wills and succession (b), bills of exchange and other negotiable instruments (c), several matters of company law (d), and violations of privacy and rights relating to personality, including defamation (e) (Art. 1(2)).

Regulation Rome I on the law applicable to contractual obligations replaces the Rome Convention in the Member States (Art. 24) and is binding in its entirety and directly applicable in the Member States of the European Union, with exception of Denmark and United Kingdom which did not take part in its adoption and are not bound by it or subject to its application (Recitals 45 and 46). This Regulation applies, from 17 December 2009 (Art. 29), in situations involving a conflict of laws, to contractual obligations in civil and commercial matters; revenue, customs or administrative matters are excluded from the scope of this Regulation (Art. 1(1)), as well as various matters, such as, for example, the status or legal capacity of natural persons (i), obligations arising out of family relationships and matrimonial property regimes, wills and succession (ii) or dealings prior to the conclusion of a contract (iii), bills of exchange and other negotiable instruments (iv), arbitration agreements and agreements on the choice of court (v), and questions governed by company law (vi) (Art. 1(2)).

General principles of conflict of laws in torts, contracts and transfer of rights

Rome II[60] provides for the principle of *universal application*, i.e. any law specified by this Regulation is to be applied irrespective

[60] Regulation (EC) No 864/2007 of the European Parliament and of the Council of 11 July 2007 on the law applicable to non-contractual obligations (Rome II), OJ L 199, 31.7.2007, p. 40. See notably L. de Lima Pinheiro, «O Direito de conflitos das obrigações extracontratuais entre a comunitarização e a globalização – uma primeira

of whether or not it is the law of a Member State (Art. 3). On the other hand, *renvoi* is excluded, meaning that the application of the law of any country specified by this Regulation refers to the rules of law in that country other than its rules of private international law (Art. 24). Moreover, concerning States with more than one legal system, comprising several territorial units, each unit is considered a country for the purposes of identifying the law applicable under Rome II (Art. 25(1)).

Taking into account that the concept of 'non-contractual obligation' varies from one Member State to another, Rome II provides an 'autonomous concept' of *non-contractual* obligation (Recital 11), so that, on one hand, damage covers any consequence arising out of tort/delict, unjust enrichment, *negotiorum gestio* or culpa *in contrahendo*[61] (Art. 2(1)), and, on the other hand, non-contractual obligations that are likely to arise are also addressed by the Regulation, including both events giving rise to damage that are likely to occur and damage that is likely to occur (Art. 2(3)). Non-contractual obligations arising out of strict liability are also covered.

As for the scope of the law applicable to non-contractual obligations under Rome II (Art. 15), it governs: (a) the basis and extent of liability, including the determination of persons who may be held liable for acts performed by them; (b) the grounds for exemption from liability, any limitation of liability and any division of liability;

apreciação do Regulamento Comunitário Roma II», *O Direito* 139/V (2007), pp. 1027 ff; A. L. Calvo Caravaca, J. Carrascosa González, *Las obligaciones extracontractuales en Derecho internacional privado. El Reglamento «Roma II»*, Granada, Comares, 2008; G. Wagner, «Die neue Rom II-Verordnung», *Praxis des Internationalen Privat- und Verfahrensrechts* (2008), pp. 1 ff.

[61] In order to overcome the differences in national law concerning the interpretation of *culpa in contrahendo*, an 'autonomous concept' is provided for in Recital 30 according to which it includes 'the violation of the duty of disclosure and the breakdown of contractual negotiations', and furthermore it is indicated that 'Article 12 covers only non-contractual obligations presenting a direct link with the dealings prior to the conclusion of a contract', so that it does not apply where, for example, a person suffers personal injury while a contract is being negotiated

(c) the existence, the nature and the assessment of damage or the remedy claimed; (d) within the limits of powers conferred on the court by its procedural law, the measures which a court may take to prevent or terminate injury or damage or to ensure the provision of compensation; (e) the question whether a right to claim damages or a remedy may be transferred, including by inheritance; (f) persons entitled to compensation for damage sustained personally; (g) liability for the acts of another person; (h) the manner in which an obligation may be extinguished and rules of prescription and limitation, including rules relating to the commencement, interruption and suspension of a period of prescription or limitation.

Rome II strikes a balance between the requirement of legal certainty and the need to do justice in individual cases, establishing rules that aim to create a *flexible framework* of conflict-of-law and to enable the court seised to treat individual cases in an appropriate manner by providing for the connecting factors which are deemed the most appropriate to achieve these objectives. Accordingly, Rome II provides for a general rule but also for specific rules and, in certain provisions, for an 'escape clause' which allows a departure from these rules where it is clear from all the circumstances of the case that the tort/delict is manifestly more closely connected with another country (Recital 14).

As for the *general rule*, the law of the country in which the damage occurs (*lex loci damni)* is provided for in Article 4(1), 'irrespective of the country in which the event giving rise to the damage occurred and irrespective of the country or countries in which the indirect consequences of that event occur'. E.g. in cases of personal injury or damage to property, the country in which the damage occurs is considered to be, respectively, the country where the injury was sustained or the property was damaged (Recital 17)[62]. An exception to

[62] It is understood that the connection with the country where the direct damage occurred (*lex loci damni*) strikes a fair balance between the interests of the person

the general rule is provided for in Article 4(2), which creates a special connection where the parties have their habitual residence[63] in the same country at the time when damage occurs, so that the law of that country applies. Moreover, where it is clear from all the circumstances of the case that the tort/delict is manifestly more closely connected with another country, the law of that country applies according to the 'escape clause' (Recital 18) provided for in Article 4(3).

On the other hand, Rome II lays down *specific rules* for special torts/delicts where it is understood that the general rule does not allow a reasonable balance to be struck between the interests at stake (Recital 19). Such special torts/delicts are product liability, unfair competition and acts restricting free competition, environmental damage, infringement of intellectual property rights, and industrial action (Arts. 5 to 9). These special rules are not considered exceptions but rather specifications or 'clarifications' of the general rule (*lex loci damni).* For example, in matters of **unfair competition**, Article 6(1) provides for the connection to the law of the country where competitive relations or the collective interests of consumers are, or are likely to be, affected. This conflict-of-law rule is aimed to protect competitors, consumers and the general public and to ensure that the market economy functions properly (Recital 21). Then, concerning restrictions of competition, it is established the law of the country where the market is, or is likely to be, affected,

claimed to be liable and the person sustaining the damage, and also reflects the modern approach to civil liability and the development of systems of strict liability (Recital 16), thus overcoming the uncertainty arising out of the practical application of the principle of *lex loci delicti commissi*.

[63] A notion of habitual residence is provided for according to which the place of central administration is deemed the habitual residence of companies and other bodies, corporate or unincorporated, and where the event giving rise to the damage occurs, or the damage arises, in the course of operation of a branch, agency or any other establishment, the place where the branch, agency or any other establishment is located shall be treated as the place of habitual residence (Art. 23(1)). Concerning a natural person acting in the course of his or her business, the habitual residence is his/her principal place of business (Art. 23(2)).

but in case it refers to more than one country, the claimant is able in certain circumstances to choose to base his/her claim on the law of the court seized (Art. 6(3)).[64]

Infringements of *intellectual property* rights are special torts/ delicts which the 'universally acknowledged' principle of *lex loci protectionis* is provided for under Article 8(1), i.e. the law of the country for which protection is claimed. However, concerning unitary Community intellectual property rights and only for any question that is not governed by the relevant Community instrument, the law applicable is the law of the country in which the act of infringement was committed, i.e. *lex loci delicti* (Art. 8(2)). Along copyright and industrial property rights, Recital 26 refers the *sui generis* right for the protection of databases (Directive 96/9) as an intellectual property right, so that it is not confused with unfair competition.

Some of these special criteria prevail over freedom of choice preserved in Article 14, as the law applicable under them may not be derogated from by a choice-of-law agreement (see Art. 6(4) on unfair competition and acts restricting free competition, and Article 8(3) on infringement of intellectual property rights).

Moreover, Rome II provides for in chapter III special rules where damage is caused by an act other than a tort/delict, such as unjust enrichment, *negotiorum gestio* and *culpa in contrahendo* (Arts. 10 to 13). These situations are in principle governed by the law that governs the relationship between the parties arising out of a contract or a tort/delict that gives rise to the non-contractual obligation and

[64] Recital 23 informs that the concept of restriction of competition covers prohibitions on agreements between undertakings, decisions by associations of undertakings and concerted practices which have as their object or effect the prevention, restriction or distortion of competition within a Member State or within the internal market, as well as prohibitions on the abuse of a dominant position within a Member State or within the internal market, where such agreements, decisions, concerted practices or abuses are prohibited by Articles 81 and 82 of the Treaty or by the law of a Member State.

is closely connected with it (Arts. 10(1), 11(1) and 12(1)). However, non-contractual obligations arising from an infringement of an intellectual property right are governed by the criteria laid down in Article 8 mentioned above (Art. 13).

Freedom of choice is a basic principle of private law. In order to respect the principle of party autonomy and to enhance legal certainty, the parties are allowed to make a choice as to the law applicable to a non-contractual obligation. In general, the parties may choose the applicable law by an agreement entered into force only *after* the event giving rise to the damage occurred (Art. 14(1)(a)). In case all the parties are pursuing a commercial activity, they may choose by an agreement freely negotiated before such event (Art. 14(1)(b)). In any case, the choice must be expressed or demonstrated with reasonable certainty by the circumstances of the case, with due respect to the intentions of the parties and the rights of third parties (Art. 14, 2nd period, Recital 31).

Moreover, the choice of the parties does not prejudice the application of provisions, which cannot be derogated from by agreement, of the law of a country - other than the country whose law has been chosen - where all the elements relevant to the situation at the time when the event giving rise to the damage occurs are located (Art. 14(2)). A similar limitation to freedom of choice is provided for the application of provisions of Community law, where appropriate as implemented in the Member State of the forum, in case 'all the relevant elements' are located in one or more of the Member States, other than that of the parties' choice (Art. 14(3)).

Rome II does not restrict the application of the provisions of the law of the forum in a situation where they are mandatory irrespective of the law otherwise applicable to the non-contractual obligation (Art. 16). The mandatory nature of such provisions is however not to be interpreted in a broad way, as the title of the Article indicates: *overriding mandatory provisions*. This is also stressed by

Article 26 on public policy of the forum which provides that the application of a provision of the law of any country specified by this Regulation (Rome II) may be refused only if such application is manifestly incompatible with the public policy (*ordre public*) of the forum. Recital 32 stresses this concern with the application of mandatory provisions of *lex fori*: 'Considerations of public interest justify giving the courts of the Member States the possibility, in exceptional circumstances, of applying exceptions based on public policy and overriding mandatory provisions'. And it offers a clarification for a situation of *ordre public*: noncompensatory exemplary or punitive damages of an excessive nature that would be awarded by the application of a provision of the law designated by this Regulation may be regarded as being contrary to the public policy, depending on the circumstances of the case and the legal order of the Member State of the court seized. Another example that seems to be therein implied is the Community economic *ordre public* for electronic commerce (e.g. rules on online gambling).

Rome I[65] provides for the principle of *universal application*, i.e. any law specified by this Regulation is to be applied irrespective of whether or not it is the law of a Member State (Art. 1). The scope of the law applicable to contractual obligations includes, in particular (Art. 12(1)): interpretation (i), performance (ii), within the limits of the powers conferred on the courts by its procedural law, the consequences of a total or partial breach of obligations, including the assessment of damages in so far as it is governed by rules of law (iii), the various ways of extinguishing obligations, and prescription and limitation of actions (iv), and the consequences of nullity of the contract (v). However, regard to the law of the

[65] Regulation (EC) N° 593/2008 of the European Parliament and of the Council of 17 June 2008 on the law applicable to contractual obligations (Rome I), OJ L 177, 4.7.2008, p. 7. On this Regulation see, e.g., B. Ubertazzi, *Il regolamento Roma I sulla legge applicabile alle obbligazioni contrattuali,* Milano, Giuffrè, 2008.

country in which performance takes place is required concerning the manner of performance and the steps to be taken in the event of defective performance (Art. 12(2)).

On the other hand, *renvoi* is excluded, i.e. the application of the law of any country specified by this Regulation means the application of the rules of law in that country other than its rules of private international law, unless provided otherwise in this Regulation (Art. 20). Moreover, concerning States with more than one legal system, comprising several territorial units, each unit is considered a country for the purposes of identifying the law applicable under Rome I (Art. 22(1)).

Moreover, for reasons of legal certainty, i.e. in order to enable the parties to foresee the law applicable to their situation, and unlike Regulation 44/2001 which establishes three criteria in Article 60(1) for companies and other bodies, the conflict-of-law rule proceeds on the basis of a single criterion: the place of central administration (Art. 19(1), 1st period). In case the contract is concluded in the course of operations of a branch, agency or any other establishment, or if, under the contract, performance is the responsibility of such a branch, agency or establishment, the place where they are located is treated as the place of habitual residence of the company (Art. 19(3)). Concerning a natural person acting in the course of his business activity, the *habitual residence* is his principal place of business (Art. 19(1), 2nd period). The time of conclusion of the contract is the relevant point in time to determine the habitual residence (Art. 19(3)).

Freedom of choice: the parties' freedom to choose the applicable law is one of the 'cornerstones' upon which the system of conflict-of-law rules in matters of contractual obligations was laid down in Rome I. In fact, contracts are governed by the law chosen by the parties, who can select the law applicable to the whole or to part only of the contract, provided the choice is made expressly or clearly demonstrated by the terms of the contract or the circumstances of the case (Art. 3(1)).

Furthermore, freedom of choice means that the parties may at any time agree to subject the contract to a law other than that which previously governed it, either as a result of a choice-of-law agreement or of other provisions of Rome I (Art. 3(2), 1st period). However, changes made after the conclusion of the contract do not prejudice its validity nor affect the rights of third parties (Art. 3(2), 2nd period).

Moreover, freedom of choice does not prejudice provisions which cannot be derogated from by agreement of the law of a country where all *other elements relevant* to the situation at the time of the choice are located but other than the country whose law has been chosen. The same applies *mutatis mutandis* concerning similar provisions of Community law, where appropriate as implemented in the Member State of the forum (Art. 3(3)(4)).

In the absence of choice, Rome I provides for in Article 4(1) specific criteria for different types of contracts, such as: contracts for the *sale of goods* are governed by the law of the country where the seller has his habitual residence (i); contracts for the *provision of services* are governed by the law of the country where the service provider has his habitual residence (ii); although *franchise* and *distribution contracts* are considered contracts for services (Recital 17, 2nd period), they are subject to specific rules, as franchise and distribution contracts are governed by the law of the country where the franchisee or distributor has his habitual residence (iii); contracts relating to a right *in rem* in immovable property are governed by the law of the country where the property is situated (iv).

Where the contract cannot be categorized as being one of the specified types or where its elements fall within more than one of the specified types (e.g. a contract consisting of a bundle of rights and obligations), it is governed by the law of the country where the party required to effect the *characteristic performance* has his *habitual residence* (Art. 4(2))[66]. The time of conclusion of the contract is the relevant point in time to determine the habitual residence (Art. 19(3)).

An *escape clause* is provided in Article 4(3) for such cases where it is clear from all circumstances that the contract is manifestly more closely connected with a country other than that indicated in Article 4(1) or (2), so that the law of the that other country applies. Recital 20 indicates that in order to determine that country, account should be taken, *inter alia*, of whether the contract in question has a very close relationship with another contract or contracts. Moreover where, in the absence of choice, the applicable law cannot be determined either on the basis of the fact that the contract can be categorized as one of the specified types (i) or as being the law of the country of habitual residence of the party required to effect the characteristic performance of the contract (ii), the contract is governed by the law of the country with which it is most closely connected (Art. 4(4)).

Rome I provides for specific conflict-of-law rules on contracts of carriage, consumer contracts, insurance contracts, and individual employment contracts (Arts. 5 to 8), implementing the principle of protection of the weaker party (Recital 23). For example, *consumer contracts* - i.e. contracts concluded by a natural person for a purpose which can be regarded as being outside his trade or profession (the consumer) with another person acting in the exercise of his trade or profession (the professional) – are governed by the law of the country of *habitual residence of the consumer*, provided that the professional pursues his commercial or professional activities in that country or, by any means, directs such activities to that

[66] The theory of absorption seems to be indicated to apply to mixed contracts as 'the characteristic performance of the contract' is to be determined having regard to its 'centre of gravity' (Recital 19).

country or to several countries including that country, and the contract falls within the scope of such activities (Art. 6(1)).[67] In these circumstances, despite choice of law agreements are allowed, they cannot deprive the consumer of the protection afforded to him by provisions of the country of his habitual residence that cannot be derogated from by agreement (Art. 6(2)). However, these consumer protective conflict-of-law rules meet various exceptions. In fact, they do not apply in certain cases, such as, namely, contracts for the supply of services where the services are to be supplied to the consumer exclusively in a country other than that in which he has his habitual residence (Art. 6(4)).

The application of the *overriding mandatory provisions* of the law of the *forum* is safeguarded under Rome I (Art. 9(2)). It is understood that considerations of public interest justify giving the courts of the Member State the possibility, in exceptional circumstances, of applying exceptions based on public policy and overriding mandatory provisions. However, Recital 37 indicates that 'overriding mandatory provisions' are to be distinguished from 'provisions which cannot be derogated from by agreement', so that they are construed more restrictively. Article 9(1) provides for a

---

[67] Reference to the concept of directed activity as a condition for applying the consumer protection rule is intended to achieve an harmonious interpretation of the concept both in Regulation (EC) n° 44/2001 and this Regulation, taking into account the joint declaration by the Council and the Commission on Article 15 of Regulation (EC) n° 44/2001 according to which: 'for Article 15(1)(c) to be applicable it is not sufficient for an undertaking to target its activities at the Member State of the consumer's residence, or at a number of Member States including that Member State; a contract must also be concluded within the framework of its activities'. The declaration also states that 'the mere fact that an Internet site is accessible is not sufficient for Article 15 to be applicable, although a factor will be that this Internet site solicits the conclusion of distance contracts and that a contract has actually been concluded at a distance, by whatever means. In this respect, the language or currency which a website uses does not constitute a relevant factor.' (Recital 24). See L. de Lima Pinheiro, «Direito aplicável aos contratos com consumidores», *Revista da Ordem dos Advogados* 66/1 (2001), p. 162 ff; Idem, «Direito aplicável aos contratos celebrados através da Internet», *Direito da Sociedade da Informação* VII (2008), pp. 363 ff (389).

definition of 'overriding mandatory provisions' according to which they 'are provisions the respect for which is regarded as crucial by a country for safeguarding its public interests, such as its political, social or economic organization, to such an extent that they are applicable to any situation falling within their scope, irrespective of the law otherwise applicable to the contract under this Regulation.'[68] Moreover, overriding mandatory provisions of the law of the country where the obligations arising out of the contract have to be or have been performed may only be given effect in so far as they render the performance of the contract unlawful, having in regard to their nature and purpose and the consequences of their application or non-application (Art. 9(3)). One of these consequences may be the restrictions of *free movement of goods and services* as regulated by Community instruments, notably Directive 2000/31 on electronic commerce referred to in Recital 40.

Concerning consent and *validity of contracts*, Rome I establishes, through a rule of multiple alternative links, the principle of *favor negotii*, with some exceptions, concerning namely consumer contracts and contracts the subject matter of which is a right *in rem* in immovable property (Art. 11(4) and (5)).

To begin with, the existence and material validity of a contract, or of any term thereof, is determined by the law which would govern it under Rome I if the contract or term were valid; however, if it appears from the circumstances that it would not be reasonable for a party to determine the effect of his conduct in accordance with such law, such party may rely upon the law of the country in

[68] See, e.g., Judgment of the Court (Fifth Chamber) of 9 November 2000, C-381/98, *Ingmar GB Ltd* v *Eaton Leonard Technologies Inc.* [2000] *ECR* I-09305 ('The purpose of the regime established in Articles 17 to 19 of the Directive [86/653 on self-employed commercial agents], which is mandatory in nature, is to protect, for all commercial agents, freedom of establishment and the operation of undistorted competition in the internal market, so that they must be applied where the situation is closely connected with the Community').

which he has his habitual residence in order to establish that he did not consent (Art. 10(1) and (2)).

Then, concerning *formal validity*, a contract concluded between persons who are in the same country at the time of its conclusion is formally valid if it satisfies the formal requirements of the law which governs it in substance under this Regulation or of the law of the country where it is concluded (Art. 11(1)). In case the parties are in different countries, it is also valid if it satisfies the formal requirements of the law of either of the countries where any of the parties had his habitual residence at the time of conclusion of the contract (Art. 11(2)).

The formal validity of consumer contracts is governed by the law of the country where the consumer has his habitual residence (Art. 11(4)), and, concerning contracts the subject matter of which is a right *in rem* in immovable property or a tenancy of immovable property, the requirements of form of the law of the country where the property is situated apply if by that law those requirements are imposed irrespective of the country where the contract is concluded and irrespective of the law governing the contract and cannot be derogated by agreement (Art. 11(5)).

6. Recognition and enforcement of foreign judgments and interim measures

Where Regulation Brussels I as well as Brussels and Lugano Conventions do not apply, a Portuguese court will follow the *system of judicial review and confirmation* provided for the Portuguese Código de Processo Civil (Code of Civil Procedure, hereinafter CCP), according to which, without prejudice to the provisions of international conventions, Community regulations or special legislation, no judgment on private rights given by a foreign court can have effects in Portugal, whatever the nationality of the parties, without judicial review and confirmation (Art. 1094(1)). However, revision is not required when such judgment is invoked in proceedings pending in Portuguese courts as a mere means of proof subject to the appreciation of the competent court (Art. 1094(2) CCP).

The District court of appeals of the domicile of the person against whom the judgment is to be enforced has jurisdiction over proceedings of revision and confirmation of foreign judgments (Art. 1095 CCP).

In order for a foreign judgment to be confirmed several *requirements* must be fulfilled concerning the judgment (Art. 1096 CCP): no doubt can exist as to the authenticity of the document which contains the judgment nor to the intelligibility of the decision (a); it has to be final and cannot be appealed according to the law of the country in which it has been given (b); it must be given by a foreign court the jurisdiction of which has not been caused by fraud to the law and which does not decide upon matters of exclusive jurisdiction of Portuguese courts (c); the exceptions of *lis pendens* or final decision ('caso julgado') cannot be invoked upon proceedings pending in a Portuguese court, unless the foreign court has declined jurisdiction (d); the defendant has been regularly called to the proceedings, under the law of the country of origin, and the principles of contradictory and equality of the parties have been observed in the proceedings (e); and finally it is required that the foreign judgment does not contain any decision the recognition of which leads to a result manifestly incompatible with the principles of the international public order of the Portuguese State (f).

Submitted with the application the document that contains the decision to be reviewed, the other party is notified to contest within 15 days (Art. 1098 CCP). The application can only be contested upon grounds of lack of any of the requirements that must be fulfilled for the foreign judgment to be reviewed and upon other grounds of revision provided for in the Code (Art. 1100 CCP).

At its own motion, the court checks whether the requirements laid down in Article 1096 are fulfilled and it denies confirmation where any of those requirements is not met, e.g., where proceedings have not observed the principles of contradictory and equality of the parties (Art. 1101 CCP). The decision of the court can be appealed from to the Supreme Court of Justice (Art. 1102 CCP).

A different *exequatur system* is set up under Brussels I, which lays down in Chapter III provisions on recognition and enforcement of foreign judgments and interim measures. As stated in Recitals 16 to 18, the principle of mutual trust in the administration of justice in the Community justifies judgments given in a Member State being recognized automatically without the need for any procedure except in cases of dispute (1) and demands the procedure for making enforceable in one Member State a judgment given in another to be efficient and rapid, so that the declaration that a judgment is enforceable is issued virtually automatically after purely formal checks of the documents supplied, without there being any possibility for the court to raise of its own motion any of the grounds for non-enforcement provided for by this Regulation (2).

Nonetheless, in order to respect the rights of the defense, the defendant is able to appeal in an adversarial procedure, against the declaration of enforceability, if he considers that any of the grounds for non-enforcement is present, and redress procedures are also available to the claimant where his application for a declaration of enforceability has been rejected.

Brussels I provides a comprehensive notion of *judgment* according to which '"judgment" means any judgment given by a court or tribunal of a Member State, whatever the judgment may be called, including a decree, order, decision or writ of execution, as well as the determination of costs or expenses by an officer of the court" (Art. 32). This notion of 'judgment' seems to include 'foreign interim/

preliminary measures'[69]. Settlements are to be excluded from the notion of judgment, as ruled by the ECJ: "The definition of a "judgment" given in Article 25 of the [Brussels] Convention [...] refers, for the purposes of the application of the various provisions of the Convention in which the term is used, solely to judicial decisions actually given by a court or tribunal of a Contracting State deciding on its own authority on the issues between the parties. That is not the case as far as a settlement is concerned, even if it was reached in a court of a Contracting State and brings legal proceedings to an end, because settlements in court are essentially contractual in that their terms depend first and foremost on the parties' intention."[70]

However, Brussels I provides for criteria on recognition and enforcement of settlements which are identical to those provided for authentic instruments and which follow procedures similar to those provided for judgments (Arts. 57(1) and 58).

A judgment given in a Member State is to be automatically recognized in the other Member States without any special procedure (Art. 33(1)). However, recognition is to be denied in case one or more of the following situations provided for in Article 34 occur, such as: recognition is manifestly contrary to *public policy* in the Member State in which recognition is sought[71] (a); it concerns

---

[69] These are excluded from the notion of judgment provided for in the Hague Convention, which however does not govern such measures (Art. 4(1) and Article 7). This Convention is not yet in force. The European Community has declared, in accordance with Article 30 of the Convention on Choice of Court Agreements that it exercises competence over all the matters governed by this Convention. Its Member States will not sign, ratify, accept or approve the Convention, but shall be bound by the Convention by virtue of its conclusion by the European Community'. For the purpose of this declaration, the term "European Community" does not include Denmark by virtue of Articles 1 and 2 of the Protocol on the position of Denmark annexed to the Treaty on European Union and the Treaty establishing the European Community'.

[70] Judgment of 2 June 1994, C-414/92, *Solo Kleinmotoren GmbH* v *Emilio Boch* [1994] *ECR* I-2237.

[71] See Judgment of 11 May 2000, C-38/98, *Régie Nationale des Usines Renault SA* v *Maxicar SpA and Orazio Formento* [2000] *ECR* I-2973, ruling that 'the decision from a court of a Member State to recognize the existence of an intellectual property right

a judgment given in default of appearance, if the defendant was not served with the document which instituted the proceedings or with an equivalent document in sufficient time and in such a way as to enable him to arrange for his defence (*inaudita altera pars*), unless the defendant failed to commence proceedings to challenge the judgment when it was possible for him to do so (b); it is irreconcilable with a judgment given in a dispute between the same parties in the Member State in which recognition is sought (c); it is irreconcilable with an earlier judgment given in another Member State or in a third State involving the same cause of action and between the same parties, provided that the earlier judgment fulfils the conditions necessary for its recognition in the Member State addressed (d).

Moreover, in case recognition is contested by an interested party - either as the principal issue in a dispute or as an incidental question (Art. 33(1)(2)) -, a judgment is not to be recognized if it was given by a court without jurisdiction, according to Brussels I, concerning namely matters relating to insurance, consumer contracts, and proceedings subject to exclusive jurisdiction (Art. 35(1)). In the examination of such grounds of jurisdiction, the court or authority applied is bound by the findings of fact on which the court of the Member State of origin based its jurisdiction (Art. 35(2)). However, this justification for non-recognition of the judgment is not to be raised by the courts of their *own motion*, because the jurisdiction of the court of the Member State of origin may not be reviewed and the test of public policy may not be applied to the rules relating

in car body parts, and to confer on the holder of that right protection by enabling him to prevent third party trading in another Member State from manufacturing and commercializing in that State, cannot be considered to be contrary to public policy'. See R.M. de Moura Ramos, «Public Policy in the Framework of the Brussels Conventions: Remarks on two Recent Decisions by the European Court of Justice», *Yearbook of Private International Law – YPIL* II (2000), pp. 25-40.

to jurisdiction (Art. 35(3). Moreover, under no circumstances may a foreign judgment be reviewed as to its substance (Art. 36).

Concerning *enforcement* in other Member States, the judgment must be declared enforceable in the Member State of origin on the application of any interested party, to be submitted to a specific court or competent authority (Arts. 38(1) and 39(1)), which issues the declaration of enforceability 'immediately' on completion of certain formalities and without any review of the impediments of recognition (Art. 41). I.e., the courts are not to raise of their own motion the grounds for non-enforcement. Nonetheless, the decision on the application for a declaration of enforceability may be appealed against by either party (Art. 43(1)). A *declaration of enforceability* is to be refused or revoked by the competent court of appeal (Arts 43 and 44) only on one of the grounds that justify non recognition (Arts 34 and 35) [72], but under no circumstances may the foreign judgment be reviewed as to its substance (Art. 45(1)(2)).

A *settlement* which has been approved by a court in the course of proceedings and is enforceable in the Member State in which it was concluded is to be enforced in the State addressed under the same conditions as authentic instruments (Art. 58). It means, *ex vi* Article 57(1), it must follow the same procedure as provided for judgments: the settlement must be declared enforceable in the Member State of origin on the application of any interested party, to be submitted to a specific court or competent authority (Arts. 38(1) and 39(1)), which issues the declaration of enforceability "immediately" on completion of certain formalities and without any review of the impediments of recognition (Art. 41).

However, as provided for authentic instruments (Art. 57(1), 2nd period), in case an appeal is lodged, the competent court can refuse

[72] See Tribunal da Relação de Lisboa (Lisbon Court of Appeals), Judgment of 16 December 2008, Proc. 10053/2008-1 (available at www.dgsi.pt/jtrl).

or revoke a declaration of enforceability only in case enforcement of the instrument is manifestly contrary to public policy in the Member State addressed. It means that a declaration of enforceability cannot be refused or revoked upon any other grounds that justify non-recognition.

Under Brussels I, recognition of judgments and provisional measures handed down after *ex parte* proceedings[73] is to be denied where it concerns a judgment given in default of appearance, if the defendant was not served with the document which instituted the proceedings or with an equivalent document in sufficient time and in such a way as to enable him to arrange for his defence (*inaudita altera pars*), unless the defendant failed to commence proceedings to challenge the judgment when it was possible for him to do so (Art. 34(b)). Moreover, in case recognition is contested by an interested party - either as the principal issue in a dispute or as an incidental question (Art. 33(1)(2)) -, a judgment is not to be recognized if it was given by a court without jurisdiction, according to Brussels I, concerning namely proceedings subject to exclusive jurisdiction (Art. 35(1)). However, this cause of non recognition is not to be raised by the courts of their own motion. I particular, the test of public policy may not be applied to the rules relating to jurisdiction (Art. 35(3).

Furthermore, in order to be enforced in the other Member States, judgments and provisional measures handed down after *ex parte* proceedings must be declared enforceable in the Member State of origin on the application of any interested party, to be submitted to a specific court or competent authority (Arts. 38(1) and 39(1)),

---

[73] '*Ex parte measures* mean, in the context of provisional measures, temporary orders issued by the court based on one part's request without hearing from the other side' – Green Paper on the Review of Council Regulation (EC) No 44/2001 on Jurisdiction and the Recognition and Enforcement of Judgments in Civil and Commercial Matters, COM (2009) 175 final, p. 8, fn. 13.

which issues the declaration of enforceability 'immediately' on completion of certain formalities and without any review of the impediments of recognition (Art. 41).

The decision on the application for a declaration of enforceability may be appealed against by either party (Art. 43(1)). A declaration of enforceability is to be refused or revoked by the competent court of appeals (Arts 43 and 44) only on one of the grounds that justify non recognition (Arts 34 and 35), but under no circumstances may the foreign judgment be reviewed as to its substance (Art. 45(1)(2)).

Under Brussels I, judgments given by the courts of Ireland or the United Kingdom pose specific problems. On one hand, in general, for a court of a Member State in which recognition is sought of a judgment given in another Member State to stay the proceedings, it is required that an ***ordinary*** appeal against the judgment has been lodged (Art. 37(1)). However, concerning a judgment given in Ireland or the United Kingdom the court may stay the proceedings if enforcement is suspended in the State of origin by reason of an appeal (Art. 37(2)). On the other hand, concerning enforcement, in general, a judgment given in a Member State and enforceable in that State is enforced in another Member State when, on the application of any interested party, it has been declared enforceable there (Art. 38(1)), registration not being required. However, in the United Kingdom, for such a judgment to be enforced in England and Wales, in Scotland, or in Northern Ireland, it must have been registered for enforcement in that part of the United Kingdom on the application of any interested party (Art. 38(1)).

Finally, any form of appeal available in Ireland or the United Kingdom is treated as an ordinary appeal for purposes of Article 46(1), which provides for that the court with which an appeal is lodged under Article 43 or Article 44 may, on the application of the party against whom enforcement is sought, stay the proceedings if an ordinary appeal has been lodged against the judgment in the Member State of origin or if the time for such an appeal has not yet expired; in the latter case, the court may specify the time within which such an appeal is to be lodged.

6. Intellectual property conflict of laws rules and international jurisdiction

There is no domestic rule specially designed for international jurisdiction over intellectual property issues. Nonetheless, Brussels I (as well as the Brussels and Lugano Conventions) provides for a special rule of international jurisdiction, regardless of domicile, for proceedings concerned with the *registration or validity* of patents, trademarks, designs, or other similar rights required to be deposited or registered, according to which the courts of the Member State in which the deposit or registration has been applied for, has taken place or is under the terms of a Community instrument or an international convention deemed to have taken place, have *exclusive* jurisdiction (Art. 22(4)). Choice of court agreements contrary to this rule of exclusive jurisdiction have no legal force (Art. 23(5)), and a court of a Member State must declare of its own motion that it has no jurisdiction in case it is seized of a claim which is principally concerned with such a matter over which the courts of another Member State have *exclusive jurisdiction* (Art. 25).

The case is rather sensitive concerning European patents granted for several Member States, which could even justify the jurisdiction of the courts of a Member State in which a person is domiciled, where he is one of a number of defendants, as the claims would be so closely connected that it would be expedient to hear and determine them together to avoid the risk of irreconcilable judgments resulting from separate proceedings (Art. 6(1))

It might be argued, a *contrario sensu*, that in case a claim concerned with such a matter is only incidentally raised and jurisdiction is not contested, the court could give a judgment over such questions the effects of which would be limited to *inter partes* provided such judgments are possible under *lex fori*, as suggested by CLIP[74]. Within these constraints choice of court agreements - e.g. within license agreements - would also be admitted to confer jurisdiction over such matters where incidentally raised to the chosen court (as provided for under the Hague Convention).

However, Portuguese courts are not expected to depart from the ECJ restrictive rulings[75], which have been later confirmed by the revision of the Lugano Convention (Art. 22(4)), even if they may evidence 'shortcomings of the current system'[76]. In fact, Portuguese

---

[74] CLIP - European Max-Planck Group for Conflict of Laws in Intellectual Property, Exclusive Jurisdiction and Cross Border IP (Patent) Infringement. Suggestions for Amendment of the Brussels I Regulation (20.12.2006), *EIPR* (2007) p. 193 ff. For the US, see American Law Institute, *Intellectual Property: Principles Governing Jurisdiction, Choice of Law, and Judgments in Transnational Disputes*. As Adopted and Promulgated by the American Law Institute at San Francisco, California May 14, 2007, St. Paul, Minnesota, American Law Institute Publishers, 2008 (ALI Principles).

[75] Judgment of the Court (First Chamber) of 13 July 2006, C-4/03, *Gesellschaft für Antriebstechnik mbH & Co. KG (GAT)* v *Lamellen und Kupplungsbau Beteiligungs KG (LuK)* [2006] *ECR* I-6509, and concerning Article 6(1), Judgment of the Court (First Chamber) of 13 July 2006, C-539/03, *Roche Nederland BV and Others* v. *Fredrick Primus and Milton Goldberg* [2006] *ECR* I- 06535. On the impact of this jurisprudence see notably A. Kur, «A farewell to cross-border injunctions? The ECJ decisions GAT v. LuK and Roche Nederland v. Primus and Goldenberg», *International Review of Industrial Property and Copyright Law* IIC 37 (2006), pp. 844 ff; P. A. Miguel Asensio, «Cross-Border Adjudication of Intellectual Property Rights and Competition between Jurisdictions», *Annali Italiani del Diritto d'Autore, della Cultura e dello Spettacolo* - AIDA XVI (2007) p. 1.

[76] Green Paper on the Review of Council Regulation (EC) No 44/2001 on Jurisdiction and the Recognition and Enforcement of Judgments in Civil and Commercial Matters, COM (2009) 175 final, question 4, p. 7. See also Report from the Commission to the European Parliament, the Council and the European Economic and Social Committee on the application of Council Regulation (EC) No 44/2001 on jurisdiction and the recognition and enforcement of judgments in civil and commercial matters, COM(2009) 174 final, Brussels, 21.4.2009; B. Hees et al., *Report on the Application of Regulation Brussels I in the Member States*, Study JLS/C4/2005/03, Final Version September 2007.

courts normally base their application of Brussels I upon the ECJ jurisprudence. For example, the Supreme Court of Justice ruled that an international license to broadcast football matches is not to qualify as a contract for the provision of services within the meaning of the second indent of Article 5(1)(b) of Brussels I[77].

Moreover, concerning choice of court agreements, this court held that domestic law cannot add formal requirements to those provided for under Brussels I[78], and another court decided Brussels I does not provide the courts with the possibility to *control the grounds of jurisdiction* of a court chosen by agreement, namely as *forum non conveniens*[79].

There is also 'case-law' of the Supreme Court of Justice holding that a choice of court agreement concerning a *license contract* does not include litigations concerning the termination of the contract and tort liability caused by unlawful acts committed by the plaintiff in Portugal[80]. However, the same Court ruled, in a different case, that a choice of court agreement concerns any dispute that arises out of the main contract and therefore jurisdiction of the chosen court includes all issues, either contractual or tort, that result thereof[81]. Furthermore, taking into consideration that a choice of court agree-

---

[77] Supremo Tribunal de Justiça (Supreme Court of Justice), Judgement of 21 May 2009, Proc. 4986/06.3TVLSB.S1 (available at www.dgsi.pt/jstj). See Judgment of the Court (Fourth Chamber) of 23 April 2009, C-533/07, *Falco Privatstiftung and Thomas Rabitsch* v *Gisela Weller-Lindhorst*, OJ C 141/15, 20.6.2009.

[78] Judgment of 8 October 2009, Proc. 5138/06.8TBSTS.S1, available at ww.dgsi.pt/jstj. See Judgment of 24 June 1981, C-150/80, *Elefanten Schuh GmbH* v *Jacqmain*, *ECR* 1981 01671.

[79] Tribunal da Relação de Lisboa (Lisbon Court of Appeals), Judgment of 21 May 2009, Proc. 8748/2008-6 (available at www.dgsi.pt/jtrl). See Judgment of the Court of 1 March 2005, C-281/02, *Andrew Owusu* v *N.B. Jackson, Trading as Villa Holidays Bal In Villas and others* [2005] *ECR* I-1383, par. 37-40.

[80] Supremo Tribunal de Justiça (Supreme Court of Justice), Judgment of 12 April 1997, Proc. 98B292 (available at www.dgsi.pt/jstj).

[81] Judgment of 8 October 2009, Proc. 5138/06.8TBSTS.S1 (available at www.dgsi.pt/jstj).

ment can allow a party to depart from such agreement, this court accepted that such a party could apply before a court the issuance of provisional measures, even if that court does not have jurisdiction over the substance of the action.[82] Finally, there is Portuguese jurisprudence holding that an *international arbitration agreement* does not exclude the international jurisdiction of Portuguese courts concerning related *interim provisional procedures*[83].

Law applicable to intellectual property issues

Under domestic law, intellectual property is subject to a special provision of the Civil Code (Art. 48), according to which: the law applicable to copyright is the law of the first publication of the work and, in case it is not published, the personal law of the author, without prejudice of special legislation; the law applicable to industrial property is the law of the country of its creation. However, international conventions and Community regulations render this domestic provision almost irrelevant[84].

According to well-established interpretation of Article 5(2), 2nd period, of the Berne Convention, copyright is governed by *the law of the country for which protection is claimed* (*lex loci protectionis*). In this sense is Article 63 of the Copyright Act to be interpreted, as it provides that the copyright protection claimed for Portugal is determined by Portuguese law. However, this principle meets several exceptions concerning namely copyright ownership and issues related to copyright contracts[85].

---

[82] Judgment of 17 December 2004, Proc. 04B4076 (available at www.dgsi.pt/jstj).

[83] Tribunal da Relação de Lisboa (Lisbon Court of Appeals), Judgments of 2 December 2003 and 13 March 2007 (available at www.dgsi.pt/jtrl).

[84] Cf. L. de Lima Pinheiro, «A lei aplicável aos direitos de propriedade intelectual», *Revista da Faculdade de Direito Universidade de Lisboa* 42 (2001), pp. 63 ff; See D. Moura Vicente, op. cit. n. 41, pp. 230.

[85] On this issue see Lima Pinheiro op. cit. n. 84, p. 63; D. Moura Vicente, «Direito internacional de autor», *Estudos em Homenagem à Professora Doutora Isabel*

To begin with, the Supremo Tribunal de Justiça (*Supreme Court of Justice*) has ruled[86] that *copyright ownership* is governed by the law of the country of origin of the work as defined by the Berne Convention (Art. 5(4)). This solution is expressly provided for copyright ownership of software[87] and databases[88]. However it's been argued that it should not apply to moral rights[89]. Moreover, the Berne Convention provides for in Article 14-*bis*(2)(a) that copyright ownership 'in a cinematographic work shall be a matter for legislation in the country where [i.e. for which] protection is claimed' (*lex loci protectionis*).

Then, concerning issues related to *copyright contracts*, including copyright ownership of works created by employees or works made for hire, these are considered to be governed by *lex contractus* or *lex loci laboris.*[90] Moreover, the law applicable to copyright, either *lex loci protectionis, lex originis or lex contractus,* meets several limitations, concerning namely the principle of reciprocity[91], overriding mandatory provisions and *ordre public* (e.g. renunciation to moral rights).

Industrial property is also governed, in general, by *lex loci protectionis*, i.e. the law of the country for which protection is claimed (Paris Convention, Arts. 4-bis(1), 6(2)(3) and 6-quinquies(B). This

---

Magalhães Colaço, I, Coimbra, Almedina, 2002, pp. 469 ff; P. Torremans, «Authorship, Ownership of Right and Works Created by Employees. Which Law Applies?» *EIPR* 27/6 (2005), pp. 220 ff.

86 STJ, Judgment of 10 January 2008, available at www.dgsi.pt/jstj.

87 Software Copyright Act, Decree-Law 252/94, Article 17(4).

88 Databases Copyright Act, Decree-Law 122/2000, Article 2(4).

89 Cf. Lima Pinheiro, op. cit. n. 84, p. 63; D. Moura Vicente, op. cit. n. 41, pp. 230-1, 236-7.

90 See also Labour Code, Article 6. An application of this provision has been given by Tribunal da Relação de Lisboa (Lisbon Court of Appeals), Judgment of 2 April 2008 (available at www.dgsi.pt/jstj).

91 Berne Convention, Article 6(1), see also, concerning the *droit de suite*, Article 14-ter(2), and Directive *droit de suite*, Article 7(1).

solution applies also to non-registered well-known trademarks which are to be protected according to the Paris Convention (Art. 6-bis). However, matters of *registration and validity* of industrial property rights are governed by *lex originis*, i.e. the law of the country of registration (Civil Code, Art. 48(2)). Moreover, the Supremo Tribunal de Justiça (Supreme Court of Justice) has decided that the law chosen by the parties to govern their license contract can also apply to torts related to such a contract (e.g., in case the use of the licensed right exceeds the terms of the license)[92]. Finally, the law applicable to industrial property litigations meets also several limitations, namely *ordre public* of *lex fori* (e.g., the right of the inventor to be identified in the patent title[93]).

Regulation Rome II on the law applicable to non-contractual obligations establishes specific criteria for torts/delicts concerning *infringement* of intellectual property rights. These criteria prevail over freedom of choice preserved in Article 14, as the law applicable under them may not be derogated from by a choice-of-law agreement (Art. 8(3) Rome II). Instead of the general rule which designates the law of the country in which the damage occurs irrespective of the country in which the event giving rise to the damage occurred and irrespective of the country or countries in which the indirect consequences of that event occur (Art. 4(1)), the 'universally acknowledged' principle of *lex loci protectionis* is provided for in Article 8(1) Rome II, i.e., the law of the country for which protection is claimed[94]. This solution corresponds to

---

[92] Supremo Tribunal de Justiça, Judgment of 16 October 2002, I *Colectânea de Jurisprudência / Acórdãos do Supremo Tribunal de Justiça - CJ/ASTJ* (2002) p. 11.

[93] D. Moura Vicente, op. cit. n. 41, p. 279.

[94] See e.g. N. Boschiero, «Infringement of Intellectual Property Rights. A Commentary on Article 8 of the Rome II Regulation», *Yearbook of Private International Law* – YPIL IX (2007), p. 87; G. Palao Moreno, «La proteccion de los derechos de propiedad intelectual en Europa: el artículo 8 del Reglamento Roma II», *Revista Jurídica de Deporte y Entretenimiento* 22 (2008), p. 557.

the Berne Convention (Art. 5(2), 2nd period) as well as to the Paris Convention (Arts. 2(2), 4-bis(1), 6(2)(3) and 6-quinquies(B)).

However, concerning *unitary* Community intellectual property rights and only for any question that is not governed by the relevant Community instrument, the law applicable is the law of the country in which the act of infringement was committed – *lex deliciti comissi* (Art. 8(2) Rome II).

Concerning the law applicable to IP issues related to *contractual obligations* under Rome I, the parties may choose the law applicable to contractual obligations concerning intellectual property rights within the conditions laid down in Article 3 of Rome I. Portuguese courts did already accept that the law chosen by the parties to govern their license contract can also apply to torts related to such a contract (e.g., in case the use of the licensed right exceeds the terms of the license)[95].

In the *absence of choice*, Regulation Rome I provides for in Article 4(1) specific criteria for different types of contracts. It is not clear however whether or how would these criteria apply to IPR contracts. Should a contract for *transfer* of intellectual property rights qualify as a contract for the sale of goods, then the law of the country where the seller has his habitual residence would apply. Moreover, should a contract of *work made for hire* qualify as a contract for the provision of services, then the law of the country where the service provider has his habitual residence would apply. These may however be disputed qualifications. For special contracts which normally comprehend intellectual property rights, namely franchise and distribution contracts and despite they are considered contracts for services (Recital 17, 2nd period), Rome I provides specific rules, as franchise and distribution contracts are

[95] Supremo Tribunal de Justiça (Supreme Court of Justice), Judgment of 16 October 2002, I *CJ/ASTJ* (2002) p. 11.

governed by the law of the country where the franchisee or distributor has his habitual residence. Nonetheless, the ECJ held that the second indent of Article 5(1)(b) of Regulation Brussels I "is to be interpreted to the effect that a contract under which the owner of an intellectual property right grants its contractual partner the right to use that right in return for remuneration is not a contract for the provision of services within the meaning of that provision"[96].

For reasons of consistency between Brussels I and Rome, this ECJ judgment should be taken into account. It means that, in the absence of choice, intellectual property license contracts would be governed by the law of the country where the *licensor* has his habitual residence.

In case the contract cannot be categorized as being one of the specified types or where its elements fall within more than one of the specified types (e.g. a contract consisting of a bundle of rights and obligations), it is governed by the law of the country where the party required to effect the characteristic performance has his *habitual residence* (Art. 4(2)), and it is indicated that 'the characteristic performance of the contract' is to be determined having regard to its 'centre of gravity' (Recital 19). An 'escape clause' is provided for in Article 4(3) for such cases where it is clear from all circumstances that the contract is manifestly more closely connected with a country other than that indicated in Article 4(1) or (2), so that the law of the that other country applies. Recital 20 indicates that in order to determine that country, account should be taken, *inter alia*, of whether the contract in question has a very close relationship with another contract or contracts. The same law applies where, in the absence of choice, the applicable law cannot be determined either on the basis of the fact that the contract can

[96] Judgment of the Court (Fourth Chamber) of 23 April 2009, C-533/07, *Falco Privatstiftung and Thomas Rabitsch* v *Gisela Weller-Lindhorst*, OJ C 141/15, 20.6.2009.

be categorized as one of the specified types or as being the law of the country of habitual residence of the party required to effect the characteristic performance of the contract (Art. 4(4)).

Literature

Intellectual Property: Ascensão, José de Oliveira, *Direito Civil – Direito de Autor e Direitos Conexos* (Coimbra, Coimbra Editora, 1992); Gonçalves, Luís Couto, *Manual de Direito Industrial - Patentes, desenhos ou modelos, marcas, concorrência desleal*, 2ª ed. (Coimbra, Almedina, 2008); Marques, João Paulo Remédio, *Biotecnologias e propriedade intelectual* (Coimbra, Almedina, 2007); Olavo, Carlos, *Propriedade Industrial*, I, 2.ª ed. (Coimbra, Almedina, 2005); Pereira, Alexandre L. Dias, *Direitos de Autor e Liberdade de Informação* (Coimbra, Almedina, 2008); Rebello, Luiz Francisco, *Código do Direito de Autor e dos Direitos Conexos anotado*, 3ª ed. (Âncora Editora, 2002); Serens, Manuel C. Nogueira, *A Monopolização da Concorrência e a (Re-) Emergência da Tutela da Marca* (Coimbra, Almedina, 2007).

Jurisdiction and international private law: Correia, António Ferrer, *Lições de Direito Internacional Privado*, I (Coimbra, Almedina, 2000), *Direito Internacional Privado – Alguns Problemas* (Coimbra, 1997); Machado, João Baptista, *Lições de Direito Internacional Privado*, 2ª ed. (Coimbra, Almedina, 1982); Pinheiro, Luís de Lima, *Estudos de Direito Internacional Privado. Direito de Conflitos, Competência Internacional e Reconhecimento de Decisões Estrangeiras* (Coimbra, Almedina, 2006), II *Contratos, Obrigações Extracontratuais, Insolvência, Operações Bancárias, Operações sobre Instrumentos Financeiros e Reconhecimento de Decisões Estrangeiras* (Coimbra, Almedina, 2009) - *Direito Internacional Privado* (Coimbra, Almedina, I, 2008, 2ª ed.; II, 2002 (2ª ed.), vol. III 2002, 2ª ed.); Ramos, Rui

Manuel de Moura, *Estudos de Direito Internacional Privado e de Direito Processual Civil Internacional – II* (Coimbra, Coimbra Editora, 2007) - *Direito Internacional Privado e Direito Comunitário. Termos de uma Interacção*, in Nos 20 Anos do Código das Sociedades Comerciais Homenagem aos Professores Doutores A. Ferrer Correia, Orlando de Carvalho e Vasco Lobo Xavier, III, (Coimbra, Coimbra Editora, 2007); *Da lei aplicável ao contrato de trabalho internacional* (Coimbra, Almedina, 1991); Santos, António Marques dos, *Direito Internacional Privado. Introdução*, I (Lisboa, AAFDL, 2001) - *As normas de aplicação imediata no Direito Internacional Privado. Esboço de uma teoria geral*, 2 vols. (Coimbra, Almedina, 1991); Soares, Maria Ângela Bento Soares, e Rui Manuel de Moura Ramos, *Contratos Internacionais - Compra e Venda, Cláusulas Penais, Arbitragem* **(Coimbra, 1995)**; Sousa, Miguel Teixeira de, e Dário Moura Vicente, *Comentário à Convenção de Bruxelas de 27 de Setembro de 1968 relativa à competência judiciária e à execução de decisões em matéria civil e comercial e textos complementares* (Lisboa, Lex, 1994); Vicente, Dário Moura, *Direito Internacional Privado: Problemática Internacional da Sociedade da Informação – Relatório* (Coimbra, Almedina, 2005) - *Da responsabilidade pré-contratual em Direito Internacional Privado* (Coimbra, Almedina, 2001)

International jurisdiction, conflict of laws and intellectual property: *Intellectual Property on the Internet: A Survey of Issues* (WIPO/OMPI, Geneva, 2002) - *Primer on Electronic Commerce and Intellectual Property Rights* (WIPO/OMPI Geneva, May 2000); *Intellectual Property and Private International Law* (ed. Josef Drexl and Annette Kur, Oxford/Portland, Hart Publishing, 2005); *International Litigation in Intellectual Property and Information Technology* (ed. Arnaud Nuyts, Wolters Kluwer, Austin, 2008); *Internet: Which Court Decides? Which Law Applies?*, (ed. Katharina Boele-Woelki and Catherine Kessedjian, The Hague, Kluwer, 1998); *Intellectual Property and Private International Law* (ed. Stefan Leible and Ansgar Ohly,

Tübingen, Mohr Siebeck, 2009); Vicente, Dário Moura, *A Tutela Internacional da Propriedade Intelectual* (Coimbra, Almedina, 2009) – *La propriété intellectuelle en droit international privé* (Leiden/ Boston, Martinus Nijhoff Publishers, 2009).

II – Case studies

1 - General / special grounds of jurisdiction

A is an international pop-music idol who has just released a new single. At a point in time when sales of the new single have increased B, the publisher of a monthly music journal, inserts a headline article claiming that the new single of A is a mere adaptation of a song released in the 1950's.

A files a defamation suit.

1) Would a court of your country have international jurisdiction if the defendant B had its residence in your country? Would the decision regarding international jurisdiction of the court of your country differ if the defendant was a corporation having its main place of business in a third country X, but a branch was located your country?

1.1. Under Brussels I, a Portuguese court would have jurisdiction if defendant B had its residence in Portugal. To begin with, defamation suits are not excluded from the scope of application of Brussels I (Art. 1). Then, this Regulation provides for the general criterion of jurisdiction of the EU **country of domicile of the defendant** (Art. 2(1)), regardless of his nationality (Art. 2(2)). Finally, in order to ascertain whether a litigant has domicile in the territory of the Member-State before which courts an action is submitted, the judge applies its internal legislation (Art. 59(1)), and the Portuguese Código Civil (Civil Code) provides for that a person has domicile at the place of her usual residence (Art. 82(1)).

1.2. Despite legal persons are deemed to have domicile at the place of their head office, main administration, or main establishment (Art. 60(1) of Brussels I), the decision regarding international jurisdiction of the Portuguese court would not differ if the defendant is a corporation having its main place of business in a third country X, but the dispute arises out of the operations of a **branch** situated in Portugal (Art. 5(5) of Brussels I).

2) Would a court of your country have international jurisdiction if the copies of the journal were distributed in your country in the language which is officially spoken? Would the decision differ if the journal was printed in your country for distribution in neighboring country X (in a language which is not spoken in your country)?

2.1. If copies of the journal were distributed in Portugal in Portuguese language, the **harmful event** would be deemed to have occurred in Portugal and consequently Portuguese courts would have international jurisdiction, under Brussels I, provided the defendant had domicile in any Member State (Art. 5(3)).

2.2. The decision would not differ if the journal was printed in Portugal for distribution in neighboring country X in a language which is not spoken in Portugal, because, as the ECJ already held, 'the defendant may be sued, at the option of the plaintiff, either in the courts for the place where the damage occurred or in the courts for the place of the event which gives rise to and is at the origin of that damage.'[97] Therefore, reading Brussels I in accordance with this relevant case-law, a Portuguese court would have international jurisdiction under Article 5(3)).

3) Under the law of your country, would residence of the defendant be necessary for a court to have international jurisdiction over A's claim for the overall damage sustained in all countries where the journal was published?

In case the defendant is established in Portugal Portuguese courts would have international jurisdiction over A's claim for the **overall damages** sustained in all countries where the journal was published. According to the ECJ,

'the victim of a libel by a newspaper article distributed in several Contracting States may bring an action for damages against the publisher either before the courts of the Contracting State of the place where the publisher of the defamatory publication is established, which have jurisdiction to award damages for all the harm caused by the defamation, or before the courts of each Contracting State in which the publication was distributed and where the victim claims to have suffered injury to his reputation, which have jurisdiction to rule solely in respect of the harm caused in the State of the court seized.'[98]

---

[97] Judgment of the Court of 30 November 1976, 21-76, *Handelskwekerij G. J. Bier BV* v *Mines de potasse d'Alsace SA* [1976] *ECR* 01735 ('Where the place of the happening of the event which may give rise to liability in tort, delict or quasi-delict and the place where that event results in damage are not identical , the expression "place where the harmful event occurred", in article 5(3) of the Convention of 27 September 1968 on jurisdiction and the enforcement of judgments in civil and commercial matters , must be understood as being intended to cover both the place where the damage occurred and the place of the event giving rise to it .').

[98] Judgment of the Court of 7 March 1995, C-68/93, *Fiona Shevill et. al.* v *Presse Alliance SA* [1995] *ECR* I-415.

Obs.: *Answers to questions 1), 2) and 3) would not differ in cases where intellectual property rights are at stake.*

2 – Subject-matter jurisdiction

A court of country X is dealing with a dispute between A and B concerning an infringement of a foreign patent issued in country Y. During the course of infringement proceedings, B makes a counter-claim that the patent is invalid.

Assuming that a court of your country is the court of country X:

1) Would it have international jurisdiction and would it decide the question of the infringement of foreign intellectual property rights?

Despite a Portuguese court could, under Brussels I, have international jurisdiction and decide the question of the infringement of foreign intellectual property rights namely in case the defendant had domicile in Portugal (Art. 2(1)) or in case the harmful event occurred or might occur in Portugal (Art. 5(3)), as B made a **counterclaim**, during the course of infringement proceedings, that the patent is invalid, a Portuguese court would have to, according to relevant ECJ case-law on Article 25 of Brussels Convention, declare of its own motion that it has no jurisdiction because it is seized of a claim which is principally concerned with a matter over which the courts of another Member State have **exclusive jurisdiction** by virtue of Article 22. In fact, the ECJ held that

'Article 16(4) of the [Brussels] Convention [...] is to be interpreted as meaning that the rule of exclusive jurisdiction laid down therein concerns all proceedings relating to the registration or validity of a patent, irrespective of whether the issue is raised by way of an action or a plea in objection.'[99]

2) Would the court have international jurisdiction to decide upon the issues of validity (and registration) of foreign intellectual property rights? If so what would be the legal effects (inter partes or erga omnes) of such a decision? Would the decision differ with regard to registered and non-registered intellectual property rights?

2.1. The Portuguese court would not have international jurisdiction to decide upon the issues of validity (and registration) of foreign intellectual property rights addressed in the case. In fact, under Brussels I, the validity of patents (and other industrial property rights for which registration or deposit is required) is an issue of **exclusive competence** of the courts of the Member State in which territory registration has been requested or taken place, according to a Community or international instrument (Art. 22(4)). Moreover, the wording of Article 22(4), 2nd paragraph, is rather restrictive, as it provides for that the courts of each Member State have exclusive jurisdiction, regardless of domicile, in proceedings concerned with the registration or validity of any European patent granted for that State, without prejudice to the jurisdiction of the European Patent Office under the Convention on the Grant of European Patents, signed at Munich on 5 October 1973.

Furthermore, according to the ECJ, 'the rule of exclusive jurisdiction laid down [in Article 16(4) of the Brussels Convention] concerns all proceedings relating to the registration or validity of a patent, irrespective of whether the issue is raised by way of an action or a

[99] Judgment of the Court (First Chamber) of 13 July 2006, C-4/03, *Gesellschaft für Antriebstechnik mbH & Co. KG (GAT)* v *Lamellen und Kupplungsbau Beteiligungs KG (LuK)* [2006] *ECR* I-6509.

plea in objection.'[100] The 2007 revision of the Lugano Convention has expressly included this understating into the international instrument: 'irrespective of whether the issue is raised by way of an action or as a defence' (Lugano Convention, Art. 22(4), 2nd paragraph, *in fine*).

2.2. As a Portuguese court would not have international jurisdiction to decide upon the issues of validity of foreign patents, the issue of the **legal effects** (*inter partes* or *erga omnes*) of its decision would not arise. The possibility suggested by CLIP to allow decisions that would not affect the validity or registration of registered intellectual property rights 'as against third parties' would not apply to this case, because the issue of patent validity has been made by defendant B as a 'counterclaim'.[101]

2.3. The decision would differ with regard to registered and non-registered intellectual property rights, because the criterion of exclusive jurisdiction applies only to registered IP rights. It means that a Portuguese court could have international jurisdiction over both **infringement** and **validity** issues of non-registered intellectual property rights.

3) What would be the decision of a court if the question of the validity of a foreign intellectual property right arose as a preliminary question and remained unchallenged by the parties?

---

[100] Judgment of the Court (First Chamber) of 13 July 2006, C-4/03, *Gesellschaft für Antriebstechnik mbH & Co. KG (GAT)* v *Lamellen und Kupplungsbau Beteiligungs KG (LuK)* [2006] *ECR* I-6509.

[101] *Exclusive Jurisdiction and Cross Border IP (Patent) Infringement: Suggestions for Amendment of the Brussels I Regulation*, *EIPR* (2007) pp. 195 ff (suggested Art. 22(4)(b): 'The provisions under lit. (a) do not apply where validity of registration arises in a context other than by principal claim or counterclaim. The decisions resulting from such proceedings do not affect the validity or registration of those rights as against third parties.').

If the question of the validity of a foreign intellectual property right arose as a preliminary question and remained unchallenged by the parties, a Portuguese court could decide to give a judgment both for registered and non-registered intellectual property rights. In fact, Article 25 of Brussels I provides for that a court of a Member State has to declare of its own motion that it does not have jurisdiction where it is seized of a claim which is principally concerned with a matter over which the courts of another Member State have exclusive jurisdiction by virtue of Article 22. Moreover, the ECJ ruling on *GAT* v *LuK* judgment does not provide that 'the rule of exclusive jurisdiction' concerns all *questions* that arise in proceedings but rather 'all *proceedings* relating to the registration or validity of a patent, irrespective of whether the issue is raised by way of an action or a plea in objection' [*emphasis added*]. A *contrario sensu*, in proceedings in which the question of patent validity arises only as a preliminary question and remains unchallenged by the parties, i.e., in proceedings not relating to the registration or validity of a patent, it seems reasonable that the court would not have to declare of its own motion that it does not have jurisdiction, so that it could give a judgment with *inter partes* effects. One could even wonder whether the amendment to Brussels I suggested by CLIP is not already implied by the ECJ *GAT* v *LuK* judgment[102].

3 - Consolidation of proceedings

A is a holder of identical patents in countries X, W, Y and Z. B, C and D are competitors of A and are located in countries X, Y and Z respectively. A finds that B, C and D infringe its patents in

[102] See also ALI Principles (§ 221(2)).

countries X, Y and Z. A institutes patent infringement proceedings against alleged infringers before the courts of countries X, Y and Z. A's main place of business is in country W; due to high litigation costs A seeks the consolidation of claims forum of country W.

1) Assuming that the court of country W is a court of your country, would it have jurisdiction to join claims against defendants B, C and D? Would the decision of a court differ if A was a licensor and the claims were raised against licensees B, C and D on the ground of the infringement of a contract?

1.1. A Portuguese court would not have jurisdiction to join claims against defendants B, C and D because, even if they were domiciled in a Brussels country and despite 'the claims are so closely connected that it is expedient to hear and determine them together to avoid the risk of irreconcilable judgments resulting from separate proceedings', none of the defendants is domiciled in Portugal, as required under Article 6(1) of Brussels I.

Nonetheless, as these may be related actions pending in the courts of different Member States (Art. 28 (3)), a Portuguese court could have jurisdiction to join claims against defendants B, C and D only in case it is the *court first seized* and the courts of the other countries stay their proceedings (Art. 28(1)) or, 'where these actions are pending at first instance', such courts, on the application of one of the parties, namely A, decline jurisdiction, provided the Portuguese court has jurisdiction over the actions in question and its law permits the consolidation thereof (Art. 28(2)); however, the later situation would not be possible, because Portuguese courts do not have jurisdiction: neither the domicile of the defendants nor the place where the harmful event occurs or, according to the facts of the case, might occur, is located in country W, i.e. Portugal (Arts. 2, 5(3) and 6(1)).

1.2. If A was a licensor and claims were raised against licensees B, C and D on the ground of the infringement of a contract, Portuguese courts would have jurisdiction in case the defendants were domiciled in a Brussels country and Portugal was the *place of performance* of the obligation in question, either by virtue of agreement or by a connection provided for in Article 5(1). In absence of agreement, it may be disputed whether, for purposes of establishing the connection, **license contracts** should qualify as sale of goods or rather as provision of services.

According to the relevant ECJ jurisprudence, despite 'the national court's jurisdiction to determine questions relating to a contract includes the power to consider the existence of the constituent parts of the contract itself, since that is indispensable in order to enable the national court in which proceedings are brought to examine whether it has jurisdiction under the Convention'[103], the second indent of Article 5(1)(b) of Brussels I "is to be interpreted to the effect that a contract under which the owner of an intellectual property right grants its contractual partner the right to use that right in return for remuneration is not a contract for the provision of services within the meaning of that provision"[104].

In Portugal, the Supremo Tribunal de Justiça (Supreme Court of Justice) has applied this jurisprudence to an international license to broadcast football matches[105].

In short, license contracts should not qualify as provision of services, and the court should establish its jurisdiction by virtue of the connection of the place in a Member State where, under the

[103] Judgment of the Court (First Chamber) of 4 March 1982, C-38/81, *Effer SpA* v *Hans-Joachim Kantner* [1982] *ECR* 00825.

[104] Judgment of the Court (Fourth Chamber) of 23 April 2009, C-533/07, *Falco Privatstiftung and Thomas Rabitsch* v *Gisela Weller-Lindhorst*, OJ C 141/15, 20.6.2009.

[105] Supremo Tribunal de Justiça (Supreme Court of Justice), Judgment of 21 May 2009, Proc. 4986/06.3TVLSB.S1 (available at www.dgsi.pt/jstj).

contract, the goods were delivered or should have been delivered, as this criterion applies to sale of goods as well as to any other contract that does not qualify as provision of services (Art. 5(1)(c))[106]. The place where, under the contract, the goods were delivered or should have been delivered is, in absence of agreement concerning the place of delivery, determined by national law. Under Portuguese law, the general principle is the **domicile of the debtor**, i.e., the licensor (Civil Code, Article 772(1)), which is also the place of performance of the obligation of payment (Civil Code, Art. 885(1)).

Therefore, a Portuguese court would have jurisdiction to join claims against defendants B, C and D on the ground of infringement of the license contract, because Portugal would be deemed the place of performance of the obligations of delivery and payment of the license.[107] However, as well as on matters relating to tort[108], jurisdiction is limited to 'matters relating to a contract', i.e.,

---

[106] Considering that the wording 'goods' and 'services' of Article 5(1)(b) of Brussels I concern corporeal activities capable of delivery or provision, Tribunal da Relação de Lisboa (Lisbon Court of Appeals), Judgment of 17 December 2008 (available at www.dgsi.pt/jtrl).

[107] However, it should be noted that, for purposes of the law applicable to contractual obligations, where the licensee has the obligation to explore the license, as it happens in patent licenses, this is considered to be the characteristic obligation (see D. Moura Vicente, op. cit. n. 41, pp. 294-6). And the place where the licensee does have to explore the license is not the domicile of the licensor, but the territory or territories established under the contract. Moreover, copyright edition contracts as well as patent licenses of production and distribution have relevant similarities with to franchising contracts which are to be governed by the law of the country of the franchisee according to Regulation Rome I. In order to achieve consistency with Brussels I, perhaps this should be considered, otherwise, for purposes of jurisdiction, the connection is limited to the place of delivery of the license, i.e., the licensor's domicile (as the licensor is the debtor of the obligation of delivery). See also L. Lima Pinheiro, op.cit. n. 84, p. 73.

[108] Judgment of the Court (Fifth Chamber) of 27 September 1988, C-189/87, *Athanasios Kalfelis* v *Bankhaus Schröder, Münchmeyer, Hengst and Co. and others* [1988] *ECR* 05565 ('The expression "matters relating to tort, delict or quasi-delict" contained in Article 5(3) of the [Brussels]Convention must be regarded as an independent concept covering all actions which seek to establish the liability of a defendant and which are not related to a "contract" within the meaning of Article 5(1). A court which has jurisdiction under Article 5(3) over an action in so far as

obligations 'freely accepted by the parties'.[109] Accordingly, jurisdiction of Portuguese courts would be limited to *matters related to the contract*, and not extend to infringement claims arising out of the license contracts.

This solution has been criticized due to the fragmentation of jurisdiction, and it has been argued[110] that it should be reviewed according to the CLIP suggestion: 'In disputes concerned with infringement claims arising out of a contractual relationship between the parties, a court having jurisdiction with regard to the contract shall also have jurisdiction in respect of the infringement' (2:201(c)). A similar solution is provided for the Hague Convention on choice of court agreements (Art. 2(2)(a)), unless the agreement is null and void under the law of that State (Art. 5(1))[111].

In Portugal, the Supreme Court of Justice did already accept that the law chosen by the parties to govern their license contract can also apply to torts related to such a contract (e.g., in case the use of the licensed right exceeds the terms of the license)[112]. More recently, the same court ruled that a choice of court agreement concerns any dispute that arises out of the main contract and

---

it is based on tort or delict does not have jurisdiction over that action in so far as it is not so based').

[109] Judgment of 17 June 1992, C-26/91, *Jakob Handte & Co. GmbH* v *Traitements Mécano-chimiques des Surfaces SA* [1992] *ECR* I-3967. See also Judgment of 17 September 2002, C-334/00, *Fonderie Officine Meccaniche Tacconi SpA* v *Heirinch Wagner Sinto Maschinenfabrik GmbH* [2002] *ECR* I-10087 ('In circumstances such as those of the main proceedings, characterized by the absence of obligations freely assumed by one party towards another on the occasion of negotiations with a view to the formation of a contract and by a possible breach of rules of law, in particular the rule which requires the parties to act in good faith in such negotiations, an action founded on the pre-contractual liability of the defendant is a matter relating to tort, delict or quasi-delict within the meaning of Article 5(3) of the [Brussels] Convention [...].').

[110] Cf. D. Moura Vicente, op. cit. n. 41, p. 411.

[111] See also ALI Principles, § 211(1)).

[112] Supremo Tribunal de Justiça (Supreme Court of Justice), Judgment of 16 October 2002, I *CJ/ASTJ* (2002) p. 11.

therefore jurisdiction of the chosen court includes all issues, either contractual or tort, that arise thereof [113].

2) Assuming that B, C and D are members of a group of a corporation and takes identical steps in infringement of A's patents, A seeks to consolidate the proceedings before a court of country X where the coordinator of infringing activities has its main place of business. Assuming that the court of country of X is a court of your country would (and if so under what conditions) it consolidate the proceedings if it was to decide upon the request of A? Would the decision change if B, C and D raised counterclaims that A's patents are invalid?

2.1. As the coordinator of infringing activities has its main place of business in Portugal he is considered to be domiciled in Portugal. Therefore, he could be sued in Portuguese courts under the general criterion of the defendants' domicile (Art. 2(1)). Moreover, B, C and D, as members of a group of a corporation that take identical steps in infringement of A's patents, could also be sued in a Portuguese court under Article 6(1) of Brussels I as the claims would be so closely connected that it would be expedient to hear and determine them together to avoid the risk of irreconcilable judgments resulting from separate proceedings. Furthermore, under Brussels I (Art. 28(3)), A could apply for *consolidation of proceedings* in the Portuguese court if this had been the court first seized. This could be a situation of 'spider in the web'.

---

[113] Judgment of 8 October 2009, Proc. 5138/06.8TBSTS.S1 (available at www.dgsi.pt/jstj). This court had previously ruled that, for jurisdiction purposes, a choice of court agreement concerning a license contract does not include litigations concerning the termination of the contract and tort liability caused by unlawful acts committed by the plaintiff in Portugal (judgment of 12 April 1997, Proc. 98B292, available at www.dgsi.pt/jstj).

However, taking into account Community jurisprudence, Portuguese courts would deny jurisdiction to consolidate proceedings. In fact, the ECJ has rejected the possibility under Article 6(1) of the Brussels Convention of joint proceedings over patent infringement against companies in relation of group based upon *concerted infringement* by these companies against a bundle of patents issued for several Contracting States to the European Patent Convention. The Court argued that not only the events were not the same, but also joint proceedings would affect legal certainty and promote forum shopping, as well as it would not prevent fragmentation of *fora* whenever the issue of patent validity is raised as an incidental question, as it remained a matter of exclusive competence of the courts provided for in Article 16(4). In summary: "Article 6(1) of the [Brussels] Convention (...) must be interpreted as meaning that it does not apply in European patent infringement proceedings involving a number of companies established in various Contracting States in respect of acts committed in one or more of those States even where those companies, which belong to the same group, may have acted in an identical or similar manner in accordance with a common policy elaborated by one of them. Since neither the patent infringements of which the various defendants are accused nor the national law in relation to which those acts are assessed are the same there is no risk of irreconcilable decisions being given in European patent infringement proceedings brought in different Contracting States, since possible divergences between decisions given by the courts concerned would not arise in the context of the same factual and legal situation."[114]

---

[114] Judgment of the Court (First Chamber) of 13 July 2006, C-539/03, *Roche Nederland BV and Others* v. *Fredrick Primus and Milton Goldberg* [2006] *ECR* I-06535. In the US, the situation is similar. The United States Court of Appeals for the Federal Circuit, in *Voda v. Cordis* of 1 February 2007, decided that for reasons of independence of patent rights, comity, judicial economy, *forum non conveniens*

2.2. If B, C and D raised counterclaims that A's patents are invalid, the court would have to deny jurisdiction at its own motion (Brussels I, Art. 25).[115] As mentioned above, the ECJ ruled that the rule of exclusive jurisdiction concerns 'all *proceedings* relating to the registration or validity of a patent, irrespective of whether the issue is raised by way of an action or a plea in objection'[116].

4 - Choice of court

A, who holds a bundle of patents in different countries, entered into a non-exclusive license agreement with B pursuant to which B received a license to make, use or offer for sale and otherwise dispose licensed products. B paid the initial license fee but later refused to pay other fees arguing inter alia that its products do not fall under the scope of the licensed patents.

A filed a suit against B seeking patent infringement damages and refers to the choice of forum clause which the parties agreed upon in the license agreement. B objects to the enforcement of such a choice of forum clause arguing that the issue is related to foreign patents and thus the asserted choice of court clause is not enforceable.

---

and Act of State, the court of first instance exceeded its supplemental jurisdiction in appreciating the validity of foreign patents, despite such patents had been issued under the PCT (Patent Cooperation Treaty). On this decision see e.g. J.K. Voda, «*M.D.* v. 'Cordis Corporation', *Gewerblicher Rechtsschutz und Urheberrecht - Internationaler Teil* - GRUR Int. 56/5 (2007), pp. 442-447.

[115] See Judgment of the Court (Fourth Chamber) of 15 November 1983, C-288/82, *Ferdinand M.J.J. Duijnstee v Lodewijk Goderbauer* [1983] *ECR* 03663 ('Article 19 of the Convention of 27 September 1968 requires the national court to declare of its own motion that it has no jurisdiction whenever it finds that a court of another contracting state has exclusive jurisdiction under Article 16 of the Convention, even in an appeal in cassation where the national rules of procedure limit the court's reviewal to the grounds raised by the parties.').

[116] Judgment of the Court (First Chamber) of 13 July 2006, C-4/03, *Gesellschaft für Antriebstechnik mbH & Co. KG (GAT)* v *Lamellen und Kupplungsbau Beteiligungs KG (LuK)* [2006] *ECR* I-6509.

Assuming that A and B are not nationals of your country and do not have any place of business in your country:

1) Would such a choice of court clause of the license agreement be enforceable? Would the decision differ if parties made (new) choice of court agreement at the time when the dispute arose?

1.1. Despite A and B are not Portuguese nationals and do not have any place of business in Portugal, the choice of court clause which the parties agreed upon in the license agreement would be enforceable under Brussels I in case one of them is domiciled in a country of Brussels I. According to Article 23(1): 'If the parties, one or more of whom is domiciled in a Member State, have agreed that a court or the courts of a Member State are to have jurisdiction to settle any disputes which have arisen or which may arise in connection with a particular legal relationship, that court or those courts shall have jurisdiction. Such jurisdiction shall be exclusive unless the parties have agreed otherwise.' Moreover, if none of the parties is domiciled in a Member State, the courts of other Member States have no jurisdiction over their disputes unless the court or courts chosen have declined jurisdiction (Art. 23(3)).

Such a choice of court agreement would not have legal force if, as provided for in Article 23(5), the courts whose jurisdiction they purport to exclude have exclusive jurisdiction by virtue of Article 22. However, as far as patents or other similar rights required to be deposited or registered are concerned, this rule of exclusive jurisdiction is limited to proceedings concerned with their **registration** or **validity** (Art. 22(4)). Accordingly, the fact that the issue is related to foreign patents does not exclude the enforceability of such a choice of forum clause as the suit filed against B seeks patent infringement damages.

Moreover, according to ECJ relevant jurisprudence[117], a Portuguese court has recently ruled that Brussels I does not provide the courts with the possibility to control the grounds of jurisdiction of a court chosen by agreement, namely as *forum non conveniens*[118]. Nonetheless, it should be taken into account that the court can declare null and void a choice of court agreement that is an unfair standard term even if concluded between professionals[119].[120]

---

[117] Judgment of the Court of 1 March 2005, C-281/02, *Andrew Owusu* v *N.B. Jackson, Trading as Villa Holidays Bal In Villas and others* [2005] *ECR* I-1383, par. 37-40 ('No exception on the basis of the *forum non conveniens* doctrine was provided for by the authors of the Convention').

[118] Tribunal da Relação de Lisboa (Lisbon Court of Appeals), Judgment 21 May 2009, Proc. 8748/2008-6 (available at www.dgsi.pt/jtrl).

[119] Unfair Standard Terms Act, approved by Decree-Law 44/85 of 25 October, and as last amended by Decree-Law 249/99 of 7 July, Article 19(g). Considering the use of unfair terms as tort for purposes of Article 5(3) of the Brussels Convention, ECJ Judgment of 1 October 2002, C-167/00, *Verein fur Konsumenteninformation* v *K.H. Henkel* [2002] *ECR* I-8111.

[120] Concerning consumer contracts, the ECJ ruled that the court shall decline of its own motion the jurisdiction conferred on it by virtue of an unfair term. See Judgment of the Court of 27 June 2000, Joined cases C-240/98 to C-244/98, *Océano Grupo Editorial SA v Roció Murciano Quintero (C-240/98) and Salvat Editores SA v José M. Sánchez Alcón Prades (C-241/98), José Luis Copano Badillo (C-242/98), Mohammed Berroane (C-243/98) and Emilio Viñas Feliú (C-244/98)* [2000] *ECR* I-04941, para. 24, 29, 32 ('1. Where a jurisdiction clause is included, without being individually negotiated, in a contract between a consumer and a seller or supplier and where it confers exclusive jurisdiction on a court in the territorial jurisdiction of which the seller or supplier has his principal place of business, it must be regarded as unfair within the meaning of Article 3 of Directive 93/13 on unfair terms in consumer contracts in so far as it causes, contrary to the requirement of good faith, a significant imbalance in the parties' rights and obligations arising under the contract, to the detriment of the consumer. / 2. The protection provided for consumers by Directive 93/13 on unfair terms in consumer contracts entails the national court being able to determine of its own motion whether a term of a contract before it is unfair when making its preliminary assessment as to whether a claim should be allowed to proceed before the national courts. The national court is obliged, when it applies national law provisions predating or postdating the said Directive, to interpret those provisions, so far as possible, in the light of the wording and purpose of the Directive. The requirement for an interpretation in conformity with the Directive requires the national court, in particular, to favour the interpretation that would allow it to decline of its own motion the jurisdiction conferred on it by virtue of an unfair term').

1.2. Article 23(1) of Brussels I provides for that the 'parties, one or more of whom is domiciled in a Member State, may agree that a court or the courts of a Member State are to have jurisdiction to settle any disputes *which have arisen* or *which may arise* in connection with a particular legal relationship' [*emphasis added*]. Therefore, the decision would not differ if parties made (new) choice of court agreement only at the time when the dispute arose, provided nevertheless that such an agreement is in writing or evidenced in writing (with the equivalence of any communication by electronic means which provides a durable record of the agreement), or in a form which accords with practices which the parties have established between themselves, or in international trade or commerce, in a form which accords with a usage of which the parties are or ought to have been aware and which in such trade or commerce is widely known to, and regularly observed by, parties to contracts of the type involved in the particular trade or commerce concerned (Art. 23(1) 2nd period).

According to relevant ECJ jurisprudence, no other formal requirements, including language, can be provided for under domestic law[121]. This ruling has recently been followed by the Portuguese Supremo Tribunal de Justiça (Supreme Court of Justice)[122].

---

[121] Judgment of 24 June 1981, C-150/80, *Elefanten Schuh GmbH* v *Jacqmain* [1981] *ECR* 01671 ('Since the aim of article 17 of the Convention is to lay down the formal requirements which agreements conferring jurisdiction must meet, contracting states are not free to lay down formal requirements other than those contained in the Convention. When those rules are applied to provisions concerning the language to be used in an agreement conferring jurisdiction they imply that the legislation of a contracting state may not allow the validity of such an agreement to be called in question solely on the ground that the language used is not that prescribed by that legislation.').

[122] Judgment of 8 October 2009, Proc. 5138/06.8TBSTS.S1 (available at ww.dgsi.pt/jstj).

2) Would the court enforce an exclusive choice of court clause if the defendant raised a counter-claim that patents are invalid?

Should the defendant raise a counterclaim that patents are invalid, the court would not enforce an exclusive choice of court clause because, under Brussels I, patent validity is a matter of *exclusive jurisdiction* and cannot be excluded by choice of court clauses (Art. 23(5)). As the issue of validity of patent is raised by the defendant as a *counterclaim*, under Brussels I, either as it stands or as read in accordance with the CLIP suggestion, a Portuguese court would not enforce such choice of court clause[123].

3) Would the court assert jurisdiction if the choice of court agreement was made in patent infringement proceedings?

Under Brussels I, choice of courts may be agreed to 'settle any disputes which have arisen or which may arise in connection with a particular legal relationship' (Art. 23(1)).

However, according to the ECJ jurisprudence, jurisdiction is limited to 'matters relating to a contract', i.e. obligations 'freely accepted by the parties'.[124] Therefore, jurisdiction of Portuguese courts would be limited to matters related to the contract, and not extend to *infringement claims* arising out of the *license contracts*. The Portuguese Supreme Court has already held that, concerning intellectual property contracts, a choice of court clause agreed upon

---

[123] See also the Hague Convention, which does not apply to choice of court agreements concerning the validity of intellectual property rights other than copyright and related rights (Art. 2(2)(n)), except where they 'arise merely as a preliminary question and not as an object of the proceedings. In particular, the mere fact that a matter excluded under paragraph 2 arises by way of defence does not exclude proceedings from the Convention, if that matter is not an object of the proceedings' (Art. 2(3)).

[124] Judgments of the Court of 17 June 1992, C-26/91, *Jakob Handte & Co. GmbH* v *Traitements Mécano-chimiques des Surfaces SA* [1992] *ECR* I-3967, and of 17 September 2002, C-334/00, *Fonderie Officine Meccaniche Tacconi SpA* v *Heirinch Wagner Sinto Maschinenfabrik GmbH* [2002] *ECR* I-10087.

in a license agreement does not include litigations concerning the termination of the contract and tort liability caused by unlawful acts committed by the plaintiff in Portugal[125].

This restrictive solution has however been criticized due to the *fragmentation of jurisdiction*, and it has been argued[126] that it should be reviewed according to the CLIP suggestion (2:201(c)): 'In disputes concerned with infringement claims arising out of a contractual relationship between the parties, a court having jurisdiction with regard to the contract shall also have jurisdiction in respect of the infringement'. A similar solution is provided for the Hague Convention on choice of court agreements (Art. 2(2)(a)), unless the agreement is null and void under the law of that State (Art. 5(1)).

In Portugal, the courts did already accept that the law chosen by the parties to govern their license contract can also apply to torts related to such a contract (e.g., in case the use of the licensed right exceeds the terms of the license)[127]. However, for jurisdiction purposes, the Portuguese Supreme Court hold that a choice of court agreement concerning a license contract does not include litigations concerning the termination of the contract and tort liability caused by unlawful acts committed by the plaintiff in Portugal[128]. However, more recently, the same Court grounded its jurisdiction over tort liability arising out of illegal termination of a concession contract and compensation for good-will under Article 5(1)(a) of Brussels I[129], and moreover it ruled, in a different case, that a choice of court agreement concerns any dispute that arises out of the main

---

[125] Supremo Tribunal de Justiça (Supreme Court of Justice), Judgment of 12 April 1997, Proc. 98B292 (available at www.dgsi.pt/jstj).

[126] D. Moura Vicente, op. cit. n. 41, pp. 387-97.

[127] Supremo Tribunal de Justiça (Supreme Court of Justice), Judgment of 16 October 2002, I *CJ/ASTJ* (2002) p. 11.

[128] Supremo Tribunal de Justiça (Supreme Court of Justice), Judgment of 12 April 1997, Proc. 98B292 (available at www.dgsi.pt/jstj).

[129] Judgment of 9 October 2008, Proc. 08B2633 (available at www.dgsi.pt/jstj).

contract and therefore jurisdiction of the chosen court includes all issues, either contractual or tort, that result thereof[130]. Therefore, according to this new ruling of the Supremo Tribunal de Justiça (Supreme Court of Justice), a Portuguese court would assert jurisdiction even if the choice of court agreement was made in patent infringement proceedings. However, the conformity of this approach with ECJ relevant jurisprudence may be disputed.

4) Would parties' arbitration agreement be enforceable under the law of your country? Could the arbitration tribunal decide upon the validity of intellectual property rights? If so, what would be legal effects of such decision?

4.1. Under Portuguese Arbitration Act[131], *arbitration agreements* are not allowed where they are mandatorily subject to court decision or concerning rights which the parties cannot dispose of (Art. 1(1)). Arbitration agreements contrary to this prohibition are deemed null and void (Art. 3). Arbitration tribunals can decide upon their own jurisdiction (Art. 21(1)), but their decisions can be annulled in case such litigation cannot be decided by arbitration (Art. 27(1)(a)).

4.2. The exclusive jurisdiction rule provided for in Article 22(4) of Brussels I is interpreted as an exclusion of the possibility of submitting those matters to arbitrage[132]. Accordingly, the validity of intellectual property rights subject to registration, such as patents or marks, could not be decided by the arbitration tribunal. Concerning other intellectual property rights, such as copyright, the arbitra-

---

[130] Judgment of 8 October 2009, Proc. 5138/06.8TBSTS.S1 (available at www.dgsi.pt/jstj).

[131] Law 31/86 of 29 August (Lei da Arbitragem Voluntária).

[132] Cf. D. Moura Vicente, op. cit. n. 41, pp. 426-7 (with further references such as with a different understanding, L. Lima Pinheiro, *Arbitragem internacional*, Coimbra, Almedina, 2005).

tion tribunal could decide upon their validity insofar as they can be disposed of by the parties, as it would be the case concerning economic rights. Arbitration agreements have to be concluded in writing[133] and comply and specify the legal relationship concerning the litigation (Art. 2).

4.3. A decision of an arbitration tribunal has the same legal effects as a decision of a court of first instance (Art. 26(2)) and therefore the parties have to comply with it, unless an action of annulment is brought before the court.

5 - Parallel proceedings

A owns two product patents in countries X and Y. B who is located in country Z produces the identical product to that for which A has patents and exports that infringing product to the countries X and Y. Having found out about the infringing activities A files an infringement suit before the court of country Z. However, before A brings a suit in country Z, B launches actions in countries X and Y seeking declarations that B is not liable for the infringements of patents owned by A.

Assuming that the court of country Z is a court of your country:

1) What procedural steps would a court of a country Z take having regard pending proceedings in countries X and Y? Would the decision of a court of country Z be different if the dispute was related to intellectual property rights that are not subject to registration?

1.1. Having regard to *pending proceedings* in countries X and Y, a Portuguese court would have to stay its proceedings until such

---

133 See Supremo Tribunal de Justiça (Supreme Court of Justice), Judgment of 27 March 2003, Proc. 03B3145, available www.dgsi.pt/jstj

time as the jurisdiction of the court first seized is established, according to Article 27(1) of Brussels I concerning proceedings involving the same cause of action and between the same parties which are brought in the courts of different Member States. In fact, actions launched by B in countries X and Y seeking declarations that B is not liable for the infringements of patents owned by A would have the 'same cause of action' and the 'same parties' as the infringement suit brought by A before the Portuguese court according to the broad interpretation of Article 21 of the Brussels Convention given by the ECJ, so that it covers all situations of '*lis alibi pendens*' before courts in Member States.[134]

Even if the courts of countries X and Y lacked jurisdiction and regardless of the excessive duration of their proceedings, a Portuguese court, according to ECJ jurisprudence[135], would have to stay its proceedings until such time as the jurisdiction of the court first seized is established. Then, where the jurisdiction of the court first seized (court of country X) is established, both the courts of country Y and the Portuguese courts would have to decline jurisdiction in favor of that court (Art. 27(2)).

In order to escape from such 'torpedo'[136], A could argue abuse of right and contest jurisdiction. However, according to the ECJ jurisprudence, "Without prejudice to the case where the court second

[134] Judgment of 26 June 1991, C-351/89, *Overseas Union Insurance Limited e.a.* v *New Hampshire Insurance Company* [1999] *ECR* I-3317. See also Judgment of the Court (Sixth Chamber) of 8 December 1987, C-144/86, *Gubisch Maschinenfabrik KG* v *Giulio Palumbo* [1987] *ECR* 04861 ('The terms used in article 21 of the Convention of 27 September 1968 in order to determine whether a situation of *lis pendens* arises must be regarded as independent. *Lis pendens* within the meaning of that article arises where a party brings an action before a court in a contracting state for the rescission or discharge of an international sales contract whilst an action by the other party to enforce the same contract is pending before a court in another contracting state.').

[135] Judgment of the Court of 30 November 1976, C-21/76, *Handelskwekerij G. J. Bier BV* v *Mines de potasse d'Alsace SA*, [1976] *ECR* 01735.

[136] M. Franzosi, *Worldwide Patent Litigation and the Italian Torpedo, EIPR* (1997) p. 7.

seised has exclusive jurisdiction under the [Brussels] Convention and in particular under Article 16 thereof, Article 21 of the Convention must be interpreted as meaning that, where the jurisdiction of the court first seised is contested, the court second seised may, if it does not decline jurisdiction, only stay the proceedings and may not itself examine the jurisdiction of the court first seised."[137]

Nonetheless, it should be noted that, regardless of A having domicile in countries X or Y[138], the courts of these countries would also have jurisdiction over B' claims for declarations of non-liability for the infringements of patents owned by A, because countries X and Y, as the place of destination of the infringing products, were the place where the harmful event occurred for purposes of Article 5(3) of Brussels I.

1.2. The decision of the Portuguese court (as a court of country Z) would not be different if the dispute was related to intellectual property rights that are not subject to registration. In any case, the exclusive jurisdiction rule does not apply because the issue of patent registration or validity is not in question.

2) What procedural steps would the court in country Z take if B brought a suit before a court of a third country W challenging the validity of patents in countries X and Y?

---

[137] Judgment of 26 June 1991, C-351/89, *Overseas Union Insurance Limited e.a.* v *New Hampshire Insurance Company* [1991] *ECR* I-3317.

[138] Judgment of 26 June 1991, C-351/89, *Overseas Union Insurance Limited e.a.* v *New Hampshire Insurance Company* [1991] *ECR* I-3317 ('Article 21 of the [Brussels] Convention [...] must be interpreted as meaning that the rules applicable to *lis alibi pendens* set out therein must be applied irrespective of the domicile of the parties to the two sets of proceedings.'). See however the Italian Supreme Court decision of 12 December 2003 (*Macchine Automatiche* v *Windmoller & Holscher KG*) and the Milan Court of First Instance decision n. 3773 of 26 March 2007, according to which a cross-border claim for a declaration of non-infringement of a European patent is unlikely to succeed before an Italian court unless it is brought against an Italian domiciled party.

If B brought a suit before a court of a third country W challenging the validity of patents in countries X and Y, the cause of action would not be the same, but rather there would be, under Brussels I, a situation of **related actions**, i.e. actions that are so closely connected that it is expedient to hear and determine them together to avoid the risk of irreconcilable judgments resulting from separate proceedings (Art. 28(3)). For these, Article 28(1) provides for that, where related actions are pending in the courts of different Member States, any court other than the court first seized may stay its proceedings. Article 28(2) adds that, where these actions are pending at first instance, any court other than the court first seized may also, on the application of one of the parties, decline jurisdiction if the court first seized has jurisdiction over the actions in question and its law permits the consolidation thereof.

Because a court of country Z has jurisdiction over the proceedings on patent infringement under the general rule (domicile of the defendant, Art. 2) and a court of a third country W does not have jurisdiction over the proceedings on patent validity, as such jurisdiction is exclusive of the courts of countries X and Y, a Portuguese court of first instance may not, on the application of the parties, decline jurisdiction in favor of a court of country W. Nonetheless, it may *stay proceedings* according to Article 28(1).

6 - Principle of territoriality (choice of law)

A owns a patent over an engine in country X. B produces separate parts of the patented engine and exports them separately to its customers in countries Y and Z. Customers of B can easily assemble the parts of the patented engine in a very short time.

Having found out about B's activities, A files a suit in country X requesting an injunction and recovery of damages for patent in-

fringement. B argues that the export of separate parts of an invention does not amount to patent infringement and that the patent statute of country X does not extend to activities abroad.

1) Assuming that the court of country X is a court of your country, could it apply the patent statute for allegedly infringing acts occurring in country Z?

A Portuguese court could apply the patent statute (Código da Propriedade Industrial) for allegedly infringing acts occurring in country Z as events that give rise to infringing acts likely to occur in Portugal. Torts arising out of infringements of intellectual property rights are a special tort for which Article 8(1) of Regulation Rome II provides the 'universally acknowledged' principle of *lex loci protectionis*, i.e. the law of the country for which protection is claimed. Protection may be claimed for a country in which the infringing acts are likely to occur[139]. Accordingly, a Portuguese court could apply the Portuguese patent statute in case protection is claimed for Portugal, as allegedly infringing acts occurring in country Z could be considered, for purposes of an **injunction**, as events that give rise to infringing acts likely to occur in Portugal, i.e. as evidence of an 'imminent commission' of a tort or delict[140] which the application of Portuguese patent law would prevent.

2) Assuming, firstly, that the claim for the infringement of patent granted in country X is brought before the court of country Z and, secondly, that the court of country Z is a court of your country,

---

139 See S. Ricketson & J. Ginsburg, *International Copyright and Neighbouring Rights: The Berne Convention and Beyond*, 2 vol., 2nd ed., Oxford, Oxford University Press, 2006, pp. 320-321.

140 Judgment of 1 October 2002, C-167/00, *Verein fur Konsumenteninformation* v *K.H. Henkel* [2002] *ECR* I-8111.

could the court apply the patent statute of country X for allegedly infringing acts that occur in country Z?

A Portuguese court could only apply the patent statute of country X for allegedly infringing acts that occur in Portugal if it considers such acts, for purposes of an injunction, as events that give rise to infringing acts likely to occur in country X in order to prevent an 'imminent commission' of a tort or delict therein.

7 - Infringement of intellectual property rights

Three IT students A, B and C have created a website which facilitates speedy exchange of digital files (music, videos, software etc.) among users from all over the world. After several months when the website became very popular A, B and C introduced an additional paid service: the speedy exchange of big capacity digital files. Although A, B and C know that some files that are stored in the server of their website are illegal, they do not take any actions to somehow prevent infringements of intellectual property rights.

Major international entertainment industry companies file an infringement suit against A, B and C requesting to close the website and pay damages.

Assuming that the court of your country has international jurisdiction in such a case:

1) What law would be applied to determine the liability of A, B and C for direct infringement acts? Would parties be allowed to agree on the applicable law (infringement and remedies)?

1.1. The law that would be applied to determine the *liability* of A, B and C for direct infringement acts would be the law of the country for which protection is claimed according to the special criterion provided for IPR torts under Article 8(1) of Regulation

Rome II. The scope of the law applicable includes namely the determination of the persons whom liability can be attributed to due to their actions as well as the existence, nature and evaluation of damages or requested compensation and other provisions on remedies (Art. 15(a)(d)). Accordingly, Portuguese courts would apply the law of each country for which protection is claimed.

1.2. The parties would not be allowed to agree on (a different) applicable law (infringement and remedies) because the law applicable to infringement of intellectual property rights may not be derogated from by an agreement (Rome II, Art. 8(3)).

2) Would the choice of law differ if the claim for damages was brought against the internet service provider (ISP) as a secondary infringer? Would parties be allowed to agree on the applicable law (infringement and remedies)?

Under Rome II, the choice of law would not differ if the claim for damages was brought against the internet service provider (ISP) as a secondary infringer (Art. 15(a)(b)), and the parties would not be allowed to agree on the applicable law (Art. 8(3))[141].

3) Could the court decide on the ubiquitous infringement (where the infringement occurs in multiple places/countries) of intellectual property rights? If so, what would be the applicable law? Would the

---

[141] It has been suggested that the application of the law of the country of origin (introduction into the network) could apply in terms similar to the solution provided for by the Satellite and Cable Directive (Art. 1(2)). Cf. D. Moura Vicente, op. cit. n. 41, p. 226. However, this community instrument does not apply to making available on the Internet (different from webcasting) and moreover the principle of origin established for information society services under Directive 2000/31 on e-commerce does not apply to intellectual property matters. Nonetheless, by analogy with ECJ *Fiona Shevill* ruling, it might be argued that a Portuguese court could apply the Portuguese Copyright Act for the overall ubiquitous infringement in case any of the defendants were established in Portugal.

parties' choice of law be allowed? How would the court of your country define ubiquitous infringement of intellectual property rights?

3.1. The court could decide on the *ubiquitous infringement*, i.e. where the infringement to intellectual property occurs in multiple/ places rights, concerning defendants domiciled in any Member State (Brussels I, Art. 6(1)).

3.2. The law applicable to such infringements would be the law of each country for which protection is claimed. It is disputed, however, whether the mere *accessibility* of an internet website is enough to establish a substantial connection with the law of a country[142] . For reasons of consistency with jurisdiction under Brussels I, concerning ubiquitous infringement on the Internet, the mere accessibility of a website in a country may not be enough to establish jurisdiction in case the defendant does not direct his activity to that country nor engage in activities therein. According to the ECJ, 'the jurisdictional rules [are to be] interpreted in such a way as to enable a normally well-informed defendant reasonably to predict before which courts, other than those of the State in which he is domiciled, he may be sued'[143].

Therefore, the applicable law should be reasonably *predictable* by a 'normally well-informed defendant'. That would be the case where the defendant does not exclude a country from his 'stream

[142] Two cases are pending at the ECJ for a preliminary ruling on the issue of whether the mere accessibility of a website is enough connection with the law of a country to establish its application (C-509/09, BGH; C-161/10, TGI Paris). On the issue D. Moura Vicente, *Direito Internacional Privado: Problemática Internacional da Sociedade da Informação*, Coimbra, Almedina, 2005, p. 320; G. Palao Moreno, «Competencia judicial internacional en supuestos de responsabilidad civil en Internet», *Cuestiones Actuales de Derecho y Tecnologías de la Información e la Comunicación (TICs)*, coord. J. Plaza Penadés, Cizur Menor, Thomson Aranzadi, 2006, pp. 275 ff (293-5); A. Dias Pereira, op. cit. n. 14, p. 360-1.

[143] Judgment of 17 June 1992, C-26/91, *Jakob Handte & Co. GmbH* v *Traitements Mécano-chimiques des Surfaces SA* [1992] *ECR* I-3967.

of commerce'[144]. A reasoning closer to the criteria on the law applicable to consumer contracts provided for under Rome I should arguably be taken into consideration[145]. This implies, as indicated in Recital 24 of this Regulation, 'a reference to the concept of directed activity', as well as, quoting a joint declaration by the Council and the Commission on Article 15 of Brussels I, "the mere fact that an Internet site is accessible is not sufficient for Article 15 to be applicable, although a factor will be that this Internet site solicits the conclusion of distance contracts and that a contract has actually been concluded at a distance, by whatever means. In this respect, the language or currency which a website uses does not constitute a relevant factor."

In the case, A, B and C, the IT students who have created a website which facilitates speedy exchange of digital files (music, videos, software, etc.) among users from all over the world and, after the website became very popular, have introduced an additional paid service for the speedy exchange of big capacity digital files, knowing that the files they store in the server of their website are illegal but do not taking any actions to somehow prevent infringements of intellectual property rights, it is fair that they could reasonably predict the application of copyright law of any of the countries to which they did not actually exclude their commercial activities. Accordingly, a Portuguese court would apply the law of each of such countries for which protection is claimed.[146]

---

[144] On the 'stream of commerce' doctrine, see US Supreme Court *International Shoe Co.* v *Washington*, December 3, 1945; 326 US 310 (1945) and, concerning the interactivity of a website as a relevant connection, *Zippo Manufacturing Co.* v *Zippo Dot Com, Inc.* U.S. District Court of Pennsylvania January 16, 1997, 952 F. Supp 119. See e.g. M. Lemley et al., *Software and Internet Law*, 2nd ed., New York, Aspen, 2003, pp. 584-605.

[145] See ALI Principles, § 204(3) and CLIP Principles (Art. 2:202).

[146] However, applying the ECJ *Fiona Shevill* ruling by analogy, it might be argued that a Portuguese court could apply the Portuguese Copyright Act for the overall ubiquitous infringement in case any of the defendants was established in Portugal.

3.3. The parties' choice of a different law would not be allowed because the law applicable (*lex loci protectionis*) may not be derogated from by a choice-of-law agreement (Art. 8(3) of Rome II).

3.4. No reported Portuguese court decision defining ubiquitous infringement of intellectual property rights has been found. Nonetheless, a Portuguese court could define it as an infringement that may occur at the same time in different places arising out of the same causal event.

8 – Applicable law to initial ownership

A is a foreign visiting researcher in B's laboratory. Soon after being employed, A made several significant inventions using the equipment of B's laboratory. B's is now making huge profits by granting licenses to a number of companies to use the inventions of A. A files a suit for compensation arguing that he is the initial owner of the inventions and B should not have granted licenses without A's consent. Assuming that A files a claim before a court of your country:

1) What law would the court of your country apply to determine who is the initial owner of the invention? Would the parties' choice of law clause concerning initial ownership be enforceable in your country?

1.1. For reasons of consistency with ECJ jurisprudence concerning rules on jurisdiction[147], in order to determine who the *initial*

[147] Judgment of the Court (Fourth Chamber) of 15 November 1983, C-288/82, *Ferdinand M.J.J. Duijnstee v Lodewijk Goderbauer* [1983] *ECR* 03663 ('3. The term 'proceedings concerned with the registration or validity of patents' contained in Article 16 (4) of the Convention of 27 September 1968 must be regarded as an independent concept intended to have uniform application in all the contracting states. 4. The term 'proceedings concerned with the registration or validity of patents' does not include a dispute between an employee for whose invention a patent has

owner of the invention is, a Portuguese court would apply the law applicable to individual employment contracts provided for in Article 8 of Rome I[148].

Accordingly, Portuguese courts would apply either the law chosen by the parties or, in the absence of such an agreement, the law of the country in which the employee habitually carried out his work in performance of the contract (*lex loci laboris*), i.e., the law of the country in which the laboratory is established (Arts. 8(1) and (2)). However, in this case, as the inventor is carrying his work as a visiting researcher, it falls under Article 8(2), 2nd period, which provides for that a country where work is habitually carried out shall not be deemed to have changed if he is temporarily employed in another country. Therefore, the court would apply the law of the country where the visiting researcher habitually carried out his work.

In case it is not possible to determine such country, the court applies the law of the country where the place of business through which the employee was engaged is situated (Art. 8(3)). However, where it appears from the circumstances as a whole that the contract is more closely connected with a country other than the country of performance of the contract (*lex loci laboris*) and the country where is the place of business of the employer, the law of that other country applies (Art. 8(4)).[149]

1.2. The parties' choice of law clause concerning initial ownership would be enforceable in Portugal under Rome I if it did

been applied for or obtained and his employer, where the dispute relates to their respective rights in that patent arising out of the contract of employment .).

[148] Cf. D Moura Vicente, op. cit. n. 41, p. 266.

[149] Concerning European patents, the European Patent Convention provides for a special rule in Article 60(1) according to which the right to patent is governed by the law of State in which the employee carries out his main activity, or, in case it cannot be determined, the law of the country where the place of business through which the employee was engaged is situated.

not have the result of depriving the employee of the protection afforded to him by provisions that cannot be derogated from by agreement and that would apply pursuant to any of the alternative connection points provided for in Article 8 (Art. 8(1), 2nd period). In case Portuguese law, in the absence of choice, would have been applicable pursuant to any of these connection points, namely as *lex loci laboris,* then the parties' choice of law concerning initial ownership would not be enforceable to the extent that it would deprive A of his *inventor's rights.* Under Portuguese patent law an inventor cannot renounce in advance to the rights recognized to him concerning patent ownership (Code of Industrial Property, Art. 59(9)). Nevertheless, under Portuguese law, patent ownership is attributed to the company in case an invention is made during the performance of an employment contract in which the inventive activity is included and the inventor is entitled only to a right of remuneration in harmony with the importance of the invention in case the inventive activity is not particularly remunerated (Art. 59(1) (2), Code of Industrial Property)).

2) Would the decision differ if A made an invention in joint collaboration with other researchers?

The decision would not differ if A made an invention in joint collaboration with other researchers concerning the law applicable to initial ownership in the absence of choice, but it could differ concerning the enforceability of the parties' choice of law on initial ownership in case of different provisions that cannot be derogated from by agreement and that would apply to other researchers pursuant to any of the alternative connections points indicated above.

3) Would the applicable law differ in case of initial authorship or initial title to trademark?

In general, copyright ownership is governed by the law of the country of origin of the work[150]. However, copyright ownership of works created by employees or works made for hire is governed by *lex contractus* or *lex loci laboris*. Therefore, the applicable law would not differ in case of initial authorship concerning works created by employees. Moreover, a parties' choice of law clause would be enforceable in Portugal if it did not have the result of depriving the employee of the protection afforded to him by provisions that cannot be derogated from by agreement and that would apply pursuant to any of the alternative connection points provided for in Article 8 of Rome I (Art. 8(1), 2nd period). In case Portuguese law, in the absence of choice, would have been applicable pursuant to any of the connection points, e.g., as *lex loci laboris,* then the parties' choice of law concerning initial authorship would not be enforceable to the extent that it would deprive A of his author's rights. Under Portuguese copyright law, despite copyright is configured as a unitary right of economic and moral rights, while economic rights can be assigned, moral rights, namely the right of paternity and the right of integrity, are always attached to the creator and cannot be disposed of nor waived (Arts. 9, 42 and 52(2) of Copyright Act). Moreover, in case of works created by employees or works made for hire, the parties may agree the transmission of the economic rights, which is presumed if the name of the creator is not mentioned in the work or in the usual place for purposes of authorship identification (Art. 14(1)(3) of Copyright Act)[151]. In case of transmission, the intellectual creator

---

[150] Supremo Tribunal de Justiça (Supreme Court of Justice), Judgment of 10 January 2008 (available at www.dgsi.pt/jstj). However, the Berne Convention provides for in Article 14-*bis*(2)(a) that copyright ownership 'in a cinematographic work shall be a matter for legislation in the country where [i.e. for which] protection is claimed' (*lex loci protectionis*)

[151] See also Law 1/99 of 13 January, as amended by Law 94/2007 of 6 November, concerning authorship and ownership of works of journalists (Art. 7-B).

will be entitled to a special remunerative compensation (Art. 14(4), see also Art. 49 of Copyright Act). Concerning a work created by several persons, copyright belongs jointly to its creators, unless it is deemed a collective work, where copyright is assigned by law to the natural or legal person that organizes and directs its creation and in the name of which it is published (Arts. 16 to 19 of Copyright Act).

The law applicable to the initial title to trademark is the law of the country of registration (*lex originis)*, according to the special criteria provided for under the Portuguese Civil Code (Art. 48(2)), the Paris Convention (Art. 6-*quinquies*, A)(1)) and the Code of Industrial Property (Art. 254)[152].

4) *What law would the court of your country apply if A raised a claim arguing that B did not pay reasonable compensation for patents obtained by B in a number of foreign countries?*

Concerning such foreign patents, a Portuguese court would apply the law applicable to each individual employment contract provided for in Article 8 of Rome I, i.e. either the law chosen by the parties or, in the absence of such an agreement, the law of the country in which the employee habitually carried out his work in performance of the contract (*lex loci laboris*), i.e., the law of the country in which the laboratory is established (Arts. 8(1) and (2)): or, In case it is not possible to determine such country, the law of the country where the place of business through which the employee was engaged is situated (Art. 8(3)); or, where it appears from the circumstances as a whole that the contract is more closely connected with a country other than the country of performance of the contract (*lex loci laboris*) and the country

[152] Cf. D. Moura Vicente, op. cit. n. 41, pp. 260-261, 265-6.

where the place of business of the employer, the law of that other country applies (Art. 8(4)).[153]

Moreover, the law chosen by the parties to govern each employment contract could not have the result of depriving the employee of the protection afforded to him by provisions that cannot be derogated from by agreement and that would apply pursuant to any of the alternative connection points provided for in Article 8 (Art. 8(1), 2nd period), which would therefore be applied by the Portuguese court.

9 – Applicable law to the transfer of rights agreements

A is a rising popular music band. After one of the concerts in country X, a representative of foreign recording company B and A orally agreed to release A's albums in the future. After the release of the debut album, B has made some arrangements of the debut single for the distribution of the album in country Y. A files a suit before a court in country X arguing that the moral right of integrity of a work has not been transferred and thus infringed. Assuming that a court of your country is a court of country X:

1) Would the court enforce the parties' choice of law clause regarding the transfer of economic and moral rights of authors?

Under Rome, I, for a Portuguese court to enforce the parties' choice of law regarding the transfer of economic and moral rights of authors the choice would have to be made expressly or clearly demonstrated

[153] Concerning European patents, the European Patent Convention provides for a special rule in Article 60(1) according to which the right to patent is governed by the law of State in which the employee carries out his main activity, or, in case it cannot be determined, the law of the country where the place of business through which the employee was engaged is situated.

by the terms of the contract or the circumstances of the case (Art. 3(1)). Moreover, the court would enforce such choice of law in so far as it does not prejudice the provisions which cannot be derogated from by agreement of the law of a country other than the country whose law has been chosen where all other elements relevant to the situation at the time of the choice are located (Art. 3(3)).

In this case, we infer from the question that such choice of law is made expressly or clearly demonstrated by the terms of the contract or the circumstances of the case. Otherwise, the court would not enforce it. Assuming that there is such a choice of law, the court would have to check the existence and validity of the consent of the parties, in special the issue of *formal validity*, as the agreement was orally concluded. Under Article 3(5) of Rome I, the formal validity of choice of law clauses is determined in accordance with the provision on formal validity of the main contract, i.e., Article 11, which provides for in paragraph (1) that 'a contract concluded between persons who, or whose agents, are in the same country at the time of its conclusion is formally valid if it satisfies the formal requirements of the law which governs it in substance under this Regulation or of the law of the country where it is concluded'. Under Portuguese law, as the law of the country where the contract is concluded (country X), such contract would not be formally valid, because a public deed is required for the complete and final transfer of economic rights, otherwise it is null and void (Article 44 of Copyright Act). However, it may be formally valid under the law which governs the transfer in substance under Rome I, i.e., the law chosen by the parties (Art. 3(1)).

Assuming that it is, a Portuguese court would still have to check whether the enforcement of such choice of law does not prejudice the provisions which cannot be derogated from by agreement of the law of a country other than the country whose law has been chosen where all other elements relevant to the situation at the time of the choice are located (Art. 3(3)). As the contract has been concluded after one of the concerts in Portugal and assuming that A is a Portuguese resident, the court would have to check whether such choice of law does prejudice the relevant provisions of Portuguese copyright law that cannot be derogated from by agreement. In particular, concerning the transfer of moral rights, the Copyright Act expressly provides for in Article 56(2) that moral rights are not transferable (alienable), and that any modification to be introduced into the work requires an express agreement of its intellectual creator and can only take place within the agreed conditions (Art. 15(2)). These are *mandatory provisions*, i.e., provisions that cannot be derogated from by agreement of the parties, otherwise such an agreement is null and void (Civil Code, Article 294).

2) How will the court deal with the issue of transferability?

The court will deal with the issue of *transferability* taking into account the provisions of Portuguese copyright law that cannot be derogated from by agreement (Rome I, Art. 3(3)). As for the transfer of moral rights, the Portuguese Copyright Act expressly provides for in Article 56(2) that they are not transferable (alienable), and that any modification to be introduced into the work requires an express agreement of its intellectual creator and can only take place within the agreed conditions (Copyright Act, Art. 15(2)). These are mandatory provisions, i.e. provisions that cannot be derogated from by agreement of the parties, otherwise such an agreement is null and void (Civil Code, Article 294). And even if Portugal is not considered the country where all other elements relevant to the situation at the time of the choice are located, for purposes of safeguarding its provisions which cannot be derogated from by agreement and that would be prejudiced by the law chosen by the parties, a Portuguese would still apply those provisions on transferability of moral rights as 'overriding mandatory provisions' -

despite these are to be construed more restrictively than the notion of provisions which cannot be derogated from by agreement (Rome I, Recital 37) -, because moral rights are attached to the human personality of authors.

As for the transfer of *economic rights*, where complete and final, despite it is allowed under the dualistic Portuguese copyright system, public deed is required, otherwise it is null and void (Copyright Act, Article 44). Nevertheless, in case the contract is formally valid under the law which governs it in substance, i.e., under the law chosen by the parties, then the formal requirements of Portuguese copyright law cannot oppose to the transferability of the economic rights. Moreover, under Rome I, such formal requirements would not be considered as overriding mandatory provisions (Art. 9) and the application of the law chosen by the parties rendering the transfer of economic rights formally valid would not be manifestly incompatible with the public policy (*ordre public*) of the forum (Art. 21).

3) What would be the applicable law in a case where there is no choice of law made by the parties?

The applicable law in case where there is no choice of law made by the parties would be, under Rome I, the law of the country where A has its *habitual residence* at the time of the conclusion of the contract (Arts. 4(1)(a) and 19(3)). Actually, in the absence of choice, Rome I provides for in Article 4(1) that the applicable law is determined in accordance with the rule specified for the particular type of contract, such as, namely, contracts for the sale of goods, contracts for the provision of services, as well as franchise and distribution contracts. Transfer of rights agreements, where final and against a price (e.g. a sum lump), should qualify as a sale contract. At least they are not to qualify as provision of services, for reasons of consistency with the ECJ relevant jurisprudence on Brussels

I[154]. Accordingly, it would be governed by the law of the country in which the seller (A) has his habitual residence (Art. 4 (1)(a)).

A, as a rising popular music band, could qualify as a body, corporate or unincorporated, so that its habitual residence would be the place of central administration (Art. 19(1), 1st paragraph). However, in case where A is a natural person acting in the course of his business, the principal place of his business is considered his habitual residence (Art. 19(1), 2nd paragraph).

10 – Recognition and enforcement of foreign judgments

A court of a foreign country X decides a case between the parties A and B ruling that A is the owner of a patent registered in your country. A refers to a court of your country asking to recognize and enforce the foreign judgment.

1) Could the foreign judgment concerning the ownership be recognised in your country? How would the recognising court assess the international jurisdiction of the rendering court?

1.1. Under Brussels I, the foreign judgment concerning the ownership of a patent registered in Portugal could be recognized in Portugal if it is given by a court of a Brussels country and its jurisdiction is not contested by an interested party either as the principal issue in a dispute or as an incidental question. In fact, in case country X is a Brussels I country, a judgment given by a court of such country is to be automatically recognized in the

[154] Judgment of the Court (Fourth Chamber) of 23 April 2009, C-533/07, *Falco Privatstiftung and Thomas Rabitsch* v *Gisela Weller-Lindhorst*, OJ C 141/15, 20.6.2009 ('a contract under which the owner of an intellectual property right grants its contractual partner the right to use that right in return for remuneration is not a contract for the provision of services within the meaning of that provision').

other Member States without any special procedure (Article 33(1)). However, recognition is to be denied only in case one or more of the situations 'exhaustively listed'[155] under Article 34 occurs (e.g. if such recognition is manifestly contrary to public policy in Portugal) or, in case recognition is contested by an interested party - either as the principal issue in a dispute or as an incidental question (Art. 33(1)(2)) -, the judgment was given by a court without jurisdiction, concerning namely matters relating to insurance, consumer contracts, and proceedings subject to exclusive jurisdiction (Art. 35(1)).

Even if patent ownership was to be decided by the court of the country of registration, the recognizing country is not to raise such question at its own motion. Moreover, in case B or any other interested party would contest recognition arguing that the judgment was given by a court without jurisdiction as such matter would be of *exclusive jurisdiction* of Portuguese courts under Article 22(4) of Brussels I, such claim would not meet the relevant ECJ jurisprudence. In fact, considering that "The term 'proceedings concerned with the registration or validity of patents' contained in Article 16(4) of the Convention of 27 September 1968 must be regarded as an independent concept intended to have uniform application in all the contracting states', the Court held that such term 'does not include a dispute between an employee for whose invention a patent has been applied for or obtained and his employer, where the dispute relates to their respective rights in that patent arising out of the contract of employment'[156].

---

[155] Judgment of 2 June 1994, C-414/92, *Solo Kleinmotoren GmbH* v *Emilio Boch* [1994] *ECR* I-2237, par. 10 ('Articles 27 and 28 of the [Brussels] Convention list exhaustively the grounds for refusing to recognize such a judgment').

[156] Judgment of the Court (Fourth Chamber) of 15 November 1983, C-288/82, *Ferdinand M.J.J. Duijnstee* v *Lodewijk Goderbauer* [1983] *ECR* 03663. See *supra* Case 8, 1.1.

1.2. In the examination of such grounds of jurisdiction, the court applied is bound by the findings of fact on which the court of the Member State of origin based its jurisdiction (Art. 35(2)). Since the jurisdiction of the court of the Member State of origin may not be reviewed and the test of public policy (Art. 34) may not be applied to the rules relating to jurisdiction (Art. 35(3)), this ground for non recognition of the judgment is not to be raised by the courts of their own motion. In other words, the issue has to be raised by the defendant (or by any other interested party). In any case, Article 36 provides for that under no circumstances may a foreign judgment be reviewed as to its substance.

2) Wouldn't the parties be required to re-litigate the dispute in order to have the ownership decision registered in registry of a recognising country?

Under Brussels I, if the defendant (or any other interested party) does not contest the recognition, the parties are not required to re-litigate the dispute in order to have the ownership decision registered in registry of a recognizing country. In the examination of such grounds of jurisdiction, the court or authority applied is bound by the findings of fact on which the court of the Member State of origin based its jurisdiction (Art. 35(2)). Moreover, the jurisdiction of the court of the Member State of origin may not be reviewed and the test of public policy (Art. 34) may not be applied to the rules relating to jurisdiction (Art. 35(3)). So, this justification for non recognition of the judgment is not to be raised by the courts of their own motion, and under no circumstances may a foreign judgment be reviewed as to its substance (Art. 36).

3) Assuming that the judgment is recognised, what procedural steps have to be taken to enforce the judgment in your country?

Would the enforcement judgment be necessary or would it suffice to present the original judgment to the enforcing authority?

3.1. Brussels provides for that, in order to be enforced in Portugal, the judgment must be declared enforceable in the Member State of origin on the application of any interested party (Art. 38(1)). This application is to be submitted to a specific court or competent authority (Art. 39(1)), which issues the declaration of enforceability 'immediately' on completion of certain formalities and without any review of the impediments of recognition; the party against whom enforcement is sought cannot at this stage of the proceedings make any submissions on the application (Art. 41).

Moreover, the decision on the application for a declaration of enforceability is to be brought to the notice of the applicant and served on the party against whom enforcement is sought, accompanied by the judgment, if not already served on that party (Art. 42), and may be appealed against by either party (Art. 43). A declaration of enforceability is to be refused or revoked by the competent court of appeal (Arts. 43 and 44) only upon one of the grounds that justify non recognition (Arts. 34 and 35), but under no circumstances may the foreign judgment be reviewed as to its substance (Art. 45(1)(2).

3.2. The applicant has to produce a copy of the original judgment which satisfies the conditions necessary to establish its authenticity (Art. 53(1)) as well as a certificate issued by the court or competent authority of the Member State where a judgment was given using a specific standard form (Art. 54 and Annex V). In case this certificate is not produced the enforcing authority may specify a time for its production or accept an equivalent document or, if it considers that it has sufficient information before it, dispense with its production (Art. 55(1)). The enforcing authority may also require the production of a translation of the documents, which has to be certified by a person qualified to do so in one of the Member States (Art. 55(2)). For these documents as well as for the copy of the judgment no legalisation or other formality is required (Art. 56).

11 – Provisional measures and injunctions

A owns a worldwide famous accessories trademark. After finding out that B is selling fake goods which infringe A's trademark on an internet auction A files an infringement suit also asking the court to issue an injunction to stop infringing activities and seize infringing goods. Assuming that both A and B are resident in your country and the main infringing activities take place there:

1) Would a court of your country have jurisdiction to issue provisional measures/injunction (regarding infringing acts and counterfeited goods located in different countries) which would also have extraterritorial effects? Would the situation change if the court of your country did not have jurisdiction over the main dispute (e.g., if B was resident in country Y and infringing acts were made in country Y)?

1.1. A Portuguese court would have jurisdiction to issue provisional measures/injunction (regarding infringing acts and counterfeited goods located in different countries) which could also have extraterritorial effects to some extent. In fact, the Code of Industrial Property provides for such provisional measures as required under the TRIPS Agreement (Art. 50) and the Enforcement Directive (Art. 9). In the case, since both A and B are resident in Portugal and the main infringing activities take place there, Portuguese courts would also have jurisdiction over the main dispute under Brussels, as the courts of the country of either the domicile of the defendant (Art. 2(1)) or of the place where the harmful event occurred or may occur (Art. 5(3)), considering that A owns a world-wide famous accessories trade mark and that B is selling fake goods which infringe A's trademark on an internet auction. Moreover, Portuguese courts could have jurisdiction concerning such provisional, including protective, measures as may be available under Portuguese law, even if the courts of another Member State have jurisdiction as to the substance of the matter (Brussels I, Article 31).

However, the extraterritorial effects of these measures are limited as a 'real connecting link' between the object of such measures and the country of the forum is required under ECJ jurisprudence[157]. In summary: "The granting of provisional or protective measures on the basis of Article 24 of the [Brussels] Convention is conditional on, *inter alia*, the existence of a real connecting link between the subject-matter of the measures sought and the territorial jurisdiction of the Contracting State of the court before which those measures are sought."[158]

1.2. According to this jurisprudence, if B was resident in country Y and infringing acts were made in country Y, Portuguese courts would not have jurisdiction to issue provisional measures/injunctions where the internet auction of the counterfeited goods actually excluded the Portuguese market, because there would not be 'a real connecting link between the subject-matter of the measures sought and the territorial jurisdiction' of the forum. Despite under Article 31 of Brussels I Portuguese courts might have jurisdiction concerning such provisional, including protective, measures as may

[157] See CLIP Principles (Art. 2:202) and ALI Principles (§ 214).

[158] Judgment of the Court of 17 November 1998, C-391/95, *Van Uden Maritime BV, trading as Van Uden Africa Line* v *Kommanditgesellschaft in Firma Deco-Line and Another* [1998] *ECR* I-07091.

be available under Portuguese law, even if the courts of another Member State have jurisdiction as to the substance of the matter, the ECJ *Van Uden* ruling has limited the possibility of **cross-border injunctions**. In fact, if B was resident in country Y and infringing acts were made in country Y, then the courts of country Y would have jurisdiction as to the substance of the matter as the courts of the country of domicile of the defendant (Art. 2(1)) or of the place where the harmful event occurred or may occur (Art. 5(3)). Nevertheless, under Article 31 of Brussels I Portuguese courts might have jurisdiction concerning such provisional, including protective, measures as may be available under Portuguese law. However, the ECJ ruling has conditioned such jurisdiction to the existence of 'a real connecting link between the subject-matter of the measures sought and the territorial jurisdiction' of the forum, in order to prevent abuses of cross-border injunctions that were facilitated namely by the so-called *kort geding* procedures of Dutch courts as they imposed no time limit to the initiation of the main proceedings therefore rendering definitive what was supposed to be merely provisional protection measures.

However, if B was resident in country Y and infringing acts were made in country Y, a Portuguese court would still have jurisdiction not only as to the substance of the matter but also to issue provisional measures/injunction, in case infringing acts made in country Y were events that give rise to infringing acts likely to occur in Portugal, i.e., as evidence of an 'imminent commission' of a tort (or delict) in Portugal. That would be the case if the internet auction of fake goods did not actually exclude the Portuguese market. According to the ECJ, it is "not possible to accept an interpretation of Article 5(3) of the Brussels Convention according to which application of that provision is conditional on the actual occurrence of damage. Furthermore, it would be inconsistent to require that an action to prevent behaviour considered to be unlawful[...] whose principal aim is precisely to prevent damage, may be brought only after that damage has occurred."[159]

2) Could a court issue an injunction/protective measures if the trade mark for which the protection is sought was registered abroad?

If the trademark for which the protection is sought was registered not in Portugal but abroad, then the claimant would not provide the required elements of proof of ownership of the trademark right in Portugal (Code of Industrial Property, Art. 338-I (2)[160]). However, unregistered worldwide famous trademarks can be protected under unfair competition law and benefit from similar provisional and protective measures (Art. 317(2) of of Code of Industrial Property), which can be issued against any internet intermediary whose services are used by third parties to infringe industrial property rights (Art. 338-I (3) of Code of Industrial Property). Accordingly, on grounds

---

[159] Judgment of 1 October 2002, C-167/00, *Verein fur Konsumenteninformation* v *K.H. Henkel* [2002] ECR I-8111, par. 48. See also, on Article 50 of TRIPS, which provides for that judicial authorities shall have the authority to order prompt and effective provisional measures namely to 'to prevent an infringement of any intellectual property right from occurring, and in particular to prevent the entry into the channels of commerce in their jurisdiction of goods, including imported goods immediately after customs clearance' (Art. 50(1)(a)) as well as the authority to adopt 'provisional measures *inaudita altera parte* where appropriate, in particular where any delay is likely to cause irreparable harm to the right holder' (Art. 50(2)). See Joined cases C-300/98 and C-392/98, Judgment of the Court of 14 December 2000, *Parfums Christian Dior SA* v *TUK Consultancy BV and Assco Gerüste GmbH and Rob van Dijk v Wilhelm Layher GmbH & Co. KG and Layher BV* [2000] *ECR* I-11307 ('In a field in which the Community has not yet legislated and which consequently falls within the competence of the Member States, the protection of intellectual property rights, and measures adopted for that purpose by the judicial authorities, do not fall within the scope of Community law. Accordingly, Community law neither requires nor forbids that the legal order of a Member State should accord to individuals the right to rely directly on the rule laid down by Article 50(6) of the TRIPs Agreement or that it should oblige the courts to apply that rule of their own motion').

[160] Effective protection requires registration of the mark at the Industrial Property Office according to the registration procedure (Arts. 233 ff. CPI) and, on the other hand, the court shall demand the applicant of a provisional measure to provide elements of proof to demonstrate that he is the holder of the industrial property right, or that he is authorized to use it, and that an infringement takes place or is imminent.

of unfair competition, a Portuguese court could issue protective measures/injunction despite the trademark for which the protection is sought is registered abroad.

Concerning Community trademarks, Portuguese courts as the courts of the place of infringement would have 'exclusive jurisdiction to grant provisional and protective measures which, subject to a necessary procedure for recognition and enforcement pursuant to Title III of Brussels I Regulation, are applicable in the territory of any Member State' (Community TM Regulation, Art. 103(2), and Art. 96(a)).

3) Would a court in your country require the person seeking issuance of provisional measures to grant a guarantee?

A Portuguese court could at its own motion require the person seeking issuance of provisional measures to grant an adequate *guarantee* where the judge finds it convenient, according to the circumstances of the case (Art. 390(2) of Code of Civil Procedure, by remission of Article 338-P of Code of Industrial Property). Concerning the issuance of provisional measures to preserve evidence, the court may also require the person seeking issuance of such measures to grant an adequate guarantee also aimed to assure the compensation for damages that the defendant may be entitled to, under certain circumstances, as a result of the issuance of such measures (Art. 338-G(1) of Code of Industrial Property).

4) Would a court of your country be pre-empted from issuing an injunction if the parties had submitted the dispute to arbitration proceedings?

A Portuguese court would not be pre-empted from issuing an injunction if the parties had submitted the dispute to arbitration proceedings. Brussels I does not apply to arbitrage and neither the Arbitration Act[161] nor the Código de Processo Civil

[161] Law 31/86 of 29 August (*Lei da Arbitragem Voluntária*).

(Code of Civil Procedure) provide an answer to this question. Nonetheless, a Portuguese court of appeal held that an international arbitration agreement does not exclude the international jurisdiction of Portuguese courts concerning related interim provisional procedures[162]. This domestic jurisprudence is in conformity with ECJ *Van Uden* ruling. In summary: "On a proper construction of Article 5, point 1, of the [Brussels] Convention [...], the court which has jurisdiction by virtue of that provision also has jurisdiction to order provisional or protective measures, without that jurisdiction being subject to any further conditions. However, where the parties have validly excluded the jurisdiction of the courts in a dispute arising under a contract and have referred that dispute to arbitration, it is only under Article 24 of the Convention that a court may be empowered to order such measures, since it cannot do so as the court having jurisdiction on the substance of the dispute. In that connection, where the subject-matter of an application for provisional measures relates to a question falling within the scope *ratione materiae* of the Convention, that Convention is applicable and Article 24 thereof may confer jurisdiction on the court hearing that application even where proceedings have already been, or may be, commenced on the substance of the case and even where those proceedings are to be conducted before arbitrators."[163]

It could be added that, considering that a choice of court agreement can allow a party to depart from such agreement, the Supremo Tribunal de Justiça (Supreme Court of Justice) accepted that such a party could apply before a court the issuance of provisional

[162] Tribunal da Relação de Lisboa (Lisbon Court of Appeals), Judgments of 2 December 2003 and 13 March 2007 (available at www.dgsi.pt/jtrl).

[163] Judgment of the Court of 17 November 1998, C-391/95, *Van Uden Maritime BV, trading as Van Uden Africa Line* v *Kommanditgesellschaft in Firma Deco-Line and Another* [1998] *ECR* I-07091.

measures, even if that court does not have jurisdiction over the substance of the action.[164]

5) If the claimant asked to issue an injunction to cease infringing acts, would a court in your country conceive of an injunction to cease as a procedural or substantive measure?

If the claimant asked to issue an injunction to cease infringing acts a Portuguese court would conceive of an injunction to cease not as a substantive but rather as a *procedural measure.* In Portugal injunctions to cease infringing acts are conceived as procedural measures. The Code of Civil Procedure provides for in Article 383(1) that the provisional/protective measure is always dependent upon the action caused by the protected right. The procedural nature of these measures is evidenced by the fact that the provisional procedure is extinguished and, where ordered, the provisional measure ceases if one of the grounds provided for in Article 389(1) of the Code of Civil Procedure occurs, such as, for example, the plaintiff does not initiate the main proceedings within 30 days (a), or the defendant is not convicted (d) or the protected right is extinguished (e).

12. Securities in intellectual proper

In order to get loan from Bank B, A decides to use intellectual property rights and royalties from those intellectual property rights as a collateral. A fails to repay the loan. Assuming that A is a national of country X and B is a bank in country Y:

1) Could intellectual property rights be used as a collateral pursuant to the law of your country?

---

[164] Judgment of 17 December 2004, Proc. 04B4076 (available at www.dgsi.pt/jstj).

Pursuant to Portuguese law, intellectual property rights can be used as a collateral. Economic copyrights and industrial property rights can be object of usufruct rights (*usufructus*) and can be given as a guarantee (*penhor*) (Copyright Act, Arts. 43, 45, 46 and 215(1)(a); Industrial Property Act, Arts. 6, 30(1)(c) and 356(1)(l)).

2) *What law would be applied to such issues as the creation, effectiveness against third parties, priority and the enforcement of these security rights?*

Insofar as such issues concern the legal status of IP rights they would be governed by the law of the country for which protection is claimed, i.e. *lex loci protectionis* (Berne Convention, Art. 5(2); Paris Convention, Arts. 4-bis(1), Art. 6(2)(3))[165]. However, the formal validity of the transactions would be governed by the law of the country designated according to Article 11 of Rome I.[166]

3) *Would a court of your country apply the same law to registered and non-registered intellectual property rights?*

A Portuguese court would apply the law of the country for which protection is claimed both to registered and non-registered intellectual property rights. However, concerning registered intellectual property rights, the jurisdiction of a Portuguese court could be

[165] See D. Moura Vicente, op. cit. n. 41, pp. 222-3, 254-5, 305, 377.

[166] Note that, under Rome I, security rights over claims are included within the concept of voluntary assignment and this relationship is governed by the law applicable to the contract between the assignor and assignee, including the assignability of the assigned claim, the relationship between the assignee and the debtor, the conditions under which the assignment can be invoked against the debtor and whether the debtor's obligations have been discharged (Art. 14(1)(2)(3)). The law applicable to the assignor and the assignee can be chosen by the parties (Art. 3). In the absence of choice, such an assignment of an intellectual property right should qualify, taking into account the ECJ judgment of 23 April 2009 (C-533/07, *Falco Privatstiftung and Thomas Rabitsch* v *Gisela Weller-Lindhorst*), as a contract for the sale of goods, and therefore the law of the country where the seller (assignor) has his habitual residence would apply.

contested if the question of registration or validity of such rights were raised according to Brussels I (Art. 22(4)) and the relevant ECJ jurisprudence.

References

European Court of Justice (ECJ)

Judgment of the Court of 30 November 1976, 21-76, *Handelskwekerij G. J. Bier BV* v *Mines de potasse d'Alsace SA* [1976] *ECR 01735*

Judgment of the Court of 24 June 1981, C-150/80, *Elefanten Schuh GmbH* v *Jacqmain* [1981] *ECR 01671*

Judgment of the Court (First Chamber) of 4 March 1982, C-38/81, *Effer SpA* **v** *Hans-Joachim Kantner* [1982] *ECR 00825*

Judgment of the Court (Fourth Chamber) of 15 November 1983, C-288/82, *Ferdinand M.J.J. Duijnstee v Lodewijk Goderbauer* [1983] *ECR* 03663

Judgment of the Court (Sixth Chamber) of 8 December 1987, C-144/86, *Gubisch Maschinenfabrik KG* v *Giulio Palumbo* [1987] *ECR* 04861

Judgment of the Court (Fifth Chamber) of 27 September 1988, C-189/87, *Athanasios Kalfelis* v *Bankhaus Schröder, Münchmeyer, Hengst and Co. and others* [1988] *ECR* 05565

Judgment of the Court of 26 June 1991, C-351/89, *Overseas Union Insurance Limited e.a.* v *New Hampshire Insurance Company* [1999] *ECR* I-3317

Judgment of the Court of 17 June 1992, C-26/91, *Jakob Handte & Co. GmbH* v *Traitements Mécano-chimiques des Surfaces SA* [1992] ECR I-3967

Judgment of the Court of 2 June 1994, C-414/92, *Solo Kleinmotoren GmbH* v *Emilio Boch* [1994] *ECR* I-2237

Judgment of the Court of 7 March 1995, C-68/93, *Fiona Shevill et. al.* v *Presse Alliance SA* [1995] *ECR* I-415

Judgment of the Court of 17 November 1998, C-391/95, *Van Uden Maritime BV, trading as Van Uden Africa Line* **v** *Kommanditgesellschaft in Firma Deco-Line and Another* [1998] *ECR I-07091*

Judgment of the Court of 11 May 2000, C-38/98, *Régie Nationale des Usines Renault SA* v *Maxicar SpA and Orazio Formento* [2000] *ECR* I-2973

Judgment of the Court of 28 March 2000, C-7/98, *Dieter Krombach v André Bamberski*, [2000] *ECR* I-1935

Judgment of the Court of 27 June 2000, Joined cases C-240/98 to C-244/98, *Océano Grupo Editorial SA v Roció Murciano Quintero (C-240/98) and Salvat Editores*

SA v José M. Sánchez Alcón Prades (C-241/98), José Luis Copano Badillo (C-242/98), Mohammed Berroane (C-243/98) and Emilio Viñas Feliú (C-244/98) [2000] *ECR* I-04941

Judgment of the Court (Fifth Chamber) of 9 November 2000, C-381/98, *Ingmar GB Ltd* v *Eaton Leonard Technologies Inc.* [2000] *ECR* I-09305

Judgment of the Court of 14 December 2000, joined cases C-300/98 and C-392/98, *Parfums Christian Dior SA* v *TUK Consultancy BV and Assco Gerüste GmbH and Rob van Dijk v Wilhelm Layher GmbH & Co. KG and Layher BV* [2000] *ECR I-11307*

Judgment of the Court of 17 September 2002, C-334/00, *Fonderie Officine Meccaniche Tacconi SpA* v *Heirinch Wagner Sinto Maschinenfabrik GmbH* [2002] *ECR* I-10087

Judgment of the Court of 1 October 2002, C-167/00, *Verein fur Konsumenteninformation* v *K.H. Henkel* [2002] *ECR* I-8111

Judgment of the Court of 1 March 2005, C-281/02, *Andrew Owusu* v *N.B. Jackson, Trading as Villa Holidays Bal In Villas and others* [2005] *ECR* I-1383

Judgment of the Court (First Chamber) of 13 July 2006, C-4/03, *Gesellschaft für Antriebstechnik mbH & Co. KG (GAT)* v *Lamellen und Kupplungsbau Beteiligungs KG (LuK)* [2006] *ECR* I-6509

Judgment of the Court (First Chamber) of 13 July 2006, C-539/03, *Roche Nederland BV and Others* v. *Fredrick Primus and Milton Goldberg* [2006] *ECR* I- *06535*

Judgment of the Court (Fourth Chamber) of 23 April 2009, C-533/07, *Falco Privatstiftung and Thomas Rabitsch* v *Gisela Weller-Lindhorst*, OJ C 141/15, 20.6.2009

National Courts

Supremo Tribunal de Justiça (Supreme Court of Justice, Portugal): Judgments of 31 April 1988, 12 April 1997, 15 December 1998 (BMJ 482 (1999) p. 266), 16 October 2002 (CJ/ASTJ (2002) p. 11), 27 March 2003 (Proc. 03B3145), 17 December 2004 (Proc. 04B4076), 31 March 2005, 14 March 2006, 3 October 2007 (Proc. 07S922), 10 January 2008, 9 October 2008 (Proc. 08B2633), 21 May 2009 (Proc. 4986/06.3TVLSB.S1), 8 October 2009 (Proc. 5138/06.8TBSTS.S1) (www.dgsi.pt/jstj).

Tribunal da Relação de Coimbra (Coimbra Court of Appeals): Judgments of 29 October 1985 (CJ IV/1985, pp. 86-89), 12 June 2007 and 27 November 2007 (www.dgsi.pt/jtrc)

Tribunal da Relação de Lisboa (Lisbon Court of Appeals): Judgments of 2 December 2003, 17 February 2005, 24 October 2006, 18 January 2007, 13 March 2007, 2 April 2008, 25 September 2008, 16 December 2008 (Proc. 10053/2008-1), 17 December 2008, 13 January 2009, 21 May 2009 (Proc. 8748/2008-6) (www.dgsi.pt/jtrl)

Tribunal da Relação do Porto (Porto Court of Appeals): Judgment of 30 September 2008 (www.dgsi.pt/jtrp)

Literature

American Law Institute, *Intellectual Property: Principles Governing Jurisdiction, Choice of Law, and Judgments in Transnational Disputes*. As Adopted and Promulgated by the American Law Institute at San Francisco, California May 14, 2007, St. Paul, Minnesota, American Law Institute Publishers, 2008 (ALI Principles)

Asensio, P.A. Miguel,Cross-Border Adjudication of Intellectual Property Rights and Competition between Jurisdictions', *Annali Italiani del Diritto d'Autore, della Cultura e dello Spettacolo* - AIDA XVI (2007) p. 1.

Boschiero, N. 'Infringement of Intellectual Property Rights. A Commentary on Article 8 of the Rome II Regulation', *Yearbook of Private International Law* – YPIL IX (2007), p. 87

Calvo Caravaca, A.L., Carrascosa González, J. *Las obligaciones extracontractuales en Derecho internacional privado. El Reglamento «Roma II»*, Granada, Comares, 2008

CLIP – European Max-Planck Group for Conflict of Laws in Intellectual Property, 'Exclusive Jurisdiction and Cross Border IP (Patent) Infringement. Suggestions for Amendment of the Brussels I Regulation (20.12.2006)', *EIPR* (2007) p. 193

Correia, A. Ferrer - *Direito Internacional Privado – Alguns Problemas,* Coimbra, 1997

European Commission - *Green Paper on the Review of Council Regulation (EC) No 44/2001 on Jurisdiction and the Recognition and Enforcement of Judgments in Civil and Commercial Matters*, COM (2009) 175 final - *Report from the Commission to the European Parliament, the Council and the European Economic and Social Committee on the application of Council Regulation (EC) No 44/2001 on jurisdiction and the recognition and enforcement of judgments in civil and commercial matters*, COM(2009) 174 final, Brussels, 21.4.2009 -

Franzosi, M. *Worldwide Patent Litigation and the Italian Torpedo, EIPR* (1997) p. 7.

Kur, A. 'A farewell to cross-border injunctions? The ECJ decisions GAT v. LuK and Roche Nederland v. Primus and Goldenberg', *International Review of Industrial Property and Copyright Law* IIC 37 (2006), p. 844

Palao Moreno, G. 'La proteccion de los derechos de propiedad intelectual en Europa: el artículo 8 del Reglamento Roma II', *Revista Jurídica de Deporte y Entretenimiento* 22 (2008), p. 557 - 'Competencia judicial internacional en supuestos de responsabilidad civil en Internet', *Cuestiones Actuales de Derecho y Tecnologías de la Información e la Comunicación (TICs),* coord. J. Plaza Penadés, Cizur Menor, Thomson Aranzadi, 2006, p. 275

Pereira, A.L.D. *Direitos de Autor e Liberdade de Informação,* Coimbra, Almedina, 2008 - «A Jurisdição na Internet segundo o Regulamento 44/2001 (e as alternativas extrajudiciais e tecnológicas)», *Boletim da Faculdade de Direito Universidade de Coimbra* LXXVII (2001), pp. 633-687 – 'A via electrónica da negociação (alguns aspectos)', *Estudos de Direito do Consumidor* 8 (2006/2007), p. 275

Pinheiro, L. de Lima – 'Direito aplicável aos contratos celebrados através da Internet', *Direito da Sociedade da Informação* VII (2008), p. 363 - 'O Direito de conflitos das obrigações extracontratuais entre a comunitarização e a globalização – uma primeira apreciação do Regulamento Comunitário Roma II', *O Direito* 139/V (2007), p. 1027 - *Arbitragem internacional,* Coimbra, Almedina, 2005 - 'Direito aplicável aos contratos com consumidores', *Revista da Ordem dos Advogados*

66/1 (2001), p. 162 - 'A lei aplicável aos direitos de propriedade intelectual', *Revista da Faculdade de Direito Universidade de Lisboa* 42 (2001), p. 63

Ramos, R.M. de Moura – 'Public Policy in the Framework of the Brussels Conventions: Remarks on two Recent Decisions by the European Court of Justice', *Yearbook of Private International Law – YPIL* II (2000), pp. 25-40

Ricketson S., & Ginsburg, J. *International Copyright and Neighbouring Rights: The Berne Convention and Beyond*, 2 vol., 2nd ed., Oxford, Oxford University Press, 2006

Torremans, P. 'Authorship, Ownership of Right and Works Created by Employees. Which Law Applies?' *EIPR* 27/6 (2005), p. 220

Ubertazzi, B. *Il regolamento Roma I sulla legge applicabile alle obbligazioni contrattuali,* Milano, Giuffrè, 2008

Vicente, D. Moura - *A Tutela Internacional da Propriedade Intelectual*, Coimbra, Almedina, 2009 – 'Sources and General Principles of Portuguese International Private Law: An Outline', *Yearbook of Private International Law* – YPIL IX (2007), p. 257 - *Direito Internacional Privado: Problemática Internacional da Sociedade da Informação*, Coimbra, Almedina, 2005, p. 320 - 'Direito internacional de autor', *Estudos em Homenagem à Professora Doutora Isabel Magalhães Colaço*, I, Coimbra, Almedina, 2002, p. 469 - Competência Judiciária e Reconhecimento de Decisões Estrangeiras no Regulamento (CE) n.° 44/2001», *Scientia Iuridica* (2002), p. 347

Wagner, G. 'Die neue Rom II-Verordnung', *Praxis des Internationalen Privat- und Verfahrensrechts* (2008), p. 1

Voda, J.K. '*M.D.* v. 'Cordis Corporation', *Gewerblicher Rechtsschutz und Urheberrecht - Internationaler Teil* - GRUR Int. 56/5 (2007), pp. 442-447

MONDIALISTION ET INTERNET AU PORTUGAL*

I/ Mondialisation, Internet et les droits des individus

A. Comment sont protégées dans votre droit les données personnelle?

1. Les données à caractère personnel sont définis dans la loi n. 67/98 du 26 octobre comme «toute information de tout type, quel que soit le support, y compris le son et l'image, concernant une personne physique identifiée ou identifiable (personne concernée) », i.e., une personne qui peut être identifiée directement ou indirectement, notamment en se référant à un certain nombre d' identification ou à un ou plusieurs facteurs spécifiques comme physique, physiologique, mentale, économique, culturelle ou identité sociale» (art. 3, al. a). Cette définition transpose l'art. 2, al. a), de la directive 95/46/CE du Parlement Européen et du Conseil du 24 octobre 1995 relative à la protection des personnes physiques à l'égard du traitement des données à caractère personnel et à la libre circulation de ces données, la jurisprudence de la CJUE y ayant donc un rôle important: voire e.g. les arrêts *Lindqvist* (6.11/2003)[1]

---

* *La mondialisation, Journées allemandes*, Tome LXVI/2016, coll. «Travaux de l'Association Henri Capitant», Berlin, 2017, p. 881-894, Éditions Bruylant.

[1] Affaire C-101/01, ECLI:EU:C:2003:596 (« L'indication du fait qu'une personne s'est blessée au pied et est en congé de maladie partiel constitue une donnée à caractère personnel relative à la santé »).

e *Worten c ACT* (30.5. 2013)[2]; v. aussi les documents de travail de l' «Art. 29 Working Party».[3]

2. La loi n. 67/98 ne consacre pas un droit de propriété sur les données. Il s'agit plutôt d'un droit à la protection de la vie privée concernant l'information des individus. Le code civil prévoit le droit à la protection de la personnalité (art. 70) et des droits spéciaux de personnalité, comme le droit à l'image et le droit au respect the l'intimité de la vie privée (arts. 70 e 80)[4], la protection des données à caractère personnel en étant assimilé.[5] La Cour suprême du Portugal a utilisé la désignation, provenant de la doctrine allemande, de « droit fondammental à l'autodétermination informationelle »[6].

Nonobstant, la Constitution de la république portugaise autonomise la protection des données à caractère personnelle au regard du droit à la vie privée dans un art. sur l'utilisation de l'informatique (art. 35). Dans le même sens la Charte des droits fondamentaux de l'Union Européenne prévoit un art. spécial pour garantir la protection juridique des données à caractère personnelle (art. 8).

D'ailleurs, au Portugal, la loi n. 12/2005 du 26 janvier sur l'information génétique et personnelle de santé établi que cette information est propriété de la personne concernée, y compris les données cliniques registrées, les résultats des analyses et des autres examens subsidiaires (art. 3/1).

---

[2] Affaire C-342/12, ECLI:EU:C:2013:355 (registre du temps de travail).

[3] À partir du 25 mai 2018 Il s'applique le règlement (UE) 2016/679 du Parlement européen et du Conseil du 27 avril 2016 relatif à la protection des personnes physiques à l'égard du traitement des données à caractère personnel et à la libre circulation de ces données, et abrogeant la directive 95/46/CE (règlement général sur la protection des données).

[4] CAMPOS, D. Leite de (1991). Lições de Direitos da Personalidade. BFDUC 57.

[5] PINTO, P. Mota (1993). O direito à reserva sobre a intimidade da vida privada. BFDUC 69: 479-585.

[6] Arrêt du 16 octobre 2014, affaire 679/05.7TAEVR.E2.S1: <www.dgsi.pt>

En prévoyant l'information de santé comme objet d'une propriété la loi a ouvert une nouvelle branche des droits exclusifs sur des biens incorporels, en plus du droit d'auteur, de ses droits voisins et de la propriété industrielle.

3. Le traitement des données à caractère personnel peut être licite sans un accord de l'internaute dans les cas prévus dans la loi n. 67/98 (art. 6, en transposant art. 7 de la directive 95/46), i.e., si le traitement est nécessaire notamment à l'exécution d'un contrat auquel la personne concernée est partie ou à l'exécution de mesures précontractuelles prises à la demande de celle-ci ou à la réalisation de l'intérêt légitime poursuivi par le responsable du traitement.

4. Les « données sensibles », c'est à dire, des catégories particulières de données. Selon la constitution, «l'ordinateur ne peut pas être utilisé pour le traitement des données concernant les croyances philosophiques ou politiques, le parti ou l'appartenance syndicale, les croyances religieuses, la vie privée ou l'origine ethnique, à moins que par consentement exprès du titulaire, prévue par l'autorisation de la loi avec des garanties de non-discrimination ou de traitement données statistiques non identifiables individuellement» (art. 35/2).

En outre, le traitement des données personnelles relatives aux croyances philosophiques ou politiques, parti ou à un syndicat, les croyances religieuses, la vie privée et l'origine raciale ou ethnique et le traitement des données relatives à la santé ou la vie sexuelle, y compris les données génétiques (loi 67/98 art. 7/1; cf. art. 8 de la directive 95/46).

Toutefois, le traitement des « données sensibles » est licite si, en étant assurées les mesures adéquates, selon certaines conditions, notamment la personne concernée a donné son consentement explicite à un tel traitement (art. 7/2) ou le traitement est nécessaire à la protection des intérêts vitaux de la personne concernée ou d'une autre personne dans le cas où la personne concernée n'a pas la capacité physique ou juridique pour donner son consentement (art. 7/3, al. a).

D'ailleurs, le traitement des données sensibles peut être autorisé par disposition légale ou par la Commission nationale de protection des données (CNPD) quand il est indispensable par des raisons d'intérêt public important pour l'exercice des compétences légales ou statutaires du responsable par le traitement (art. 7/2, de la loi n. 67/9, en conformité avec l'art. 7/4, de la directive 95/46). Par exemple, le traitement des données relatives aux infractions, aux condamnations pénales ou aux mesures de sûreté doit être autorisée par la CNPD, et doit être nécessaire à l'éxécution des finalités légitimes de son responsable (art. 8/2).

Le traitement nécessaire aux fins de respecter les obligations et les droits spécifiques du responsable du traitement en matière de droit du travail, prévue par la directive (art. 7/2, al. b), est disciplinée dans Code du travail portugais (art. 17), et se conforme avec la jurisprudence de la CJUE (*Worten c. ACT*).

5. Portugal fait partie de l'Union européenne. Le Conseil et le Parlement européen ont chargé la Commission de déterminer, sur la base de l'art. 25/6, de la directive 95/46/CE, quels sont les pays tiers qui assurent un niveau de protection adéquat en raison de sa législation interne ou des engagements internationaux qu'il a conclus.[7]

Le 6 octobre 2015[8], la CJUE a jugé l'invalidité de la décision 2000/520/CE de la Commission du 26 juillet 2000 « EU-US Safe-Harbour ».

---

[7] Liste des pays y compris (seulement en anglais) : http://ec.europa.eu/justice/data-protection/international-transfers/adequacy/index_en.htm

[8] Affaire C-362/14, Maximillian Schrems v Data Protection Commissioner. ECLI:EU:C:2015:650.

Le 2 février 2016, la Commission européenne et les États-Unis ont convenu d'un nouveau cadre pour les transferts de données transatlantiques: l'UE-U.S. « Privacy Shield ».[9]

6/7. Au Portugal aucune exception n'est prévue pour le cloud computing, donc la legislation en vigueur, notamment la loi 67/98, doit être respectée.

Le règlement général sur la protection des données remplacera la directive 95/46 en modernisant la protection des données à caractère personnel pour l'environnement de la nuage et du « Big Data ». Selon l'information du *Consilium*[10], le règlement prévoit comme droits de la personne concernée notamment « la nécessité d'obtenir de la personne qu'elle indique clairement qu'elle consent au traitement des données à caractère personnel » et « les droits à la rectification, à l'effacement des données et à l'oubli ».

8. Un droit à l'oubli a été proposé comme manifestation du droit général de personnalité[11], mas il n'est pas prévu dans la loi ni affirmé par la jurisprudence interne.

La loi 67/98 établi le droit d'accès selon lequel toute personne concernée a le droit d'obtenir du responsable du traitement, notamment, selon le cas, la rectification, l'effacement ou le verrouillage des données dont le traitement n'est pas conforme à cette loi, notamment en raison du caractère incomplet ou inexact des données [art. 11/d); correspond à l'art. 12, al. b) de la directive 95/46].

---

[9] http://ec.europa.eu/justice/data-protection/files/privacy-shield-adequacy-decision_en.pdf

[10] http://www.consilium.europa.eu/fr/policies/data-protection-reform/data-protection-regulation/

[11] CARVALHO, Orlando de (1973). Les droits de l'Homme dans le Droit Civil Portugais. BFDUC 49: 1-24.

La jurisprudence de la CJUE dans l'arrêt *Google Spain*[12] a consacré le droit à l'oubli en jugeant que « l'exploitant d'un moteur de recherche est obligé de supprimer de la liste de résultats, (...) également dans l'hypothèse où ce nom ou ces informations ne sont pas effacés préalablement ou simultanément de ces pages web, et ce, le cas échéant, même lorsque leur publication en elle-même sur lesdites pages est licite. »

En mai 2015 il y avait au Portugal plus de 2000 applications d'élimination de presque 9000 URL, mais seulement peu plus que 25% avait été supprimés.[13]

9. Le transfert des données à caractère personnel est discipliné par la loi 67/98, en transposant la directive 95/46 (arts. 25 e 26).

La circulation des données à caractère personnel est libre entre les États-membres de l'UE, sans préjudice des dispositions communautaires de nature fiscale ou des douanes (art. 18). Le transfert des données pour des pays tiers démande que ces pays assurent un niveau de protection adéquat, ce que la Comission nationale de protection des données (CNPD) decide (art. 19/1-2-3). En tout cas le transfert des données pour un pays tiers dont la protection n'est pas adéquate selon la Commission européene est strictement interdit (art. 19/5)

Malgré le pays tiers n'a pas un niveau de protection adequat le transfert des données peut être authorisé par la CNPD selon les conditions prévues dans l'art. 20/1, notamment si la personne concernée ait indubitablement donné son consentement au transfert envisagé, ou le transfert soit necessaire par exemple à l'exécution d' un contrat entre la personne concernée et le responsable du traitement. En outre, la CNPD autorise le transfert des données qui

---

12 Arrêt du 13 mai 2014, affaire C131/12, ECLI:EU:C:2014:317.

13 <http://www.computerworld.com.pt/2015/05/13/um-ano-apos-o-direito-ao--esquecimento-no-google/>

respect les clauses contractuelles types ayant les garanties suffisantes selon la Commission européenne (art. 19/5).[14]

10. Au niveau de l'Union européenne c'est compétent la Commission européenne. Au niveau national c'est compétent la CNPD (Commission nationale de protection des données), une autorité administrative indépendante qui fonctionne auprès du Parlement (art. 20 de la loi 67/98). Cette Commission a le pouvoir notamment d'appliquer des amendes établies pour les infractions à la loi des données (art. 41).

B. / La liberté d'expression sur Internet

1. La Constitution consacre la liberté d'expression et d'information (art. 37/1-2). L'entité regulatrice des media (ERC) a rendu décisions contre sites de racism et xenophobie (le 27 june 2001), canibalism et d'autres violences gothiques (le 25 aout 2004) hebergés par un serviteur web établi au Portugal.[15]

2. Il y a plusières arrêts des tribunaux sur l'abus de la liberté d'expression. La jurisprudence de la Cour d'appel du Porto est particulièrement expressive. Dans l'arrêt du 5 juin 2015, affaire 101/13.5TAMCN.P1, la Cour a decidé que la publication en *Facebook* d'une photographie avec l'image du personne contre sa volonté est un acte incriminé dans le Code pénal (art. 199/2).

Dans l'arrêt de la Cour suprême du 16 novembre 2012 (affaire 54/11.4TASVC.L1 – 3), il s'agissait d'un texte ironique et critique publiée dans une page personnelle au Facebook d'un homme politique qui exprimait des jugements. La Cour a estimé que l'agent n'attentait personnellement contre son adversaire politique et donc

---

[14] La notion de transfert de données a été interpretée dans l'arrêt *Lindqvist* (6.112003), affaire C-101/01, ECLI:EU:C:2003:596.

[15] <http://www.erc.pt/pt/deliberacoes>

il n'y avait pas de diffamation. Selon la cour, il y a plus tolérance versée aux jugements de valeur que celui accordée à des imputations personnelles et ses limites sont plus larges quand il s'agit d'un homme politique agissant en sa qualité de personnage public, que lorsqu'on se réfère à un seul particulier.[16]

Parfois le licenciement de travailleurs est justifié à cause de messages qu'ils ont publiée dans ses pages du Facebook et qui portent atteinte contre l'image et la réputation de l'employer. Selon les tribunaux les pages du Facebook ne sont pas normalement reservées aux amis intimes, mais assez ouvertes aux amis des amis ou même publiques.[17]

3. Ceux qui estiment d'être victimes d'un atteint peuvent demander ordinnance par la Cour d'une injonction selon le Code de procédure civil (art. 362). Il s'agit d'une injonction non spécifiée dans le Code, comme par exemple, ordonner l'éffacement de la page ou le blocage d'accès à la publication. D'ailleurs, la victime peut demander les remèdes prévus dans le Code civil, comme le payment des dommages-intérêsts causés et bien aussi que l'agent ne poste plus le contenu diffamatoire ou injurieux, sous peine d'une astreinte (arts. 483, 829 e 829-A du Code civil).

C/ Autres droits

1. La liberté de presse et des media est protégée par la Constitution (art. 38), et la compétence pour régulation de la communication

---

[16] Voir aussi l'arrêt du 13 avril 2016, l'affaire 471/15.0T9AGD-A.P1 (la page Facebook comme publication), et arrêts du 25 novembre 2015, affaire 848/13.6TAVRF. P1, et du 16 décembre 2015, affaire 886/14.1PBAVR.P1 (le Messenger est communication privée).

[17] Voir Cour d'appel de Lisbonne, l'arrêt du 29 septembre 2014, affaire 431/13.6TTFUN.L1-4. Voir aussi les arrêts de la Cour suprême du 13 avril 2016, affaire 471/15.0T9AGD-A.P1 (la page Facebook comme publication), du 25 novembre 2015, affaire 848/13.6TAVRF.P1, et du 16 décembre 2015, affaire 886/14.1PBAVR.P1 (le Messenger est communication privée).

sociale est attribuée à une autorité administratif indépendante (art. 39), en espèce la ERC.

Le balance entre la liberté de presse et le droit au respect de la vie privée fait objet d'abondante jurisprudence national[18] et international, en particulier la jurisprudence de la Cour européenne des droits de l'homme (CEDH)[19].

Dans l'arrêt du 8 mai 2013, affaire 1755/08.0TVLSB.L1.S1, la Cour suprême a décidé que la révélation du domicile d'une personne avec projection publique dans un reportage publiée par un journal en ligne n'était pas justifié par le fin d'information et alors constituait un abuse de liberté de presse. Le Code civile prévoit le droit au respect de la vie privée selon la nature du cas et la condition des personnes (art. 80). Par analogie avec le droit à l'image, il est accepté de publier des informations sur la vie privée des personnes en fonction de leur notoriété ou profession, ou par des exigences de justice, finalités scientifiques, didactiques ou culturelles, ou quand l'image est dans places publiques ou des faits d'intérêt public ou des évènements publiques (art. 79/2).

2. La loi du commerce électronique – décret-loi n. 7/2004 du 7 janvier - prévoit un méchanisme de « *notice and take down* » (art. 18). La personne qui s'estime lesée peut démander au fournisseur d'hébèrgement (ou des moteurs de recherche) le blocage d'accès aux contenus illicites. Si l'illicéité n'est pas manifeste, le fournisseur d'Internet n'a pas le devoir de bloquer l'accès. En ce cas, l'interessé peut demander à l'entité de supervision – en espèce, l'entité régulatrice de la communication (ERC) -, laquelle doit produire une décision provisoire dans 48 heures et la communiquer par moyen électronique aux parties. Quand-même, si le fournisseur d'Internet

[18] V. par ex. l'arrêt de la Cour Suprême du 29 janvier 2015, affaire 24412/02.6TVLLSB.L1.S1

[19] < http://echr.coe.int/Documents/Research_report_internet_FRA.pdf >

décide le blocage d'accès, l'interessé en mantenir de contenu disponible peut appeller pour l'entité de supervision. La décision de l' entité de supervision fait objet d'appell judiciare. Le fournisseur d'Internet n'a pas aussi aucune responsabilité si l'illiceité n'est pas manifeste. Parfois le contenu illicit se trouve dans les commentaires des lecteurs, voire par exemple la déliberation n. 19/CONT-I/2012 du 26 septembre 2012 de l'entité régulatrice de la communication.[20]

3. Les droits de propriété intellectuelle sont fragilisés par Internet. Par ex., la mise en circulation dans le web des œuvres protégées, l'utilisation des marques et des autres signes distinctifs comme noms de domaine ou mots clé.

Selon la directive 2004/48/CE du Parlement européen et du Conseil du 29 avril 2004 relative au respect des droits de propriété intellectuelle « Le développement de l'usage de l'Internet permet une distribution instantanée de produits pirates dans le monde entier » (cons. 9). La directive 2004/48 (*enforcement*) a été transposée par la loi n. 16/2008 du 1 avril, qui a modifié le code du droit d'auteur et le code de la propriété industrielle.

En autre, la directive 2001/29/CE du Parlement européen et du Conseil du 22 mai 2001 sur l'harmonisation de certains aspects du droit d'auteur et des droits voisins dans la société de l'information, considère que « Les services d'intermédiaires peuvent, en particulier dans un environnement numérique, être de plus en plus utilisés par des tiers pour porter atteinte à des droits. Dans de nombreux cas, ces intermédiaires sont les mieux à même de mettre fin à ces atteintes. (...) » En conformité, l'art. 8/3, de la directive 2001/29 dispose que « Les États membres veillent à ce que les titulaires de droits puissent demander qu'une ordonnance sur requête soit rendue

[20] <http://www.erc.pt/>

à l'encontre des intermédiaires dont les services sont utilisés par un tiers pour porter atteinte à un droit d'auteur ou à un droit voisin. »

La directive 2001/29 a été transposée par la loi n. 50/2004 du 24 aout qui modifie le code du droit d'auteur et des droits voisins ; en particulier, l'ordonnance est prévue dans l'art. 227/2, du code do droit d'auteur. La configuration de cette ordonnance (injonction) dans le droit interne des États membres a suscité des arrêts de la CJUE, notamment l'arrêt *Scarlet* (24.11 2011)[21] au quel la Cour n'a pas accepté des filtres préventifs par temps indéterminé et aux frais exclusif du fournisseur d'Internet. Plus récemment, dans l'arrêt *Telekabel* (27.3.2014)[22], la Cour a jugé que « Les droits fondamentaux reconnus par le droit de l'Union doivent être interprétés en ce sens qu'ils ne s'opposent pas à ce qu'il soit fait interdiction, au moyen d'une injonction prononcée par un juge, à un fournisseur d'accès à Internet d'accorder à ses clients l'accès à un site Internet mettant en ligne des objets protégés sans l'accord des titulaires de droits, (...) »

D'abords, le rôle des fournisseurs d'Internet touche des autres droits de propriété intellectuelle, comme le droit des marques. L'interprétation de la loi interne en transposant des instruments de l'Union normalement s'accorde avec la jurisprudence de la CJUE. En particulier, l'arrêt *Google c Louis Vuitton* (23.3.2010)[23] clarifie la responsabilité du prestataire d'un service de référencement sur Internet vis-à-vis l'utilisation des marques comme mot clé – question laissée ouverte par la directive du commerce électronique - en décidant que « Le prestataire d'un service de référencement sur Internet qui stocke en tant que mot clé un signe identique à une

[21] Affaire C70/10, ECLI:EU:C:2011:771. V. aussi l'arrêt du 16.2. 2012, affaire C360/10, SABAM c. Netlog NV. ECLI:EU:C:2012:85.

[22] Affaire C-314/12, ECLI:EU:C:2014:192.

[23] Affaires jointes C236/08 à C238/08, ECLI:EU:C:2010:159.

marque et organise l'affichage d'annonces à partir de celui-ci, ne fait pas un usage de ce signe ».

À propos de la protection des marques vis-à-vis les enregistrements spéculatifs et abusifs, de 'mauvaise foi', des domaines .eu, disciplinés par le Règlement (CE) n° 874/2004, voir l'arrêt *Internetportal* (3.6.2010) de la CJUE.[24] Au Portugal le règlement des noms de domaine .pt incorpore les recommandations de l'OMPI contre l'enregistrement abusif des marques comme noms domaine. En particulier, le règlement prévoit que la mauvaise-foi peut être prouvée par exemple par le fait que le nom de domaine a été enregistré ou acquis en vue de leur cession ultérieure à la requérante. La Cour suprême a décidé que l'enregistrement peut porter atteinte aux droit des marques même s'il est en conformité avec le règlement de noms de domaine .pt.[25]

D/ Aspects de droit international privé

1. Les règles de compétence judiciaire en matière de cyber-délits privés sont établies dans le code de procédure civile[26] (arts. 59 et suivants) e dans certains instruments internationaux et européens, notamment le règlement (UE) n. 1215/2012 du Parlement européen et du Conseil du 12 décembre 2012 concernant la compétence judiciaire, la reconnaissance et l'exécution des décisions en matière civile et commerciale (Brussels refonte).

Dans les matières couvertes par le règlement, la règle générale c'est le *forum domicilii*, ça veut dire, «les personnes domiciliées sur le territoire d'un État membre sont attraites, quelle que soit leur nationalité, devant les juridictions de cet État membre» (art. 4/1).

Toutefois, pour les matières contractuelles, délictuelles et d'autres, le règlement Brussels prévoit des compétences spéciales. Les cy-

[24] Affaire C-569/08, ECLI:EU:C:2010:311.

[25] Arrêt du 29 janvier 2015, affaire 1222/06.6TYLSB.L1.S1.

[26] Loi n. 41/2013 du 26 juin.

ber-délits ne sont pas une catégorie autonome. Les cyber-délits concernent les violations par Internet des droits absolus, comme les droits de personnalité ou les droits de propriété intellectuelle, et bien aussi les infractions par l'internet aux intérêts protégés par la loi. Donc, selon l'art. 7/2 du règlement Brussels, le tribunal compétent en matière délictuelle ou quasi délictuelle, est celui du lieu où le fait dommageable s'est produit ou risque de se produire (*forum delicti commissi*).

2. La jurisprudence de la CJUE en fait la distinction entre action en responsabilité au tire de l'intégralité du dommage causé (1) et action devant les juridictions de chaque État membre sur le territoire duquel un contenu mis en ligne est accessible ou l'a été (2). [27]

Dans le premier cas la personne qui s'estime lésée peut choisir le tribunal de l'État membre du lieu d'établissement de l'émetteur de ces contenus ou le tribunal de l'État membre dans lequel se trouve le centre de ses intérêts. Dans la deuxième situation, le tribunal compétent c'est celui de chaque État membre sur le territoire duquel un contenu mis en ligne est accessible ou l'a été, mais seulement pour connaître du seul dommage causé sur le territoire de l'État membre de la juridiction saisie.

Cette jurisprudence concerne des atteintes aux droits de personnalité, mais elle serait aussi valide pour des atteintes à d'autres droits absolus, comme le droit d'auteur et les droits voisins ou le droit des marques. Toutefois, la jurisprudence de la CJUE est assez restrictive à admettre un super-forum en matière des droits patrimoniaux à cause du principe de territorialité de ces droits. Selon l'arrêt de la *Pinckney* (3.10 2013), la juridiction saisie «n'est compétente que

[27] Arrêt du 25 octobre 2011, affaires jointes C509/09 et C161/10, eDate Advertising, ECLI:EU:C:2011:685.

pour connaître du seul dommage causé sur le territoire de l'État membre dont elle relève.» [28]

3. Le Code civile contient des dispositions sur la loi applicable (arts. 25 et suivants), y compris un art. sur la responsabilité extracontractuelle. D'ailleurs, cette matière est disciplinée par le règlement (CE) n. 864/2007 du Parlement européen et du Conseil du 11 juillet 2007 sur la loi applicable aux obligations non contractuelles (« Rome II »), qui a précédence sur les règles du code civile.

Le principe général du règlement Rome II c'est la *lex loci damni* (art. 4/2). Cette règle générale s'applique « indépendamment du ou des pays où pourraient survenir des conséquences indirectes. (...) (cons. 18).

Ce principe général connait une exception: si les parties ont leur résidence habituelle dans le même pays au moment de la survenance du dommage, la loi de ce pays s'applique (art. 4/2). En chaque cas, toutefois, s'il résulte de l'ensemble des circonstances que le fait dommageable présente des liens manifestement plus étroits avec un autre pays, la loi de cet autre pays s'applique (art. 4/3) en dérogation de la *lex loci damni* ou de la *lex* du pays de résidence commun des parties.

4. Le règlement Rome II exclu de son champ d'application « les obligations non contractuelles découlant d'atteintes à la vie privée et aux droits de la personnalité, y compris la diffamation » (art. 1/2, al. g). Donc ces cas sont disciplinés par la respective disposition du code civil (art. 45): il s'applique la loi où l'activité principale a eu lieu causant des blessures (*lex loci delicti commissi*) ; si cette loi ne rend pas responsable l'agent mais la loi de l'Etat où elle a

---

[28] Affaire C170/12, ECLI:EU:C:2013:635. Voir aussi l'arrêt du 22 janvier 2015 dans l'ffaire C441/13, Pez Hejduk c. EnergieAgentur.NRW GmbH. ECLI:EU:C:2015:28.

produit les blessures le fait, cette loi s'applique à condition que l'agent doit prévoir la production de dommages dans ce pays en raison de son acte ou son omission.

D'ailleurs, le règlement contient des dispositions spéciales pour la loi applicable aux délits en matière de responsabilité du fait des produits (art. 5), concurrence déloyale et actes restreignant la libre concurrence (art. 6), et bien aussi aux atteintes à l'environnement (art. 7) et aux droits de propriété intellectuelle (art. 8). La loi applicable est celle du pays pour lequel la protection est revendiquée ou, en s'agissant d'un droit de propriété intellectuelle communautaire à caractère unitaire, la loi applicable à toute question qui n'est pas régie par l'instrument communautaire pertinent est la loi du pays dans lequel il a été porté atteinte à ce droit (art. 8/1-2 règlement II). Concernant les cyber-délits en matière des droits de propriété intellectuelle, le règlement 'préserve' impérativement (art. 8/3) le principe *lex loci protectionis*, importé de la Convention de Berne sur la protection de la propriété littéraire et artistique.[29]

II/ Mondialisation, Internet et la puissance des acteurs

1. Le droit portugais ne connait pas encore des mesures spécifiques sur l'apparente gratuité du modèle économique. Si la proposition de directive du Parlement européen et du Conseil concernant certains aspects des contrats de fourniture de contenu numérique[30] est adoptée, les contrats d'utilisation des services et applications d'Internet, comme ceux de Google ou Facebook, ne seront plus des contrats gratuits puisque l'utilisation de ces services ou applications é autorisée en exchange de données. Ça veut dire,

[29] Art. 5/2, 2ème per.

[30] COM(2015) 634 final, Bruxelles, le 9.12.2015.

les données sont considérées comme équivalent à l'argent. Selon l'exposé des motifs de la proposition « elle ne couvre pas uniquement le contenu numérique fourni contre paiement, mais aussi le contenu fourni en échange de données (à caractère personnel et autre) transmises par le consommateur » (p. 13).

2. En ce qu'il concerne la situation juridique (clause attributive de juridiction, clause de loi applicable), le Code civile prévoit la prohibition de fraude de la loi (art. 20) et la clause générale d'ordre public (art. 21).

En outre, les règlements ont des dispositions qui limitent la liberté contractuelle concernant des clauses attribution de juridiction (Brussels, arts. 15, 19, 23, 25) et clauses de loi applicable (Rome II, arts. 6/4, 8, para 3, 14, para 2). Le règlement Rome II sauvegarde que ses dispositions « ne portent pas atteinte à l'application des dispositions de la loi du for qui régissent impérativement la situation, quelle que soit la loi applicable à l'obligation non contractuelle » (art. 16).

En matière fiscale, le régime général des infractions tributaires – loi n. 15/2001 du 5 juin – incrimine la fraude fiscale (arts. 103 et 104).

3. Dans l'arrêt *Microsoft*[31] le géant nord-américain a été condamné d'abus de position dominante en se refusant de licencier le code-source de son système Windows à des concurrents dans le marché des systèmes opératifs pour serveurs qui voulaient développer des programmes compatibles avec le Windows.

Récemment, selon le communiqué de presse de la Commission européenne, du 20 avril 2016, « La Commission européenne a informé Google de sa conclusion préliminaire selon laquelle la société a, en violation des règles de concurrence de l'UE, abusé de sa position

[31] Tribunal de première instance (17.9.2007), affaire T-201/04. ECLI:EU:T:2007:289.

dominante en imposant des restrictions aux fabricants d'appareils Android et aux opérateurs de réseaux mobiles. »[32]

4. Il y a une conviction par abus de position dominante concernant la refuse par une grande entreprise de télécommunications de fournir accès à ses pipelines pour les concurrents dans le secteur de TV câble et services associés, mais l'entreprise a été acquittée par la Cour d'appel.[33]

5. La loi portugaise de la concurrence – loi n. 19/2012 du 8 mai – interdit les accords et les pratiques concertées entre entreprises, et bien aussi les décisions d'associations d'entreprises, qui sont susceptibles d'affecter la concurrence dans le marché national, et notamment ceux qui consistent à subordonner la conclusion de contrats à l'acceptation, par les partenaires, de prestations supplémentaires qui, par leur nature ou selon les usages commerciaux, n'ont pas de lien avec l'objet de ces contrats (art. 9, para 1, al. e). Toutefois, les accords sont acceptés si les entreprises font preuve qu'ils remplissent les conditions du bilan économique et, en particulier, si les accords s'encadrent dans un règlement d'exemption adopté par la Commission européenne (art. 10). Le *tying* ou *bundling* est aussi prévu comme un exemple de possible abus de position dominante, interdite par la loi de la concurrence (art. 11/1-2-e).

En outre, le règlement (UE) 2015/2120 du Parlement européen et du Conseil du 25 novembre 2015 établisse des mesures relatives à l'accès à un internet ouvert et modifie la directive 2002/22/CE concernant le service universel et les droits des utilisateurs au regard des réseaux et services de communications électroniques et le règlement (UE) 531/2012 concernant l'itinérance sur les réseaux publics de commu-

---

[32] http://europa.eu/rapid/press-release_IP-16-1492_fr.htm

[33] http://www.concorrencia.pt/vPT/Praticas_Proibidas/Decisoes_da_AdC/Paginas/lista.aspx

nications mobiles à l'intérieur de l'Union. Le fournisseur d'accès doit traiter « tout le trafic de façon égale et sans discrimination, restriction ou interférence, quels que soient l'expéditeur et le destinataire, les contenus consultés ou diffusés, les applications ou les services utilisés ou fournis ou les équipements terminaux utilisés », sans préjudice de mettre en œuvre des mesures raisonnables de gestion du trafic dans les conditions prévues par le règlement (art. 3/3).

6. Pour utiliser les services des géants de l'Internet il faut toujours accepter des conditions d'utilisation par moyen de cliquer : « Oui, je comprends et j'accepte ». Ces licences clique-wrap ne sont pas toutefois libres de vices.

Pour commencer, elles sont des conditions générales, écrites sans négociation individuelle préalable et proposées a des bénéficiaires indéterminées. En tant que tel, font objet du décret-loi n. 446/85 du 25 octobre. Inspiré sur la loi allemande (AGB), le régime a été modifié pour transposer la Directive 93/13/CEE du Conseil du 5 avril 1993 concernant les clauses abusives dans les contrats conclus avec les consommateurs.

En essence, il consiste à contrôler la formation e le contenu des conditions générale. En premier, les conditions doivent être communiquées préalablement à son destinataire, qui a aussi le droit à recevoir réponse complète à tous ses questions raisonnables. Autrefois les clauses sont exclues du contrat autant que « clauses – surprise » (arts. 5, 6 et 8). D'autre part, le contenu des clauses doit être conforme aux listes noires et grises de clauses absolument ou relativement interdites dans les contrats entre entrepreneurs ou entités similaires (B2B) ou dans les contrats avec les consommateurs (B2C). Les clauses qui font des fictions d'acceptation sont relativement interdites, et on peut se demander s'il n'est pas le cas des licences clique-wrap. En autre, la loi du commerce électronique – décret-loi n. 7/2004 du 7 janvier - interdit les conditions générales du contrat qui imposent la conclusion par voie électronique des contrats avec des consommateurs (art. 25/4).

La directive 2005/29/ce du Parlement européen et du Conseil du 11 mai 2005, relative aux pratiques commerciales déloyales des entreprises vis-à-vis des consommateurs dans le marché intérieur, a été transposée par le décret-loi n. 57/2008 du 26 mars, dont l'art. 12, al. c) prévoit comme absolument agressive se livrer à des sollicitations répétées et non souhaitées notamment par courrier électronique ou tout autre outil de communication à distance, sauf si et dans la mesure où la législation nationale l'autorise pour assurer l'exécution d'une obligation contractuelle. La gratuité des sollicitations n'empêche pas la nature commerciale des pratiques.

III/ Mondialisation, Internet et les difficultés de la répression des pratiques illicites

1. Le Code pénal incrimine l'abus sexuel, la prostitution et la pornographie des mineurs (arts. 171-176). L'acte de séduire mineurs par moyen des technologies d'information et de communication pour des rendez-vous sexuelles ou pour la pornographie est aussi incriminé (art. 176-A). D'ailleurs, la consommation intentionnelle de pédopornographie est incriminée et la pénalisation de l'exploitation de la pédopornographie avec des fins lucratives est aggravée (art. 178/5-7).

Le Code pénal a été modifié par la loi n. 103/2015 du 24 aout a fin de transposer la Directive 2011/93/UE du Parlement européen et du Conseil du 13 décembre 2011 relative à la lutte contre les abus sexuels et l'exploitation sexuelle des enfants, ainsi que la pédopornographie et remplaçant la décision-cadre 2004/68/JAI du Conseil.

2. Le Code pénal prévoit comme un délit criminel l'organisation ou le financement de participation en des activités de propagande avec des propos racistes, religieux, haineux ou sexuelles (art. 240, para 1). En dehors des activités organisées il est aussi incriminé la divulgation par les media ou système informatique des messages avec propos discriminatoires qui causent actes violence, menacent ou atteinte contre des autres à cause de leur race, religion, nationalité, ethnie ou orientation sexuelle (art. 240, para 2).

3. Les réseaux de pédopornographie en Internet ne sont pas confinés aux frontières nationaux et donc la lutte contre de telles infractions n'est toujours la plus efficace. Toutefois il y a plusieurs arrêts des tribunaux portugais.[34]

Récemment, le 29 mars 2016, un homme a été arrêté en flagrant délit, à sa résidence à Lisbonne, à cause de la forte suspicion de la pratique sur 1262 crimes de pédopornographie. Selon les éléments de preuve recueillis, l'accusé avait gardé et téléchargé des images illégales contenant l'abus sexuel des enfants de moins de quatorze ans, et ces fichiers étaient partagés contenant des images d'enfants à des actes sexuels avec des adultes.[35]

4. La soft law ou l'autorégulation est faite par les agents d'Internet avec ses conditions d'utilisation et règles (par exemple, la netiquette de Youtube). Elle existe et est respectée, autant qu'elle ne porte pas atteinte à la « hard law » (par exemple, des conditions d'utilisation excessivement restrictives en matière de liberté d'expression).

---

[34] Plus récemment voire les arrêts de la Cour suprême de justice du 12 juin 2013, affaire 1291/10.4JDLSB.S1, du 12 novembre 2014, affaire 1287/08.6JDLSB.L1.S1, du 22 avril 2015, affaire 45/13.0JASTB.L1.S1, et du 23 septembre 2015, affaire 524/13.0JDLSB.E1.S1 – < www.dgsi.pt >. Voir aussi par ex. l'arrêt de la Cour d'appel de Coimbra du 11 novembre 2015, affaire 372/12, dans lequel la Cour a estimé que ne fait pas partie du concept normatif de détention, aux fins du paragraphe 4 de l'art. 176 du Code pénal (version avant la loi n ° 103/2015, de 24-08), l'accès de l'agent à un site de pédopornographie, avec une expansion ultérieure et l'affichage des photographies des mineurs en actes sexuelles.

[35] <http://www.pgdlisboa.pt/novidades/nov_main.php?comarcas=S>

5. La loi du cyber-crime - loi n. 109/2009 du 15 septembre[36] - prévoit des dispositions processuels qui s'appliquent aux cyber-crimes mais aussi à des crimes commis par moyen d'un système informatique ou pour lesquels il faut obtenir des preuves en support électronique.

Ces dispositions processuelles comprennent la conservation rapide de données, notamment par le fournisseur des services Internet (art. 12) et la divulgation rapide de données de trafic (art. 13). Pendant le procès, les cours peuvent aussi ordonner une injonction pour la présentation ou l'accès aux données (art. 14), la recherche (art. 15) et la saisie de données informatiques (art. 16) ou, selon les dispositions du code de procédure pénale, la saisie de l'e-mail et des dossiers de communication similaires (art. 17). L'interception des communications (art. 18) et les « actions secrètes » (art. 19) sont aussi prévues dans la loi du cyber-crime pour certains types de crimes.

La loi n. 41/2004 du 18 aout[37] protège la vie privée dans les communications électroniques, en particulier les données relatives au trafic et les données de localisation. Elle sauvegarde que le régime des données relatives au trafic ne préjudice pas les dispositions processuelles de prévention et combattre la criminalité.

IV/ Mondialisation, Internet et les nouvelles opportunités

1. Au Portugal les jeux en ligne sont réglés dans le décret-loi n. 66/2015 du 29 avril.

---

[36] Cette loi transpose la décision-cadre du Conseil 2005/222 / JAI du Conseil du 24 février, sur les attaques contre les systèmes d'information, et adapte le droit national à la Convention sur la cybercriminalité du Conseil de l'Europe.

[37] Transpose en droit national la directive 2002/58 / CE du Parlement européen et du Conseil du 12 Juillet, concernant le traitement des données à caractère personnel et la protection de la vie privée dans le secteur des communications électroniques.

L'État se réserve de droit de l'exploitation des jeux en ligne (art. 8) et le concède par licence administrative à des personnes morales privées, sous la forme de société anonyme ou équivalente, établie dans un État-membre de l'Union européenne ou d'un État signataire de l'accord sur l'espace économique européen qui est lié à la coopération administrative dans le domaine de la fraude fiscale et la lutte contre le blanchiment d'argent le capital, à condition d'avoir succursale au Portugal (art. 9/1). Le fonctionnement des jeux et paris en ligne ne peut être attribué qu'à des personnes morales dont l'objet est, pendant toute la durée de l'exploration de licence, des jeux et des paris (art. 9/2).

Le principe du pays d'origine de la directive sur le commerce électronique ne s'applique pas en ce secteur[38]. L'exploitation des jeux en ligne pour les opérateurs reconnus par les autres États-membres de l'Union dépend de l'octroi d'une licence par l'entité le contrôle, l'inspection et la réglementation et ne sont pas valides au Portugal les licences ou d'autres titres habilitants octroyées par d'autres Etats (art. 9/3).

2. La loi n. 102/2015 du 24 aout établit le régime juridique du financement du « crowdfunding ». L'ordonnance n. 344/2015 du 12 octobre règle le préavis de mise en activité des plates-formes de « crowdfunding » dans les modalités de don et / ou de récompense dédiée prévus dans la loi 102/2015.

¾. L'économie de partage permise par l'Internet est connue et discutée mais il n'y a pas de loi spécifique pour la réguler.

L' «ubérisation » de l'économie est discutée, en particulier concernant les taxis et l' opérateur Uber, mais aucune loi ou décret-loi n'a pas encore été passé pour accommoder cette nouvelle économie.

---

[38] Directive 2000/31/CE du Parlement européen et du Conseil du 8 juin 2000 relative à certains aspects juridiques des services de la société de l'information, et notamment du commerce électronique, dans le marché intérieur («directive sur le commerce électronique»), art. 1/5.

INTELLECTUAL PROPERTY LAW IN MACAU*

1. Sources

As member of the World Trade Organization, Macau has enacted new legislation on intellectual property rights[1] (IPR), in order to comply with the Agreement on Trade-Related Aspects of Intellectual Property Rights.

On one hand, Decree-Law 97/99/M, of December 13, has approved the new Code of Industrial Property (hereinafter CIP) concerning patents (including the protection of new plant species), industrial designs and models, trademarks (including services marks), geographical indications (including appellations of origin), and the configuration topography of integrated circuits.

On the other hand, Decree-Law 43/99/M, of August 16, has approved the new Copyright Law (hereinafter CL). In view of the WTO/TRIPS obligations, Macau copyright law has been harmonized with the Paris Act of 1971 of the Berne Convention for the Protection of Literary and Artistic Works and the Rome Convention for the Protection of Performers, Producers of Phonograms and Broadcasting Organizations, signed in Rome in 1961.

---

* In Alexandre Dias Pereira, *In Business Law: A Code Study (The Commercial Code of Macau)*, Coimbra, 2004.

[1] See José de Oliveira Ascensão, 'A situação da propriedade intelectual em Macau', Revista da Faculdade de Direito, Universidade de Lisboa, XLII, 2/2001, pp. 691-734.

2. Patents

Patent law protects inventions. An invention is a novel idea which permits in practice the solution of a specific problem in the field of technology. In order to be protected by law ("patentable"), the idea must fulfil several requirements (CIP, arts. 61 to 68). In fact, it must be: 1. *new* in the sense that it has not already been published or publicly used; 2. *non-obvious* ("involve an inventive step") meaning that it would not have occurred to any specialist in the particular industrial field, had such a specialist been asked to find a solution to the particular problem; 3. *capable of industrial application*, i.e. it can be industrially manufactured or used.

There are however limits to the object of patent (e.g., discoveries, scientific theories and mathematical methods, as well as human cloning processes cannot be patented - CIP, arts. 61, 1-a, 3-b). Patents have to be applied for at the government office for patents (CIP, art. 77 ff.), which will issue a patent document, describing the invention and creating a legal situation in which the patent holder will be entitled with an exclusive right of economic exploitation (making, use, sale, import) of the patent (CIP, art. 104) for a period of 20 years from the filing date of the application for the grant of a patent (CIP, art. 103, 1).

3. Marks

A mark is a sign, or a combination of signs, capable of distinguishing the goods or services of one undertaking from those of other undertakings (commercial or not). In short, it must be a distinctive sign. Concerning its composition, the sign may consist of one or more distinctive words, letters, numbers, drawings or pictures, emblems, colours or combinations of colours, or may be three-dimensional, such as the form of containers or packages (provided they are not solely dictated by their function - CIP art. 199, 1-a) for the product; the sign may also consist of combinations of any of the foregoing (CIP, arts. 197 to 199). However, certain elements, such as signs or indications that have become customary in current language or in bona fide and established commercial practices cannot be granted an exclusive use, unless the signs have acquired distinctive character in commercial practice (CIP art. 199, 1-b, 2)

Generally it is necessary for effective protection that a mark be registered in the government office for marks (DES) according to the registration procedure (CIP, arts. 204 ff; however, unregistered trademarks also enjoy some protection - CIP, art. 202, see also for well-known and prestigious marks art. 214, 1-b/c, CIP). The registration of the mark will be made in respect of specified goods or services. However, registration may be refused if, e.g., the sign is deceptive or misleading, meaning that it is likely to mislead the public, namely with respect to the nature, qualities, usefulness or geographical origin of the product or service for which the trademark is to be used (CIP, art. 214, 2-a). In case it is registered, then no person or enterprise other than the owner may use it for goods or services identical with or similar to those for which the mark is registered (*principle of specialty*); moreover, any unauthorized use of a sign similar to the protected mark is also prohibited, if such use may lead to confusion in the minds of the public (art. 219, 1). The exclusive right does also include the use of the marks in documents, printed matter, computer pages, advertising and documents relative to the entrepreneurial activity of the titleholder (CIP, art. 219, 2).

However, it does not include the use of the registered trademark, whenever that be necessary to indicate the origin of a product or service, namely in respect of accessories or spare parts, provided that it is used according to the standards and honest practice applicable in industrial and commercial matters (CIP, art. 220-c). Registration lasts for 7 years, and it can be renewed (art. 218).

4. Industrial designs and models

Industrial designs are defined as creations whose appearance represents a product in whole or in part by virtue of such characteristics as lines, contours, colours, forms, textures and/or the materials used in the product itself and/or its ornamentation (CPI, art. 150). Basically, an industrial design is the ornamental aspect of a useful article. This ornamental aspect may be constituted by elements which are three-dimensional (the shape of the article) or two-dimensional (lines, designs, colours) provided that they are not dictated solely or essentially by technical or functional considerations.

To be eligible for industrial property protection, industrial designs must be original or novel (although it is not entirely novel, it can be protected in case it involves novel combinations of known elements or a different layout of already used elements that endow the respective subject matter with a unique character - art. 152, 2), and must be registered in the government office for industrial designs (see CPI, arts. 152 to 158) according to a certain application procedure (art. 160 ff.).

In case protection of an industrial design is granted, third parties without consent of the right may not make, sell or import articles bearing or embodying a design which is a copy, or substantially a copy, of the protected design, when such acts are undertaken for commercial purposes (arts. 177 and 178).

Moreover, some kinds of industrial designs can (also) be protected as works of art (works of art being objects of copyright protection) – cf. CIP art. 179, and Copyright Law, art. 2, 1(i) (original works of applied art, industrial designs or models and design works that constitute artistic creations).

5. Copyright and related rights

According to international treaties, Macau Copyright Law (CL) protects "literary and artistic works," that is, original creations in the fields of literature and arts, regardless of the form in which such works are expressed, be it words, symbols, music, pictures, three-dimensional objects, or combinations thereof as in the case of an opera or a motion picture (CL, art. 1).

The acquisition of copyright protection is independent of any formalities, such as registration or deposit (CL, art. 10), that is, copyright protection starts as soon as the work is created (CL, art. 1, 3). *Originality* is the basis of protection. A work is considered original if it results of the author's own creative effort and not merely the appropriation of another person's creation. However, even if original certain works are not protected, such as requests submitted to public authorities, political speeches and official texts (CL, arts. 5 and 6). Moreover, the protection only applies to the literary or artistic form of expression of the work (and provided that it is original), not to the ideas, processes, systems, operational methods, concepts, principles or discoveries, as such, that may be embedded in the work (CL, art. 1, 2). Examples of types of works that are protected include (see Copyright Law, arts. 2 and 3): literary works (e.g., novels and poems), including computer programs and «oral works» (i.e., works not reduced to writing), musical works (e.g., songs and operas), choreographic works; artistic works (e.g., paintings and sculptures), maps and technical drawings, photographic works (e.g., portraits); audiovisual works, i.e. "motion pictures" or "cinematographic works", as well as the so-called derivative works (translations, adaptations) and collections (compilations) of works and mere data (data bases), and "works of applied art" (e.g., artistic jewels).

Copyright protection generally means that certain uses of the work are lawful only if they are done with the authorization of the owner of the copyright: the so-called exclusive rights of economic exploitation.

Macau copyright law provides a large bundle of rights (CL, arts. 7, 55 and 56) covering the most typical uses (which are independent one from another) of works such as: 1. the right *to copy or otherwise reproduce* any kind of work; 2. the right to *distribute* copies to the public; 3. the right *to rent* copies of certain categories of works such as computer programs and audiovisual works; 4. the right to make sound recordings of the performances of literary and musical works; 5. the right to *perform in public*, particularly musical, dramatic or audiovisual works; 6. the right to communicate to the public by cable or otherwise the performances of such works and, particularly, *to broadcast*, by radio, television or other wireless means, any kind of work; 7. the right *to translate* literary works; 8. the right *to adapt* any kind of work and particularly the right *to make audiovisual works* thereof. Copyright Law provides detailed regulation for special uses such as publication stage performance, production of audiovisual works, fixation and publication of phonograms and videos, broadcasting, and communication to the public, and translations (CL, arts. 67 ff.)

In some specific cases the authors are granted not an exclusive right but a right to remuneration (see, for example, arts. 125, 2, 130, concerning publication and broadcasting of previously fixed works) or equitable compensation (see CL, arts. 62, 2-b, 137, 191, 2). However, certain uses (for example, private use and certain fair uses, such as quotations, teaching illustration, or press reviews including the use of articles on political or economic matters in other newspapers) are "copyright free", that is, they require neither the authorization of, nor remuneration for, the owner of the copyright (CL, art. 60).

In addition to economic rights, authors (whether or not they own the economic rights) enjoy "moral rights" on the basis of which authors have the right to claim their authorship and require that their names be indicated on the copies of the work and in connection with other uses thereof; moreover, they have the right to oppose the mutilation or deformation of their works as well as the right of withdrawal (CL, arts. 7-3, and 41 to 48). Although the owner of copyright may generally transfer his right or may license certain uses of his work, moral rights are, however, inalienable and cannot in principle be waived by the author.

As for the beneficiary of protection, copyright generally vests in the author of the work (CL, art. 9 - or authors, in case of works of joint authorship, art. 14). However, certain exceptions are provided. For example, the employer may be considered the owner of copyright if the author was, when the work was created, an employee and was employed for the very purpose of creating the work (CL, art. 12).

Concerning duration, copyright protection is limited in time. The general rule is a term of protection that starts at the time of the creation of the work and ends 50 years after the death of the author, thereby falling into the public domain (see CL, arts. 21 to 25).

Artistic performers, phonogram producers, broadcasting organizations and entertainment organizers are granted related or neighbouring rights (arts. 170 ff.).

6. Unfair competition

The protection of intellectual property in Macao is reinforced by the prohibition of unfair competition.

The Commercial Code of Macau (approved by Decree-Law 40/99/M, of August 3) provides the prohibition of *unfair acts of competition* in a *general clause* according to which it applies to any act of competition that is objectively against the norms and honest usage of economic activity (art. 158).

This general clause is illustrated by a series of typical acts of competition that are deemed to be, in certain circumstances, unfair competition, such as acts of confusion (risk of association by consumer is sufficient to ascertain the confusion - art. 159, 2), misleading advertising, aggressive sales, wrongful comparisons, slavish imitation and parasitism (despite the basic principle of freedom of imitation, only limited in general terms by the existence of a legal exclusive right, such as patent, trademark or copyright - art. 164, 1), breach of confidential entrepreneurial secrets (including all and any technical or commercial information that: 1. has practical use and provides economic benefits to the holder; 2. is not of public knowledge; 3. the holder of the secrets took appropriate measures to guarantee its confidentiality - art. 166, 2), instigation and exploitation of contractual breaches (e.g., having access to the entrepreneurial secrets of competitors - art. 167, 2), exploitation of economic dependence and sales at a loss (see arts. 159 to 169).

The scope of this regulation is a broad notion of competition acts: competition acts are those practiced by marketers with competition purposes regardless of their entrepreneurial nature and of the fact that marketers act in the same branch of activity (arts. 156, 1, and 157). Moreover, competition purposes are presumed whenever the acts are objectively adequate to promote or to ensure the distribution in the market of the goods of the marketer or of a third party (arts. 156, 2).

As for remedies against unfair competition, upon request of an injured party or in class actions by entities representative of the category of interested parties (art. 173), the Court may order the termination of unfair competition practices, and the unfair competitor may have to compensate damages caused with fault, which is presumed in case there is an act of unfair competition (arts. 171 to 173).

MEDIA ANALYSIS AND COPYRIGHT: EUROPEAN PERSPECTIVES VIEWED FROM THE ATLANTIC[*]

Abstract - The construction of the European information market has justified the adoption of several harmonizing measures on copyright law. The approach followed is to establish minimal standards and minimal harmonization. However, media analysis activities claim special rules of protection, having in consideration the Berne and the Rome Conventions, concerning the exclusive right of reproduction, the protection of *fait divers* and the principle of copyright fair use. Media analysis is an information service that includes monitoring and clipping activities. Some argue that these businesses could be justified under the private copy exception as mandates of their clients. However, the commercial nature of this use seems notorious. Perhaps it should be more adequate to establish a system of compulsory licenses for these activities, in exchange for an equitable compensation for copyright holders. Moreover, the free flow of information should also shed light on the interpretation of the EC Directive on database protection. In any case, the solution to the conflict of interests placed by these activities should take in due con-

---

[*] *Media e Copyright: How to Harmonize a European Issue*, Proceeddings of the EMAA - European Media Analysts Association International Conference on *Media Analysis and Copyright,* Stintino, Italy, on 23 to 25 May 1997.

sideration not only the interests of media analysis undertakings and the interests of their clients, but also the interests of the right holders and the general interest.

1. The European information market

The improvement of the European information market requires the creation of a legal framework, so that media analysis activities can be carried within this market, which has specific rules concerning free provision of services and free circulation of goods. Media analysis poses new problems in terms of copyright; their solution depends on finding the right answers using the legal instruments already provided. We will thus analyze these instruments.

To begin with, there is a legal vacuum in terms of European law: media analysis activities are not regulated at the European level. Moreover, there is a strong diversity between Member States regulations. This diversity and the absence of European regulations hinders the creation of a European information market. In the case of media analysis activities, we can evaluate the interests at stake using the metaphor of the scale. On one side, there are the interests of media analyst undertakings and their clients, which claim the lawfulness of this activity, while on the other side there are the copyright and neighboring rights holders, which claim their exclusive rights to reproduce their work. The needle of the balance is embodied by the Community's general interest, in the name of which it is possible to justify certain restrictions on the exclusivity of copyright.

There are some topics to consider when dealing with the problem of copyright in Europe. There are four main issues. Firstly, harmonized copyright measures have to respect national traditions. According to primary European law, certain countries may impose some restrictions on the free provision of services and free circulation of goods in order to safeguard their interest in terms of intellectual property. This means that harmonization should provide for minimal standards, to respect that faculty which European primary law reserves to member states. In Europe, there are different conceptions and very strong traditions in terms of copyright law. The harmonizing measures on copyright should also take into consideration other already existing measures on copyright, such as, for example, the legal protection of computer programs.

For what media analysis is concerned, it is important to consider EC Directive 92/100 on rental right, lending and certain neighboring rights and EC Directive 96/6 on legal protection of databases. These two directives already provide some legal criteria to discuss media analysis activities. For example, the EC Directive on rental rights allows the use of short fragments for information purposes, while the directive on legal protection of databases - although it does not establish any free use of works - states that the databases created by media analysis are eligible for copyright protection. These two directives address one, and the same problem: media analysis implies the creation of databases, whereas the databases thereby created may also be protected.

Other useful legal tools are International Conventions on intellectual property, in special the Berne Convention and the Rome Convention. The Berne Convention establishes a union for the protection of author's rights providing an international platform for the protection of works. It guarantees a minimal protection, which is occurs regardless of formalities. It provides the principle of equal or national treatment between the countries of the Union. A recent decision of the European Council stated that all member states have to adhere to the Paris Act of the Berne Convention. This Treaty is something like an umbrella and represents the first step to solve our problem.

2. There are three main ideas. First, media works may be protected by copyright. In economical terms this means the author has the exclusive right of reproduction, he is the only one authorized to take economical advantage of that work through its reproduction. In this context, the WIPO (World Intellectual Property Organization) conference on copyright and neighboring right questions, which took place Dec. 1996, stated that the reproduction rights set out in Article 9 of the Berne Convention and the exceptions permitted thereunder fully apply in the digital environment, in particular to the use of works in the digital form. It is understood that the storage of protected work in digital from in an electronic medium constitutes a. reproduction within the meaning of said provision. It means, for example, that electronic clipping constitutes a reproduction within the meaning of the Berne Convention, reproduction being in principle an exclusive right of the author. Therere, in principle, media analysis undertakings need an authorization from copyright holders.

However, the same the Berne Convention provides certain legal tools to deal with the problem. First, it establishes an exception to the scope of protection, as mere information items is not protected. This means that media analysts may collect items of media information even from works where this information is simply included. There is no copyright protection of raw data. Second, the principle of fair use and the system of compulsory licenses are also provided under the Berne Convention, in particular Article 10, on quotations of works, including quotations from newspaper articles in formal press summaries, but only in so far as those quotations are compatible with fair practice. In this context, the concept of fair practice allows the use of works protected by copyright.

This is close to the European Convention on human rights, which states that the free flow of information is a fundamental value in democratic societies. In the society of information, information is the 'blood' or 'oxygen' of economics, politics, and culture. Property rights over one's work have be in balance with fundamental values such as the free flow of information.

Article 10 bis, par. 2 of the Berne Convention provides for free use of media work for informative purposes and state the importance of promoting the free flow of information within the EU. This justifies the fairness, i.e. the lawfulness, of the use of protected works, which otherwise would not be allowed.

In short, media analysis activities reproduce media works with informative purposes, which can be justified by the principle of fair use. In principle, it seems that media monitoring and clipping activities have an informative nature. These activities provide an informative service, without it, this information would not flow freely. The principle of fair use thus represents an important legal tool to justify the lawfulness of reproduction of media works required by monitoring and clipping.

3. However, the fairness principle justifies mainly monitoring, clipping is harder to justify. The reproduction involved in clipping should rather be dealt with by a compulsory license system. The Berne Convention gives indications also about compulsory license systems. Article 9 states that Member Countries can establish compulsory licenses in certain cases, provided that such reproduction does not contrast with the normal exploitation of the work and does not unreasonably prejudice the legitimate interest of the author. The system of compulsory licenses is designed for the so-called private copy, i.e., reproductions made by the single consumer in order to satisfy his or her personal needs. On the contrary, unlawful reproduction means making copies for commercial use. According to the distinction between commercial use and personal uses, the harmonizing measures will have to answer the question of whether the copies of media works made by media analysts are for commercial use or whether there is not a commercial use.

Harmonizing measures could establish a compulsory license for the reproduction of works within media analysis activities, under a dualistic approach: fair use for monitoring and compulsory license for clipping.

Media analysis is something like media recycling. Considering the potential danger of prejudice and that media analysis profit from someone else's works, it reasonably follows that something should be granted as an equitable compensation. What form should this equitable compensation take?

Directly there is no commercial use of these copies. In fact, they are included free of charge on special request of the clients as proofs of the correctness of the information provided. Media analysts do not sell copies, they provide information about one's media image, advertising performances, competitors and their media strategies, but they do not to sell copies. Therefore, since these activities do not imply that copyright holders sell less relevant quantities of copies, there is not an unreasonable prejudice against the legitimate interest of the author or copyright owner. In Portugal, for example, there is a collective compensation, which comes from a levy on reproduction devices. This means that if I buy a tape recorder I shall pay a small "tax" that is deposited in a collective fund established for the benefit of authors, interpreters, and copyright holders in general.

4. In conclusion, the thread that run through my discussion and that I think should run through any discussion on harmonization concerns the development of the European information market.

This market has to respect the rules of a free market, namely free circulation of goods and free provision of services. But since the main issue at stake is that of intellectual property, any attempt to harmonize and regulate copyright will have to respect the competence of each Member State to protect its general interesta and traditions. EU harmonization should thus only provide minimal standards. The principles to be included in this minimal harmonization could be on the one hand the principle of fair use (mainly for monitoring) and, on the other hand, a compulsory license system for clipping services, all combined with an equitable compensation for copyright holders.

This brings us back to the metaphor of the scale we started from: on one dish we have copyright and on the other we have free flow of information, a fundamental right in contemporary democracies. I think that a free market in Europe should be founded upon rules that allow this freedom; the legal tools referred to seem adequate to deal with this issue and to find the balance between the two dishes of our scale.

COPYRIGHT ISSUES OF TECHNO-DIGITAL PROPERTY*

Abstract - This paper addresses some copyright issues of electronic commerce within the construction of the legal framework for the information society and its digital economy. On the one hand, it addresses the issue on circumvention of technological measures used by copyright owners to protect their works, as well as on tampering with copyright management information. On the other hand, it addresses the issue of the liability of online service providers for copyright infringement when engaging in certain activities, such as: 1. transitory communications ("mere conduit"); 2. system caching; 3. storage of information on systems or networks at direction of users ("hosting"); 4. information location tools ("browsing" and "linking").

The main legal sources which this paper is based upon are the new WIPO Treaties (Dec. 1996), the European Directive Proposal (as amended) on Copyright in the Information Society [COM(99) 250 final], the European Directive on Electronic Commerce (2000/31/CE), and the U.S. Digital Millennium Copyright Act (Oct. 1998). Moreover, the European Directives on Computer Programs (91/250/CEE), Databases Protection (96/9/CE), and Encrypted

---

* In *Intellectual Property in the Digital Age: Challenges for Asia*, ed. C. Heath & A.K. Sanders (eds.), p. 65-94, The Hague: Kluwer Law International, 2001, Wolters Kluwer.

Services (98/84/CE), as well as important case law of the E.U. Member States and the U.S. are also considered.

The study of those copyright issues of electronic commerce aims to explain how copyright has been adapted to the new technological paradigm. In other words, this paper is an essay on the adaptation of copyright to the digital computer and network technologies, in particular the Internet. As the title of this paper suggests, copyright has been transformed by legal metamorphosis into a sort of technodigital property for cyberspace. Furthermore, it aims to explain how, in this adaptation process, due to the absence of Community harmonization of unfair competition, author's rights system of Civil Law countries are importing certain copyright concepts from Common Law countries.

Finally, we will see that, instead of being replaced by the rule of technology and cyber-ethics in the brave new world of intelligent electronic agents, copyright has been called to put an end to the "electronic woodstock" and "anarchy online", establishing a legal form of property rights in Digitalia. Moreover, at the same time, copyright law is a *leit-motiv* to grant protection to the investment of producers in the digital economy by *sui generis* intellectual property rights and technological adjuncts, which can appropriate public domain information and control the freedom of expression on the World Wide Web (www).

"... there is an inherent logic to using the Internet to buy and sell intangible products that need never be more than digital "bits." At the same time, however, there is a commensurate need for effective intellectual property protection that can address the international dimensions of this commerce. [...] This commerce in intangible products raises a number of issues for intellectual property, in addition to those that would arise in respect of physical goods. For example, there is a growing role to be played by technological measures in protecting the rights of intellectual property owners."

(World Intellectual Property Organization - WIPO, *Primer on Electronic Commerce and Intellectual Property Rights*, Geneva, May 2000)

I - Introduction

1. Property in Digitalia and "The End of the Electronic Woodstock"

Information is probably the main commodity of the emerging digital economy, and it is commonplace to say that information is the new petroleum of our societies. Accordingly, the construction of the "information society" has been put forward as a major political task for the third millennium[1]. The edification of the global information infrastructure is under way. A super-highway has already created the global village. We could call it Cyberland, Internetland, or - why not? - Digitalia.

The petroleum of Digitalia is information, and information is everything that can be digitized. Information could be a free good

---

[1] See, in the E.U., *Europe and the Information Society*, Bangemann Report, 26.V.1994; Council Resolution of 21 November 1996 on *New Policy-priorities regarding the Information Society* (96/C 376/01). For the origins of the "Information Society" in the language of the European Commission, see the White Paper on *Growth, Competition and Employment* [Growth, Competitiveness, Employment: The Challenges and Ways Forward into the 21st Century - White Paper; COM(93)700, 5 December 1993]. Since then the European Commission has presented several documents on the construction of the Information Society. See, more recently, *Green Paper on public sector information in the information society*, COM(98)585 final, adopted on 20 January 1999. At the national level, see, for example, in Germany, the BMWi Report, *Die Informationsgesellschaft*, Bonn, 1995, and, in Portugal, *Livro Verde Para A Sociedade da Informação Em Portugal*, Missão para a Sociedade da Informação 1997.

like oxygen. The founders of cybernetics, namely Wiener[2], have argued that the free flow of information is of vital interest for human societies. The digital revolution could be of unprecedented contribution to this ideal. However, many things that can be reduced to bits are not *res communes omnium*. Intellectual property rights, in particular copyright and related rights, are one of the most important legal forms of appropriation of information. Information that otherwise would flow free as the wind is subject to *ius excluendi omnes alios*. One can exclude all from exploiting and using the petroleum of Digitalia.

The concept of property has a major role in Digitalia, and it seems to make sense. However, some argued that the new wine could not fit in the "old bottles"[3]. The new wine would be digital information and technologies, and the "old bottles" would be traditional legal concepts, in particular copyright and other forms of intellectual property. Moreover, it was questioned the ability of Law to deal with this brave new world of electronic communications. It should be replaced by some kind of "Cyber-Ethics" and technology would do the rest. In particular, since copyright was an "artefact of Gutenberg" and therefore a product of the atom economy, it would

---

[2] Wiener, *Cybernetic or the Control and Communication in the Animal and the Machine*, 1948. According to Prof. Miguel Baptista Pereira: "Toda a informação armazenada fica também esclerosada e isolada e, por isso, Wiener formulou o princípio da circulação, que transforma a informação num processo, de cuja paralisação decorreria a decadência social, porque a informação é o cimento da sociedade. A conversão da informação em mercadoria armazenada com fins lucrativos é sinónimo de degradação e de enfraquecimento da corrente contínua, que deve irrigar a sociedade." (M. Baptista Pereira, *Filosofia da Comunicação Hoje*, in *Comunicação e Defesa do Consumidor*, Actas do Congresso Internacional organizado pelo Instituto Jurídico da Comunicação da Faculdade de Direito da Universidade de Coimbra, de 25 a 27 de Novembro de 1993, IJC: Coimbra, 1996, p. 65).

[3] See Barlow, *Selling Wine Without Bottles. The Economy of Mind on the Global Net*, in B. Hugenholtz (ed.), *The Future of Copyright in a Digital Environment*, 1996, p. 169. For the state of the discussion before the new WIPO Treaties, see Ficsor, in M. Dellebeke (ed.), *Copyright in Cyberspace: Copyright and the Global Information Infrastructure*, 1997, p. 29

be completely outdated in the digital age and, probably, "the answer to the machine" would be "in the machine" itself [4]. Nevertheless, one can wonder whether a strict technologist approach of the rule of technology and cyber-ethics wouldn't be pursuing the dream of a digital world free of Law.

However, one's dream is often another's nightmare. For information owners, a technologically self-ruled cyberspace could be nothing but an anarchist vision, since there would be no legal remedies for infringement. Digitalia is "no man's land", they argued, and therefore traditional legal concepts such as property and privacy should be called to play a major role in the construction of the legal framework for the information society. In short: *ubi societas, ibi ius.*

But in this process something else is happening. The question is not only of enforcing traditional rights in the digital environment. Law in Digitalia went further and deeper. The purpose of constructing an information society has served to create new legal forms of private and public appropriation of information.[5] The question of

---

[4] See Negroponte, *Being Digital*, 1995, p. 58; Clark, *The Answer to the Machine is in the Machine*, in B. Hugenholtz (ed.), *The Future of Copyright in a Digital Environment*, 1996, p. 139.

[5] In fact, information owners have pursued in official reports and legislation drafts the so-called "maximalist agenda" based upon the following commands: *1. The exclusive right to read: copyright control over every use of copyrighted works in digital form by interpreting existing law as being violated whenever users make even temporary reproductions of works in the random access memory of their computers. 2. The exclusive right to transmit: copyright control over every transmission of works in digital form by amending the copyright statute so that digital transmissions will be regarded as distributions of copies to the public. 3. The end of fair-use rights: eliminate fair-use rights whenever a use might be licensed. 4. Eliminating first-sale rights for digitally transmitted documents: deprive the public of the "first sale" rights it has long enjoyed in the print world. 5. Helping documents spy on you: attach copyright management information to digital copies of a work, ensuring that publishers can track every use made of digital copies and trace where each copy resides on the network and what is being done with it at any time. 6. Outlawing decryption: protect every digital copy of every work technologically (by encryption, for example) and make illegal any attempt to circumvent that protection. 7. Turning online service providers into cops: force online service providers to become copyright police, charged with implementing pay-per-use rules. 8. Teaching children not to share: "Just say yes to licensing"*. Samuelson, *The Copyright Grab*, Wired, 1996.

whether there would be room left for copyright in the "brave new world of technical systems", or whether it could be "unimportant on the Internet"[6] seems to have been answered already. The fact is that the Internet is a global marketplace. If it were just a limited community of computer maniacs, probably there would be no special problems. There would be no need to care, as long as they didn't abuse too much. As the Romans used to say, *de minimis non curat praetor.*

However, the World Wide Web is huge. The new "golden goose" is called electronic commerce, in particular direct electronic commerce. In the name of the new economy, global efforts are being made to eliminate the "malign hacker-culture" and to put an end to "anarchy online". Of special importance is the work undertaken at the international level by International Organizations such as the UNCITRAL, WIPO, OECD[7]. Moreover, in the European Union and its Member States[8], the creation of the legal framework for electronic commerce in the information society is under way. In the U.S. the emerging digital economy is at the heart of much legislation and case-law[9].

---

[6] See Vinje, EIPR 1996, p. 431; Schlachter, BTLJ 1997, p. 15.

[7] See, more recently, WIPO Premier on *Electronic Commerce and Intellectual Property Rights*, 2000; OECD Forum on *Electronic Commerce: Progress Report on the OECD Action Plan for Electronic Commerce*, Oct. 1999; Recommendations of the OECD Council Concerning Cryptography Policy (1997); *Uncitral Model Law On Electronic Commerce 1996 (with additional article 5 bis as adopted in 1998)*, and its *Guide To Enactment.*

[8] See *European Initiative for Electronic Commerce*, Communication of the Commission, COM (97) 157 final. See also, for example, Green Paper on the *Convergence of the Telecommunications, Media and Information Technology Sectors, and the Implications for Regulation - Towards an Information Society Approach*; COM(97)623. At the national level, see, in Portugal, the *Iniciativa Nacional para o Comércio Electrónico* (Resolução do Conselho de Ministros n.° 115/98) and its *Documento Orientador* (Resolução do Conselho de Ministros n.° 94/99).

[9] See William J. Clinton & Albert Gore, Jr., *A Framework for Global Electronic Commerce*, 1997; *The Emerging Digital Economy*, U.S. Department of Commerce, Secretariat on Electronic Commerce, 1998.

Law has a preference for legitimate interests. There are many legitimate interests in the digital environment of electronic network communications. Regarding interests protected under copyright, there are several agents involved, such as: individual creators, copyright owners, and users (1); service providers, computer software, motion picture, music, broadcasting, electronic, publishing and other information and entertainment industries (2); the academic, research, library and legal communities (3). Several official reports contain efforts to clarify the value of all these different interests in the process of adaptation of copyright to the digital environment[10]. At the same time, this issue has been the subject of intensive study and debate[11], demonstrating that copyright is one of the most important

---

[10] See *Green Paper On Intellectual Property And The National Information Infrastructure, Working Group On Intellectual Property,* 1994, and *Intellectual Property and the National Information Infrastructure, The Report of the Working Group on Intellectual Property Rights,* Bruce Lehman, Ronald Brown, September 1995 (U.S.A); *Predicted Problems and Possible Solutions for Administering Intellectual Property Rights in a Multimedia Society*, IIP, Juin 1995 (Japan); *Highways to change: Copyright in the new Communications Environment, Report of the Copyright Convergence Group*, August 1994 (Australia); *Rapport Sirinelli — Industries culturelles et nouvelles technologies*, septembre 1994 (France); *Copyright and the Information Highway, Final Report of the Copyright Sub-Comittee*, Ottawa, March 1995 (Canada); *Green Book on Copyright and the Challenge of Technology*, COM(88) 172 final; *Green Book on Copyright in the Information Society,* COM(95), 382 final, and *Following,* COM(96) 568 final, 20.11.1996; *Green Paper combating counterfeiting and piracy in the Single Market*, COM/98/0569 final of 15 October 1998 (Europe); Schricker (Hrsg.), *Urheberrecht auf dem Weg zur Informationsgesellschaft*, 1997 (Germany).

[11] See, *inter alia, L'informatique et le droit d'auteur*, ALAI, 1989; WIPO *Worldwide Symposium on the Impact of Digital Technology on Copyright and Neighboring Rights*, Harvard 1993; *Num Mundo Novo do Direito de Autor?*, I, II, Lisboa 1994; Goldstein, *Copyright's Highway*, 1994; Becker/Dreier, *Urheberrecht und digitale Technologie*, 1994; Heymann (Hrsg.), *Informationsmarkt und Informationsschutz in Europa*, 1995; Fiedler/Ullrich (Hrsg.), *Information als Wirtschaftsgut*, Köln, 1996; Hugenholtz (ed), *The Future of Copyright in a Digital Environment*, 1996; Dellebeke (ed.), *Copyright in Cyberspace*, 1997; Boyle, *Software, Shamans, and Spleens*, 1997; Merger/Menell/Lemley/Jorde, *Intellectual Property in the New Technological Age*, 1997; Lee/Davidson, *Intellectual Property for the Internet*, 1997; Schricker (Hrsg.), *Urheberrecht auf dem Weg zur Informationsgesellschaft* (Dreier, Katzenberger, v. Lewinski, Schricker), 1997; Strowel/Triaille, *Le droit d'auteur, du logiciel au multimedia*, 1997; Vivant (dir.), *Les créations immatérielles et le droit*, 1997; Samuelson, *The Information Society and the Role of Copyright in It*, 1998; Lessig, *Code and Other Laws of Cyberspace*, 1999.

legal fields of the Electronic Revolution, playing a major role within the so-called Information Society Law or Internet or Cyberlaw[12].

The emerging digital law is supposed to serve the creation of the information society. Nevertheless, it can reasonably be said that in this emerging digital law it is of greater importance to begin with establishing property rights in Digitalia. In short, to clarify who owns what in cyberspace, in particular who owns information. This was the major task of the new WIPO Treaties on Copyright and certain Related Rights (December 1996)[13]. The mission cannot be said to have been fully accomplished, since several issues remained open, such as liability of online service providers and *sui generis* intellectual property for databases. Moreover, the WIPO Treaties did not provide ready answers on the use of copyright defeating devices.

The WIPO treaties have answered to questions such as: Why should online transmission of copyrighted works be considered distribution of copies, when there's always a copy left behind which can be used? If a copyright owner can get paid for every access to his encrypted electronic book, why shouldn't the circumvention of technological

---

[12] See, *inter alia*, Katsch, *Law in a Digital World*, 1995; Perritt Jr., *Law and the Information Society*, 1996; Bensoussan (dir.), *Internet, aspects juridiques*, 1996; Demnard-Tellier (dir.), *Le multimedia et le droit*, 1996; Iteanu, *Internet et le droit*, 1996; Hilty (Hrsg.), *Infomation Highway (Beiträge zu rechtlichen und tatsäschlichen Fragen)*, 1996; Lopes Rocha/Macedo, *Direito no Ciberespaço*, 1996; Becker (Hrsg.), *Rechtsprobleme internationaler Datennetze*, 1996; Bender, *Computer Law*, 1997; Lehmann (Hrsg.), *Internet- und Multimediarecht*, 1997; Sédallian, *Droit de l'Internet*, 1997; Piette-Coudol / Bertrand, *Internet et la loi*, 1997; Hoeren, *Rechtsfragen des Internet*, 1998; Loewenheim/Koch (Hrsg.), *Praxis des Online-Rechts*, 1998; Bartsch/Lutterbek (Hrsg.), *Neues Recht für neue Medien*, 1998; Roßnagel, *Recht der Multimedia-Dienste: Kommentar*, 1999; *As Telecomunicações e o Direito na Sociedade da Informação*, IJC, 1999; *Direito da Sociedade da Informação*, FDUL/APDI, I, 1999. See also Katsch, *The Electronic Media and the Transformation of Law*, 1989; Giannantonnio (ed.), *Law and Computers*, I, 1989, II, 1991; Forester, *The Information Technology Revolution*, 1990; Egan, *Information Superhighways*, 1991; Vivant (sous la responsabilité de), *Lamy Droit Informatique*, 1992; Scott, *Multimedia: Law and Practise*, 1993; Egan, *EC Information Technology Law*, 1995; Webster, *Theories of the Information Society*, 1995; Tinnefeld/ Phillips/Heil (Hrsg.), *Informationsgesellschaft und Rechtskultur in Europa*, 1995.

[13] On the new WIPO Treaties see, for example, Françon, RIDA 1997, p. 3; Vinje, EIPR 1997, p. 230.

protection measures be considered unlawful? If a copyright owner can patrol the Web in order to find unlawfully disseminated copies of his books, why shouldn't the tampering of information management systems be considered unlawful? Other issues, however, remained open at the international level: Why should "mere conduit", caching, hosting, or browsing be lawful, when online service providers know that these acts contribute to copyright infringement? Why should anyone be free to extract and re-utilize information content from electronic databases, when the production of such databases required substantial investments?

2. Copyright Issues of Electronic Commerce: Basic Legal Framework

The European Union has constructed a legal framework for the information society. The major Recently, a major step has been taken with the approval by the European Parliament of the Directive on electronic commerce[14]. This Directive deals with one of the most important copyright issues of electronic commerce: the liability of online service providers for copyright infringement when engaging in certain activities.

Another major step would be the adoption of the Proposal for a European Parliament and Council Directive on the harmonization of certain aspects of copyright and related rights in the Information Society, that the Commission transmitted to the Parliament and the Council on 21 January 1998[15]. In the amended proposal for a

---

[14] Directive 2000/31/EC of the European Parliament and of the Council of June 2000 on certain legal aspects of information society services, in particular electronic commerce, in the Internal market ("Directive on electronic commerce"), OJ L 178, 17.07.2000.

[15] COM(97)628 final of 10.12.1997, OJ C 108, 7.4.1998, p. 6.

Directive, the Commission has considered the Parliament's opinion regarding several aspects[16]. This Proposal aims to implement a number of the new international obligations, mainly the new WIPO Treaties[17], dealing respectively with the protection of authors and the protection of performers and phonogram producers.

Those Treaties, which have been adopted by the Diplomatic Conference held under the auspices of the World Intellectual Property Organization (WIPO) in December 1996[18], update the international protection for copyright and related rights with regard to the so-called "digital agenda", and improve the means to fight piracy world-wide. Among other aspects, they provide prohibitions on circumvention of technological measures used by copyright owners to protect their works[19], and on tampering with copyright management information[20]. The Community and a majority of Member

---

16 Amended proposal for a European Parliament and Council Directive on the harmonisation of certain aspects of copyright and related rights in the Information Society, COM(99) 250 final. On the initial draft Directive [COM(97) 628 final, 10.12.1997] see, for example, Reinbothe, Dietz, ZUM 1998, p. 429, p. 438. The legal concept of copyright proposed to serve the construction of the information society is the concept of intellectual property as a form of property.

17 The WIPO Copyright Treaty (WCT) and the WIPO Performances and Phonograms Treaty (WPPT), December 1996.

18 WIPO Copyright Treaty, Articles 11 and 12; WIPO Performances and Phonograms Treaty, Articles 18 and 19. Those Treaties have already been implemented in Brazil (Lei n.° 9.610, de 19 de Fevereiro de 1998) and in the U.S. (*The Digital Millennium Copyright Act of 1998*), where the prohibition circle has been enlarged to marketing activities of devices which main purpose is to circumvent technological protection measures. See on *www.digital-forum.net* (JURINET), Oliveira Ascensão, *O Direito de Autor no Ciberespaço* (<=> Separata de Portugal-Brasil Ano 2000, Boletim da Faculdade de Direito, Studia Ivridica, Coimbra, 1999) / *A recente lei brasileira dos direitos autorais, compilada com os novos tratados da OMPI* (1999).

19 Article 11 of the WCT states that "Contracting Parties shall provide adequate legal protection and effective legal remedies against the circumvention of effective technological measures that are used by authors in connection with the exercise of their rights under this Treaty or the Bern Convention and that restricts acts, in respect of their works, which are not authorized by the authors concerned or permitted by law." See also Article 18 of the WPPT.

20 Article 12 of the WCT states that Contracting Parties shall provide adequate and effective legal remedies against any person knowingly performing any of the following acts knowing, or with respect to civil remedies having reasonable

States have already signed the Treaties and the process of making arrangements for the ratification of the Treaties by the Community and the Member States is under way.

On the other side of the Atlantic, the new WIPO Treaties have already been implemented by the Digital Millennium Copyright Act (DMCA)[21]. In fact, title I of the DMCA[22] implements the WIPO Treaties where they oblige member states to provide legal protection for the exploitation of works on digital networks, which serves as "technological adjuncts" to the exclusive rights granted by copyright law. Accordingly, title I creates two new prohibitions, and it adds civil remedies and criminal penalties for violating the prohibitions. Of the new prohibitions, one covers the circumvention of technological measures used by copyright owners to protect their works, and another one the tampering with copyright management information.

Moreover, title II of the DMCA[23] deals with another very important copyright issue of electronic commerce: the liability of online service providers for copyright infringement. In fact, Title II of the DMCA creates limitations on the liability of online service providers for copyright infringement when engaging in certain activities. This title adds a new section to the Copyright Act to create four new limitations on liability for copyright infringement by online service providers based on the following categories of acts, such as: 1. transitory communications ("mere conduit"); 2. system caching; 3.

grounds to know, that it will induce, enable, facilitate or conceal and infringement of any right covered by this Treaty or the Bern Convention: (i) to remove or alter any electronic rights management information without authority; (ii) to distribute, import for fabrication, broadcast or communicate to the public, without authority, works or copies of works knowing that electronic rights management information has been removed or altered without authority." See also Article 19 of the WPPT.

[21] The Digital Millennium Copyright Act (DMCA) of 1998, Pub. L. No. 105-304, 112 Stat. 2860 (Oct. 28, 1998). On the DMCA, see: Ginsburg, RIDA 1999, p. 21; Samuelson, BTLJ 1999, p. 520.

[22] The WIPO Copyright and Performances and Phonograms Treaties Act of 1998.

[23] The Online Copyright Infringement Liability Limitation Act.

storage of information on systems or networks at direction of users ("hosting"); 4. information location tools ("browsing", "linking").

It is important to study these copyright issues of electronic commerce for they have been dealt under different approaches from legislation and case-law.

To begin with, as far as the copyright defeating devices are concerned, in Europe there were mainly two approaches to the question of the legal protection of technological protection measures. For example, while in Germany case law held the sale and distribution of copyright defeating devices as well as other devices designed to circumvent technological protection measures to be unfair competition under §1 UWG[24], in Common Law countries these acts may be dealt with under the principle of contributory infringement under copyright law[25], i.e., acts of inducing, causing and providing the means to carry out the infringement, knowing or having reason to know of the infringement. The secondary infringement approach has been adopted at the European level for harmonization purposes[26].

---

[24] See: OLG Stuttgart, "Feilhalten von Hardlock-Entfernen", 10.2.1989; OLG München, "Unprotect", 3.11.1994; LG München, "Dongle", 1.12.1994; OLG Frankfurt am Main, "Piratenkarten", 13.6.1995; BGB, "Dongle-Umgehung", 9.11.1995. The decision LG Manheim, "Dongle", 20.1.1995, has considered it lawful under copyright to circumvent a technological protection measure in order to correct errors of a program. In Holland case law deems those acts to constitute tort liability: See: Hague District Court, "FilmNet v. Planken", 20.11.1986; Court of Appeal, "Esselte v. Ten", 2.5.1991; Supreme Court, "Groeneveld v. Television Distribution Systems NV - TDS", 17.12.1993. See Lehmann, Grosheide, in Dellebeke (ed.), *Copyright in Cyberspace*, Amsterdam, 1997, p. 364-5, p. 408-9.

[25] See: UK Copyright, Designs and Patents Act of 1988, Part VII, § 296; U.S. Communications Act of 1988 [47U.S.C § 605(e)(4)] and Audio Home Recording Act of 1992 [Serial Copy Management System, 17 U.S. Code § 1002(c)]. See also NAFTA, Art. 1707; TRIPS Agreement (Art. 46); NII Copyright Protection Act of 1995 [§ 1201. Circumvention of Copyright Protection Systems; § 1202. Integrity of Copyright Management Information].

[26] See Art. 7.° of the Council Directive 91/250/EEC of 14 May 1991 on the legal protection of computer programs (OJ L 122, 17.5.1991, p. 42, as amended by Directive 93/98/EEC). See also, at the European level, *Green Paper on copyright and the challenge of technology - copyright issues requiring immediate action*, COM(88)172; *Green Paper on Copyright and Related Rights in the Information Society*; COM(95)382 (Sec. XI); *Follow-Up of the Green Paper on Copyright and Related Rights in the Information Society*, COM(96) 586 final, 20.11.1996.

Regarding the issue on liability of on-line services providers, in Europe two Member States (Germany[27] and Sweden[28]) have adopted specific legislation. However, in other member States, the situation of case-law is one of uncertainty. There is case law regarding liability of service providers for privacy infringement and providing access to defamatory material[29]. But there's also case law establishing no monitor obligation for online intermediaries[30]. In comparison, in the United States on-line intermediaries have been sued for copyright infringement, either for direct infringement[31], contributory infringement[32], and vicarious infringement[33].

3. Information Society Services: Notion and Examples

Electronic commerce is based upon the so-called information society services. Before entering into the discussion of those copyright issues of electronic commerce, it is important to find a definition of those services.

The *acquis communautaire* already provides a definition of information society services. In other words, the definition of Information Society services already exists in Community law. It

---

[27] Federal Act Establishing the General Conditions for Information and Communication Services (*Informations-und Kommunikationsdienste-Gesetz*-IuKDG), August 1 1997.

[28] Act on Responsibility for Electronic Bulletin Boards (1998:112).

[29] *Estelle Haliday v. Valentin Lacambre*, February 1999, Cour d'Appel de Paris (confirming the decision of the Tribunal de Grande Instance de Paris of June 1998); *DEMON*, London High Court, March 1999 (obliging host service providers to monitor content).

[30] See *UEJF v. Calvacom, Compu-serve and others*, TGI Paris, 12 June 1996.

[31] *Playboy Enters., Inc v. Frena*, 839 F. Supp. 1552 (M.D. FLA. 1993).

[32] *Sega Enterprises v. MAPHIA*, 948 F. Supp. 923 (N.D. CAL. 1996.

[33] *Religious Technology Center v. Netcom On-line Communication Services*, Inc, 907 F. Supp. 1361 (N.D. Cal. 1995).

is provided by Directive on Technical Standards[34], and it has been adopted by Directive on Conditional Access Services[35] and Directive on Electronic Commerce[36].

According to this definition, "Information Society services" are *any service normally provided for remuneration* (1), *at a distance* (or without the parties being simultaneously present) (2), *by electronic means* (or sent initially and received at its destination by means of electronic equipment for the processing - including digital compression- and storage of data, and entirely transmitted, conveyed and received by wire, by radio, by optical means or by other electromagnetic means) (3) *and at the individual request of a recipient of services* (provided through the transmission of data on individual request) (4).[37] In short, this definition covers any service normally provided for or against remuneration, at a distance, via networks, by means of electronic equipment for the processing (including digital compression) and storage of data, and at the individual request of a

---

[34] Directive 98/34/EC of the European Parliament and the Council of 22 June 1998 laying down a procedure for the provision of information in the field of technical standards and regulations (OJ L 204, 21.7.1998, p.37), as amended by Directive 98/48/EC of the European Parliament and the Council of 20 July 1998 (OJ L 217, 5.8.1998, p.18).

[35] Directive 98/84/EC of the European Parliament and of the Council of 20 November 1998 on the legal protection of services based on, or consisting of, conditional access (OJ L 320, 28.11.1998, p.54).

[36] Directive on electronic commerce, Art. 2(a) [Directive 2000/31/EC of the European Parliament and of the Council of June 2000 on certain legal aspects of information society services, in particular electronic commerce, in the Internal market ("Directive on electronic commerce"), OJ L 178, 17.07.2000].

[37] In Germany, a similar notion is provided for by §2 TDG (*Teledienstgesetz*) under Article 1 of the *Informations- und Kommunikationsdienste-Gesetz* (IuKDG), from August 1, 1997. Telecommunication services as such (§3 TDK, Telekommunikationsgesetz, July 25, 1996) and broadcasting are excluded. See Engel-Flechsig, ZUM 1997, p. 106. In Portugal, the Act on cable distribution provides interactive services of addressed nature accessible either on individual (such as Internet services and video-on-demand) or on adhesion. See Decree-Law n.° 241/97 of 18 September 1997. Moreover, the definition of information society services as provided for by Directive on Technical Standards (98/34/EC) has been introduced into national law by Decree-Law n.° 58/2000 of 18 April 2000 which implements that Directive.

recipient of a service. Services which do not imply data processing and storage are not covered by this definition.

Information Society services span a wide range of activities of the so-called digital economy. In particular, those economic activities can consist of: selling goods on line (1), offering on-line information or commercial communications (2), providing tools allowing for search, access and retrieval of data (3), online activities via telephony and telefax (4), transmitting information via a communication network (5), providing access to a communication network (5) or hosting information provided by a recipient of the service (6)[38].

Accordingly, services that are transmitted point to point, such as video on demand or the sending of commercial communications by e-mail are Information Society services. By contrast, television broadcasting within the meaning of the Directive on Television Broadcasting Directive[39], and radio broadcasting are not Information Society services because they are not provided at individual request. Other examples of non- information society services are: the use of electronic communication or equivalent individual communications for instance by natural persons acting outside their trade, business or profession including their use for the conclusion of contracts between such persons (1); the contractual relationship between an employee and his employer (2); activities which by their very nature cannot be carried out at a distance and by electronic means, such

---

[38] The DMCA provides a definition of service provider for "mere conduit" activities, according to which a service provider is an entity offering the transmission, routing, or providing connections for digital online communications, between or among points specified by a user, of material of the user's choosing, without modification to the content of the material as sent or received [Sec. 512(k)(1)(A)]. For other activities (system caching, hosting, browsing), a service provider is defined as a provider of online services or network access, or the operator of facilities thereof [Sec. 512(k)(1)(B)].

[39] Directive 89/552/EEC of 3 October 1989 on the co-ordination of certain provisions laid down by Law, Regulation or Administrative Action in Member States concerning the pursuit of television broadcasting activities (OJ L 298, 17.10.1989, p.23). Directive as amended by Directive 97/36/EC of the European Parliament and of the Council (OJ L 202, 30.7.1997, p. 60).

as the statutory auditing of company accounts or medical advice requiring the physical examination of a patient (3)[40].

II - Circumvention of Technological Protection Measures and Integrity of Copyright Management Information

1. "Technological Adjuncts" to the Exclusive Rights

New opportunities to exploit works or other subject matter in the framework of on-line services are provided by new communication technologies. However, at the same time, these new technologies bring about new risks of piracy. Chapter III of the Directive Proposal on Copyright provides for protection of technological measures (1) and rights-management information (2), in order to implement the new WIPO Treaties.

It is understood that a common search for technical measures to protect works and to provide the necessary information on rights are essential insofar as the ultimate aim of these measures is to give effect to the principles and guarantees laid down in law. It means that technological protection measures and information management systems are not meant to create a sort of *technological or digital property*[41] that would grant rightholders more power than recognized by copyright law. For example, decompilation of a computer program for purposes of interoperability is a lawful act, and therefore the legal protection of technological measures shall not make it unlawful to circumvent that protection for purposes

---

[40] See Recital 18 of the Directive on Electronic Commerce (2000/31/EC).

[41] On the so-called "digital property rights" see Stefik, BTLJ 1997, p. 137.

of decompilation. The same applies, *mutatis mutandis*, to back-up copies of computer programs or lawful access to databases.

However, "gray zones" such as private copying are dealt in a different way. In fact, private copying is not deemed to be a user's right. Accordingly, it is considered that when applying the exception on private copying, Member States shall take due account of technological and economic developments, in particular with respect to digital private copying and remuneration schemes, when effective technological protection measures are available, since such exceptions shall not inhibit the use of technological measures or their enforcement against circumvention.

In the U.S., title I of the DMCA[42] implements the WIPO Treaties. These Treaties oblige member states to provide legal protection for the exploitation of works on digital networks, which serve as "technological adjuncts" to the exclusive rights granted by copyright law.

Accordingly, title I of the DMCA creates two new prohibitions, and it adds civil remedies and criminal penalties for violating the prohibitions. The new prohibitions are, one on circumvention of technological measures used by copyright owners to protect their works, and another one on tampering with copyright management information.

The DMCA[43] makes it a criminal offense to violate, willfully and for purposes of commercial advantage or private financial gain, the prohibition of circumvention of technological protection measures (section 1201) and the protection of the integrity of copyright management information (section 1202). Under Section 1204, penalties may range up to a $500,000 fine or up to five years imprisonment for a first offense, and up to a 1,000,000 fine or up to 10 years

[42] The WIPO Copyright and Performances and Phonograms Treaties Act of 1998.

[43] The Digital Millennium Copyright Act of 1998, Pub. L. No. 105-304, 112 Stat. 2860 (Oct. 28, 1998).

imprisonment for subsequent offenses[44]. These criminal penalties have been adopted to implement the WIPO Treaties[45] obligations to provide adequate and effective protection against circumvention of technological measures used by copyright owners to protect their works, and to prevent tampering with the integrity of copyright management information.[46]

2. Circumvention of Technological Protection Measures

Technological development allows rightholders to make use of technological measures, namely SCMS and "cryptographic envelopes", designed to prevent and inhibit the infringement of any copyright or any rights related to copyright, including the so-called *sui generis* rights provided by law. The danger, however, exists that illegal activities might be carried out in order to enable or facilitate the circumvention of the technical protection provided by these measures.

The Directive Proposal on Copyright is based upon the understanding that there is a need to provide for harmonized legal protection against any activity enabling or facilitating the circumvention without authority, whether granted by the rightholders or conferred by law, of such measures. Accordingly, such a legal

[44] Courts are also given the power to grant a range of equitable and monetary remedies similar to those available under the Copyright Act, including statutory damages, and they have the discretion to reduce or remit damages in cases of innocent violations, where the violator proves that it was not aware and had no reason to believe its acts constituted a violation (section 1203). Regarding nonprofit libraries, archives and educational institutions, on one hand, they are entitled to a complete remission of damages where they prove that they were not aware and had no reason to believe their acts constituted a violation; on the other hand, they are entirely exempted from criminal liability.

[45] The WIPO Copyright Treaty (WCT) and the WIPO Performances and Phonograms Treaty (WPPT) , December 1996.

[46] Arts. 11, 12 WCT, Arts. 18,19 WPPT.

protection is provided to technological measures that effectively inhibit and/or prevent the infringement of any copyright, rights related to copyright or *sui generis* rights provided by law, without, however, preventing the normal operation of electronic equipment and its technological development.

However, according to the Recitals of the draft Directive, such legal protection:

- implies no obligation to design devices, products, components or services to correspond to technological measures (1);
- respects proportionality and does not prohibit those devices or activities which have a commercially significant purpose or use other than to circumvent the technical protection (2);
- does not hinder research into cryptography (3);
- does not affect the specific provisions of protection provided for by Directive on Computer Programs[47], and, in particular, it does not inhibit decompilation permitted by Art. 6.° of that Directive (4).

Regarding this last aspect, the draft Directive makes it clear that the prohibition on circumvention of technological protection measures ("copyright busting devices") does not affect the reverse engineering exception, having regard of the importance of the imperative of interoperability for the promotion of global electronic communication systems. It is expressly considered that important progress has been made in the international standardization of technical systems of identification of works and protected subject matter in digital format. Moreover, in an increasingly networked environment, differences between technological measures could

[47] Council Directive 91/250/EEC of 14 May 1991 on the legal protection of computer programs (OJ L 122, 17.5.1991, p. 42.). On this Directive see, *inter alia*, Franceschelli, RDI 1991, p. 169; Lehmann, GRUR Int. 1991, p. 327; Vivant, JCP 1991, p. 485.

lead to an incompatibility of systems within the Community. In order to encourage compatibility and interoperability of the different systems and to encourage the development of global systems[48], it is expressly considered that the legal protection of technological protection measures shall not inhibit decompilation permitted by Directive on Computer Programs.

In our opinion, the terms under which this Directive provides for the lawfulness of reverse engineering[49] do include hard-, soft- and dataware interoperability, according to the definition of interoperability thereby provided ("the ability to exchange information and mutually to use the information which has been exchanged"). In the digital environment there is no "wine" (data) without "bottles" (software). If one has "the right to drink the wine", then *a fortiori* one should be entitled "to open the bottle", and *vice versa*. And one should also be allowed to manufacture and market devices for opening the bottle. The same applies, for example, for back-up copies, error correction, and "other legitimate purposes". I also argue that even if genetic software code (algorithms and so on) is to be protected by patent law or trade-secret law[50], *the imperative of interoperability in electronic communications, as provided for by Directive on Computer Programs, should prevail over such legal forms of protection*. In fact, the decompilation exception is not a strict copyright exception, but indeed a intellectual property exception *tout court.*[51].

---

[48] An example of the importance of interoperability in electronic communications is provided by Decision n.° 1720/1999/EC of the European Parliament and of the Council of 12 July 1999 adopting a series of actions and measures in order to ensure interoperability of access to trans-European networks for the electronic interchange of data between administrations (IDA).

[49] See Lehmann, *Die europäische Richtlinie über den Schutz von Computerprogrammen*, in M. Lehmann (Hrsg.), *Rechtsschutz und Verwertung von Computerprogrammen*, 2.Aufl.,1993, p. 4.

[50] See the Report of the European Commission, COM(2000) 1999 final, 10.04.2000.

[51] See my *Informática, direito de autor e propriedade tecnodigital*, Coimbra 1998, §§ 52, 54, 55.

Regarding the obligations as to technological measures (Art. 6), the Directive Proposal on Copyright obliges to provide adequate legal protection against the circumvention and against circumvention related activities.[52] On one hand, Member States are required to provide adequate legal protection against the circumvention without authority of any effective technological measures designed to protect any copyright or any rights related to copyright as provided by law or the *sui generis* right provided for in Chapter III of Directive on Databases[53], which the person concerned carries out in the knowledge, or with reasonable grounds to know that he or she pursues that objective[54]. On the other hand, they are required to provide adequate legal protection against any activities, including the manufacture or distribution of devices, products or components or the provision of services, carried out without authority, which are promoted, advertised or marketed for the purpose of circumvention of (1), or have only a limited commercially significant purpose or use other than to circumvent (2), or are primarily designed, produced, adapted or performed for the purpose of enabling or facilitating the circumvention (3)[55] of, any effective

[52] The initial Proposal was not directed simply against the circumvention of technological measures as in the WIPO Treaties, but covered only any activity, including preparatory activities such as the manufacture and distribution, as well as services, that facilitate or enable the circumvention of these devices. In fact, it was considered that the real danger for intellectual property rights would not be the single act of circumvention by individuals, but the preparatory acts carried out by commercial companies that could produce, sell, rent, or advertise circumventing devices. This was also the original Proposal of the NII Copyright Protection Act of 1995 (§ 1201).

[53] Directive 96/9/EC of the European Parliament and of the Council of 11 March 1996 on the legal protection of databases (OJ L 77, 27.3.1996, p. 20). On this Directive see, *inter alia*, Lehmann, NJW-CoR 1996, p. 249; Cornish, in Dellebeke (ed.), *Copyright in Cyberspace*, 1997, p. 435.

[54] A similar expression ("knowingly or having reasonable grounds to know") is already used in the provisions on enforcement in the WTO/TRIPS Agreement (Art. 45.°). It excludes from protection those activities which are carried out without the knowledge that they will enable circumvention of technological protection devices.

[55] This solution ensures that general-purpose electronic equipment and services are not outlawed merely because they may also be used in breaking copy protection or similar measures.

technological measures[56] designed to protect any copyright or any right related to copyright as provided by law or the *sui generis* right provided for in Chapter III of Directive on Databases (4).[57]

The draft Directive extends the prohibition on circumvention of technological protection measures to this intellectual property *sui generis* right created by the European legislator[58]. This result is not currently admitted in the U.S. in view of the *Feist* decision[59], which

---

[56] For purposes of this provision "technological measures" are defined as any technology, device or component that, in the normal course of its operation, is designed to prevent or inhibit the infringement of any copyright or any right related to copyright as provided by law or the *sui generis* right provided for in Chapter III of Directive on Databases. Moreover, those technological measures shall be deemed "effective" where the access to or use of a protected work or other subject matter is controlled through application of an access code or any other type of protection process which achieves the protection objective in an operational and reliable manner with the authority of the right holders. Such measures may include decryption, descrambling or other transformation of the work or other subject matter.

[57] Moreover, the protection of technological measures provided for by Directive Proposal on Copyright is complemented by Directive on Conditional Access Services (Directive 98/84/EC of the European Parliament and of the Council of 20 November 1998 on the legal protection of services based on, or consisting of, conditional access). Protection is granted to the following services, where provided against remuneration and on the basis of conditional access: television broadcasting (1) radio broadcasting (2), and information society services (3); or the provision of conditional access to the above services considered as a service in its own right (4). The legal protection of service providers against illicit devices which allow access to these services free of charge is deemed necessary in order to ensure the economic viability of the services. According to the Directive, Member States are required to provide appropriate legal protection against the placing on the market, for direct or indirect financial gain, of an illicit device which enables or facilitates without authority the circumvention of any technological measures designed to protect the remuneration of a legally provided service. Those commercial activities which concern illicit devices include commercial communications covering all forms of advertising, direct marketing, sponsorship, sales promotion and public relations promoting such products and services. In this sense, certain activities are considered infringing: the manufacture, import, distribution, sale, rental or possession for commercial purposes of illicit devices (1); the installation, maintenance or replacement for commercial purposes of an illicit device (2); and the use of commercial communications to promote illicit devices (3). Regarding the private possession of illicit devices, this Directive is without prejudice to the application of any national provisions which may prohibit the private possession of illicit devices. See *Green Paper on the Legal Protection of Encrypted Services in the Internal Market*, COM(96)76, March 1996

[58] See Chapter III (*sui generis* right) of the Directive 96/9/EC of the European Parliament and of the Council of 11 March 1996 on the Legal Protection of Databases.

[59] *Feist Publications Inc. v. Rural Telephone Service Co. Inc.* (1991).

requires that for a database to be copyrightable it must be original in the sense that it must have "a modicum of creativity". The same applies to the integrity of copyright management information.

Accordingly, if the investment in the production of a database is worth protecting under the *sui generis* right, the maker will have the right to prevent access to, extraction from and re-utilization of his database content to every one without authority, *even if that content is purely made of public domain information*. And the same applies to the integrity of management information of his "*sui generis*" right. Nonetheless, it is considered that Article 10 (1) of the Bern Convention is not affected by this Directive[60], in order to leave some room left, although minimal if one considers the exceptions to the *sui generis* right, for the free flow of information.

In the U.S., the obligation to provide adequate and effective protection against circumvention of technological measures used by copyright owners to protect their works is implemented in new section 1201. This section divides technological measures into two categories. On one hand, measures that prevent unauthorized access to a copyrighted work. On the other hand, measures that prevent unauthorized copying, distribution or public performance of a copyrighted work.[61]

First, the act of circumvention is prohibited in the first category of technical measures (*access*), but not the second (*copying*). The act of circumventing a technological measure that prevents copying is not prohibited not only because the copying of a work may be fair use under certain circumstances, but also because it was to assure that the public will have the continued ability to make fair use of copyrighted works.

Second, the act of circumventing a technological measure in order to gain access is prohibited, because the fair use doctrine is not a

---

[60] See Recital 37 of the Directive on Database Protection.

[61] See *The Digital Millennium Copyright Act of 1998*, U.S. Copyright Office Executive Summary, December 1998.

defense to the act of gaining access to a work. The prohibition on the act of circumvention of access control measures does not take effect until October 28, 2000.

Third, making or selling devices or services that are used to circumvent either category of technological measures is prohibited, where they are primarily designed or produced to circumvent (1); they have only limited commercially significant purpose or use other than to circumvent (3); they are marketed for use in circumventing (4).[62]

Nonetheless, the prohibition on circumvention of technological measures meets several exceptions[63]. Law enforcement, intelligence and other governmental activities are exempted from the prohibition of circumventing both access and copying technological measures. Other exemptions are provided in respect with the category of technological measures that control access to works, such as exceptions for: nonprofit libraries, archives and educational institutions (1), reserve engineering (2), encryption research (3), protection of minors (4), personal privacy (5), security testing (6). In comparison with the European draft Directive on Copyright, the DMCA expressly codifies these several exceptions into the Copyright Law, instead of only considering their lawfulness in the Recital. The European way doesn't not follow a "copyright-based" approach to the issues of electronic communications, since most of them are horizontal issues in the sense that they do not affect only the interests of copyright owners. Nevertheless, the DMCA has the advantage of removing doubts as to the lawfulness of several activities on circumvention of technological

---

[62] There's however a "no mandate" general rule, according to which the prohibition on circumvention devices does not require manufacturers of consumer electronics, telecommunications or computer equipment to design their products to respond to any particular technological measure. Moreover, two general saving clauses are provided according to which the new prohibitions do not affect rights, remedies, limitations or defenses to copyright infringement, including fair use, nor enlarge or diminish vicarious or contributory copyright infringement.

[63] See DMCA, Sec. 1201(a)(d)(f)(g)(h)(i)(j).

protection measures, although it is not clear whether the fair use clause of the Copyright Act still continues to apply to the "access right".

3. Integrity of Copyright Management Information

The distribution of works, in special on networks, has been facilitated by digital technologies. Consequently, in order to render easier the management of rights attached to them, rightholders need to better identify the work or other subject matter, the author or any other rightholder, and to provide information about the terms and conditions of use of the work or other subject matter. However, illegal activities may be carried out in order to remove or alter the electronic copyright-management information attached to it ("digital watermarking"), or otherwise to distribute, import for distribution, broadcast, communicate to the public or make available to the public copies from which such information has been removed without authorization.

In view of this, the European draft Directive on Copyright aims to provide for harmonized legal protection against any of those activities. Article 7 imposes obligations concerning rights-management information[64]. First, they shall provide for adequate legal protection against any person performing without authorization any of the following acts: the removal or alteration of any electronic rights-management information (1); the distribution, importation for distribution, broadcasting, communication or making available to the public, of copies of works or other subject matter protected under this Directive or

[64] "Rights-management information" is defined as any information provided by rightholders which identifies the work or other subject matter referred to in the Directive or covered by the *sui generis* right provided for in Chapter III of Directive on Databases Protection, the author or any other rightholder, or information about the terms and conditions of use of the work or other subject matter, and any numbers or codes that represent such information.

under Chapter III of Directive on Databases from which electronic rights-management information has been removed or altered without authorization (2), if such person knows, or has reasonable grounds to know, that by so doing he is inducing, enabling or facilitating an infringement of any copyright or any rights related to copyright as provided by law, or of the *sui generis* right provided for in Chapter III of Directive on Database Protection[65].

It should be noted that one of the conditions is that the information has been removed or altered without authorization. Without authorization means, for example, that the provision does not cover the removal or alteration of rights-management information done with the permission of the rightholder (or his intermediary) or permitted or even required by law, such as for data protection reasons according to the Directive on Data Protection[66]. In particular, the Directive Proposal on Copyright considers that these technical means, in their technical functions, should incorporate privacy safeguards in accordance with Directive on Personal Data.

This last aspect is of greater importance. In fact, any such "rights-management information systems" referred to above may, depending on their design, at the same time process personal data about the consumption patterns of protected subject matter by individuals and allow for tracing of on-line behavior . Actually, in the world of digital technology and global networks, users often leave behind long-lasting "electronic footprints", that is, digital records of where they have been, what they

[65] In fact, the forbidden activity, in order to benefit from protection, shall lead to, or be preparatory to, an infringement of an intellectual property right provided by law, since the provision does not cover complementary activities such as the fraudulent communication of rights-management information to a public authority.

[66] Directive 95/46/EC of the European Parliament and of the Council of 24 October 1995 on the protection of individuals with regard to the processing of personal data and the free movement of such data (OJ L 281, 23.11.1995, p. 31). See also Directive 97/66/EC of the European Parliament and of the Council of 15 December 1997 concerning the processing of personal data and the protection of privacy in the telecommunications sector (OJ L 24, 30.1.1998, p. 1).

spent time looking at, the thoughts they aired, the messages they sent, and the goods and services they purchased. These data tend to be detailed, individualized and computer-processable, especially the so-called "cookies", which are small data packets created by a Website server and stored on the user's hard drive.

In the U.S., the obligation to protect the integrity of copyright management information (CMI) is implemented in section 1202. CMI is defined as identifying information about the work, the author, the copyright owner, and in certain cases, the performer, writer or director of the work, as well as the terms and conditions for use of the work. Information concerning users of works is explicitly excluded.

On one hand, regarding false CMI: the knowing provision or distribution of false CMI is prohibited, if done with the intent to induce, enable, facilitate or conceal infringement. On the other hand, as for the removal or alteration of CMI: the intentional removal or alteration of CMI without authority, as well as the dissemination of CMI or copies of works, knowing that the CMI has been removed or altered without authorization, is prohibited.[67]

III. Liability of Online Service Providers

1. The Right of Reproduction and The "Three Step Test"

The European Directive on electronic commerce[68] deals with one of the most important copyright issues of electronic commerce:

[67] Limitations on the liability of broadcast stations and cable systems for removal or alteration of CMI are provided in certain circumstances where there is no intent to induce, enable, facilitate or conceal an infringement.

[68] Directive 2000/31/EC of the European Parliament and of the Council of June 2000 on certain legal aspects of information society services, in particular

the liability of online service providers when engaging in certain activities, notably "mere conduit", "system caching" and "hosting". In the U.S., title II of the DMCA[69] creates limitations on the liability of online service providers for copyright infringement based on the following categories of acts: 1. transitory communications ("mere conduit"); 2. system caching; 3. storage of information on systems or networks at direction of users ("hosting"); 4. information location tools ("browsing", "linking"). The issue on liability of online service providers[70] is related to the definition of the scope of the reproduction right. The Diplomatic Conference that led to the adoption of the new WIPO Treaties could not answer this issue.

At the European level, the draft Directive on Copyright provides the exclusive right to authorize or prohibit direct or indirect, temporary or permanent reproduction by any means and in any form, in whole or in part; at the same time, however, it makes clear that access and service providers would be exempted from reproduction rights for certain incidental temporary "caching" copies arising during transmission over the Internet. It means that, despite the broad definition of the right of reproduction, those copies which are of a mere technical nature (1), are an integral part of another act (2), and have no separate economic significance (3), are excluded from the reproduction right, and therefore do not require authorization of the rightholder. Nonetheless, according to the WIPO Treaties, the Directive Proposal on Copyright applies the "three step test" to this exception to the reproduction right.

---

electronic commerce, in the Internal market ("Directive on electronic commerce"), OJ L 178, 17.07.2000.

[69] The Online Copyright Infringement Liability Limitation Act.

[70] On this issue, see, *inter alia*, Koch, CR 1997, p. 193; Strowel, A&M 1998, p. 296; Julia-Barcelo, EIPR 1998, p. 453; Nathenson, JOLT 1998, p. 60; for a comparison of the EU draft directive on electronic commerce and the US DMCA, see also, in particular, R. Julià-Barceló, *On-Line Intermediary Liability Issues: Comparing EU and U.S. Legal Frame-works*, ECLIP EP 27028 16 December 1999 1.

The question as to whether the scope of the reproduction right should be adapted or clarified to explicitly cover electronic reproductions was subject of discussions in the course of the negotiations which took place in the framework of WIPO and which led to the adoption of the new WIPO treaties.

Regarding the definition of what constitutes an act of reproduction, particularly concerning temporary or incidental reproductions in the electronic environment, no new provisions were considered necessary for authors' right, because the concept of this right is not limited by reference to particular technologies or formats of creation. The definition contained in Article 9(1) of the Bern Convention[71] was considered equally valid in the digital environment and was incorporated accordingly into the WIPO obligations[72].

In this sense, a statement adopted by the Diplomatic Conference, which adopted the new WIPO Treaties clarifies that the existing international rules are sufficiently wide to cover reproductions made in the digital environment[73]. According to this statement, "the reproduction right as set out in Article 9 of the Bern Convention, and the exceptions permitted thereunder, fully apply in the digital environment, in particular to the use of works in digital form. It is understood that the storage of a protected work in digital form in an electronic medium constitutes a reproduction within the meaning of Article 9 of the Bern Convention."

---

[71] Art. 9(1) Bern Convention provides that "authors of literary and artistic works protected by this Convention shall have the exclusive right of authorizing the reproduction of these works in any manner or form".

[72] See Article 1(4) WCT. The broad definition of Article 9(1) Bern Convention has also been used for the definition of the reproduction right of performers and phonogram producers (Articles 7 and 11 WPPT), in more precise terms than the wording of the respective provisions in the Rome Convention and the WTO/TRIPs Agreement.

[73] See Agreed Statements to the WCT concerning Article 1(4), and to the WPPT concerning Articles 7, 11 and 16.

Regarding limitations of and exceptions to the rights, both the new WIPO Treaties refrain from listing particular exceptions. They, however, make the “three step test” of Article 9(2) Bern Convention applicable to all exceptions concerning authors’ rights granted by the Treaty[74]. It was understood that these provisions permit Contracting Parties to carry forward into, and to devise new exceptions and limitations that are appropriate in the digital environment, provided that these comply with the standards set out in the Bern Convention[75]. According to the “three steps test”, limitations to the reproduction right are allowed in “certain special cases” (1), which do not “conflict with a normal exploitation of the work” (2) and do not “unreasonably prejudice the legitimate interests of the author” (3).

This result differs from the Basic Proposal[76], according to which, it would be a matter for legislation in Contracting Parties subject to the “three step test” to limit the right of reproduction in cases where a temporary reproduction has the sole purpose of making the work perceptible or where the reproduction is of a transient or incidental nature, provided that such reproduction takes place in the course of use of the work that is authorized by the author or permitted by law. According to this proposal, the “three step test” could not allow limitations to the reproductions right for incidental, technical, and in some cases technically indispensable instances of reproduction which form part of another use of a protected work, if that use was not authorized or otherwise lawful. If this proposal were to be adopted, public access to the WWW would be reduced since on-line intermediaries would be held liable for any use not authorized

[74] See Article 10 WCT, and *mutatis mutandis* Article 16 WPPT.

[75] See Agreed Statements to the WCT concerning Article 10.

[76] Article 7(2) (Scope of the Right of Reproduction, Limitations) of the Basic Proposal for the Substantive Provisions of the Treaty on Certain Questions Concerning The Protection of Literary and Artistic Works To Be Considered By the Diplomatic Conference.

by recipients of their services. First, online intermediaries would be obliged to monitor the material flowing through their systems. Second, this would increase the costs of operating online services due to investments in monitoring technologies and insurance. Third, these costs would be supported by their users, who at the same time would have their privacy invaded.

For these reasons, supported by intensive lobbying, liability of on-line service providers is not included in the provisions of the WIPO Treaties, and service and access providers have confirmed their support for the WIPO Treaties in their present form, i. e., without any provision on liability. Despite the proposal, it was common view during the Conference that these Treaties do not alter the existing national regimes on liability and that the issue should be left to the national or domestic legislator.

2. The European Legal Framework and the U.S. DMCA

At the European level, neither the existing E.U. copyright Directives nor the draft Directive on Copyright include provisions concerning liability of online service providers. It is viewed as a horizontal issue concerning not only copyright but also issues as defamation, privacy, unfair competition, trademarks, misleading advertising, pornography and racist and violent content.

It is considered that this problem would be addressed horizontally in Directive on Electronic Commerce[77] and that these provisions

[77] See also the initial and the amended Proposals: COM(1998)586 final of 18.11.1998; COM(99) 427 final. The European horizontal approach differs from the U.S., where copyright issues are dealt by the DMCA and other issues are dealt by the Communications Decency Act of 1996 (CDA), which gave providers of Internet services immunity against liability claims derived from defamatory material placed in or disseminated by their facilities. See *Blumenthal v. Drudge*, 992 F.Supp. 44 (D.D.C. 1998).

relating to liability in the context of electronic commerce should come into force within a time scale similar to that of the Directive on Copyright, since they should provide a harmonized framework of principles and provisions relevant to *inter alia* important parts of this Directive[78]. Nevertheless, the provisions of the draft Directive on Copyright make clear that access and service providers would be exempted from reproduction rights for certain incidental temporary "caching" copies arising during transmission over the Internet because they have no separate economic significance.

On one hand, the draft Directive on Copyright provides the exclusive right to authorize or prohibit direct or indirect, temporary or permanent reproduction by any means and in any form, in whole or in part (Art. 2). This provision sets out a broad, comprehensive definition of the reproduction right covering all relevant acts of reproduction, and follows the approach of the *acquis communautaire* for computer programs[79] and electronic databases[80]. In fact, the scope of the acts covered by the reproduction right are defined with regard to the different beneficiaries in conformity with the *acquis communautaire*, and a broad definition of these acts is considered to be needed to ensure legal certainty within the Internal Market.

But, on the other hand, temporary acts of reproduction are exempted from the reproduction right, such as transient and incidental acts of reproduction which are an integral and essential part of a technological process, including those which facilitate effective functioning of transmission systems, whose sole purpose is to enable use to be made of a work or other subject matter, and which have no independent economic significance (Art. 5, 1).

---

[78] Directive Proposal on Copyright, Recital 12.

[79] Article 4 of Council Directive 91/250/ECC on the legal protection of computer programs (OJ L 122, 17.5.1991, p. 42).

[80] Article 5 of the European Parliament and Council Directive 96/9/EC on the legal protection of databases (OJ L 77, 27.3.1996, p. 20).

It means that, despite the broad definition of the right of reproduction, those copies which are of a mere technical nature (1), are an integral part of another act (2), and have no separate economic significance (3), are excluded from the reproduction right, and therefore do not require authorization of the rightholder. Nonetheless, in accordance with the WIPO Treaties, the Directive Proposal on Copyright stipulates the "three step test" be applied to this exception to the reproduction right, albeit limited to certain specific cases and it shall not be interpreted in such a way as to allow their application to be used in a manner which unreasonably prejudices the right holders' legitimate interests or conflicts with the normal exploitation of their works or other subject matter (Art. 5.°, 4).

The question then is which "certain specific cases" would pass the "three step test". For example, certain forms of "browsing" or "caching" may not be subject to the control of the rightholder.

The Directive Proposal on Copyright provides that the exclusive right of reproduction should be subject to an exception to allow certain acts of temporary reproduction, such as transient and incidental reproductions, forming an integral part of, and essential to, a technological process carried out for the sole purpose of enabling the use of a work or other protected subject matter and which have no separate economic value on their own. And Recital 23 clarifies that under these conditions this exception should include acts of caching or browsing[81]. Therefore, according to the Copyright Proposal, despite the broad definition of the right of reproduction, copies which are of a mere technical nature, are an integral part of another act, and have no separate economic significance, are excluded from the reproduction right, and therefore do not require authorization of the rightholder, insofar as

---

[81] See Recital 23.

they pass the "three step test". Acts of caching and browsing are considered to pass this test.[82]

These principles are implemented in the Directive on Electronic Commerce. This Directive provides in detail the "certain specific cases" which pass the "three step test" and therefore are exempted from the right of reproduction. Three groups of "certain specific cases" are provided: "mere conduit", "caching", and "hosting". Another group of cases, "browsing", is referred for further study in what concerns liability of providers of hyperlinks and location tool services, although it is considered in the Copyright Proposal as a case capable of passing the "three step test". In any case, this test will not be passed by providers of information society services, such as on-line travel agencies or on-line bookstores. If they post infringing copyright material on their Websites, they are to be regarded as content providers, to whom no limitation is provided in terms either of the right of reproduction or the right of communication to the public.[83].

---

[82] Moreover, regarding the right of communication to the public, Article 3(4) also provides that the mere provision of physical facilities for enabling or making a communication does not in itself amount to an act of communication to the public, according to the Agreed Statement adopted by the Diplomatic Conference concerning Article 8 WCT.

[83] The WIPO Treaties define the right of communication to the public as the exclusive right of authorizing any communication to the public of their works, by wire or wireless means, including the making available to the public of their works in such a way that members of the public may access these works from a place and at a time individually chosen by them. See Article 8 WCT. See also Articles 10 and 14 WPPT. These "on-demand transmissions" are characterized by the fact that a work or other subject matter stored in digital format is made available to third parties interactively, i.e. in such a way that they may access it and request its transmission individually regarding time and place. Economically, the interactive on-demand transmission is a new form of exploitation of intellectual property, and, in the end, it was generally accepted, in legal terms, that the distribution right only applies to the distribution of physical copies and does not cover the act of transmission. See Agreed Statements adopted by the Diplomatic Conference concerning Articles 6 and 7 WCT and Articles 2(e), 8, 9 and 13 WPPT.

The classification of on-demand digital transmissions within the right of communication to the public has been proposed by the European Commission [see *Following of the Green Paper*, COM(96) 586 final, p. 12-4], having in regard that

In comparison, in the U.S., the DMCA creates four new limitations on liability for copyright infringement by online service providers, based on four categories of conduct by a service provider: transitory communications ("mere conduit") (1); system caching (2); hosting (3); information location tools (4). We will analyze each of these categories of conduct as they are provided for in Directive on Electronic Commerce as well as in the U.S. DMCA.

3. "Mere Conduit" (Transitory Communications: Carriers and Access Providers)

Cases of "mere conduit" include two different situations[84]. First, the transmission in a communication network of information provided by the recipient of the service. In this situation, ISS providers act as *carriers* of information in communication networks transmitting information provided by third parties[85]. Second, the provision of access to a communication network, such as the Internet. In this situation, ISS providers act as *access providers*.

In these two situations of mere conduit the ISS provider's liability is excluded on condition that he: does not initiate the transmission (1); does not select the receiver of the transmission (2); and does not select or modify the information contained in the transmission (3). For example, where an end user requests to forward an e-mail

Directive on Databases Protection covers on-demand transmission of the content of a database because it protects any form of making available to the public all or a substantial part of the contents of the database by on-line or other forms of transmission under the *sui generis* rights (Article 2(2)(b)). However, the initial approach was to include on-demand transmission within the right of distribution (See *Green Paper*, COM(95)382 final, p. 59; NII White Paper, p. 213).

[84] See Directive on Electronic Commerce, Article 12.

[85] This is usually carried out by telecommunications operators and consists of providing facilities for the transmission of data such as cables, routers and switches.

to a mailing list, and the provider transmits the message to each one of the addresses contained in the mailing list, the provider will not be considered to have initiated the transmission or selected the recipient.

Moreover, those acts of "mere conduit" (transmission and provision of access) include the automatic, intermediate and transient storage of the information transmitted in so far as this takes place for the sole purpose of carrying out the transmission in the communication network, and provided that the information is not stored for any period longer than is reasonably necessary for the transmission. This rules applies to the so-called process of "packet switching transmission", during which acts of reproduction technically take place countless times in the course of routing and transmission to the end user.

In the U.S., the DMCA also provides a limitation for transitory communication[86], which covers not only acts of transmission, routing, or providing connections for the information, but also the intermediate and transient copies that are made automatically in the operation of a network. This limitation for transitory communication limits the liability of service providers in circumstances where the provider merely acts as a data conduit, transmitting digital information from one point on a network to another at someone else's request.

In detail, those circumstances are: the transmission must be initiated by a person other than the provider (1); the transmission, routing, provision of connections, or copying must be carried out by an automatic technical process without selection of material by the service provider (2); the service provider must not determine the recipients of the material (3); any intermediate copies must neither ordinarily be accessible to anyone other than anticipated recipients nor be retained for longer than reasonably necessary (4).

---

[86] See DMCA, Sec. 512(a).

4. "System Caching"

Cases of "caching" are those where an IIS consists in the transmission in a communication network of information provided by a recipient of the service, with the automatic, intermediate and temporary storage of that information being performed for the sole purpose of making more efficient the information's onward transmission to other recipients of the service upon their request.

In this group of cases, the service provider (in particular, the local server) retains the material so that subsequent requests for the same material can be fulfilled by transmitting the retained copy, rather than retrieving the material from the original source on the network. In other words, caching consists of storing to a local server copies of high demand material that originates on remote servers, so that when an end-user requires certain material, it is transmitted from the local server rather than from the source computer, and therefore data has less distance and time to travel. It means that caching allows a quicker and more efficient use of the Internet, because it reduces the service provider's bandwidth requirements and reduces the waiting time on subsequent requests for the same information.

Despite this benefit, caching can result in the delivery of outdated information to subscribers and can deprive website operators of accurate "hit" information (information about the number of requests for particular material on a website) from which advertising revenue is frequently calculated. For this reason, the person making the material available online may establish rules about updating it, and may utilize technological means to track the number of "hits".

In view of this, the Directive on Electronic Commerce provides a "caching" liability limitation[87] on condition that: the provider does not modify the information (1); the provider complies with

[87] See Directive on Electronic Commerce, Article 13.

conditions on access to the information (2); the provider complies with rules regarding the updating of the information, specified in a manner consistent with industrial standards (3); the provider does not interfere with the technology, consistent with industrial standards, used to obtain data on the use of the information (4); and the provider acts expeditiously to remove or to bar access to the information (5) upon obtaining actual knowledge of the fact that: the information at the initial source of the transmission has been removed from the network (5.1); access to it has been disabled (5.2); a court or an administrative authority has ordered such removal or disablement (5.3).

In the U.S., the DMCA establishes a limitation for system caching[88], which applies to acts of intermediate and temporary storage, when carried out through an automatic technical process for the purpose of making the material available to subscribers who subsequently request it, provided that: the content of the retained material is not modified (1); the provider complies with rules about "refreshing" material (replacing copies of material with material from the original location) when specified in accordance with a generally accepted industry standard data communication protocol (2); the provider does not interfere with technology that returns "hit" information to the person who posted the material, where such technology meets certain requirements (3); the provider limits users' access to the material in accordance with conditions on access (e.g., password protection) imposed by the person who posted the material (4); any material that was posted without the copyright owner's authorization is removed or blocked promptly once the service provider has been informed that it has been removed, blocked, or ordered to be removed or blocked, at the originating site (5).

[88] See DMCA, Sec. 512(b).

5. "Hosting" (Information Residing on Systems or Networks at the Direction of Users)

Cases of "hosting" are those where an information society service consists in the storage of information provided by a recipient of the service, and the information is stored at the request of a recipient of the service. In this group of cases, the server provider rents space to users for their content upon the server (e.g., a Web page), which may include different materials (software, text, graphics, sound). In short, hosting has to do with infringing material on websites (or other information repositories) hosted on the service providers' systems.

The Directive on Electronic Commerce provides this "hosting limitation"[89] to ISS providers on condition that: the provider does not have actual knowledge that the activity is illegal and, as regards claims for damages, is not aware of facts or circumstances from which illegal activity is apparent (1); the provider, upon obtaining such knowledge or awareness, acts expeditiously to remove or to disable access to the information (2).[90]

In the U.S., the DMCA establishes a limitation for information residing on systems or networks at the direction of users[91]. This limitation is provided if the ISP: does not have a requisite of knowledge[92] (1); does not receive a financial benefit directly attributable to the infringing activity, and has the right and ability to control it (2); takes down or blocks access to the material expeditiously, upon receiving proper notification of proper infringement (3).

---

[89] See Directive on Electronic Commerce, Article 14.

[90] These hosting cases will fall outside de three step rule when the recipient of the service is acting under the authority or the control of the provider (Art. 14.°, par. 2).

[91] See DMCA, Sec. 512(c).

[92] The knowledge standard means that he does not have actual knowledge of the infringement (1), is not aware of facts or circumstances from which infringing activity is apparent (2), or upon gaining such knowledge or awareness, responds expeditiously to take the material down or block access to it (3).

Regarding this last condition, a service provider must have filed with the Copyright Office a designation of an agent to receive notifications of claimed infringement, and a detailed "notice and takedown procedure" is provided[93].

6. No Monitor Obligation and The Knowledge Standard

In any group of cases ("mere conduit", "caching", "hosting"), the Directive on Electronic Commerce imposes no general obligation on providers to monitor the information which they transmit or store, nor a general obligation actively to seek facts or circumstances indicating illegal activity.[94]

However, this no general obligation to monitor does not affect the possibility for Member States to require service providers, who host information provided by recipients of their service, to apply duties of care, which can reasonably be expected from them and which are specified by national law, in order to detect and prevent certain types of illegal activities. Moreover, Member States may establish obligations for information society services providers promptly to inform the competent public authorities of alleged illegal activities or information undertaken by recipients of their service or obligations to communicate to the competent authorities, at their request, information enabling the identification of recipients of their service with whom they have storage agreements.[95]

Then, the Directive on Electronic Commerce does not provide a "notice and takedown procedure" similar to the procedure provided

[93] See DMCA, Sec. 512(c)(3) (procedures for proper notification and rules as to its effect)

[94] See Directive on Electronic Commerce, Art. 15, 1.

[95] Directive on Electronic Commerce, Recital 48 and Art. 15, 2.

for, in the US by the DMCA[96]. It doesn't say, for example, what is the effect regarding the subscriber of removing material or disabling access to it after receiving notice that it is infringing.

Without an obligation to monitor and a notice and takedown procedure how are online service providers going to be considered to have awareness of the facts and circumstances from which the illegal activity is apparent?

The Directive on Electronic Commerce is meant to constitute the appropriate basis for the development of rapid and reliable procedures for removing and disabling access to illegal information. However, the Directive considers that such mechanisms are to be developed on the basis of voluntary agreements between all concerned parties, since it is considered to be in the interest of all parties involved in the provision of information society services to adopt and implement such procedures[97]. Nevertheless, the attribution of liability following the taking down of content is one of the aspects the Commission shall re-examine in its report[98].

Moreover, the Proposal was also not meant to preclude the development and effective operation, by the different interested parties, of technical systems of protection and identification and of technical surveillance ("cookies") instruments made possible by digital technology within the limits laid down by Directives 95/46/EC and 97/66/EC[99]. However, technical screening devices, such as

---

[96] See DMCA, Sec. 512.

[97] See Directive on Electronic Commerce, Recital 49.

[98] Article 21, 2, of the Directive on Electronic Commerce states: "In examining the need for an adaptation of this Directive, the report shall in particular analyze the need for proposals concerning the liability of providers of hyperlinks and location tools services, "notice and take down" procedures and the attribution of liability following the taking down of content."

[99] Confidentiality of electronic messages is guaranteed by Article 5 of Directive 97/66/EC. According to that Directive, Member States must prohibit any kind of interception or surveillance of such electronic messages by others than the senders

filtering mechanisms, have not shown to work properly, meaning that not only they may not detect all illicit material and but also they can filter out some legitimate material. But even if they did work properly, it is not certain whether online service providers themselves will use those monitoring systems: online services providers are most likely to obtain the requisite of knowledge through notices from third parties, since software manufacturers and other copyright owners, such as phonogram producers, are regularly patrolling the Web to identify sites containing infringing material. Moreover, the implementation of filtering software and rating systems do not provide host service providers with the required level of knowledge since editorial control involves the use of judgment, and no computer program has such capacity[100].

Unlike the DMCA, the Directive on Electronic Commerce does not clarify what constitutes an adequate notice to provide the host intermediary with the required level of knowledge, and it does not address the scope of liability that host service providers will face as a result of removing material incorrectly believed to be illegal.

In the U.S., the DMCA establishes a procedure for notification of the existence of illegal material. In particular, it requires that copyright owners who notify an on-line intermediary of allegedly infringing material include a list of specified elements that, *inter alia*, will permit the on-line intermediary to identify the material. If the notification rules are complied with, the on-line intermediary will be regarded as having the required level of knowledge. If, upon receiving proper notification, the host provider removes or blocks access to the identified material, then the provider will benefit from

---

and receivers and abstain from prohibiting or restricting the use of cryptographic methods or tools for protecting confidentiality or ensuring authenticity of the information transmitted or stored.

[100] See *Lunney v. Prodigy Services Company* (1998 N.Y. App.). See also, however, *Stratton Oakmont v. Prodigy*, 1995 (N.Y. Misc. Lexis, 229, N.Y. Sup. Ct Nassau, 1995).

the liability limitation provided the host provider has notified the owner of the site access to which has been blocked. In addition, the person who misrepresents that material as infringing will be liable for damages incurred by a host service provider or a user as a result of the information's having been removed or access disabled.[101]

Instead of establishing a statutory "notice and take-down" procedure like the DMCA, the Directive on Electronic Commerce only includes an obligation to re-study the need for legislation on "notice and take-down" procedures within three years after adoption of the Directive, and relies upon and promotes self-regulation and private solutions for notice and take-down. The result of this legal uncertainty could be that, to avoid liability, European service providers would take down material upon receipt of almost any type of notice, and they would include provisions in their users' agreements permitting them to remove material at their discretion. In view of this legal uncertainty, it's arguable that freedom of expression and fair competition on the Web might be compromised.

However, the Directive on Electronic Commerce[102] provides that mere conduit, caching and hosting limitations do not affect the possibility for a court or administrative authority, in accordance with Member States' legal systems, to require the service provider to terminate or prevent an infringement[103]. Regarding hosting activities it goes further to leave the possibility for Member States to establish procedures governing the removal or disabling of access to information[104].

It seems that those orders from courts or administrative authorities will fulfill the knowledge standard regarding the service provider.

---

[101] See DMCA, Sec. 512(c)(3)/(g)(1)/(f).

[102] Directive 2000/31/EC of the European Parliament and of the Council of June 2000 on certain legal aspects of information society services, in particular electronic commerce, in the Internal market ("Directive on electronic commerce") (OJ L 178, 17.07.2000).

[103] See Directive on electronic commerce, Article 12, 3, and Article 13, 2.

[104] See Directive on electronic commerce, Art. 14, 3.

After notification from these authorities the intermediary will be regarded as having the required level of knowledge. Moreover, upon receiving that notification, if the host provider removes or blocks access to the identified material, then he should benefit from the liability limitation provided the host provider has notified the owner of the site to which access has been blocked.

7. Information Location Tools (Browsing, Crawling, Linking)

1. The Directive on Electronic Commerce does not address the search engine function carried out by information location tool providers, which allow information to be easily located and accessed by Internet users. It means that, if an on-line intermediary provided both access and hosting services, he could benefit from the limitations of liability for "mere conduits" and for "hosting"; however, if he provided also a search engine he would not be able to benefit from any liability limitation provided by Directive on Electronic Commerce, which does not exempt any activity involving selection, modification or creation of material by the ISS provider itself.

Information location tools, such as "crawlers" and other search engines, identify and index Web sites according to "meta tags" contained in the respective HTML or XML documents, and display a list of links to Web sites where the request information is located. Examples of famous search engines are Euroseek, Lycos, Altavista, Yahoo. Despite its important role in the Internet, providing links to Web sites may raise some legal questions.

To begin with, crawlers may link to Web sites with copyright infringing content and the ILT provider may know about that[105]. In

---

[105] See, for example, *Church of Scientology v. several Internet Providers,* the District Court of the Hague, 9 June 1999 (the Court found that knowingly giving

the U.S., the DMCA provides an answer to this question. Section 512 (d), relating to hyperlinks, online directories and search engines, limits liability for the acts of referring or linking users to a site that contains infringing material by using such information tools, if the provider does not have actual knowledge that the material is infringing or, in the absence of such actual knowledge, is not aware of facts or circumstances from which the infringing activity is apparent (1); or upon gaining such knowledge or awareness, acts expeditiously to take the material down or block access to it (2); does not receive a financial benefit directly attributable to the infringing activity, in a case where the service provider has the right and ability to control such activity (3); and upon proper notification of claimed infringement responds expeditiously to remove, or disable access (4).[106]

In Europe, the Directive on Electronic Commerce doesn't answer the question of linking to infringing sites. Nevertheless, it is provided a "re-examination procedure", under which the Commission will have three years following adoption of the Directive to re-evaluate the importance of addressing the scope of liability of information location tool providers and hyperlink providers[107]. This is a delicate question, because it implies a compromise between different legal traditions of Member States[108]. In *droit d'auteur* countries the ques-

access to or hosting links that upon activation by an end-user displayed Church of Scientology's copyright material is a copyright infringement).

[106] See DMCA, Section 512 (d).

[107] Directive on electronic commerce, Article 21 (Re-examination) states: 1. Not later than three years after the adoption of this Directive, and thereafter every two years, the Commission shall submit to the European Parliament, the Council and the Economic and Social Committee a report on the application of this Directive, accompanied, where necessary, by proposals for adapting it to developments in the field of Information Society services (...). 2. In examining the need for an adaptation of this Directive, the report shall in particular analyze the need for proposals concerning the liability of providers of hyperlinks and location tool services, notice and take down procedures and the attribution of liability following the taking down of content. (...).

[108] See Ellins, *Copyright Law, Urheberrecht und ihre Harmonisierung in der Europaïschen Gemeinschaft*, Berlin, 1997.

tion could be solved as a matter of unfair competition, while in the United Kingdom, the CPDA 1988 would provide a basis to impose liability for linking to infringing material: the secondary infringement, which requires knowledge. So, if the Directive were to establish rules similar to the DMCA, it would probably enlarge the copyright notion of secondary infringement to *droit d'auteur* countries.

On the other hand, it could be argued that there would be infringement of any of the rights of the copyright owner of a Web site where an information location tool provider provides a link to that site without the site owner's permission[109]. However, the mere provision of links to another Web site should not be deemed copyright infringement. Linking interactive documents is the very heart of the new interactive media, notably the Internet, and mere linking means that the information location tool provider is simply pointing the user at that Web site by providing the means by which the browser can make his own copy. Temporary copies made by the Internet user when browsing the Web (RAM copies) are excluded from the scope of the reproduction right. In other words, browsing the Web falls outside the right of reproduction, since it only makes copies which are of a mere technical nature (1), are an integral part of another act (2), and have no separate economic significance (3): acts of caching and browsing pass the "three step test"[110].

However, there are certain linking techniques of interactive documents, such as linking to an internal part of a Web page ("deep-linking") or merging the content of a linked site to the Web site of another ("in-linking"), which might be considered infringing. In fact, these techniques may cause the owner of the linked site

[109] See *Washington Post v. Total News* case [No. 97 Civ. 1190 (S.D.N.Y. 1997) (the defendant provided several links to the plaintiff's news sites, and, once activated, the links incorporated the content of the second site into frames of the primary site, instead of sending the browser to the linked sites).

[110] See Directive Proposal on Copyright, Art. 5, 1, and Recital 23.

to lose revenue from advertising posted on its homepage and are capable of creating confusion as to the identity of the site owner[111]. Nonetheless, these are not strict problems of copyright law. The same applies, *mutatis mutandis*, to "pagejacking" and "mouse-trapping"[112].

Conclusion

In this paper we have addressed two major copyright issues of electronic commerce within the construction of the legal framework for the information society and its digital economy.

First, we he have addressed the issue on circumvention of technological measures used by copyright owners to protect their works, as well as on tampering with copyright management information. Second, we have addressed the issue on the liability of online service providers for copyright infringement when engaging in certain activities, such as: 1. transitory communications ("mere conduit"); 2. system caching; 3. storage of information on systems or networks at direction of users ("hosting"); 4. information location tools ("browsing", "crawling", and "linking").

The main legal sources which this paper was based upon are the new WIPO Treaties (Dec. 1996), the European Directive Proposal (as amended) on Copyright in the Information Society [COM(99) 250 final], the European Directive on Electronic Commerce (2000/31/CE), and the U.S. Digital Millennium Copyright Act (Oct. 1998). Moreover, the European Directives on Computer Programs (91/250/CEE), Databases Protection (96/9/CE), and Encrypted Services

[111] See *TicketMaster, Inc v. Microsoft Corp* , Civ. 3055 (C.D. CAL.); *Shetland Times Limited v. Shetland's News.*

[112] See *Federal Trade Commission v. Pereira*, U.S. District Court of Eastern Virginia, 20 September 1999.

(98/84/CE), as well as important case law of the European Union's Member States and the U.S. have also been considered.

With the analisis of those copyright issues of electronic commerce we aimed to explain how copyright has been adapted to the new technological paradigm. In other words, this paper essayed to study some solutions already provided by the process of adaptation of copyright to the digital computer and network technologies, in particular the Internet. As the title of this paper suggests, copyright has been transformed by legal metamorphosis into a sort of technodigital property for cyberspace. Furthermore, in this adaptation process and in the absence of Community harmonization of unfair competition, we have identified a tendency according to which author's rights system of Civil Law countries are importing legal categories from the copyright concept of Common Law countries.

Finally, it seems that copyright law will play a major role in the construction of the information society and in the improvement of electronic commerce. Instead of being replaced by the rule of technology and cyber-ethics in the brave new world of intelligent electronic agents, copyright has been called to put an end to the "electronic woodstock" and "anarchy online", establishing a legal form of property rights in Digitalia. However, at the same time, the adaptation of copyright to the digital environment shows that copyright law is being used as a *leit-motiv* to grant protection to the investment of producers in the digital economy. In other words, copyright law, at least in the sense of European *droit d'auteur*, is being "taken-over" by *sui generis* intellectual property rights and technological adjuncts, which can be used to appropriate public domain information and control access to information and the freedom of expression within electronic communications.

EUROPEANA CONNECT - NATIONAL TERM OF PROTECTION RULES (PORTUGAL)*

1. Legal act which governs the term of protection of copyright and related rights

The legal act which governs the term of protection of copyright and related rights is the Code of Author' Right and Related Rights (Código do Direito de Autor e dos Direitos Conexos) - brevis causa, Copyright Act -, Chapter IV (Articles 31 to 39 and Article 183) as amended by Decree-Law 334/97 of 27 November in order to implement Council Directive 93/98/CEE of 29 October (now repealed by EU Directive 2006/116/EC of 12 December 2006). The term of protection for databases is governed by the Database Act enacted by Decree-Law 122/2000 of 4 July which has implemented EU Directive 96/9/EC of 11 March. Hereinafter the Articles referred to belong to the Copyright Act, unless otherwise stated.

The general term of protection is 70 years after the death of the intellectual creator even where the work has only been published *postmortem auctoris* (Art. 31). The term of protection occurs after January 1 of the year following the year in which the term has been completed (Art. 3 of DL 334/97).

---

* Questionnaire on the Implementation of the Term Directive in EU Member States, ed. Lucie Guibault & Christina Angelopoulos, Institute for Information Law (IViR), University of Amsterdam. Date: 24/11/2010.

2. Works of joint authorship, collective works, anonymous and pseudonymous works and works published in parts, instalments, issues or episodes

In relation to works of joint authorship the term is 70 years after the death of the author who dies in the last place (Art. 32(1)). In relation to collective works, the term is 70 years after the first lawful publication or divulgation, unless the human persons who have created the work have been identified in the versions of the work made available to the public (Art. 32(2)). The term of copyright concerning individual and separable contributions to the collective work is the general term, i.e., 70 years after the death of the intellectual creator, even if the work has only been published postmortem (Art. 32(3) and Art. 31). In relation to anonymous and pseudonymous works, the term is 70 years after the publication or divulgation (Art. 33(1)), unless the pseudonymous used leaves no room for doubts concerning the identity of the author or in case he/she reveals it within such term, as the term will correspond to the term of works published or divulgated under his/her own name (Art. 33(2)). Concerning works published in parts, installments, issues or episodes, for each of them the term is separately calculated (Art. 35(1)). This applies also to parts or issues of periodical collective works such as newspapers and publications alike (Art. 35(2)).

3. Distinction made between works of joint authorship, collective works and compilations

Portuguese copyright law distinguishes works of joint authorship (*obras em colaboração*) from collective works (*obras colectivas*). Compilations can be works equivalent to original works (Art. 3) and/or composite works (*obra compósita*).

Works of joint authorship are defined as those which are a creation of a plurality of persons and are divulgated or published under the name of them or some of them, whether or not the individual contributions can be discriminated (Art. 16(1)(a)). So, joint authorship does not presuppose that the contributions of several authors are inseparable and each author may individually exercise the rights corresponding to his/her personal contribution, when it can be discriminated and without prejudice to the joint exploitation of the work of joint authorship (Art. 18(2)). The same applies, mutatis mutandis, to collective works (Art. 19(2)).

Collective works are defined as those which are a creation of a plurality of persons when it is organized by the initiative of a human or legal person and published under his/her/its own name (Art. 16(1)(b)). Compilations as composite works are those which incorporate, in whole or in part, a preexisting work with the authorization but without the collaboration of its author (Art. 20).

4. Co-written musical works as works of joint authorship or multiple separate works?

Co-written musical works, as such, are considered to be, in principle, works of joint authorship. Several works are legally deemed to be works of joint authorship such as broadcasted works (Art. 21), cinematographic works (Art. 22) as well as phonographic and video works (Art. 24). Journals and other periodical publications are legally deemed to be collective works (Art. 19(3)), as well as computer programs and databases created within an enterprise (Decree-Law 252/94 of 20 October, Art. 3(2), and Decree-Law 122/2000 of 4 July, Art. 5(2)). Compilations include namely dictionaries, encyclopedias and anthologies (Art. 3(1)(b)(c)) which are also considered collective works.

5. Legal person as the original author of a work of copyright?

Portuguese copyright law belongs to the family of *droit d'auteur*. Article 29(1) of the Copyright Act apparently implies that a legal person can be the original author of a work. Moreover, some provisions seem to imply an original assignment of the copyright to legal persons, such as Art. 32(2), Art. 36 (computer programs), and Art. 6(2) of DL 122/2000 (databases). Those would be mainly the cases of works made for hire and collective works organized by and published under the name of a legal person. In short, author would be the original owner of copyright according to legal provisions. However, dogmatically, this derogation to the principle of authorship is rather controversial as legal persons are deprived of the capacity of intellectual creation, which is recognized only to human persons. Moreover, despite the dualistic system of Portuguese copyright law (meaning that economic rights can be independently disposed of by act *inter vivos*), it is also controversial whether the original owner of the copyright can be someone else but the creator as, according to well established jurisprudence, the originating fact of copyright is the act of creation itself.

6. Co-authorship of cinematographic or audiovisual works

Together with the director there are other co-authors assigned to cinematographic or audiovisual works namely the author of the script, the author of the dialogues, and the author of the musical composition (Art. 22). Similar co-authors are assigned for specific audiovisual works such as broadcasted and video works (Arts. 21(2) and 24). The term of protection is 70 years after the death of the last surviving person assigned as co-author (Art. 34). There is legal opinion holding that the typical creative input in cinematographic works is provided for by the director and the other persons are legally assigned as co-authors for reasons of convenience.

7. Official documents?

Official documents (e.g. legal texts, court decisions) are not protected by copyright in Portugal (Art. 8(2) and Art. 3(1)(c)).

8. Duration of related rights

Article 3 of the Term Directive on the duration of related rights has been implemented into Article 183 of the Copyright Act by Decree-Law 334/97 of 27 November. According to Article 183(1), the term of protection of related rights is 50 years after: the performance by the interpreting or performing artist (a), the first fixation of phonogram, video or movie by the producer (b), the first emission by the broadcasting organization whether by means of wire or wireless, including cable or satellite (c). However, in case the fixation of the protected performance, phonogram, video or movie are legally published or publicly communicated within such period, the term of protection starts with these facts (Art. 183(2)). By movie it is understood a cinematographic or audiovisual work as well as any sequence of motion pictures (moving images) together or not with sound (Art. 183(3)). Owners of related rights whose country of origin is a non EU country are afforded the term of protection of their country of origin provided it does not exceed the above mentioned term of protection (Art. 183(4) and Art. 37).

9. Previously unpublished works

The term of protection, limited to economic rights, is 25 years after the publication or divulgation of previously unpublished works which have come into the public domain (Art. 39(1)).

10. Critical and scientific publications of works into the public domain

Critical and scientific publications of works which have come into the public domain are protected under Portuguese copyright law for a term of 25 years after lawful publication (Art. 39(2)).

11. Non-original photographs

Non-original photographs are not protected under Portuguese copyright law (Art. 164), and no specific term of protection is provided for original ones.

12. Original and unoriginal databases

The term of protection for original databases is 70 years after the death of its intellectual creator (Art. 6(1) of DL 122/2000). In case protection is originally attributed to other entities (e.g. in case of databases created within an enterprise or made for hire) the term is for 70 years after its first publication or public divulgation (Art. 6(2) of DL 122/2000). The term of protection of the database producers' sui generis right is for 15 years after the conclusion of its production starting on the January 1st of the year following the year of its date of production (Art. 16(1) of DL 122/2000). Non-original databases can have only this term of protection. Each substantial modification to the content of a database which qualifies as a substantial investment gives rise to a term of protection of its own.

13. Different term of protection for other categories of works

Broadcasting, reproducing in phonogram or video, filming or exhibiting of public performances of protected works is subject to authorization also of the promoter of the public show (Art. 117). However, there is no rule on the term of protection for this 'atypical' related right.

14. Relations with third countries. international obligations granting a longer term of protection to non-Community nationals

Works whose country of origin is a foreign non EU country and whose author is not a national of an EU country are afforded the term of protection of the legislation of the country of origin provided it does not exceed the term of protection established by the Copyright Act (Art. 37). Owners of related rights whose country of origin is a non EU country and who are not nationals of an EU country are afforded the term of protection of their country of origin provided it does not exceed the term of protection established by the Copyright Act (Art. 183(4) and Art. 37). No record has been found concerning the acceptance by Portugal, prior to the adoption of the Term Directive, of any international obligations granting a longer term of protection to non- Community nationals than that foreseen by Article 7(1) and (2) of the Term Directive.

15. Moral rights

Moral rights may be considered relatively perpetual as they are enjoyed by the author, regardless and even after the transmission or extinction of the economic rights (Art. 9(3)). Moreover, the 'moral right' is inalienable, has no term of protection and is perpetuated after the death of the author (Art. 56(1)), meaning that while it does not come into the public domain it is exercised by the heirs of the author (Art. 57(1)) and once into the public domain the protection of the integrity of the work is done by the State (Art. 57(2)). According to relevant copyright literature, this means that, once into the public domain, only the right of integrity seems to be perpetual but no longer as an author's right but rather as a right of the State concerning the protection of the country's cultural heritage.

16. Date of amendment of copyright Act and ressuscitation of previously expired rights

In order to implement the Term Directive (93/83/CEE) the Copyright Act has been amended by Decree-Law 334/97 of 27 November. The provisions of this Act became applicable since 1 July 1995 and to any work, performance or production protected on that date in any country of the European Union (Art. 5(1)). No transitional provisions have been introduced. There were cases of resuscitation because the heirs of the author enjoyed the reactivation of rights arising thereof (i.e., provided that protection existed on that date), but without prejudice to the acts of exploitation already practiced and rights acquired by third parties (Art. 5(2)).

17. Relevance of the class of the beneficiary to whom copyright or related rights pass after the death of the rightholder

The term of protection does not vary according to the class of the beneficiary to whom the copyright or related rights pass after the death of the copyright holder, except in what concerns the perpetual 'right of integrity' which is conferred to the State (Art. 57(2)).

18. Domaine Public Payant?

Portuguese copyright law does not provide a *Domaine Public Payant*. There is however discussion whether legislation on access to and reuse of administrative documents as well as on the protection of cultural heritage could provide the foundations of such a regimen.

INTELLIGENCE ARTIFICIELLE ET DROIT D'AUTEUR AU PORTUGAL*

I. Partie introductive

1. Contexte législatif

1. La propriété intellectuelle, y compris les droits d'auteur et la propriété industrielle, est désignée à l'article 1303 du Code civil portugais comme un type spécial de propriété, qui protège le droit général de propriété réglementé par législation spéciale, qui se compose de deux instruments principaux: le code de la propriété industrielle et le code du droit d'auteur et des droits voisins (propriété littéraire et artistique). Les droits de propriété sont donc couverts par l'article 62/1 de la Constitution de la République portugaise, qui protège le droit général à la propriété[1].

Plus directement, le droit d'auteur portugaise est expressément prévue dans la Constitution au deuxième paragraphe de l'article 42,

---

* RRDDIS – *Revista Rede de Direito Digital, Intelectual & Sociedade*, Curitiba, vol. 1/1 (2021), p. 69-100 (relatório elaborado, com a colaboração de PEDRO DE PERDIGÃO LANA para as jornadas internacionais sobre «Inteligência Artificial e Direito» da Associação «HENRI CAPITANT», em Seul, Coreia do Sul).

[1] Les droits moraux sont aussi compris dans le droit constitutionnel au développement de la personnalité, selon article 26, 1 de la CRP. Cf. Cour Constitutionnel, arrêt n. 577/11 du 29/11/2011, rapporteur José Borges Soeiro. Avant, cf. arrêt n. 491/2002 du 26/11/2002.

qui aborde la liberté de création culturelle. La source juridique principale de la propriété littéraire et artistique au Portugal c'est le code du droit d'auteur et des droits voisions (CDA), adoptée par le décret-loi n. 63/85, du 14 marche (mise à jour plusieurs fois). Au dehors du code du droit d'auteur, il-y-a d'autres législations spéciales concernant par ex. la protection juridique des logiciels (décret-loi n. 252/94, du 20 octobre) et des bases de données (décret-loi n. 122/2000, du 4 juillet), la transmission par satellite et la retransmission par cable (décret-loi n. 333/97, du 27 novembre), la compensation pour la copie privée (loi n. 62/98, du 1 septembre, mise à jour plusieurs fois), etc.

La législation portugaise reçoit au droit national des traités internationaux, comme la Convention de Berne pour la protection des œuvres littéraires et artistiques, adoptée en 1886 (et mise à jour plusieurs fois), la Convention internationale sur la protection des artistes interprètes ou exécutants, des producteurs de phonogrammes et des organismes de radiodiffusion, faite à Rome le 26 octobre 1961, ou l'accord sur les aspects des droits de propriété intellectuelle qui touchent au commerce (ADPIC 1994). Autrement, depuis 1991, la propriété littéraire et artistique au Portugal a devenu fortement configurée par le droit d'auteur de l'Union Européenne, surtout par la transposition des directives d'harmonisation du droit d'auteur et des droits voisins, comme, par ex.: directive 96/9/CE du Parlement européen et du Conseil, du 11 mars 1996, concernant la protection juridique des bases de données (JO L 77 du 27.3.1996, p. 20); directive 2000/31/CE du Parlement européen et du Conseil du 8 juin 2000 relative à certains aspects juridiques des services de la société de l'information, et notamment du commerce électronique, dans le marché intérieur (directive sur le commerce électronique) (JO L 178 du 17.7.2000, p. 1); directive 2001/29/CE du Parlement européen et du Conseil du 22 mai 2001 sur l'harmonisation de certains aspects du droit d'auteur et des droits voisins dans la société de l'information (JO L 167 du 22.6.2001, p. 10); directive 2006/115/CE du Parlement européen et du Conseil du 12 décembre

2006 relative au droit de location et de prêt et à certains droits voisins du droit d'auteur dans le domaine de la propriété intellectuelle (JO L 376 du 27.12.2006, p. 28); irective 2009/24/CE du Parlement européen et du Conseil du 23 avril 2009 concernant la protection juridique des programmes d'ordinateur (JO L 111 du 5.5.2009, p. 16); directive 2012/28/UE du Parlement européen et du Conseil du 25 octobre 2012 sur certaines utilisations autorisées des œuvres orphelines (JO L 299 du 27.10.2012, p. 5); directive 2014/26/UE du Parlement européen et du Conseil du 26 février 2014 concernant la gestion collective du droit d'auteur et des droits voisins et l'octroi de licences multiterritoriales de droits sur des œuvres musicales en vue de leur utilisation en ligne dans le marché intérieur (JO L 84 du 20.3.2014, p. 72), etc.

2. Portugal c'est un pays de droit civil et de droit d'auteur. Le droit d'auteur au Portugal protège des œuvres originales, c'est-à-dire les créations intellectuelles dans les domaines littéraires ou artistiques exprimées sous toute forme perceptible, quels que soient leur objet ou leurs mérites (article 1 (1) CDA). L'originalité est la base de la protection. Une œuvre est considérée comme originale si elle résulte de l'apport créatif de l'auteur et non simplement de l'appropriation de la création de la nature ou d'une autre personne. Le concept normatif des œuvres protégées est illustré par un catalogue ouvert d'exemples (art. 2 CDA), similaire a la convention de Berne. Les œuvres dérivées (par ex. traductions) et les compilations peuvent également être protégées en tant qu'œuvres originales (art. 3 CDA). La protection du droit d'auteur prend effet dès la création de l'œuvre et est indépendante de toute formalité, telle que l'enregistrement ou le dépôt (art. 12 CDA), à l'exception des titres des œuvres periodiques ou non publiées (art. 4 (3) CDA). La protection du droit d'auteur ne s'étend pas aux idées, procédures, méthodes opérationnelles ou concepts mathématiques en tant que tels (art. 1 (2) CDA), ni aux informations ou rapports de faits ou discours politiques (art. 7 (1) CDA).

3. Bien que le droit d'auteur soit configuré comme un droit unitaire comprenant à la fois des droits économiques et des droits moraux[2], les droits économiques peuvent être cédés, tandis que les droits moraux, à savoir le droit de paternité et le droit à l'intégrité, sont toujours attachés au créateur et ne peuvent être ni abandonnés ni cédés (arts. 9, 42 et 52 (2) CDA). Néanmoins, le droit à l'intégrité vise à protéger l'honneur et la réputation du créateur intellectuel en tant que tel (art. 56 (1) CDA), l'auteur peut convenir d'une identification de la paternité (art. 28 CDA) et il peut consentir à des modifications l'œuvre (art. 15 (2) et 59 CDA). D'autres droits moraux comprennent le droit de ne pas publier l'œuvre ainsi que le droit de retirer l'œuvre de la circulation (art. 62 CDA). Le droit de suite prévu pour certaines œuvres artistiques (art. 54 CDA) ne peut pas non plus être cédé ni supprimé.

4. Le droit d'auteur appartient au créateur intellectuel de l'œuvre, c'est-à-dire l'auteur, qui est en principe la personne identifiée comme telle (art. 11 et 27 CDA)[3]. Cependant, dans le cas d'œuvres créées par des employés ou sous commande, les parties peuvent convenir de la transmission des droits patrimoniaux, ce qui est présumé si le nom du créateur n'est pas mentionné dans l'œuvre ou à l'endroit habituel à des fins d'identification de l'auteur (art. 14 (1) (3) CDA). En cas de transmission, le créateur intellectuel aura droit à une rémunération

---

[2] Cf. arrêt n. 216/2015 du 08/04/2015, rapporteur ANA GUERRA MARTINS. Dans la doctrine, voir JOAQUIM JOSÉ GOMES. CANOTILHO, "Liberdade e Exclusivo Na Constituição." In IDEM, *Estudos Sobre Direitos Fundamentais*, 217–32. Coimbra: Almedina, 2004.

[3] Sur le principe du créateur dans le droit portugais, voir ALEXANDRE DIAS PEREIRA, *Direitos de Autor e Liberdade de Informação*. p. 436-439, 2008a; ALBERTO DE SÁ E MELLO, *Manual de Direito de Autor e Direitos Conexos*. 2 ed. Coimbra: Almedina, 2016. p. 47–48; JOÃO PAULO REMÉDIO MARQUES e MANUEL NOGUEIRA SERENS, "Criações Publicitárias - a Atribuição Do Direito Patrimonial de Autor e a Utilização Das Criações Protegidas Por Parte Dos Anunciantes" In *Direito Da Sociedade de Informação,* v. VII, Coimbra: Coimbra Editora. 2008. p. 230-233.

supplémentaire (art. 14 (4) - voir aussi art. 49 CDA). Concernant une œuvre créée par plusieurs personnes, le droit d'auteur appartient conjointement à ses créateurs, sauf s'il est considéré comme une œuvre collective, lorsque le droit d'auteur est attribué par la loi à la personne physique ou morale qui organise et dirige sa création et au nom de laquelle elle est publié (arts 16 à 19 CDA). Certains types d'œuvres sont réputés être des œuvres en collaboration, à savoir les œuvres cinématographiques, de sorte que la paternité est accordée à plusieurs personnes (art. 22 CDA).

5. La protection du droit d'auteur commence dès la création de l'œuvre, aucun dépôt ni enregistrement n'est requis, et dure en principe pendant la vie de l'auteur plus 70 ans *post mortem auctoris* (art. 31 CDA). Il-y-a des critères spéciaux pour certaines catégories d'œuvres, à savoir les œuvres communes et les œuvres orphelines (art. 32 à 34 CDA). Après la durée de la protection, le droit d'auteur expire et l'œuvre tombe dans le domaine public (art. 38 CDA). Toutefois, un «droit d'auteur» spécial est accordé pendant 25 ans à l'éditeur d'une œuvre non publiée pour laquelle la durée de protection a déjà expiré (art. 39 CDA).

6. Les droits patrimoniaux sont des droits exclusifs et disposables: le titulaire du droit d'auteur a non seulement le droit exclusif d'autoriser l'utilisation de l'œuvre par des tiers, mais également le droit de transférer et d'utiliser à titre de garantie, en tout ou en partie, les droits patrimoniaux (art. 40 CDA). Les autorisations (licences) d'utiliser des œuvres protégées par le droit d'auteur doivent répondre à certaines exigences, à savoir qu'elles doivent être faites par écrit et préciser les utilisations autorisées et les conditions de temps, de lieu et de paiement de celles-ci. Malgré la réglementation du prototype normatif des contrats d'autorisation de droit d'auteur prévoyant que le contrat d'édition est nul et non avenu s'il n'est pas conclu

par écrit (art. 87 CDA), il est cependant de jurisprudence stable que l'exigence de document écrit pour les autorisations de droits d'auteur n'a qu'une valeur de preuve (formalité *ad probationem*).

Des transferts partiels de droits d'auteur sont possibles pour des droits économiques spécifiques mais doivent être effectués par écrit et sont soumis à la reconnaissance notariale des signatures, sauf peine de nullité (art. 43 (1) (2) CDA). De plus, la transmission complète et définitive des droits patrimoniaux peut avoir lieu par contrat, à condition que l'œuvre et le prix soient indiqués et conclus par écriture public redigée par le notaire (formalité *ad substantiam*); sinon, elle est nulle (art. 44 CDA). La jurisprudence portugaise n'étend pas cette exigence de forme aux œuvres réalisées sous contrat de commande, mais le cas de la transmission du droit d'auteur sur les œuvres futures n'est pas clair (art. 48 CDA)[4].

7. Le droit d'auteur confère un droit exclusif et disposable d'exploitation économique de l'œuvre sous toute forme connue ou développée ultérieurement (art. 67 et 68 (1) CDA). Le droit exclusif comprend un ensemble de droits indépendants qui couvrent les utilisations les plus typiques telles que, conformément à l'article 68, paragraphe 2, du CDA, le droit de copier ou de reproduire d'une autre manière l'œuvre (a), le droit de distribuer des copies, y compris la vente, la location et le prêt public (b), le droit d'exécuter en public, notamment des œuvres musicales, dramatiques ou audiovisuelles (c), le droit de communiquer au public par câble et de diffuser, par radio, télévision ou autre moyen sans fil (d), le droit de mettre à disposition au public sur le réseau informatique (e), le droit de traduire et le droit de s'adapter (f).

---

[4] Pour les détails de cette discussion, cf. TIAGO BESSA, "Direito Contratual de Autor e licenças voluntárias de exploração da obra". *Revista da Ordem dos Advogados*, ano 72, IV, 2012. p. 1185-1191.

La réglementation de ces droits patrimoniaux est complétée par une législation spéciale concernant des droits spécifiques tels que la location et le prêt public ainsi que la radiodiffusion par satellite et la retransmission par câble. La loi sur le droit d'auteur prévoit au chapitre III un règlement détaillé pour des utilisations spéciales, telles que l'édition, la représentation sur scène, la production d'œuvres audiovisuelles, la fixation et la publication de phonogrammes et de vidéos, la radiodiffusion, la communication au public et les traductions. Les droits patrimoniaux peuvent être exercés directement par les titulaires des droits d'auteur ou par le biais d'entités de gestion collective (art. 71 à 74 CDA). Cependant, dans certaines situations, comme le droit de retransmission par câble, la gestion collective du droit d'auteur est obligatoire (décret-loi n. 333/97, du 27 novembre).

8. Le droit exclusif répond à certaines limitations et exceptions. Tout d'abord, le droit de reproduction ne s'applique pas à l'activité de simple conduit, de mise en cache, d'hébergement, de navigation et de liaison exercée par des prestataires de services de la société de l'information agissant comme de simples intermédiaires (art. 75 (1) CDA). Ensuite, la copie privée et d'autres utilisations telles que les revues de presse, les citations, les illustrations pédagogiques sont des exemples d'utilisations libres énumérées à l'article 75 (2) CDA, c'est-à-dire qu'elles n'entrent pas dans le champ d'application du droit exclusif, à condition toutefois que ces utilisations n'entrent pas en conflit avec une exploitation normale de l'œuvre et ne portent pas indûment préjudice aux intérêts légitimes du titulaire du droit (art. 75 (4) CDA). Ces utilisations libres sont considérées comme des droits obligatoires de l'utilisateur, car elles ne peuvent être dérogées par contrat (article 75 (5) CDA).

En outre, les titulaires de droits d'auteur ont droit à une compensation équitable pour certaines des utilisations libres (art. 76

CDA). En particulier, un système de compensation equitable est prévu pour les reproductions à usage privé (art. 82 CDA et loi n. 62/98, du 1 septembre, mise à jour plusieurs fois),).

9. Le titre III de la loi sur le droit d'auteur prévoit les droits dits voisins (*direitos conexos*). Les artistes interprètes ou exécutants, les producteurs de phonogrammes, les organismes de radiodiffusion et les organisateurs de spectacles bénéficient de droits voisins. Il s'agit de droits économiques similaires au droit d'auteur, mais la durée de protection est limitée à 50 ans après l'occurrence qui les a créés (art. 183 CDA). De plus, un droit moral limité est conféré aux artistes interprètes ou exécutants (art. 182 CDA).

En plus de ces droits connexes «typiques», d'autres droits connexes sont identifiés, tels que le droit de représentation conféré au promoteur de spectacles publics (art. 117 CDA). Le droit *sui generis* accordé au producteur d'une base de données pour protéger ses investissements substantiels dans la production de la base de données (chapitre III du décret-loi n. 122/2000, du 4 juillet) pourrait également être ajouté à cette liste de droits connexes «atypiques» dans le sens où il n›est pas inclus dans le cadre d›un traité international[5].

10. Les atteintes au droit d'auteur et aux droits voisins sont considérées comme des infractions non seulement de droit civil, mas aussi comme délits pénales: usurpation, contrefaçon, violation du droit moral et utilisation d'œuvres littéraires contrefaites (art. 195 à 202 CDA). La loi sur le droit d'auteur prévoit aussi des dispositions spéciales d'exécution concernant notamment la collecte

[5] Certains commentateurs classent les droits voisins de manière extensive et énumèrent un éventail plus large de titulaires, y compris, par exemple, certains types d'éditeurs. Cf. NUNO SOUSA E SILVA, "Direitos Conexos (ao Direito de Autor)", *Revista Da Ordem Dos Advogados*, Ano 76, p. 355–445, 2016.

et la conservation des preuves et des mesures provisoires (art. 209 à 211-B CDA). Il en va de même pour la protection des mesures techniques de protection et l'intégrité des informations de gestion du droit d'auteur (titre VI, art. 217 à 228 CDA). Par exemple, le fait de contourner (ou de faciliter le contournement) les mesures de protection technologiques utilisées par les titulaires de droits d'auteur et de droits voisins constitue une infraction pénale, y compris le droit sui generis du producteur de la base de données (art. 217 à 219 CDA). Cependant, la protection des mesures techniques est limitée par certains des limitations et exceptions autant que des droits obligatoires de l'utilisateur (art. 221 CDA).

0.2. Protection alternative

1. Les systèmes d'intelligence artificielle exigent d'autres droits de propriété intellectuelle en plus du droit d'auteur, comme c'est le cas pour les brevets d'inventions liées aux programmes informatiques dans le secteur de la robotique.

Les breves sont réglés par le nouveau Code de la propriété intelectuelle, approuvé par le décret-loi n. 110/2018, du 10 décembre (version mise à jour). Les inventions nouvelles, qui impliquent une activité inventive et sont susceptibles d'application industrielle, sont protégées par le droit des brevets (art. 50). Les brevets concernent des inventions techniques, c'est-à-dire des œuvres de l'esprit sur des problèmes techniques et qui ne sont pas seulement des formules mathématiques ou logiques. Les inventions techniques doivent être nouvelles, au vu de l'état de la technique, et résulter d'une activité inventive, en ce sens qu'elles ne résultent pas manifestement de l'état de la technique. L'invention doit quand-même être susceptible d'application industrielle, c'est-à-dire qu'elle peut être utilisée dans l'industrie ou l'agriculture.

L'objet du brevet ne couvre pas toutes les œuvres de l'esprit. En vertu de l'article 52/1 CPI, ne peuvent pas faire l'objet du droit des brevets les découvertes, les théories scientifiques et les méthodes mathématiques, (a), les matières ou substances déjà existantes dans la nature et les matières nucléaires (b), les créations esthétiques (c), les projets, principes et méthodes d'exercice d'activités intellectuelles dans le domaine des jeux d'argent ou dans le domaine des activités économiques, ainsi que des programmes informatiques, en tant que tels, sans aucune contribution (d), et les présentations d'informations (e). Cependant, la norme de la Convention de Munich sur le brevet européen qui sous-tend ledit régime interne n'a pas empêché l'Office européen des brevets de délivrer des brevets pour des inventions liées à des programmes informatiques, en particulier dans le secteur des dispositifs médicaux.

2. Outre les droits d'auteur et les brevets, il convient également de mentionner la protection éventuelle du logiciel comme coeur de l'intelligence artificielle[6], en tant que secrets commerciaux ou savoir-faire. Les secrets commerciaux sont protégés dans Code de la propriété industrielle, qui transpose la directive (UE) 2016/943 du Parlement européen et du Conseil du 8 juin 2016 relative à la protection du savoir-faire et des informations commerciales confidentielles (secrets d'affaires) contre leur acquisition, leur utilisation et divulgation illégale. Les informations commerciales confidentielles sont considérées comme (1) des informations secrètes (en ce sens que, dans leur ensemble ou dans la configuration et la connexion exactes de leurs éléments constitutifs, elles ne sont généralement pas connues des personnes dans les cercles qui traitent normalement du

[6] COMISSÃO EUROPEIA, "Livro Branco Sobre a Inteligência Artificial - Uma Abordagem Europeia Virada Para a Excelência e a Confiança." COM(2020) 65 Final. 2020. p. 16.

type d'informations en question,); (2) ayant une valeur commerciale parce qu'ils sont secrets; (3) et qui ont fait l'objet d'une diligence raisonnable, compte tenu des circonstances, à garder secret par la personne qui exerce légalement leur controle (art. 313).

Le secret commercial est protégé contre l'accès, appropriation ou copie non autorisée de documents, objets, matériaux, substances ou fichiers électroniques, qui sont légalement sous le contrôle du détenteur du secret commercial et qui contiennent ce secret ou dont il est déductible, et contre toute autre conduite qui, dans les circonstances spécifiques dans lesquelles elle se produit, est considérée comme contraire aux pratiques commerciales honnêtes (art. 314/1). Plusiers autres actes sont interdits, notament d'utiliser ou de divulguer un secret commercial obtenu illégalement ou en violation d'un accord de confidentialité ou toute autre obligation de ne pas divulguer le secret commercial, ou une obligation contractuelle ou toute autre obligation de limiter l'utilisation des secrets d'affaires (art. 314/2).

Enfin, la protection des topographies de produits semi-conducteurs peut être mentionnée, ce qui au Portugal suppose un caractère *sui generis* entre le droit d'auteur et la propriété industrielle[7], bien qu'il semble y avoir une plus grande approximation de cette dernière, étant prévue aux articles 153 et suivants du Code de la Propriété Industrielle.

3. Les droits de la personnalité constituent un autre domaine d'application pertinent de l'intelligence artificielle, notamment dans le domaine des données personnelles. La personnalité juridique s'acquiert au moment de la naissance et de la vie, et cesse avec la mort (art. 66 et 68 du code civil). La personnalité juridique implique

[7] ALEXANDRE DIAS PEREIRA. "Circuitos integrados: protecção jurídica das topografias de produtos semicondutores". In *Direito Industrial*, vol. II, p. 309-340, 2002.

immédiatement un droit général de la personnalité (art. 70) qui se déploie dans des droits spéciaux de la personnalité, y compris le droit au nom, le droit à l'image, le droit à la création culturelle ou le droit de réserver l'intimité de la vie toilette. Par ailleurs, une partie minoritaire de la doctrine affirme que le droit d'auteur est essentiellement un droit de la personnalité, en raison de ses aspects moraux[8].

Outre la protection de ces personnalités prévue par le droit civil et le droit pénal, la protection des données des personnes physiques a été développée dans une législation autonome, qui correspond actuellement au Règlement (UE) 2016/679 du Parlement européen et du Conseil du 27 avril 2016 sur la protection des des données à caractère personnel et à la libre circulation de ces données, et abrogeant la directive 95/46 / CE (Règlement général sur la protection des données), et à la loi n. 52/2019, du 8 août, applicable à la mise en œuvre, dans l'ordre juridique interne, du règlement (EU) 2016/679.

0.3. Législation et projets spécifiques

Il n'existe pas de lois ou de règles spécifiques sur l'intelligence artificielle et le droit d'auteur au Portugal, et il n'y a pas non plus de décisions de justice spécifiques sur cette question.Toutefois, la note de bas n. 18 de l'arrêt de la Cour Suprême de Justice du 07/05/2012, affaire n° 855/07.8TVPRT.P1.S1, indique que «dans la mesure où les techniques de l'intelligence artificielle permettront la création de l'œuvre exclusivement par machine, nous ne traiterons naturellement pas d'œuvres protégées par le droit d'auteur, car il n'y a pas d'auteur. «Dans la mesure où les techniques de l'intelligence

[8] Notamment, ORLANDO DE CARVALHO, "Direito de Personalidade de Autor." In *Num Novo Mundo Do Direito de Autor? II Congresso Ibero-Americano de Direito de Autor e Direitos Conexos,* Tomo II. Lisboa: Edições Cosmos, 1994.

artificielle permettront la création de l'œuvre exclusivement par machine, nous ne traiterons naturellement pas d'œuvres protégées par le droit d'auteur, car il n'y a pas d'auteur. Dans tous les cas, cependant, lorsque c'est une personne qui est à l'origine de l'œuvre, elle peut être protégée par le droit d'auteur». La doctrine adopte presque unanimement des variantes de cette position[9].

Comme le Portugal fait partie de l'Union européenne, il est encore nécessaire de suivre les débats au niveau européen. Dans la résolution du Parlement européen sur les dispositions de droit civil relatives à la robotique (2015/2103(INL)[10]), il est recommandé à la Commission d'établir «des critères pour une «création intellectuelle propre» en relation avec les œuvres protégées par le droit d'auteur produites par des ordinateurs ou des robots». Le 20 octobre 2020, le Parlement européen a publié une nouvelle résolution (2020/2015(INI)[11]), qui n'indique pas encore de voie plus concrète à suivre, mais qui réitère la primauté du «niveau élevé de protection» du système européen de propriété intellectuelle et l'importance d'équilibrer les intérêts en jeu. Elle a également réaffirmé la possibilité que de telles œuvres ne soient pas protégées en raison du principe d'originalité et de son lien avec la personnalité de l'auteur en tant que personne naturelle.

---

[9] JOSÉ DE OLIVEIRA ASCENSÃO, *Direito Civil - Direito de Autor e Direitos Conexos*, Coimbra: Coimbra Editora, 1992, p. 76-77; JOSÉ ALBERTO VIEIRA, "Obras Geradas Por Computador e Direito de Autor." In *Direito Da Sociedade de Informação*, vol. II, 2001. p. 128–37; ALBERTO DE SÁ E MELLO, *Op. Cit.* 2016. p. 50-61; ALEXANDRE DIAS PEREIRA, "A Proteção Jurídica de Software Executados Por Robots (e Obras Geradas Por I.A.)." In IDEM, *Direito Da Propriedade Intelectual & Novas Tecnologias,* vol. I, 25–37. Coimbra: Gestlegal, 2019; TITO RENDAS & NUNO SOUSA E SILVA, *Direito de Autor Nos Tribunais*. 2. Ed. Lisboa: Universidade Católica Editora, 2019. p. 98; PEDRO DE PERDIGÃO LANA, "A Questão Da Autoria Em Obras Produzidas Por Inteligência Artificial." *Estudos Doutoramento & Mestrado*. Coimbra: Instituto Jurídico da FDUC, 2019; DARIO MOURA VICENTE. "Economia Criativa e Equilíbrio de Interesses no Direito Autoral." In *Direito Autoral & Economia Criativa*, Curitiba: GEDAI, 2012; LUÍS MANUEL TELES DE MENEZES LEITÃO, *Direito de Autor.* Coimbra: Almedina, 2018. p. 61;

[10] https://www.europarl.europa.eu/doceo/document/A-8-2017-0005_FR.html

[11] https://www.europarl.europa.eu/doceo/document/TA-9-2020-0277_FR.html

1) Les données d'entrée – exploration de données

1.1. Existence d'un acte de reproduction

Le droit exclusif couvre la reproduction directe ou indirecte, temporaire ou permanente, par tout moyen et sous quelque forme que ce soit, en tout ou en partie (art. 68/1-i) CDA). Toutefois, les actes de reproduction temporaire transitoires, épisodiques ou accessoires sont exclus du droit de reproduction s'ils font partie intégrante et essentielle d'un processus technologique et dont le seul but est de permettre la transmission sur un réseau entre des tiers, par un intermédiaire, ou une utilisation légitime d'une œuvre protégée et n'ont pas, en elles-mêmes, une importance économique, y compris, dans la mesure où elles remplissent les conditions fixées, les actes permettant la navigation sur les réseaux et le stockage temporaire, ainsi que ceux qui permettent le fonctionnement efficace des systèmes de transmission, à condition que l'intermédiaire ne modifie pas le contenu de la transmission et n'interfère pas avec l'utilisation légitime de la technologie selon les bons usages reconnus par le marché, pour obtenir des données sur le l'utilisation de l'information et, en général, les processus de transmission purement technologiques (art. 75/1 CDA).

Selon la directive 2001/29, cette exclusion couvre des actes tels que la navigation (*vide* le considérant 33, *in fine*). La directive 2001/29 inclut la reproduction temporaire dans le droit de reproduction (art. 5/1). La Cour de justice, dans l'ordonnance du 17 janvier 2012 (proc. n. C-302/10 - *Infopaq II*), a considéré exclus les actes de reproduction temporaire effectués au cours d'un processus appelé «saisie de données» qui font partie intégrante et essentielle d'un processus technologique, malgré le fait qu'ils introduisent et terminent le processus et impliquent une intervention humaine, qui ne permettent qu'une utilisation légitime de l'œuvre et qui n'ont pas de signification économique en eux-mêmes, car ils ne permettent pas de réaliser un profit supplémentaire, qui va au-delà de celui obtenu de l'utilisation légitime de l'œuvre protégée, et n'entraîne pas une altération de l'œuvre.

Il en va de même, *mutatis mutandis*, pour le droit d'extraction du producteur de la base de données. Le décret-loi n. 122/2000 transpose la directive 96/9/CE relative à la protection juridique des bases de données. Le droit *sui generis* du producteur de la base de données c'est le droit d'autoriser ou d'interdire l'extraction et / ou la réutilisation de tout ou partie substantielle, appréciée qualitativement ou quantitativement, du contenu d'un base de données, lorsque son obtention, sa vérification ou sa présentation représente un investissement substantiel d'un point de vue qualitatif ou quantitatif (art. 12/1)[12]. L'extraction c'est le transfert, permanent ou temporaire, de tout ou partie substantielle du contenu d'une base de données à un autre support, que ce soit par des moyens ou sous quelque forme que ce soit (art. 12/2-a).

Cependant, la reproduction temporaire effectuée par l'IA peut faire une valeur économique supplémentaire et, dans cette mesure, est couverte par le droit de reproduction. Il s'agit de la «fouille de textes et de données» (prospection), définie par la directive 2019/790 comme «toute technique d'analyse automatisée visant à analyser des textes et des données sous une forme numérique afin d'en dégager des informations, ce qui comprend, à titre non exhaustif, des constantes, des tendances et des corrélations.»

Le préambule de la directive 2019/790 précise que la recherche de textes ou de données implique des actes de reproduction de matériel protégé par le droit d'auteur ou l'extraction de contenu à partir de bases de données protégées par la loi spéciale du fabricant

---

[12] La Cour de Justice des Communautés Européennes (qui a précédé la CJUE) fournit certains paramètres pour expliquer ce qu'est un «investissement substantiel» dans les arrêts Fixtures (C-46/02, C-203/02, C-338/02 et C-444/02). Dans la doctrine, voir NUNO SOUSA E SILVA, *Op. Cit.* 2016. p. 393-395.

(rec. 9). Il précise en outre que dans les cas où les chercheurs ont un accès légal au contenu, par exemple par le biais d›abonnements à des publications ou de licences en libre accès, les conditions des licences peuvent exclure la prospection de textes et de données (rec. 10). Compte tenu de l›importance de l›exploration de données pour la recherche scientifique, la directive n›inclut pas le droit de reproduction et le droit d›extraire le contenu des bases de données, ainsi que le droit de reproduction en général du droit d›auteur et des droits voisins, reproductions et extractions effectuées par des organismes de recherche et des institutions responsables du patrimoine culturel pour la prospection de textes et de données sur des œuvres ou autres matériels protégés auxquels ils ont légalement accès à des fins de recherche scientifique (art. 3/1).

L'exception n'est établie qu'en faveur des organismes de recherche et des institutions responsables du patrimoine culturel. Parmi les premiers figurent les universités, y compris leurs bibliothèques, instituts de recherche ou toute autre entité dont l'objectif principal est de mener des recherches scientifiques ou d'exercer des activités éducatives impliquant également la réalisation de recherches scientifiques à but non lucratif ou de réinvestir tous les bénéfices de la recherche scientifique, ou dans le cadre d'une mission d'intérêt public reconnue par un État membre, de sorte que l'accès aux résultats de cette recherche scientifique ne puisse, à des conditions préférentielles, bénéficier à une entreprise qui exerce une influence déterminante sur cet organisme (art. 2/1). Ces derniers comprennent les bibliothèques ou musées accessibles au public, les archives ou les institutions responsables du patrimoine cinématographique ou sonore (par exemple, la Cinémathèque portugaise).

Le recital 14 clarifie la notion d'accès legal comme englobant l'accès au contenu basé sur une politique d'accès libre ou par le biais d'accords contractuels entre les titulaires de droits et les organismes de recherche ou les institutions responsables du patrimoine culturel, tels que les abonnements, ou par d'autres canaux juridiques; l'accès légal devrait également couvrir l'accès au contenu disponible gratuitement en ligne. Par raisons de securité et d'intégrité du système, l'accès légal peut demander la validation des adresses IP ou l'authentification des utilisateurs (rec. 16).

L'exception ou la limitation de la fouille (prospection) de textes ou de données à des fins d'investigation scientifique est obligatoire et impérative, et une prospection plus complète des textes et données à d'autres fins (art. 4) n'est applicable que tant que l'utilisation des œuvres et les autres éléments protégés n'ont pas été expressément réservés par les titulaires de droits respectifs de manière appropriée, en particulier par lecture optique dans le cas de contenus mis à la disposition du public en ligne (art. 4/3). Selon le recital 18, dans le cas d'un contenu qui a été rendu public en ligne, il ne devrait être considéré comme approprié de réserver ces droits qu'en utilisant des moyens de lecture optique, y compris les métadonnées et les conditions générales d'un site ou d'un service Internet.

1.2. Exceptions non spécifiques

La directive 2019/790 semble limiter les exceptions et limitations au droit de reproduction impliqué dans la fouille de textes et de données à la poursuite de fins de recherche scientifique. Dans cette mesure, les exceptions ou limitations restantes, prévus à l'article 75 du code du droit d'auteur et des droits voisins[13], ne bénéficieront pas de la liberté de fouille des textes ou des données, sauf si cela n'a pas été réservé par les titulaires de droits[14].

---

[13] Les exceptions et limitations concernant les bases de données sont prévues à l'art. 10 et à l'art. 15 (en relation avec le droit spécial du fabricant) du Décret-loi 122/2000.

[14] NUNO SOUSA E SILVA, "Subsídios para a transposição da Diretiva 2019/790". *Revista de Direito Intelectual*, n.1, 2020. p. 251-252.

1.3. Exceptions spécifiques

Il n'y a toujours pas de projet de transposition de la directive 2019/790 dans le droit portugais, ni de règles ayant une signification et une portée similaires dans le domaine du droit d'auteur. En tant qu'utilisation à des fins privées ou pour d'autres utilisations autorisées par la loi, l'exploration de données devrait également être soumise à une rémunération ou à une compensation, en particulier en ce qui concerne une compensation équitable pour la reproduction à usage privé. Cependant, la loi sur la copie privée ne discrimine pas ce nouvel usage. En outre, le préambule de la directive 2019/790 considère que les dommages potentiels causés par cette nouvelle exception aux titulaires de droits sont minimes, car c'est limitée à des institutions de la recherche scientifique. Cela va encore plus loin, considérant que: «Les États membres ne devraient, dès lors, pas prévoir de compensation pour les titulaires de droits en ce qui concerne les utilisations relevant des exceptions en matière de fouille de textes et de données introduites par la présente directive» (rec. 17).

1.4. Équilibre et justification

Le régime juridique portugais ne prévoit pas expressément l'utilisation de systèmes d'intelligence artificielle. Le code du droit d'auteur a été modifié pour transposer les directives de l'Union européenne, mais la directive 2019/790 n'a pas encore été transposée. En général, les exceptions ou limitations au droit d'auteur ne couvrent pas les utilisations à des fins commerciales, directes ou indirectes. En outre, le principe est que les droits sont réservés par la loi et que, par conséquent, le titulaire du droit n'a pas la charge de réserver les utilisations soumises à son autorisation[15]. Dans cette mesure, considérer que la prospection de textes ou de données extrait une valeur économique des reproductions qu'elle implique et imposer ensuite au titulaire de droits la charge de réserver cet usage revient à tout le moins à renverser la logique du système en faveur des utilisateurs de systèmes d'intelligence artificiel. D'autant plus que les géants de l'internet qui exploitent de grandes plateformes de partage de contenus numériques établissent dans les conditions générales du service le droit de prospecter des textes et données téléchargés par les utilisateurs de leurs services. En d'autres termes, dans la pratique, le droit de s'opposer à la prospection aura peu de valeur dans la relation avec les grandes sociétés Internet (GAFA), qui finissent ainsi par bénéficier de ce droit face à une concurrence à moindre pouvoir de négociation.

D'autre part, en limitant la liberté de recherche de textes et de données à des activités de recherche scientifique à but non lucratif ou menées dans le cadre d'une mission d'intérêt public, la directive 2019/790 désavantage d'autres secteurs bénéficiant traditionnellement d'exceptions, comme les médias, qui facent la concurrence des grandes entreprises Internet en ce qui concerne l'accès à la principale matière première de ce marché, à savoir l'information, le divertissement et d'autres contenus audiovisuels.

1.5. Conception du corpus de départ

Un ensemble de données composé spécifiquement pour servir de données d'entrée peut bénéficier de la protection juridique

[15] Nous avons développé ce sujet en mettant l'accent sur l'équilibre intrinsèque du droit d'auteur dans le système de l'Europe continentale et du *copyright* dans ALEXANDRE DIAS PEREIRA, "Fair use e Direitos de Autor (entre a regra e a exceção)". In *Estudos em Honra do Professor Doutor José de Oliveira Ascensão*, vol. I. Almedina: Coimbra, 2008b. p. 853-859.

des bases de données, protégées par le décret-loi no. 122/2000, qui transpose la directive 96/9/CE. Base de données signifie «la collecte d'œuvres, de données ou d'autres éléments indépendants, organisée de manière systématique ou méthodique et susceptible d'accès individuel par voie électronique ou autre» (art. 1/2). Les bases de données qui, par la sélection ou la disposition des contenus respectifs, constituent des créations intellectuelles sont protégées par le droit d'auteur (art. 4/1). Ainsi, si le choix des données d'entrée est original, la structuration de ces données sera protégée par le droit d'auteur.

En revanche, le fabricant de la base de données se voit accorder un droit spécial, qui consiste en le droit d'autoriser ou d'interdire l'extraction et / ou la réutilisation de tout ou partie substantielle, appréciée qualitativement ou quantitativement, du contenu d'une base de données; données, lorsque leur collecte, vérification ou présentation représente un investissement substantiel d'un point de vue qualitatif ou quantitatif (art. 12/1).

1.6. Étendue des données protégées

En effet, le droit d'auteur ne protège pas les œuvres non originales, ni la simple information, ainsi que le style ou un genre littéraire ou artistique. Cependant, les possibilités d'imitation du style littéraire ou artistique apportées par l'IA peuvent justifier l'approfondissement de l'objet de protection du droit d'auteur. En plus de la forme d'expression externe, la forme interne doit également être prise en compte[16]. Dans tous les cas il est impératif

[16] ALEXANDRE DIAS PEREIRA, Música e electrónica: «sound sampling», obras de computador e direitos de autor na internet". *In Direito da sociedade da informação*, vol. 5, Coimbra: Coimbra Editora, 2004.

de préserver la dichotomie idée-expression, afin de sauvegarder la liberté des idées et, finalement, la liberté de pensée elle-même et la liberte d'imagination.

Le droit spécial du fabricant ne couvre pas la création des données, mais seulement le contrôle de l'extraction ou de la réutilisation[17]. Un droit sur la création de données non personnelles a même été proposé dans la communication de la Commission «Construire une économie européenne des données» (SWD(2017) 2 final), mais a été rejeté.

Pour cette raison, il peut être plus approprié de rechercher la protection de ces éléments chez la concurrence déloyale[18]. L'article 311 du code de la propriété industrielle définit la concurrence déloyale comme «tout acte de concurrence contraire aux règles et usages honnêtes de toute branche d'activité économique». Le catalogue des actes illustrant une concurrence déloyale comprend, entre autres, «ceux susceptibles de créer une confusion avec la société, l'établissement, les produits ou services des concurrents, quel que soit le moyen employé», et aussi les références non autorisées faites pour bénéficier du crédit ou de la réputation d'un nom, d'un établissement ou d'une marque étranger, etc.

D'ailleurs, les droits de la personnalité, tels que le nom et l'image, au sens du code civil et du régime des données personnelles, au sens du RGPD et du droit interne, peuvent s'avérer des moyens de protection valables et efficaces contre le parasitisme par «imitation».

---

[17] MARIA IGLESIAS, SHARON SHAMULIA. AMANDA ANDERBERG, *Intellectual Property and Artificial Intelligence - A Literature Review*. Luxembourg, European Union Publications, 2019. p. 9.

[18] Il convient de noter que dans le monde, des propositions ont déjà été faites pour protéger les œuvres créées par l'intelligence artificielle par des régimes modifiés de concurrence déloyale JANI IHALAINEN, "Computer Creativity: Artificial Intelligence and Copyright." *Journal of Intellectual Property Law & Practice*, v. 13, n. 9, 2018. p. 727-728.

1.7. Géstion collective

Les entités de gestion collective enregistrées au Portugal n'offrent pas encore de licences spécifiques pour l'IA. Voire p.ex. https://www.spautores.pt/usuarios/tabelas

2) Le système d'intelligence artificielle

2.1. Algorithme de départ

En droit portugais, les programmes d'ordinateur sont protégés par le droit d'auteur en vertu du décret-loi n. 252/94 du 20 octobre, qui transpose la directive 91/250/CEE (remplacée entre-temps par la directive 2009/24/CE). Les programmes d'ordinateur à caractère créatif bénéficient d'une protection similaire à celle accordée aux œuvres littéraires, le matériel de conception préliminaire du programme étant equiparé au programme d'ordinateur (art. 1/2-3). L'algorithme, en tant que racine logique du programme informatique, peut être protégé comme matériau de conception préliminaire, dans la mesure où il ne s'agit pas simplement d'une idée, d'un principe ou d'une découverte[19].

2.2. Connaissance accumulée.

En effet, le corpus de données auquel recourt l'algorithme du système d'intelligence artificielle pour prendre une décision et donc

[19] JOÃO PAULO REMÉDIO MARQUES, "Patentes de Programas de Computador de Sistemas Informáticos de Jogos Eletrônicos / Patentes de Métodos de Exercício de Actividades Econômicas?" *PIDCC,* v. 10, n. 01, 2016. p. 3-5.

génèrer son propre «savoir» et sa «connaissance» est protégéable par les droits de propriété littéraire, notamment en tant que base de données.

La protection jurídique des bases de données établie par le décret-loi no. 122/2000, qui transpose la directive 96/9/CE, definit como base de données «la collecte d'œuvres, de données ou d'autres éléments indépendants, organisée de manière systématique ou méthodique et susceptible d'accès individuel par voie électronique ou autre» (art. 1/2). Les bases de données qui, par la sélection ou la disposition des contenus respectifs, constituent des créations intellectuelles sont protégées par le droit d'auteur (art. 4/1). Ainsi, si la sélection ou disposition des données accumulées est originale, la structure de la base sera protégée par le droit d'auteur.

En autre, le fabricant de la base de données se voit accorder un droit spécial, qui consiste en le droit d'autoriser ou d'interdire l'extraction et / ou la réutilisation de tout ou partie substantielle, appréciée qualitativement ou quantitativement, du contenu d'une base de données; données, lorsque leur collecte, vérification ou présentation représente un investissement substantiel d'un point de vue qualitatif ou quantitatif (art. 12/1). Si l'utilisation d'un système d'intelligence artifielle est considerée un investissement substantial, le droit sui generis du producteur sera applicable[20].

2.3. Algorithme développé (*deep learning*)

Le development et l'amélioration d'un algorithme a partir de l'analyse des données et des résultats par le système d'intelligence artificielle c'est une evolution du programme informatique et au-

[20] Comme indiqué dans la note de bas n. 12.

tant que tel c'est protégéable comme version derivée du logiciel par le droit d'auteur s'il a du character creative. Neamois, le «deep learning», notamment les bases de données et le code généré par la IA, semble produit de la machine ele-même et donc ne sera pas original au sens du droit d'auteur.

3) Le produit de l'intelligence artificielle

3.1. Protection des créations de l'intelligence artificielle.

Le résultat produit de manière autoneme par une système d'intelligence artificielle n'est pas protégé par les droits d'auteur selon la législation portugaise[21]. Le droit d'auteur protège les œuvres littéraires ou artistiques en tant que formes d'expression originale générées par l'auteur dans l'exercice de sa liberté de création culturelle. La création artistique digne de protection doit résulter du libre choix de l'auteur en tant que personne humaine. Les créations naturelles, telles que les sons d'animaux ou les constellations d'étoiles, ne sont pas protégées par le droit d'auteur, quelle que soit leur valeur esthétique. Seuls les humains, en tant qu'êtres dotés de conscience et de libre arbitre, ont la capacité de créer des œuvres littéraires ou artistiques aux fins de la protection du droit d'auteur[22].

Cependant, à côté du droit d'auteur, la loi établit les droits voisins de l'artiste interprète ou exécutant, du producteur phonographique ou vidéographique et du diffuseur. En particulier, il nous semble

---

[21] PEDRO DE PERDIGÃO LANA, *A Autoria das Obras Autônomamente Geradas por Inteligência Artificial e o Domínio do Público* (Dissertation de masters non publiée), Universidade de Coimbra, 2020.

[22] JOSÉ ALBERTO VIEIRA, *Op. Cit.* 2001. p. 113-45.

que le résultat produit par un système d'intelligence artificielle peut être protégé par le droit connexe du producteur phonographique ou vidéographique, entendue comme «la personne physique ou morale qui fixe en premier les sons d'une exécution ou de toute autre, ou des images de toute source, accompagnées ou non de sons» (art. 176/3 CDA). Le droit connexe du producteur aux sons et/ou images provenant d'un système d'intelligence artificielle ne requiert qu'ils soient originaux en tant que fruits de la liberté de création culturelle[23], parce que leur fixation ou leur enregistrement dans un phonogramme ou un vidéogramme c'est suffisante.

3.1.1. Aspect moral

Contrairement aux œuvres littéraires ou artistiques protégées par le droit d'auteur, le produit d'intelligence artificielle n'exprime pas de personnalité et, dans cette mesure, ne justifie pas la reconnaissance de droits moraux, en tant que droits de personnalité de l'auteur fondés sur sa liberté de création culturelle. Toutefois, la protection au titre du droit du producteur de phonogrammes ou de vidéogrammes exige l'identification des phonogrammes et vidéogrammes dans toutes les copies autorisées et dans l'emballage respectif au moyen d'une mention constituée du symbole P (la lettre P entourée d'un cercle), accompagnée de l'indication de l'année de la première publication ainsi que l'identification du producteur ou de son représentant (art. 185 / 1-2 CDA), à supposer que c'est celui ci dont le nom ou la dénomination figure comme tel dans les exemplaires autorisés et dans l'emballage respectif (185/3 CDA).

---

[23] Cf. AIPPI. "Resolution - 2019 Study Question - Copyright in Artificially Generated Works." London, 2019.

3.1.2. Aspect economique

Les droits patrimoniaux de l'auteur incitent à la création culturelle, en garantissant à l'auteur le droit exclusif d'exploiter ses créations intellectuelles. De même façon, la protection des produits d'intelligence artificielle par le droit connexe du producteur phonographique ou vidéographique peut stimuler ou encourager l'investissement dans les systèmes d'intelligence artificielle et la production culturelle en général. Même si le système informatique n'a pas besoin d'incitations économiques, celles-ci peuvent être nécessaires pour promouvoir l'investissement dans l'IA, en conférant des droits exclusifs sur les produits artificiels à ceux qui investissent dans l'IA[24].

3.2. Titulaire des droits

« Le droit d›auteur appartient au créateur intellectuel de l›œuvre », prévoit l›article 11 du Code du droit d›auteur, en ajoutant « sauf disposition expresse au contraire ». À son tour, l›article 27/1 établit que, « sauf disposition au contraire, l›auteur est le créateur intellectuel de l›œuvre ». Ainsi, en principe, le droit d'auteur appartient au créateur intellectuel de l'œuvre, c'est-à-dire à l'auteur, en présumant « l'auteur dont le nom a été indiqué comme tel dans l'œuvre, selon l'usage établi, ou annoncé sous toute forme de communication au public » (art. 27/2 CDA). Cependant, le terme auteur est utilisé plus

---

[24] Décrivant plus en détail la nécessité de récompenser cet investissement, voire JANI MCCUTCHEON. "The Vanishing Author in Computer-Generated Works: A Critical Analysis of Recent Australian Case Law." *Melbourne University Law Review* 36 (3), 2013. p. 954-957; RUSS PEARLMAN. "Recognizing Artificial Intelligence (AI) as Authors and Inventors under U.S. Intellectual Property Law." *Richmond Journal of Law & Technology*, v. 24, n. 2, 2018. p. 1-4.

largement dans la loi[25], couvrant également, p.ex., le successeur et le cessionnaire des droits (art. 27/3 CDA).

Les conventions sur la propriété du droit d'auteur concernant des travaux réalisés sur commande ou pour le compte d'autrui sont admises, soit dans le quadre d'une obligation fonctionnelle, soit d'un contrat de travail (art. 14/1 CDA). En d'autres termes, dans le travail réalisé sur commande ou pour le compte d'autrui, il est possible de céder la propriété du droit d'auteur au mandant ou à l'employeur. En l'absence de convention, le droit d'auteur sur l'œuvre réalisée pour des tiers est présumé appartenir à son créateur intellectuel (art. 14/2 CDA), à moins que son nom ne soit pas mentionné dans l'œuvre ou n'apparaisse pas à l'endroit prévu pour l'effet selon l'usage universel, car dans ce cas la présomption est inversée en faveur de l'entité pour le compte de laquelle l'œuvre est réalisée (art. 14/3 CDA).

Pour certains comentators, s'il existe une convention de propriété des droits en faveur du mandant ou de l'employeur ou si le créateur intellectuel n'est pas identifié, le droit d'auteur appartient au mandant ou à l'employeur et à titre original[26]. Ce serait le cas d'une disposition expressément contraire à l'appartenance originelle du droit d'auteur au créateur intellectuel. Dans cette situation, le travail subventionné et le travail collectif le seraient encore.

Neanmois, le droit d'auteur appartient au créateur intellectuel pour le simple fait de la création intellectuelle, étant reconnu indépendamment de l'enregistrement, du dépôt ou de toute autre formalité (art. 12). Donc, à notre avis, si le droit d'auteur est concédé à une personne autre que le créateur intellectuel, il faut comprendre que seuls les droits patrimoniaux sont en jeu, puisque les droits moraux et autres droits inaliénables restent au titre du créateur

[25] JOSÉ DE OLIVEIRA ASCENSÃO, *Op. Cit.* 2012. p. 105.

[26] ALBERTO DE SÁ E MELLO, *Contrato de Direito de Autor: a autonomia contratual na formação do direito de autor*. Coimbra: Almedina, 2008a. p. 69.

intellectuel même après la transmission ou extinction des droits de propriété (art. 9/3 et art. 56 CDA)[27]. Une telle attribution de droits patrimoniaux peut être convenue ou présumée par la loi, comme c'est le cas pour les travaux effectués pour le compte d'autrui sans identification de l'auteur.

Mais il est important de clarifier les termes de cette attribution. S'il y a une convention, c'est une attribution par contrat. En l'absence de convention, opère une présomption légale fondée sur l'anonymat de l'œuvre, donc à notre avis le régime de l'œuvre d'un auteur anonyme est applicable, en vertu duquel quiconque «divulgue ou publie une œuvre avec le consentement de l'auteur, sous un nom qui ne le révèle son identité ou de manière anonyme, il se considère comme le représentant de l'auteur, lui confiant le devoir de défendre les droits respectifs devant des tiers, sauf si l'auteur exprime sa volonté contraire »(art. 30/1), e celui peut à tout moment révéler son identité et la paternité de l'œuvre, et à partir de ce moment les pouvoirs de représentation cessent (art. 30/2). Ainsi, le droit d'auteur relatif à l'œuvre d'un auteur anonyme appartient vraisemblablement au mandant ou à l'employeur en tant que représentants légaux de l'auteur. Il s'agit donc d'une attribution de portée légale et limitée, et non de la propriété originale et complète du droit d'auteur, même s'il fusse limitée aux droits économiques.

La même compréhension est valable pour l'oeuvre dit collectif. Elle est considérée comme «la création d'une pluralité de personnes [...] lorsqu'elle est organisée à l'initiative d'une entité singulier ou collective et diffusée ou publiée en leur nom» (art. 16/1-b CDA). C'est un type de création plurielle, avec l'oeuvre réalisée en collaboration, qui consiste en ce qui est «diffusée ou publiée au nom des collabo-

---

[27] Pour les détails de la discussion, voir ALEXANDRE DIAS PEREIRA. *Informática, Direito de Autor e Propriedade Tecnodigital*. Coimbra: Coimbra Editora, 2001. p. 274-302.

rateurs ou de l'un d'entre eux, qu'ils puissent discriminer ou non les contributions individuelles» (art. 16/1-a CDA). Les différences de mode de divulgation ou de publication de ces œuvres se reflètent dans la propriété des droits. Dans l'œuvre réalisée en collaboration, en tant qu '«unité», le droit d'auteur appartient à tous ceux qui y ont collaboré, régissant son exercice commun en copropriété et considérant les parties indivises des auteurs comme égales, sauf autrement accordé par stipulation écrite (art. 17/1-2 CDA). Cependant, si l'œuvre est divulguée ou publiée au nom d'un ou de certains des collaborateurs et si les autres ne sont pas explicitement désignés dans une partie quelconque de l'œuvre, il est supposé que les non-désignés ont cédé leurs droits à celui ou à ceux au nom desquels l'œuvre a été divulguée ou publiée (art. 17/3 CDA).

Harmonisant cette présomption de cession de droits avec ce que nous avons dit de l'attribution de droits d'auteur sur des œuvres «anonymes» réalisées pour d'autres, il nous semble également que les auteurs désignés dans l'œuvre réalisée en collaboration sont considérés comme auteurs de l'œuvre en tant que représentants légaux des auteurs «non désignés», selon les termes du régime de l'œuvre de l'auteur anonyme. De plus, la loi préserve les droits individuels des auteurs d'une œuvre réalisée en collaboration sans faire de distinction entre les auteurs désignés et les auteurs non désignés, à condition que chacun d'entre eux «puisse demander la divulgation, la publication, l'exploitation ou la modification d'une œuvre réalisée en collaboration, étant, en cas de divergence, la question résolue selon les règles de la bonne foi » (art. 18/1 CDA); et, en outre, sans préjudice de l'exploitation conjointe, ils peuvent exercer individuellement les droits liés à leur contribution personnelle, quand elle peut être discriminée (art. 18/2 CDA). La loi considère comme des œuvres réalisées en collaboration l'œuvre radiodiffusée, l'œuvre cinématographique et l'œuvre phonographique ou vidéographique, en identifiant la contribution typique de chaque auteur à ces œuvres.

Alors que dans l'œuvre en collaboration, le droit d'auteur est attribué à ceux qui y ont collaboré en tant qu'auteurs, dans l'œuvre collective, le droit d'auteur «est attribué à l'entité singulière ou collective qui a organisé et dirigé sa création et au nom de celui qui a divulgué ou publié» (art. 19/1 CDA). En d'autres termes, la loi cède le droit d'auteur non aux créateurs intellectuels qui y ont collaboré, mais plutôt à l'organisateur de l'œuvre au nom duquel elle a été divulguée ou publiée et qui peut être une entité individuelle ou collective. Comme dans le contrat de copyright en faveur du mandant ou de l'employeur, ici la loi elle-même attribue le droit d'auteur à une personne autre que le créateur intellectuel, et qui peut etre une personne juridique (par ex. une société commerciale).

Cependant, il est important de mieux comprendre l'oeuvre collective. À ce titre, les journaux et autres publications périodiques sont présumés des oeuvres collectives, et le droit d'auteur appartient aux sociétés respectives (art. 19/3 CDA). Il en va de même pour les programmes informatiques et les bases de données créés au sein d'une entreprise (art. 3/2 du décret-loi n. 252/94 et art. 5/du décret-loi n. 122/2000). Les dictionnaires et les encyclopédies sont également considérés comme des œuvres collectives.

La protection du titre de l'œuvre non publiée, ainsi que du titre des journaux et d'autres périodiques, dépend de l'enregistrement (art. 214 CDA). Lors de l'enregistrement des titres de ces œuvres, des entités naturelles ou collectives, généralement des entreprises des media, acquièrent des «droits d›auteur» dont la logique est plus proche de celle des droits voisins. La protection des titres a des exigences qui sont étrangères au droit d›auteur classique.

Cependant, le droit d'auteur sur l'œuvre collective ne se limite pas au titre, car il couvre également le contenu de l'œuvre, par exemple articles de journaux ou entrées d'encyclopédie. La loi se réserve le droit d'auteur sur la production personnelle de certains ou de certains collaborateurs discriminables dans l'ensemble de l'œuvre collective, en les renvoyant au régime de l'œuvre réalisée en collaboration (art. 19/2 CDA). En d'autres termes, même dans l'œuvre collective, le créateur intellectuel n'est pas complètement dépouillé de son droit d'auteur, bien que son silence semble compter comme un consentement à la publication de l'œuvre sans désignation de la paternité et «cession» des droits à l'entité qui organise et publie l'œuvre[28].

Cette compréhension du régime de propriété du droit d'auteur fondé sur le principe de la paternité est également valable pour les programmes informatiques et les bases de données - qui, de plus, sont présumés œuvres collectives lorsqu'elles sont créées dans une entreprise. La loi établit que les droits appartiennent au destinataire du programme (ou de la base) lorsqu'il est créé par le travailleur dans le cadre d'un contrat de travail ou par un travailleur indépendant dans le cadre d'un contrat de commande, sauf possibilité de stipulation contraire ou résultat différent selon les finalités du contrat (art. 3/2 du décret-loi n. 252/94 et art. 5/3 du décret-loi n. 122/2000; pour le travail photographique réalisé en exécution de contrat de travail ou par arrêté, le droit d'auteur est présumé appartenir à l'employeur ou au mandant - art. 165 CDA). Le droit d'auteur naît *ipso facto* avec la création intellectuelle et dans la sphère juridique du créateur de l'œuvre. Cependant, par convention ou règle légale, des droits patrimoniaux peuvent être attribués à l'employeur ou au mandant.

Dans tous les cas, l'œuvre générée par un système d'IA n'est pas protégée par le droit d'auteur car elle ne résulte pas de choix libres et créatifs, mais du fonctionnement automatique d'algorithmes et de logiciels. Lors de l'enregistrement d'images ou de sons, l'œuvre peut être protégée par le droit du producteur phonographique ou viodegraphique, ou par le droit du producteur de la base de don-

---

28 ALEXANDRE DIAS PEREIRA, *Op. Cit.* 2008a. p. 260-261

nées (contre l'extraction et la réutilisation d'une partie importante des données de la base). La durée de protection de est plus courte, mais rien n'empêche le producteur d'être une personne morale, comme dans la plupart des cas.

3.3. Opportunité d'une protection des produits d'intelligence artificielle

3.3.1. Protection par le droit d'auteur

Compte tenu de la capacité de production presque infinie de l'IA, il est possible que la protection du droit d'auteur de ces œuvres dévaste l'espace de la liberté de création intellectuelle, perturbant l'équilibre entre la création de la machine et la création humaine. Il existe, en effet, un risque que l'IA dépasse les capacités de création littéraire et artistique des humains. En ce sens, le créateur intellectuel humain peut devenir obsolète et jetable face aux capacités promises par l'IA[29].

Toutefois, les œuvres artificielles peuvent déjà être protégées sous forme de vidéogrammes ou de phonogrammes, les droits sur ces enregistrements appartenant aux producteurs respectifs. En ce sens, comme le producteur de phonogrammes ou de vidéogrammes, la production IA doit contenir l'identification du «producteur» à protéger par ce droit connexe, en indiquant la source respective. Le marquage des œuvres d'IA sera important dès le départ pour que

---

[29] JESUS MANUEL ZATARAIN, "The Role of Automated Technology in the Creation of Copyright Works: The Challenges of Artificial Intelligence." *International Review of Law, Computers and Technology*, v. 31, n. 1, p. 91–104, 2017; BENÔIT MICHAUX, "Singularité Technologique, Singularité Humaine et Droit d'auteur." In *Droit, Normes et Libertés Dans Le Cybermonde*. Bruxelles: Larcier, 2018. p. 418.

le public sache s'il s'agit d'œuvres à usage gratuit ou soumises au droit du producteur. La maximisation de l'offre culturelle est importante et l'IA contribuera certainement à accroître l'offre culturelle.

3.3.2. Protection par un régime autonome

Le créateur intellectuel est la raison d'être et le protagoniste du régime juridique du droit d'auteur, au moins dans la tradition juridique de l'Europe continentale. L'application des règles de droit d'auteur faites pour les humains au système d'IA n'implique pas la dénaturation de ces règles, au contraire, elle aide à clarifier le sens et les limites de la protection conférée par le droit d'auteur au sens propre[30].

Cependant, autor du droit d'auteur, le système connaît les droits voisins, à savoir celui du producteur du phonogramme et / ou du vidéogramme, des éditeurs de publications de presse pour l'utilisation en ligne (article 15 de la Directive (UE) 2019/790, non encore transposée dans non encore transposée dans le droit portugais) et des bases de données. Actuellement, bien que la loi portugaise ne interdire pas la création d'un droit voisin spécifique pour les œuvres générées de manière autonome par des intelligences artificielles[31], le développement de l'IA ne semble pas exiger un nouveau droit connexe, en plus de ceux que la loi prévoit déjà, sauf peut-être dans le domaine des arts plastiques (par exemple peinture, sculpture). Mais même dans le domaine de ce dernier, le travail de l'IA

---

[30] PEDRO DE PERDIGÃO LANA, *Op. Cit.* 2020. p. 142-148

[31] Cependant, les États membres de l'Union européenne ne peuvent pas créer de nouveaux droits voisins nationaux, et il existe plusieurs exigences pour la création d'un nouveau droit connexe dans le droit d'auteur communautaire. Cf. ANA RAMALHO,"Beyond the Cover Story – An Enquiry into the EU Competence to Introduce a Right for Publishers", *IIC International Review of Intellectual Property and Competition Law,* v. 48, n. 1, p. 71–91, 2017.

peut être assimilé au travail de la nature ou au travail généré par des animaux, qui ne sont protégés par le droit d'auteur, ni comme d'art aléatoire, sauf dans la mesure où l'animal est un élément du processus de création esquissé par l'auteur (humain)[32].

En outre, le Code civil spécifie comme cas de spécification «l'écriture, la peinture, le dessin, la photographie, l'impression, la gravure et autres actes similaires, réalisés avec l'utilisation d'autres matériaux» (art. 1338). Le fait que ces activités soient menées par IA n'empêche pas l'application du Code civil, qui distingue la spécification de bonne foi de la spécification de mauvaise foi. Dans la première situation, la personne qui donne une nouvelle forme, à travers son travail, à une chose mobile appartenant à une autre personne, fait sienne la chose transformée, si elle ne peut pas être restaurée à sa forme originale ou ne peut être restaurée sans perdre la valeur créée par la spécification, ayant le propriétaire de la matière, dans ce dernier cas, le droit de conserver la chose, si la valeur de la spécification ne dépasse pas celle de la matière. En tout cas, si celui qui garde la chose est obligé de compenser l'autre de la valeur qui lui appartient (art. 1336). Dans la seconde situation, la chose spécifiée est restituée à son propriétaire dans l'état dans lequel elle se trouve, avec dommages et intérêts, sans que le propriétaire soit obligé d'indemniser le prescripteur, si la valeur augmentait de plus du tiers de la valeur de la chose spécifiée; si l'augmentation est plus élevée, le propriétaire de la chose doit remplacer ce qui excède ledit tiers (art. 1337).

Le cadre juridique actuel n'a pas empêché le développement de nouvelles technologies et, par conséquent, à notre avis, une harmonisation plus poussée au niveau européen ou international n'est pas encore nécessaire, sauf peut-être en ce qui concerne la protection des œuvres d'art générées par l'IA (par ex. logiciel créatif avec

---

[32] JOSÉ ALBERTO VIEIRA, *op. Cit.*, 2001. p. 132.

autonomie d'impression 3D). Mais, le droit connexe du producteur semble capable d'assurer un certain niveau de protection et de rémunération pour plusiers productions de l'IA[33]. En le combinant avec d'autres formes de monétisation caractéristiques de la société de l'information, en plus d'autres droits de propriété intellectuelle (tels que la concurrence déloyale et les secrets d'affaires), l'objectif de stimuler économiquement le développement de ce type de technologie semble être suffisamment rempli, sans qu'il soit nécessaire de modifier les éléments structurels du droit d'auteur.

Bibliographie sur le droit d'auteur au Portugal

AA.VV. - Direito de autor: que futuro na era digital? Lisboa : Guerra e Paz, 2016

AA.VV - Revista de Direito Intelectual, APDI (2014-)

AA.VV. – Direito da Sociedade da Informação, 10 vols., Coimbra Editora, 1999/2012.

AA.VV. - Num Novo Mundo do Direito de Autor? 2 Tomos, Cosmos, 1994.

AKESTER, Patrícia - Direito de Autor em Portugal, nos PALOP, na União Europeia e nos Tratados Internacionais, Almedina, 2013

ASCENSÃO, José de Oliveira - Direito Civil - Direito de Autor e Direitos Conexos. Coimbra: Coimbra Editora, 1992 - Estudos sobre Direito da Internet e da Sociedade da Informação, Almedina, 2001

CORDEIRO, Pedro - Direito de Autor e Radiodifusão, Almedina, 2004.

LEITÃO, Luís Manuel Teles de Menezes – Manual de Direito de Autor, 3.ª ed. Almedina, 2020

MELLO, Alberto de Sá e - Manual de Direito de Autor, 4-ª ed. Almedina, 2020 - Contrato de Direito de Autor A autonomia contratual na formação do direito de autor, Almedina, 2008

PEREIRA, Alexandre L. Dias - Direito da propriedade intelectual & novas tecnologias - Estudos, vol. 1, Gestlegal, 2019 - Direitos de Autor e Liberdade de Informação. Almedina: Coimbra, 2008 - Informática, Direito de Autor e Propriedade Tecnodigital, Coimbra Editora, 2001

REBELLO, Luiz Francisco – Código do Direito de Autor e dos Direitos Conexos Anotado, 3ª ed., Âncora, 2006 - Introdução ao Direito de Autor, Vol. I. D. Quixote: Lisboa, 1994

[33] ANA RAMALHO, "Beyond the Cover Story – An Enquiry into the EU Competence to Introduce a Right for Publishers." *IIC International Review of Intellectual Property and Competition Law* 48/ (2017), p. 71–91.

RENDAS, Tito, SILVA, Nuno Sousa e - O Direito de Autor nos Tribunais, Lisboa, 2ª ed., UCP, 2019.

TRABUCO, Cláudia - O Direito de Reprodução de Obras Literárias e Artísticas no Ambiente Digital, Coimbra Editora, 2006

VICENTE, Dário Moura – A Tutela Internacional da Propriedade Intelectual, 2.º ed. Almedina, 2019

VIEIRA, José Alberto – A Protecção dos Programas de Computador pelo Direito de Autor, Lex, 2005

VITORINO, António de Macedo - A Eficácia dos Contratos de Direito de Autor, Almedina, 2005

A TDM Copyright for AI in Europe: A View from Portugal*

Abstract: The development of Artificial Intelligence (AI) justified the harmonization in the European Union (EU) of a new copyright exception regarding text and data mining (TDM) for purposes of scientific research conducted by research organizations and entities responsible for cultural heritage. This exception is binding and mandatory, as Member States have to provide it in domestic law and cannot be excluded by contract nor by technical measures. In addition to this exception for sicentific purposes, a general TDM exception is also provided, which is also binding but applies only by default, meaning that it can be excluded by contract and/or by technical measures. The defaulft TDM exception also applies to computer programs, rasing the question of whether acts allowed under the Sofware Directive can now be excluded by contract and/or technical measures. It is far from clear whether the new regime extends or, on the contrary, restricts freedom of innovation in AI, and whether and how the TDM copyright will contribute to the development of AI and encourage 'machine learning' in Europe. The Portuguese implementation of the new 'TDM Copyright' has been faithful to EU law, and therefore AI development in Portugal will be carried

* Journal of Intellectual Property Law & Practice, vol. 18 / 12, p. 900-906, 2023, published by Sweet & Maxwell (imprint of Thomson Reuters).

out under the copyright terms of Directive 2019/790, which seeks a fair balance between the principle of high level protection of rightholders, users' fundamental rights and freedoms, and the good functioning of the digital market in the EU.

1. Introduction: TDM copyright for 'the encouragement of machine learning'?

Artificial Intelligence (hereinafter AI) was identified by the European Commission as a critical sector for Europe, considering that 'the increase in computational capacity, the availability of data and the evolution of algorithms have made AI one of the most strategic technologies of the 21st century'.[1] However, the development of AI faces legal constraints and legal uncertainty, namely with the use by AI systems of literary and artistic works protected by copyright and related rights, including computer programs and databases.

From a purely technical point of view, AI systems reproduce works and other content in the process of creating new content, be it texts, sounds and/or images and even software. In the field of databases, AI systems extract data from the database. Are these acts of reproduction or extraction subject to copyright or special rights?

During the preliminay drafting of Directive 2019/790 on copyright in the digital single market[2] (hereinafter DSM), the European Commission considered that the new mandatory exception or limitation for the use of text and data mining (hereinafter TDM)

---

[1] *Artificial Intelligence for Europe*, COM(2018) 237 final, Brussels, 25.4.2018, p. 3. Available at https://eur-lex.europa.eu/legal-content/EN/TXT/HTML/?uri=CELEX:52018DC0237

[2] Directive (EU) 2019/790 of the European Parliament and of the Council of 17 April 2019 on copyright and related rights in the Digital Single Market and amending Directives 96/9/EC and 2001/29/EC.

technologies in the field of scientific research would be of great utility for AI development.[3]

Later, after the approval of the Directive, the European Parliament adopted a resolution on intellectual property rights for the development of AI technologies[4], according to which it will be possible to protect works generated autonomously by AI with recourse to material protected by copyright, only if the copyright holder has granted permission or unless exceptions or limitations to copyright apply[5], in particular the exception relating to TDM provided for by the DSM Directive[6]. It also recalls the ethical duty of the Union to support the development of AI worldwide, facilitating cross-border cooperation in this field, in particular through limitations and exceptions with regard to cross-border research and TDM[7].

---

[3] Artificial Intelligence for Europe (n 1) at 11. For preliminary and preparatory works, European Commission, Directorate-General for the Internal Market and Services, JM d'Argenteuil, J Triaille, A Francquen, *Study on the legal framework of text and data mining (TDM)* (EU Publications Office 2014), available at https://data.europa.eu/doi/10.2780/1475; C Geiger, G Frosio, O Bulayenko, *The Exception for Text and Data Mining (TDM) in the Proposed Directive on Copyright in the Digital Single Market - Legal Aspects* (European Parliament 2018), available at https://www.europarl.europa.eu/RegData/etudes/IDAN/2018/604941/IPOL_IDA(2018)604941_EN.pdf

[4] European Parliament resolution of 20 October 2020 on intellectual property rights for the development of artificial intelligence technologies (2020), available at https://www.europarl.europa.eu/doceo/document/TA-9-2020-0277_EN.html

[5] Directive 2019/790, recital 15.

[6] Directive 2019/790, recital 17.

[7] Directive 2019/790, recital 20. It is understood that the policy of AI development cannot make a 'clean slate' of copyright, nor exempt users of AI systems from respecting copyright by means of helding Robots liable for their acts, and the risk exists that, according to M Senftleben and L Buijtelaar, 'Robot Creativity: An Incentive-Based Neighbouring Rights Approach' EIPR 42 (2020), p. 797 at 814, that: 'Instead of seeing the grant of protection as a stimulus for stronger efforts to develop the full potential of creative AI machines, robot users may eschew the right holder status to escape liability for potential infringements'. On this isue, the Members of the European Parliament (MEPs) found that generative AI (for ex. GPT) should disclose the source of the generated content, in particular designing the system by default to prevent illegal content. See DRAFT Compromise Amendments on the Draft Report Proposal for a regulation of the European Parliament and of the Council on harmonised rules on Artificial Intelligence (Artificial Intelligence Act) and amending

The DSM Directive answers the question of whether and how copyright will facilitate the development of AI in the EU, namely 'Machine Learning'. The first copyright act – the Statue of Anne[8] - was entitled 'An Act for the Encouragement of Learning'. Is this the Era of copyright for the encouragement of 'Machine Learning'?

2. TDM for scientific research purposes by research organizations and cultural heritage institutions

The DSM Directive introduced mandatory exceptions or restrictions for the use of TDM technologies, illustration for teaching in the digital environment and for the preservation of cultural heritage[9]. These are added to those already listed in Directives 96/9[10], 2001/29[11] and 2009/24[12].

The TDM exception is meant to play an important role in the development of AI. To begin with, text and data mining is considered a new type of use made possible by digital technologies and as such not yet provided for in EU legislation[13], the so-called

certain Union Legislative Acts (16/5/2023), available at https://www.europarl.europa.eu/resources/library/media/20230516RES90302/20230516RES90302.pdf

8 The Statute of Anne (1710), available at https://www.copyrighthistory.com/anne.html

9 Directive 2019/790, recital 5.

10 Directive 96/9/EC of the European Parliament and of the Council of 11 March 1996 on the legal protection of databases, OJ L 77, 27.3.1996, p. 20.

11 Directive 2001/29/EC of the European Parliament and of the Council of 22 May 2001 on the harmonisation of certain aspects of copyright and related rights in the information society, OJ L 167, 22.6.2001, p. 10.

12 Directive 2009/24/EC of the European Parliament and of the Council of 23 April 2009 on the legal protection of computer programs, OJ L 111, 5.5.2009, p. 16, articles 5(3) and art. 6. In domestic law, see articles 10(2) and 7 of Decree-Law No. 252/94 of 20 October, which implemented Directive 91/250/EEC, of the Council, of 14 May (repealed and replaced by Directive 2009/24/EC).

13 Directive 2019/790, recital 8.

automated computational analysis of information in digital format, such as texts, sounds, images or data, regarded as a very valuable tool for research and innovation, as it processes large amounts of information with the aim of obtaining new knowledge and discovering new trends. By TDM it is understood any automatic analysis technique aimed at the analysis of texts and data in digital format, in order to produce information, such as patterns, trends and correlations, among others[14].

In order to overcome legal uncertainty regarding the copyright relevance of text and data mining, the DSM Directive established that universities and other research bodies, as well as institutions responsible for cultural heritage, may carry out TDM without authorization of rightholders, e.g. when data are normalized in that process, even if these acts are protected by copyright, by related or special rights such as the *sui generis* right of the database producer or the new right of the publisher of press publications with regard to online uses.[15]

---

[14] Directive 2019/790, art. 2(2).

[15] Personal data also raises concerns about AI uses, which may be allowed for general interest scientific research purposes under Regulation (EU) 2016/679 of the European Parliament and of the Council of 27 April 2016 on the protection of natural persons with regard to the processing of personal data and on the free movement of such data, and repealing Directive 95/46/EC (General Data Protection Regulation), OJ L 119, 4.5.2016, p. 1, see Articles 9(2)(j) (processing of special categories of personal data), 14(5)(b) (information to be provided where personal data have not been obtained from the data subject), 17(3)(d) (right to erasure - 'right to be forgotten'), 21(6) (right to object) and in special Article 89 (safeguards and derogations relating to processing for archiving purposes in the public interest, scientific or historical research purposes or statistical purposes); recitals 26, 33, 50 to 53, 62, 65, 113, 156, and 157 to 160. On this issue see European Parliament, How the General Data Protection Regulation changes the rules for scientific research (EPRS Brussels 2019). Concerning non-personal data the principle is that they should be freely available in machine-readable and open formats to feed machine learning and AI. Regulation (EU) 2018/1807 of the European Parliament and of the Council of 14 November 2018 on a framework for the free flow of non-personal data in the European Union, OJ L 303, 28.11.2018, p. 59, recital 9 reads that 'The expanding Internet of Things, artificial intelligence and machine learning, represent major sources of non-personal data, for example as a result of their deployment in automated industrial production processes. Specific examples of non-personal data

The TDM exception for scientific research purposes prevails over any subscription conditions of publications or open access licenses terms that exclude it[16]. The exception is limited to the exclusive right of reproduction and to the right of database extraction, and it is provided only to universities and other research bodies, and institutions responsible for cultural heritage, although it may extend to their private partners in activities of research in the scope of public-private partnerships[17]. Moreover, the exception applies only where the beneficiaries have *legal access* to the protected content, which may be based on an open access policy or agreements (e.g. signatures) between rightholders and research organizations or cultural heritage institutions, or by other legal means, such as for ex. content freely available online[18].

In short, research organizations and institutions responsible for cultural heritage are allowed to make reproductions and extractions to carry out TDM in works or other protected material to which they have legal access for purposes of scientific investigation[19]. This exception also includes the storage of copies for the purposes of scientific research[20], including for subsequent verification of the research

include aggregate and anonymised datasets used for big data analytics, data on precision farming that can help to monitor and optimise the use of pesticides and water, or data on maintenance needs for industrial machines.' The same principle applies to the re-use of public sector information, under Directive (EU) 2019/1024 of the European Parliament and of the Council of 20 June 2019 on open data and the re-use of public sector information (recast), OJ L 172, 26.6.2019, p. 56. See also Regulation (EU) 2022/868 of the European Parliament and of the Council of 30 May 2022 on European data governance and amending Regulation (EU) 2018/1724 (Data Governance Act), OJ L 152, 3.6.2022, p. 1–44; https://digital-strategy.ec.europa.eu/en/policies/psi-open-data

[16] Directive 2019/790, recital 10.

[17] Directive 2019/790, recital 11.

[18] Directive 2019/790, recital 14. Open access is a must in research funded by the European Commission. See <https://research-and-innovation.ec.europa.eu/strategy/strategy-2020-2024/our-digital-future/open-science/open-access_en>

[19] Directive 2019/790, art. 3(1).

[20] An 'an ancillary right to digitise the works by publicly accessible libraries' had already been recognized by the Court judgment in *Eugen Ulmer* C117/13, ECLI:EU:C:2014:2196, para. 43, which, by the way, adopts the doctrine of 'users'

results, provided that the storage is done in a secure environment. It is for each Member State to decide, after discussion with relevant stakeholders, on other specific provisions for the retention of copies, including the possibility of appointing trusted bodies for this purpose. However, security conditions must not unduly restrict the application of the exception, and must be proportionate and limited to what is necessary to keep copies securely and prevent unauthorized use. Likewise, security conditions must not prevent other uses for scientific research purposes, such as scientific peer review and joint research, which are considered already covered by the exception or limitation provided for in art. 5(3), indent a), of the InfoSoc Directive[21].

Furthermore, this exception is without prejudice to other exceptions or limitations to exclusive rights. Thus, as the preamble reads[22], TDM can also be carried out in relation to the facts themselves or to data that are not protected by copyright and, in these cases, no authorization would is required under copyright law, as well as it may not concern acts of reproduction or reproductions covered by the mandatory exception of acts of temporary reproduction provided for under art. 5(1) of Directive 2001/29, which continues to apply to TDM techniques that do not imply making copies of materials beyond the scope of this exception.

The principle is that the exception for text and data mining should not be interpreted in the opposite sense to broaden the subject

rights', later confirmed in *Funke Medien* and and *Poland c. Parliament and Council*, respectively judgments of 29 July 2019, C 469/17, ECLI:EU:C:2019:623, para. 70, and 26 April 2022, C 401/19, ECLI:EU:C:2022:297, para. 88. In favor of the user's rights doctrine in the US, L. Ray PATTERSON / Stanley W. LINDBERG, *The Nature of Copyright: A Law of Users' Rights*, The University of Georgia Press, 1991, and in Portugal, Alexandre DIAS PEREIRA, *Direitos de autor e liberdade de informação*, Coimbra, Almedina, 2008, p. 649; Tito RENDAS, 'Are copyright-permitted uses 'exceptions', 'limitations' or 'user rights'? The special case of Article 17 CDSM Directive' 17 *JIPLP* 17 (2022) 54-64.

[21] Directive 2019/790, recital 5.

[22] Directive 2019/790, recital 9.

matter and content of the exclusive right, nor to tighten the scope of existing exceptions and limitations. However, it is not easy to draw the line between what was previously permitted as 'transient or incidental reproductions', including 'browsing' and 'caching'[23], and what is now covered by the TDM activities. For instance, it is not clear whether 'web harvesting of AI training data' is included in the scope of the TDM exception and, therefore, 'time will tell whether perhaps a new exception provision under copyright law is needed for the web harvesting of AI training data in Europe'[24].

The lawfulness of 'transient or incidental reproductions' under art. 5(1) of the InfoSoc Directive instrumental to 'enabling either efficient transmission in a network between third parties by an intermediary [mere conduit, caching], or a lawful use of a work or other subject-matter to be made', and in particular 'acts of reproduction concerned should have no separate economic value on their own'[25]. Once it is understood that the TDM rather implies reproductions which have 'separate economic value on their own', in light of the wide definitions of reproduction and extraction rights[26], TDM related reproductions are no longer excluded from the right of reproduction under art. 5(1) of the InfoSOc Directive. It means that copyright expands along with the economic value of the TDM

[23] Directive 2001/29, recital 33.

[24] Jan Bernd Nordemann, Jonathan Pukas, «Copyright exceptions for AI training data—will there be an international level playing field?», JIPLP 17/12 (2022), p. 973-4.

[25] Directive 2001/29, recital (33).

[26] In *Infopaq I*, the CJUE found that 'An act occurring during a data capture process, which consists of storing an extract of a protected work comprising 11 words and printing out that extract, is such as to come within the concept of reproduction in part within the meaning of Article 2 of Directive 2001/29/EC [...], if the elements thus reproduced are the expression of the intellectual creation of their author' – judgment of 16 july 2009, C5/08, ECLI:EU:C:2009:465. Moreover, in *British Horseracing*, the CJUE held that the Database Diretive provided a "wide definition" of the extraction right, in order to protect the producer against acts 'depriving him of revenue which should have enabled him to redeem the cost of the investment' - judgment of 9 November 2004, C-203/02, *British Horseracing*, ECLI:EU:C:2004:695, para 51.

activity, and therefore TDM is made subject to the rightholder's authorisation or to a statutory restriction of the exclusive right.

The same reasoning applies to copies of works or other protected material made in the context of TDM mining, which must be stored with an adequate level of security and may be kept for the purposes of scientific research, including for verifying the results of the investigation[27]. Rightholders can apply measures to ensure the security and integrity of the networks and databases in which the works or other protected material are hosted to the extent necessary to achieve that objective, and to this end, Member States shall encourage rightholders, research organizations and institutions responsible for cultural heritage to develop agreed best practices[28].

Will fair compensation be due for reproductions made within TDM for purposes of scientific research? According to the recitals, there is no justification for compensating rightholders for the uses allowed by the new exception, because the potential damage they suffer is minimal, taking into account that it is limited to entities carrying out scientific research[29]. A 'research organization' means a university, including its libraries, a research institute or any other entity whose main objective is to carry out scientific research or the exercise of didactic activities that also involve to carry out scientific research, and do not for profit

[27] Directive 2019/790, art. 3(2). Re-usability, including for verification purposes, is one of the 2016 FAIR Guiding Principles for scientific data management and stewardship ('Findable, Acessible, Interoperable, Reusable'). See https://www.go-fair.org/fair-principles/

[28] Directive 2019/790, art. 3 (3) and (4). The legal framework for computer security is established by Law No. 46/2018, of 13 August, which transposes Directive (EU) 2016/1148, of the European Parliament and of the Council, of 6 July 2016, on measures aimed at ensuring a high common level of security for networks and information systems across the European Union, , which was repealed by Directive (EU) 2022/2555 of the European Parliament and of the Council of 14 December 2022 on measures for a high common level of cybersecurity across the Union, also amending Regulation (EU) No 910/2014 and Directive (EU) 2018/1972 (not yet implemented in Portugal).

[29] Directive 2019/790, recital 17.

or reinvest all profits in scientific research or act in the context of a public interest mission recognized by a Member State, so that access to the results resulting from that scientific research cannot benefit in preferential conditions a company that exercises decisive influence over that body[30]; an 'institution responsible for cultural heritage' means a library or museum accessible to the public, an archive or an institution responsible for cinematographic or sound heritage[31].

3. TDM for purposes (and or by entities) other than sicentific research

Along with the TDM exception for scientific research purposes, the DSM Directive harmonized another TDM binding exception, according which the rights provided for in art. 5(a) and 7(1) of Databases Directive, in art. 2 of InfoSoc Directive, in art. 4(1)(a)(b) of Software Directive and in art. 15(1) of DSM Directive (right of the press publisher), do not apply to reproductions and extractions of works and other protected material that are legally accessible for TDM purposes, as well as their conservation as long as necessary for conducting TDM[32]. Importantly, rightholders may expressly reserve this TDM use in an appropriate manner, 'such as machine-readable means in the case of content made available to the public online', without prejudice to TDM for scientific research[33].

As it is stated in the preamble[34], in addition to their importance in the context of scientific research, TDM techniques are widely

[30] Directive 2019/790, art. 1(1),

[31] Directive 2019/790, art. 1(3)

[32] Directive 2019/790, art. 4(1) (2).

[33] Directive 2019/790, art. 4(3)(4).

[34] Directive 2019/790, recital 18.

used, both by public and private entities, to analyze large amounts of data in different domains of life and for various purposes, namely for public services, complex business decisions and for the development of new applications or technologies. Due to its economic value, TDM for purposes and or by entities other than scientific research may be subject to licenses by rightholders. However, no additional authorization is necessary, as the exception, which is also binding to Member Statets, applies by default, i.e., it can be excluded by rightholders. The default statutory exception is justified due to the existing legal uncertainty regarding the reproductions and extractions carried out for TDM purposes even when access to the content is legal, in particular with regard to the conditions of the temporary reproduction exception provided for in article 5(1) of InfoSoc Directive, because reproductions carried out within TDM activities for purposes (and or by entities) other than scientific research may have 'separate economic value on their own' and therefore should not be completely copyright-free.

In order to provide greater legal certainty and, at the same time, to encourage innovation in the private sector[35], the DSM Directive provided a new general exception for reproductions and extractions of works or other protected material for TDM purposes, including the storage of the copies as long as necessary for such purposes. This exception also requires 'lawful access' to the content, namely whenever it has been made available online to the public and provided that the rights holders have not adequately reserved the right to make reproductions and extractions within text and data mining activities for purposes (and or by entities) other than sicentific research.

Rightholders may therefore reserve the right to mine for data through the use of machine-readable means, including metadata

[35] Directive 2019/790, recital 18.

and general conditions of an Internet site or service, in relation to content that has been made available online to the public, or by terms of contract agreements or by a unilateral declaration in other cases. Despite rightholders can prevent TDM for purposes other than scientific research, this default cannot prejudice the mandatory TDM exception for scientific research purposes, nor the exception of temporary reproduction provided for in art. 5(1) of InfoSoc Directive.

Moreover, this default exception also applies to computer programs, the legal protection of which already provided for the freedom to analyze software as an object of scientific research, as well as the decompilation of program interfaces for interoperability purposes with other programs.[36] It has been argued that TDM should equally apply to computer programs where carried out for scientific research purposes, but nonetheless: 'While it is possible that TDM for research on computer programs can be performed on the grounds of Art 5 (3) of the Computer Programs Directive (the so called 'black box' analysis), that provision does not cover acts of translation and adaptation. [...] National lawmakers are encouraged to eliminate the disparities regarding the scope of application of the provisions of Art 3 and 4 DSMD and specifically to provide that TDM for research purposes on computer programs is also allowed'.[37]

However, when carried out for purposes (or by entities) other than scientific research, software analysis by means of TDM is is no longer mandatory[38]. Whether and how this solution fosters the development of AI in Europe is hard to tell.

---

[36] Software Directive, art. 5(3) and art. 6; in domestic law, Decree-Law no. 252/94, arts. 10(2) and 7.

[37] J Griffiths, T Synodinou, R Xalabarder, 'Comment of the European Copyright Society Addressing Selected Aspects of the Implementation of Articles 3 to 7 of Directive (EU) 2019/790 on Copyright in the Digital Single Market' *GRUR Int. 72 (2023), p.* 22, available at https://doi.org/10.1093/grurint/ikac137

[38] Software Directive, art. 8, para. 2.

4. The Portuguese implementation of the TDM exceptions

In Portugal, Law No. 11/2023 of March 22, authorized the Government to implement the DSM Directive, and in particular to add exceptions and limitations to the exercise of copyright and related rights, including rights over computer programs and databases, under the terms of the relevant articles of the DSM Directive.[39]

The implementation has been carried out by Decree-Law No. 47/2023, of 19 June, mainly by means of amending the Copyright Act[40]. With regard to TDM exceptions, the transposition consisted of introducing two new indents, v) and w), in paragraph 2 of art. 75 of the Copyright Act, and the addition of a new number 6 to the aforementioned article, to provide for the notions of 'research organization' and 'text and data mining'. Furthermore, it amended art. 76 on free use requirements, introducing new numbers, namely 4 (on safe storage of reproductions made for TDM purposes) and 5 (on security and integrity measures for networks and databases where the texts and data subject to mining are kept). In this regard, the legislator did not take advantage of the possibility of appointing trust bodies to carry out cybersecurity and network integrity measures[41], rather entrusted rightholders and research organizations to agree on best practices on cybersecurity concerning safe storage of reproductions.

On the other hand, Decree-Law 43/2023 also amended the Database Copyright Act[42], adding a new paragraph to number 1 of article 10,

---

[39] Law No. 11/2023 of March 22, art. 2.°/B.

[40] 'Código do Direito de Autor e dos Direitos Conexos', approved by Decreto-Lei n.° 63/85, de 14 de março, several times amended, mainly to implement EU Copyright Directives.

[41] The legal regime for IT security is established by Law No. 46/2018, of August 13, which implements Directive (EU) 2016/1148 of the European Parliament and of the Council of 6 July 2016 concerning measures for a high common level of security of network and information systems across the Union.

[42] Decree-Law No. 122/2000, of July 4, which has implemented Directive 96/9/EC on the legal protection of databases.

under the heading exceptions, which allows acts of reproduction and extraction of works and other legally accessible protected material for TDM purposes, as long as this use has not been expressly reserved by the respective rights holders in an appropriate manner (the default TDM exception). Furthermore, two other free uses have been added to art. 15, namely acts of reproduction and extraction carried out by research organizations and institutions responsible for cultural heritage to carry out mining from works or other protected material to which they have legal access for purposes of scientific research, on the one hand and acts of reproduction and extraction of works and other legally accessible protected material for TDM purposes, as long as this use has not been expressly reserved by the respective rights holders in appropriate manner, in particular by means of optical reading in the case of content made available to the public online, on the other - indent e) and f), respectively.

It should be noted that Decree-Law 47/2023 did not amend the Software Copyright Act[43]. The DSM Directive expressly states that Member States shall provide for an exception or limitation to the rights provided for in art. 4(1)(a) and (b) of th Software Directive, for reproductions and extractions of works and other legally accessible protected material within TDM for purposes other than scientific research or by entities that are not research organizations or institutions responsible for cultural heritage.

The transposition of the Directive was silent on this issue. The legislator possibly considered that the failure to provide the TDM exception for purposes of scientific research in the field of computer programs would mean, *a contrario*, that these acts would not be permitted. However, this free use was already be permiited under the freedom to study computer programs as objects of scientific research,

[43] Decree-Law 252/94, which implemented Council Directive 91/250/EEC, repealed and replaced by EU Directive 2009/24/on the legal protection of computer programs.

as well as the decompilation of program interfaces for the purpose of interoperability with other programs. In any case, the legislator's omission is criticizable, although it is recognized that the default nature of the TDM exception for purposes other than scientific research will contribute to curtail competitive technological innovation in software, which is a critical sector of AI.

5. Closing remarks

The policy of AI development justified the introduction of a binding and mandatory TDM exception for purposes of scientific research by research organizations and cultural heritage entities. In addition to this exception of general interest, a default TDM exception is also provided for purposes (or and by entities) other than scientific research. TDM for other purposes is a default exception, because rights holders may reserve mining as a protected use of their works insofar as it requires acts of reproduction or extraction with separate economic value on their own. Moreover, it also applies to computer programs, adding to the exceptions of reverse engineering for interoperability purposes and the analysis of computer programs as objects of scientific research. The development of AI, with regard to TDM, shifts the burden of expressly reserving this new use upon the rightholders. Otherwise, by default, it is statutorily authorized.

The rational of the TDM exception is far from obvious[44]. The InfoSoc Directive already excluded transient reproductions, merely instrumental in legitimate uses, including web browsing. The default TDM exception will limit this exclusion from the right of reproduction,

[44] See Eleonora Rosati, 'An EU text and data mining exception for the few: would it make sense?' *Journal of Intellectual Property Law & Practice*, vol. 13/6 (2018), p. 429-430.

allowing rightholders to reserve TDM as acts with separate economic value on their own. The same applies to computer programs: the analysis for research on computer programs was already pemitted, as well as decompilation, and now the new TDM exception for purposes of scientific research does not include the analysis of computer programs, and TDM of software for other purposes can be excluded by contract.

Where covering TDM, even if subject to an express reservation, the useful purpose of promoting AI development in Europe may be at risk, particularly when compared to less rigid legal environments[45], such as the North-American, marked by a general *fair use* clause that entrusts the courts with the case-by-case management of adapting copyright law to the needs of technological development, and whose transplantation into EU copyright law has been advocated[46].

---

[45] See e.g. Charlotte Gerrish and AM Skavlan, 'European copyright law and the text and data mining exceptions and limitations' *Stockholm Intellectual Property Law Review* 2 (2019), p. 60 ("By creating and maintaining a restrictive environment for TDM, which is often a key component of Artificial Intelligence ("AI") and machine learning, the EU runs the risk of losing a foothold in a growing industry, and causing an exodus of key talent to other TDM friendly jurisdictions"), available at https://stockholmiplawreview.com/wp-content/uploads/2019/12/Tryck_IP_nr-2_2019_A4_European-copyright-law.pdf. Thomas Margoni and Martin Kretschmer, 'A Deeper Look into the EU Text and Data Mining Exceptions: Harmonisation, Data Ownership, and the Future of Technology', GRUR Int. 71/8 (2022), p. 685–701, argue that "there should be no need for a TDM exception for the act of extracting informational value from protected works. The EU's CDSM provisions paradoxically may favour the development of biased AI systems due to price and accessibility conditions for training data that offer the wrong incentives. To avoid licensing, it may be economically attractive for EU-based developers to train their algorithms on older, less accurate, biased data, or import AI models already trained abroad on unverifiable data"). Holding that a strict TDM excpetion is a 'foolish' and 'harmful' option to the EU competitiveness, Tito Rendas, 'Inteligênca artificial, prospeção de dados e direito de autor', in *Propriedade Intelectual, Contratação e Sociedade da Informação. Estudos Jurídicos em Homenagem a Manuel Oben Mendes*, coord. Dário Moura Vicente, Nuno Sousa e Silva, APDI/Almedina, 2022, p. 531-562, at 559. Considering that, in view of the UK policy on AI and IP, which will not allow rights holders to charge extra specifically for the mining of their works, 'there is a risk that competition between countries will result in something more akin to a race to the bottom than to a prudent balance between the legitimate interests of harvesters and copyright holders', Jan Bernd Nordemann and Jonathan Pukas, 'Copyright exceptions for AI training data', cit., p. 974.

[46] See for ex. Vanessa Jiménez Serranía, 'Datos, minería e innovación: ¿qvo vadis, Europa? Análisis sobre las nuevas excepciones para la mineria de textos

Moreover, it is claimed that the DSM Directive would have been yet another 'missed opportunity' to modernize copyright law in the face of technology challenges, in particular Artificial Intelligence[47].

However, EU Copyright Law is governed by the 'principle of high level of protection'[48] of rightholders, strengthening their bargaining power in the relation with Media and Big-Tech-Data corporations concerning extracting value by means of TDM from their works and other protected materials. In the EU, copyright is not a 'no man's land': copyrighted works and other protected material cannot be freely used to feed new technologies and AI developers. Off course AI development is important, but it should not be on the shoulders of copyright alone, despite its nowadays gigantic proportions.

The binding and mandatory TDM exception for purposes of scientific research already paves the way to AI development, including partnerships with private entities. The binding and default general TDM exception for other purposes also shifts the burden of copyright to the hands of rightholders, who will have to reserve TDM of their works. Instead of a right to authorise, TDM copyright becomes a right to oppose, as silence means acceptance.

Probably AI developers do not find it 'liberal' enough. But, at the same time, it is possible that rightholders also feel half-expropriated

---

y datos', *Cuadernos de Derecho Transnacional*, vol. 12/1 (2020), p. 247-258 ("es realmente necesario, a nuestro entender, replantearse seriamente a nivel europeo el impulso del llamado 'flexible copyright' en la aplicación de la regla de los tres pasos (threestep rules), especialmente en aras de permitir la actividad innovadora o transformativa" – at p. 256). See Christophe Geiger, «The Role of the Three-Step Test in the Adaptation of Copyright Law to the Information Society», *e-Copyright Bulletin*, 2007; Tito Rendas, *Exceptions in EU Copyright Law: In Search of a Balance Between Flexibility and Legal Certainty*, Kluwer Law International, 2021, and Eleonora Rosati, «Copyright reformed: the narrative of flexibility and its pitfalls in policy and legislative initiatives (2011–2021)», *Asia Pacific Law Review*, vol. 31/1 (2023), p. 33-54.

[47] Theodoros Chiou, 'Copyright lessons on Machine Learning: what impact on algorithmic art?' *JIPITEC* vol. 10 (2019), p. 398-411, at p. 411 ("the DSM Directive is a missed opportunity for true modernization of the European Copyright Law").

[48] See for ex. Directive 2001/29, recital 4, 9; Directive 2019/790, recital 2.

of their right to be asked permission in the first place, and perhaps an equitable compensation could be a good remedy for them concerning TDM for purposes (and or by entities) other than scientific research.[49] The equitable compensation has been excluded for the mandatory TDM exception. But, perhaps it could be an equitable remedy to rightholders who do not want to obstruct TDM, but at the same would like to get some juice out of the fruit they have created and which feeds AI for free if they do not reserve TDM of their works. The Act of Anne for the encouragement of learning did not mean that one would learn by getting printed books for free...

The Portuguese implementation of the TDM exceptions did not provide an equitable compensation for the general and TDM default exception. It follows very closely the wording of the EU provisions, except in what concerns software analysis, which apparently has not been addressed by the national legislation despite its major role in AI development and machine learning. Perhaps the national legislator found that the software copyright law already provided equivalent rules to those of the DSM Directive on the field of software. However, in this concern, comfromity with EU law cannot be fully guaranteed.

Some years ago the question was raised of whether the notion of reproduction would not apply to human brains, as it would be already applying to 'silicon brains' and therefore copyright would become a kind of 'right to read'[49]. Indeed, reading assisted by TDM digital tools is no longer copyright-free, as rightholders can reserve TDM for purposes (and or by entities) other than scientific research. Copyright is placed among transaction costs in the European market of TDM tools and activities. Consumers and other users of such tools may have to bear the cost of a 'right to read' assisted by TDM tools, except for purposes of scientific research.

---

[49] David Nimmer, 'Brains and Other Paraphernalia of the Digital Age', *Harvard Journal of Law and Technology*, vol. 10 (1996) p. 1-46.

COMPETITION IN THE ONLINE PLATFORM ECONOMY: ONLINE SALES AND ADVERTISING UNDER EU COMPETITION RULES FOR DIGITAL MARKETS*

Abstract: The online platform economy faces regulatory and competition challenges, as some platforms dominate the market, causing concerns about unfair practices and antitrust. Online intermediation services facilitate B2B and B2C direct transactions in the digital marketplace, but online sales and advertising may be restricted by commercial policies, such as selective distribution, resale price maintenance, territorial restrictions, platform bans, and cross-border sales restrictions.This paper addresses the regulatory framework adopted by the European Union to protect competition in the online platform economy, including the Digital Markets Act and the regulation on vertical agreements block exemption.

Introduction

The online platform economy faces several challenges, in particular regulatory issues and competition concerns. Some large online platforms have achieved near-monopoly dominance in certain markets,

* European Competition Law Review, vol. 45 / 8, p. 355-359, 2024, published by Sweet & Maxwell (imprint of Thomson Reuters).

raising concerns about unfair business practices and antitrust. In particular, there are anti-competitive behavior issues, such as predatory pricing or exclusionary practices, which can harm competition and consumers, as well as the vast amounts of user data that online platforms collect and which can provide them with significant competitive advantages.

Some online platforms also control access to facilities, such as key technologies or infrastructure, which are vital for competitors to effectively compete in the market. Moreover, the lack of interoperability between platforms and restrictions on data portability can inhibit competition by making it difficult for users to switch between platforms or for new entrants to enter the market, as lock-in effects entrench the market power of incumbent platforms. Not to mention that platforms that both operate a marketplace and offer their own products or services may have incentives to prioritize their own offerings over those of third-party sellers, and that some platforms impose price parity clauses in their contracts with sellers, preventing them from offering lower prices on other platforms or their own websites, thus harming consumers by maintaining artificially high prices.

Online intermediation services play a crucial role in facilitating both B2B (business-to-business) and B2C (business-to-consumer) direct transactions in the digital marketplace. These services act as platforms that connect buyers and sellers, providing a virtual space where transactions can take place efficiently and securely. B2B digital platforms streamline the procurement process, allowing businesses to easily source products or services from suppliers around the world. Concerning B2C, online intermediation services provide consumers with access to a wide range of products and services from various sellers, often with features such as user reviews, product recommendations, and secure payment processing. These platforms have revolutionized retail, enabling consumers to browse and purchase goods, while also providing sellers with opportunities for market expansion.

However, online sales may be restricted by commercial policies, such as: a) selective distribution, where manufacturers or suppliers limit the number of retailers authorized to sell their products online or requiring online retailers to have a certain level of expertise or to maintain a dedicated website; b) resale price maintenance, where manufacturers or suppliers set minimum resale prices at which their products must be sold by retailers, usually with a view to protect brand image or to ensure quality; c) territorial restrictions, where manufacturers or suppliers prevent retailers from selling their products outside of certain geographical areas or markets, usually to prevent free-riding or to maintain brand exclusivity; d) platform bans, i.e. manufacturers or suppliers may prohibit retailers from selling their products on certain online platforms or marketplaces, in order to control brand image or distribution channels; e) cross-border sales restrictions, where retailers cannot sell their products to customers located in other countries or regions (geo-blocking).

To address competion issues in the digital market, in particular in what concerns online sales and online advertising, the European Union has adopted a complex package of legislation, including, the Digital Markets Act (DMA)[1] and the Digital Services Act (DAS)[2], on one hand, and the regulation of vertical agreements block exemption (VAR)[3], on the other. This paper provides an overview of the EU

[1] Regulation (EU) 2022/1925 of the European Parliament and of the Council of 14 September 2022 on contestable and fair markets in the digital sector and amending Directives (EU) 2019/1937 and (EU) 2020/1828.

[2] Regulation (EU) 2022/2065 of the European Parliament and of the Council of 19 October 2022 on a Single Market For Digital Services and amending Directive 2000/31/EC.

[3] Commission Regulation (EU) 2022/720 of 10 May 2022 on the application of Article 101(3) of the Treaty on the Functioning of the European Union to categories of vertical agreements and concerted practices.

regulatory framework of the online platform economy concerning restrictions to online sales and advertising as competition law issues.

The regulation of digital markets and services

The DMA aims to promote innovation and a fairer environment for emerging companies in the sector, ensuring fair competition conditions for all digital companies, regardless of their size[4]. To this end, it prohibits unfair practices by online platforms that hold the largest market share (a), expands the options of choice for professional users to improve the quality of service and prices for consumers (b), and establishes a framework of rights and obligations of large online platforms (c), the so-called 'gatekeepers' who provide 'core platform services', in order to ensure that they do not abuse their position (e.g. by favoring their own products or preventing users from installing external applications).

The online platform essential service category includes services such as intermediary services, online search engines, social networks, video sharing, operating systems, web browsers, virtual assistants, cloud computing, and online advertising[5]. It is considered that large technology companies increasingly act as access points (gateways) or access controllers (gatekeepers), controlling access to the network of companies that intend to provide their online services and take on an increasingly important role as intermediaries for most transactions between business users and end users. The main objective of the DMA is, therefore, to prevent abuse by large access controllers of their dominant position to the detriment of (economically dependent) companies that wish to access online

[4] Article 1 (1) of Regulation (EU) 2022/1925.

[5] Article 2 (2) of Regulation (EU) 2022/1925.

consumers, and for this purpose it provides *ex ante* regulation for competition in the digital markets[6].

The DMA applies to so-called 'essential platform services' (excluding services related to electronic communications networks) provided or offered by gatekeepers to professional users established in the Union or to end users established or located in the Union, regardless of the place of establishment of controllers and the law applicable to the provision of the service[7]. In the virtual world, so-called gatekeepers act as 'intermediaries' between professional users who offer content and services on the network and end users of the internet (consumers or professionals). Gatekeepers can control the information that circulates on the network, for example, by making or not making news available in an online media outlet, or eliminating information by removing a publication considered inappropriate.

Given the current complexity of cyberspace, these gatekeepers allow the user to locate information or a service that would otherwise be inaccessible. In the early days of the digital revolution it was common to say that 'what is not on the Internet does not exist'. But nowadays it is more appropriate to say that what is not in the

[6] See MJ Schmidt-Kessen, M Huffman, 'Antitrust Law and Coordination Through AI-Based Pricing Technologies', in *Multidisciplinary Perspectives on Artificial Intelligence and the Law*, ed. HS Antunes, PM Freitas, AL Oliveira, CM Pereira, EV Sequeira, LB Xavier, Springer, 2023, p. 371–395. Pricing algorithms can continuously monitor competitor prices and quantify the value delivered to customers, and then adjust prices accordingly to optimize prices to maximize revenue, taking advantage of fluctuations in customer behavior, and to remain competitive in the market. Pricing algorithms enable businesses to make data-driven pricing decisions that are more accurate, timely, and responsive to market dynamics, ultimately helping to maximize revenue and profitability. However, algorithmic decision-making raises issues such as price discrimination or anticompetitive behavior, which may infringe competition rules. On this issue see notably Autorité de la concurrence & Bundeskartellamt, *Algorithms and Competition*, November 2019; Autoridade da Concorrência, *Digital ecosystems, Big Data and Algorithms*, 2019; OECD, *Handbook on Competition Policy in the Digital Age*, 2022.

[7] Article 1 (2) of Regulation (EU) 2022/1925.

online platform or the search engine (e.g. *Google*) does not exist. This controlling position of gatekeepers gives them an increasingly stronger market power. Due to their size, access controllers benefit from significant advantages over smaller competitors and occupy a dominant position in the digital market.[8]

A company is designated as a gatekeeper where it has a significant impact on the internal market, provides an essential platform service that constitutes an important gateway for professional users to reach end users, and benefits from a rooted and lasting position in its operations or is expected to benefit from such a position in the near future[9]. A platform is presumed to be a 'gatekeeper" where it: (1) has achieved an annual turnover in the European Union equal to or greater than 7,500 million euros in the last three years, or has a market capitalization equal to or greater than 75 billion euros, (2) has at least 45 million monthly active end users, (3) has 10,000 or more professional users established in the EU, and (4) controls one or more essential platform services in at least three Member States[10]. In light of these requirements, the European Commission designated six gatekeepers, who were obliged to comply with their new obligations until March 2024, namely: *Alphabet* (*Google*), *Amazon*, *Apple*, *ByteDance* (*TikTok*), *Meta* (*Facebook, Instagram*), and *Microsoft*.[11]

The DMA is complemented by the Digital Services Act (DSA), which aims to promote a safe, predictable and reliable online environment,

---

[8] In the judgment of 14 September 2022, case T-604/18, *Google and Alphabet v Commission* ('Google Android'), the General Court largely upheld the Commission's decision condemning Google for imposing illegal restrictions on Android mobile device manufacturers and mobile network operators in order to consolidate the dominant position of their search engine. On this jurisprudence see e.g. Bernadette Zelger, *Restrictions of EU Competition Law in the Digital Age: The Meaning of 'Effects' in a Digital Economy*, Springer, Cham, 2023.

[9] Article 3 (1) of Regulation (EU) 2022/1925.

[10] Article 3 (2) of Regulation (EU) 2022/1925

[11] <https://digital-strategy.ec.europa.eu/pt/news/digital-markets-act-commission--designates-six-gatekeepers>

in order to facilitate innovation and effectively protect the fundamental rights enshrined in the Charter of the Union, including the principle of consumer protection[12]. To this end, the DSA regulates the responsibility of intermediary service providers (hereinafter ISP) and establishes due diligence obligations for them, without prejudice to other rules that regulate intermediary services, such as those contained in the directives on copyright and related rights in the information society[13], copyright in the digital market[14], consumer rights[15], and other regulations such as the General Data Protection Regulation[16]. As special law, this regulation establishes special rules for new online platform services and online search engines.

Online intermediation services under the vertical agreements regulation (VAR)

The regulation of competition in the digital single market is a major concern. Online intermediation services are facilitators of B2B or B2C direct transactions. The growth of e-commerce and

---

[12] Article 1(1) of Regulation (EU) 2022/2065.

[13] Directive 2001/29/EC of the European Parliament and of the Council of 22 May 2001 on the harmonisation of certain aspects of copyright and related rights in the information society.

[14] Directive (EU) 2019/790 of the European Parliament and of the Council of 17 April 2019 on copyright and related rights in the Digital Single Market and amending Directives 96/9/EC and 2001/29/EC.

[15] Directive 2011/83/EU of the European Parliament and of the Council of 25 October 2011 on consumer rights, amending Council Directive 93/13/EEC and Directive 1999/44/EC of the European Parliament and of the Council and repealing Council Directive 85/577/EEC and Directive 97/7/EC of the European Parliament and of the Council.

[16] Directive 2011/83/EU of the European Parliament and of the Council of 25 October 2011 on consumer rights, amending Council Directive 93/13/EEC and Directive 1999/44/EC of the European Parliament and of the Council and repealing Council Directive 85/577/EEC and Directive 97/7/EC of the European Parliament and of the Council.

the online platform economy are new market developments envisaged by the regulation of block exemptions concerning vertical agreements adopted in 2022. It focus, in particular, the provision of online intermediation services, defined as information society services within the meaning of Directive 2015/1535[17], which allow undertakings to offer goods or services: (i) to other undertakings, with a view to facilitating the initiating of direct transactions between those undertakings, or (ii) to final consumers, with a view to facilitating the the initiating of direct transactions between those undertakings and final consumers, irrespective of whether and where the transactions are ultimately concluded[18].

Vertical agreements or concerted practices are those between two or more undertakings, each of which operates, for the purposes of the agreement or the concerted practice, at a different level of the production or distribution chain, and relating to the conditions under which the parties may purchase, sell or resell certain goods or services[19]. The provision of online intermediation services are held vertical agreements as facilitators of B2B or B2C direct transactions[20].

As vertical agreements, online intermediation services are exempted from the prohibition of collusive practices provided for under Article 101(1) of the Treaty on the Functionning of the European Union. However, due to their hybrid function, online intermediation services place specific challenges. For instance, the exemption of dual distribution agreements is found not to apply where the provider of the online intermediation services is also a competing undertaking on the relevant market for the sale of the intermediated

---

[17] Directive (EU) 2015/1535 of the European Parliament and of the Council of 9 September 2015 laying down a procedure for the provision of information in the field of technical regulations and of rules on Information Society services.

[18] Article 1(1)(e) of Commission Regulation (EU) 2022/720.

[19] Article 1(1)(a) of Commission Regulation (EU) 2022/720.

[20] Recitals (10) and (11) of Commission Regulation 2022/720.

goods or services, as it may have the ability and the incentive to influence the outcome of competition on such market.[21]

On the contrary, restrictions of online sales and online advertising benefit from the block exemption, provided that they do not, directly or indirectly, in isolation or in combination with other facts controlled by the parties, have the object of *preventing the effective use of the Internet* by the buyer or its customers to sell the contract goods or services to particular territories or customers, or of *preventing the use of an entire online advertising channel*, such as price comparison services or search engine advertising, in particular where the objective of online sales restrictions is to significantly diminish the aggregate volume of online sales of the contract goods or services in the relevant market or the possibility for consumers to buy the contract goods or services online[22].

Online advertising and promotion are considered 'active sales'[23], including online media, price comparison services or advertising on search engines targeting customers in particular territories or customer groups, operating a website with a top-level domain corresponding to particular territories, or offering on a website languages that are commonly used in particular territories, where such languages are different from the ones commonly used in the territory in which the buyer is established[24].

In general, vertical agreements entered into between competing undertakings are excluded from the exemption, unless they enter into a non-reciprocal vertical agreement and a) the supplier is active at an upstream level as a manufacturer, importer, or wholesaler

---

[21] Recital (14) of Commission Regulation (EU) 2022/720.

[22] Recital (15) of Commission Regulation (EU) 2022/720.

[23] Article 2(a)(b) of Commission Regulation (EU) 2022/720. On this regulation of active sales see PA de Miguel Asensio, *Manual de Derecho de las Nuevas Tecnologías. Derecho Digital,* Aranzadi, Cizur Menor, 2023. p. 211-216.

[24] Article 1(1)(l) of Commission Regulation (EU) 2022/720.

and at a downstream level as an importer, wholesaler, or retailer of goods, while the buyer is an importer, wholesaler, or retailer at the downstream level and not a competing undertaking at the level of trade where it purchases the contract services; or b) the suplier is a provider of services at several levels of trade, while the buyer provides its services at the retail level and is not a competing undertaking at the level of trade where it purchases the contract services.

Notwithstanding, where the provider of the online intermediation services is a competing undertaking on the relevant market for the sale of the intermediated goods or services, the exemption does not apply, even if the competing undertakings enter into a non-reciprocal vertical agreement and any of those exceptions applies[25].

Hardcore restrictions - i.e. restrictions that remove the benefit of the block exemption – include, in particular, the prevention of the effective use of the internet by the buyer or its customers to sell the contract goods or services, as it restricts the territory into which or the customers to whom the contract goods or services may be sold within, in special an exclusive or selective distribution system[26], notwithstanding other restrictions that may be imposed on the buyer concerning online sales or online advertising that do have the object of preventing the use of an entire advertising channel[27].

Moreover, certain restrictions are excluded from the exemption, in particular, concerning online platforms, any direct or indirect

---

[25] Article 2(6) of Commission Regulation (EU) 2022/720.

[26] In *Pierre Fabre DermoCosmétique*, judgment of 13 October 2011, C439/09, ECLI:EU:C:2011:649, the Court of Justice of the EU found that, "in the context of a selective distribution system, a contractual clause requiring sales of cosmetics and personal care products to be made in a physical space where a qualified pharmacist must be present, resulting in a ban on the use of the internet for those sales, amounts to a restriction by object within the meaning of that provision where, following an individual and specific examination of the content and objective of that contractual clause and the legal and economic context of which it forms a part, it is apparent that, having regard to the properties of the products at issue, that clause is not objectively justified."

[27] Article 4(e) of Commission Regulation (EU) 2022/720.

obligation causing a buyer of online intermediation services not to offer, sell or resell goods or services to end users under more favourable conditions via competing online intermediation services[28]. Indeed, the exemption of online intermediation services does not apply to retail parity obligations causing buyers of such services not to offer, sell or resell goods or services to end users under more favourable conditions via competing online intermediation services[29].

Concerning exclusive or selective distribution systems, the Commission's *Guidelines on vertical restraints and online sales of distributors*[30] had already underlined, as a general principle, the freedom of online sales, so that distributors may reach a wider and more diverse clientele, albeit limited to passive sales, i.e., when the customer visits the distributor's website and following that visit the customer contacts the distributor, resulting in a sale, or when a sale results from information received by the customer (for ex., the costumer has chosen to receive the distributor's newsletter, regardless of the language options available on the website).[31]

The Commission found as serious (hardcore) restrictions on passive sales agreements between the supplier and the distributor under which, for ex., the exclusive distributor cannot sell to consumers via the Internet when the credit card information shows that the consumer does not belong to the distributor's exclusive territory, or the distributor has to limit the percentage of global sales over the Internet, or to charge higher prices for online sales ('dual pricing').[32] On the contrary, restrictions to active online sales

[28] Article 5(d) of Commission Regulation (EU) 2022/720.

[29] Recital (16) of Commission Regulation (EU) 2022/720.

[30] SEC(2010) 411, < http://ec.europa.eu/competition/antitrust/legislation/guidelines_vertical_en.pdf>

[31] *Guidelines on vertical restraints*, para. 52.

[32] *Guidelines on vertical restraints*, para. 52, pointing out however that dual pricing could be justified under Article 101 (3) where online sales entail substantially higher costs for the manufacturer than offline sales (para. 64).

would be accepted, such as for example on-line advertising targeted specifically at certain customers, through territory-based advertising banners on third-party websites, or an online advertising provider to advertise specifically to users in a specific territory.[33] Quality standards for the distributor's online site as well as the prohibition to host the distributor's website in third-party platforms (e.g. e.g. *eBay*, *Facebook*, *YouTube*) were also accepted by the Court of Justice.[34]

Conclusion

The online platform economy faces regulatory and competition challenges, with some platforms achieving near-monopoly dominance, causing concerns about unfair business practices and antitrust. Anti-competitive behavior issues, such as exclusionary practices, and the vast amounts of user data collected by online platforms can harm competition and consumers. Additionally, platforms controlling access to facilities and data portability can inhibit competition, making it difficult for users to switch between platforms or for new entrants to enter the market. Online intermediation services facilitate B2B

---

[33] *Guidelines on vertical restraints*, para. 53.

[34] In *Coty Germany*, judgment of 6 December 2017, C-230/16, EU:C:2017:941, the Court found out that: "2. Article 101(1) TFEU must be interpreted as not precluding a contractual clause, such as that at issue in the main proceedings, which prohibits authorised distributors in a selective distribution system for luxury goods designed, primarily, to preserve the luxury image of those goods from using, in a discernible manner, third-party platforms for the internet sale of the contract goods, on condition that that clause has the objective of preserving the luxury image of those goods, that it is laid down uniformly and not applied in a discriminatory fashion, and that it is proportionate in the light of the objective pursued, these being matters to be determined by the referring court. 3. [...] the prohibition imposed on the members of a selective distribution system for luxury goods, which operate as distributors at the retail level of trade, of making use, in a discernible manner, of third-party undertakings for internet sales does not constitute a restriction of customers[...], or a restriction of passive sales to end users, within the meaning of Article 4(c) of [Regulation No 330/2010]". See also *Guidelines,* para. 54.

and B2C direct transactions in the digital marketplace, but online sales may be restricted by commercial policies, such as selective distribution, resale price maintenance, territorial restrictions, platform bans, and cross-border sales restrictions.

In order to address competition issues in digital markets, the European Union has adopted several pieces of legislation, notably the Digital Markets Act (DMA) and the regulation of vertical agreements block exemption (VAR). The DMA provides *ex ante* regulation to ensure fair competition. It prohibits unfair practices by online platforms holding the largest market share, expands options for professional users to improve service quality and prices, and establishes a framework for large online platforms, known as 'gatekeepers', to prevent abuse of their dominant position.

As for the block exemption regulation, it follows the previous case-law of the Court of Justice and the Commission's *Guidelines* on vertical restraints and online sales of distributors. It addresses in special *online intermediation services*, which allow undertakings to offer goods or services to other undertakings or final consumers. These services are considered vertical agreements as facilitators of B2B or B2C direct transactions, and they raise issues due to their *hybrid function*, such as the exclusion of *dual distribution* agreements when the provider is also a competing undertaking. In short, online sales and advertising restrictions may benefit from the block exemption, provided notably that they do not prevent the effective use of the internet by buyers or customers to sell goods or services to specific territories or customers.

The Impact of the Digital Services Act on Fundamental Rights in Europe*

1. Introduction

The growth of the digital economy brought new business models and new players to the forefront acting on a global scale. The rules for the proper functioning of competition in the European market, as well as the challenges to citizens' fundamental rights and the principle of the Rule of Law itself, are entering into crisis. Although the phenomenon is not new, it was found necessary to enact specific legislation to adapt the legal regime to the new challenges of the digital economy, with the European Union assuming the main role in regulating the European market, in particular with the approval of the Digital Services Act (DSA)[1].[2]

---

* Athens Training School Human Rights and the Artificial Intelligence, 3-5/7/2024, Laboratory of Law and Informatics (L.L.I.), Athens Law School, National and Kapodistrian University of Athens.

[1] Regulation (EU) 2022/2065 of the European Parliament and of the Council of 19 October 2022 on a Single Market For Digital Services and amending Directive 2000/31/EC (Digital Services Act).

[2] The EU digital law package includes other regulations, notably the Regulation (EU) 2022/1925 of the European Parliament and of the Council of 14 September 2022 on contestable and fair markets in the digital sector and amending Directives (EU) 2019/1937 and (EU) 2020/1828 (Digital Markets Act), the main purpose of which is to prevent abuses by the main access controllers, as providers of essential platform services, in their position of dominance, to the detriment of (economically dependent) companies willing to access online consumers. On this Regulation see for ex. Pedro Alberto de Miguel Asensio, *Manual de Derecho de las Nuevas Tecnologías. Derecho Digital*, Aranzadi, Cizur Menor, 2023, p. 211-216, and Alexandre L Dias Pereira, «Competition in the online

The DSA aims to promote a safe, predictable and reliable online environment, facilitating innovation and protecting the fundamental rights enshrined in the Charter of the Union, including the principle of consumer protection (art. 1/1). To this end, the DSA regulates the liability of intermediary service providers and establishes obligations of *due diligence*, without prejudice to other rules governing intermediary services, such as those contained in the provisions on electronic commerce (e-commerce directive)[3], copyright in information society[4] and copyright in the digital market[5], consumer rights[6] or the protection of personal data[7]. More recently, the EU has also enacted the AI Act[8].

---

platform economy: online sales and advertising under EU competition rules for digital markets», *European Competition Law Review*, 45/8(2024), p. 354-358. In its judgment of 14 September 2022, Case T-604/18, Google and Alphabet v. Commission ('Google Android'), ECLI:EU:T:2022:541, the General Court largely upheld the Commission's decision convicting Google of imposing unlawful restrictions on manufacturers of Android mobile devices and mobile network operators in order to consolidate the dominant position of its search engine. On this case-law, Bernadette Zelger, *Restrictions of EU Competition Law in the Digital Age: The Meaning of 'Effects' in a Digital Economy*, Springer, Cham, 2023.

[3] Directive 2000/31/EC of the European Parliament and of the Council of 8 June 2000 on certain legal aspects of information society services, in particular electronic commerce, in the Internal Market ('Directive on electronic commerce').

[4] Directive 2001/29/EC of the European Parliament and of the Council of 22 May 2001 on the harmonisation of certain aspects of copyright and related rights in the information society.

[5] Directive (EU) 2019/790 of the European Parliament and of the Council of 17 April 2019 on copyright and related rights in the Digital Single Market and amending Directives 96/9/EC and 2001/29/EC.

[6] Directive 2011/83/EU of the European Parliament and of the Council of 25 October 2011 on consumer rights, amending Council Directive 93/13/EEC and Directive 1999/44/EC of the European Parliament and of the Council and repealing Council Directive 85/577/EEC and Directive 97/7/EC of the European Parliament and of the Council; Directive (EU) 2019/770 of the European Parliament and of the Council of 20 May 2019 on certain aspects concerning contracts for the supply of digital content and digital services, and Directive (EU) 2019/771 of the European Parliament and of the Council of 20 May 2019 on certain aspects concerning contracts for the sale of goods, amending Regulation (EU) 2017/2394; and Directive 2009/22/EC, and repealing Directive 1999/44/EC.

[7] Regulation (EU) 2016/679 of the European Parliament and of the Council of 27 April 2016 on the protection of natural persons with regard to the processing of personal data and on the free movement of such data, and repealing Directive 95/46/EC (General Data Protection Regulation).

[8] Regulation (EU) 2024/1689 of the European Parliament and of the Council of 13 June 2024 laying down harmonised rules on artificial intelligence and amending

2. Overview of the DSA

2.1. Scope of application

The DSA applies to intermediary services offered to recipients established or located in the Union, whichever is the place of establishment of the provider (article 2/1). The determining criterion is not the place where the provider is established, but where it is more likely to offer services to recipients (consumers and professionals) established or located in the Union.

However, according to the recital (6), the DSA applies only to intermediary services and does not affect the requirements established in the EU law or in national legislation in relation to products or services intermediated through intermediary services, such as, for example, platforms like *Über*, which the Court of Justice classified as transport service:[9] "an intermediation service such as that at issue in the main proceedings, the purpose of which is to connect, by means of a smartphone application and for remuneration, non-professional drivers using their own vehicle with persons who wish to make urban journeys, must be regarded as being inherently linked to a transport service and, accordingly, must be classified as 'a service in the field of transport' within the meaning of Article 58(1) TFEU. Consequently, such a service must be excluded from the scope of Article 56 TFEU, Directive 2006/123 and Directive 2000/31." For purposes of the DSA, intermediation services are thus limited to mere conduit, temporary

Regulations (EC) No 300/2008, (EU) No 167/2013, (EU) No 168/2013, (EU) 2018/858, (EU) 2018/1139 and (EU) 2019/2144 and Directives 2014/90/EU, (EU) 2016/797 and (EU) 2020/1828 (Artificial Intelligence Act).

[9] Judgment of the Court of 20 December 2017, C434/15, Elite Taxi c. Uber Systems Spain, ECLI:EU:C:2017:981

storage (caching) and virtual hosting, including online platforms (for ex. *Amazon*, *Facebook, Instagram*) and search engines (for ex. *Google*). For instance, in *Airbnb Ireland*, the Court of Justice held that "an intermediation service which, by means of an electronic platform, is intended to connect, for remuneration, potential guests with professional or non-professional hosts offering short-term accommodation, while also providing a certain number of services ancillary to that intermediation service, must be classified as an 'information society service' under Directive 2000/31" [10].

2.2. Liability of intermediary service providers

With regard to the liability of intermediary service providers, the DSA eliminated articles 12 to 15 of Directive 2000/31 and replaced them by articles 4, 5, 6 and 8 of the Regulation (Art. 89). The liability exemption regime for the ISP was preserved and incorporated into the DSA, which also clarified certain elements of this regime, taking into account, according to recital (16), the case law of the Court of Justice of the European Union developed in particular in the field of online trademark protection[11].

To benefit from liability exemptions, the service provider must act neutrally, through pure and automatic technical processing of the information provided to the recipient of the service, as the automatic processing of information using IT tools alone does not mean that the PSI acquires knowledge of illegalities or illicit content stored on its platform.

[10] Judgment of the Court of 19 December 2019, C390/18, *Airbnb Ireland*, ECLI:EU:C:2019:1112.

[11] Concerning trademarks, see Judgments of 23 March 2010, C-236/08 to C-238/08, *Google France*, ECLI:EU:C:2010:159, and Judgment of 12 July 2011, C-324/09, *L'Oréal/ eBay*, ECLI:EU:C:2011:474.

As regards B2C platforms, the exemption from responsibility of the hosting provider does not apply, within the scope of consumer protection, in relation to online platforms that allow consumers to enter into distance contracts with merchants (B2C), where the platforms make the average consumer believe that the information, the product or the service object of the transaction is provided by the platform itself online or by a recipient of the service who acts under his authority or control (Art. 6/3). According to recital (24), acting under the authority or control of the platform means, in particular, that the B2C platform: a) determines the price of goods or services offered by the merchant; b) does not clearly present the identity of the trader, refusing to reveal the his/her identity or contact until after the contract between the trader and the consumer has been concluded; c) sells the product or service under its own name, instead of using the name of the merchant who will supply this product or service.

This is a solution of strict liability for trust or appearance in order to protect not only consumers, but also trademarks, brands and other distinctive signs. In judgment *Louboutin v. Amazon*, the CJEU ruled that "the operator of an online sales website incorporating, as well as that operator's own sales offerings, an online marketplace may be regarded as itself using a sign which is identical with an EU trade mark of another person for goods which are identical with those for which that trade mark is registered, where third-party sellers offer for sale, on that marketplace, without the consent of the proprietor of that trade mark, such goods bearing that sign, if a well-informed and reasonably observant user of that site establishes a link between the services of that operator and the sign at issue, which is in particular the case where, in view of all the circumstances of the situation in question, such a user may have the impression that that operator itself is marketing, in its own name and on its own account, the goods bearing that sign. In that regard, the following are relevant: the fact that that operator uses a uniform method of presenting the offers published on its website, displaying both the advertisements relating to the goods which it sells in its own name and on its own behalf and those relating to goods offered by third-party sellers on that marketplace; the fact that it places its own logo as a renowned distributor on all those advertisements; and the fact that it offers third-party sellers, in connection with the marketing of goods bearing the sign at issue, additional services consisting inter alia in the storing and shipping of those goods."[12]

2.3. Obligations of «due diligence» of intermediary providers of digital services

The DSA establishes *due diligence* obligations on intermediary providers of digital services. Micro or small undertakings are exempted from most of them.

The DSA provides 4 layers of due diligence obligations of intermediary digital service providers: a) due diligence obligations of intermediary digital service providers in general (mere conduit, caching and virtual hosting, including online platforms and search engines); b) specific obligations for digital hosting service providers, including online platforms; c) specific obligations of B2C online platforms; d) specific obligations of Very Large Online Platforms (VLOP) and Very Large Online Search Engines (VLOSE) in order to manage systemic risks.

---

[12] Judgment of the Court (Grand Chamber) of 22 December 2022, *Christian Louboutin v. Amazon Europe Core Sàrl and Others*, ECLI:EU:C:2022:1016. See Luís Manuel Teles de MENEZES LEITÃO, «O novo *Regulamento* europeu 2022/2065 sobre os serviços digitais: o Digital Services Act (DSA)», *RFDUL* 64 (2023), n.º 1, tomo 2, p. 1449-1468, 1459.

2.3.1. Due diligence obligations of intermediary digital service providers in general

The due diligence obligations of intermediary digital service providers in general are as follows:

1.° to designate contact points or, when they are not established in the Union, a legal representative;
2.° transparency of the terms and conditions of use of the service with respect to restrictions on the information provided by recipients of the service, for example, with respect to the content moderation policy;
3.° to provide annual transparency reports on content moderation, in particular on the number of notifications sent, mainly by trusted flaggers, and on the use of automated content moderation tools

2.3.2. Specific obligations for digital hosting service providers, including online platforms

In addition, digital hosting service providers, including online platforms have specific due diligence obligations[13], such as:

1.° to provide notification and action mechanisms ("notice and withdrawal");
2.° to be aware of the effective knowledge of illegality, without the need for a detailed legal examination, of certain information that has been notified to them;

---

[13] Notwithstanding specific obligations for purposes of copyright compliance provided by the Digital Market Copyright Directive. See for ex. Alexandre L. Dias Pereira, «Upload filters for obvious copyright infringements», *European Intellectual Property Review* vol. 45/5 (2023), p. 266-269.

3.º to justify the deletion or blocking of content, explaining to the recipients the reasons for the restrictions imposed by him knowing that the information provided by them is illegal or incompatible with the terms and conditions of use of his service;

4.º to notify the authorities of the member states about alleged crimes against life or the security of people;

5.º to have an internal system for handling queries against decisions to delete/block or not delete/block content;

6.º to recognize the user's right to appeal to any extrajudicial conflict resolution body certified by the Digital Services Coordinator;

7.º to give priority to notifications sent by trusted flaggers;

8.º to adopt protection measures against the misuse of its services by recipients who frequently provide manifestly illicit content or whistleblowers who frequently present manifestly unfounded content;

9.º to deliver transparency reports, particularly on disputes in extrajudicial liquidations and account suspensions;

10.º to design and organize the interface online so as not to deceive or manipulate the recipients of the services or to distort or materially harm the capacity of the recipients of the service to make free and informed decisions.

Special *advertising rules* also establish specific obligations for providers of digital hosting services, including online platforms, such as:

1.º to identify, in real time, advertising, advertisers and parameters to determine the recipients of advertisements;

2.º to do not advertise to recipients of the service based on the creation of profiles, using special categories of personal data such as ethnic origin, religion, health, sexual orientation and when it is reasonably certain that the recipient of the service is underage;

3.º to protect minors online through appropriate and proportionate measures with a high level of privacy, protection and security;
4.º to assure transparency of recommendation systems, with respect to their main parameters and the possibility that recipients change or influence these parameters.

2.3.3. Additional obligations of B2C online platforms

Additional due diligence obligations B2C are provided for online platforms, such as:

1.º to trace traders with their information and contact details;
2.º to inform consumers as soon as they are aware that a merchant has offered an illegal product or service to consumers located in the Union through its services, including the identity of the merchant and any applicable resource;
3.º to ensure compliance by design of the online interface with pre-contractual and product security compliance, and subject to random verification (for example, the consumers' right to precontractual information in the case of digital content or services, about functionality, including technical protection measures, and pertinent compatibility and interoperability of digital content or services).

2.3.4. Specific due dilligence obligations of very large online platforms (VLOP) and very large online search engines (VLOSE) to manage systemic risks.

In addition to the listed obligations of due diligence, providers of very large online platforms and very large online search engines (VLOP/

VLOSE) have additional obligations for the management of systemic risks. Very large online platforms or search engines are those which have an average monthly number of active service recipients in the Union of 45 million or more, and are designated as such by the Commission.[14]

Additional obligations specifically tailored for VLOP/VLOSE are notably:

1.º to evaluate the systemic risks of the systems, including, for example, content moderation and recommendation algorithms, in terms of dissemination of illegal content, fundamental rights, civic discourse and electoral processes, public security, gender violence, public health and minors;
2.º to adopt measures to mitigate system risks in terms of fundamental rights, e.g., false content markers. According to recital (47), "When designing, applying and enforcing those restrictions, providers of intermediary services should act in a non-arbitrary and non-discriminatory manner and take into account the rights and legitimate interests of the recipients of the service, including fundamental rights as enshrined in the Charter. For example, providers of very large online platforms should in particular pay due regard to freedom of expression and of information, including media freedom and pluralism. All providers of intermediary services should also pay due regard to relevant international standards for the protection of human rights, such as the United Nations Guiding Principles on Business and Human Rights." The right to property, including intellectual and industrial property, is one of the fundamental rights in consideration.[15]

---

[14] The list of designated VLOP and VLOSE is available at https://digital-strategy.ec.europa.eu/en/policies/list-designated-vlops-and-vloses

[15] Recital (52) of DSA: "Those fundamental rights include but are not limited to: [...] for parties affected by illegal content, the right to human dignity, the rights of

3.º to apply the crisis response mechanism in the event of a serious threat to public health or security in the Union;
4.º to carry out an annual independent audit;
5.º to provide at least one option for each of the recommendation systems that are not based on the creation of profiles;
6.º to strengthen advertising transparency by providing a repository with advertisements, advertisers, viewing period, profiles and number of targeted recipients;
7.º to provide access to data, including algorithmic moderation and recommendation systems, to the Digital Services Coordinator or to the Commission with the aim of monitoring and evaluating compliance with the DSA;
8.º to have a compliance function, i.e., a DSA Compliance Officer;
9.º to present semi-annual or quarterly transparency reports;
10.º to pay a supervision fee no higher than 0.05% of the global annual VLOP/VLOSE net benefit from the previous financial exercise.

2.3.5. Jurisdiction and fines

In terms of jurisdiction, rights and fines, Digital Service Coordinators are responsible for supervision in the provider's country of origin. In Portugal, ANACOM is the Digital Services Coordinator, and sectorial jurisdiction is conferred to ERC and IGAC[16]. However, the Commission has exclusive competence to supervise and sanction VLOP/VLOSE, which means the Brussels forum for very large platforms and search engines.

the child, the right to protection of property, including intellectual property, and the right to non-discrimination."

[16] Decree-Law No. 20-B/2024 of February 16.

Sanctions can be fines of up to 6% of the provider's annual global turnover in the previous exercise; in relation to non-compliance with obligations, they can be up to 1% of global business volume (Arts. 51 and 52). Fines are also foreseen that do not exceed 5% of the average daily income or the average annual global turnover of the previous exercise.[17]

3. Fundamental Rights Compliance By Online Platforms And Search Engines Under the DSA

The DSA, adopted by the European Union in 2022, aims to establish a robust regulatory framework for digital platforms and search engines, ensuring they comply with fundamental rights standards. Compliance by online platforms and search engines is addressed by the DSA in several aspects, in particular by upholding freedom of expression, protecting the right to privacy and personal data and providing accountability mechanisms, as well as by protecting against harmful content, in special regarding vulnerable groups, and establishing due diligence obligations, human rights impact assessments, collaboration with public authorities, and empowerment of users. Enforecement of the regulation is pursued by jurisdiction and heavy penalties for non-compliance.

3.1. Upholding freedom of expression

Under the DSA, platforms and search engines must respect freedom of expression when moderating content. They are required

[17] Recent figures for main digital corporations (in billion US dollars): Alibaba 130; Alphabet 300; Amazon 575; Apple 385; Meta Platforms 140. See <https://www.insidermonkey.com/blog/apple-inc-facebook-inc-amazon-alibaba-300-million-value--investor-likes-only-two-of-these-510895/2/>

to provide clear reasons when content is removed or restricted, ensuring users understand why their content was affected. Content removal must be based on terms that align with EU law and fundamental rights, preventing overreach in censorship. Moreover, platforms and search engines must publish regular reports detailing content moderation activities, including the number of content removals and the reasoning behind them. This promotes transparency and ensures moderation decisions respect freedom of speech.[18]

3.2. Right to privacy and data protection

The DSA restricts platforms' and search engines' use of sensitive personal data (e.g., ethnicity, political beliefs) for targeted advertising. This enhances users' right to privacy and aligns with the General Data Protection Regulation (GDPR). Moreover, platforms must inform users about the algorithms that shape content rankings and recommendations (algorithmic transparency[19]). This gives users more control over their data and ensures that automated systems respect users' rights to fair treatment.

---

[18] On the relation between trademark protection and fundamental rights, in special freedom of expression and information, see Maria Miguel Carvalho, *Quo Vadis Direito de Marcas? Reflexão sobre a necessidade de redimensionamento do seu alcance a partir da tutela da marca de prestígio*, Coimbra, Almedina, 2023.

[19] The current importance of algorithms has led to talk of the "tyranny of algorithms" (Miguel Benasayag, *La Tyrannie des algoritmes*, Ed. Textuel, Paris, 2019), and the need to design ethical and socially responsible algorithms (Michael Kearns, Aaron Roth, *El algoritmo ético. La ciência del diseño de algoritmos socialmente responsables*, Wolters Kluwer, Madrid, 2020). To this end, the Commission has created a *European Centre for Algorithmic Transparency*, with headquarters in Seville, Spain: <https://ec.europa.eu/commission/presscorner/detail/en/ip_23_2186>

3.3. Accountability mechanisms

Platforms must provide users with accessible and fair mechanisms to contest decisions (e.g., content takedowns or account suspensions), so that users can challenge decisions that violate their rights, such as wrongful removal of content (internal complaint handling). Moreover, platforms must also guarantee external dispute resolution bodies to handle content moderation issues (independent out-of-court bodies). This allows users to resolve disputes without resorting to lengthy legal processes, ensuring efficient protection of their rights.

3.4. Protection against harmful content and protection of vulnerable groups (e.g. minors)

Platforms are required to act quickly to remove illegal content (e.g., hate speech, terrorism-related material) while balancing this obligation against the need to safeguard users' rights. The DSA emphasizes the importance of not removing content simply based on its harmfulness, unless it explicitly violates the law. Moreover, platforms and search engines classified as Very Large Online Platforms (e.g., Google, Meta) must conduct annual risk assessments to identify risks to fundamental rights, including freedom of expression, privacy, intellectual property, and discrimination (risk mitigation). They must take measures to mitigate these risks while being accountable to independent auditors.

Concerning vulnerable groups, platforms interacting with minors have to comply with stricter measures and higher standards for protection. For example, profiling and targeted advertising based on minors' data are prohibited, ensuring their right to privacy and protection from exploitation. Moreover, platforms are required to ensure accessibility for users with disabilities, allowing them to enjoy their digital rights without discrimination.

3.5. Obligations of due diligence and fundamental rights impact assessments

VLOPs are expected to carry out risk assessments on how their services impact fundamental rights, including the rights to privacy, freedom of speech, and non-discrimination. They must identify and mitigate systemic risks like the spread of disinformation or amplification of harmful content. On the other hand, independent audits ensure that platforms and search engines follow due diligence processes and adhere to the DAS fundamental rights requirements. Failure to comply can result in significant fines and penalties. Indeed, platforms that fail to comply with the DSA's human rights-related provisions can face fines of up to 6% of their global revenue. This creates a strong incentive for compliance with fundamental rights standards, without prejudice to other regulations. According to the preamble, "third parties potentially affected should be afforded the opportunity to be heard and such orders should only be issued when powers to take such measures as provided by other acts of Union law or by national law, for instance to [...] disable access to services that are being used by a third party to infringe an intellectual property right, are not reasonably available."[20]

3.6. Collaboration with public authorities and empowerment of users

Platforms are required to collaborate with EU public authorities by removing illegal content and sharing data where necessary, such

[20] Recital (119) DSA.

as in cases involving national security. However, they must balance this with protecting users' privacy rights and preventing overreach by governments. Moreover, search engines and platforms must provide users with detailed information about the operation of their services, including content moderation rules, data collection practices, and terms of service. This transparency is key to empowering users to make informed decisions about their use of digital services.

Empowerment of users is also pursued through control over algorithms. Users must be given control over content recommendations and advertising settings. For instance, platforms must offer users the option to turn off personalized recommendations based on tracking, empowering them to control how their data is used.

3.7. Disinformation and media literacy

Platforms and search engines providers are encouraged to sign up for the EU's Code of Practice on Disinformation.[21] While this is a voluntary initiative, participation in this program ensures that they are actively taking steps to combat the spread of false information while safeguarding freedom of expression. Moreover, the DSA supports initiatives to promote fact-checking and media literacy, helping users critically assess the content they encounter online.

4. Conclusion

The DSA provides a comprehensive framework for ensuring that online platforms and search engines operate in a way that respects and promotes fundamental rights, including intelectual property. The

[21] https://digital-strategy.ec.europa.eu/en/policies/code-practice-disinformation

act emphasizes transparency, user protection, and accountability, balancing the need for content regulation with the protection of fundamental rights like freedom of expression, privacy and intellectual property. It is designed to regulate digital platforms and services, with a focus on creating a safer and more transparent online environment. Its impact in terms of trademark protection will certainly be high because it introduces new obligations for platforms to prevent violations of fundamental rights, including intellectual property.

The DSA places greater responsibilities on online intermediaries, especially online marketplaces, in the management of illegal content, including products that violate fundamental rights. Platforms are now required to act more proactively to remove and prevent offences to fundamental rights, the protection of which is strengthened because the DSA requires platforms to implement efficient processes for handling notices of illegal content, ensuring faster removal of infringing products or services (notice and action mechanisms). In addition, platforms with more than 45 million users (e.g. Amazon) have stricter obligations, such as taking proactive measures against piracy and disclosing how they handle such content. This is a heightened duty of care for very large platforms.

The DSA introduces transparency and accountability obligations, requiring platforms to regularly publish transparency reports on how they deal with content moderation and infringements, including violations of fundamental rights. It also empowers "trusted flaggers" to report infringements. Since platforms must prioritise such reports, the likelihood of such action being taken against fundamental rights violations increases.

The heightened obligations of due diligence also means that platforms now have to collect and verify information about traders (i.e., "know your business customer" obligations), thereby reducing the anonymity of sellers and enabling more effective monitoring of the legality of digital marketplaces.

In short, the DSA and other EU digital law regulations are relevant steps forward to promote rule of law in cyberspace. Not so long ago it was said that: "Courts are disabled, legislatures pathetic, and code untouchable. That is our present condition."[22] A quarter of century later the EU has built a robust legal framework to deal with the challenges of the digital world, of which the DSA is a most relevant part. Hopefully law in action matches with law in the books will, and the European market and citizen are not left alone in the hands of digital moguls.

[22] Lawrence Lessig, *Code and Other Laws of Cyberspace*, Basic Books, New York, 1999, p. 221.

www.ingramcontent.com/pod-product-compliance
Lightning Source LLC
LaVergne TN
LVHW052014200926
848481LV00005B/1485